Numbers in red refer to chapters which describe the area indicated

THE COMPANION GUIDE TO
East Anglia

THE COMPANION GUIDES

GENERAL EDITOR: VINCENT CRONIN

*It is the aim of these Guides to provide a
Companion, in the person of the author,
who knows intimately the places and
people of whom he writes, and is able to
communicate this knowledge and affection
to his readers. It is hoped that the text
and pictures will aid them in their
preparations and in their travels, and will
help them to remember on their return.*

THE GREEK ISLANDS
PARIS
THE SOUTH OF FRANCE
ROME
VENICE
LONDON
FLORENCE
JUGOSLAVIA
WEST HIGHLANDS OF SCOTLAND
UMBRIA
SOUTHERN ITALY
TUSCANY

In preparation
GREECE
TURKEY
SOUTHERN SPAIN
IRELAND
SOMERSET AND WILTSHIRE

THE COMPANION GUIDE TO

EAST ANGLIA

JOHN SEYMOUR

Collins

ST JAMES'S PLACE, LONDON

First Edition 1970
Second Edition 1972

I.S.B.N. 0 00 211136 5
Maps by D. M. Yuill
© *John Seymour, 1970*
Printed in Great Britain
Collins Clear-Type Press
London and Glasgow

Contents

Illustrations

Castle Acre: West Front (*Edwin Smith*)   224

Preface

Preface

East Anglia is flat, and it is no use anybody saying anything else. Strangers to it often express wonder as to what we see in the place. And not only is it flat, they say, but large areas of it are treeless, and there are a lot of very muddy fields: why, then, do East Anglians so passionately defend it? It is my hope that this book will give at least part of the answer.

In spite of being so near to London East Anglia is still very much a country place. This fact has often been put down to the dreadful service of the old L.N.E.R. and the utter inadequacy of the A12, but I would say that it is more probably because East Anglia is not a *pretty* place. Surrey, Sussex, Kent and Hampshire have wooded hills and valleys and picturesque little villages (the latter almost entirely inhabited by people who are either retired from—or commute to—London). And further, in the winter time, over East Anglia a cold wind blows: some people say it comes straight from Siberia. True, we have rather more sun than anywhere else in England, and our summers are lovely. And our villages are not yet inhabited by commuters, but, for the most part, by true East Anglian country people. We have our weekenders, and we have our retired people, and they are accepted and welcomed into the community; but they do not overwhelm it as they tend to do south of London. East Anglia is a large lump of England, and our culture is very distinctive and very strong: until the Fens were drained, and the Essex forests cut down and made passable, East Anglia was very much cut off from the rest of England. The first time I took my wife, who is Australian, into a Suffolk pub she came out, after a long evening, and said: 'Thank God nobody asked me a question—I couldn't understand a word anybody said!'

But what has this flat and supposedly featureless country got to offer to the tourist?

In the first place it has a greater wealth of magnificent medieval building than any other area of the same size in the world.

9

Preface

Apart from Ely Cathedral, and Norwich, and King's College Chapel, there is such a plethora of superb medieval churches that, after making the East Anglian tour the traveller is bound to be disappointed in what he finds of this sort in any other part of the British Isles; and to the East Anglian a visit to some locally famous church in any other part of England is almost always a disappointment: he is apt to think: 'What is all the fuss about?' But the tourist from the south often gets no farther than the famous West Suffolk 'wool country': the Lavenhams, Long Melfords, and Bury St Edmunds. I would urge him to go farther north—to such unheard of places as Sall, Cawston, Ranworth, Trunch, and then west to that medieval merchant-adventurers' lair of King's Lynn, and farther west into the Norfolk Marshland country, where he will find a series of churches of such diversity and curious interest, with such a wealth of medieval art, that will make the churches of the Suffolk 'wool villages', in all their Perpendicular magnificence, seem stereotyped by comparison. Certainly to the lover of English Gothic architecture East Anglia is the most important place in the world.

But there is plenty in East Anglia besides churches.

There is perhaps a greater wealth of good Tudor domestic building than anywhere else. There are said to be five hundred timber-framed Tudor farmhouses in Suffolk alone and they are beautiful beyond belief. There are a hundred beautiful villages: little places no outsider has ever heard about: Coddenham, Somersham, East Harling, Old Buckenham. There are splendid little market towns in which hardly a building offends and most are lovely: Woodbridge, Eye, Wymondham, North Walsham: a score of others.

And for the lover of scenery, if his taste is subtle and mature enough, East Anglia offers enormous charm and great diversity. The *valleys*, gentle declivities though they may be, are always charming: much of the scenic charm of both Suffolk and Norfolk lies in their valleys. In Suffolk there are miles and miles of deserted coast: very difficult to attain by road and therefore still unspoilt. There is the Sandling country behind this coast: miles of wild heathland and big old light-land farms. On the other side of the county is Breckland: one of the biggest areas of wild country in England, wherein roam uncounted deer: red, fallow and roe and, quite wild, the golden pheasant. In North Norfolk, and in Suffolk too, there are miles of that lovely material: *mud*. Muddy tidal estuaries, miles of saltings, where loneliness and wildfowl rule the world. And Broadland, which people who don't know imagine to be nothing but motor boats and transistor radios is, for the most of its miles, a haven of watery, willowy, bird-haunted peace.

Of great houses East Anglia has more than its fair share: Ickworth, Holkham, Sawston, Oxborough, Blickling, Heveningham and Raynham are but a few. Cambridge is a cultural world of its own, and the student of English architecture need go no farther: for here are to be found fine examples of every style from Saxon to Concrete Brutalism. For little unspoiled country towns Suffolk and Norfolk cannot be beaten. We got over our industrial revolution in medieval times, and our lack of water power and coal saved us from the degradation and ugliness that followed in other places.

So to the tourist I would say: if what you are looking for is English countryside, English architecture, and English culture at its very best, come to East Anglia. If it's mountains you are looking for, or goats, then you would do better to go somewhere else.

As for the question 'What is East Anglia?', my answer has been: Suffolk, Norfolk, Cambridgeshire and the Isle of Ely. Historically the East Anglian kingdom did not extend south of the Stour into Essex, nor west of the Cam. I have respected the southern frontier but not the western, for I have included the whole of Cambridgeshire (though the western part in rather less detail) in the book. This is, I believe, the generally accepted definition of East Anglia among East Anglians today.

CHAPTER 1

Woodbridge to Aldeburgh

Ideally **Woodbridge** should be approached from the sea, as the first East Anglians approached it, up the beautiful Deben Estuary. Then the traveller may see the red-brick town below its church and (if his keel be not grabbed by the mud of Upper Troublesome Reach first!) be greeted by a small spinney of yacht masts growing before the big gaunt tidal mill so beloved of the artists who paint the pictures that one sees in railway carriages. The mill is now clothed in corrugated iron and not weather boarding, and driven by electricity and not the tide, but it is still beautiful. The big tidal pound has been dug out and turned into a yacht basin (thus ending England's last chance of retaining just *one* tidal mill for the wonder of future generations). There was a tidal mill there in the year 1190, when one was mentioned in a grant of land. Mrs Rodney Gardner has recently bought the mill with the intention of preserving it, as a mill and also as an art centre.

The station is within pea-shooter range of the quay, so train traveller and seafarer disembark at nearly the same spot. The motorist from the south, however, will have been subjected to the horrors of the A12 and Ipswich, and the final indignity of Kesgrave, and will have reached the conclusion that East Anglia is nothing but a long-drawn-out subtopia. He will be refreshed, then, at finding himself in the middle of Woodbridge, a splendid little Georgian country town.

Woodbridge (Anglo-Saxon *Udebryge*) is an old place, having been granted, together with the nearby royal manor of Kingston, to the monks of Ely by Edgar the Peaceable in AD 920. As the effective head of navigation on the Deben it must early have become a port. In medieval times Goseford, a now extinct town which was farther down the estuary, was the main port and shipping centre: in 1338

Goseford sent fifteen ships and 538 men and eleven boys to France in the king's name. It sent thirteen ships to the siege of Calais, but only three to meet the Armada, so by Tudor times Goseford was fading away. Woodbridge itself, being farther inland and therefore nearer to the dwindling oak forests of High Suffolk, took its place as the ship-building port and also—as the river below it was better trained and the draught of water increased—a big timber exporting town.

By the mid-seventeenth century 350 ships were registered at Woodbridge. Then the fate befell the port that has befallen all other ports in similar situations; that caused grass to grow in the streets of Amsterdam (until the invention of the steam dredger saved that place). It was not that the rivers silted up, as is generally supposed. It was that ships became larger, and of deeper draught. Fifty years ago only sailing barges came into Woodbridge (and an occasional schooner on high spring tides). The former great ship-building industry died away; but never completely—a spark remained which has now been blown again into a flourishing yacht-building industry.

The quay area still has charm, but the Victorians mauled it with their gas-works and their railway, and later people have carried on the bad work with a horrible concrete 'prom'. But as we progress up into the town we find very little that is displeasing. The town was lucky—as were so many East Anglian towns—in having had great prosperity in periods of good taste, and it has a wealth of fine eighteenth-century buildings, with a smattering of Tudor. The more immediately noticeable buildings in the latter style are the King's Head, on the Market Square, with its corbels carved as faces (and a superb room upstairs for assemblies) and the Bell and Steelyard just down New Street. The steelyard, which hangs outside the latter, with new rope rove through its blocks as though ready to hoist up and weigh the passing motor cars, took part in a 'London Street' exhibit in the 'Victorian Era Exhibition' in London in 1897, and a model of it can be seen in the Science Museum at South Kensington to this day.

The Crown is an ancient hotel. John Fox was born there in 1528. He was appointed gunner in the *Three and a Half Moons*, a merchant ship bound for Spain with a crew of thirty-eight men. The ship was attacked by eight galleys of Sultan Murad's Turkish fleet and taken, the crew sold into the galleys, and Fox pulled an oar for fourteen years, at the end of this time being the only survivor from the crew of his old ship. One winter, when the galleys were laid up in Alexandria and the slaves kept ashore under guard, Fox led a rebellion of 268 men, only two others besides himself of whom were British (William Wickney of Portsmouth and Robert Moore of Harwich) and they overpowered the guard, seized a galley and oars and escaped to sea. There eight men died of starvation but the ship eventually reached Candia in Crete where the monks welcomed them and hung Fox's rusty sword up in their church as a relic. Fox was rewarded by the Pope, and sent by him to Philip of Spain who made him Master Gunner of Valentia with a salary of £2 10s a month. In two years he returned to England, was pensioned by Queen Elizabeth, returned to Aldeburgh to command an old ship of his, the *Mary Fortune*, and he served aboard her under Admiral Lord Seymour against the Armada. After this he continued quietly trading between Blyth-borough and London, and when he died in 1594 he left £10 to the poor of Woodbridge.

Peter Pett, a Commissioner to the Admiralty in Pepys's time, sailed into Woodbridge, married the daughter of the Crown Inn, one Margaret Cole, and set up a ship-building yard in the town. He built two royal warships there in 1650. The Bull Hotel, up the road, has great associations with Edward Fitzgerald, who used to put his friends up there, including Alfred Lord Tennyson. A generation back blood horses were bred in the hotel stables. When Fitzgerald was explaining to the landlord what a famous poet Tennyson was the landlord replied: 'Well he may be a fine poet but he doesn't know a damn' thing about horses!' Tennyson was most annoyed when 'Fitz' left him to pay the hotel bill.

The church, although not one of the great Suffolk churches, is good enough. Look at the fine flint and stone flush-work around the north porch and at the base of the tower. This flush-work building with alternate knapped flint and freestone is an East Anglian speciality. The tower is 108 feet high, and as the church stands on a hill it offers a fine view over the red pantiles of the town, and also of one of the beauties of Woodbridge normally hidden from visitors, the gardens lying behind the Georgian façades of the streets.

Inside, the church has a grand airy spaciousness. There is an air of wealthy urban sumptuousness about it, conferred by present and recent parishioners. The gilded, green, blue and scarlet font cover may be recent, but it is magnificent nevertheless, and so are the polished brass candelabra, reminiscent of those found in Danish and Swedish churches. The monument (in the chancel on the north side) to Thomas Seckford is interesting because Seckford had so much to do with Woodbridge that he can practically be said to have created it as it is today. He was Master of the Court Rolls in Elizabeth I's day, and his ghost may be seen by ghost-lovers at Seckford Hall in high hat and splendid period costume, carrying his wand of office, bemoaning the fact that most of the money he left for the poor has in fact been appropriated by the rich. The three-storied monument in the south chapel depicts, in a life-like way, Jeoffrey Pitman, his two wives, and his two sons.

The churchyard is an oasis of bosky charm. The Market Hall has hardly a jarring note to it. The Shire Hall, which is said to have been built by Thomas Seckford in 1570, once had its lower floor open to the wind to be used as a market. This floor was bricked in in Regency times and converted to a corn exchange, and now the buildings are used as a court room. The English word 'tawdry' is said to come from the old fair which used to be held in Woodbridge market on Saint Audrey's Day, 23rd October. The goods sold there were describable by our present word 'tawdry', a corruption of the name of the blessed saint.

Outside the town **Seckford Hall** is worth visiting. As well as the chance of a sight of Thomas Seckford's ghost excellent food may be had there, and rooms from 42s 6d a night with breakfast, for the place has been turned into a very good hotel. The beautiful Tudor façade was built in about 1530 by Thomas Seckford's father. A nice Seckford relic is the small Seckford library, now housed in the drawing-room of Miss Redstone, whose house is next to the County Library in Seckford Street, Woodbridge (new premises are now being constructed for the County Library). This is a collection of books relating to the area, arranged in a charming antique room looking out on an idyllic small garden. A perfect place for the study of Woodbridge, or Sutton Hoo, or Edward Fitzgerald.

Fitzgerald, who leapt to fame with the sudden popularity of his translation of *The Rubaiyat of Omar Khayyám*, was a splendid Victorian eccentric, who sailed the seas in small and somewhat scruffy yachts, dressed in a top hat which he tied on in gales with a scarf which went under his chin, and making huge friends with Suffolk sailors and fishermen, until he was even able to write a book on their *Suffolk Sea Phrases*. Although of Irish blood he loved his Suffolk, and was seldom able to tear himself away from it for long. He once sailed to the Maas in his little yacht intending to see some paintings at

Rotterdam, but on a fair wind springing up from home he immediately gave orders to his skipper to sail home again, back to the Deben Estuary, and he never clapped eyes on canvas (excepting that over his head). Tales about him are endless, and of the 'Woodbridge Wits', the small coterie of civilized people with whom Fitzgerald associated. His admirers may wish to make a small pilgrimage to Boulge churchyard, but a couple of miles to the north, where 'Fitz' lies buried with a rose of Naishapur over his grave. On Thursday evenings Mr Green, late of Barclay's Bank, plays the organ there, very often in strong competition with the nightingales in the great trees nearby.

> *By heaven! the bold sun*
> *Is with me in the room*
> *Shining, shining!*
> *Then the clouds part,*
> *Swallows soaring between;*
> *The spring is alive,*
> *And the meadows are green!*
> *I jump up like mad,*
> *Break the old pipe in twain,*
> *And away to the meadows,*
> *The meadows again!*

One of Fitzgerald's closest associates—in fact his father-in-law, for 'Fitz' married this man's daughter in a misguided fit of sentimentalism and the marriage only really lasted one night if it can be said to have lasted that—Bernard B arton, was a Quaker bank clerk and a minor poet. He was beloved of everybody in Woodbridge, and so much so that the Woodbridge ship owners named a ship after him. He remarked, on hearing that he had been thus honoured: 'If my Bardship never gets me on the muster-roll of Parnassus, it will get me into the Shipping List.'

Thomas Churchyard was a solicitor of the town, a collector of early English landscapes, and a not-negligible painter in his own right. He was much influenced by Constable but carried impressionism somewhat further. He painted with great gusto and a very sure eye. There is a good collection of his watercolours in Christchurch Mansion, Ipswich. He died in 1865, and a contemporary wrote of him: 'His manner was polished and gentlemanly in the extreme, his conversation full of wit and anecdote to overflow;

while his varied information, especially on matters connected with art, made his company at all times amusing and delightful.'

Melton's ugly new church has an old and beautifu' sacrament font in it.

A short excursion should be made from Woodbridge to **Ufford**, which has the finest font cover in England. When Smasher Dowsing, the Cromwellians' church-basher, came to Ufford to do his hatchet-work, he was forcibly kept out of the church by the church wardens, and thus the latter saved this cover, and probably at the risk of their lives. Apart from this treasure the little church is interesting. There are good fifteenth-century bench-ends. Local benefactors give money to have some of the hideous Victorian glass in the windows removed from time to time, and their excellent actions are commemorated by glass engravings on the new clear glass executed by an Ipswich engraver, Mrs Sheila Elmhurst. The north wall of the nave has herring-bone and stratified masonry of the eleventh century. At the Lion public house, down the road, live the Chilvers family, famous thatchers in 'Norfolk reed'. Ufford is a little showplace of a village now, with most of its houses restored by wealthy Woodbridge people. The village stocks by the churchyard gate are no longer used.

But the searcher for East Anglia will probably wish to strike out towards the sea; and on his way he will pass close by the very cradle and beginning of this ancient kingdom.

It is known from the writings of Bede that the first kings of all East Anglia, the members of the Wuffinga dynasty, had their Great Hall at **Rendlesham**, a tiny village north-east of Woodbridge, dominated nowadays by an American-occupied aerodrome. There is little to see there now, save a great park and woods and peace (the latter only when the planes are grounded), and the winding Deben valley, and nobody knows where the Great Hall was, although various 'Saxon' remains have been dug up. But certainly the kings (such of them as died at home) were buried at **Sutton Hoo**, which is, by the way, now a hot rival to Hoxne as a candidate for the probable site of St Edmund's martyrdom.

A track which leads straight off to the right from the junction of the Hollesley and Shottisham roads on Sutton Common leads straight to the eleven barrows of Sutton Hoo. Four barrows have been excavated.

All you see there is the sandy ridge on which you stand and the wood in front of you which cuts off your view of the Deben Estuary. Before this wood grew up there must have been a fine view, for the ridge is a hundred feet above the mud and salt water of the estuary. Here, over thirteen hundred years ago, a ship eighty-nine feet long (as long as an East Coast sailing barge) was carried or dragged on skids up the hill, a treasure chamber was built in her and filled with a priceless treasure, and she was buried deep in the sand. In *Beowulf* is described just such a ship burial; and the treasure is still there for all to see, in its golden splendour, but safe inside the King Edward VII gallery at the British Museum.

Mr Basil Brown, then a young man on the staff of Ipswich Museum, was given the task of opening some of the barrows in 1938. He started on the smaller mounds. The first had some bones in it. The second some bones, some pieces of bronze, some pottery, and a Frankish throwing axe. The third contained a boat. Not much of a boat, and not much left of it.

Next year, in April, Brown attacked the biggest of the barrows, and thereafter he went from excitement to excitement until he realized that he was the discoverer of the greatest archaeological find that has ever been made in England or is ever likely to be made. On the 8th of June the Office of Works took over the responsibility for the dig and put Mr C. W. Phillips in charge. Mr Basil Brown went on working under him. Mrs E. M. Pretty, the owner of the land, generously gave what was found to the nation.

The great ship, with holes for thirty-eight oars, was laid bare. Little was left of the wood of her, except its perfect imprint in the sand, and nearly all her iron rivets and roves. Of human remains there was no sign.

There were some large, lavishly ornamented but inferior pieces of silver from Mediterranean lands (one huge bowl had the stamp of the Emperor Anastasius on it), a helmet and shield of Swedish design, some Celtic hanging-bowls with the Christian fish symbol, a bewildering mass of Anglo-Saxon jewellery—most of it gold set with garnets and worked with intricate designs. There was a gold-mouthed purse filled with Merovingian gold coins, there were buckles and mounts, all bullion, a great sword with scabbard and harness, a shield, an iron battle standard, a ceremonial whetstone (symbol of the king—the Swordgiver of his people? Recently pottery sherds were unearthed at the site of Ipswich Co-operative Society with heads on them *exactly* like the strange pear-shaped heads on the great whet-

stone). There were angons, spear heads, the mountings of a great
drinking-horn. There was a gold-mounted harp, and one can look at
it and hear the author of *Beowulf* sing:

> . . . the harp music, and the clear voice of the poet, singing how
> Man was made long ago, and how God made the world a bright
> sea-enriched plain, made the sun and moon to light its inhabitants,
> clothed the earth with leaves and branches, gave life to all moving
> things.

But the digging up of history was interrupted by history in the
making. Once more East Anglia was threatened by Germanic
invasion. The great dig was completed a few days before World
War Two broke out, and it was not until after the war that the finds
could be properly examined and evaluated, and even now much
work remains to be done.

Dating can be done fairly accurately from coins and other arte-
facts, and this places the burial in the middle of the seventh century.
Which king was it who had this mighty funeral in his honour?
Wehha, Wuffa, Tyttla, Raedwald were all too early. (It was
Raedwald (died AD 624) who—converted to Christianity in AD 619
—prudently installed two altars in his church at Rendlesham—one
pagan and one Christian.) Great research has gone on, and so far
Aethelhere, who died in battle on the Winwaed (AD 654) fighting
in the Mercian army against the King of Northumbria, is considered
most likely. The fact that he died far from home would account for
his body not having been found in his burial ship. The site was re-
excavated in 1966-7.

All this country between the A12 road and the sea is marvellous
walking country. It is called **the Sandlings**, by reason of its being
light and sandy. Here are great open sandy heaths with a blaze of
yellow gorse and broom blossom in summer (and gorse blooms all
the year, of course—when gorse is in bloom kissing's in season.
There's a Suffolk saying about what to do with a reluctant maiden:
'Git her up agin' a whin bush bor! She 'on't back away then!').
There is heather and ling. Nowadays great acres of former heathland
have been ploughed up and they grow fair crops of rye, poor crops of
barley, and acres and acres of carrots. Large stretches are under the
Forestry Commission, and planted with Scots and Corsican pine:
the great stretches of the Rendlesham and Tunstall Forests put one
in mind of Siberia and packs of wolves. One can walk or ride a horse

through these forests, which after all belong to the people of Britain; but the fire peril is intense. A cigarette-end can destroy a million trees.

It is not quite a flat country. It is a low table-land cut into by river valleys and estuaries. Seabirds wheel and shout over saltings and marshes. It is a sparse, little inhabited, country. Farms are few and huge. It is not a country of fine buildings: most farmhouses and cottages seem to have been built in the last couple of centuries, of brick, and to a nondescript architecture. Here is little timber framing—there never was much timber. The churches are of flint (as they are all over Suffolk) and some of the cottages near the sea are of beach pebble.

This coast is much the same from the Orwell Estuary, in the south, to Lowestoft and the Norfolk border in the north where it comes to an end. The country being treeless by nature, and well drained, it was a natural habitation for Stone Age people, and worked flints are everywhere. The Romans looked upon it as a barren coast-line to be defended against the Saxons, under the command of the 'Count of the Saxon Shore'. When the Romans left, the first East Anglians seem to have sailed for the Wash, and left their boats, and moved inland to settle as farmers in scattered communities. It was not until Raedwald and his kin arrived, and settled near the Deben Estuary, and retained their ships and their command of the sea, that East Anglia was united and began to take on a name and character of its own. These Anglo-Saxons, like the Stone Age people, found the Sandlings easy to farm; but they slowly hacked their way into the great elm and oak forests of High Suffolk, with its heavy, intractable, but exceedingly fertile, land.

In the Middle Ages the Sandlings were given over to the sheep. You will see the word 'walks' all over the map: Sutton Walks, Alderton Walks, Hinton Walks, Westleton Walks. This means sheep walks, large areas of uncultivated ground supporting sheep and wandering shepherds.

Then, late in the eighteenth century, began the pheasant craze. Rich men from the cities bought up vast tracts of the Sandlings, great estates were formed, and the whole country given over to the cult of the pheasant. The inhabitants had either to become game-keepers or other estate servants or get out. Pheasants were bred, pheasants were preserved, and pheasants were shot in vast numbers. The pheasant cult reached its peak in Edward VII's reign: but still you will see more pheasants in the Sandlings than anywhere else in England—the Brecklands not excepted.

Hitler's war brought about the next change in the Sandlings country: it introduced arable farming. New methods of cultivation and artificial fertilizers, and now more and more piped irrigation, are making these sandy acres profitable to plough, but wind erosion is becoming severe, and in a dry spring roads are blocked with sand that has blown off the arid fields.

Ramsholt is a good little place to go to see the Deben Estuary. You climb the red crag hill there, over the road from the pub, and get a fine view down to the south of the river, and can imagine the Wuffing king and his seafarers sounding their way in over the bar to reach the shelter of the estuary and found a kingdom.

Farther downstream Bawdsey is given over to the Royal Air Force, who play with radar in the great manor house on the cliff. Here radar was first developed. They will sometimes take you over the river in their ferry, but not your car.

North is **Hollesley** (we say 'Hosely') with its huge open Borstal prison, in a superb position overlooking the mouth of the Ore. Here is one of the last hold-outs of the Suffolk Punch: the finest heavy horse ever produced. Suffolks still do most of the heavy work on the farms attached to the Institution. In years gone by Hollesley was the 'Colonial College', and Canada, Australia and New Zealand are full of the descendants of men who trained there, before going overseas.

Follow the road over the marshes and you will come suddenly to **Shingle Street**. This is well named, excepting that there is no 'street' in the accepted modern sense. But there is plenty of shingle—in fact little else. There is a row of cottages built along the top of a shingle bank, with the sea down the slope in front of them and the wide marshes at their back. I can only think of one other place in England so uncompromisingly spare and bleak, and that is Boulmer, in Northumberland, but there each little cottage has a fishing coble drawn up in front of it. At Shingle Street you will see a few fishing boats: not cobles but the famous 'punt' of this coastline, and anything less like a punt would be hard to imagine. These boats are beamy, full-bilged, clinker-built, transom-sterned, always white painted, and they are built to come through the breakers to the shore bow-on (unlike cobles which come through stern-on). They are then hauled up the steep shingle beach on skids with a windlass.

23

But these boats belong to part-time fishermen. More and more of the houses at Shingle Street belong to week-enders, but Norman Scarfe, the scholarly author of the *Shell Guide to Suffolk* (the best of the series so far) lives in one of them.

It is fun to walk along the beach, northwards, to the mouth of the Ore, which is there a great flood, and very swift. At low tide steep-sided islands are revealed in the mouth, showing how easily the navigator may come to grief when trying to enter this difficult river.

To avoid further confusion let it here be said that the Ore is the same river as the Alde. The lower reaches are called the Ore, as is that branch of the headwaters which runs by Framlingham. The rest of it is called the Alde. It is as improbable that the men of Orford would submit to calling *their* river the Alde as it is that the men of Aldeburgh should call *theirs* the Ore, so it has to go by both names.

The coast here has the loneliness and desolation of a desert shore: the yellow horned poppy, the sea bindweed and maritime thistle among the sparse flora. You can, if you like, walk right along the river wall to Chillesford, and for a naturalist, or a lover of lonely places, what a superb walk.

If you are travelling by car though, go back to Hollesley and turn right through Boyton (simply to see the fine brick almshouses, the central range built in 1736) and then through a lovely land of ridges and marshy valleys to **Butley**. If you pass Butley Church note the fine roof of 'Norfolk' reed thatch, in fact very Suffolk reed, because it was cut within sight—almost spitting-distance—of the church. This was put on by the Chilvers family, whom we have met in the Lion Inn at Ufford. Then you must go to look at the gate house of Butley Abbey.

The gatehouse is now a private residence, but if you can get permission to see the outside of it do so, for here is one of the best pieces of flush-work in East Anglia, which means in the world, for this is very much an East Anglian art. And here it is seen in splendid exuberance: a great many marvellously done heraldic shields, which indicate a date of the early fourteenth century making this one of the earliest examples of flush-work in the country, besides one of the best. The freestone, as opposed to the flint, was brought from France, and the track of a canal has been traced leading to the priory from the Butley River (just as a canal was dug from the Wensum to Norwich Cathedral). This stone is said to have come from the valley of the Yonne, a tributary of the Seine. Much stone in East Anglian buildings came from Caen in Normandy, but as you get into Norfolk more and more Northamptonshire stone is found, particularly of course in that part of the country drained by the rivers which run into the Wash.

More fascinating perhaps than this gatehouse—a poor remains of a great religious house—is the 'Register or Chronicle of Buttley Priory, Suffolk, 1510 to 1535', which has been edited by A. G. Dickens and turned into understandable English (there is a copy at the Seckford Library, Woodbridge). This gives a splendid look at the everyday life of a religious house just before the Dissolution. It is mundane and intimate. The writer shows humane concern when a hard winter kills off birds and rabbits, pleasure when a good herring harvest fills the poor people's bellies. He enjoys recounting how Mary, Queen Dowager of France, and her husband Charles Brandon, Duke of Suffolk, used the priory rather like a hunting box, following the hounds in nearby Staverton Forest, or picnicking in Brother Nicholas's garden only to be driven indoors—into the church—by a scatter of rain. The list of servants at the priory is fascinating. Cooks, pantrymen, launderers, dairy maids, bakers and maltsters, warreners, a cooper, a slaughterman, ploughwrights and cartwrights, shepherds and carters and many others, including a 'keeper of swannys and pulleyn'. The continuity of life in England is nicely illustrated by the fact that a great modern farmhouse now straddles the site of the old priory and the lands which once supported a great religious community now support the family of a modern farmer, who owns an uncounted number of combine harvesters. There is a local legend that a silver coffin is hidden somewhere at Butley containing the remains of Michael de la Pole, killed at Agincourt.

Turn sharp left past the priory and you will come to Staverton Thicks, a dense and ancient wood of oak and holly, the oaks stunted by the poorness of the land. Some say it was planted by the Druids, others that it was planted by Butley monks who—having been given permission to take *one crop* off the land—planted oaks! There is a pleasant book about this haunted ancient forest: *The Cottage in the Forest* by Hugh Farmar (Hutchinson).

The pub at Butley is a favourite of mine for it is still completely unspoilt. Nowadays one lives in terror of fine country pubs being 'tarted up', but the Oyster has not had a penny mis-spent upon it, either by the brewers or the landlady. The company to be found in it are foresters and farm workers, and here you will hear the purest coastal Suffolk, the sweetest English, and far closer to the language of Chaucer than any English you will find in a town. If the seeker wishes to find the heart of East Anglia he must learn to know East Anglian countrymen, learn to appreciate the richness of their dialect and understand their wry humour.

On a fine summer's evening you may be lucky at Butley to see the old game of quoits—the true game as it was played in Shakespeare's time. The quoit is of steel, and heavy, and flung a long distance into a pad of clay. A few Suffolk parishes still have teams, and Butley is one of them.

A little farther along the road, the lane to Butley Mill, is Mounts Field—just an ordinary field, but from it a Neolithic village of the 'Beaker' period has been dug up, Bronze Age axes have been found, Iron Age material, Roman material, and the foundations of a 'Saxon' house. What more can you ask of one field?

Chillesford is a tiny hamlet but a name familiar to geologists, because here can be seen the Chillesford Beds and the Coralline Crag. In the latter (a Pleistocene deposit until recently thought Pliocene) can be found four hundred different species of mollusc shell, 142 of which are extinct. They were laid down in a warm sea, some 2,000,000 years ago, in between forty and fifty fathoms of water. The much thinner Chillesford Beds consist of fine micaceous sands and clays containing estuarine fauna. The thirty-one-foot long vertebral column of a whale was found in the old brick-works just along from the church (the last brick-maker, Mr Chittleburgh, died only a few years ago). There is a crag quarry just in front of the church, but the Corraline Crag can be seen without looking into it, for the tower of the church is built of it (as is the tower of the eleventh-century church of Wantisden, now lost to an airfield).

It is now but a short walk to **Orford**. The walker should go by Friar's Walk, a lane that takes off just beyond the Mill Lane junction and leads past Sudbourne Hall. Within living memory Sudbourne Hall employed twenty-two gamekeepers and a tailor to make green liveries for them to wear. Within living memory a whole row of cottages was pulled down in Orford because the doctor complained to the squire that the inhabitants made too much noise near his house. Within living memory it was usual for six thousand pheasants to be shot here in one day. The estate is partially broken up now though, and the great house pulled down.

Orford is a curious little town. The Market Square (no longer a market) is attractive, but for one hideous modern house. Quay Street is a quite charming village street, with a long strung-out green. The church is noble, and could house all Orford's inhabitants and the people for miles around. The castle really does 'stand sentinel', as so many castles have stood in so many guide books throughout the ages. Climb to the top of it (costs a shilling) and you have a great view of the strange geographical phenomenon of the Ore and Alde River, with its narrow ten miles long shingle bank which separates it from the sea. The army used the castle as an observation post during the last two wars, and no doubt its military uses are not over yet, despite its eight hundred years.

Alas, only the keep remains, the great tower that was the heart and citadel of the castle. But this is in fine order, one of the finest keeps in England. A drawing done of the castle in 1601 by John Norden shows its former huge ramifications. The mystery to me is where all this stone has gone to. You don't see much stone in the buildings round about, and most of what you do see came from the old Austin Friary, fragments of which can be seen next door to Chantry Farm.

The castle was built for Henry II in 1165 and onwards, the work supervised by the then equivalent of the Ministry of Works: a gentleman named Alnoth. The keep was revolutionary in its day, being the first in England built polygonal in shape, not square. This was to counter the nasty habit of attackers of undermining the corner of a square thus causing it to collapse: it was later that round keeps came into vogue, better still. Orford also has pointed windows instead of Norman round ones, showing the influence of the new Gothic ideas. Inside is a chapel, and garderobes, and a great hall, and a cellar below with a well in it. We are told (by Ralph of Coggeshall) in *Chronicon Anglicanum*, fifteenth century, and quoted by Camden, that a Wild Man was held in the dungeon. He was taken in nets from the sea by fishermen, and was half man, half fish, but although put to torments he could not be made to talk like a Christian, and finally he escaped to the sea again. A modern portrait of him can be seen over a shop which sells coffee and oysters and smoked salmon in the square. Hubert de Burgh, of 'Heat me these irons hot' fame in Shakespeare's *King John*, was a warden in Orford Castle, and it seems just possible that the 'Room in a Castle' in which poor little Arthur was immured was here.

The stone that the keep is built of is interesting: much of it septaria, dredged out of the sea off Felixstowe and Harwich. Orford has been patched up recently with ugly sandstone: ignore that.

The church has a ruined Norman chancel standing to the east of it, with splendid twirly and dog-tooth decoration on the forlornly standing piers. The existing nave, aisles and west tower are Decorated of the finest, and the church has a wide, grand air. Several of Benjamin Britten's works have had their first-ever performances here, and every year during the Aldeburgh Festival some work of music is performed. The tower was repaired recently (the top fell off in 1830) and is unfinished. There are many fine brasses, all of about 1500.

At the bottom of Quay Street the Jolly Sailor beckons—one of the very fine old waterside pubs and except for the 'big room' (unused but for courting couples and rock enthusiasts) quite unspoiled. The tap room (called here 'the kitchen') has fine wooden bench backs, and it is a tradition that locals do not use the front door. There is a brass bar by the fireplace which shows where the sea came in the 1953 flood, when Syd Harper, the landlord, nobly dived into the cellar to rescue the beer, the customers meanwhile sitting on the table with their legs up secure in the knowledge that licensing laws were unlikely to be enforced that night. When the roof was lifted off the pub by a private whirlwind in 1963 a customer was heard to say: 'What the hell is a'gooin' to happen in 1973—an aarthquake?' But the supply of beer never fails in these disasters. Ask Mr Harper to show you the 'Chinese muff dogs', and look at the tiny 'Captain's Room' at the north end of the building. In here, tradition has it, the body of Will Laud the smuggler was laid, after he had been shot by the Preventive men on Orford beach, and Margaret Catchpole swounded. Will Laud may never have existed, but Margaret Catchpole certainly did, and the Jolly Sailor for long had a copy of the handbill offering a reward for her capture. There is still a facsimile in the pub—the original is in Christchurch Museum, Ipswich. The Reverend James Cobbold's novel *Margaret Catchpole, a Suffolk Lass* recounts all these doings, and the Margaret Catchpole legend is strong all along this coast. This was the smuggler's coast *par excellence*, and not a village for miles but has its stories.

Most of the activity down at the quay is connected with the Atomic Weapons Research Station on 'The Island' over the river. The 'Island' is not an island, being connected by shingle to the mainland at Slaughden. It has huge concrete installations and is wrapped in secrecy.

Orford was a great port in Elizabethan times, and thereafter until the seventeenth century. She sent wool to the Continent. The port decayed when ships became of deeper draught; but old men can still tell of the time when Orford had her own fleet of schooners, ketches and boomy barges, her brewery (Mr Rope's), her bakers and butchers, blacksmiths and wheelwrights, tailors, carpenters, millers and builders.

Above all ask to see the Town Regalia, which is magnificent, and unique in England. There are miniature oars, made of silver, which were once carried by the Portmen, who enforced the rights of Orford over the fisheries in the River Ore. You still may not trawl in that river unless you pay a licence fee to the Orford Town Trust (Mr George Brinkley, to be found sometimes at the Jolly Sailor, will take your money). The Town Charter, too, is famous, and has been studied by students of constitutional matters from afar. Major Stewart Gratton, who lives in Quay House right down by the quay, has charge of the regalia, and is a mine of information.

The road north to **Iken** gives grand views of the River Alde. The river turns inland (if you are following it upstream) at Aldeburgh, and widens out there so that at high tide it resembles a wide lake and is very beautiful. The late Julian Tennyson wrote of Iken, in his one book, *Suffolk Scene*: 'Everyone wants to lie in his own country: this is mine. I shall feel safe if I have the scream of the birds and the moan of the wind and the lapping of the water all round me, and the lonely woods and marshes I love so well.' He lies, though, not at Iken but in the Burma jungle, having been killed there in the war against Japan. Reading his book is a big step towards understanding East Anglia. He would scarcely know Iken now, all the beautiful heathland has been ploughed up and the place is encompassed with 'No Trespassing' notices. The National Trust is acquiring some of this estuary.

Blaxhall, a few miles inland, is an untouched and remote village, scattered about former common land. It has a Youth Hostel, a book written about it (*Ask the Fellows who cut the Hay*, by George Ewart Evans, an excellent report of what Blaxhall was like in the early memories of old men and women), and a pub named the Ship, which is one of the last hide-outs of the country song in England. Here you can still hear men sing *The Dark Eyed Sailor, The Larks they* *sang Melodious*, *The Bonny Bunch of Roses Oh*, and many scores of other songs as good and as old.

Snape Maltings, just before the bridge over the River Alde—once a bridge famous for its beauty and beloved of artists but, alas, pulled down by vandals a few years ago—are a happy amalgam of several periods of very good industrial building and well covered with virginia creeper. They worked as maltings until 1965 when the malting firm succumbed to the pressure of the giant monopolies. I have seen sailing barges lying at the Malting's Quay discharging American barley, which the barges had loaded from ship-side in London River, and the Maltings owned two venerable steam barges. The sea-borne traffic was knocked out in World War Two by the revival of barley-growing in England, when barley began to be bought locally and brought by road. Now the quay is a fine place to sail to in a small boat—but beware the sailor who is not used to navigating in tidal waters and over mud—and part of the maltings are to be used as a concert hall by the Aldeburgh Festival having been beautifully converted by the Swedish firm of Ore Aarup, burnt down in 1969, but now rebuilding. There is a 'Sailor's Walk' right along the north bank of the Alde from Snape to Aldeburgh, one of the most beautiful walks in England. Let no-one dispute your right of way along it—sailor or no. It goes in front of a huge Victorian mansion, very ugly but in a most beautiful position, one of the houses belonging to the Wentworth family.

In the Crown Inn, in Snape, is a secret chamber, once used by smugglers. Snape Church is a long way north of the village; and half a mile to the east of it, in 1862, an Anglian ship was dug up, 48 feet in length: the burial has been dated between AD 635 and 650.

Aldeburgh can hardly fail to please. Now a holiday and residential town for people with money and good taste it was an ancient port which rivalled Orford. One enters past the church, a large and interesting one (the south porch is pierced to allow of ceremonial circumambulation without stepping on unhallowed ground). Straight down to the sea you come to the Moot Hall, which is splendid and early sixteenth century: now right on the sea, it was once in the centre of the town. The rest of Aldeburgh has gone—having been devoured by the sea, including all of Roman Aldeburgh.

The beach has many boats, or 'punts', and a strong force of professional fishermen. It is famous for its 'long-shore' herring, and for the best sprats in England in November and December. The lifeboat stands poised like a fish eagle—ready to swoop down into the breakers if there is need. Even in days of oar and sail the lifeboat never failed to launch when called—in spite of the terrific seas which hit this beach in easterly gales. On one occasion she launched, was overturned, and every member of the crew was drowned. The two towers on the beach are the watch towers of the now-extinct 'beach companies', salvage companies that pre-dated the Royal National Lifeboat Institution. Watch was kept from them for wrecks in bad weather, and boats stood ready to crash the breakers and put to sea. Walk south until you come to the place where the River Alde nearly meets the sea, where there is a yacht club, and the most northerly of all Martello Towers in East Anglia.

Benjamin Britten (a Lowestoft man) has made Aldeburgh famous by founding the *Aldeburgh Festival of Music and the Arts*. The first festival (in which Eric Crozier had a big part) was in 1948, and it takes place every year in June. (Programmes may be had from S. C. Reiss, Esq, Festival Officer, Aldeburgh, Suffolk.) Some 3,000 people attend the event every year, some of them commuting from London because the hotels then are packed out. Every event is always completely sold out in advance (the Jubilee Hall, in which most events are held, only holds 330 people), but there are overflow events in Aldeburgh Church, Orford, Framlingham, Blythburgh, and sometimes in Ely Cathedral, and the new concert hall in Snape Maltings will hold many people when it is rebuilt.

When we observe the teeming music lovers, all looking very fashionable and metropolitan in this rustic setting, the women in the very latest and least practical of hats, and the least sensible of shoes, hastening between concerts, exhibitions, wine tastings and plays, or savouring briefly the sea breezes along the Crag Path by the shingly beach, we may feel that it is a far cry from the Aldeburgh depicted by George Crabbe, inhabited by:

> . . . *a wild amphibious race,*
> *With sullen woe displayed in every face;*
> *Who far from civil arts and social fly,*
> *And scowl at strangers with suspicious eye.*

Crabbe, born in Aldeburgh the son of a salt tax collector, sailed away from the place (aboard a fish carrier) to London to become a poet. Before this he had unsuccessfully tried to become a doctor. His

CHAPTER

Woodbridge to Southwold

The A12 road running north from Woodbridge quickly brings you to **Wickham Market**, which has a fine watermill, the water wheel still working, astride the River Deben, and opposite Mr Mullins, the basket-maker, who grows and cuts his own withies and weaves good willow hurdles besides making baskets. The market of Wickham is now by the railway, at the village of Campsey Ash, and market day is Monday.

Strike north-east for **Leiston**. Leiston is, at first sight, like a piece of the industrial Midlands flung down in the Suffolk countryside. In 1728 the local blacksmith, a Mr Garrett, decided to step aboard the Industrial Revolution by setting up a works for making blades and agricultural implements. The 'Leiston Works' grew, built steam rollers and other things in peace, tanks and shells during the wars, and attracted workers from the Midlands. It still works—rises up huge and gaunt in the middle of the little town, and has spawned streets and streets of ugly brick industrial housing: outside of Ipswich the only blemish of this kind on the beauty of East Suffolk. Leiston Church is a wonder of Victorian ingenuity and ebullience, and should be visited by all carpenters.

Mr A. S. Neill's world-famous school, 'Summerhill', where the children can do what they like, is in Leiston, just over the railway line, the first-ever 'progressive school' and the pattern for all others. It still flourishes, although so many of its ideas have been incorporated in traditional education that it does not seem so different as it once did. Many of the sixty-odd pupils are from America.

North of Leiston you will see, standing up out of the open fields on your left, the romantic ruins of **Leiston Abbey**. Enough remains of this Premonstratensian abbey for it to be well worth going off the road for. The Lady Chapel is the only complete building left of the grand church, having been preserved because it was useful as a granary after the Dissolution. It was restored in 1920 as a chapel, and was restored again, and more elaborately, after being used as a furniture store for displaced persons during the Hitler war. It is now a place of peace and great beauty, open to all, and Holy Communion is celebrated there every Wednesday morning at 8.30 in the winter and 8 in the summer. An altar has been built over the site of the original high altar of the abbey, now under the sky amid the ruins, and Holy Communion is celebrated there on the last Saturday of every May.

The great barn belonging to the abbey is a thing worth visiting for itself. The dwelling house, too, which was built after the Dissolution, encroaches on the abbey buildings, and is built partly of the material of the ravaged church. It is beautiful and interesting, dating from 1536, with a large Georgian addition and not altogether happy twentieth-century alterations. It is used now as a Conference and Retreat House by members of the Church of England, and parties of retreatants are living in it during most of the year. The Lady Warden will always welcome those truly interested. Upstairs, in this grand old farmhouse, you can see the hanging knees of ancient ships, broken out of some wreck of long ago and incorporated into a new roof. The abbey was founded in 1182, but was then down at Minsmere, on the coast, now a bird sanctuary belonging to the Royal Society for the Protection of Birds. It was moved to its present place 'from its swampy site near the sea' in 1365, burned down about 1380 and rebuilt on a grander scale. It flourished until the Dissolution when it was quarried for its stone, and such buildings as were left standing were used for cow houses, stables and granaries by the adjoining farm.

Not three miles away, on the coast at **Sizewell**, is Britain's largest atomic power station. It pumps 580,000 kilowatts of electrical power to the Midlands along monstrous cables and pylons which cut the country in half, and it raises the temperature of the sea water in its vicinity by ten degrees, so that if you wish to bathe, but cannot face the rigours of the unimproved North Sea, you might try plunging in just down-tide of the cooling water outlet tower. Near Leiston, too, if you can find it by careful map-reading, is the pleasant little Eel's Foot public house in the hamlet of **Eastbridge**, made famous years ago by broadcasts of folk singing put out by the BBC.

This is the last corner of England—Suffolk and Norfolk, but the Sandling country of Suffolk in particular—where men still sing 'folk songs' without being conscious that they are 'folk songs', and where the melodeon may be heard, and old English 'step dancing' may be seen, in many a village pub. I know a man—and quite a young one too—who claims to know a song for every day in the year. Eastbridge has a pumping windmill too, and a fine little old brick bridge in the marshes. There is a superb walk from here northwards to Westleton.

But back to the main road which runs north from Leiston, and we come to the three villages of Theberton, Middleton and Westleton. All three are delightful—their houses scattered as if they were built haphazard on common land years ago, and then strung together by roads. **Theberton** has the prettiest little church, from the outside, that you could find in England: thatched roof, round tower with an octagonal top to it. A piece of shot-down Zeppelin hangs in the porch, and over the road, in the new graveyard, is a board commemorating the fact that sixteen German airmen were buried there, after their airship had been shot down by a fighter in June 1917. They were recently moved to where they must lie in some gigantic war cemetery, anonymous and forgotten. While they laid at Theberton their graves were decorated with flowers once a year, at dead of night, by some undiscovered person, and on their common headstone was written: 'Who art thou that judgest another man's servant? To his own master he standeth or falleth.'

At Theberton Hall, in 1843, Charles Montagu Doughty was born. He wrote *Travels in Arabia Deserta*, which some think the best travel book that has ever been written. He developed a new language, almost, to write it, a compound of the English of the Revised Version, Arabic, and—I like to think—Suffolk. It is a superb prose— rich and powerful, and once you attune your ear to it it will carry you along through some of the strangest and most desperate adventures ever man had. A thing which sets him high above most other travellers is the instant sympathy he seems to have felt for everyone he met—whether king or camel driver.

Westleton is a big and fine village. It stands about a fine green, with a horse pond and all. The once famous windmill has, alas, lost its sails. The large pub opposite the church serves good meals all summer. But one of Westleton's uniquenesses (besides the very lively fair held every summer when barrels are rolled down the main street to the consternation of the police) is the fact that it contains the world's leading clematis specialist, Mr James Fiske. A local boy, he started work in big nurseries in other places, fell in love with clematis, started growing them on his own at home and now grows a hundred and fifty different varieties and sends them to all parts of the world, making his remote and otherwise little-known village, to clematis lovers at least, world famous. Another, older, source of fame is the witch's stone near the priest door of the huge thatched barn-like church, over which no grass will ever grow, and if you put your handkerchief in the grating of the wall and run eastwards, northwards, and back again by the west end of the church (circumambulating widdershins) you will be vouchsafed the sound of the Devil clanking his chains below the grating. The present writer has not tried it.

A short road through the lonely Sandlings (where there are notices which say: 'Beware of Adders') takes you to **Dunwich**. Here is little to see, but much to think about. Nearly all of the Dunwich that mattered has been swallowed up by the sea. Even when Domesday was written the sea had carried away (*mare abstulit*) one of the three carucates of cultivated land there. Domesday records 236 burgesses in Dunwich, making it a far bigger town than Ipswich with 110. It also records twenty-four Frenchmen, 178 poor men, and eighty mere men. At that time the town rendered 68,000 herrings a year as tax. But it was in the Middle Ages that Dunwich grew to what was then a great city.

The visitor will now find a tiny hamlet behind the cliffs of the seashore. On the top of the cliffs at one point is a walled quadrangle now used as a smallholding: once the wall of a priory. If he explores the foot of the cliffs below where All Saints Church used to be, before it totally disappeared from view, he will find human bones in plenty: local children are fond of digging these up to embellish their bedrooms. Dig with care, though: a family was buried alive—and unburied dead—some few years ago. They were sitting in a cave at the bottom of the steep crumbling cliff. Better still, leave the remains of our ancestors in peace.

Nowhere else in England has so great a place come to so little. It was at Dunwich that Christianity came finally to rest in East Anglia. The Burgundian missionary, Saint Felix, may have been bishop there, and there he crowned Sigebert, half brother to Eorpwald, son of Raedwald of Rendlesham, King of East Anglia. Sigebert built his palace at Dunwich in AD 630 to 631. Later there was a monastery of Dominicans and another of Friars Minor. There was a lazar-house and a Maison Dieu hospital, a church of the Knights Templar, three other chapels and a cell of Eye Priory. At one time there were nine churches in Dunwich, and it was a great port owning—in the thirteenth century—eighty 'great ships'.

Of all this greatness and beauty what is left? There is the Norman apse of the Lazar Hospital moved to a new position inland and with an ugly vault built next to it and the curtain wall of Grey Friars which was used as an anti-aircraft gun site during the Second Great War. The church is new. The tower of the last of the nine churches fell into the sea in 1918 (there are photographs of this in a tiny museum).

Dunwich has a tenuous link with New York. John Daye, the printer, was born there, and the modern publishing firm, John Day of New York, was named after him. The first John Daye invented Saxon type-face, and printed Foxe's *Book of Martyrs* and other religious works. Edward Fitzgerald loved Dunwich, where he was wont to visit the artist Edwin Edwards, who had a house there, and in this house Charles Keane of *Punch* taught him to play Spanish Dominoes. Dunwich is nowadays a place of Roman Catholic pilgrimage, and the sea is blessed there every September.

But what can we do there now? There is a good pub which serves good meals. There are Westleton Walks to the southward, marshes and pine woods to the north. There is a fine sweeping view on a clear day across Sole Bay to Southwold. You can stand on the cliffs and gaze down into the sea and imagine streets and houses, and harbour works, and those nine churches and an unrecorded number of pubs. You can imagine you hear, as fishermen coming home in their boats at night have imagined they have heard, the sound of bells coming up from the waters.

There must at one time have been a capacious natural harbour at Dunwich: now there is no trace of a coastal formation which could have been a harbour at all. But not many hundreds of years ago there was a natural inlet of the sea. Defoe records that in his day Dunwich was still exporting butter, cheese and corn, and that a local rhyme had it:

> *Swoul, and Dunwich, and Walderswick*
> *All go in at one lousie creek.*

Swoul meant—and still means locally—Southwold. The creek was 'lousie' presumably because the sand bar which strangled Dunwich was already forming across its entrance.

A walk of three miles along the beach northwards brings us to **Walberswick**, or Walhbert's village, the habitation of the Walberswig Whisperers, men noted for their loud voices, which could be heard across the river and the marshes in Southwold.

Many people are rude about Walberswick, lamenting the fact that what was once a fine little fishing village is now a kind of seaside Hampstead Garden Suburb. It is, indeed, the haunt of ex-theatrical folk and lady water-colourists, but it is very attractive nevertheless. An attractive position, with its small sandy beach, Sole Bay on one side and the rushing tidal River Blyth on the other, full of fishing boats, marshes to the south, heathland to the west. The church has a noble tower, built in 1426 by Richard Russel of Dunwich, and Adam Powle of Blythburgh, masons. The contract of these two men can be seen in Gardner's *Dunwich*. It specifies that the 'steeple' should be like that of Tunstall, the west door like that of Halesworth, likewise the windows. The two masons were to find all material, and were to be paid forty shillings and a cade of herrings every year. One imagines that they did not become rich men. In Cromwell's time 'Smasher' Dowsing did a thorough job here—destroying forty windows and defacing all the tombs, thus earning a different sort of immortality from that of Messrs Russel and Powle. The tower, the south aisle, and the porch are all that are left of this once mighty church, besides the ruins of the rest of it.

The village is the remains of a much bigger place. There are lovely greens, big houses—many of them old and beautiful, some, on the outskirts, modern and bogus-timbered. There is a fine eighteenth-century building near the middle which is now one of the best contemporary pottery shops in the country. Walberswick is a paradise for children who do not yearn for the pin-tables and what the butler saw, but can find their fun on the sands, the marshes, the river and the sea.

Sometimes a fisherman will row you across the mouth of the Blyth. If not there is a Bailey footbridge a mile upstream. This was once the bridge of the now-defunct light railway between Southwold and Halesworth, a railway locally famous because the carriages for it had been manufactured for the Emperor of China. They were not delivered, owing to some war or financial difficulty, but were sent to the Halesworth-Southwold Railway instead, and it is said that the imperial dragons could sometimes be seen under the paintwork. A collection of comical cartoons concerning this railway can be seen in the Sailor's Reading Room in Southwold, about which more later; and meanwhile the walk along the old railway track from Southwold to Halesworth is a delightful experience. It takes you up the lovely Blyth valley, and through **Wenhaston**, the church of which is famous for its Doom: a quite marvellous panel.

But just over the Bailey bridge is the Harbour Inn: one of the very finest of Suffolk's several fine waterside inns. It stands on the river wall, with marshes close behind it and the strongly tidal river in front. The scene is very Dutch, and the town of Southwold, just under a mile away over the flat marshes, looks like a town of Zeeland. These marshes were flooded in 1953 and many people drowned. The river is furnished on both banks with wooden stages, at the ends of which lie fishing boats. Many of these belong to week-enders, working men or farmers who fish in their spare time, trawling or drifting in professional fashion, but about ten are manned by full-time fishermen, who make a living at the job. But we will deal with Southwold Harbour (it is Southwold Harbour although it is much nearer to Walberswick than it is to Southwold) when we come to Southwold itself.

Assuming that we are mechanized, and at Walberswick, and wish to continue northwards, we will have to strike inland to the first vehicle bridge across the River Blyth, which is at Blythburgh.

Blythburgh is a strange and interesting little village on the edge of marshes, and the tidal waters from the sea come right up to it. It is the remains of a much bigger place: indeed a place that centuries ago was of some importance. Besides the cluster of fine old village houses, the magnificent White Hart Inn, with its 'Dutch' gables and moulded and carved ceilings that was once a court house, the scant remains of an Augustinian priory in somebody's garden, there is a church of a size suitable for a place perhaps a hundred times as large. The church is best first seen from across the marshes from the north. It stands there barnlike and huge, very graceful, but with its tower out of proportion to the rest of it, for the church is 128 feet long and the tower but 83 feet high. It is a fine church whichever way you look at it, but seen from the distance from far away across the marshes it is one of the grandest sights in Suffolk.

Entering the church one is struck by its lightness and whiteness

1. EAST ANGLIAN CASTLES. *Above left*, Castle Rising (p. 200), a Norman keep within earthworks that are said to be Roman. *Right*, Orford, of which only the keep remains, was built for Henry II as a counter to Framlingham (*below left*), which was the stronghold of turbulent barons: the Bigods, Mowbrays and Howards. Framlingham is an example of a castle influenced by returned crusaders: with a huge curtain-wall. *Right*, Caister Castle, built by Sir John Fastolf in the 1440's

2. The entrance hall at Heveningham Hall, by James Wyatt in the style of Adam

and emptiness and grand proportions. There is the air of a Continental church about it, with large areas of uncluttered stone-flagged floor. Simply to wander in, and savour the sense of space, of light, of simplicity and massiveness, is an experience; but do not miss the backless benches with their carvings of Deadly Sins, such as Gluttony, Drunkenness (very rightly in the stocks to sober up), Sloth (in bed), Hypocrisy (praying with eyes open), Avarice (sitting on a chest), and one particularly deadly sin which some prude has censored with a hammer. There are fifteenth-century poppy heads, and in the south aisle are the Seasons, including a very large man in a very small boat. Outside are carved dripstones, including a very amiable chained bear. The painted roof is very noteworthy, and the carved angels, their wings much shot away by Cromwell's enthusiasts but replaced by the generosity of some Americans. The font, according to legend, was shattered by the Devil.

On Sunday the 4th of August 1577, while the minister was reading the second lesson, a 'strange and terrible tempest' 'strake' down through the wall of the church, toppled the spire down through the roof so that it shattered the font, tumbled the bells and the Jack o' the Clock (he was repaired, and is still there), killed a man and a boy and scorched many members of the congregation. It was known that this visitation was of the Devil, because as he fled out of the north door on his way to Bungay his fingermarks were revealed, and the truth of the legend verified. If you search in the choir, near the organ, you will find the carved signature of Dirck Lowensen van Stockholm, aged twelve, AD 1665. Dirck was one of the children of a Dutch community imported from Holland to reclaim marshes in the Blyth and correct the course of the river. In the seventeenth century as in the twentieth, wherever in Northern Europe there was a difficult drainage or sea defence job to be done, there were Dutchmen there to do it. Over the South Porch is a small oratory, or priest's room.

A king was killed near Blythburgh, and buried in the church. According to the *Liber Eliensis* (Ely Chronicle) King Anna and his son were slain at the battle on Bulcamp Hill (where now stands a vast eighteenth-century workhouse) and their bodies brought to Blythburgh Church and buried. King Anna's remains were later removed to Bury St Edmunds, and after that to Ely, where his daughter Aethelthryth or Etheldreda (wife of the King of Northumbria) had founded a convent.

41

Anna, we are told by Bede, was a good man and had good and pious offspring. He founded Blythburgh monastery, and embellished the monastery founded by the Irish monk Fursey at Burgh Castle. His eldest daughter, Sexburgh, became Queen of Kent and later Abbess of Ely in succession to her sister Aethelthryth. Another daughter, Aethelberg, became Abbess of Brie, in France, so Anna had no reason to complain of the lack of piety of his daughters. Anna himself was son of Eni, and Eni was brother to the famous King Redwald or Raedwald, who had the prudence to install both pagan and Christian altars in his temple at Rendlesham. Anna was brother to the Aethelhere whose death is thought to have been commemorated in the Sutton Hoo ship burial. Anna was killed here at Blythburgh fighting against Penda, King of Mercia, who was a pagan and a tireless warrior. The battle took place in AD 654 and in that same year Anna's brother Aethelhere was slain fighting beside Penda against the Northumbrians at the Battle of the Winwaed.

Blythburgh was more important, once, than it is today—a mere hamlet on the A12 road. It suffered the fate of most early ports. As ships became too deep draughted to reach its docksides the latter decayed, and trade was removed from it to places with deeper water. (Boston, Lincs, too, nearly died from the same cause.)

Blythburgh now is one of the purest of places, but according to an ancient rhyme this was not always so:

> *Beccles for a Puritan,*
> *Bungay for the Poor;*
> *Halesworth for a Drunkard,*
> *And Bliborough for a Whore.*

A road follows the north bank of the Blyth to **Southwold**: which is built on an island. Buss Creek cuts it off from the mainland to the north-east (*buss* was a square-rigged herring smack) as the Town Marshes and the Blyth do from the south-west, and the sea completes the triangle.

I cannot think of anything bad to say about Southwold. It is a real town, with good shops and good hotels. It is all that a small seaside resort should be. It has fine cliffs, a long sandy beach, a little harbour in the mouth of the Blyth, and a wealth of good houses, many of them Georgian.

The church is one of the great ones, even for Suffolk. The Victorian glass was all blown out in World War Two (except the west window), and now light floods into the superb Perpendicular-style building. Take note of the splendid flush-work and freestone work of the exterior, particularly the south porch, the loftiness and fine proportions of the nave roof and clerestory, the slenderness of the pillars. The pulpit is magnificent, a most rare fifteenth-century one, brightly painted. The organ case is exuberant Victorian work. The early sixteenth-century screen is one of the finest painted screens there is, even if the angels and blessed saints were touched up in Victorian times, making them, it is said, resemble the members of the Town Council. Reading from the north on this fine screen there are visible:

Angel with Trinity Shield.
Gabriel with sceptre of authority as God's messenger.
Archangel with sword and scales.
Potestates, with scourge and chained dragon.
St Andrew with saltire cross.
St Peter with keys.
St Paul with sword.
St John with poisoned chalice.
St James the Great, with a scallop shell on his pilgrim boat.
St Bartholomew with book and knife.
St Jude with boat.
St Simon with oar.

As in Blythburgh Church, there is a splendid Jack o' the Clock—a little wooden man in armour who strikes the bell on the hours. The church is filled with good wood carving. The hammerbeam roof is new, but fine nevertheless, there are two Brasyer bells, there is a door at the top of the stairs leading to the chamber over the porch which has a secret latch and a wealth of other interesting detail; but this church is a fine bright jewel without, and is flooded with light and magnificence within.

There is a broken tombstone without, to Samuel Charles May, who died in 1923. On it is inscribed:

> *His Anchor was the Holy Word,*
> *His Rudder Blooming Hope,*
> *The Love of God his Maintops'l*
> *And Faith his Sailing Rope.*

There is a small museum in Southwold, well worth seeing if you can ever find it open, but the nicest place for me is the Sailor's Reading Room.

This is open to all; but there is a box there for the landlubber to drop in small contributions for the upkeep of the place. In the winter there is a good coal fire, and generally some retired fisherman, or non-retired ones waiting for the weather to improve. (There is a local legend that—in sailing days—a fisherman would pop a candle out of his bedroom window when he woke up in the morning. If there was enough wind to blow the candle out—it was too rough to venture forth. If not enough wind—then not enough wind to sail. In either case the fisherman went back to bed. There is even a song about it, the refrain of which is: 'So I open the pane and pop out the flame, to see how the wind do blow!')

But the walls of the Reading Room are covered thick with paintings and prints and photographs, and the tables with models. There is a fine scale-model of the yawl *Bittern*, a most famous rowing and sailing boat.

The 'beach yawls' were built in some numbers around the coasts of East Anglia for the purpose of taking men out to ships in the North Sea to put pilots aboard them, or assist them when in trouble, or rescue the men in them when the ships were *in extremis*. The yawls were the property of the 'beach companies', the members of which kept watch in foul weather, and vied with each other in launching their open boats to row or sail them to the scene of wrecks or ships in trouble. They were the precursors of the modern lifeboat. Their function was not solely humanitarian: salvage was their mainstay. They would carry an anchor off for a ship aground on the sands so that she could winch herself off—but not for nothing of course. Hundreds of lives were saved by the beach yawls before the days of steam and radar, for it is a poor seaman who will not drop everything else if another man's life is at stake. The *Bittern* was said to be the fastest of these boats, whether under sail or oar. She was 49 feet long, and built in 1890, one of the last. Her crew challenged the schooner *America*, of America's Cup fame, to a race, but the captain of the latter would not accept the challenge except for a prohibitive stake. The yawls carried shifting ballast in the form of bags of shingle which could be shifted by the large crew up to windward, and it is probable that—in hard weather—the *Bittern* would have left the *America* standing. Her lines were very close to those of the Viking ships.

44

Up on Gun Cliff, on one of Southwold's beautiful greens, stand six eighteen-pounder guns with the emblems of the Tudor Rose and Crown on them. These are rare pieces in that they were very large for their early period. They are said to have been captured by Prince Charles Edward from Edinburgh, recaptured by the Duke of Cumberland at Culloden and later presented by him to Southwold. They had to be buried in the 1914–18 war, because the Germans bombarded Southwold from the sea on their account, claiming that it was a fortified place.

Southwold was early renowned for its fishery. Domesday records an annual rent of 25,000 herrings a year, and that it had a *sea-weir*. (A weir was a wicker fence built out at sea to entrap fish, and generally paid a rent to the lord of the manor. A local song, which describes which fish are taken on the days of the week, has a line: 'Weir-fish for Wednesday, swell the net full!' This was because on Wednesday you got 'Wind from the northard—wind from the east' and therefore no fish could be caught at sea, so the weir was resorted to. There are no fish weirs left in East Anglia—on the other side of the North Sea there are hundreds.) But it was in the sixteenth century that Southwold rose to great importance as a port. In 1750 the Free British Fishery was created, in an attempt to seize back the herring fishing monopoly from the Dutch. This had its headquarters in Buss Creek, and at its zenith there were fifty great 'busses', or square-rigged herring vessels, there. The company came to grief, however, in 1792, and the fishermen returned to fishing their small beach punts again. In 1757 the River Blyth Navigation Act was passed, part of the great spate of canal-fever legislation all over England, and the river was canalized and locked as far as Halesworth, to which inland town wherries could then sail. The harbour failed, however, when the saltings up-river were enclosed by landowners, which reduced the scouring action of the tides.

In 1898 the harbour was vested in Southwold Corporation, the Government voted £21,500 to improve it, in 1908 herring curing began again; seventy big Scottish drifters used the port and Southwold was full of Scottish fisher girls. The little railway reached the harbour in 1880, and then there was a great hope of Southwold becoming a rival to Harwich as a port for the Continent. None of the hopes were fulfilled, however. The herring industry went back to Lowestoft and Great Yarmouth, the railway is closed down, and a merciless gravel bar comes and goes over the harbour mouth, often practically bottling it up altogether. A couple of dozen small motor fishing boats still use it, though, and there is a good little yacht club; and ever and anon a new scheme is propounded for improving the harbour entrance and making Southwold a port again.

But Southwold's greatest excitement was the Battle of Sole Bay.

At Whitsun, 1672, a British fleet of seventy-one ships, mounting 4,000 guns, and manned by 23,500 men, lay at anchor just off Southwold, together with the allied French fleet. As it was Whitsun many of the English sailors were ashore getting drunk. Prince James, Duke of York, was aboard his flagship and in command of the Red, and the Earl of Sandwich (who lived at Shrubland Park, near Ipswich) commanded the Blue. Nobody had any expectation of the enemy, but at 2.30 on the morning of the 28th of March a French frigate sailed in with news that the Dutch were advancing from the south.

Great confusion immediately prevailed among the Allied fleets. The French ships slipped their cables, sailed away to the northward, and did not return. The British were left to face the Dutch fleet of sixty-one ships, commanded by de Ruyter, aboard his *Seven Provinces*.

The Dutch sailed right in among the British fleet and a battle ensued, the noise of which could be heard for many miles inland. The people of Southwold lined the cliff tops watching the carnage, and the commander of the town ordered that the bridge over Buss Creek should be destroyed to prevent people from leaving, so that, in the event of disaster, there should be English manpower enough to defend the town.

The *Great Holland*, of 62 guns, was pressed by the tide against the still-anchored *Royal James*, which had the Earl of Sandwich aboard. Sandwich ordered a boarding party away but three more Dutch ships drove in to help the *Great Holland*, the *Royal James* was set on fire, and later Sandwich's body was washed up on Clacton beach, and recognized by a ring that he was wearing. Van Ghent, the commander of the *Great Holland*, was also killed. One British ship was taken by the Dutch and the remnants of the crew battened down under hatches as prisoners, but one man—seeing that his Dutch captors were hard-pressed on deck—led his fellow prisoners to arise and together they overpowered the Dutch and took back the ship.

Altogether it was a most terrible and bloody battle: 800 wounded men were carried into Southwold, thousands were killed, great destruction was wrought to both fleets, and nobody really won. Ten years later England had a Dutch king, and Great Britain and Holland were happily engaged in waging war against the French.

Adnam's beer is brewed in Southwold, long recognized as the best beer in England.

CHAPTER 3

Woodbridge to Eye

Strike north from Woodbridge and you come quickly into one of the remote back-blocks of Suffolk, where no tourist ever goes and where the villages have names like Dallinghoo, Monewden, Cretingham, Kettleburgh and even Hoo. The charm of this sort of country lies in its utter unselfconsciousness. Such villages are not subject to guide book treatment. Most of them have pretty little churches, all have fine farmhouses (estimates of the number of Tudor or earlier farm-houses in Suffolk vary between five and six hundred); they all bear quiet exploration, on foot, on wheels, or on horseback, by the stranger looking for unexpected beauty that does not depend upon dramatic effect or over-statement. Most of such villages have good little pubs. This is heavy-land arable country I must add, and for the most part the traveller is confined to the tarred roads.

At **Brandeston** (which has a most attractive little white-washed church standing up by its tiny valley) lives Mr Hector Moore, who does fine wrought-iron work at the Old Forge, and in 1646 John Lowes was burnt, for that he 'travelled with Satan'.

Framlingham, beyond this back-block, is a little town of the first interest and importance. Most visitors head straight for the castle, but I would suggest a walk round the town first, and then the church, with the castle to round the day off with.

Clustered on its little hill, with the tiny River Ore flowing through the marshes beside it, Framlingham still has something of the air of a fortified town; although there was never a town wall: the place was surrounded by a ditch. But there is a compactness, a jumbling of the streets, an antiquity. Taken together with its castle and its church it is clear that this was once a splendid place, where knights and squires rode in fine array, where armies gathered—a centre of power. Now, however, we have a charming little country town, with

good shops, at least one excellent hotel, and the best agricultural hardwear supplier for many miles around. There is a book shop of real distinction, most unexpected in a tiny remote Suffolk town, and plenty of good and ancient pubs: the Crown goes back many centuries and is still a good place to stay. The landlord of the Castle has ancient musical instruments which he will sometimes show to the curious. There are two good saddlers and harness-makers: Mr Clements, one of them, is a horse-breaker to boot, and a mine of equine information.

The nave of the big church is somewhat bleak to my taste, although there is a fine chestnut roof with hammerbeams concealed under fan vaulting (as at St Peter Mancroft, Norwich). But the chancel is amazing to behold. For it is crammed full of great monuments to the illustrious departed.

And before we go any further here, to describe these tombs and adumbrate their occupants, it will be convenient to list the owners of Framlingham from the earliest that we know down to the present day.

There was an important fortified dwelling here in East Anglian times: recently Anglian graves have been dug up near the moat. Hinvar and Ubba, the wild sons of old Lothbroc (Leather-breeches) are said to have captured the place when they raided England with some twenty-thousand other Scandinavians in 865, entering the castle by a secret passage revealed to them by a prisoner. King Edmund is said to have hidden here during his celebrated flight from the Danes, before he fled north to Hoxne, but the evidence for this story appears to be pretty slight—if indeed existent.

After the Conquest Henry I granted whatever there was of Framlingham to Roger Bigod, and it remained in the turbulent hands of the Bigod family until the last one died out and Edward II gave it to his half-brother Thomas de Brotherton. It went to the latter's widow, thence to her aunt, thence to the aunt's daughter, and thence to the latter's husband John Mowbray. John died in 1368 and it remained with the Mowbray family (with occasional seizures by various kings) until the line died out in 1476 when it passed by marriage to the Howards, Dukes of Norfolk. These kept it (also with occasional surrenders to the Crown) until 14th May 1635, when Theophilus Howard sold it, and its estates, for £14,000, to a lawyer named Sir Robert Hitches, who could think of nothing better to do with it but try to pull it down. The great curtain wall was too much for his resources, however, and still stands. When he died he bequeathed the carcase to Pembroke College, Cambridge, and, in the ripeness of time, this body handed it over to the Ministry of Works.

So let us return to the church with its chancel full of monuments.

The chancel was rebuilt in mid-sixteenth century, much larger than it had been before and in fact out of proportion with the rest of the church. It is actually wider than the nave. It was built in the time of the Howards—by Thomas Howard, 3rd Duke of Norfolk. Thomas Howard is buried under the great block of stone to the south of the altar. This man only escaped having his head cut off by order of Henry VIII because that monarch died the night before it was due to happen, and thus on the collar of his effigy is written: 'By the Grace of God I am what I am.' Above his monument may be seen hung high up on the wall, the helmet worn by the 2nd Duke at the Battle of Flodden, where the 2nd Duke successfully commanded the English. It is said that a rector tried to sell it once to an American for £500, but that the present Duke of Norfolk prevented him.

The 3rd Duke's son was not so lucky as his father for, imprisoned at the same time, his head fell the day before Henry VIII all too tardily died and England lost a good poet, and, from all that we hear of him, a civilized man. It will be seen that his coronet is carved lying beside the head of his effigy on the monument, in significance of the fact that he was beheaded.

Poor Henry Howard, Earl of Surrey, the beheaded poet, was imprisoned at Windsor, before his death, and he had known Windsor in happier circumstances in his gilded youth:

> *So Cruell prison how could betide, alas,*
> *As proude Windsor? where I in lust and joy,*
> *With a kinges sonne, my childishe yeres did passe,*
> *In greater feast than Priams sonnes of Troy:*
> *Where eche swete place returns a taste full sower,*
> *The large grene courtes, where we were wont to hove,*
> *With eyes cast up into the maydens tower.*

But being now imprisoned and ill-treated in this place of his former happiness:

> *Thus I alone, where all my fredome grewe,*
> *In prison pyne, with bondage and restrainte,*

And with remembrance of the greater greefe,
To banish the less, I find my chief releefe.

His body was brought from the Tower, and it lies at Framlingham next to the body of his countess, Frances de Vere.

The 4th Duke of Norfolk also had the misfortune to be beheaded, this time by order of Elizabeth I. The tomb in the north chancel aisle is for his two wives: Lady Mary, daughter of Fitz-Alan, Earl of Arundel (her effigy is the one with its head on a horse couchant and its feet on a hart at layes), and Lady Margaret, daughter of Thomas Lord Audley, Baron of Walden and Lord Chancellor of England. The head of her effigy is on a tiger collared and chained, and there is a wivern, or dragon, at her feet.

It may be noticed that there is a space between the effigies of these two ladies. It is said that this was intended for no less a person than Mary, Queen of Scots. The 4th Duke had the intention of marrying her, and then overthrowing Elizabeth and putting his new wife on the throne instead. It was this duke's marriage, incidentally, to the daughter of Arundel that brought Arundel Castle into the ownership of the Norfolk family, and the present Duke of Norfolk still lives at Arundel. There is a large and ornate tomb chest with shields round it, stories from Genesis, and four charming guardian angels. It is for Henry Fitzroy, Duke of Richmond, son of Henry VIII by Lady Elizabeth Mount, or Talbois, who was Maid of Honour to Henry's Queen Catharine of Aragon. Henry Fitzroy was the 'King's sonne' in Surrey's poem, childhood friend and confidant to the Earl of Surrey and also half brother-in-law, for Henry married Surrey's sister Lady Mary Howard, who is buried beside him at Framlingham. In his life he lived at Blackwell in Essex and Henry VIII 'loved him like his own soule' and made him Knight of the Garter, Duke of Richmond and of Somerset, and, then having no legitimate male offspring, obviously intended him for the throne. When the lad died, however, at the age of seventeen, he was already out of favour with his father and was buried at Framlingham with no pomp or ceremony.

This is an astonishing collection of fine Renaissance stone carving to find in a tiny and remote English township. Only at Fotheringhay, in Northamptonshire, can we see anything comparable. The church still has its eighteenth-century reredos—a rare survival.

The castle is best seen for the first time from a distance, preferably from the Dennington Road, across the flat vale of the Ore. It stands proudly on its hill, one of the most impressive military buildings in England, and certainly the most impressive in East Anglia.

Alas, when you get inside there is not much there. There is the 'Poor House', built up against the great shell of the castle on the west side. This is a fine enough hall, the south wing of it 1636 and the centre early eighteenth century. Three of the west windows are left from the medieval hall on the site of which the Poor House was built. The hall is now being restored by the Ministry of Works, and will, it is hoped, be used as a museum. There are traces, and traces only, up against the inside of the east curtain wall, of the Bigods' hall and their chapel (although what such hell-raking fellows as the Bigods wanted with a chapel is hard to see—their *prison* still exists, stuck outside the castle on a limb to the west, well out of earshot of the noble owners). But the great curtain wall with its thirteen towers is most of what there is to see.

Framlingham was one of the first fortresses in England built thus as a curtain wall, instead of with a predominant keep, as at Orford. The tower-studded curtain wall idea came to England with the returning Crusaders, copied from the castles of the Saracens. One must imagine the castle extending southwards with an inner bailey (a pond, on which swim muscovy ducks of a piercing ugliness, opposite the Castle Inn, may be where the moat once was), and an outer bailey comprising most of what is now the town of Framlingham. It was a tremendous fortification, one of the strongest in Europe.

We may wonder where all this enormous quantity of stone came from, in this stoneless country. The answer is it all came up the Ore in boats (anchors have been dug out of the mud beside the now-tiny trickle of a stream), and it came from Barnack in Northamptonshire. It is oolitic limestone, of the sort that made houses from the Cots-wolds to Lincolnshire, and it all came by sea.

The most rewarding thing to do is to climb up to the 'wall walk', which runs right round the curtain wall, and admire the view. From here you can gaze over the little red-roofed town to the southward, and the elm and oak hedged fields of heavy-land Suffolk in other directions. It is not difficult, while standing up there in the wind, to imagine Suffolk as it was when the castle was first built: a great forest in which men were only beginning to hack for themselves clearings to live in.

53

It would not be too absurd to say that the history of Framlingham reflects every stage of the history of England, at least up until the Industrial Revolution which one must admit has not impinged upon it much, excepting in so far as the Ministry of Works is one of the results of that cataclysm.

The first post-Conquest owners, the Bigods, were a desperate lot of fellows. We get the impression that their contract with the English people around them was very simple: 'If you give us what we want we won't beat you up!' On the other hand a reading of the Anglo-Saxon Chronicle makes us realize that by that time the English people were probably only too anxious to give anybody anything if only they could be protected from the Danes. As for the Bigods' relations with their kings, these left a lot to be desired.

The second Bigod (his elder brother was drowned in the White Ship) was created Earl of Norfolk or of the East Angles by the king, presumably to keep him quiet. But he helped Stephen usurp the crown from Princess Maud, or Matilda, then spent much of his life intriguing against Stephen. He supported Henry II against Stephen, then rebelled against Henry II. He harboured Robert de Beaumont, Earl of Leicester, and his Flemish troops, when these landed on the East Anglian coast, helped them to attack Orford (unsuccessfully), and when Leicester was captured Bigod took refuge in Framlingham, defended it against the king, but finally had to surrender it. It was then that, according to William Camden (b.1551), he shouted down from the castle wall: 'Were I in my castle of Bungay, upon the waters of Waveneye, I would ne care for the King of Cockneye!'

But he wasn't, and he had to care, and his castle was dismantled by Alnoth the Engineer (the man who built Orford Castle), at the cost of £14 15s 11d. What is surprising is that Henry did not have Bigod dismantled too.

Hugh died in 1178, and his son Roger re-fortified the castle. He entertained King John in it, but later was prominent among the barons in forcing the king to sign Magna Carta. Afterwards, however, the king had his revenge by attacking Framlingham, in 1215, and reducing it once more.

Roger, the 4th Earl, defied Henry III and actually challenged him to try and take Framlingham but the king declined. The 5th Earl, also a Roger (and the nephew of the 4th Earl) was ordered by Edward I to serve with his army abroad. It is recorded that the king said to him: 'By the eternal God you shall march or be hanged!'

to which he answered: 'By the eternal God I shall neither march nor be hanged!' And he neither marched nor was hanged. But he was the last of a turbulent race: he died without heir and left the castle to the king (it has been said merely to prevent his own brother from getting it).

The Mowbrays were also a turbulent lot. The first (1st Duke of Norfolk) died in exile, the third was beheaded, together with Richard Scrope, Archbishop of York, for intriguing against the king. The fourth left the castle to Lady Anne Mowbray, who was married, at the tender age of *three* (some say four), to the five (some say four-and-a-half-) year old Duke of York, who was later one of the princes to be murdered in the Tower. Little Anne died in 1481 when she was eleven: her husband was murdered a few years later. In January 1965 a small lead coffin was dug up from a building site in Stepney and was found to contain her remains. The site was once occupied by a nunnery of the Order of St Clare (the Minories), and Anne's coffin had been moved to there from Westminster Abbey to make way for the Henry VII Chapel. She was returned to her former grave in the Abbey (after her bones had been examined by radiologists, osteologists and dentists).

Of the Howard family, John was killed at Bosworth Field, Thomas, as we have seen, led the English at Flodden, the 3rd Duke gave his niece (Catherine Howard) in marriage to Henry VIII, she was executed and he would have been executed himself, as we have seen, had the king not died the day before this was due to happen.

Queen Mary came to Framlingham after the death of her brother Edward VI and raised her standard against the supporters of Lady Jane Grey, and to her came a great army from the countryside: 13,000 armed men. It was then that she was said to have kept a lookout across the forests to Orford Castle, so as to be informed about shipping, not knowing whether she was to keep her crown or have to flee the country. Unfortunately for nearly everybody she became queen (the Earl of Arundel came riding up to the castle gate to inform her that her rights as Queen of England were established) and she set about exterminating as many as she could of the people who did not agree with her. There was a nasty rumour (put about by Protestants?) that, while waiting in the castle, she gave birth to a baby, but that it was a monster, and she killed it by bashing out its brains against the castle walls.

Thomas, the son of the poet Earl of Surrey, was also executed—

but this time by Elizabeth I. His son, too, Philip, Earl of Arundel, was sentenced to death for praying for the success of the Armada, and he died in the Tower.

After this Framlingham retired from its turbulent place on the stage of history. In Elizabeth's reign it was used as a prison for recusants, and when Sir Robert the lawyer left it to Pembroke College he did so on condition that they built a Poor House in it, and this still exists.

Perhaps it is fitting that the last use of this mighty building should have been that of sheltering the poor. For centuries it sheltered people who tyrannized the poor. And perhaps, as we stand on its walls, we should shift our thoughts from the nobles who postured and intrigued and glorified themselves within the gates, and think of the real East Anglians without, who were busy through the centuries hacking their way into the forests with their soft iron axes, pit-sawing the hard oak to build houses and ships, ploughing the land which is the support of all human life.

Let us go north to **Dennington**, which must have been something of a suburb to the metropolitan grandeur of Framlingham.

This church is supposed to have been erected on the site of a 'Druidical Temple' on an ancient Way that ran north and south through the forests. Whether or no, it is a superb church, with some of the finest wood carving in the country: the bench-ends are justly famous, there is a seventeenth-century three-decker pulpit, a pyx canopy over the altar (made of one piece of wood in the early sixteenth century), superb parclose screens forming the south and north chapels—these are infinitely worth looking at. The south chapel is the Bardolph Chapel, or chantry. Here is Lord Bardolph's tomb (which was cleaned not long ago and revealed to be of ala-baster: it had been painted to make it look like stone). The sarcophagus and effigies are very beautiful: the latter more so, perhaps, than any of the effigies of Framlingham. Lord Bardolph was one of the 'happy few' who fought with Henry V at Agincourt. There is a sciapod carved on a bench-end in this church (south side of centre aisle) said to be the only one in England. The sciapod had one great foot which it held over its head for shade against the African sun. Pliny records that these creatures were 'great leap-ers'.

But no list of contents can give any idea of the gracious beauty of this church, when you enter it, and of its lightness and sense of well

3. Cratfield, Suffolk

4. Part of the great 14th century retable in the tiny thatched church of Thornham Parva, which stands apparently lost in the muddy fields

enclosed and well formed space. This is one of the churches that even the architecturally incurious should not miss.

Saxtead Green, west of Framlingham, has a beautifully restored post windmill which one is allowed to visit because, like Framlingham Castle, it is controlled by the Ministry of Works. (There is a larger and better post mill at Friston, alas, being allowed to fall into decay because nobody can be bothered to look after it.)

North of Dennington Laxfield, Heveningham and Cratfield are well worth visiting. At **Laxfield** a 'simple unlearned man', a shoe-maker named John Noyes, was burned at the stake in Bloody Mary's reign. He was taken before the Bishop of Norwich, refused to recant, taken back to Laxfield and there burnt. His neighbours, on the day, doused all their household fires, save one man, and his door was burst open and fire obtained. Noyes kissed the burning faggot before it was applied to the heap of incendiary material among which he stood, and his last words to his neighbours were: 'They say they can make God of a piece of bread—believe them not!'

As much to Laxfield's discredit as Noyes was to its credit was that other native son, 'Smasher' Dowsing. William Dowsing was employed under the egregious Earl of Manchester, during the Commonwealth, 'for the defacing, demolishing, and quite taking away of all images, altars, or tables turned altar-wise, crucifixes, superstitious pictures, monuments, and reliques of idolatry, out of all churches and chapels'. He is damned by his diaries, for he left copious accounts of his works of vandalism: hardly a church in Suffolk but suffered at his hands, and acres of medieval stained glass ('superstitious pictures') are lost to us for ever. There was a Dowsing among the men who burned John Noyes: was he an ancestor of William? There is still a Dowsings' Farm in the parish.

But before we condemn such men outright we should remember that they were activated, not by mere lust for destruction, but by intense religious fervour. To us the stone carving and the stained glass would have been priceless and irreplaceable works of art: to Dowsing and his friends they were works of idolatry that stood between Man and God. Dowsing went to work with his hammer in the spirit of those other East Anglians who charged the enemy at Marston Moor and at Naseby with the psalm rolling from their lips.

Heveningham Hall, recently opened to the public, was built by Sir Gerald Vanneck, to replace a Queen Anne house already existing on the site. Sir Robert Taylor, King George III's architect, designed it, in a fine and magnificent Palladian style, James Wyatt did the interior, and 'Capability' Brown the gardens in 1781-2. Wyatt designed the interior 'after' Robert Adam, and his grand entrance hall has been called the finest neo-classical room in England. He also designed the famous Orangery. The dining-room was burnt out in 1949, but was restored to the original plans which were still in existence. This is one of the most beautiful—and liveable-in—big houses in East Anglia, and to visit it is like a dip into time to the eighteenth century.

Cratfield is interesting in that its parish accounts are very complete and in a fine state of preservation for as far back as 1490. Religion was apparently a much merrier affair in those days: frequent mention is made of 'church ales', or *potationes ecclesiasticae.* Such days occurred on Passion Sunday, Pentecost, All Saints' Day, Plough Monday and the Fourth Sunday in Lent, which still is sometimes called 'Refreshment Sunday'. On top of this, numerous legacies made provision for the purchase of ale for 'church ales' on other, non-official days. Seven and sixpence seems to have been a fairly usual sum for the provision of a 'church ale', and we can suppose that in those days that would have bought a very decent amount of beer. For the 10th of October 1553 expenses are listed for providing one soldier to help guard Princess Mary at Framlingham Castle, and most of the expenses for this come under the heading or 'Drinke', although there was also a firkin of butter which cost a shilling. At Armada time 23s 7d is charged for the expenses of 'trayned sougers'.

Stradbroke is a pretty little place—a large village. A small art gallery has recently been opened there, there is a fine arbutus in the churchyard and a magnificent weathercock on top of the church tower.

Fressingfield is the place to eat if you like superb food and can pay for it. The Fox and Goose Inn, to the south of the church, is famous over England among gourmets, but it pays to book a day or two ahead, and specify what you want to eat. People come from as far as Yorkshire to Fressingfield—just for the *eating*. The inn building was the old guildhall, and has fine timbering. The church is one of the finest-looking small churches in Suffolk, both within and without. There is an array of superb fifteenth-century bench-ends— perhaps the best collection in England—all unstained oak, and the marvellous hammerbeam roof is of unstained oak too. Look in the

eastern arch of the south arcade for the remains of the block and
girder of the *rotula*, a ring of light which used to hang before the
Rood. The initials 'A.P.' on a bench are those of Alice de la Pole,
grand-daughter of the poet Chaucer. Prince Edward, later King
Edward I, came hunting here once and fell in love with one 'Fair
Margaret'. He left her in the tender care of the Earl of Lincoln, who
cared for her so well that he married her himself.

At **Worlingworth** is a great font cover, which was formerly in the
Abbey Church of Bury St Edmunds, before this was pulled down.

At **Hoxne** (pronounced *hoxen*) legend stubbornly holds that King
Edmund was slaughtered by the Danes. There is still a plaque in a
building beside Goldbrook Bridge, which conveys the information
that Edmund was discovered hiding beneath the bridge (presumably
not the ugly structure we have here now)—given away by a pair of
lovers who saw the glint of his golden spurs. The best account of this
tale that will ever be is recorded in his book *Suffolk Scene*, by the
late Julian Tennyson as from the mouth of a Hoxne roadman; but
readings from the Anglo-Saxon Chronicle, Abbot of Fleury, and
other sources, convey the following story, less colourful than the
roadman's although no less packed with action:

In AD 869 and 870 Hinvar and Ubba and twenty thousand Danes
laid waste Bardney, Crowland, Thorney, Peterborough, Ramsey,
Ely, Stuntney and Thetford. Hinvar sent a message to the young
King Edmund telling him to submit but Edmund refused to do so, in
spite of the advice of his Bishop Humbert. The Danes attacked,
Edmund fled, was eventually found hiding under a bridge given
away by his spurs, was offered his life if he renounced Christianity,
refused, and was killed. Days later a voice was heard coming from
his dismembered head crying: 'Here! Here! Here!' A friendly wolf
was found guarding the head, which was retrieved, and became the
chief relic of Bury Abbey. For half a century following this East
Anglia was completely under the heel of the Danes, and not until 918
did Edward the Elder (King Alfred's son) drive them out.

Hoxne Church, incidentally, is dedicated to St Aethelbert, as is
Hereford Cathedral. Aethelbert was an East Anglian prince who
was murdered in Herefordshire when he went there with the intention of marrying Offa's daughter. The pleasantest thing now about
Hoxne is its churchyard, a deliciously unkempt jungle of huge
cedars, yews, and other trees and shrubs, some of them overturning
with their roots the Victorian tombstones. Inside the church are old

bench-ends, one of them of St Edmund's head being carried by the wolf, and there are interesting murals of the Seven Deadly Sins with the sinners, nicely labelled, being eaten by dragons growing out of a tree; and of the Works of Mercy: clothing the naked, giving drink to the thirsty, visiting prisoners, feeding the hungry, visiting the sick and burying the dead. The tower of the church is very grand. In 1797 John Frere discovered Acheulian hand axes in this parish.

Wingfield should be walked to, from Hoxne, for this is a most delicious walk and it is a crime to travel the distance in a motor car. Wingfield has a castle, but you cannot go into it unless you know the owner, for it is a private house. Not much can be seen from the road, save a good brick and timber-framed Tudor house joined to the outer front and gatehouse of a castle and a large notice saying 'No Admittance'.

William atte Pool founded the city of Kingston upon Hull (where he set up as a merchant) in the reign of Edward I. He is thought not to have been of Norman stock, but he came from the Continent. His grandson, Michael, came to Suffolk and married Katherine Wingfield of Wingfield. The Wingfields were an Anglian family:

> *Wynkefelde the Saxon held Honor and Fee*
> *Ere William the Norman came over the sea.*

Michael was created Earl of Suffolk in 1385. His grandson, also Michael, fell at Agincourt, as Shakespeare observes:

> *Where is the number of our English dead?*
> *Edward the Duke of York, the Earl of Suffolk,*
> *Sir Richard Ketly, David Gam, esquire;*
> *None else of name; and of all other men*
> *But five and twenty.*

and rumour has it that he lies buried in a silver coffin at Butley. This Michael's brother married Alice, daughter of Thomas Chaucer and widow of the Earl of Salisbury.

The de la Poles were a boisterous lot, rather like the Bigods. Michael, the First Earl, who built the castle, had to flee to Paris on one occasion disguised as a poulterer, Michael the second died of a fever at Harfleur, and his eldest son fell at Agincourt. William led the English against Joan of Arc at Orleans, and then came very near to having supreme power in England. He did this by arranging the marriage of Henry VI to Margaret of Anjou, having captured that lady at Orleans. Then, with the help of the queen (who was almost certainly his mistress) he became the power behind a very weak throne. Shakespeare makes him say (in *Henry VI*):

> *Margaret shall now be queen, and rule the King;*
> *But I will rule both her, and King, and realm.*

He overreached himself, principally by arranging for the murder of the virtuous Duke of Gloucester near Bury while Parliament was meeting there, and he was impeached and banished to France. While on his way there his boat was arrested at Dover, and he was taken ashore and beheaded over the gunwale of a boat. Shakespeare makes the sea-captain who commanded his death say:

> *Pole! Sir Pole! Lord!*
> *Ay, kennel, puddle, sink; whose filth and dirt*
> *Troubles the silver spring where England drinks.*
> *Now will I dam up this yawning mouth*
> *For swallowing the treasure of the realm:*
> *Thy lips, that kissed the queen, shall sweep the ground . . .*

All of which seems a long way from the sleepy little village of Wingfield today.

Wingfield Church you are allowed to look at, and it is fine. It stands on the edge of a little valley, overlooking rolling heavy-land country, and there is a mounting-block before it, and a parson's shelter within (to shelter the parson at funerals, while his flock took what weather was coming to them). There is a monument to Sir John Wingfield in the wonderfully medieval-looking north chapel, which was built in the middle of the fourteenth century when Sir John was founding a college here and this church was the collegiate church. The south chapel, which is fine indeed, was built by Michael, the 2nd Earl, who died in 1415 and contains his magnificent monument. Note among the lavish decorations the *wings* of the East Anglian Wingfields, the *leopard heads* of the de la Poles, and the *knots* of the Staffords, to whom the family was joined by marriage.

Just to the south of the church is College Farm, a lovely house of the mid-eighteenth century, on the site of the old college. Opposite the church is a perfect pub, unspoiled, simple, truly rural, and hospitable.

Eye is an absolutely lovely little town. Pevsner calls the tower of the church 'one of the wonders of Suffolk', and so it is, 101 feet of

Companion Guide to East Anglia

marvellous flush-work. Approach from the Stradbroke direction and
you get a shock of surprise and beauty as you suddenly see the
church, and the Norman castle on its high steep little hill beyond it,
and then discover the early sixteenth-century guildhall. Then
you come into the fine little town with its ancient houses and maze
of streets, its Victorian town hall (really a corker!) and its ancient
pubs. Remains of a priory can be seen in a farmyard not far from the
church. The castle was built by William Mallet of Graville, Normandy, one of the Conqueror's trustiest men at Hastings. He died
later fighting against Hereward the Wake. Go inside the church and
see the rood screen with its triple cornice. The loft and rood are
1925: the screen is medieval and has, reading from the north, St
Paul, St Helen, St Edmund, St Ursula concealing virgins under her
cloak, Henry VI, St Dorothy with roses, St Barbara with tower,
St Agnes with sword at throat and lamb, Edward the Confessor,
St John, Catherine and wheel, William of Norwich with cross and
nails (but read *A Saint at Stake* by M. D. Anderson, which is about
this doubtful martyr), St Lucy with eyes on book, St Blaise (patron
saint of wool combers), St Cecilia with sword in throat and roses at
waist, and an effaced saint thought to be Peter. In the porch of the
church, south wall, is a dole table, on which loans of money were
made, and a nice verse of 1601 of advice to lenders.

In the north of Eye there is an exuberant fish and chip shop,
tricked out like a smuggler's cave. Opposite is a crinkle-crankle wall:
that kind of brick wall peculiar to Suffolk which is built in waves, or
corrugations.

Out in the woolly back-block to the west are the Thornhams,
Magna and Parva.

Both of these parishes contain much thatch, and very good too,
and very much signed by the thatcher, Mr Fuller of Gisleham. The
White Horse Inn is half in Thornham Magna and half in Stoke
Ash, so that the landlord pulls his beer from the latter parish and
sells it in the former. This inn, incidentally, serves food and is a good
lorry drivers' pull-in (and good for any other kind of driver, too, for
the matter of that).

In **Thornham Magna** were the Killigrews. James was a sea-
captain, and killed in an engagement with the French off Sardinia.
Thomas was in exile with Charles II and was ordered to leave
Venice because he was too debauched even for that place. After the
Restoration he founded Drury Lane Theatre and wrote indecent

plays while Lady Shannon, née Killigrew, bore Charles II a child. At Thornham Magna Church Peals of Minor on six bells of 10,080 changes were rung in 1928.

Thornham Parva has a most famous retable in its church. The latter is a tiny thatched building standing out in the middle of a field, and it is often locked to protect its most valuable content.

The retable is of *circa* 1300 in framing of the same date. The figures on it are said by Munro Cautley to be, from the north: St Dominic, St Catherine, St John the Baptist, St Peter, the Crucifixion with the B.V.M. on the left of the Cross and St John the Evangelist on the right, St Paul, St Edmund, St Margaret of Antioch and St Peter Martyr in the robes of a Dominican and with his scimitar lodged in his throat. But the painting, against good gesso work, is superb, the figures all slender and willowy and with graceful drapery—inspired by the very spirit of the Middle Ages. It is an astonishing experience to come across this great work of art out in the middle of a muddy Suffolk field. The retable was discovered, incidentally, in the stable of Lord Henniker among a load of junk which he had just bought from Rookery Farm, Stradbroke, a farm which had for long been occupied by Catholics. It still has an auctioneer's label stuck on it which reads *Second Day Lot* 171. This church also has wall paintings and is well worth going to see.

Wetheringsett, south-east across the Norwich-Ipswich Road, is notable for two of its past parsons.

One was Richard Hakluyt, who was Rector from 1590 to 1616, and he wrote *Principall Navigations, Voiages, Traffiques and Discoveries of the English Nation*, a book of endless fascination.

The other was not really a parson at all. He was George Wilfrid Ellis, first a tailor of Brighton, then butler to a bishop, and then bogus clerk in holy orders and incumbent of Wetheringsett from 1858 to 1883. He was industrious and very popular, but alas he was unmasked. A special Act of Parliament had to be passed to validate the marriages that he had solemnized for many were the respectable citizens of Wetheringsett who discovered that they had, all unknowingly, been born 'the wrong side of the blanket'.

CHAPTER 4

Ipswich, Stowmarket

Ipswich is a town of great antiquity and historic interest, but, alas, practically nothing remains to show for either. The Ipswichians seem to have made a decision in the past, and to have kept to it most assiduously, to erase every building of antique beauty and interest, and to turn Ipswich into, at every succeeding period, a 'modern' town. Unfortunately the search for 'modernity' is ever doomed to failure, for what is modern in one decade is horribly dated in the next. Thus Cornhill, the heart of the town, is a hugger-mugger of derivative styles, all started in 1812 when the ancient Moot Hall and the two hundred year old Market Cross were pulled down. There are mock-Gothic, mock-Renaissance, mock-Italianate, mock-Classical. At least now Ipswich seems to have turned its back on these imitations of former glories and much resolutely 'contemporary' building is going up. The new Civic College, in the old demolished Rope Walk (which used to be a slum area of wonderful liveliness) is a fine slab of glass and concrete. The Ipswich Hospital, at the top of Berner Street, is itself not a building of notable beauty but the new boiler house and cooler tower designed by Peter Barefoot are very spirited, and deservedly won the RIBA's bronze medal for 1960–63. Fison's office building, down by the station, is something of a *tour de force*: its occupants sit up in a great glass case on show like canaries and so slender are the concrete Vs which hold it up that one wonders why the whole edifice does not collapse at the first puff of wind. The glass engravings by John Hutton on the downstairs walls are very effective.

Another new building is the office of the *East Anglian Daily Times* in Lower Brook Street, which is decorated with terra-cotta arabesques. (This might be the place to say that East Anglia is better served than any other rural area in England with provincial newspapers: both the

East Anglian Daily Times of Ipswich, and the *Eastern Daily Press* of Norwich, are models of regional journalism; together they help greatly to create a climate of cultural autonomy in East Anglia.)

Much new building, too, is going up in the large area of slum clearance going on south-east of Cornhill—in particular the Underground Spiral Car Park, which is a gigantic affair and should be visited by all car park lovers. This was the first of its kind in this country, 180 feet in diameter and 46 feet deep with an entirely new method of concrete construction. Hard by is the new Civic Centre, and the Civic Drive.

But of ancient buildings in Ipswich, of the tiny scattering that there are left it can only be said that they are still there because nobody has yet got round to the business of pulling them down. As late as 1960 the old Half Moon Inn, which had a marvellous carved corner-post depicting a friar in fox's clothing preaching to geese, and which itself was pre-Elizabethan building and of great beauty, was ruthlessly bull-dozed. It was not in the way and so far nothing has been put in its place. It was old, that is all.

Ipswich is situated at a point which could not help but be the site of an important settlement, in very early times as at the present day. The River Orwell, which leads up to it, is the one easily navigable river in Suffolk: ships can enter or leave at any state of the tide or set of the wind. The site of Ipswich is at the limit of navigability of this river, and also at the lowest possible ford. Thus any road going from the south to the east of East Anglia perforce went through Ipswich, and any merchandise bound in or out of the hinterland could more conveniently be embarked or disembarked at Ipswich than at any other place: here sea-borne vessels were able to penetrate deep inland.

The Vikings found the place of great use to them. In 991 Olaf landed at Ipswich from ninety-three ships, overran the town, and then went off to fight and win the famous Battle of Maldon. In 1010, according to the Anglo-Saxon Chronicle:

... the army (Danes) came to East Anglia after Easter and landed at Ipswich, and went straightway to where they had heard that Ulfcetel was with his army. That was on Ascension Day and at once the East Angles fled. The men of Cambridgeshire stood firm against them. The king's son Athelstan was killed there, and Oswig and his son, and Wulfric, Leofrine's son, and Eadwig, Aefic's brother, and many other good thegns and a countless number of the people ... The Danes had control of the field, and they were provided with horses and afterwards had control of East Anglia, and ravaged and burnt the country for three months and even went into the wild fens; and there they burnt down Thetford and Cambridge.

The place where the battle was fought on Ascension Day was Ringmere Heath, over in the Breckland country.

By Domesday there were 110 burgesses and a hundred 'poor men' in Ipswich. In the Middle Ages a great area of woollen industry around Lavenham. By Henry VIII's reign it was a very important town, and would have become more important still had it not been for the downfall of Wolsey.

Wolsey was an Ipswich man, and he spent his boyhood next door to where now stands that seedy-looking building, the old Hippodrome, now given over to Bingo. His father was a butcher, grazier and cloth merchant, and he owned an inn and was fined for allowing it to become a resort of 'friars and women of loose character' and also for selling beer at excessive prices. He was, nonetheless, a churchwarden.

Wolsey, in his hour of greatness, planned a great college at Ipswich, a College of Secular Canons. He began the buildings in Black Friar's Street, and incorporated the already existing Ipswich School. On his downfall the college crashed too, and all that is left of it is a brick gateway; but the school was re-incorporated by Henry VIII, ratified by Elizabeth I, and is now up in Henley Road, in a vast brick building put up in Victorian times but Elizabethan regardless.

Henry VIII once stayed in Ipswich, as the guest of a nobleman in Silent Street, and he attended Mass at the Our Lady of Grace Chapel in what is still called Lady Lane. This was a place of national pilgrimage, but at the Dissolution Henry VIII had it pulled down, and the effigy was burnt in London.

After Elizabeth Ipswich waxed strong as a shipping town, and by the seventeenth century had captured most of the coal trade between the north and London. Defoe, in his *Particular and Diverting Account of whatever is Curious and worthy Observation*, says that Ipswich-built colliers were 'so prodigious strong that they would reign forty or fifty years or more'. These ships were laid up all winter in Defoe's time, their topmasts struck, and they lay at moorings in the Orwell: 'as safe as in a wet dock, and it was a very agreeable sight to see perhaps 200 sail of ships of all sizes lie in that posture every winter All this while . . . the masters lived calm and secure with their families in Ipswich, and enjoying plentifully what in the summer they had got laboriously at sea, and this made the town of Ipswich a very populous place in the winter, for as the masters so most of the men, especially their mates, boatswains, carpenters, etc., were of the same place and lived in their proportions, just as the masters did, so that in the winter there might be perhaps a thousand men in the town more than in the summer, and perhaps a greater number.' But by 1720 Defoe saw a great falling-away: 'It was melancholy to hear that there were now scarce 40 sail of good colliers that belonged to the whole town.'

It was Dutch ships that were, then as now, helping to knock out native English coastal shipping. As you roam around Ipswich docks now you will see Dutch, German and Belgian ships aplenty, and but a few English ones. The Wet Dock was built in 1839–42 by seventy-two gentlemen who constituted themselves as the River Commissioners, and was, when it was built, quite revolutionary and the biggest wet dock in the country. If you walk farther down the river you will come to berths for much bigger ships, unloading at Fison's big fertilizer factory, or the big modern power station. For the Port of Ipswich is expanding by building more tidal berths for bigger ships outside the old Wet Dock area.

Ipswich lost the coastal coal trade completely, to the rising County Durham and Northumberland ship-owning interests, but in the times of the big sailing ships it became an important port of entry for these, the very biggest having to lie at Butterman's Bay, down the river, and lighter themselves into sailing barges before proceeding up to the Wet Dock. Ipswich also became one of the biggest of the sailing barge ports, the big mills, Cranfields and Pauls, owning large fleets. The Industrial Revolution brought heavy industry, in the form of engineering works, boiler-makers, plough-makers and agricultural machinery makers: Ransomes, Sims and Jefferies still make farming machinery and Ransome and Rapier make cranes, and hydraulic machinery. You will see the name of Ipswich on the sluice gates of the mile-long Lloyd Barrage over the Indus in Pakistan, and on many other hydraulic works under a foreign sun. The first lawn mower was made at Ipswich (this would be disputed by the citizens of Stroud, Gloucestershire), printing started in 1548 (with John Bale's *Summary of the Illustrious Writers of Great Britain*) and W. S. Cowell Ltd. still carry on printing just off the Buttermarket, and are one of the best printers in Britain.

As for what there is to see today in Ipswich for the sightseer the story is soon told.

Old Ipswich was a timber-built town, but very few good timber-frame houses remain today. In Oak Lane, north of Tavern Street, is the old Royal Oak Inn, now offices, which has fine timber framing and Renaissance carving on its angle-posts—one of them depicting a smith at his anvil. South of this is the Great White House, in which Mr Pickwick had many of his adventures, and it is still a very good inn, and so is the Crown and Anchor in Westgate Street. The latter has an undistinguished modern front but old building of some charm inside.

The **Ancient House**, in the Buttermarket, is the pride of Ipswich. This was the home of the Sparrowe family for 200 years: merchants and grocers. They were staunch Royalists in the Civil War period (unusual for East Anglians) and there is a yarn, which must be quite untrue, of course, that Charles II slept in the Ancient House. Charles II certainly hid around, as Elizabeth I slept, but he certainly did not hide here, although recently a secret chamber was discovered upstairs.

This house is fifteenth century, but the amazing pargetting, or plaster moulding, on the exterior is Restoration. This pargetting symbolizes the four continents (the others had not been discovered at that time) and at one corner is depicted a scene from the 1st Eclogue of Virgil: the shepherd Tityrus sleeping under a tree. This is a building of great interest and beauty, which has had a vast and hideous red-brick cinema built right up against it. The Ancient House now houses a good book shop, and one is allowed to inspect the building. There is a great Elizabethan picture of Hercules on the staircase.

Skirting **the docks** are still some old buildings: warehouse-cum-dwelling houses, such as No. 80 Fore Street and the nearby Old Neptune Inn (an inn no longer). These buildings had their backs to the river, for the unloading of merchandise, had store rooms and also living accommodation within (accommodation for apprentices as well as the master and his family) and withal a shop in front on the street. These merchants engaged in all forms of trade, importing goods from other countries in bulk, and selling it in pennyworths over the counter in the shop. It is interesting to compare these warehouses with those at King's Lynn.

Fore Street, in fact, has a busy, lorry-bustling charm. College Street, near it, still has Cardinal Wolsey's gate: Tudor brick on which the arms of Henry VIII can be seen. The Customs House, by the Wet Dock, is famous. It is of 1843–4, designed by J. M. Clark, a local man.

Of churches, Ipswich is in a county of fine churches (probably we can say *the* county) but itself has little of interest to offer. St Margaret's is Decorated and very beautiful; St Mary-le-Tower, the civic church, was hideously restored in 1860, nay rebuilt; St Mary at the Elms has a Norman south doorway and an early Tudor brick tower and has charm.

Perhaps the most interesting and unusual place of worship in Ipswich is the **Old Meeting House** in Friar's Street. This was built in 1699 by Joseph Clarke, who was a house carpenter, and is of wood. Without windows and inside furnishings the building cost £257, which also had to pay for 'four barrels of good small beers for to drink while imployed in said building', those early Presbyterians evidently not objecting to liquor—at least for their workmen. At the end of the eighteenth century the congregation turned to Unitarianism and the Meeting House became Unitarian, which it still is. Inside are four great wooden pillars always said to have been ships' masts, a candelabrum, thought to be Dutch and seventeenth century, which weighs 200 pounds, very fine and solid box pews, all original, with some 'wig pews' in the galleries. There is a spy-hole in the door facing St Nicholas Street through which a watch could be kept for the Trinitarian mob in troubled times, and there is a sumptuous pulpit carved—if not by Grinling Gibbons himself—at least by his pupils. Defoe praised the building in 1720.

There are two museums in Ipswich. One in a Victorian brick building at the top of High Street, the **Ipswich Museum**, and it has the best collection in the world of fossils from the Crag (which it should have, for this deposit is a Suffolk speciality), very sound archaeological collections, and is one of the best museums for Early Paleolithic material in England. Much important research has been carried out by the staff of the museum (Basil Brown, of Sutton Hoo fame, only recently retired from the staff). Don't be put off by the antique show-cases and general air of lack of money. In this extremely wealthy county borough this museum suffers terribly from lack of funds.

A former curator was notable for the fact that he used to keep his bottled beer in the belly of the stuffed rhino.

The other museum is **Christchurch Mansion**, in the middle of a beautiful park. It has thirty-six rooms, all full of interest.

The house is on the site of an Augustinian priory. The latter was suppressed in 1537; the king had the lead taken off the roof and sold the house to a man named Sir Thomas Pope; this man sold it at a profit to a London merchant, Paul Withipoll, who wanted it for his son Edmund, who was having to get out of his house in Walthamstow because he had killed a French man-servant in a brawl. Edmund built the beginnings of the present house. Queen Elizabeth visited him twice.

In 1642 the house passed by marriage to the Hereford family and belonged to the Herefords until sold to Zachary Fonnereau, a Huguenot refugee. The Fonnereaus built many more rooms on to it. In 1892 they sold it and (this being Ipswich) it was immediately proposed to pull it down and to turn the surrounding parkland (one of the most beautiful parks in the country) into a housing estate. However, in the nick of time one of the brewing Cobbold family intervened, bought it, and most magnificently gave the money to start the present excellent collection. It is perhaps the one thing that really makes the visit to Ipswich worth while.

The museum contains good collections of domestic furniture of various periods: the kitchen is particularly interesting. There is much carved woodwork from the many ancient houses that have been pulled down recently in Ipswich, and a most rare twelfth-century font of black Tournai marble. Two fine brasses from the bombed-out church of St Mary-at-the-Quay are noteworthy (particularly the brass to Thomas Pounder and his family), there are Fitzgerald relics, and a most interesting collection of Margaret Catchpole relics—including handbills for her recapture after she had escaped from prison, letters home (very illiterate and not at all like the letters made up by the Reverend Cobbold in his book about her) and the *stuffed lyre bird* that she sent home to her old mistress, Mrs Cobbold, from Van Diemen's Land. There is the sword of Tipoo Sultan captured by the Suffolks when they stormed the fort of Seringapatam in 1799, to rescue British officers immured there, and some fine ship models—including those beautiful ones made of bone by French prisoners of war in Napoleonic times. There is a panelled and painted room, Elizabethan, from Hawstead Place. There are many Elizabethan wall paintings, and a most interesting panorama of Ipswich, with giant cabbages in the foreground, in the eighteenth century, by James Cleverly.

Most early writers praised Ipswich. Tusser likened it to Paradise, no less. Cobbett said: 'Fine, populous, beautiful, substantially built, well paved, everything good and solid, no wretched buildings to be seen on its outskirts.' From one point near it he could see the spinning sails of seventeen windmills. He noted that in 1830 wheat was 6s a quarter more in Ipswich than it was in Norwich, simply because Ipswich was a safe sail in any weather away from London and therefore it was cheaper to carry wheat there. Now Ipswich, this capital of England's chief wheat-growing area, imports more wheat than she exports.

Great energy and prosperity in Victorian times wiped away old Ipswich, and the town as it is is largely Victorian. But vast twentieth-century suburbs are spreading in nearly every direction from it and the Planners are threatening to double its population in the next few decades. It is to become a mere limb of London. Foxhall quarry, east of the town, is a classic site for the Palaeolithic, and in **Belstead**,

Newbell's Farm • Gipping • Saxstead Green •
Haughley • DEBENHAM • Crows Hall • FRAMLINGHAM
STOWMARKET • Little Stonham • Mickfield • Brandeston • Kettleburgh
Pains Hill • Stonham Aspal • Cretingham • Hoo • Easton
Earl Stonham • Angel Hill • A1120 • Helmingham • Monewden
Combs • Coddenham • Otley • Dallinghoo
NEEDHAM MARKET • Shrubland Park • Barham • Grundisburgh • Ufford
Offton • Claydan • B1077 • B1079 • Melton
Somersham • Westerfield • WOODBRIDGE
Aldham • Christ Church Park • Kesgrave
Hall • Hintlesham • IPSWICH • A12
Washbrook • Orwell Park • Nacton • Levington
Little Wenham Hall • Freston • Wolverstone • Hall • Broke Hall
Tattingstone • Hall • Pinmill • RIVER ORWELL
East Bergholt • Holbrook Royal Hosp. School • Brantham
Stratford St Mary • Valley Farm • Hall • Erwarton • Walton • FELIXSTOWE
Dedham • Flatford Mill • Cattawade • Xylonite Works • Shotley Gate • Bloody Pt.
MANNINGTREE • Mistley • RIVER STOUR • HARWICH • Landguard Fort • Landguard Point
A137 • B1352 • Ramsey
Little Bromley • A604 • A136
Great Bromley • Great Oakley • Pennyhole Bay

0 miles 4

south, Mr Malcolm Tricker recently unearthed five early Iron Age torques, or gold collars, with an excavator. They are in the British Museum, replicas in Ipswich Museum, and Mr Tricker got £45,000.

It is well worth going down the left bank of the Orwell to Nacton and Levington. At **Nacton** is Orwell Park, now a boys' preparatory school, in the old home of Admiral Vernon, who captured Portobello for George II with six ships and the loss of but seven men, but who failed, alas, to capture Cartagena: episodes described in *Roderick Random*. Vernon was known as 'Old Grog' from his habit of wearing grogram breeches and when he introduced the institution of the rum ration into the navy rum was named *grog* after him. He died in 1775 and is buried in Nacton churchyard.

Broke Hall, farther down the river, still a private house, was the home of another seafaring gentleman, Sir Philip Broke. He commanded HMS *Shannon* when she captured the United States frigate *Chesapeake* on the 1st June 1813 within easy sight of Boston.

The *Shannon* (39 guns) issued a personal challenge to the *Chesapeake* (44 guns) which was then lying in Boston harbour. The latter accepted the challenge and sailed out to battle, a battle which was watched by the entire population of Boston.

During a very short engagement 62 men were killed and 83 wounded aboard the *Chesapeake*, her captain, James Lawrence, falling in the first broadside, and the *Shannon* lost 43 killed and 39 wounded. The *Chesapeake* struck her colours and was taken. Even the boys in both ships, some mere children, climbed the rigging and slaughtered each other with pistols.

Levington is a charming little village, with lovely views of the estuary, and with the unspoilt Ship Inn near its church.

Farther on comes **Felixstowe**, an excellent seaside resort, very Edwardian in flavour, with a fine south-facing beach and a Fun Fair. It has little of the charm of Southwold or Aldeburgh, being a different sort of place, but in its way none the worse for that. Aqualung divers can visit the Roman fort at Walton Castle, for this is now under the sea and a couple of hundred yards from the shore. Landguard Fort, hard by, is a strange piece of military architecture, which has been adapted anew for each war, including the last one. The Dutch, under de Ruyter, attacked it in 1665, and made a landing; but withdrew to their ships before the Ipswich Militia could come at them.

An interesting part of Felixstowe is the Dock, round the corner and on the Orwell. A fine little artificial harbour, and being developed fast. Most of the Danish lager that comes into this country comes through this port. Like the other little ports of East Anglia it is booming as a result of the slow strangulation of the Port of London by restrictive practices.

To the other side of Felixstowe the land comes to a halt again at **Felixstowe Ferry**, a hamlet of shingly charm, with some lobster fishing boats, an RAF ferry running to Bawdsey on the other side (p23), the swiftly tidal and beautifully clean River Deben running out to sea over its sand bar. A place which combines very well the interest of sea and tidal river. There is a good anchorage here, west of the Horse Sand, for small yachts, and a good steep dry landing at all states of the tides on the shingle bank. Entering or leaving the river, though, requires local knowledge.

But to see the best of the Orwell Estuary, follow the right bank down from Ipswich: take, in fact, the Shotley Road. A marvellous walk is to be had from Ipswich right down to Shotley along the shore, but even from a motor car fine views can be obtained of what is one of the most beautiful estuaries in England. The Orwell compares very well with anything that Devon or Cornwall have to offer.

Shortly after leaving the industrial area of Ipswich by crossing the Bourne Bridge we come to a stretch of road from which we obtain incomparable views over the water. The road then leaves the river to climb **Freston Hill**, so if we wish to follow the river from here we have to walk. The tower in Freston Park was built in the 1550s supposedly by a member of the Latimer family (some say the Goodings). The Latimers left shields in the windows of Freston Church. One story is that it was a watch tower, for looking out for ships inward bound up the estuary. The other that a father built it as a school for his daughter. She studied different subjects on each floor—ending up with astronomy on the roof. What she studied in the basement is not recorded. **Woolverstone** hall was built in 1776, and was the seat of the Berners family, before it became what it is now, an LCC school. The Royal Harwich Yacht Club has its headquarters in the grounds, there is a boat yard, and the *cat house*. This latter is a little Gothic cottage, built 1793, with a white cat painted in the window which overlooks the Orwell. The legend is that the silhouette of a cat was placed there in times gone by to show approaching smugglers that the coast was clear. The legend is firmly believed throughout Suffolk, and there is no reason that I know of to suppose that it isn't true. It is pleasant that the tradition of the cat is still maintained by the present owners.

Following downstream through the magnificent park one comes to **Pin Mill**. This hamlet has had the misfortune to become known as a 'beauty spot' (which indeed it used to be), and on fine week-ends in summer, when there is a line of parked cars and chara-bancs standing half a mile up the lane, the place has all the beauty of the North Circular Road. But in off-seasons it is still pretty, with charming old terraced cottages down in a dell, a tiny group of single cottages clustered together on the 'Grindle' (a tiny sparkling stream), a rough common dotted with stranded boats, the Butt and Oyster— a noble waterside pub (one can sail a boat up to it at high water springs and buy a pint through the window). The anchorage in the estuary is very crowded these days, and most inconvenient. There is half a mile of soft mud at low water, traversed by a rough 'hard', and the shore-going yachtsman develops a sixth sense which tells him—as he comes ashore in the afternoon—just where the water will be lapping at pub-closing-time, and there he leaves his dinghy.

Generally there are some wooden sailing barges pulled up on the mud being repaired (the Webb family are the last remaining barge-wrights). Forty years ago Pin Mill was all barge folk: skippers and mates and barge repairers. Now most of the cottages have been bought up by week-enders and retired people. Once a great gang of dockers worked from Pin Mill, for the sailing ships from the Americas and the Continent were unable to get right up to Ipswich and so used to lie at Butterman's Bay, just below Pin Mill, and discharge their cargoes into sailing barges for the last stage of the journey. There was also a great fleet of *stone drudgers*. These were heavy fishing smacks which used to *drudge* (dredge in received English) the stone called septaria for the manufacture of 'Roman cement', which antedated Portland.

We can walk on downstream, first along a steep wooded cliff, at the foot of which great trees lie felled by tidal erosion, to a river wall, with marshes behind it, and along this to **Shotley**.

The old village of Shotley is set well away from the Shotley Road, on a hill overlooking the marshes and the mouth of the estuary.

> *Shotley Church—no steeple,*
> *Dirty Parson—wicked people!*

—no longer holds true, if it ever did, except in its description of the church. Shotley Church is a romantic place, set up on this lonely marsh-bound hill, among old brick cottages, not yet 'discovered' by anybody, and with a rare view out to the North Sea. The church is a strange building, with a Georgian chancel. Many hundreds of sailors are buried in the churchyard, including the entire ship's company of HMS *Gypsy*, which struck a magnetic mine in the Orwell, almost within a stone's throw of where the men are now buried.

At Shotley Hall, where the stables were once full of grand Suffolk horses, lives Mr Donald Wrinch, a Suffolk farmer of the old school. He used to own a fleet of five sailing barges, to sail his produce up to London and return laden with 'London Muck', or stable manure, thus carrying on a beneficent two-way traffic in fertility between town and country, now, alas, non-existent.

Shotley Gate, on the Stour Estuary—a few hundred yards from Bloody Point where the Stour joins the Orwell—is a modern village, completely dominated by HMS *Ganges*, the shore-based naval training station. The *Shell Guide to Suffolk* talks of the 'immemorial ferry' plying across the Stour to Harwich. Immemorial it may have been, but it has taken our own age to abandon it. British Railways closed it down, and to get to Harwich—a mile away—you now have to travel twenty.

The Black Prince was left ashore at Shotley as a small boy, when his father sailed away to the Battle of Sluys, in 1346—to send home the first-ever British naval dispatch, announcing victory and the capture of 230 ships.

The original HMS *Ganges* was an actual ship, built of teak in India in 1821, mounting 84 guns, the fourth ship to bear the name and the last sailing ship in the Royal Navy to fly an admiral's flag. In 1898 she was berthed off Shotley and used as a training ship, but in 1905 the shore station was commissioned under the same name, the real *Ganges* towed away to Chatham, and the boy sailors moved ashore.

Now 1,600 boys are trained each year for the Royal Navy, one can watch them rowing races in cutters and whalers in the two rivers, and clambering up their great mast to perch perilously on the very truck. There is a Nelson Museum, and the two water towers that stand up so conspicuously are built on the top of old Martello towers built to keep away Napoleon.

Not far away is the tiny village of **Erwarton**, the hall of which belongs to the Admiralty and is used as the private residence of the captain of HMS *Ganges*. The house is fundamentally Elizabethan, the front of it being of bricks laid in the old English bond. There is a most beautiful and striking gate house, dated at 1549. The gardens are kept up by working parties from *Ganges*. One feels that their Lordships of the Admiralty do the captain proud.

The church of Erwarton is of that strange rock dredged out of the sea, septaria, like much of Orford Castle. It is said that the heart of Anne Boleyn was buried in this church. Her aunt, Amata Boleyn, married a Calthorpe at the Hall and Anne spent much of her childhood there. Henry VIII is supposed to have visited her, during their courtship, by yacht. In the church also are two fourteenth-century canopied monuments: much neglected.

Bearing on westward one comes to the village of **Holbrook**, with a pub nicely named The Compasses, an almost too-picturesque watermill, and the Royal Hospital School.

The latter was founded at Greenwich in 1715, but transferred to Holbrook in 1933. Admission to the school is restricted to sons of officers and men of the Royal Navy, Royal Marines, Mercantile Marine and Lifeboat Service. A man named Gifford Sherman Reade, of Holbrook, gave land and money for the new school, and the architects were H. T. Buckland and W. Hayward. The architecture has been described as 'neo-Wren'. It is vast, sprawling, symmetrical, bright red brick faced in places with stone, with concrete cupolas here and there, and a huge cold-looking chapel with murals by Eric Gill. Whatever else one sees about the vast buildings, in term time or vacation, one never sees a boy, and one draws the impression that, if A. S. Neill's Summerhill School at Leiston is at one extreme end of the disciplinary spectrum, Holbrook is at the very extremity of the other. Superb views are to be had from the school over the mile-wide Stour Estuary.

If you do happen to diverge to **Tattingstone**, and see a row of cottages with one end built to look like a ruined church, this is the 'Tattingstone Wonder'. It was built by a squire because he said his neighbours were always wondering at nothing so he would give them something to wonder at.

Farther west the **Brantham** Bull is a noble pub, and down the hill by the river one comes to the 85 acre B.X. Plastic Works, perhaps the most severely functional set of buildings in England.

The place looks like nothing so much as 85 acres of tortured writhing, steel pipes. It is built on the marshes, and protected from a return of the 1953 floods by a high wall. Uncompromising though it may be in appearance it is historically interesting. In 1876 British Xylonite made Celluloid in London: the first 'plastics industry'. The firm moved to Brantham in 1887, and until recently the factory was supplied with raw materials by sailing barge. Even now a few little motor coasters unload chemicals there. Two thousand people are employed, and the factory makes a very wide range of plastic raw material. Thomas Tusser farmed at Brantham Hall, where he wrote, four hundred years ago, his *100 Points of Good Husbandry*.

Cattawade Bridge, which leads out of the ancient kingdom of East Anglia into Essex, is a fine old brick arch over the Stour. Just upstream is an ancient tidal mill, perhaps the last to work in England, after the last war a spice mill and now a factory for the manufacture of plastic-covered wire rope. The great tidal water wheel will, alas, turn no longer.

We are now on what has become hallowed ground, for this is John Constable's country. When the artist himself was travelling to it once in a carriage, a fellow-traveller who did not know him tapped him on the knee and said: 'Look out of the window, Sir—this is Constable's country!'

Constable wrote: 'I love every stile and stump and lane in the village; as long as I am able to hold a brush I shall never cease to paint them . . . The beauty of the surrounding country, its luxuriant meadow flats sprinkled with flocks and herds, its well cultivated uplands, its woods and rivers, with numerous scattered villages and churches, farms and picturesque cottages, all impart to this particular spot an amenity and elegance hardly anywhere else to be found.'

The village is **East Bergholt**. If you can get there, through the summer columns of charabancs and cars, you will find many fine Georgian houses and a most unusual church, with its broken remains of an unfinished tower and its bells housed in the wooden sixteenth-century bell house next door. The story is that every time the builders built more on to the tower during the day the Devil came along and cast it down at night. Another story, less picturesque, is that Wolsey was financing the building of the tower, and when he crashed the tower had to be abandoned. Anyway, the incomplete tower is most romantic, and the bell house quite unique.

The bells (a very fine peal) are rung by hand, without the aid of ropes, and the bell-ringers must be nearly deafened. East Bergholt Place has a garden made by Charles Eley, author of *Gardening for the Twentieth Century*.

The little lane down to **Flatford Mill** is so thronged with traffic in the summer that I would not recommend it. But in off-seasons Flatford Mill is charming, although no more so than a score of other old watermills in Norfolk and Suffolk. On the way down, if you are very clever, you may be able to spot the place on which Constable stood to paint 'The Cornfield'. In the mill-house itself he was born, in 1776. His father, Golding Constable, owned two watermills on the river, besides East Bergholt windmill. The little group of buildings comprise the mill, mill-house, Willy Lott's cottage, and Valley Farm, all much painted by the artist, and painted so many times since by amateurs that it is a wonder they have not all been painted right away. The buildings stand unaltered: one sees them with a jolt of recognition if one is used to looking at the paintings. They now belong to the National Trust, and are rented to the Council for the Promotion of Field Studies (Flatford Mill Field Centre). There is hostel accommodation for fifty students. There is a vast car park and a thronged café. If Constable came back and saw it all on a fine Sunday afternoon it would be interesting to hear what he would say.

A popular game is trying to spot the places where the artist sat or stood to paint his famous pictures, and then see what the scene is like today. This is rendered difficult by the artist's readiness to shift, say, Dedham Church a half a mile or so if it suited his composition. But the country has altered little over the years. Fewer trees, more houses, more wire (or at least wire, where there was no wire).

Constable fell in love with Maria Bicknell, grand-daughter of the Rector of East Bergholt, one Dr Rhudde. They wished to marry in 1800, but Rhudde persistently opposed their marriage, and they did not reach the altar until 1816, when Constable was forty. Maria died in 1829, leaving John the rest of his life to regret the sixteen years of happiness they might have had together had it not been for the stupidity of his grandfather-in-law.

Stratford Saint Mary has recently had a vast by-pass road made round it, and not before time; for this nice little Tudor village was being choked by the roaring traffic of the A12. It has long been partially spoiled by a Water Board pumping station of such revolting aspect that, fascinated, one cannot wrest one's eyes off it to look at

79

the beautiful Weaver's House and other buildings. The embattled Perpendicular church looks like a wedding cake: note the fine flush-work alphabet around its walls, and the arms of Chaucer quartered with those of de la Pole. The first Duke of Suffolk, a de la Pole, married Geoffrey Chaucer's grand-daughter. There is a headstone in the graveyard of Anne Richardson, who died in 1803 aged sixty-six. She was the last daughter of Samuel Richardson, the father of the English novel (*Pamela*). There are still several Richardsons living about Stratford St Mary. Stratford St Mary was a staging place in Roman times, on Route 9 of Antonine's 'Itinerary'.

Proceeding Ipswichwards again we can make a detour off the A12 to look at **Little Wenham** Hall. This solid little castle (it is a fortified house actually, but it looks like a castle to me) is of great interest because it was one of the first buildings in post-Roman times to have been built of brick (but compare Polstead Church). It was built at the latter end of the thirteenth century, and looks today quite unchanged. There is a great hall in it, kept furnished by the present owner, a chapel and a spiral staircase, and a fine view from the battlemented roof. One can stand there and imagine this very level country as it was when it was all one great hard-wood forest. There is a fine sixteenth-century tithe barn nearby, with brick nogging (an in-filling of bricks set at an angle to the horizontal) in timber framing and a thatched roof. But there are hundreds of such barns in East Anglia, great timber-framed barns are so common as to be commonplace. Many have been converted to twentieth-century uses, and serve as well now as they did when they were built. It's worth looking into the church just to see the early fourteenth-century wall paintings.

We might now work northwards, and circumnavigate Ipswich to the west and north.

Hintlesham used to be famous for its festivals which occurred every year for most of July. Mr Anthony Stokes, who owned the hall and was the prime mover, alas died in 1970. Mr Stokes was one of the passing breed of English eccentrics, and the festivals were a great asset to the locality. They were joyous occasions and did not take themselves too seriously. There was the occasion when a ballet dancer fell through the stage in an excess of en-thusiasm, and the other occasion when Mr Stokes opened a parcel solemnly presented to him after his closing speech and found that it contained a live frog. The village is charming and tree-shaded, the Hall magnificent. In the pretty little, very country, church is a memorial to Captayne John Timperley made of black stone inlaid with white stone to resemble a brass. It is floridly ornamented, with a Roundhead helmet and other warlike regalia. On the corbels 'in the way of' (as a sailor would say) the rood screen there are fine grotesque heads—one pulling his mouth open in a rude gesture. The Timperleys built the Hall in Elizabeth's time (they were recusants and had to flee the country), but a Georgian façade has been built in front of the old Tudor one, thus making a corridor immediately inside the front door ideal for exhibitions of paintings.

Washbrook has Mr John Budgen, the famous restorer of barrel, and other, organs.

Northward brings you over the chalk uplands, with many exceedingly pretty villages, to the valley of the Gipping, the river that turns into the Orwell at Ipswich. The Gipping valley started on the road to industrialism when the river was canalized in 1793, and horse barges, followed by steam ones, connected Stowmarket and other places cheaply to Ipswich Docks. The East Union Railway killed this goose in 1847 (you will still see the picturesquely decaying lock gates even from the road) but Stowmarket has now got a large chemical factory, besides several other works. The valley is much dominated by the A45, which runs from Felixstowe to Birmingham.

Needham Market has a roof in its church which Cautley in his *Suffolk Churches* calls 'the culmination of the English carpenter'. It is worth spending some time looking at this roof from the inside, working out how the various pieces are put together and how the thrusts are taken. A carved wood covering conceals the arch braces which support the hammerbeams, as at Framlingham, St Peter Mancroft, Norwich, and Ringstead, Norfolk. The church was originally fifteenth century. Much of the timber of the roof is Victorian, although no doubt a close copy of the original.

Stowmarket is a good little market town, becoming industrialized, and much spoiled by the A45. Much of the church is Decorated —always a relief in Perpendicular East Anglia. It is a jolly church. There are Tyrrell monuments, and a seventeenth-century inscription on a brass to eight-year-old Ann Tyrrell which is a most distinguished piece of verse. New at Stowmarket is a Rural Industries Museum. At **Shelland,** in the Church of King Charles the Martyr, is a barrel organ which is played at services. It was made in 1800 and plays thirty-six hymn tunes, which have not been changed since it was made (map, p349). At **Gipping** stands the private chapel of the Tyrrell family, by the site of their now vanished mansion. Sir James confessed himself to have been the murderer of the Princes in the Tower (the bride of one of whom we discussed at Framlingham), and his ancestor, Sir Walter, is said to have shot the arrow into the heart of William Rufus while the two were hunting in the New Forest. Sir James built the beautiful little private chapel, one of the most perfect Perpendicular buildings in the country, but this did not prevent him from being executed by Henry VII.

At **Haughley** is a motte and bailey castle (Haughley is an attractive village with cottages amid the apple trees) and the experimental station of the Soil Association at New Bells Farm. New Bells Farm may be said to be the world centre of what has become known as the Organic Movement, and is visited by organic farming enthusiasts from all over the world. The quite large typically Suffolk farm is divided into three sections: one farmed with stock and the use of no inorganic manure, one farmed with stock plus added 'artificial' or inorganic manure, and the third with no stock but plenty of inorganic manure. The results of many years of this treatment are studied and the three sections compared. The manager of the farm lives in the lovely Tudor farmhouse which is but typical of so many hundreds in this part of Suffolk. Visitors are welcomed, but there are open days in the summer when they are more particularly welcomed, and details of these may be had from The Manager, New Bells Farm, Haughley, Stowmarket.

Earl Stonham Church is a stunningly beautiful little country church: inside and out it has the utmost grace and elegance. Tiny although it is, it is cruciform, and has a clerestory. The roof is breathtaking—a single hammerbeam roof of sumptuously carved chestnut dating from the mid-fifteenth century. There are angels alternating with carved pendant bosses, and it has a massive solidity about the roof: it is built like a ship. The choir stalls are interesting, there is a triple hourglass in the south transept and there are remains of ancient wall paintings.

Stonham Aspall is a little lost village in this moated country. Stonham Hall is a typical completely moated fine Tudor house, and it still has its stew ponds and pigeon loft—and kept in use, too. It has for long been the house of the Chevallier family. Anne Francis Chevallier was the mother of Lord Kitchener. The family came to

England as Huguenot refugees and became famous farmers. The farming writer Arthur Young praised their husbandry, and a variety of barley they bred, 'Chevallier', is known to every farmer in the land and has only recently been superseded. When the family came from Normandy they brought their cider mill with them—a granite trough around which rolls a huge stone wheel and is thought to date from the time of the Conquest. This mill is still there, and people intent on buying cider may see it, but the apples are nowadays crushed by a small motor-driven crusher. Cider is still made, and is for sale, and is some of the best cider in the country.

I call this heavy-land country between the A45 and the A12 the 'moated country' because so many of its farmhouses are surrounded by deep moats. These have been explained in various ways. One is drainage: every field hereabouts is surrounded by a deep ditch, which must be kept constantly cleaned out, otherwise cultivation becomes impossible. The siting of the homestead on an island of land isolated by a deep moat kept it well drained. Another is defence, perhaps in the times of the Danish invasions. Another is as stew ponds. Certainly carp and other fish were bred in them for the table. It is easy to see that this country was once all hard-wood forest—oak and elm. Indeed even today, looking over the fields, one gets the impression of fields in a forest, so many hedges have big elm or oak trees growing in them.

Crow's Hall, Debenham, is a magnificent example of these moated mansions, although grander than most of them. Built about 1508 of brick (more typical is timber framing and lath and plaster) it has a wide and deep moat on which the owner's children and their friends skate in the winter, inside is a great wealth of wonderful old oak—a great staircase every step of which is an oak beam, oak panelling everywhere and enormous panelled oak doors. The marvellous range of farm buildings before you come to the Hall are known as 'the Barracks', and the place was a Cavalier stronghold in the Civil War. It is now a private house, and the centre of a bunch of farms and a pedigree Jersey herd. Debenham is as beautiful a little Suffolk town as you will find: completely free from tourists although far more picturesque than plenty of tourist-ridden places farther south. The church is beautifully placed, nestling among the ancient houses, but over-restored within. It has, though, a massive rood beam, and a monument to a very pious-looking double-chinned gentleman named John Sheppard flanked by two very well-fed urchins old beyond their years. On the 18th October 1890, we are told, a peal of 5040 Bob Triples was rung at Debenham, and on 3rd December 5056 changes of Superlative Surprise were rung in three hours and two minutes. The fine bells, cast in 1761, were re-hung on ball bearings in 1932 and are famous among bell-ringers. There are two incontestably Anglo-Saxon windows on the south of the tower. There is a butcher's shop in Debenham, 'F. E. Neave', with a most colourful and beautiful sign; and the Debenham Rush Weavers turn out rush table mats, carpets, baskets, and other rush materials at the other end of the town.

Shrublands is a great mansion in a great garden, the latter one of the grandest in East Anglia. The hall was built, or rebuilt, in Elizabeth I's reign by Edward Bacon, the brother of the famous Francis, who had married into the property. Beyond a window and a few details little of this remains. The last of the Bacons, the Reverend Nicholas, who died in 1795, commissioned James Paine to build a new house between 1770 and 1772. In 1830 William Fowle Middleton, the then owner, added two wings, a terrace and a conservatory, designed by J. P. Gandy Deering. In 1848, having made the Grand Tour (which went to his head as it did to the heads of so many English magnates) he commissioned Sir Charles Barry to Italianate the whole thing up. The park and gardens were turned into an Englishman's idea of Italy or a copy of the gardens of the Villa d'Este. The gardens were extensively remodelled, and simplified, by William Robinson in 1888.

They are still very fine. There is a sumptuous staircase leading down from a terrace to a fountain and parterre, and thence a vista to an ornate loggia. There are fine vistas and fine trees, and Italianate gatehouses around the walls. Six Roman roads are said to meet in the park, and they have been retained in the form of tree-lined avenues.

As for the house today, it is a health clinic, where you may undergo Kneipp Water Therapy (wherein you are subjected to water from high-pressure hoses), sauna baths, colonic irrigation, fasting and dieting, and chiropractic manipulation.

Barham Manor, over the road, is Elizabethan, but much more modest than Shrublands. The Barham Sorrel Horse, on the Norwich Road, is a famous road inn, and always has been. Behind it is a vast place where they slaughter chickens.

Coddenham's one street, up the hill, is like a fairy-tale village:

it is a place with hardly a jarring note in it. Starting at the bottom of the hill Gryffon House was until recently the Crown Inn—alas strangled by the licensing laws like many another fine country inn. According to story it was once the house of an archer named Wodehouse, knighted by Henry V after the Battle of Agincourt. Certainly it looks ancient enough for this to have been true. Up the street there are several oversailing half-timbered houses, with pargetted walls: the pink-washed post office, which is in Lodge House, was once a pub called the Live and Let Live, and above it is the one pub still open, the George. Bickers' Garage is run by Dave Bickers, the nationally famous motor-cycle scrambling ace, and his father is the village blacksmith.

Near Debenham lives Mr Hugh Barrett, who has written a very fine book on Suffolk country life, *Early to Rise*.

Norwich

'A fine old city, truly, is that, view it from whatever side you will; but it shows best from the east, where the ground, bold and elevated, overlooks the fair and fertile valley in which it stands. Gazing from those heights, the eye beholds a scene which cannot fail to awaken, even in the least sensitive bosom, feelings of pleasure and admiration.' Thus George Borrow, in *Lavengro*. '. . . the fine old city, perhaps the most curious specimen at present extant of the genuine old English town.'

And he could say the same today. In spite of the sad if necessary removal of the cattle market from the Castle Bailey to the suburbs, and the building in the last year or two of vast skyscrapers containing a myriad insurance workers, and the throwing up of that—to me— hideous city hall (many good judges like it—I think it looks like a gigantic public convenience, which I suppose is what it is) Norwich is still a fine city, and an ancient one, and bids fair to become a great centre of provincial culture, a bastion against the overwhelming and deadening metropolitanism that afflicts this land. For many centuries it was the second city of England, and although now far overtaken in size by the midland and northern parvenues it is still one of the finest and withal the most lovable. To a miraculous degree it has retained its ancient charm while adapting itself to the exigencies of the twentieth century.

Yes, there it spreads from north to south, with its venerable houses, its numerous gardens, its thrice twelve churches, its mighty mound, which, if tradition speaks true, was raised by human hands to serve as a grave-heap of an old heathen king, who sits deep within it, with his sword in his hand, and his gold

86

PLACES OF INTEREST
1 Strangers Hall
2 Bridewell Hall
3 King Edward the Sixth School
4 Music House
5 Guildhall
6 Art School (Boot & Shoe Dept)

CHURCHES
7 St. Peter Mancroft
8 St. Gregory's
9 St. John the Baptist
10 St. Peter Parmentergate
11 St. John de Sepulchre
12 St. Michael-at-Coslany
13 St. Michael-at-Plea
14 Unitarian Octagon Chapel

0   mile   ¼

and silver treasures about him. There is a grey old castle upon the top of that mighty mound . . .

There still is, and it contains probably the best provincial museum in England.

. . . and yonder, rising three hundred feet above the soil, from among those noble forest trees, behold that old Norman master-work, that cloud-encircled cathedral spire, around which a garrulous army of rooks and choughs continually wheel their flight.

Behold it still.

Norwich owes its individual character to the fact that it has always been an isolated city, cut off from the Midlands by the Wash and the Fens (almost unpassable until the nineteenth century) and a long way from London. It is a port, moreover, with close connections with the Continent. Until the railway age it would have been quicker for a Norwich man to have gone to Antwerp or Rotterdam than to any English city. Thus there is an isolationist feeling about the place, and a strong Continental influence. Isolation makes for self-sufficiency; and Norwich has always had a great variety of industry, made necessary by remoteness. As a shopping and marketing centre it is excellent, by reason of the fact that it serves a vast hinterland, and is the only first class shopping centre for fifty miles.

I love to wander round the streets of Norwich, penetrating the jumble of medieval streets in the old walled city, looking into the occasional deserted church (there are far too many churches for the inhabitants), looking also into the seldom deserted pubs. When I was a boy it was said that you could go to a different church every Sunday of the year in Norwich, and a different pub every night. And I know of no city in England with better pubs. Not the grand pubs, or the pretentious ones, but the little back-street pubs and the working men's pubs (and working women's too, for there are very few traditionally men-only pubs in Norwich—the women earn with the men, in the many industries that employ them). There are pubs full of jolly old factory women who love 'a laugh and a joke', and don't care very much what the joke is about. There are pubs full of market stall-holders, pubs full of settled 'Travellers', or Gypsies, for there is a strong community of this brotherhood in Norwich, descendants, certainly some of them, of George Borrow's Petulengro, pubs full of the sailors who come up the Yare, pubs where the most unusually jolly ladies of joy await their gentlemen friends (Norwich has the jolliest harlots of any city I know—most of the sisterhood are woefully dull), pubs full of lorry drivers, pubs full of rich farmers in from the Norfolk countryside, pubs full of burglars.

A burglar told me, in one of the latter, how, when robbing a warehouse he had had a vision of God. He couldn't remember the exact words that the Deity spoke to him, but gathered that the meaning of them was: 'Lay off the stuff!' However, my friend heeded not the words, and pinched a carpet (more or less out of habit), and the police were waiting for him outside in the street and he got eighteen months.

Still a great deal of the social life of Norwich centres round its pubs, and always did do. Old Crome, the father of the Norwich School of Painting '. . . was a simple man, of genial company. To the end of his life he used to go of an evening to a public-house as to an informal club. In the privileged bar-parlour, behind the taps and glasses, he sat with his friends and the shop-keepers, talking of local things.' (The Rifleman, Colegate, was where he sat. Alas, it is closed now.) But before we lose ourselves completely in the pubs, let us go and look at **the Castle.**

The East Angles certainly had a fortified place at Norwich (though the Danes twice burned it down). At the time of the Conquest Gyrth Godwinsson, brother of King Harold, was Earl of the East Angles, and probably lived there. He was killed at Hastings, and the year after the battle the Normans pulled down a hundred houses in Norwich and built an earth and wood castle using the forced labour of the inhabitants.

Early in the twelfth century the wooden castle was replaced by the present stone structure. This looks, today, brand new; the reason being that it was refaced with Bath stone in 1834, by Salvin. But even before that date it must have been well preserved. The new keep was more than just a last-ditch refuge, but was the main residential part of the castle, and the fifth largest keep in England.

The first Norman to control it, under the king, was William Fitzosbern. A few years later Ralph Guader, Earl of Norfolk and Suffolk, was the Constable but plotted with other barons at his wedding feast to overthrow King William ('That Wedding Ale, Was many Man's Bale'), was forced to flee to Brittany, leaving his wife in charge of the castle. This lady for three months withstood the king's forces so valiantly that she was granted a free pardon and allowed to join her husband in exile.

The Bigods (see Framlingham, p48) then became constables of the castle for the king, and kept the job, in spite of many intrigues, until they displeased King John by plotting against him, and were replaced by Hubert de Burgh (see Orford, p27), of 'heat me these irons hot' fame. The castle was attacked and taken by Hugh Bigod and his Flemish allies in 1174, but later re-taken by the king. In 1220 it was demilitarized and turned into the county jail, which it remained right up until 1887 after which it was transformed into a museum.

In Norman times the castle and the area around it were completely outside the jurisdiction of the city, and there was much friction between the Norman garrison within and the East Anglians without. The castle formed a foreign enclave within the city, and the cathedral and priory another. It was not until 1345 that Edward III consented to the citizens of Norwich renting land inside the castle fee, and thus one of the foreign enclaves was dissolved.

Whatever else you miss in the castle, do not miss the doorway which leads to the outer building known as Bigods' Tower from the main body of the keep. Around this is superb Norman carving. This door was once the only way into the keep. Have patience, too, to wait for the time of day when you can join a guided party to the castle ramparts, if only for the fine views over the great city, and the strong sense of a romantic past.

As might be expected in the bird-rich county of Norfolk **the museum** in the castle has a fine collection of stuffed birds, including such rarities as the last of Norfolk's Greater Bustards (would that they had been left flying around) and a Greater Spotted Cuckoo. But the stuffed-bird-lover will discover such delights for himself. The 'Norfolk Room' is a triumph of museummanship, with magnificent dioramas of various types of Norfolk countryside: Broadland, Breckland, and the ordinary indiscriminate countryside in between. These six great displays are really excellent of their kind.

There are ten galleries of paintings, most of them, quite rightly, filled with the products of the Norwich School. There is a Crome Gallery and a Cotman Gallery. John Crome ('Old Crome') was born in 1768, the son of a weaver. At twelve he became an errand boy to a doctor, then an apprentice to a painter of coaches and of inn signs, and in this employment he learnt to grind and use colours. He met another apprentice, a boy named Ladbrooke, who supplemented his income by painting portraits of people for five shillings a head. Crome was thus encouraged to paint, and began doing landscapes at thirty shillings each. Ladbrooke and Crome married a pair of sisters, and remained close friends. Crome did his seven years as an apprentice, started the 'Norwich Society of Artists', in 1803, and founded the Norwich school of painting which in its time was famous throughout Europe and for a time was in the van of European landscape art. Crome and Cotman to a certain extent anticipated the Impressionists. Both were among the first to get away from a photographic reproduction of every leaf and twig, and to come close to catching the essence of the scene they were striving to depict. Cotman, perhaps more than Crome, seems surprisingly modern even when we see his work today.

But it was Crome who captured the feeling of Norfolk as no other artist has, and who realized—like John Constable—that it is the working and homely things that make up our old countryside that are beautiful: the old mills and cottages, the work boats and working horses, the nature, water and the trees. Crome could never make a living by his painting alone, but was forced all his life to teach, to support his large family, including his son John ('Young Crome') who also became a painter.

John Sell Cotman was fourteen years younger than Crome, the son of a silk mercer. He went to London to paint at an early age, nearly starved, but was appointed, in the nick of time, Professor of Drawing at London University, and thus survived. He was a superb draughtsman, particularly of buildings; and his *Specimens of Archi-tectural Remains* are unsurpassed. Cotman's house can be seen at St Martin's-at-Palace Plain, next door to the White Lion. It was here, in 1824 that he opened his 'School of Drawing and Painting in Water Colour'. Tuition fees were one guinea and a half per quarter. His son, J. J. Cotman, was another good artist.

There is still a lively Norwich Art Circle. Their work is often exhibited in the beautiful Assembly House, in Theatre Street (built 1754 by Thomas Ivory), where incidentally the most excellent cold collations can be had at lunch time on weekdays, not expensive.

For the rest there is much in this museum to instruct and amuse, including dioramas of what Norfolk may (or may not) have looked like during Mesolithic times and later, 'Snap', the ceremonial dragon such as that used by the St. George's Guild (which was established in the fourteenth century and extinguished in 1732), the 'Parliament Chair', carved with cherubs, in which the newly elected Member was wont to be carried through the streets of Norwich, and flung painfully and perilously into the air at intervals, Lord Nelson's hat, some Lowestoft porcelain and much else.

While on museums, go, by all means, to the **Strangers' Hall**, in Norwich's Charing Cross. This contains furniture and domestic utensils of many different periods, and if the lover of Victoriana wishes to know just where his *outré* tastes may lead him, if he indulges them in full, let him take a look at the three Victorian rooms here. I always leave with a conviction that the art of living has steadily retrogressed since Tudor times. It is important not to become so engrossed in the fine exhibits as to notice the house itself, a marvellously preserved medieval mansion. The undercroft is early fourteenth century, the Great Hall (the splendid open crown-post roof was added in the sixteenth century) mid-fifteenth.

The Hall has been inhabited by a succession of rich merchants (note the Grocers' Arms on the screen near the door—put there for Nicholas Sotherton, who moved in about 1525). Roman Catholic priests inhabited the place during much of the nineteenth century, then a private family, and it was presented to Norwich in 1922.

The other museum which the stranger should not miss is the **Bridewell**. The north wall of this is an example of squared flint at its perfection (a rather black and sombre perfection perhaps) put up in the fourteenth century. The museum has local industries and crafts. Particularly interesting are examples of old building methods, brick making, the first wire-netting machine (Norwich led the world in making this useful stuff—it is difficult to see how people kept chickens without it), a Jacquard machine on a loom of amazing complexity, a beautiful wooden aeroplane propeller (that high summit of the wood-worker's art), fine models of windmills and a Norfolk wherry. These are the things that catch my eye there— there is very much more. And not least, contained in the Bridewell, is the secret of the Norwich canary.

Norwich has for long been so famous for canaries that the very word canary has become to mean a Norwich man. The Norwich City football team (which so often wins its matches) is called 'The Canaries'. For many years canary fanciers up and down the land were yellow with envy at the *colour* of the Norwich breeders' canaries, which was yellow of the very yellowest. Then, in the year 1875, one W. Blackston let the cat, if not the bird, out of the bag. He published the secret of the Norwich canary fanciers to the astonished world. It was simply that they fed their canaries on cayenne pepper. (They now feed them on Spanish red pepper, or *Capsicum annum.*) Thus the Norwich fanciers lost their great advantage over all others, although not their supremacy; and still, for many, the annual canary show at Norwich is the highlight of the year. I once asked a Norwich man in a pub which party was going to win the General Election. 'Election?' he said. 'What election? It's the Canary Show I'm worried about.'

The other museum is the old church of **St Peter Hungate**, which contains examples of ecclesiastical art, including weird and wonderful musical instruments, and much else of interest including part of a manuscript of a 'Wycliffe' Bible.

As for the churches of Norwich, if you try to see all of them you will suffer from a severe surfeit of ecclesiastical architecture.

But **St Peter Mancroft**, up in the Market Place, must be inspected, for it is one of the great buildings of East Anglia. The finest Perpendicular, this church is noble and stately, in a perfect position dominating the lovely market place (dominating it in spite of the much bigger modern City Hall), set off wonderfully by gaily painted old houses that cluster around its foot. Inside you see a timber roof like that of Framlingham (but much bigger), a hammerbeam roof with the hammerbeams concealed by fan vaulting. There is a rare timber baptistry, one of only three in England (one is at Trunch, where we shall go). The bottom part of this is fifteenth century, but the upper part was restored (well) in the nineteenth. The High Altar was made at Exeter in 1885, but the lower part, with Christ in Glory and Saints Alban, Augustine, Columba and Felix—the first to try to convert the heathen English—was built to the design of Sir Ninian Comper in 1930, to mark the church's five hundredth birthday.

Sir Thomas Browne (1605–82—*Religio Medici* and *Urn Burial*) has two tablets let into the wall south of the altar: one put there by his wife, when he was buried in the chancel, and the other in 1922 after his skull was decently re-buried after having been dug up by grave diggers in 1840, hawked around as a curio, and finally put in a medical museum. Sir Thomas's statue, with him depicted as contemplating a piece of urn, is just south of the church.

But it is the building itself that is noteworthy. Particularly look at the tower arch, as you stand in the nave and look west. It is a miracle of strength with economy. And the clerestory is lovely, whether viewed from within or without. The church plate is as good as there is, and there are Browne relics. In the group of houses just east of the church is the best grocer's in Norwich.

To describe all the other churches in this city would be for another book, and another writer. Things which have pleased me have been: the painting of St George clad as a medieval knight on the west wall of the north aisle of **St Gregory's, Pottergate**. (Pottergate is a nice street to wander in anyway, and Old 'Snap', the dragon like the one in the Castle Museum, used to be kept in St Gregory's, for it was here that the St George Society used to hold their revels. There is a fine eagle lectern, too, dated variously 1493 or 1496.) The ancient glass in **St Andrew's Hall** in the north side, and particularly the bishop dancing with Death at the west end of the south aisle of St Andrews church. St Andrew's Hall is a fine building, splendid Perpendicular, with portraits in it, including the last one made of Nelson and one by Gainsborough. This is now used for concerts and flower shows and such like; would that more redundant churches were. It was once part of the church of the 'Sackites' (called so because they used to dress up in old sacks), or Friars of the Penance of Jesus Christ. When these mendicants were suppressed in 1307 their convent was granted to the Dominicans, and they in their turn were suppressed in 1538. At one time the always separated choir of their church (called Blackfriar's Hall) was used by the Dutch community in Norwich, and a Dutch service was held there once a year until recently. (It was in 1336 that Edward III, with his Dutch wife, brought the first parcel of Hollanders to England, in an attempt to turn the country from a wool exporting country into a cloth exporting one, for the Dutch were ahead of the English in fine weaving.) These two halls are among the very few friars' buildings left in England.

I like the arms of Good Old Sir Thomas Erpingham in the clerestory of **St John the Baptist, Timberhill**, for Sir Thomas fought at Agincourt (his tomb is in the cathedral). I also like a brass in **St Andrew's Church** commemorating the thrifty Alderman Gardiner, who departed this life in 1508. But before he went he sent a priest to Rome with instructions to obtain a Bull granting three hundred days' indulgence to anyone who would pray for him by his tomb—*provided the Bull could be obtained for not more than a fiver!*

I like the *names* of:

St Peter Permountergate, King Street (it has old wooden stalls).
St John de Sepulchre, Ber Street (good font).
St Michael-at-Coslany, Colegate (marvellous panelled flint work).
St Michael-at-Plea, Bank Plain (it had fine fourteenth-century panel paintings of the Resurrection, but these are now an altarpiece in the chapel at the east end of Norwich Cathedral).
St Michael-at-Thorn (bombed).

Nor are the Nonconformists to be ignored. Norwich was a 'hotbed' of Nonconformity, and still is. The Unitarian **Octagon Chapel**, off Colegate Street (a very interesting old industrial street over the river) is unique besides being octagonal, and was designed by Thomas Ivory, the local architect who also did that marvellous Georgian building, the Assembly House. It was built by the Presbyterians in 1756 but became Unitarian. The famous John Taylor preached there (causing it to be called 'a cucumber house for the forcing oi Nonconformists'), and Harriet Martineau, the writer, was of the congregation. The **Old Meeting House,** just round the corner, is to my mind far more attractive. This was built in 1693, by the early Congregationalists. These had fled from persecution to Holland (many others went to America, and founded Norwich, Connecticut, there) but returned when they could, after the Act of Toleration, to build the Dutch-looking Old Meeting House, up an alley so that it could be defended against rioters. This is one of the very early Nonconformist chapels.

The first Quaker meeting-house to be built in Norwich was in 1679, in Goat Lane. The famous Gurney family attended here. The Gurneys are a Norman family, still with a branch in Normandy. A present-day Gurney owns Walsingham Abbey. They were great bankers, and a highly talented and intellectual family. Elizabeth Fry, the prison reformer, was née Gurney, and one of seven lovely and spirited sisters. Harriet Martineau wrote of them: 'They were then a set of dashing young people, dressed in gay riding habits and scarlet boots, as Mrs Fry told us afterwards, and riding about the country to balls and gaieties of all sorts.' The new University of East Anglia is centred on the Gurneys' old home, Earlham Hall: most fitting, for Earlham Hall was a centre for lively and progressive ideas, a centre in the fight against the slave trade, and a resort of Wilberforce.

While on the subject of Nonconformity, the site of Lollard's Pit may still be seen, next to Bishop's Bridge, marked today by a plate on a cottage; and I must quote George Borrow in *Lavengro* again: '. . . we are not far from hallowed ground. Observe ye not yon chalky precipice, to the right of the Norman bridge? On this side the stream, upon its brow, is a piece of ruined wall, the last relic of what was of old a stately pile, whilst at its foot is a place called Lollard's Hole; and with good reason, for many a saint of God has breathed his last beneath that white precipice, bearing witness against popish idolatry, midst flame and pitch; many a grisly procession has advanced along that suburb, across the old bridge, towards the Lollard's Hole: furious priests in front, a calm, pale martyr in the midst, a pitying multitude behind. It has had its martyrs, the venerable old town!'

At the junction of Unthank Road and Earlham Road is a stupendous piece of Victorian Gothic. The Roman Catholic **pro-cathedral of St John the Baptist**, given to Norwich by the 15th Duke of Norfolk (see Framlingham, p50), built in neo-Early English, and a riot of flying buttresses, turrets, gables and gargoyles. It is 275 feet long, and only not a cathedral because it is not the seat of a bishop. It is not to be missed, being filled with really striking craftsmanship, none the worse because it is not old.

And at last we must come to the glory of Norwich, and in the eyes of an East Anglian of England too: the **Cathedral Church** of the most Holy and Undivided Trinity.

To enter this building and look along **the nave** and up at the glory of the stone vaulted roof is to feel dumbfounded at the skill, daring, and inspiration of the men who built it. One tends to be so overwhelmed by the grandeur of the interior that it is hard to give much attention to the marvellous details: the 1200 carved illustrative stone bosses in the cathedral and cloisters (328 in the nave alone), the sixty fine carved misericords in the choir and the canopies over the choir stalls, the marvellous fifteenth-century glass. The bosses in the nave (set up there by Bishops Lyhart and Nix in the fifteenth and sixteenth centuries) illustrate the entire Bible story, but you would need a powerful telescope or helicopter to see them properly, for they are seventy feet above your head.

You could spend a day looking at the wood carving in the choir

5. IPSWICH: The port (*above*) still flourishes as it has done for a thousand years. The Customs House was built in 1843–44. *Below,* flush-work on the tower of St. Margaret's and pargetting on the Ancient House

6. *Above left*, a "Boston Prawner" – one of the fleet which fishes in the Wash for pink shrimps. *Right*, one of the fleet of "pair fishing" boats working out of Wells. *Below left*, a King's Lynn cockling smack aground in the Wash several miles from land. The crew are waiting for the tide to turn and float her again. *Right*, a Wells whelker – built to go 30 miles out to sea and then carry in a ton of whelks over the shallow Wells Bar

alone. The carvings on the misericords represent commonplace life as it was lived in the reign of the Tudors as seen through the eyes of honest craftsmen.

The walls of the nave rise up in three tiers of the finest Norman stone, massive, solid and beautiful. The bishop's throne, in the Norman apse behind the High Altar, is, in part, the original one built by Bishop Losinga when the foundations of the cathedral were laid. It is the only bishop's throne of its kind north of the Alps.

Bishop de Losinga started the building in 1096, by order of the Pope, as a penance because he had committed the sin of simony: he had paid William Rufus £1900 to make him a bishop. Before this he had been Abbot of Ramsey, in the Fens. Rufus made him Bishop of Thetford, he went and confessed to the Pope and the Pope ordered him to move the seat of the see to Norwich and build a cathedral there, and also to build churches at King's Lynn and Yarmouth, which he did. In his life he completed the presbytery, with its apse and ambulatory, the beginnings at least of the central tower, the transepts, and part of the nave. The rest was completed after his death. A spire was built in the thirteenth century, but collapsed in 1362: the present spire is fifteenth century, the second highest in England (after Salisbury), and the golden weathercock is 315 feet from the ground!

The fire of 1509 that burnt the timber roofs saved the cathedral in June 1942, for the timber was replaced by stone and German incendiaries failed to ignite it.

The dull (in my opinion) Perpendicular west window was put in by Bishop Alnwich in the fifteenth century. The famous flying buttresses were set up to hold the high vaulted roof of the presbytery, which is one of the architectural wonders of this world. This cathedral manages to get the best of all the worlds: it combines the clean massive simplicity of the Norman with the springing elegance and daring of later ages.

Outside, **the cloister** is the biggest in England, and it is interesting to notice the transition of styles in its building, with a long break for the Black Death. The east walk is fourteenth century and Decorated: the north walk is Perpendicular built after 1430. Over the cloister is housed the cathedral library, one of the most notable libraries in Britain with seven thousand rare and old books including some of the earliest printed in England.

At the east end of the cathedral, outside the new chapel built as a memorial to the men who were killed in the First World War, is the grave of a Norfolk girl, Nurse Edith Cavell.

Daughter of the Rector of **Swardeston** (a small village south-west of Norwich on the New Buckenham road where are Cavell relics and a window) she was born on the 4th of December 1865, reared on the strictest of Victorian lines, became a nurse at twenty-two, at forty-one became matron at a clinic in Belgium, was suffered to remain there by the Germans when they occupied the country in 1914, was arrested 5th August 1915 and charged with aiding Allied soldiers to escape to Holland. She was shot by orders of the German High Command on 12th October 1915, and before her death she said to the Reverend Stirling Gahan, the English Chaplain in Brussels: 'I know that patriotism is not enough. I must have no hatred or bitterness towards anyone.' After the war her body was brought home and given a funeral service of almost royal proportions in Westminster Abbey and then actually buried under the walls of Norwich Cathedral, on the plot of land known as Life's Green. There is a dreadfully ugly statue of her in front of the Maid's Head Hotel.

The route of a canal can be traced, leading to the cathedral from the River Wensum. Up this the thousands of tons of stone were shipped from France, and without it it would have been impossible for such a vast building to have been built in a stoneless country.

The **cathedral close** is made noisome with motor cars, having been turned into a car park: a tragedy for Norwich. At one side of it is the old chapel of the **Edward the Sixth School,** originally the chantry chapel of St John, with a statue of Nelson looking at it (he attended there for a short time, and it seems unfair to have his statue eternally gazing at his erstwhile prison). The school is no parvenu, having been founded as Carnary College, with its chapel, in 1316 and made into a school by Edward VI. George Borrow went there and was soundly whacked (he ran away once but was dragged back), so did Lord Justice Coke (see Holkham p217), so did the Rajah of Sarawak (he ran away too—and stayed away) and two botanists, Sir William Jackson Hooker and John Lindley.

These last two were concerned with the farcical business of the naming of the giant water lily (*Victoria amazonica*) about which a comic opera could well be written. The business split the nation in half: even the Cabinet was involved; and there was a chase across Europe by no less than four Victorian gentlemen, sponsored by

NORWICH CATHEDRAL

various warring scientific societies, the gentlemen all in deep disguise, to seek out an old German who was found sitting in his garden next to a pool containing a vast, and flowering, *amazonica*, which had been there for years while scientists were battling through the jungles of the Amazon looking for what was half believed to be a myth. A good account of this can be read in *Some Ancient Gentlemen*, by Tyler Whittle, who lives at Old Buckenham (p174).

John Lindley was the son of a market gardener and nurseryman of Catton, just by Norwich. He was born 5th February 1799, was the first Professor of Botany at London University and was mainly instrumental in getting Kew Gardens opened to the public. He arranged for his old school-fellow Hooker to be made the first director. Hooker, son of a Norwich merchant, botanized in wild Scotland and was arrested there as a spy, botanized in Iceland and was shipwrecked on his return, his luggage, when it was rescued, was found to contain nothing but his journals and an Icelandic girl's wedding garments, was Professor of Botany at Glasgow, and was made a Knight of Hanover for his services to botany. Norwich was once rich in botanists: Clarke Abel, a Norwich surgeon, went with Lord Amherst's embassy to China in 1816 and was also shipwrecked on his return and all his specimens were lost. Sir James Edward Smith, born and buried in Norwich, founded the Linnean Society of London. And of course Sir Thomas Browne was one of the first of botanists, and is buried at St Peter Mancroft.

The gates to the cathedral close are most noteworthy. There is St Martin's, or Bishop Alnwick's, round the corner, but the best ones are, first, **St Ethelbert's Gate**, which has an unsuitable flush-work gable plonked on top of its fourteenth-century self, and was built by the townspeople as a penance, some years after one of their periodic attacks on the monks. On this occasion they had set fire to the cathedral, in a small way.

The other is **Erpingham Gate**, a memorial to Sir Thomas, who lived near St Martin-at-Palace. This is said to be one of the finest Perpendicular monuments in England. In deep moulding are the twelve apostles, the twelve virgin saints to keep them company, and Sir Thomas in the niche above:

'Good morrow, old Sir Thomas Erpingham:
a good soft pillow for that good white head
Were better than the churlish turf of France.'

'Not so, my liege: this lodging likes me better,
Since I may say, "Now lie I like a king".'

Tucked away in a side street behind the cathedral is the Adam and
Eve Inn, a splendid little ancient place to go and quench one's thirst
after gazing up at all those bosses.

For other noteworthy inns, the Maid's Head, in **Tombland**, is
famous although the exterior has been horribly and badly modernized. But inside is still fine. Queen Elizabeth slept there in 1578 (she
was half an East Anglian: her grandfather, Sir William Boleyn, is
buried in the cathedral), Sir John Paston mentioned the inn in one
of the famous Paston Letters in 1472. The Bell, on Castle Meadow,
is a fine old coaching inn. Norwich has been restrained about
pulling down good old buildings, but I can never forgive it for
bulldozing the Buff Coat, on Market Hill. It was a place where some
of the spirit of Merry England still survived, and I once stabled my
horse there.

Magdalen Street is a long street of very old buildings with new
shops in them, and in 1958 it was the first street to be re-decorated
by the Civic Trust. A gay and harmonious colour scheme was
designed by good architects, and the shop keepers of the street
persuaded to conform. The idea has spread to other streets in
Norwich, and other towns. Holt is a good example of the latter. The
garrets of hand weavers may be seen above many of the buildings.

King Street is ancient and interesting. It leaves Prince of Wales's
Road and first passes garages and a brewery, and then has several
fine old buildings in it. The Old Barge Inn, once the Three Merry
Wherrymen and before that the Meddeyz Inn, has a Perpendicular
outer door and a Decorated ogee inner one, a fine tap room, and
wooden partitioned cubicles for lorry drivers (and writers of guide
books) upstairs. The Ferry Inn, farther down, is a seafarers' pub,
presided over by Mrs ('Motty') Warminger, well known to and
loved by coastal sailors all round Britain. At the bottom of her
garden is the River Wensum, filled with shipping, unloading corn
for the mills, coal for the coal yards, and loading scrap metal for
Middlesbrough.

At the end of King Street the **Carrow Works** makes Colman's
Mustard. It was built where it is to make use of the river for its
traffic, on the site of a Benedictine nunnery, which probably contained the cell of Saint Julian, or Mother Juliana, a fourteenth-

century mystic who wrote *XVI Revelations of Divine Love*. Colman's offices are now in what was the old Colman home, part of which was the Prioress's residence, built in the sixteenth century. Mother Juliana's shrine is the rebuilt (after bombing) church of St Julian, where she spent most of her life as anchoress, up the street. It is tended by the nuns who live at Ditchingham.

The **'Music House'**, once called the 'Jew's House', is in King Street, and perhaps the oldest private dwelling house in England. Behind the stone façade of the early seventeenth century most of the remains are twelfth century, but the magnificent timbered roof in the great hall was put there by Sir John Paston (probably) and he bought the house in 1487. Sir Edward Coke (pronounced *cook*), Lord Chief Justice under James I, married Bridget Paston, and thus came to live there. In Queen Elizabeth's time the City Waits used to meet there, hence the new name. 'Jew's House' is older. (There is an item of city expenditure for fitting out the City Waits to sail round the world with Sir Francis Drake.)

Elm Hill, off Tombland, is one street preserved out of hundreds without much alteration, and is cobbled and now lined with antique dealers. The Briton's Arms on the corner, now an exceedingly good though not expensive buffet restaurant (try their Swedish herrings), was a pub, but after that the headquarters of the Norwich Wherry Trust. Just around the corner from it, on your right as you face the top of the hill, is an ugly brick Victorian building, with ecclesiastical overtones, which is used by the shoe manufacturing department of the City College This was once the home of that strange prophet, Father Ignatius, but Norwich became too hot for him and he took his community off to live in the fastnesses of the Black Mountains, at Llantony, Capel y ffin Augustine Steward's house, now a good tailor's shop, is in Tombland, and should be noticed. Steward was Deputy Mayor during the difficult days when Kett and his men lay on Mousehold Heath (see p181).

The **Maddermarket Theatre**, between Charing Cross and Pottergate, is perhaps the most famous amateur theatre in the world. It was the first to go back to an Elizabethan apron stage, and has a tradition of anonymity among its actors, who are generally admitted to be the best amateur company in the country. It owes its success to the inspiration of the late Nugent Monk.

Up on the **Market Place**, and Gentleman's Walk, are the various market stalls, with their awnings of various colours: certainly the most picturesque market place in England and one of the most ancient. Originally the market was in Tombland, but was moved to its present position when the Normans came. The cattle market was hard by the castle, but it was moved into the suburbs in 1960 and is said to be the most modern and up-to-date cattle market in the world: the sales rings look like astronomical observatories and cattle go through them thousands a day, many to be sent to the Continent for beef. Norwich has always had one of the greatest cattle markets of the country, for here was the centre for the distribution of all the store (i.e. unfatted) cattle that were brought in from Ireland and Wales, and down from the North of England and Scotland, for East Anglia, and subsequently the gathering place for the cattle newly fattened in the yards of the great arable farms and on the lush marshes. Mr Smith, the Clerk of the Markets in Norwich, claims to be the holder of the oldest municipal office in England. There are continuous records of his office going back to 1456, though it may be considerably older.

The **Guildhall** is a perfect little Gothic building somewhat restored but the lovely east end, completed in 1535, is older. There is a magnificent sword inside. It belonged to the Spanish admiral Winthuysen, but was captured by Nelson at the Battle of St Vincent, and presented to Norwich. The Guildhall was built in the first half of the fifteenth century, in 1511 the roof fell in, in 1634 the place was nearly undermined by saltpetre diggers, in 1861 Thomas Barry, the City Architect (who built the controversial porch on St Andrew's Hall) clapped a police station on the south side of it, and in 1908 it was proposed to pull it down! You can go inside it in the afternoons between 2 and 4 p.m.

The vast modern **City Hall** is an unhappy amalgam of brick and stone: some of the bricks having been carted all the way from Buckinghamshire (though there was a perfectly good yard making hand-made bricks just outside Norwich). The roof, we are told, is of concrete and asbestos, supported on steel beams. The design is said to have been inspired by Ostberg's Stockholm Town Hall. Heraldic lions are stuck on the walls, outside, looking less East Anglian than Babylonian. There is a fine collection of civic plate inside. The City Hall was opened in 1938 and looks it.

The new **City Library**, next door, is an example of good, unobtrusive, modern architecture, and it seems that modern architecture to be good must be unobtrusive, for this age cannot carry off the grand statement. They have gone to the trouble of panelling the outer walls with flint, the traditional East Anglian material, and the result is very pleasing. The building includes the American Memorial Library, given by the 2nd Air Division, USAAF, in memory of their men who died serving from East Anglia in the Second World War.

Norwich is a thriving and striving modern industrial city, although most of its industries have at least their roots far back in the past. The boot and shoe industry was old in Norwich in the Conqueror's time, it suffered some eclipse during the great days of the cloth industry, but came into its own again when the cloth industry fled to the North of England in search of coal. Then the thousands of skilled hands in Norwich, bereft of employment, turned to boot making. I asked an official of Norvic's factory how long he had been in the industry, and he said: 'Well I know my great-grand-father was a garret-master.' Until recent years garret-masters organized the work of shoe workers who worked at home, but now all the work is done in factories.

There is heavy engineering and light, electric motors, chocolate biscuits, insurance, and a factory which did the metal work for the airship R101. The BBC has a studio in All Saints' Green, in a fine Georgian house.

If you want a good view over the city go up on **Mousehold Heath**. This, like Lollard's Pit, is holy ground to lovers of liberty, for here Sir Roger Bacon and Geoffrey Lister stood up for the freedom of Englishmen in 1381, and Robert Kett and his men for the same cause in 1549 (see North Walsham and Wymondham, pages 149 and 179).

CHAPTER 6

The Yare

Broadland is basically three main rivers: Waveney in the south, forming the border between Norfolk and Suffolk, Yare in the middle, forming the sea water route between Norwich and the sea, and Bure in the north. Bure ('the North River' to all Broadsmen) is the most characteristic of the three, winds the most, connects with most 'broads', and has most tributaries.

The way to see Broadland is by boat and there's an end to it. Roads avoid the waters. The rivers wind, and are cut off from dry land by miles of soggy marshes, alder carrs and reed beds. Norwich itself is a Broadland city, and Broads pleasure boats come up Yare and Wensum to within a quarter of a mile of the cathedral.

At **Thorpe St. Andrew**, John Sell Cotman, one of the fathers of English landscape painting, was born in 1782. Thorpe has been called the Norfolk Richmond, and indeed this riverside suburb has an urbanity and some good eighteenth-century dwelling houses, and modern flat buildings, but is spoiled rather by being cut off from the water by an urgent motor road. The river is placid and tree-flanked, and on it float motor yachts of the plushier kind. Joseph Stannard's painting 'Thorpe Water Frolic', in Norwich Castle Museum, depicts the place in lustier days.

Brundall, farther downstream and also on the north bank, is also a place of select riverside residence, with an Edwardian air and plenty of very typical Broadland marshes and reed beds to the south of it. There is a tradition that the Romans had a shipyard here.

Strumpshaw, besides having a comic little hill from which you can see both Norwich and the German Ocean, has a church with a good fifteenth-century screen.

Cantley is blessed with a sugar beet factory, the smoke of which can be seen during the autumn and winter 'sugar campaign' from many miles up and down the Yare and, indeed, all over the Broadland. The factory was built where it is so that beet could be transported to it by water, but alas, short-sighted counsels have prevailed, and the factory now uses only road and rail, and the narrow winding Broadland lanes are now made perilous by lurching sugar beet lorries.

The traveller will before this have noted that the sugar beet is one of East Anglia's chief crops, generally the only 'root break' among the constant succession of white straw crops, chiefly barley. Sugar beet is a laborious crop to grow. After the seed has been drilled in early spring the little plants must be singled out, and this is still generally done with the hand hoe at a big cost to the farmer. Tractor hoeing is then necessary at least once, and a second hoeing by hand, and then the beet must be lifted, either with an expensive machine which often breaks down, or by hand. When harvested by hand the operation is known as 'knocking and topping', for two beet are knocked together to shake off the mud, and subsequently topped with the topping knife. In the autumn, and right through until after Christmas, much of the rural population of East Anglia is out in the fields 'knocking and topping'. Factories such as the one at Cantley then extract the sugar, and the remaining waste material is bagged as 'pulp' and returned to the farmers to make a very good cattle feed.

A 'Blytheburghes boat' foundered in the river at Cantley in 1343. She was laden with sea-coal, salt, iron, Baltic timber, onions, and salt herring and, of course, was bound for Norwich.

Norton Staithe has a fine drainage windmill, restored in 1962 by the Norfolk County Council and now looked after by the National Trust.

Reedham is a most excellent place. It spreads along the broad river (big steamers come past for Norwich or the sea), and seen from the water it is one of the most attractive water fronts you could find. There are several good pubs, and an hotel, and another very good pub too down at Reedham Ferry, and even if you never wish to cross the river there make an excuse to do so, for the voyage in the chain ferry is an experience not to be missed, and the only way you can get a car across the Yare between Norwich and Yarmouth. Reedham is supposed to have been a seat of East Anglian kings, and it is here that Lothbroc, old Leather-breeches and a Danish prince, is supposed to have been murdered by the English king's falconer, but this story has been told once and for all time by the road-mender in Julian Tennyson's *Suffolk Scene* and I will not repeat it here (see Hoxne, p59).

Acle has a flourishing little market, famous among local breeders of store pigs because these animals fetch such good prices there. The church is thatched, has a Norman tower, and a font of 1410 with lions and nice wodewoses, or wild men. Messrs Smithdales of Acle are the last firm of millwrights in East Anglia and are currently engaged in repairing windmills.

Halvergate is a big village depending for its existence on many square miles of marshes to the east of it. The marshland, all reclaimed from the sea, is much cut up by dikes and studded with the remains of old pumping windmills now replaced by electric pumps. Much of the grazing is parish-owned and auctioned off to graziers every year; but there is currently a move of big graziers to 'enclose' much of this grazing, making the grazing of each area the prerogative of one man only, so that he can feel that he can spend capital on developing it. Fine fattening cattle are to be seen on the marshes of the three Broads rivers every summer, but in the winter the whole unpopulated area is given over to the snipe and wild duck, the curlew and the heron. The fattening of cattle on these Norfolk marshes is an age-old pursuit. A hundred years ago kilted High-landers used to walk down from their fastnesses driving skinny cattle, to be sold in Norwich market for fattening. Norwich market has waxed fat on 'store' cattle (thin cattle ready for fattening) to be sold to the graziers, and then again from the very same cattle, duly fattened, brought in to be sold to the butchers. This traffic still goes on unabated. In 1723 Daniel Defoe wrote:

> These Scots runts, so they call them, coming out of the cold and barren mountains of the Highlands of Scotland feed so eagerly on the rich pasture in these marshes, that they thrive in an unusual manner, and grow monstrously fat; and the beef is so delicious for taste, that the inhabitants prefer 'em to the English cattle, which are much larger and fairer to look at. Some have told me there are above 40,000 of these Scots cattle fed in this country every year, and most of them in the said marshes between Norwich, Beccles and Yarmouth.

The other traditional activity of Norfolk farmers, fattening cattle in the winter time in yards, on straw and roots and imported 'cattle-cake', is now in disfavour, as artificial fertilizers have taken the place of the 'muck' which was produced by these yarded beasts and without which, once, our arable farming could not have been conducted. But there appears to be, now, a renaissance in another form of this ancient arable activity in the fattening of 'barley-beef', very young animals kept in large and very crowded yards and fed so quickly on barley-meal that they can go to the butcher a year old.

Breydon Water is a large stretch of tidal salt water or of mud, depending on the time of the day. It is a desolate place in winter, with cormorants sitting on the big posts planted in the mud which mark the narrow channel for the big ships. Many and many a Broads hire cruiser goes ignominiously on to the mud here, in the passage from the 'North River' to the Waveney or the Yare.

This might be the place to discuss the Norfolk Wherry, for at one time big fleets of these vessels used to race each other across Breydon Water on their way up from the ships in Yarmouth harbour to the quayside of Norwich, or back again with Norwich goods for export. Of all the sailing vessels evolved by use and time for a highly specialized purpose, the Norfolk Wherry was perhaps the most famous. She had to be capable of sailing very close to the wind (for it is difficult to 'tack' in very narrow rivers), of being brought about single handed and with great ease, of navigating very shallow broads and rivers, of dropping her mast with great facility to shoot the many bridges, of being propelled by man-power when the wind failed or was a dead header down a narrow reach, of pushing through reeds, and of carrying a good weight of cargo.

The Broadland rivers form a close network of water roads in a highly populated and very productive country, and thus a big fleet of these cargo vessels came into being and there was strong competition to evolve the most efficient form. The end result was a vessel some 58 feet long by 14 feet beam and 4 feet draught, with a soft-chined hull, a long straight keel (which in some cases could be dropped on the river bottom so that the boat could penetrate a very shallow creek, to be picked up again on coming out), with sweet lines, a mast 40 feet high but quite unstayed except for the heavy fore-stay used for lowering the mast down and hauling it up. Owing to its being unstayed the mast had to be strong, and was some 12 to 15 inches in diameter. So that it could be lowered it was in a tabernacle, and had three-quarters of a ton or more of iron or lead at its heel to act as a counter-weight. A child could raise or lower this enormous spar with his hand. A big wherry would carry 40 tons.

The sail plan was simple: one large, black, high-peaked mainsail, bent to a long gaff but boomless, and nothing else. The height of the sail made it efficient for catching the breeze over high trees (very necessary in Broadland), the shape made it efficient for sailing into the wind. The shape of the hull, particularly the bow section, gave the wherry the extraordinary power of 'shouldering' along a lee bank, when sailing near the wind, pushing a cushion of water between herself and the bank as she sailed. A wherry could sail straight for a bridge—drop mast and sail all standing—shoot through—and have her mast and sail up again, sail drawing, losing hardly any speed. When wind failed, the wherrymen supplied a 'shoulder breeze', punting with long poles called 'quants' (they are called 'spreets' in the Fenland waterways), shoved from the shoulder as the wherrymen walked from forward to aft along the deck. The men were a race apart. They lived in their little warm cabins, drove their craft into every nook and cranny of their maze of rivers, got their food off land and water as they could, formed a floating community of their own. Now there is one sailing wherry left, the 'Albion', owned by the Norfolk Wherry Trust. Many an old wherryman is still alive, though, and willing to tell the stranger, in the pubs of Broadland, of the days and the life that are gone. Most of their sons have become lorry drivers.

The A47 runs straight as a ruler across the flat marshes to **Great Yarmouth.** Yarmouth is supposed by many people to be nothing but fat cockney women in funny paper hats jostling each other along the crowded prom. It is that, but many other things too. To the sailor it is an exciting harbour entrance, and many a good ship has smashed herself against the South Pier, or missed the harbour and rammed the beach to north or to south of it, or—in sailing-ship days —been forced to beach herself on the 'spending ground' round the bend of the harbour in desperation. To the Broads pleasure sailor Yarmouth is a long 'marina' where the Bure meets the Yare, where he can tie up preparatory to making the (to him) perilous crossing of Breydon Water. To the lover of ancient places it is a big town of narrow streets and 'rows', old buildings, and much history—which is nearly all connected with herrings.

In Roman times the site of Yarmouth may not have existed, or at best was a sand-bank surrounded by sea. The Romans had their town to the north of it, at Caister, and their great fort and naval base at the top of Breydon Water at Burgh Castle. What is now Broadland was then under a tidal sea, and Norwich was practically a seaside town.

In Anglo-Saxon times Yarmouth was a scattering of huts on a sand-bank, occupied by migratory fishermen. In Norman times, and just before, the fishermen of Rye and Dover and the other Cinque Ports used to come there in force every year for the 'herring voyage', and Edward the Confessor granted rights to the Barons of Hastings to control the annual 'Herring Fair' to which buyers came from far and wide to buy salt herrings. For six hundred years the 'Portsmen', or bailiffs of the Cinque Ports, came to Yarmouth to control the Herring Fair and protect their fellow citizens. As time went on, and Yarmouth became an important place in its own right, their arrival led to friction and resentment, and silly arguments as to who should sit in the front pew in church; but in the seventeenth century the thing was settled amicably and the institution lapsed. The banner that the Portsmen were wont to have borne before them is still preserved at Dover, though, and the brazen horn with which their heralds announced their presence is at Romney.

To the rest of England, and indeed northern Europe, Yarmouth meant herrings. Henry appointed a Provost who received an annual rent of 10,000 of these fish. In 1238 there was a disastrous drop in price because the Swedish buyers were prevented from coming to the Fair—by the fact that the Tartars were at Sweden's gates. In 1357 the Statute of Herrings was enacted, which defined a 'last' as 10,000, a 'hundred' as 6 score, which fixed maximum prices, enforced a free market and made it compulsory for boats to moor inside the harbour before discharging their herrings, thus ensuring Yarmouth's monopoly.

But in the sixteenth century Yarmouth was falling upon hard times. She was forced to sell the church plate, also the bells and vestments, in order to pay for yet another attempt to keep the harbour mouth open. The common mouth of the three rivers was always trying to break through in another place, and the old channel was often silting up: Yarmouth was for ever fighting for its very existence to keep the channel clear. Further, there was stiff competition from the Netherlands. Dutch 'busses', or herring ships, sailed into Yarmouth with their catches, and undersold the English, and when denied the use of Yarmouth as a base they salted their herrings at sea (as indeed they still do) and took them straight back to Europe to undermine the Yarmouth export trade. For ever since the herrings mysteriously departed from the Baltic in the early Middle Ages, northern Europe had become used to buying this important fish from Yarmouth. Charles I ordered that the Dutch fishermen should be driven from our waters; Cromwell carried on this policy, and so did Charles II.

In October 1797 the men of Yarmouth watched Admiral Duncan and Onslow bring in the captured Dutch ships of the line after Camperdown, and after that Dutch power in the North Sea began to decline and Yarmouth had a revival. The Sunday nearest Michaelmas was for years celebrated after this as 'Dutch Sunday', a fair was held on the South Denes, and the ceremony of 'wetting the nets' performed there.

In the nineteenth century the Dutch boats were seen no longer in Yarmouth, but Scots ones came instead. Every year a huge fleet of 'Scafies' and 'Zulus' sailed from the north, then came steam drifters, and nowadays motor boats, many of them 'pair fishermen'. 1913 was the heyday, with a thousand vessels fishing the Yarmouth herring voyage, Scots and English, and thousands of Scots fisher girls gutting the herrings on the South Denes.

But, with modern gear, notably 'mid-water trawlers' from Continental countries, principally Russia, the fishermen have become too good for the fish. The North Sea shoals of herring have dwindled to very nearly nothing. The mid-water trawl, unlike the drift net, takes spawn and immature fish. The North Sea has become fished out. Most years for a decade now have been financial failures for the Yarmouth herring voyage, Scots boats come in fewer and fewer numbers and there are fewer and fewer East Anglian drifters and most of what there are fish in the Irish Sea or other waters. And, for trawlers, Yarmouth has been far outpaced by Lowestoft, which has built up a powerful mid-water fleet.

But Yarmouth still flourishes as a trading port. Ships from all the Baltic countries, from London, and from the North of England, lie along her long straight quays. However she is no longer the great ship-owning port that she was. In 1702 no less than 211 colliers were registered in Yarmouth—all carrying coal from the north: more colliers than had any other port including London. In 1776 Parson Woodforde wrote in his Diary (he was Rector of Weston Longville near East Dereham):

Nothing can beat what we saw today—immense sea room, ships and boats passing and re-passing—the wind being rather high, the waves being like mountains coming into shore . . .

In the evening we took a walk on the quay—as fine a one as ever was seen . . . we got on board an English vessel and were treated with wine, gin, etc. The sailors behaved very civil to us; had a difficult matter to make them take anything. She was a collier, and soon going back to Sunderland.

Major E. R. Cooper wrote that in October 1838:

. . . there were nearly 2,000 vessels lying wind-bound in Yarmouth Roads. They got underway on November 1, and were followed by another 1,000 from the southward; all 3,000 sail went through the Roads in five hours, so that the sea could hardly be seen for ships.

Yarmouth still owns some ships, which visitors might do worse than take passage aboard. There is *Queen of the Broads* (built in Yarmouth 1889 and powered by a beautiful compound steam engine), *Yarmouth* (built 1895 and very similar to the *Queen*), *Resolute*, a youngster built at Millwall in 1901, and some motor boats of less character. These take passengers out to the Scobie Sands to see the seals, or up the Broadland rivers. The afternoon trip to Reedham is well worth making.

Yarmouth was sadly smashed in the World Wars, particularly in the second one (both by bombing and shelling), and many of the famous 'rows' were destroyed. These were very narrow alleyways running at right-angles to the shore. There were special hand-carts once for carrying goods in them. The market place in Yarmouth is fun, in the summer, and there you can buy such delicacies as cow's udder, cow heel, tripe, and huge Portuguese oysters at a shilling apiece. The fourteenth-century Tolhouse should be visited. It is now a museum, and one of the oldest municipal houses in England and has a fine timbered roof to its main hall. It is open 10 a.m. to 5.30 p.m. but not on Saturdays. The old merchant's house at Row 117, South Quay, is seventeenth century with fine woodwork and iron-work and is open every day of the year excepting Christmas and Boxing Day, for sixpence. Numbers 6, 7 and 8 of Row 111 have been restored by the Ministry of Works, and are also examples of small seventeenth-century houses. 4 South Quay is a merchant's house of 1596 and contains exhibitions of domestic life. Open May to September, but not on Saturdays.

The Priory and Parish Church of **St Nicholas** was founded by Bishop de Losinga as one of his penances for the sin of simony. Alas, it was bombed in the Second World War, but has been rebuilt within the remains of its old walls in a lavish way. The church-knower may or may not like it; but should certainly go and see it. It is one of England's numerous 'largest parish churches in England', and certainly it has wide aisles, an enormously wide nave, and a floor area of 23,000 square feet. The modern electric lighting is one of its best features: the fittings are well designed and meet for their job and not made to look like anything but electric light fittings, and seen in depth across that vast expanse they look impressive. There is some modern glass by Mr Brian Thomas and five noteworthy and very spiky modern wall paintings by Meneer Ru van Rossem, done while he was teaching at Yarmouth Art School. The patron saint, St Nicholas, is patron also of seafarers, children and pawnbrokers (who all have in common innocence of heart, perhaps?), there are Tufa stones from the Rhine in the Norman tower brought hither as ballast in Norman ships, and the word 'holy-stones' used by sailors for the rough stones with which they scrub the decks is supposed to derive from stones from the fabric of St Nicholas, and therefore holy as well as good for scouring. In the churchyard there is an interesting tombstone commemorating the loss of life when a new suspension bridge over the Yare collapsed in 1840. The Eye of God can be seen in the relief looking down at the disaster in some surprise.

For better or for worse Anna Sewell, author of *Black Beauty*, was born in Great Yarmouth, and Sarah Martin is locally revered because she used to read the Prayer Book to the inmates of the dungeons in the Tolhouse jail. Dickens, of course, wrote marvellously of Great Yarmouth in *David Copperfield*. His description of a gale there is superb.

Apart from its garish sea-front Yarmouth is a wonderful town, and most worthy of exploration. It is terribly sad that so much of the old town was smashed up in the wars, and that more has been bulldozed since to make room for worse things. Yarmouth is now in process of becoming an oil boom town, as it is used as a base for drilling operations being conducted in the North Sea.

The East Anglian Maritime Museum was recently established in Great Yarmouth and is well worth visiting. Down on the front there is a waxworks show and a place where you can watch 'Yarmouth Rock' being made, in all sorts of strange shapes, some of them bizarre, not to say rather ghoulish.

And I cannot resist quoting from the works of that dissolute Elizabethan Thomas Nashe, although he was a Lowestoft man, on the chief product of Yarmouth. It was in an orgy with Nashe, incidentally, of Rhenish wine and pickled herrings, that a Yarmouth man called Robert Greene overreached himself and died of over-indulgence. But thus Nashe:

The puissant red herring, the golden *Herperides* red herring, the red herring of Red Herrings Hal, every pregnant peculiar of whose resplendent laude and honour to delineate and adumbrate to the ample life were a woorke that would drinke drie fourscour and eighteene Castalian fountaines of eloquence, consume another *Athens* of facunditie, and abate the haughtiest poetical fury twixt this and the burning Zone and the tropike of Cancer . . . But no more winde will I speed on it but this: Saint Denis for Fraunce, Saint Iames for Spaine, Saint Patrike for Ireland, Saint George for England, and the red Herring for Yarmouth.

Gorleston, over the Yare and down near the mouth of it, has some very interesting old streets and still some of the atmosphere of an old seaport, and it has a lifeboat station with a tradition of heroic rescues. Whether rightfully or not Gorleston men are called 'Kill-Jews' by some of their less reverent neighbours: in recognition of the fact that they are supposed to be very thrifty. It is implied that even a member of a mercantile race would find it impossible to get a living among them. The *Gorleston Psalter*, a lovely early fourteenth-century illuminated manuscript, is now in the British Museum.

Three miles inland (we here dip into Suffolk) is **Burgh Castle**, with the Roman fort of Gariannonum, once one of the chief naval bases of the *Comes Litoris Saxonici*, the Count of the Saxon Shore. We know that the Emperor Carausius once held this title, and that a Provost's command of African cavalry was stationed at Burgh Castle. They must have found the east wind a bit raw.

The fort was complementary to Caister, which was a Roman town and port northwards over the great estuary which has now dwindled to Breydon Water. A contour map will enable one to imagine this country in Roman times, when all that is now sea-level marsh was then sea, and the sand-bank on which Yarmouth now stands was only then being formed. Burgh Castle was thus on a wide arm of the sea. All there is now is a quadrangular field surrounded on three sides by walls and open on the other. The flint rubble has eroded badly, leaving the harder, or better bonded, tile upper courses to stand out, and thus many fragments of the wall stand up like so many vast mushrooms. It is difficult to imagine what the fort must have been like, beyond that it was large (620 feet by 383 feet), but it is fascinating to stand there and try to fill in the details of this great fortress looking over miles of shallow water to the low wooded hills of Norfolk, with fleets of war galleys at anchor, and Gallic trading ships sailing in—bound upstream to yet another Roman Caister—that near Norwich.

Besides plenty of Roman coins and pottery, Saxon relics have been found; and Burgh is supposed to have been the site of the Cnobheres-burg mentioned by Bede, where the Irish missionary St Fursey settled and founded a monastery, in the reign of Sigebert, about AD 640. St Fursey later became an anchorite, sensibly removed to France to get away from pagan invasion from Scandinavia, founded a monastery at Lagny, near Paris, and his body is at Peronne, where it is said to have defied corruption, and is still an object of reverence and pilgrimage.

St Olaves Priory, near the bridge across the Waveney, was founded by Roger Fitz Osbert in Henry III's time, and was of Austin canons. It has an early fourteenth-century undercroft with a brick vaulted ceiling, unusual at so early a time. It is open all the year, but not Sunday mornings, and entry costs sixpence. One Sirek was the ferryman at St Olaves in Edward I's time, and the bridge over the Waveney was built in the fifteenth century by the wife of Chief Justice Hobart, of London. The owner of St Olaves is still always called 'The Prior'. There are two good drainage windmills at **Herring fleet**, where St Olaves Priory stands, both smock mills, and one of them has been repaired by the East Suffolk County Council, and is to be preserved as an example of one of the hundreds of windmills which once pumped water up from the low marshes into the high wall-enclosed rivers of the Broads country. Now this work is done by oil and electricity. Strangers sometimes express wonder why, if so many pumping windmills were necessary (and still survive in ruin) in Broadland, then are no such windmills in the far greater area of the Fens, where the water has to be lifted from the low land to the high rivers in just the same manner. The explanation of this is that in Broadland the mills could be put on hard foundations, and therefore were substantially built of brick. In Fenland they had to be built on peat, and the level of the peat was constantly altering. Consequently it was the fashion to build them of a temporary wooden framework so that they could be easily moved. Hence none survive. At Manor Farm, Herringfleet, is a superb great thatched barn with Tudor flint and brickwork, and the church has a tower which looks Saxon but which is said to be in fact early Norman, and some colourful German glass.

Fritton is famous for its Decoy, a beautiful tree-surrounded lake three miles long (once Gunhilde's Mere, after an aunt of King Canute). The practice of duck-decoying, still practised in one or two places but no longer at Fritton, involves luring wild duck down from the sky by feeding barley and also by keeping a flock of tame duck. The tame duck are trained (by feeding) to swim into a large netting funnel, on the signal of a whistle from the operator and (surprisingly) the appearance of a small white dog. The wild duck swim after the tame, the entrance of the funnel is closed, and the wild duck have their necks wrung and are sent to Smithfield and other places.

Fritton has a queer asymmetrical thatched church, with a low and dark semi-circular Norman chancel, a Saxon base to the tower and Roman bricks. Still to be seen are the iron rings, 700 years old, between nave and chancel on which the Lenten Veil was once hung. Here one can still imagine something of the ancient rites and mysteries of the early Church, when religion was a magical affair.

Somerleyton has a vast neo-Elizabethan hall, built on the shell of a genuinely Elizabethan one by Samuel Peto, a man who had made a vast amount of money out of railways, and who had a hand in building Lowestoft Harbour. He also did a thorough job of the village and the church, and the place is interesting, perhaps, as a period piece. There are large, lush gardens, and a maze. The hall can be viewed on Thursday and Saturday afternoons, for 3s throughout the summer.

Haddiscoe (we are back over the Waveney in Norfolk now) is known to sailors for its Cut: a straight artificial canal joining the Yare with the Waveney and cutting off some miles of navigation including Breydon Water. This canal was made in Victorian times by the men of Lowestoft, who were busy trying to cut Yarmouth's throat by forcing through an entrance to the sea for Norwich at Lowestoft instead of at Yarmouth. They succeeded physically in making their channel but financially the thing was never a success. It came to little, and recently even the lock between Lake Lothing and Oulton Broad, a vital link in the waterway, collapsed, and is only to be repaired after a great fight to save it from being filled in. Haddiscoe Church is famous for its round Saxon tower, good Norman south doorway (note figure over it) and a floorstone in the nave for Jan Piers, a Dutch dikemaster who drained many of the surrounding marshes.

We might make a detour through Wheatacre and Burgh St Peter and Aldeby, for this is a remote countryside, much cut-off from the world by being in a loop of the River Waveney. **Burgh St Peter** has a church a long way from the village, remarkable for its strange brick tower which is shaped like a square telescope, and is a great landmark to sailors on the Waveney. Beside it is an hotel, in a fine position and with a jetty into the river. Sailing up the river here very early in the morning I once saw many score of coypu. These still exist in Broadland, in spite of the cold winter of 1962–63 which killed most of them off. They are rodents, as large as spaniels, at home in the water as on land, rat-like in appearance but with the extraordinary feature that the teats of the females are along their backs and the young ones cling on to these when the mothers are swimming and thus are dragged along the top of the water.

Aldeby was Aldeburgh in Domesday, and thus is Anglo-Saxon, not Norse. There was a priory there, founded by Ralph de Beaufon immediately after the Conquest, and a tablet in the wall of the church commemorating one Will Slater, a coach driver, in these terms:

> *True to his business and his trust,*
> *Always punctual, always just.*
> *His horses could they speak, would tell*
> *They loved their good old master well.*
> *His up-hill work is chiefly done;*
> *His stage is ended—race is run.*
> *One journey is remaining still,—*
> *To climb up Zion's holy hill.*
> *And now his faults are all forgiv'n*
> *Elijah-like drives up to heav'n;*
> *Takes the reward for all his pains,*
> *And leaves to other hands the reins.*

Raveningham has a fine Georgian hall with Cotman and Turner watercolours inside it, and paintings by Constable and Gainsborough.

Loddon is a delightful old East Anglian town, once a Broads port, with a watermill even now on the River Chet which connects with the Yare. There is a pleasure boat yard, and the headquarters of a famous seed firm, Cannells of Loddon. The church is large and fine and fifteenth century, standing grandly in a vast graveyard, and has a painted screen unusual in that it depicts scenes instead of just people. It has a representation of St William of Norwich, bound saltire-wise to stakes, with Jews catching the blood which is gushing from his side in a basin. Anti-racialists will be glad to know that recent historical research has completely discredited this gory legend. These screen panels may have come from the older, Norman church, and have been moved to the present building when it was built, which was between 1480 and 1490. (Dr Tudor-Craig says they are not pre-1480.) A relic of an even earlier church—the Anglo-Saxon one—is the alms box on the pillar facing the door. This is hewn of one piece of oak, like a dug-out canoe; and is supposed to be one of the oldest in England. It may well be old, for there is a legend that Loddon Church was founded in AD 630 by St Felix himself, the East Anglian apostle.

When the present Perpendicular church was built it was paid for by Sir James Hobart, Attorney-General to Henry VII and ancestor of the man who built Blickling. This man has his altar tomb in the sanctuary, and in the south aisle, near the door, his portrait is painted on a panel with that of his wife, Francis. Loddon Church and St Olave's Bridge are depicted with them: he paid for the church and she for the bridge.

For those who admire the constructions of the eighteenth and early nineteenth centuries Loddon is a gem of a little town. How nice to have seen it when the stately sailing wherries reached up the little River Chet, and lay and loaded and unloaded at the old wharfs. But for people interested in our present age Loddon is important too. This century has seen our country defaced from one end to the other with ugly, boring, tasteless council houses. The ones built since Hitler's war are not quite so crassly hideous as the ones built before, but they are bad enough. But at Loddon, and in the area controlled by Loddon RDC, the recent council housing has been designed by a firm of Lowestoft architects, Taylor and Green, and it is (or should be) a model for council housing for the world. Keeping well within the financial limits set by the council housing, obeying even the ludicrous laws of proportion (which legislate for a race of giants, or giraffes) these architects have managed to design homes which blend in beautifully with their surroundings, which continue in the tradition of East Anglia without slavishly aping the past, which do not strive ridiculously into a space-age future, which have unity and yet diversity, which in every case are pleasing to the eye, and which are said by the inmates to be pleasant to live in. It is well worth seeking out these little estates wherever they are to be found, and every architect in the country should be made to go and look at them.

At **Langley** are the flint remains of a Premonstratensian abbey. At **Rockland St Mary** is the New Inn, well known to Broads sailors who venture into Rockland Broad. Rockland is a perfect little broad, reed and tree-surrounded, connected to the Yare by a long narrow shallow channel along which, at one place, a line of old wooden sailing wherries have been sunk to form a bank. One can look down into the water-filled cabins and think of the bright coal fires that once burned in the stoves and of the life that was once lived there.

Into Rockland New Inn are brought reeds, in the winter, cut notably by Mr 'Fudgy' Stone, who uses the traditional Broads reed punt to carry them in. The reeds are cut in standing water (the Yare here is still slightly tidal), often in snow and ice (ice makes it easier, for the reed beds then are firmer walking). The reeds in winter are thick and brown and shoulder-high—one can easily cut oneself on them, and the clothes of the reed-cutters last but a short time. The reeds are tied into bundles, brought by punt to dry land, and sold to thatchers at prices which become higher and higher every year and make thatching with Norfolk reed a very expensive business (£200 or £300 for a very small roof). But a Norfolk reed roof should last seventy years, except for the ridge, which is generally done in the more flexible wheat straw and which needs renewing every twelve years. A kind of sedge grows in Broadland, however, which is some-times used for ridging, and which will last nearly as long as the reed itself. An extensive example of this latter can be seen in the big shooting lodge on Hickling Broad. Hardly anyone now remembers that the downy tops of the reeds were at one time stripped off as 'fledge', and used to stuff cushions, horse collars, and other things that needed stuffing.

Surlingham has a nature reserve, under the control and owner-ship of that excellent Norfolk naturalist, Mr E. A. Ellis. Here is Broadland life to be seen in its fullness and perfection.

CHAPTER 7

The Waveney

From Norwich one might advantageously begin the journey to the Waveney by going down the valley of the River Tas.

Arminghall, just south-west of **Trowse**, is the site of a large Neolithic temple, discovered from the air in 1929, excavated in 1935, and consisting of significant depressions in the ground best seen from a flying machine. It was a sort of wooden Stonehenge, 270 feet in diameter, and late Neolithic: dated *c.* 2500 BC.

Venta Icenorum was the Roman town at present-day **Caistor St Edmunds**, or Caistor-by-Norwich. This is well seen from an aeroplane too, for from above the complete street-plan of the Roman town can be descried—public baths, forum and all.

From the air it can be seen that the streets of the Roman town extend beyond the walls, as though they were built before the walls and the latter were superimposed on them. Roman occupation is supposed to have begun about AD 70 (mid-first-century pottery has been found), and then streets were laid out on the grid-iron pattern. It can be imagined (from the name as much as anything) that Venta was at first simply a trading station in the country of the Iceni tribe, probably much like a nineteenth-century Red Indian trading station. About AD 100 public buildings of more durable material were built: forum, basilica (Town Hall) and public baths with water brought from the Tas by wooden pipes. The walls were built about AD 200. These were substantial: an outer ditch some 80 to 100 feet wide crossed by wooden bridges at the gates, a wall 11 feet thick and 20 feet high, with towers at intervals, backed by a thick earthen rampart, and built of flint rubble faced with brick and dressed flint. There was a gate in each of the four walls. In the third century two temples were built near the forum: in 270 the forum and basilica were rebuilt, but smaller, on the old foundations. About AD 300 glass-making started in Caistor, and there was a pottery. After 360 the town began to decline, and the presence of a large Anglian cemetery outside the east gate has given rise to the belief that Anglian mercenaries were brought in to defend the town against Saxon pirates. Evidence indicates that the Romans, or Romano-British, lingered on until the early fifth century. For most of the above information I am indebted to Miss Barbara Green, of Norwich Museum.

What we see at Caistor now is romantic in the extreme. There is a farouche little church crouching down low behind the huge grass-grown east wall of the Roman town, far from any village and only just holding its own, one feels, against the pagan ghosts that beleaguer it. The path into the church passes through what was the east gate of the Roman town, and there are blocked Saxon windows in the south wall of the nave and a fine fifteenth-century Four Evangelists font. On this are the arms of Edward the Confessor, (probably thought up posthumously since Saxons didn't have arms) and it is thought that there was a west gallery in the church built about 1050 for no less a person than the king himself: for the church was in his gift before he gave it to Bury St Edmund's Abbey. The inside of the church is simple and has an indefinable air of great antiquity. The scrubbed quarry-tile floor is pleasant, and so are the white high plain walls—but ruined by the *scandalous* electric heaters slung up on both sides.

Much of the charm of East Anglia lies in its valleys, and the valley of the Tas is no exception. The Tas villages are as charming as their names: Stoke Holy Cross, Swainsthorpe, Newton Flotman, Flordon and Tasburgh. At **Newton Flotman** is a medieval bridge, and a monument in the church to his forebears put up by Thomas Blandevyle in 1571. Blandevyle was famous in his day as a writer on such diverse subjects as astronomy, navigation, logic and horse-manship. There is also Eric Master's bakery (oil-fired ovens and most excellent bread) (map, p106). **Long Stratton** is a pretty village and the church is the only church in England save Yaxley in Suffolk to have a sexton's wheel. This is in fact two wheels which counter-rotate. The upper had strings attached to it—one string for every day of the year sacred to the Virgin Mary. A person wishing to keep a Lady Fast, or Madonna's Fast, would ask the sexton to spin the wheels, and the string of the upper wheel which caught in

the lower wheel indicated on which of the six possible days the supplicant might propitiously keep the fast.

Tivetshall St Margaret has a monstrous Royal Arms of Elizabeth I over the chancel arch—a truly spectacular piece of work. **Pulham St Mary** is notable for its double-storied porch, said by some to have been built by William of Wykeham and others by John Morton, Archbishop of Canterbury, Lord Chancellor of England, and Cardinal of Rome in Henry VII's reign. The porch has carved pinnacles, traceried stone between bands of quatrefoils, small windows in front, niches under canopies, angels, and embattled beams in the roof. It is a gem of stone work, and well worth going off the road to see. There is an Early English piscina in the church, like three intersecting stone rainbows.

Pulham Market is a charming little town, still substantially unspoilt.

Harleston (Saxon *Herolfston*) is actually in the Parish of Redenhall with Harleston and Wortwell. It is one of Norfolk's many good small, predominantly eighteenth-century towns. It sadly needs by-passing for there can be little peace or pleasure in a small town cursed by through-traffic. But there are pleasant little closes with names like Keeling's Yard and Shipp's Close which one should look into, and a minaret over the Midland Bank from which, momently, one expects to see the manager lean forth and utter the Call to Prayer. Harleston church is Victorian, but the dressed flint is worth looking at, for it belies the contention that men have lost the art of working in dressed flint. It is very good. (Whether men could do it *now* though is open to question.)

The Swan Inn is Georgian, and mellow, and pleasant to go into.

Redenhall (Saxon *Radahalla*) has an old church, and a very fine one: the Norfolk historian Blomefield described its fifteenth-to-sixteenth-century tower as 'The finest tower of any country parish church in the country'. Certainly its proportions are beautiful, and the relationship of tower to nave. If you went to Wingfield, over the river, you would recognize the leopards carved on the base of the tower, for these are the de la Pole emblem. The roses with them are for Brotherton. If you clamber up the tower you will get a fine view of the Waveney Valley, and also see the rebus of a former rector, carved on the south-east pinnacle, a shell and a tun, for his name was Shelton. The modern crossword addict had his counterpart in the sixteenth century. The west door has horseshoes, farrier's pincers and a hammer carved on it, and a bullet hole fired by a man who was very rightly transported to Australia for this peccadillo. The double eagle lectern is fine, and about 1500, and you should not miss the fifteenth-century Venetian vestment chest, which has paintings of a square rigger and galleys inside the lid. It is a noble church altogether, but as there is an excellent little guide book (obtainable in St John's at Harleston if not here) I shall say no more about it.

From here on, downstream, the **Waveney Valley** is extremely beautiful. If John Constable had been born at Harleston, instead of at East Bergholt, we would have processions of motor coaches along the Waveney instead of along the Stour. As it is, the Waveney is frequented only by people who have business there, or the rare few who know of its beauty and go for pleasure. But certainly Constable's Stour has nothing the Waveney has not got, except Constable.

At **Homersfield** (in the Parish of St Mary South Elmham otherwise Homersfield) there is a pub by the river bridge which serves very good food, at the bar as in the dining-room. And—if the landlord likes the look of you but not unless—you may get a room. The Waveney about here is, incidentally, a coarse fisherman's paradise. The plaque on the bridge with a red hand on it is the emblem of the Adairs. From here one may well strike southward into the Saints' Country.

The **Saints' Country** is real back-block of East Anglia, a hill-billy land into which nobody penetrates unless he has good business, and that is always connected with agriculture. The reason why it is called Saints is that it contains the following parishes: St Mary South Elmham, St Cross South Elmham, St Margaret South Elmham, St Nicholas South Elmham, St James South Elmham, St Michael South Elmham, St Peter South Elmham, All Saints South Elmham, Ilketshall St Margaret, Ilketshall St John, Ilketshall St Andrew, Ilketshall St Lawrence, and All Saints Mettingham. So beware of getting lost: it is really not much good asking anyone the way. There are purists who will tell you that the Saints' Country only includes the South Elmhams and not the Ilketshalls, and that the latter are part of the 'Seven Parishes' and include All Saints Mettingham and the two parishes of Bungay. But actually, to most local people it is all 'Saints'. The South Elmhams were a deanery, in the manor of Almar Bishop of East Anglia. The Ilketshalls belonged once to Ulfketle, Earl of East Anglia in the eleventh century.

But, apart from perhaps liking to see a very remote and lost (if not particularly beautiful) farming country we go to the Saints to see **South Elmham Minster.**

There is an Elmham in Norfolk and, as we have seen, a whole rash of them in Suffolk; and the men of both counties have long been eager to claim for *their* Elmhams the honour of being the seat of the second East Anglian bishopric (Dunwich being the first). Alas for Suffolk: research indicates that North Elmham probably wins the day. But, whatever South Elmham Minster was, and whatever it was used for, it is a most romantic place to go to and should not be missed. (At the time of writing excavations are being made here.)

One proceeds from Homersfield to Elmham St Cross, keeps straight on through the little village, and on to Hall Farm. Here one must ask permission to go farther, for the holy place is on private ground; but the farmer (Mr Anderson) is a courteous man and admits the truly interested. The Hall itself is a good sixteenth-century house with a stepped gable and several older stone arches inside: built originally, it is said, by de Losinga to be a summer palace for the Bishops of Norwich. There is a stone building in the garden (by the moat) called the chapel, although whether it was one or not none can say: certainly there are no specific ecclesiastical features.

From the Hall it is expedient to *walk*—south across the fields— and you will come to the Minster surrounded by high and beautiful trees, elms and hornbeams, around which, in the nesting season, rooks wheel and shout. The situation is lonely and romantic. Inside the square of trees, growing from a deep ditch and bank, stand the ruins of an ecclesiastical building nearly, if not quite, a thousand years old. There are no Ministry of Works sign-boards, litter baskets, nor indeed litter, and you are unlucky indeed if you find anyone else there. The ruin is just over a hundred feet long. It was long thought to be seventh century, very early Anglian; but excavations carried out by Ipswich Museum in 1964 date it as eleventh century (although a ninth-century gravestone was found under the foundations). Still to be seen are the remains of a semi-circular apse, a short, aisleless nave and a third division of the church, either the sub-structure of a tower or a narthex. This latter was an anti-nave used in early Christian churches for lesser breeds such as catechumens, penitents, and the excommunicated. Such an arrangement can be seen today in the Syrian Christian churches of the Nestorians or Thomists in southern India.

It would be hard to go to South Elmham Minster, alone, and not feel a sense of mystery and of awe: and what of a night vigil at the time of the full moon! This was a holy place very far back in our East Anglian history, and its complete desolation today makes it the more impressive.

Bungay is the most interesting town in the Waveney Valley, and one of the most beautiful in East Anglia.

One theory of the derivation of its name is that it comes from *Bon Eye*—good island; but Professor Schram says that it derives, in fact, from *Bun-incga-haye*, meaning the Enclosure of the Tribe of Bonns. The town still retains, and has done certainly for a thousand years, a Town Reeve and Feoffees. Town Reeve is a much older title than the upstart Mayor, which only came in with the Normans.

But Bungay is certainly a long-inhabited place (apart from the fact that the skull of a hairy rhinoceros was dug up nearby). Before the sea receded from Broadland it must have been open to navigation—probably at the head of navigation on the river, and also it was on an easily defensible island. The fosse to the west of the castle is supposed to be Ancient British. Bungay was an important river crossing for the Romans (whose Stone Street ran through it to Venta), when the Normans came there was already a castle and an important settlement, and the Normans quickly made it a very strong place.

The first Norman owner was William de Noyers who had it from the Conqueror in 1070. In 1103 it went to our old friend Roger Bigod (see Framlingham, p50) and Hugh, Roger's son, built a keep with walls 18 feet thick and probably 90 feet high in 1165. When Hugh rebelled against Henry II in 1174 the latter ordered his castle at Bungay to be dismantled, but Bigod paid a fine (the old ballad has it of 'three score sacks of gold', but the history books say 1000 marks). Henry forbore and the castle was spared. Sir Hugh's defiance lingers on in song and story in Suffolk and Norfolk, and until recently—and who knows, perhaps even still?—children sang rhymes about it:

When the Bailey had ridden to Bramfield Oak,
Sir Hugh was at Ilketshall Bower
When the Bailey had ridden to Halesworth Cross
He was singing in Bungay Tower:
'Now that I am in my castle of Bungay

> Upon the River of Waveney
> I will ne care for the King of Cockney.'

Another rhyme has it, though, that he was actually in his castle of Framlingham when forced to surrender to 'the King's Bailey' and shouted down from the walls:

> Were I in my castle of Bungay . . .
> I would ne care for the King of Cockney.

The visitor can see, under the south-west corner of the ruins of the keep, a mine-gallery: indeed he can creep through it if he likes. This small tunnel goes from the west side diagonally across to the fore-building on the south side, and in the middle of it are two small cross-cuts (as a miner would say) running north-east and south-west into the masonry. This could be nothing else but an unfinished sapper's tunnel driven with the intention of causing that corner of the castle to collapse. The practice was to drive such a tunnel, shoring perforce with timber as you went, and then, at the appropriate moment, set fire to the timber and wait for the whole thing to come down. It is supposed that this sap was driven by Henry II's engineers (could it be supervised by Alnoth—the builder of Orford Castle and the dismantler of Bigod's other castle at Framlingham?) but discontinued when the ransom was payed up. It is also recorded that King Stephen attacked and captured *Castellum de Bunie* at Whitsuntide 1140.

Roger Bigod (another Roger) completely rebuilt the castle in 1294 (in 1281 Edward had given him 'the right to crenellate') as a big curtain wall in the Near-Eastern style brought back by the Crusaders, much like Framlingham. In 1483 the castle, by then long abandoned, passed to the Howards, Dukes of Norfolk, in whose possession it still is. The vast extent of the defended works is indicated by 'Castle Hills': some earthworks which can still be seen (rather mixed up with a bus depot and other things) to the southward. These marked part of the wall of the outer bailey. Beyond them, too, is the Town Ditch which was certainly Anglo-Saxon if not, indeed, Celtic.

It is a sad fact that in stoneless East Anglia castles do not last long. When they become redundant they are too often quarried for their stone; and this is what has happened to Bungay. All that is left of that massive keep of the Bigods are the stumps of a couple of towers

7. NORWICH. *Above left*, Elm Hill; *right*, the Keep. *Below*, the Cathedral nave

8. EAST ANGLIAN COTTAGE ARCHITECTURE. *Above left*, pargetting at Clare; *right*, Bishop Bonner's Cottages, near East Dereham. *Below*, Willie Lott's Cottage, Flatford Mill. John Constable lived next door and painted the cottage often

and a few banks and foundations. As at Orford one is puzzled as to where all that stone has gone to. We know that Bungay was thoroughly quarried in the eighteenth century (when so much quarrying was done) by a local builder named Mickleburgh, and that after this a folly cottage was built between the two towers by a romantic lady named Mrs Bonhote who wrote a novel called *Bungay Castle*, but the cottage has since been pulled down. The two existing towers were each side of the bridge pit, and the latter has recesses meant to accommodate a drawbridge (there is now a modern wooden bridge there). Beyond the towers can be seen the foundations of the two-chambered keep and the fore-gallery, which can now best be entered by crawling through the famous sap, or mine gallery. The ruins stand in a small green, surrounded by a fence; and the key can be obtained from the King's Head or, for teetotallers, from Norman's shop in Earsham Street.

Bungay is a famous printing town. There have been times when 80,000 books have come off the presses there in a week. In 1795 John Brightly, a school master, set up a wooden press. A grocer's assistant from Norwich, J. R. Childs, joined him, and drove all over England with a tandem and cart selling the books published by Brightly. Childs consolidated his position by marrying Brightly's daughter, and subsequently the firm became John and R. Childs. Childs became, locally, a great man. George Borrow and Edward Fitzgerald used to go all the way to Bungay to dine with him.

In 1837 Childs, a strict Nonconformist, was sent to prison for refusing to pay the church rates, but released after a great liberal agitation to return in triumph to Bungay. Because of his immurement the church rate was abolished. In 1866 the firm printed the second edition of *Alice in Wonderland*, and it still holds Sir John Tenniel's original wood blocks. John Childs, incidentally, was a phrenologist and notable for his grisly collection of skulls.

There is a fine Butter Cross in the centre of Bungay, a domed octagonal shelter surmounted by a lead figure of Justice. This was built to replace an earlier market cross after the great fire which consumed Bungay in 1688. Under the Butter Cross stands, not a butter-wife, but a fish salesman; and he sells very good fish and is locally popular. In 1964 the local council tried to move him, to make room for a bus stop. But the fishmonger (he doubles as a publican) pleaded the fact that a market and fair was established in Bungay in 1199 by Hugh Bigod, and he waved his arm above him to the figure of Justice, and he won the day. He still stands there selling his fish, and the buses have to stop where they can.

Near the Butter Cross is an electric light standard with the Black Dog of Bungay depicted on it, on a leaden panel (the lead was part of the now defunct Corn Cross). A bronze plate at the base of the standard quotes these words:

> *All down the Church in midst of fire*
> *The hellish monster flew;*
> *And passing onwards to the Quire*
> *He many people slew.*

This is in memory of that Sunday in August, 1577, when Old Shuck or Black Shuck, the terrible Black Dog of East Anglia, appeared in the church during a thunderstorm (the same one in which the Devil left his mark in Blythburgh Church), and wrought great havoc. Sightings of Shuck are common in East Anglia, nowadays as in the past.

The chief, and very grand, church in Bungay is St Mary's, and it was the church of the Benedictine nunnery founded by Gundreda, wife of Roger de Glanville, in the middle of the twelfth century. Ruins of the nunnery can still be seen to the east of it. The lower part of the great tower (which has been compared to Redenhall) was built about 1450, the upper part after the great fire of Bungay of 1688.

St Edmund's, just down the road, is red brick and stone, 1892, Roman Catholic, and covered all over with statuary inside and out. It is nothing if not lavish. Holy Trinity, the other parish church, south-east of St Mary's, had a very early round tower with some Saxon work in it. Both Anglican churches have interesting church-warden's books: that of St Mary's dating from 1523, excellently preserved, and written in the greatest detail. It is a mine for local historians. There is a Druid's Stone to the west of St Mary's and if you dance round it, on the right night and in the right frame of mind, you will raise the Devil.

Modern Bungay is dated by the 1688 fire, for then Tudor Bungay was wiped out, with the exception of the odd house like the one in St Mary's Street which has Samson and Delilah carved on the window sill, and which is early sixteenth century. The other big factor in the building of modern Bungay was the rendering of the Waveney navigable, after the Navigation Act of 1670. The lock was built at Geldeston, the river canalized, and wherries came up in their hundreds. Many fortunes were made in Bungay water-borne trade. Bungay was a weaving place until as late as 1855: hemp was grown in the locality, many houses had hand looms in them, and 'Bungay Canvas' was famous for sails.

A Bungay industry is the working of leather. The firm of Nursey and Son Ltd was started in 1790, and is still in the hands of Nurseys. It processes sheep skins and turns them into wind-defying coats, slippers, hats, gloves, mittens and much else. Some work is done in the factory with modern machinery, but over 200 people are employed in the countryside round about hand-stitching skins in their own homes: the sort of local industry that does nothing but good to the countryside. Mr George Sneed, of Bacon Barn, Bungay, runs another good local industry: he is a turner and woodworker, and from him you can buy very good things.

Chateaubriand spent part of his life in Bungay: at the house of the Ives family (where he fell in love with beautiful Charlotte Ives). George Crabbe went to school at Bungay, and down by the river stands the Falcon Inn, once a merry place of wherrymen; and the man who kept it until recently was named Septimus Wildgoose. Over the river another pub is named the Triple Plea, and its sign depicts three men arguing over the body of a woman with the Devil looking on. The men are a lawyer, a doctor, and a divine. The origin of the sign lies in a piece of verse which starts in lively calypso style:

> *Law, Physic and Divinity,*
> *Being in dispute could not agree*
> *To settle which among them three*
> *Should have the superiority.*

It ends:

> *But if men fools and knaves will be*
> *They'll be ass-ridden by all three.*
> *Now if these three cannot agree*
> *The Devil shall ride them three times three.*

The Falcon and the Plea are not in Bungay, but in **Ditchingham,** in Norfolk. Here Rider Haggard used to live, and there is now an Anglican community of nuns at a house called All Hallows. These sisters tend the shrine of Mother Juliana, the medieval mystic and author, in St Julian's Church, King Street, Norwich. They also run a school, and nurse in hospital, and keep bees.

The Bungay-Beccles road south of the river takes you to **Mettingham,** where there is an old castle. A gatehouse remains, with two towers, and traces of a barbican. This was a house fortified by Sir John de Norwich, when he was licensed to crenellate in 1342 as a reward for having commanded the English forces at the Battle of Sluys (see Shotley, p75). For this service he was also made a baron. He was one of England's first great sea commanders, saw service against the Spanish as well as the French, was Admiral of the Northern Fleet and Bailiff of Yarmouth.

From Mettingham perhaps it would be best to go north except that it would be a pity to miss **Barsham,** with its round-towered church and seventeenth-century parsonage forming a lovely group set back amid tall trees. A curate of Barsham was the father of Horatio Nelson. Dr Joseph Arnold was born at Barsham, in 1784. Together with Sir Stamford Raffles he discovered *Raffiesia arnoldi,* the largest flower in the world. It will hold 12 pints of water, 15 pounds, has a foul odour of bad horse meat and attracts flies—if, indeed, it attracts nothing else.

But cut back and cross to the north of the river by Ellingham bridge, for there is a pretty watermill there, as pretty as Constable ever painted. Turn right then for Geldeston, but before you come to that place turn down a muddy track across the marshes to **Geldeston Lock.** Here there is the most superbly-sited little pub in Norfolk, where the beer has to be brought by boat from Beccles (when indeed the river is not frozen up and then it cannot be brought at all) and there is a charming Scottish landlady and an ancient lock overhung by willow trees. It is impossible to imagine a better place for a picnic or a fresh water bathe. The derelict lock is the present head of navigation on the Waveney: we may hope that the lock will soon be repaired and Bungay become a port again.

Beccles has a solidly comfortable waterfront which smacks to me of Edwardian gentlemen in white flannel trousers, blue jackets with brass buttons, and blue peaked yachting-caps. Nice gardens run down to the private staithes at which the smart varnished motor launches are tied up. The houses at the tops of the gardens are not Edwardian though, but solidly Georgian as are those of Bungay and for the same reason. Beccles also was burnt out—by a number of fires—and there is little of Tudor Beccles left. Beccles also had its heyday in the great days of the Norfolk Wherry, and was then a most flourishing port. A sailing barge with an auxiliary engine can still sometimes be seen tied up just below the Ship Inn, discharging grain into the mill there, and the last *billyboy* (one of the bluff-bowed sailing ships from Yorkshire which used to trade to every hole and corner of the East Coast) put in there in 1924. There is no lock between Beccles and the sea, and Beccles could be a seaport again if she chose to be.

But, as it is, Broadland cruisers lie tied up along the staithes, in serried ranks sometimes, and the town enjoys short visitations from women with comic shorts and men with funny woollen hats.

Beccles Church is impressive. It is simply impossible to ignore the churches in East Anglia. Each town or village that one comes to has a church of such beauty and grandeur that it is impossible to pass it by. Beccles church stands on an eminence, impressive for a flattish country, and it commands the valley to the west and north. Its south porch is worth going to East Anglia to see. It is double-storied, mid-fifteenth century, marvellously detailed, one of the finest porches in existence Inside the door the church is dull. The tower is separate from the church and a huge block of a Perpendicular edifice: a mighty mass of stone.

Beccles—now bigger than Bungay—was once much smaller, but the place is no parvenu. Domesday records that it rendered 10,000 herrings a year to the Abbey of St Edmunds. This reminds us that at that time it was almost a sea-port, for Broadland was still flooded. One notices again and again in East Anglia that only the places that are near navigable water have great churches, with vast amounts of imported freestone in them, such as Beccles. It was easier to sail a freight of stone from Normandy to the heart of East Anglia up one of her rivers, than it was to move it a few miles overland. The native flint—and later brick—was everywhere available, 'freestone' from France or Northamptonshire became more expensive every mile it had to be dragged from the nearest staithe.

One could spend some time wandering around Beccles, absorbing the urbane atmosphere of its eighteenth-century buildings. But, like Bungay, it is cursed with through traffic; Adrian Bell has written a book about Northgate, the street that runs down to the river, *A Street in Suffolk*, and in it he complains of the never-ceasing heavy traffic that shakes the old houses to their foundations.

Beccles is a growing small industrial town, with a printer, a factory that makes winches for trawlers and another which makes machinery. But you might live in Beccles and not know that there was a factory there.

Worlingham has a hall built early in the nineteenth century by Francis Sandys, of Ickworth fame, described by Norman Scarfe as 'perhaps the most beautiful house of manageable size in Suffolk', but the inside is far more beautiful than the outside. It is in a nice situation, with parkland and woodland going down to the Waveney marshes. (Map, p106).

Oulton Broad is a great place for small boat sailing, but made hideous from time to time (too often) by screeching speed boats. Sir John Fastolfe's funerary brass used to be in the church, but was robbed by a scrap-metal dealer in 1857.

George Borrow lived on an estate by Oulton Broad for the latter part of his life, and there he wrote several of his few books. He welcomed gipsies to stay on his land, a fact which enraged his landed neighbours, who showed Christian charity by persecuting these people as so many land-owners do today. Borrow was grandly eccentric at Oulton, striding about in a splendid cloak, leaping fully clothed into the Broad when he felt like it and swimming across it; joining in great parties with his Romany friends, quarrelling with his neighbours, being rude to poor Agnes Strickland when she tried to present him with her 'Queens of England' ('for God's sake don't, Madam. I should not know where to put them or what to do with them') and fighting (unsuccessfully) the railway company when they wanted to build their railway across his estate. Nothing remains of his house now. (Map, p106).

Lowestoft, like Yarmouth, is a great mixture. It has its big seaside resort element, more solid and 'respectable' than that of Yarmouth where the comic paper hat tends to be the order of the day. There are large and (to me) rather forbidding hotels and boarding-houses along the front at South Town. But the fishing harbour is the heart of Lowestoft.

On the opening-up of the Dogger Bank as a trawling ground, and especially with the discovery of the fantastically sole-rich 'Silver Pit', the big West Country trawling fleets moved round to the East Coast. The arrival of the railway in Lowestoft (unprevented by George Borrow) soon knocked out the great London trawling fleet based on Barking; for it was quicker to sail fish from the Dogger to Lowestoft and rail it to Billingsgate than to sail it all the way there.

(Hull and Grimsby benefited by the same factors.) From the pattern of the famous West Country 'Brixham Trawler' was evolved the equally famous 'Lowestoft Trawler', a heavy and powerful vessel, with a 'cod-fish bow and mackerel stern', ketch-rigged, often equipped with a steam winch for hauling the trawl, capable of holding the sea in any weather at all. It was almost never that a Lowestoft trawler was overwhelmed by weather alone, and they ranged all over the North Sea. As 'fleet fishing' was developed (the practice of letting the trawlers stay out on the grounds for months at a time, while 'fleet carriers' ferried the fish to market) the sailing smacks never saw port for months together, nor did the men.

There are no sailing trawlers left now, but a growing fleet of motor ones (including some of the very latest 'stern trawlers'—built at Lowestoft, for Lowestoft is still a considerable ship-building port). It is well worth taking a walk about the fish harbour, which is one of the best in Britain. For yachtsmen there is the famous 'Royal Norfolk and Suffolk Yacht Club'. There is a story that when Queen Victoria sent her royal consent for it to become a royal club the Secretary forgot to answer the letter, and it took years of lobbying by Edward Prince of Wales to get her to renew the favour.

See also the kipper-curing houses and net-drying frames. Lowestoft kippers were once famous, and some are still cured in the old fashion, with real oak smoke and not dye and 'smoke substitute'. The real ones can be recognised by being of a light buff colour. The best of the kippers are from the fresh herring that run in the autumn, and after smoking kippers should never be frozen.

Lovers of the best in modern architecture might look at Barclay's Bank building in Lowestoft, and also the interior of the Prince Albert Inn, both by that triumphant Lowestoft firm Tayler and Green.

Lowestoft Ness is the most easterly land in the British Isles, and Lowestoft is a most exhilarating place to be. It has the real flavour of the sea about it, and—in spite of heavy bombing and shelling in both World Wars—the old alleys called 'scores' (cf. the 'rows' of Yarmouth) running down to the Denes have great character. The lighthouse is open to the public from 1 pm on weekdays, and sea and river trips may be had from the Swing Bridge and the Yacht Basin.

Pakefield men were once known as the 'Roaring Boys', and were notable smugglers. The Reverend Francis Cunningham, one of their vicars, is said to have read the burial service over a coffin filled with contraband lace under the eye of the revenue men. The coffin was interred, but later dug up and the lace distributed. Another parson, evidently not so accommodating to the Free Trade, is said to have been buried alive by his parishioners. Nowadays the people of Pakefield are much more settled.

CHAPTER 8

The Bure and the Coast to Mundesley

Wroxham is the capital of **the Broads.** Here both banks of the Bure are deeply indented with artificial basins, in which—all winter —hundreds if not thousands of Broads boats lie waiting for their season of usefulness. Roys—the 'biggest village store in the world'— throngs all summer with people buying tinned food and woolly hats (indeed you can buy practically anything there), and the boatyards hum the year through with band-saw and planing machine as more and yet more Broads hire craft come off the production lines. And— every Saturday morning throughout the summer—a great army of strong-armed cleaning women descends upon the place, to clean the returning hire craft, swab them, scour them, turn them upside down and inside out and get them ready for the afternoon's new lot.

Horning, just down the river, on the north bank, with a ferry, is another great Broadland place but less resolutely commercial and it has more substantial Edwardian-type river-lodges with green lawns coming to the water's edge and thatched boat-houses. In its way it is a pleasant place—given over to the charm of lapping water.

It would be as well to warn here—if you love peace and solitude do not go cruising on the Broads in July and August. The ratio of motor boat to sail has, alas, altered very much for the worse in recent years, and the Bure can have all the quietness and solitude of the Southend Road on a bank holiday. I do not say that you *cannot* get away from the motorized and transistorized rabble, for there are plenty of quiet corners on the hundred odd miles of waterways of the Broads (Broads promoters always say there are two hundred, but I think there are only that if you go all the way and back!) And the two South Rivers are relatively unfrequented: most of the ordinary hirers start on the North River and cannot bring themselves to face the terrors of Breydon Water.

For years the origin of the Broads, these strange shallow lakes, or meres, which lie along the sides of the Broadland rivers and offer such marvellous opportunities for small boat sailing, bird watching, and pike fishing, remained a mystery. One would have thought that the first Dutchman who clapped eyes on them (particularly if he came from that part of his country known as Randstad Holland) would not have been in a moment's doubt; for his part of Holland has exactly the same kind of meres, but on a much larger scale, and it has always been known how *they* were formed. Indeed they are still being formed. But various and ingenious were the explanations—geological, hydraulical, and plain mystical—until somebody came up with the theory that they were just dug.

They were peat diggings. Then evidence flooded in. The comparison with Holland was at last made, a great amount of historical evidence was brought forward to show that the digging of peat was a great industry in late Saxon and early Norman times (until in fact the shipping of 'sea coal' from the North of England supplanted it), and soundings were taken that proved conclusively that the Broads were artificial. And indeed the merest glance at a map would indicate that they were. No natural movement of water, or anything else not man-aided, could have formed those basins of regular depth, each one connected by a straight artificial cut to the nearest river, obviously with the purpose of shipping the peat out. And I would here advance a further theory. For many centuries Great Yarmouth supplied the whole of Northern Europe with salt herring. Where did the salt come from? Certainly not all the way from the Cheshire salt measures. It must have come from the sea, and what more likely than that peat, so easily available and so conveniently connected to Yarmouth by water, was used to fire the brine pans?

It would be hard to describe to the uninitiated the abiding *charm* of the Broads. In a land where the difference in level between land and water is often only a few inches, where 'land' tends to consist of flooded reed beds or alder swamps so that it is difficult to say where water ends and land begins, where mysterious little channels open off the rivers and widen out into tree-surrounded lakes, where, in other places, the rivers run for miles between banks so that the sailor looks down on the backs of grazing cattle, and where the little villages are almost without exception beautiful: in such a land you must travel yourself, and by water, to find the meaning of this particular kind of charm. It is a new experience, and only to be

NORTH SEA

Sidestrand
Northrepps
Trimingham
Southrepps
Gimingham
Mundesley
A149
Trunch
Paston Street
Knapton
Bacton
Broomholme Priory
R. Walsham
Happisburgh
NORTH WALSHAM
Felmingham
Honing
Dilham Canal
Happisburgh Common
North Gap
Lessingham
Cart Gap
Swanton Abbot
Worstead
Sea Palling
Dilham
Ingham
Waxham
Stalham
R. Ant
Hickling
Sutton
Horsey
Barton Turf
Barton Broad
Catfield
Hickling Broad
N.T.
Coltishall
Neatishead
Potter Heigham
Horstead
B1354
Winterton
Frettenham
Hoveton
Ludham
Horning
B1150
WROXHAM
R. Thurne
Martham
Ferry
Hemsby
Woodbastwick
St. Benet's Abbey
Ormesby Broad
Salhouse
Ranworth
Thurne
Rollesby
Scratby
A1151
Walsham Broad
B1152
A1064
Ormesby
South Walsham
Filby
Hemblington
Upton
Caister Hall
Acle Bridge
Caister
Thorpe
A47
Acle
R. Bure
A47
Brundall
Strumpshaw
0   miles   4
Breydon Water

equalled by sailing the rivers and meres of Friesland, the Malabar Backwaters of South India, or other rare places, and somehow even these, though they may be fascinating, do not quite capture the subtle quality of the Norfolk Broads.

Again we are driven, willynilly, into the churches.

Where but in East Anglia will you again and again come to some tiny village, miles away from any big place and far from a major road, and find some masterpiece of medieval art? **Ranworth**, south of the Bure (it has two superb broads near it, but one chained off and private) has a fifteenth-century screen without a peer in the country. It is complicated with two projecting wings which serve as retables for two nave altars and two wings east and west to form the sides of these two chapels. The painting is in oils, and is said to show Spanish influence. The various figures on it have been identified thus:

North Retable: Saints Etheldreda, Agnes (with lamb), John the Baptist, Barbara.

Centre: Simon (with fish), Thomas, Bartholomew, James the Less, Jude (with boat), Matthew.

South Wing: Two small figures, Lawrence, Thomas, Michael (with feathered body).

South Retable: Mary with her two children James and John, the Virgin and Child, Mary of Cleophas with her two children (one of them is Jude, holding a boat), Margaret.

The faces, alas, are defaced; but nothing can convey the delicacy of the painting which remains: the red and green and gold of the flowers on their white ground, the hunting scenes—dogs and swans and ducks and lions. The whole thing was covered over at some time with whitewash, and discovered and cleaned in the last century.

Then, there is the *Sarum Antiphoner*: a sheepskin book written and illuminated by the monks of Langley Abbey in the fourteenth century, and a fine example of East Anglian illumination. It was lost in the reign of Edward VI, discovered by a Victorian collector, sold to a bookseller who offered it to Ranworth—whence it had come—for fifty guineas. This was raised by public subscription. The illuminations, of vegetable dyes and burnished gold, are as brilliant now as when they were first laid on. It is said that the gold leaf was burnished by rubbing it with agates.

Notice, too, the fifteenth-century oak lectern, which was probably used up on the rood loft before the Reformation put a stop to all that. One of its two desks has the plainsong notation of the Gloria painted on it, the other the eagle of St John. And climb up the tower for a magnificent aerial view of the North Broads. The church is now in good repair; not long ago umbrellas had to be used, inside, by the congregation.

Half a mile along the lane one comes to **South Walsham Broad**, beautifully tree-surrounded. South Walsham itself is a lovely little village. **Upton** is a scattered, lost place near an amphibious never-never land called, lugubriously, The Doles. It has a fine church with a marvellous fourteenth- or fifteenth-century font with dogs fighting, lions twisting their tails together, a dragon, and a man with a branch in his mouth. How it makes one wish to meet the artist! Acle we have seen, but north-east is **Acle Bridge**, where Broads sailing boats must lower their masts, and good sport is provided on windy days leaning over the bridge rail watching them do it. It is surprising what entertainment is provided. **Filby** and **Ormesby Broads** are not accessible by water from the Broads system, Muck Fleet, which ought to make them so, being silted up. They make together a great and beautiful stretch of water, and being crossed by two motor roads on causeways are easily seen by the motorist. Filby is another place with a good screen in its church: lions, birds, dogs and a hare being stooped at by a falcon adorn the gorgeous robes of fifteenth-century saints. (The upper carved part is nineteenth century, just in case anybody should be led to enthuse too loudly about it.)

And so we come to the coast again and Caister, Caister-on-Sea.

As one may infer by its name this was another Roman station: a very important naval base of the Count of the Saxon Shore. It once stood on the north side of the great sea-inlet which ran into Broadland from where Yarmouth now stands. The remains of the Roman town have been excavated, and can be seen; although as with most Roman remains, there is little enough to see.

Caister Castle (a mile inland) is all muddled up with Sir John Fastolf, or Fastolfe, Sir John Falstaff, and the Paston Letters (see p147).

Sir John Fastolf came back from fighting in the French wars, in the 1440s, having made a very good thing out of them. He led the English archers at Agincourt, helped to besiege Caen and Rouen, fought against Joan of Arc, took a big part in the political settlement after these events, and accumulated a lot of gold. With this he built Caister Castle, in which he spent the rest of his life in peace. He had made a great many enemies, but was a friend and helper to the

Pastons, and this has ensured his immortality, for he is mentioned again and again in the famous Letters.

Another oblique sort of immortality was given him by Shakespeare, who modelled his Falstaff partly on Fastolf. (The latter even owned a pub in Eastcheap called The Boar's Head.)

On Fastolf's death his castle went to the Pastons (the will was in doubt, as John Paston was the executor of it). Ten years after, the Duke of Norfolk, who apparently hadn't got enough castles of his own, laid claim to Caister, and—after a year's siege in which he had to bring up eventually three thousand men—he took it, and kept it until his death, when it was re-occupied by the Pastons. They kept it until the seventeenth century when they sold it to a London business-man who immediately set about pulling it down. But enough remains of it to give a lofty view over the countryside. The castle is open all round the year, the fine Hall near it April to September, 2 to 6 pm; entry a shilling.

Caister is notable for its lifeboat, and the vigorous long-shore fishing community that centres around it. The Ship is a delightful pub, much frequented by this nautical community, and there are medals in it which were presented to the men of Caister by the Tsar of Russia, for saving men off Russian ships. As at nearly every lifeboat station on the East Anglian coast there have been frightful disasters, the mortality figures of lifeboating make it, far and away, the most dangerous occupation in the world. In 1885 at Caister a 'beach yawl' (the precursor of the modern lifeboat) went down with all hands, and the RNLI lifeboat overturned in the surf in 1901. There is a lady in Caister today who will tell you how—when she was seven years old—she was sent off early in the morning to fetch the milk. When she got back her aunt (her mother was dead) said to her: 'Your father was drowned last night.' She ran down to the boat house, looked inside, and saw nine figures lying under blankets. Her father was one and her two uncles others. The boat had put out the night before into an impossible on-shore gale, been driven some miles down the coast and overturned in the breakers. In the morning the watchers on the shore had managed to drag out the bodies. When at the enquiry afterwards, the chairman of the Board asked one of the three survivors why, on seeing the impossible nature of the gale, the boat had not turned back, the man addressed said the words which have become the motto of Caister fishermen: '*Caister men never turn back!*'

At **Hemsby Gap** there is Bingo.

Winterton is a wind-swept little place of much character. The Fisherman's Return is a fine pub, marred only by a juke box, and again there is a fine community of fishermen. Winterton men have, for years, gone away to sea in Yarmouth trawlers or drifters, or else fished off their own beach in little boats. There is an old rhyme in Winterton which I don't think does the place justice:

> *Pakefield for Poverty*
> *Lowestoft for Poor,*
> *Gorleston for Pretty Girls*
> *Yarmouth for Whores,*
> *Caister for Water Dogs*
> *California for Pluck:*
> *Beggar old Winterton—*
> *How Black she do look!*

There are several old men in Winterton who remember the sailing trawler days (the most famous was Mr Sam Larner, who knew a thousand songs and broadcast some of them frequently on the wireless. Alas, he died in 1965). They will tell you of the days when the smacks sailed out of Yarmouth northward-bound, and raced each other to the South Shields fishing grounds:

> *First the Dudgeon,*
> *Then the Spurn.*
> *Flamberry Head*
> *Come next in turn.*
> *Scarboro' Castle*
> *Standing high*
> *Whitby Rocks*
> *Lie Northerlie!*
> *Sunderland*
> *Lay in a Bight*
> *Canny ol' Shields*
> *Afore Dark that Night!*

If they had a fair fresh of wind on their beam or abaft of it the great smacks would 'sail like the Devil' and leave steamers far behind.

Defoe went to Winterton, and wrote that half the village was built from the timbers of wrecked ships, and that 200 coal ships were lost off it one winter's night, and thousands of lives. Before the RNLI station was closed down the boat, in its short career, had saved 500 lives.

The church is splendid: on a height, and its **great** tower (127 feet) is a famous landmark for sailors (as is Caister water tower). The church has a fine stone porch, and an anchorite's cell in the wall. The names of many perished fishermen are written up in the church.

Horsey stands where the Broads come to within a couple of miles of the sea, on what must at one time have been a very narrow, low, and apparently sea-threatened strip of land—a neck providing land communication to Roman Caister. Roman coins have been dug up there, and there is Saxon work in the church. One can sail into Horsey Mere with a Broads boat, and take a short walk to the beach and have a bathe in the North Sea. It is here that at very high tides the sea has broken into the Broads and flooded thousands of acres.

Happisburgh is pronounced 'Haisboro', and gives its name to the dreaded sand-bank a dozen miles out, which stretches parallel with the Norfolk coast. There is a lonely lighthouse on a cliff, and the beautifully proportioned fifteenth-century church tower is no less than 110 feet high. Probably, like other coastal church towers, it was built high to be both watch tower and landmark for sailors. Lights were often put in church towers before the days of Trinity House. There is a beautiful octagonal font.

In the churchyard are buried 32 men off HMS *Peggy* which went on the sand in 1770, 119 men of HMS *Invincible*, wrecked 1801, all hands of HMS *Hunter*, wrecked 1804, twelve men of the barque *Young England*, wrecked 1876, and three German airmen from Hitler's war.

The coast makes its transition about here from being low-lying and protected by sand-dunes only (compare the Netherlands) to high ground with cliffs.

Instead of following the coast north of Winterton it might be desired to strike inland to **Potter Heigham**. Here is a famous medieval bridge, again a marvellous place for the land-lubber to lean on the parapet and watch the Broads sailor making a fool of himself below, for here the latter must lower his mast and negotiate the old road bridge, which is villainously low, and also the railway one. There are generally some real working wherries to be seen lying at Potter Heigham, their huge masts recumbent and their sails all removed. They are motorized now, and used mostly for carrying mud. The old village of Potter Heigham is a mile north of the bridges and the growing Broads settlement by them, and was the site of a

Roman pottery. Great piles of wood ashes from the kilns have been found. The church has a beautiful roof, with embattled hammer-beams, a rather defaced fifteenth-century screen, and some interesting wall paintings. Harry Cox, perhaps the most famous real folk singer in the world, lives at Potter Heigham. He is a retired farm worker.

Ludham, more inland, has a church that—anywhere but in East Anglia—would be famous. Ludham is beautifully situated on high ground between the Rivers Thurne, Bure, and Ant. Womack Water connects it to the Thurne, and Ludham Bridge is over the Ant. On the Bure are the remains of St Benet's Abbey, which must indeed have been in a swamp. One imagines that the monks must have suffered terribly from the rheumatism, if not indeed from the shaking ague. There is little to see there now, although every Broads sailor is familiar with the stump of a windmill growing out of the remains of the Abbey gate right by the water's edge, with cattle grazing the lush pastures around it. Because at the Dissolution the reigning Abbot became Bishop of Norwich, and surrendered the cathedral estates to the Crown while retaining those of the Abbey, the Bishop of Norwich still draws his revenues from the old estates of the Abbey, and is still the Abbot: the only mitred Abbot in the House of Lords. Consequently, once a year, on the first Sunday of August, the Bishop visits the ruined Abbey by water (it is difficult to get there by land) and holds a service. It is worth going there, in a boat, to watch him.

Hickling has a famous broad and gave its name to a punt designed for wildfowling. However the broad is now owned by the Norfolk Naturalists Trust and is a National Nature Reserve. It is a great pike-fishing water. Down the lane which goes to the White Slea (a division of the broad—a sort of Sea of Okhotsk) is the famous 'Royal Shooting Lodge', built almost in the water, and beautifully thatched with Norfolk reed and ridged with sedge grass. Inside the lodge are many paintings by local bird artists and the place has a marvellous period atmosphere. The 'Pleasure Boat' at Hickling Staithe, at the other end of the Broad, is a fine inn and a good place to sail to, or to get to in any other way. Mr Edwin Vincent is king of the Hickling pike fishermen, and once caught a 31 pounder.

Barton Broad is a beautiful reed-ringed broad on the River Ant, almost unapproachable by land. West of it is the tiny village—so small that it doesn't really exist—of Barton Turf, in the church whereof is perhaps the second best rood screen in England. Here there is a fine set of the orders of angels fourteenth century:

Potestates: armed, with a devil on a chain and a scourge.

Vertutes: 4 winged, with cap, sceptre, and feathered body.

Dominaciones: 4 winged, triple-crowned and with chasuble.

Seraphim: 6 winged, feathered body, fire girdle, censer.

Cherubim: 6 winged, many-eyed, feathered, girdled, with outspread hands.

Principatus: 4 winged, belt with bells, vial and palm.

Troni: 6 winged, long-sleeved robe, holding a church and a pair of scales.

Archangeli: in alb, alms box at girdle, spear, 2 naked souls a' praying.

The angels are beautifully painted, and really most alluring.

There is a later, fifteenth century, section of the screen with Henry VI, King Edmund, Edward the Confessor, and a Dane with a battle axe and two loaves of bread.

Stalham has one of the finest fonts in England. It has a small boatyard connected by what is obviously a canal to the Ant. There is a mill there, still working, but alas trading by road now, instead of by wherry as it used to.

A country road due north brings us to **Bacton**. Here we are getting well into the flint country, which stretches westward along the Norfolk coast (and well inland too) until it merges with the carrstone country of N.W. Norfolk. Many of the villages, we shall find, are predominantly built of flint, and this lends the whole countryside a distinctive character: the villages have a hard, speckled, almost 'tweedy' texture. **Bromholm Priory,** at Bacton, was in the Middle Ages one of the holy places of Europe.

There is still a gateway, and some ruins of a choir and conventual buildings, now part of a farmstead as Mother Shipton prophesied they would be. Some of the ruins were turned into a fortification in Hitler's war and there are concrete and loopholes. It all looks desolate enough, surrounded by flinty hedgeless Norfolk fields and with tractors and combine-harvesters standing about amid the ruins.

Bromholm is mentioned at least twice in *Canterbury Tales* and once in *Piers Plowman*. 'By the Holy Rood of Bromholm!' was a binding medieval oath. Originally a small and very poor Cluniac House, founded in 1113, it was visited early in the thirteenth century by a wandering priest, who had a portion of the True Cross. He had been chaplain to Baldwin of Constantinople, had filched this relic (it was carved into the form of a double crucifix) and had hawked it all round Europe but found nobody who would pay his price. The monks of Bromholm would though, and promptly raised no fewer than thirty-nine people from the dead with it, and cured blindness, leprosy, possession by the Devil, and many lesser evils. Pilgrims began to stream in (among them Henry III) and the priory became enormously rich, and for a time rivalled even Walsingham.

Paston is a tiny hamlet, where the famous Paston family lived, before they moved to Oxnead, Norwich, Caister, and other places. The most notable sight there is the famous Paston Barn, built in Elizabethan times of flint and thatch and with an alternate hammer-beam and tie-beam roof. In the church is a Paston monument, said to be that of the John Paston who was the executor of Sir John Fastolf's will. He was supposed to have been buried in the priory, but was removed to Paston at the Dissolution.

At this point we will mention the Paston Letters. The most extraordinary collection of intimate, private writing from the Middle Ages, these letters tell us not only a great deal about East Anglia but also much about the History of England.

The Paston men spent much of their time in London going to Law, or else at home defending their enlarging properties from various attackers. The lawlessness of the times (fifteenth century) is shown by such passages as this, in a letter from Margaret Paston to her husband John in London—a passage thrown in among demands for groceries and cloth at 44d the yard—'. . . Pray you to get some crossbows and windacs to bind them with, and quarrels; for your houses here be so low that there may none man shoot out with no long bow, though we have never so much need.' And she goes on to ask for short pole-axes and jacks. (Jacks were armoured jackets, quarrels were the bolts to be fired from crossbows.)

John Paston sent a petition to the king, saying that Lord Moleyns had seized his manor of Gresham, storming it with a thousand men 'arrayed in manner of war, with cuirasses, briganders, jacks, sallets, glaives, bows, arrows, pavises, guns, pans with fire and teynes burning therein, long cromes to draw down houses, ladders, picks with which they mined the walls, and long trees with which they broke up gates and doors'.

The men may have been, nay were, hard and worldly; probably they had to be to exist: but one is struck again and again by the gentleness, high education and good common sense of the women.

What could be more tender than this, from a wife to a husband? From Margaret to John her husband, who was then ill and Mayor of Norwich:

> By my troth, I had never so heavy a sickness till I wist of your sickness til I wist of your amending ... if I might have had my will, I should have seen you ere this time: I would ye were at home lever than a gown, though it were of scarlet.

(*Lever* is still a common East Anglian word.) And what husband would not be moved to forgiveness by this:

> Right worshipful husband, I recommend me to you, beseeching you that ye be not displeased with me, though my simpleness caused for you to be displeased with me. By my troth, it is not my will neither to do nor say that should cause for you to be displeased; and if I have done, I am sorry therefore, and will amend it. Wherefore I beseech you to forgive me, for your displeasance should be to heavy for me to endure with.

(She then goes on that she wishes him to send her some herrings and eels.)

Probably the most famous love letter ever written was by a Paston girl to her father's farm bailiff with whom she had fallen in love. But there are plenty of references to weightier matters, such as the detailed account by one Wm. Lomner to John Paston about the cutting off of the Duke of Suffolk's head with a rusty axe at Dover (see Wingfield, p61).

Paston Windmill has been repaired by the County Council.

Mundesley is a good solid respectable seaside town, and that is all there is to say about that. **Knapton** Church has the best double hammerbeam roof in Norfolk.

Trunch is a little inland village worth seeing for at least one thing: the magnificent four-poster font cover, or baptistry. I will not describe it, but merely advise the reader to go and see it, for it is a marvel of medieval wood working. Again much of its impact rests on the apparent remoteness from 'civilization' of its setting.

Trunch also has a noteworthy group of farm buildings, with flint walls patterned with brick. We are really drawing into the flint country here, and there are few sights more solidly satisfying than a good group of farm buildings: farm house, bullock yards, stables, piggery, implement shed and mighty barn: all built of the grey flint, and standing grouped together like a medieval fortress. At Trunch lives a famous builder of organs, just as at Cley, farther along the coast, lives one of violins (the making of which he doubles with boat-building).

North Walsham, yet farther inland, was pretty well wiped away in the great fire of 1600 (how much of Tudor East Anglia went up in flames!) and what is there now is a little town replete with Georgian prosperity. Much of the latter was due to the digging of the North Walsham and Dilham Canal, which connected the town with the River Ant and the Broads and thus with world commerce. But North Walsham was prosperous before Tudor times too, and was a famous wool weaving town: hence the great empty church, with its ruined tower 150 feet high, and all that stone from Barnack in Northamptonshire. It is an interesting and beautiful little town today, completely unselfconscious and unspoiled, with little winding alley-ways to explore. The Market Cross was put there by a Bishop of Norwich in 1550. The arms of Edward III and John of Gaunt are carved in the pinnacled porch of the church, and there is a good fifteenth-century font cover with a pelican feeding her young at the top of it, and the ghost of a fifteenth-century screen. There is Sir William Paston's tomb, for this is Paston country. But the most notable aspect of the church is the fine uncluttered vista inside that huge nave and chancel.

Sir William Paston founded the Paston Grammar School in 1606, and it is still working, although rebuilt in 1765. Nelson went to it, from the age of ten to when he went away to sea in the *Raisonnable*, with an uncle. North Walsham must have had a lot to do with the forming of his character.

There are several crosses about the country near North Walsham, and one about a mile south of the town is known as the monument to the Peasants' Revolt of 1381. The Black Death led to a shortage of labourers, thence to the Statute of Labourers which was to make labourers labour, thence to the 1379 Poll Tax, thence to unrest and Wat Tyler and—in East Anglia—Sir Roger Bacon and Geoffrey Lister. On 17th of June 1381 a mob met on Mousehold Heath, marched on Norwich, and killed the commander of that city, Sir Robert de Salle. They were counter-attacked by Henry Despencer, the Bishop of Norwich, at the head of a strong force. The Bishop drove them from the city, attacked their main body on North

Walsham Heath, and defeated them. Geoffrey Lister fled to the sanctuary of North Walsham Church. The Bishop had him dragged from the altar and drawn and quartered, but first was as good as to grant him absolution.

The village of **Worstead** has given its name to a cloth. At the beginning of the fifteenth century William Paston wrote to a cousin: 'I pray you will send me hither two ells of Worsted for doublets, to happen this cold winter, and that ye enquire when William Paston bought his tippet of fine worsted cloth, which is almost like silk, and if that be much finer than that ye should buy me after seven or eight shillings, then buy me a quarter and a nail thereof for collars, though it be dearer than the others, for I shall have my doublet all Worsted, for the glory of Norfolk.'

Worstead was known for cloth before Edward III brought his Flemings over to 'exercise their mysteries' and to teach Englishmen how to make fine cloth; but it is probable that worsted cloth was made by the Flemings from the first, for there was some immigration right from the time of the Conquest. Worstead was undoubtedly a town before it was a village, and had two churches. With the passing of the woollen trades to the North of England it dwindled away; but there are still weavers' houses to be seen there, with tall ceilings to take the looms, and cellars to store the wool.

The present church is one of the grand ones of Norfolk. The tower is 109 feet high, with elegant detail: the Victorian pinnacles were happily struck by lightning and removed. Note the vault in the lower story of the porch, with the Coronation of the Virgin in the centre boss and the symbols of the evangelists around it. The lovely flowing tracery of the east window is late fourteenth century: the chancel clerestory and the two chapels perhaps a century later. The chancel screen dates itself as 1512. The lettering which names the painted figures is Victorian and possibly inaccurate but certainly the southernmost figure is that stubborn virgin St Uncumber, who miraculously grew a beard to stop her father from marrying her off, whereat he, reprehensibly if perhaps with some justification, crucified her. She is the Patron Saint of beards. William of Norwich stands—with his pair of nails and a dagger—beside her, beatified in the cause of anti-Semitism; and twelve other figures probably represent the Apostles. At the west end is a ringers' gallery, but the screen below it is much repainted by the Victorians. The font cover, fine if nearly rebuilt in 1954.

Coltishall is a little place of simple enchantment, and near it there is magnificent coarse fishing in the River Bure.

Frettenham is remarkable for the enlightened, and so far as I know unique, action of a Victorian squire who gave half an acre of land to every householder on his estate, thus anticipating Sri Vinobe Bhave: the Indian apostle of land reform.

CHAPTER 9

Aylsham, Cromer, East Dereham

There are two rules to follow in East Anglia to ensure the pleasantest travelling: one is to stay in the river valleys, the other is to avoid main roads. From Norwich to Aylsham we might follow the former rule by going back along the Coltishall road as far as Horstead and then travelling up the Bure. This will take us through the village of **Buxton** where Thomas Cubitt was born, the man who, some might think for worse, built more of nineteenth-century London than anybody else. The other rule would take us out of Norwich through Drayton and Reepham.

Drayton has its Old Lodge, built by the redoubtable Sir John Fastolf, left, like Caister, to the Pastons and attacked while in their hands by the greedy Duke of Suffolk and therefore mentioned in the Letters. **Felthorpe** has Mr Royal Cooper, the farmer poet and philosopher, who sells his books of verse at his farm gate as another farmer might sell eggs.

Reepham is another of the scores of good little eighteenth-century towns in Norfolk and Suffolk. It has two churches and the remains of a third, for the parishes of Hackford and Whitwell had their churches in the same churchyard as Reepham. Hackford's was burnt down in 1543, Whitwell's is still there and has a good Jacobean pulpit. Reepham's is a fine building, with an altar-tomb to Sir Roger de Kerdiston who died in 1337. This is a beautiful piece of carving, exquisite in detail, and has fine moustaches. There are good bench-ends too, which should not be missed.

This is a good day for the church-hound, for just east of Reepham is **Cawston** which I think is my favourite church of all. It has a superb tower all faced with freestone. Whence all that stone so far from a navigable river? The cost of over-land haulage must have been immense. But the story is that it came from Normandy, up

Bure to Coltishall, and then each parish through which it had to go over-land did the cartage free. It has a beautiful wodewose (wild man) and a dragon carved over the west door, there is a good screen with saints galore (St Peter is a splendid old gentleman!) and no-one less than Sir Gilbert Scott said that the hammerbeam roof of the nave was the finest in England. As if all this were not enough there is a Plough Gallery in the west arch. The gallery was placed there by the Ploughman's Guild. There is still a fine plough in the church underneath it, the kind of heavy wheel plough that came to England from Holland in the sixteenth century. In old days the Ploughman's Guild would drag a plough around the village on Plough Monday (the Twelfth Day of Christmas) and collect 'largesse' (their word for contributions) from the householders, who gave it freely, realizing as they did that their very lives depended on the Plough.

> *That Bread may not be wanting*
> *Behold the Painful Plough!*

The money thus gained would be spent, in an appropriate fashion, at the nearby Plough Inn, and on the following day the ploughmen would go to work again for the first time after the twelve days rest of the Christmas Holiday. The Plough Inn at Sygate in Cawston was, unfortunately, closed down in May 1950 (the old inn sign still hangs in the church under the Plough Gallery) but this used to be called, it is said, the Plough Lights Inn—the lights referred to being the ones kept burning by the ploughmen in their Plough Gallery in the church.

Ask to see the stamped leather Chalice case, which is very beautiful, and fourteenth century like the chancel of the church. The church was paid for largely by Michael de la Pole the 1st Earl of Suffolk (see Wingfield, p60), and his picture is on the wall of the transept, dedicating the church to St Agnes. The arms of the de la Pole family are displayed over the west doorway: besides de la Pole, Morely, Wingfield, Stafford and Brotherton. Most of the church is fifteenth century. It must not be forgotten, while seeing these mighty churches in what are now small villages, that this was Norfolk's wool country. The lightish land of North Norfolk was sheep country *par excellence*, the little villages grew into weaving centres, and the great churches of the Perpendicular period were paid for by wool.

Just outside Cawston is a stone which marks a duel fought on

Cawston Heath in 1698 between Sir Henry Hobart of Blickling, 4th Baronet, and Oliver le Neve. Le Neve was left-handed, and ran the Baronet through the body, whereat he died. Sir Henry had served on King William's staff at the Battle of the Boyne.

Lest you should think that Cawston Church is the final word for Norfolk village churches pass on to **Sall** or Salle, a couple of miles to the west. For here is a church even grander than Cawston's, grander than many cathedrals in fact, although Sall is such a tiny village that it can hardly be said to exist.

This time the stone is Barnack, from Northamptonshire (the same oolitic limestone as the Cotswold villages are built of: it runs in a slanting line right across England); but the great tower is partly of flint, and not all of freestone as the tower of Cawston. Three immensely wealthy families contributed to the building of Sall Church: the Briggs, the Fountaines, and the Boleyns. Anne Boleyn, Elizabeth I's mother, is said by some people to have been buried in Sall Church; although a more general opinion is that she was buried in the Tower of London, and that her exhumed body there was identified by having six fingers on one hand, a peculiarity taken by enemies in her lifetime to indicate that she was a witch.

There are two lovely scaly angels swinging censers over the west door, and as you walk inside the church your eye is immediately taken by the marvellous upward-striving lines of the seven sacrament font and its cover, the latter most beautiful in spite of the fact that the Puritans ripped all the carvings out of it. The sacraments depicted are: Holy Communion, Holy Orders, Holy Baptism, Confirmation, Penance, Holy Matrimony, Unction, and the eighth panel, on which all the carving is defaced, represented the Crucifixion. These seven sacrament fonts are very much an East Anglian speciality; only two of the thirty-nine which are said to exist are not in Norfolk or Suffolk. Below the panels on Sall font are angels holding symbols of the particular sacrament above, and round the base of the font the four evangelists once sat on chairs, with their symbols: one can still make out the extremities of Mark's lion and Luke's ox. It is interesting to compare these symbols with the vehicles, also animals, of the members of the Hindu pantheon.

The nave arcade is famous, with its lofty slender piers and great dimensions. The roof is a marvel of engineering. The arch braces of this very wide and lofty roof come down to rest on corbel brackets which are themselves the ends of the rafters of the aisles—brought through the nave walls for the purpose. Thus the outward thrust of the mighty nave roof is taken partly by the walls of the aisles, an ingenious idea and one that works.

There is a powerful feeling of lofty dusty emptiness and lack of use about the interior: how could there not be inside such a great building in a tiny, almost non-existent parish? But there are great artistic riches for the seeking out. Down the centre of the nave are good brasses: the most westerly is to William and Margaret Fountain, died 1505 and 1519, the fifth from the west end is to a Boleyn, one Simon, who was a priest and whose will is still in existence showing that he left money for the light of the three guilds, the light of the Holy Cross on the rood, to each Virgin's light and to each plough light. Simon, who died in 1482, also left his black cloak to the parish clerk 'if he pays what he owes me; otherwise not'.

The Boleyns were small farmers until one of them, Geoffrey, went to London, made money, became Lord Mayor, and was knighted in 1457. It was he who bought the Blickling estate from Sir John Fastolf. Sir Geoffrey's grandson, Thomas, was created Earl of Wiltshire and Viscount Rochford by Henry VIII when the monarch was courting his unfortunate daughter.

The pulpit is interesting: fifteenth-century 'wine glass' pulpit which was 'rose up' (heightened) in the seventeenth century into a three-decker, at the expense of Thomas Knyvett, who was one of the men who unmasked Guy Fawkes when the immortal man was intent upon blowing up the Houses of Parliament.

The north transept of the church was restored by Sir Alfred Jodrell after 1910, and contains the Jodrell vault. The glass in the windows is by Mr H. Bryans of London, with traces of old glass incorporated in the new designs. The north window of the transept was blocked up to provide a site for a monument to Edward Hase in 1801, and this led to a lawsuit because Hase's heirs had no legal right to place the monument there without permission of the rector or the bishop. However, it is still there right or wrong. There is a most amusing brass to Thomas Rose, his wife Katrina, and children no less than a round dozen, being eight tiny boys grouped by their father and four slightly larger girls grouped by their mother. Rose paid for the chapel in this transept and it was known as Rose's Chapel. We know where at least some of the money came from, for Rose was censored in the Cawston Court Roll in 1425 for 'grazing 500 sheep on Causton Common where he ought not to graze more than 200'. This is just an illustration of the fact that Sall Church was built upon the fleeces of sheep, not on weaving as were the great West Suffolk churches, but upon grazing and shearing. Rose lived before the height of the Enclosures that turned North Norfolk from a populous arable country into a depopulated sheep-run, but the process was even then being well advanced.

The Lady Chapel over the north porch should be seen, with its fine ceiling, and massive oak bar to secure the door.

The south transept was added by Thomas Brigg, who died in 1444. The timber roof is beautiful, and so is the empty niche in the west corner. The base of the chancel screen has paintings of those learned Latin doctors, viz: Saints Thomas, James, Gregory, Jerome, Augustine, Ambrose, Philip and Bartholomew. The top of this screen was sawn off in the sixteenth century. The chancel is magnificent, with the original fifteenth-century stalls and miserere seats, and nine scenes from the life of Jesus carved on the bosses of the roof: the Annunciation, Nativity, Circumcision, Epiphany, Entry into Jerusalem, Last Supper, Crucifixion, Resurrection, Ascension. The mighty east window has some patches of old glass in it.

Nobody should contemplate going to Norfolk without seeing Sall Church. It is perhaps the almost total depopulation of the countryside in which it was built that gives it its immense austerity and dusty dignity. There it is—a vast, cathedral-like building—standing forlorn and empty among the deserted fields. There is a rusty wheel-plough standing in the porch, which ought to be better looked after.

Moor Hall, on the Reepham Road, is medieval although very much altered to turn it into a shooting box in later times. It has good flint walls (cracking in places), a fine gloomy staircase and a spacious Gothic downstairs W.C. Bees are apt to hive in a cavity over the front door.

Animal-lovers should not miss **Great Witchingham**, for here lives Philip Wayre with his Norfolk Wildlife Park and Ornamental Pheasant Trust. Here he and his family and staff keep and observe and train such things as pheasants threatened with extinction in their own lands, eagles, otters, badgers, foxes, deer, barbary sheep, coypu, and a Malayan sun bear which once chased, and flung to earth, a producer of the BBC. There are many other animals besides, teas and light lunches are provided, and the Park is open all the year round.

Aylsham provision market is a charming place, with old buildings of brick with Dutch gables. It is said that wherries came to Aylsham, up the Bure (they certainly could not in these days) and if so that would account for the town's former prosperity. In the Middle Ages it was noted for worsted cloth and for linen. At Burgh-next-Aylsham, just down the river, is a most splendid watermill.

According to Domesday 'Elesham' was held by Guert (a Dane) in the reign of the Confessor, as sixteen ploughlands (a ploughland was land that could be ploughed by a team of eight oxen) and had woodland for 300 pigs (at about two acres per pig). At Guert's time there were twenty villeins, at the time of Domesday eleven. There were formerly eighty-eight bordars, later sixty-five, then two serfs and at Domesday three, and there were two mills.

Guert may have been 'Gurth', Earl of East Anglia and younger brother of King Harold (who lived very near at Blickling: according to Domesday he held that manor). Gurth was killed at Hastings, and the manor of Aylsham bestowed on Ralph Guader, Earl of Norfolk. This man rebelled in 1075, and the king kept the manor.

Later it went to John of Gaunt, who may or may not have spent part of his time there, and who is supposed to have founded the church, in about 1380. The church is substantially unaltered since Gaunt's day. The wonderful font is fairly undamaged, there is a copy of the 'Breeches Bible' (in this 1611 edition of the Geneva Bible is written, in Genesis III 7: 'they sewed fig leaves together and made themselves breeches'). Humphrey Repton (1752–1818), famous landscape gardener, architect and partner of John Nash, is buried under his own epitaph, and roses are still grown on his grave.

> *Not like Egyptian tyrants consecrate*
> *Unmixed with others shall my dust remains.*
> *But mold'ring, blending, melting into earth*
> *Mine shall give form and colour to the Rose,*
> *And while its vivid blossoms cheer Mankind,*
> *Its perfumed odours shall ascend to Heaven.*

Fanny Burney's younger sister Charlotte lived in Aylsham, with her husband Clement Francis, surgeon and ex-secretary to Warren Hastings. Clement Francis read Fanny's first novel, *Evelina*, in India, fell in love with the authoress *in absentia*, and hastened home to introduce himself to Dr Burney at King's Lynn and woo his daughter. But, arriving there, he fell in love with Charlotte instead, married her, and set up as a practising doctor in Aylsham. Fanny stayed with them on 8th November 1792, just after Charlotte had

had a son. There is a mural tablet to Dr Francis in the south transept of the church, by John Ivory of Norwich.

It is but a short way to **Blickling Hall**. One can scarcely see Blickling in less than a full afternoon. The house and garden, belonging to the National Trust, are open from May until the end of September from 2 pm to 5.30 pm on every Wednesday, Thursday, Sunday and Bank Holiday. Entry costs adults three shilling: children one and six.

The first glimpse of Blickling is a great *coup d'œil*. The little tree-bordered lane from Aylsham is apparently leading you into one of those uninhabited deserts of barley and sugar beet of North Norfolk —about as far from civilization as you can get—when, without warning, Blickling appears: a church, an iron railing, behind it perfect lawns and—symmetrically flanked by two wings of out-buildings—the great begabled and bepinnacled hall of the reddest brick only spoiled, for me at least, by a quite incongruous white clock tower in the middle looking like a howdah on an elephant's back. This tower which is wood and early nineteenth century, fortunately leaks and so may well be pulled down (although my latest information indicates that it has been repaired by the National Trust).

This great façade, impressive though it be, gives no impression of the size of the house; for Blickling is long and deep and the front is narrow. This shape was imposed upon the Jacobean building by the moat of its medieval predecessor.

As we saw while discussing Aylsham, Blickling Manor belonged to King Harold—the last of the true English kings and a true East Anglian. William the Conqueror bestowed it on a chaplain whom he created Bishop of Thetford, and thus it became a home of the bishops of East Anglia and Herbert de Losinga, when he moved the See to Norwich, frequently resorted to Blickling. Bishop Everard, de Losinga's successor, bestowed the southern half of the manor to a soldier, John FitzRobert. It passed to Sir Nicholas Dagworth who was Captain of Aquitaine under Richard II and he built a hall which was probably on the site of the present mansion. Sir Thomas Erpingham, whom Shakespeare immortalized if Sir Thomas didn't do it for himself, and whom we have met with his great gate and tomb in Norwich, had the house at the beginning of the fifteenth century, and he sold the place to Sir John Fastolf, whom we noticed while discussing Caister (p141). Geoffrey Boleyn, whom as we have seen lived at Sall, went to London rather as Dick Whittington did and became Lord Mayor (helped, it is believed, by Sir John Fastolf whose favourite he was) and bought the house from Sir John. Three generations of Boleyns lived there until after Anne's barbarous execution by Henry VIII, the house then passed to the Clere family of Ormesby by marriage, and was then sold to Sir Henry Hobart about 1616.

Sir Henry was Lord Chief Justice, and baroneted by James I when that monarch founded his new order of baronets. Sir Henry's portrait, painted by Daniel Mytens, hangs over the fireplace in the State Bedroom; it shows a man of apparently great strength of character, thoughtful and not unkindly, with slender sensitive hands: the portrait either flatters the man or he was a fine fellow. He died in 1625, but not before he had begun the building of the present Blickling Hall. His son Sir John, the 2nd baronet, finished the building, but died with no heir, and so the place went to a grandson of the 1st Baronet, another John, who was an eager parliamentarian in Cromwell's Upper House but found that his conscience could encompass his turning an equally eager royalist at the Restoration. He even entertained Charles II and Queen Catherine at Blickling in 1671. Sir Henry, his son, was the man slain in a duel on Cawston Common. Sir Henry's son, John, was given the Earldom of Buckinghamshire by George II: it is said not for his own talents, but for those of his attractive sister, Henrietta Howard and later Countess of Suffolk. This lady was a noted wit and intellectual, well known to Pope and Swift, and generally thought to have been the king's mistress.

The 2nd Earl of Buckinghamshire, John, was described by Horace Walpole as: 'The Clearcake. Fat, Fair, sweet, and seen through in a moment.' Hardly the man, one would have thought, to have been sent Ambassador to Catherine of Russia, but sent he was. He brought back the greatest treasure of Blickling from this appointment: the splendid tapestry (described below) that hangs in the Peter the Great Room and which was presented to him by the Empress. The Hobarts had a habit of marrying well, and the 2nd Earl married a lady who died at the age of twenty-nine leaving him £50,000.

His lordship died twenty-four years later (of the gout), leaving a bevy of four daughters. The first one ran away from her husband, and so the second inherited Blickling. She had no issue, so the

9. THE NORFOLK BROADS. *Above*, Somerleyton Mill, with the bird-haunted solitude of the remoter broads. *Below*, boats running before the wind down the River Bure

10.   The Abbey Church of Wymondham

property went to her great-nephew who happened to be the 8th
Marquis of Lothian. This was 1850. There is an effigy of the 8th
Marquis by G. F. Watts in Blickling Church, which is well worth
going to see for lovers of Victorian sculpture. Lady Lothian lived on
until 1901, long after her husband's death, and she is still spoken
about with respect by the older residents. The family moved away
from Blickling until Philip Kerr, the 11th Marquis, returned to it,
in the intervals of his being such things as the Ambassador to the
United States (which he was when he died in 1940). There is a most
charming hidden garden made by him, which few visitors find, with
a summerhouse, where he used to sit at peace with his Foreign
Office dispatches, or, one likes to think, occasionally without them.

Lord Lothian left the Hall to the National Trust, with the wish
that, although open to the public, it should also be a private
residence. It is the latter, being at present the home of a curator.

As for the architecture of the house, careful detective work has
shown that it was probably designed by Robert Lyminge, who was
largely responsible for designing Lord Salisbury's Hatfield House.
Much of the detail of the two houses is very similar. Unlike Hatfield,
Blickling lacks a great hall, which was a feature of most big houses
put up in its time; but a splendid staircase occupies the position that
a Great Hall would normally have occupied. The present staircase is
not all Lyminge's work, but probably added in the eighteenth
century by Thomas Ivory, the Norwich architect who designed the
Norwich Assembly Rooms and many other buildings.

One enters the rooms that are open to the public by the south-east
turret, which gives way into the **south drawing room.**

This was once the 'Eating Room', and one imagines simpler and
more down-to-earth. It was re-decorated by the 2nd Earl about
1765, but he left the amazing ceiling with its pendants hanging down
like fruity stalactites. The pictures are mostly portraits of members
of the family, or of other great Norfolk families: there is one of Sir
Robert Walpole, 1st Earl of Orford (1676-1745). Another Henrietta
Howard, Countess of Suffolk, whose father was the man killed in a
duel on Cawston Common. Henrietta was the lady who is supposed
to have been the mistress of George II, and the portrait indicates
that she was indeed a lady of intellect and character, as all who
described her averred. The lady and her daughter in another picture
are thought to be of Mary Anne, 2nd Countess of Buckinghamshire,

the heiress who brought £50,000 into Blickling and died so young. The picture is attributed to Francis Coates.

From here one passes into the **ante-room**, which has a most interesting ceiling of moulded plasterwork. Constantly, at Blickling, one is forced to admire the work of the plasterer, whose art was at its zenith when most of the house was decorated or re-decorated, and whose art looks very much, in these days, like dying out. The **grand staircase** must be looked at, particularly the newel figures. The two bearded men on the bottom flight among the newel figures are said to be originals—the rest were added by the 2nd Earl of Buckinghamshire: the Ambassador to Russia. He also installed the wooden carvings of Anne Boleyn and her daughter, Elizabeth I. Poor Anne is dressed in eighteenth-century clothes, and has the information written underneath her that she was born here. It is the fashion now to say that Anne Boleyn was not born at Blickling, but I cannot think where else she is likely to have been born, since her mother and father certainly lived there. Not in the present house, of course, but on its present site. The pictures again give us an insight into the former occupants of the great house: there is poor Sir Henry who was killed in a duel, by Kneller, there is Sir James Hobart, whose portrait and whose altar-tomb we saw in Loddon Church: as the Blickling portrait shows him in seventeenth-century clothing and he was a fifteenth-century man one must suppose that the Loddon portrait is more likely to be a true resemblance. Then there are two really superb portraits: one of Elizabeth I in full finery, and one of Sir Philip Sidney, looking gallant and grand.

Back through the ante-room we come into the **long gallery**, which is the *pièce de résistance* of the house. It runs the whole length of the east front from the ante-room onwards, and is 120 feet long. Alas, the whole west wall was covered, in Victorian times, with bookcases surmounted by weird painted patterns: a Ruskinesque delving into some age of chivalry which certainly never existed; but the ceiling—the ceiling!—must be one of the grandest stretches of moulded plasterwork in the world! I can never contemplate it without thinking with awe of the neck-breaking labour of putting it all up there. So beautiful was it (it was made early seventeenth century) that even those dreadful Victorians kept their hands and hammers off it, although it accords so ill with their pseudo-medieval caperings of the west wall that the juxtaposition looks absurd. On the Victorian shelves are several thousand venerable and valuable books, some Anglo-Saxon. There is the state chair sat on by James II in Dublin, and brought back as a relic by the 2nd Earl of Buckinghamshire after he had been Lord Lieutenant of Ireland, which he was after his mission to Catherine the Great. Jacob, the smooth man, and Esau, the hairy man and mighty hunter before the Lord, meet on a seventeenth-century Brussels tapestry over the fireplace (the latter is a modern fireplace put there to replace the mock Gothic monster that the Victorians put up in place of the earlier marble fireplace).

Turning left along the north end of the house brings us into the **Peter the Great Room**, with its splendid and spirited tapestry of the Tzar prancing along on his horse, under his eagle, with the slaughter and carnage of Poltawa going on well in the background. There is a big Gainsborough each side of the beautiful marble fireplace, one of the 2nd Earl, and the other of his second wife, Caroline Conolly, whom the earl married but eight months after the death of his first, who left him so much money. There is some notable eighteenth-century furniture.

Straight through is the **state bedroom**, with the noble and most striking portrait of the founder of present day Blickling Hall: Sir Henry Hobart, painted by Daniel Mytens.

The **gardens** are beautiful, but certainly there is not the space to describe them fully here. I would urge the visitor not to miss the Orangery (probably by William Ivory—son of Thomas) with its statue of Hercules which was brought from the Pastons' seat, Oxnead Hall, by the 2nd Earl, likewise the fountain just east of the house which also came from Oxnead. There is also a lovely clump of oriental plane trees, looking strange and exotic north-east of the house, there are the marvellous crossing and radiating rides and avenues—each planted with a different species of tree (in two places you can stand at the intersection of eight roads), the Temple, which cuts off the view down the magnificent vista which looks from the house east-south-east: a vista bordered most beautifully by azaleas and rhododendrons. North-west of the Hall is a pyramidal mausoleum, designed by Joseph Bonomi, in which the remains of the 2nd Earl lie with his two wives in marble sarcophagi. The loveliest thing in the grounds is the large lake, which winds away out of sight so that one can imagine it much bigger than it is, with great beech trees growing on the high ground beyond it. There is good coarse fishing in the lake, reserved by the London Anglers' Association.

And just outside the main gates is the Buckinghamshire Arms. At the nearby village of **Itteringham**, for teetotallers, vegetarians, or ordinary people just wanting a cup of tea, is the most gloriously situated Mill House, which is a vegetarian guest-house. The occupant besides accommodating guests, serves teas and sells volumes of his own poetry. He also sells little wire devices of his own manufacture for the holding of tit-bits for tits.

Erpingham is not far away. It is a pleasant, if feudal-looking, small village, with a mighty church tower built by Sir Thomas of Shakespeare's *Henry V* fame. There is a very good military brass indeed inside the very fine church—but to Sir John, Sir Thomas's father, who died in 1370.

Sir Thomas Erpingham was a knight whose story might appeal to anybody. He went to France to join the exiled Bolingbroke—after the latter's father John of Gaunt had died—came back to land at Ravenspur ('the baked shore at Ranspurg'—it was somewhere near Spurn Head) and helped to wrest the crown from the head of the effete Richard II. Later he fought at the Battle of Agincourt and cheered the king up on the eve of the battle to such effect that Henry said to him (according to Shakespeare): 'God-a-mercy, old heart, thou speakest cheerfully.' Besides the tower of Erpingham Church he built the famous Erpingham Gate at Norwich Cathedral, and, as we have seen, in the Cathedral is his tomb.

Aldborough is a village with a fine great green, on which is played much village cricket, and on which the most lively horse fair takes place every summer at the very time of the more rarified junketings at Aldeburgh, Suffolk.

And so we come to the sea again, **at Cromer,** a medium-sized, compact, predominantly railway-age seaside resort surrounding an ancient fishing village which sits within it like a pearl within an oyster. It has a simply grand Perpendicular church with one of the highest towers in Norfolk (160 feet) which served as the lighthouse before the real one was built. The church is a great building from the outside, but over-restored within: it had fallen into complete decay in the eighteenth century, so this was inevitable. There is some corking modern and recent glass: the east window of the south aisle is after Burne-Jones.

The little streets that radiate out from the church square are pretty if hellish for the motorist. The sea-front is most impressive, being backed by high, hotel-crowned cliffs, surmountable by stone steps, and very reminiscent of the Tower of Babel.

Cromer's glory is her Number One Lifeboat (she has two boats), and her hero the late Henry Blogg. About the latter a book has been written, he has been painted by an RA, and there are memorials to him both inside and outside the church. He was the most decorated of any lifeboatman in the British Isles, being awarded the 'Lifeboatman's Victoria Cross' (the RNLI's Gold Medal) no less than three times, the George Cross once, and the British Empire Medal. Most of the rescues he carried out were away on the Haisboro' Sands, and the tales of his daring as a coxswain are hair-raising. On one occasion—the wreck of the sailing barge *Sepoy*—he drove the lifeboat —in a breaking surf—right over the barge's deck on an enormous wave—thus giving the barge's crew time to jump from the rigging in which they were clinging to safety onto the lifeboat's deck. He would drive the lifeboat right into the crashing surf on the Haisboro', or on the 'Main' (mainland) until his crew wondered if they were afloat or already on the bottom. He carried this on right up to his death in 1954, thus demonstrating that a tough old 'un is as good as a tough young 'un. His nephew, Henry Davies, 'Shrimp' to his friends, is now coxswain of Cromer Number One and well carries on the great tradition.

Except for the paid full-time mechanic, all the lifeboatmen are part-time volunteers (Spurn Head has the only full-time lifeboat crew on the East Coast): during most of their lives they are fishermen, and at Cromer the fish they catch are chiefly crabs.

Cromer crabs are famous among all crab-lovers, and are undisputedly the best in England (with them I would include Sheringham ones, which are just the same). The little boats that catch them are worth examining—indeed cadging a trip in—for they are unique.

The Sheringham and Cromer crab boat is a very small, double-ended, clinker-built boat, with a straight keel, great beam, and very full bilges. She is lightly constructed ('like a basket') with numerous but very light frames. Her lines undoubtedly descend from those of Shetland boats which used to come down after the herring. So suitable is she for beach work that her lines have been sent to such far places as West Africa and the Falkland Islands, by the Colonial Office, to be copied by native fishermen.

The technique of crab fishing is to shoot long lines—called 'shanks' —of baited pots made of tarred string whipped round iron frames out on the rocky ground off-shore, pick them up next day, remove the crabs, and re-bait. The fishermen haul the shanks by hand using the technique known as 'overrunning'—or letting the boat drive down over the shank carried by the swift tide. This calls for great skill and strength, and it is quite true that nobody can do it unless they are used to it. The line-hauler must haul like a madman to keep up with the pace of the tide; and the man who removes the crabs, and the baiter, must work like lightning otherwise the pot is snatched out of their grasp by the relentless progress of the boat. The pots, having been shot one day, *must* be looked at the next—even if a gale is raging. Collectively they are worth hundreds of pounds, and cannot be left out on the bed of the ocean at risk. Whatever the weather, practically, the men go to sea off their harbourless beach, and to watch them do it—or come running in afterwards—in a strong on-shore wind, is breathtaking. Returning they run straight for the beach, the helmsman gives the boat a sheer just before she strikes, the crew fling their weights to the inshore side of the boat just in time—thus throwing her over and allowing the waves to bash (it is hoped) harmlessly up against her bottom. Meanwhile men ashore get a hook on from the tractor and drag the boat out of harm's way. Naturally there are accidents. 'Shrimp' Davies lost two brothers when their boat overturned shortly before the war.

For people seeking a quiet seaside holiday of the traditional kind, I cannot think of a better place than Cromer—unless it be Sheringham. They both have the pleasantest atmosphere, impressive cliffs, good beaches, modest amusements such as repertory theatre and concerts, good friendly Norfolk inhabitants, and crab-salads.

Sheringham, four miles west of Cromer, is much like it. It too has a fossilized flint-built fishing village inside the growing brick shell of the railway-age seaside resort, it too has a lifeboat and vigorous crabbing community. When the fishing is bad the Sheringhamers pick pebbles off the beach: the pebbles go to be ground up for such things as pottery glazes and shellac to put on motor cars.

It is said that the Sheringham fishermen incline towards Salvationism, while those of Cromer to—shall we say—more secular pursuits. Mr 'Downtide' West is king of the Sheringham fishermen. Besides going to sea he runs a very good fish restaurant in the High Street, and a crab-potting factory behind it. His father was given the title 'Downtide' after he had, as a little boy, gone long-lining with *his* father. One of the hooks of a long-line caught in his father's hand —his father shouted to the boy (who was at the oars): 'Turn her up-tide! Turn her up-tide!' The boy turned the boat *down*tide instead, thus dragging the hook deep into his father's hand and earning himself his hereditary title. Recently yet another little 'Downtide' was christened, so the name is here to stay. But indeed there are so many Wests among the fishermen of Sheringham that everyone has to have a nick-name for identification.

The Sheringham and Cromer crabbers were for long sworn enemies; and their meetings at such places as Aldborough horse fair always led to a fight—nor were they above occasionally cutting each other's shank ropes at sea. The Cromer men contemptuously used to refer to the Sheringhamers as 'Shaddocks'. But in 1928 a Sheringham boat (out whelking) was caught in a gale, the Cromer lifeboat went out to her (for Sheringham at that time did not possess a motor lifeboat) and just as she got alongside a great wave came and 'pitchpoled' the Sheringham boat—flinging her right over—stern over bows. Jack Davies, from the Cromer lifeboat, jumped overboard and got a line round two of the three Sheringhamers and these were saved, since then the two communities have (generally) been friends.

Sheringham, too, has fine cliffs (many fossils of large animals have been dug out of Sheringham and Cromer cliffs), and behind the cliffs is high ground which for Norfolk is extremely well wooded. Indeed the country there is very un-East-Anglia-like, more like the North Downs of Kent. The road that goes to Holt passes through lovely country: a picnicker's paradise. The un-East Anglian character of this ridge of hills is explained by the fact that it is not East Anglian. It is a series of moraines left by the glaciers which advanced across what is now the North Sea from the north. It contains rocks from as far away as Scandinavia, although in fact most of its substance derives from what has now become north-east England and the bed of the North Sea. Near Holt are masses of chalk: not laid down where it still is as in other parts of England, but dragged there by the bellies of great glaciers. It is this moraine which gives the Cromer Cliffs their great variety of rock and structure. The ridge is being attacked savagely by the sea, and the cliffs are crumbling away perhaps faster than any other stretch of the English coast, with the possible exception of Holderness. It is the destruction of these cliffs that releases the great masses of shingle that—dragged south by the scour of the tide—collects to form the shingle banks such as Orford Ness. Sheringham Park has a Humphrey-Repton-designed landscape garden with fine rhododendrons.

Holt is a lovely little town. It was one of the first places to apply the technique first developed along Norwich's Magdalen Street of persuading householders to beautify their frontages according to a unified colour scheme, at the same time removing the uglier of the town furniture and replacing it with better designed. The result is a little town of clean gay colours, which blend well together and with the wall here and there that has been left grey flint. Holt is well-known for Gresham's School, founded by Sir John Gresham in 1555 when he was Lord Mayor of London, and administered by the Fishmonger's Company. It is now a public school and one of the most progressive and enlightened in the country.

Castle-lovers might make the journey to **Baconsthorpe Hall**, three miles south-east of Holt. The road goes by a superb watermill, but you must then leave the tar and go along a very muddy farm lane. The Hall was a fortified manor house built by Sir Henry Heydon in 1486. There is quite an amount of ruin left, the gatehouse is fairly complete, there are curtain walls, the remains of a seventeenth-century dwelling hall, and an eighteenth-century Gothic mansion built in front of the castle mainly from the castle stone. The place stands forlornly in the muddy Norfolk fields, near a big farmstead.

Melton Constable has another of the great halls of North Norfolk, built (financially) on sheep and wool. The Astley family enclosed the park by charter in 1290; there is a lake, deer, and a mansion of 1670. The church is full of Astleys, who lasted a long time. It was an Astley who prayed before the Battle of Edgehill: 'Lord Thou Knowest how busy I must be this day—if I forget Thee do not Thou forget me!' He was a Royalist, unusual for an East Anglian, for they were almost solidly Roundhead at least until *after* the triumph of the Glorious Revolution. Then, it is true, many of them turned 'agin' the Government' again.

Farther south is **North Elmham**, where there should be far more to see, considering that here was probably the East Anglian Cathedral. In pre-Danish days North Elmham became a bishopric, St Edmund may have been crowned king there, the Danes are supposed to have laid the place waste in 866, the see was re-established in 955 but after this was removed to Thetford, and thence de Losinga took it to Norwich, where it still is. There is a great earthwork north of the present church, and it is evident that this was a heavily fortified place. The existing earthworks are supposed to have been built in the fourteenth century by Bishop Despencer. The cathedral has recently been excavated to a depth of about eight feet and the foundations can be seen.

South again—**East Dereham** where George Borrow was born at Dumpling Green, just outside. Here are the first words of *Lavengro*:

> On the evening of July, in the year 18—, at East D——, a beautiful little town in a certain district of East Anglia, I first saw the light.
>
> I love to think on thee, pretty, quiet D——, thou pattern of an English market town, with thy clean but narrow streets branching out from thy modest market place, with thine old-fashioned houses, with here and there a roof of venerable thatch . . . Pretty quiet D—— with thy venerable church, in which moulder the mortal remains of England's sweetest and most pious bard.

Except for the motor cars Borrow would find it much the same today.

Borrow mentions: 'a mouldering edifice, inclosing a spring of sanatory waters'. This is Withburga's Well, in the churchyard.

Withburga was a daughter of King Anna (see Blythburgh, p41) —a monarch who had several sainted daughters, and who founded a convent at East Dereham. She was buried there, miracles were wrought at her shrine and the presence of her body would have assured great prosperity to Dereham. But alas in AD 984 the Abbot of Ely came, with his wily monks, on a visit to Dereham, managed to get the burghers of the town drunk (perhaps no difficult matter?) and made away with the body of the saint. The men of Dereham pursued the monks and would have caught them, had the monks not reached the sanctuary of the waters of the Fens near Brandon, boarded a boat, and got away across the flood. The remains of Withburga were buried at Ely beside the remains of her sainted sister Aethelthryth, or Etheldreda, the founder of Ely monastery and, in her life, wife of the King of Northumbria. A spring burst out from the site of Withburga's desecrated grave.

The mortal remains of 'England's sweetest and most pious bard' are those of William Cowper, who died at East Dereham and is buried in the church. There is an unfortunate window to him, and a monument by Flaxman. The Congregational Chapel is built on the site of the house in which he died, and wood from the latter is incorporated in it. The story of Cowper's death at East Dereham is melancholy in the extreme, and Mary Unwin, the widow whom he would have married and who cared for him until she herself broke down, is buried at East Dereham too.

Dereham Church is enclosed nicely by the churchyard and has great mellowness and peace. There is a chest in the church which is supposed to have belonged to the Howards, Dukes of Norfolk. It resembles somewhat the tomb of Thomas, 3rd Duke and father of the poet, Surrey, but it is Flemish, and sixteenth century.

Most of Dereham was burned down in post-Tudor times, but the cottages near the church with pargetting, or moulded plasterwork, are early sixteenth century, and called 'Bonner's Cottages' because here Bishop Bonner lived when he was still a curate. He afterwards made a great reputation by sending so many Protestants to the burning pyres (see p356).

At Dereham lives Canon Noel Boston, an expert on barrel organs.

On his way Norwichwards the traveller might seek out **Elsing** to see, in the church, Sir Hugh Hasting's marvellous brass memorial, one of the most lavish and elaborate brasses in East Anglia. The little figures on either side of Sir Hugh depict his more aristocratic relations, including Edward III, Warwick, Lancaster, Pembroke, Stafford. Sir Hugh died in 1347. Elsing Hall is 1460–70, much restored, but still a very fine moated manor house with oriel windows in its great hall.

North Tuddenham has a lonely church, which has very good fifteenth-century glass in many of the windows. There are saints on the remnant of the screen—including St Geron, whose likeness is in only one other church in the country: Suffield, in Suffolk. Geron was murdered by the Danes while proselytizing in the Low Countries.

One might alternate between the rivers Tud and Yare, and certainly have a look at **Bawburgh**, which is a pretty little village indeed and which has everything a village should have including a patron saint. Farm workers will wish to strike north to **Costessey Woods** to find St Walstan's Well. For St Walstan is the patron saint of their profession. He is supposed to have been a prince among the Anglians, but he threw off his princely robes to become a farm worker. He laboured all his life at Taverham—just north across the Wissey— and was noted for his saintliness. In the year 1016, while he was mowing a hayfield, an angel appeared to him and announced to him the hour of his death. He went on quietly mowing until he died, and his body was placed on a bier drawn by his own yoke of oxen. The oxen walked down to the Wissey, crossed that river by walking on the water (their hoof marks could still be seen on the surface of the water up until the Reformation), walked into Costessey Woods and there rested, and where they rested up sprang this well of water. For centuries this was a place of pilgrimage for farm workers, and there have been suggestions quite recently of cleaning the place up and repairing the shrine.

If the traveller wishes to see what the saint looked like, let him go to **Barnham Broom** Church, for there is a portrait of St Walstan on the fine screen.

CHAPTER 10

Norwich to Wymondham

Leaving Norwich on the New Buckenham Road one passes (or does not pass?) the **Swainsthorpe** Dun Cow, which is late seventeenth century and mellow brick. In a land stacked full of ancient inns I only mention this comparatively new one because it is particularly attractive (map, p123). **Mulbarton** is one of the many villages that have 'the biggest village green in Norfolk', and in the church is a curious memorial put up by a former rector, Daniel Scargill, to his dead wife. It is in the form of a copper book which can be opened to reveal some seventeenth-century verse which although perhaps stilted and artificial after the manner of the time, expresses very touchingly the bereavement and pious hope of the widower. Scargill was expelled from Cambridge for losing his faith, but he managed to find it again and became a parson (map, p123).

Forncett St Peter has a church with a tower that is Anglo-Saxon right up to the top, with circular windows. Most of our Anglo-Saxon towers have had Norman or later tops added to them. There is a long and involved story about a John of Forncett who did—or did not, according to which theory you care to accept—compose *Sumer is i-cumen in* while he was a monk at Reading Abbey, early in the thirteenth century.

South Norfolk differs from the north of the county in that it is heavier land (like the heavy old Suffolk boulder clay) and therefore is not suitable for sheep farming, as is the north. This meant that the Enclosures were not so complete here, and many small farmers and owner-farmers survive and there are few great estates. Farming in the north to this day is mainly conducted on huge farms—getting huger and huger as amalgamation follows amalgamation. Here in the south the small yeoman still holds his own, giving a different character to the landscape, and a feeling of much more independence

to the people. Forelock-pulling is nothing like so common in the south as it is in the north.

I must mention the Farrier's Arms at **Carleton Rode**, simply because it is such an excellent little pub (it is called 'The Crow' by its habitués), has such pleasant landlord and landlady, and such good and truly rural company.

New Buckenham may have been new in 1145, when the second William d'Albini built a castle there, replacing the one he already had at Old Buckenham. At least, the situation is complicated; for 'New Buckenham Castle' is really within the parish boundary of Old Buckenham, so is New Buckenham cemetery, and the parson of New Buckenham is peculiar in that he sleeps with his head in one parish and his feet in the other. The town of New Buckenham grew up around the new castle, and it was actually laid out like any 'over-swill' town in East Anglia today: the first recorded example of English town planning—fifteenth century in fact. The result is a very civilized village, and it does not rush headlong into the space age— the History School of the new University of East Anglia has been carrying out research in the parish and amongst other discoveries has found 'an attitude to affairs which can only be described as eighteenth century!'

Of the castle only a moated mound remains, and the foundations of what is said to be the first circular keep in England. There are reasons for thinking that the Norman castle may have been antedated by a Roman one, or even an earlier. The main fabric was dismantled during the Civil War.

There is a seventeenth-century Market House in New Bucken-ham, with a whipping-post inside and carved boards out. There is a good village baker with a magnificent cast-iron bread oven in his front room. And John Eldred was born in New Buckenham. He went to Baghdad and came away from that place with 4,000 camels loaded with merchandise from the fabulous east, which he shipped home from Tripoli. The jaunt made him rich for life and he built 'Nutmeg Hall' at Saxham, in Suffolk.

In complete contrast to New is **Old Buckenham**, where nobody ever did any town planning. The village is a straggle of old houses and cottages, strung out around a rough old village green which is so large that you can hardly see across it and which makes it a long walk to visit your 'neighbour' over the road. As with many large villages Old Buckenham is divided into hamlets; and these are some of their names: Loss Wroo (Middle English for 'Linx Corner'), Hog's Snout, Puddledock, Chattergate, Stacksford, Cake Street and Hungry Hill. Hungry Hill by the way is as flat as a pancake. At Hungry Hill is a ford through a tiny river—the grandmother of the Thet—where the ultra-protestant sect of Sandemanians used to immerse each other totally, bestowing such names as Uzziah, Absalom and Karen-happuch, some of which still survive. Looking at the stream nowadays it is difficult to see how any but the most minute Sandemanian could be accommodated in it, but most East Anglian streams have shrunk during the last half century. Just by the ford is a smallholding where a lady lives with three children, and where she ferments a potent, delicious and unusual wine from the tendrils of the grape.

Old Buckenham Church is thatched, and has a fine Norman north door and beside it a 'consecration stone', carved with the crowned monogram of the Blessed Virgin (there is one like it two piers from west in the north aisle of Wymondham, but stuck in back-to-front). The church has a polygonal tower and a well-kept churchyard with fine roses. The incumbent is an excellent writer under at least two names, and we have noted one book of his in the Norwich chapter: *Some Ancient Gentlemen*. (Since this was written he has resigned the living.)

There is little to see of the first William d'Albini's castle, except a mound, and a scrap of ruin near Abbey Farm which is all that remains of the Augustinian priory which was built with the remains of the old castle. The shape of the foundations of the latter has led people to believe that the Normans built on a Roman site. The d'Albini to whom the Conqueror granted the manor is said to have come over from France as the monarch's butler.

Old Buckenham Hall has a famous cricket pitch: the turf for it was brought by Lionel Robinson all the way from Australia, and Jack Hobbs used to say that it was his favourite ground. McLaren, the great cricketer, lived nearby at Warren Cottage. In the network of tiny roads towards Wilby is a pub which sells only cider and 'British wine'. The cider is excellent.

We might strike south to **Winfarthing**, because it has such a strange name. There used to be a sword there, which had the power of finding lost horses, and if a wife burnt a candle before it every Sunday of the year she would get rid of her husband. Just down the road **Shelfanger** has an even stranger name than Winfarthing.

Diss is a splendid little town, but stands under the shadow of 'development', and what East Anglian people call 'overswill'. However, as it was spared the fires which wiped out so much of Tudor East Anglia, maybe it will be spared this. It even kept the Railway Age at arm's length—Diss insisted that the railway station should be at least a mile away, and it is, joined to the beautiful little town by a hideously ugly road.

Diss, partly Tudor, is built around a six acre mere, or lake. The name Diss comes from Anglo-Saxon *dice*, meaning standing water, so the mere is old although it looks strangely artificial. (In East Anglia a ditch is still commonly called a 'dick'.) There are many fine pubs in Diss, notably the Greyhound and the Saracen's Head. There is a corking Italianate two-towered Baptist chapel, and a fine medieval church. John Skelton, from Diss, was Poet Laureate to Edward, wrote 'Philip Sparrow', and taught Henry VIII to spell. John Wilbye was a Diss man also, born 1574, and wrote many madrigals which people still sing. What about a Madrigal Festival in Diss in 1974? In the museum of Falsterbo, in Sweden, there is an early seventeenth-century map of the Baltic countries and North Atlantic on which the British Isles are shown as a shapeless blob, and marked on them are three towns. One is Rochester, one is Chatham, and the other is Diss. **Billingford** has a splendid tower-mill.

Westward, **Bressingham** is of the very first interest to lovers of hardy perennials and steam engines. Bressingham Gardens have been carved out of a large parkland by Mr and Mrs Alan Bloom, who are large producers of hardy perennials and Alpine plants. The plants grow in 'island beds', amid the beautiful parkland, all labelled and clear to see, and there are over 5000 species of them! Then there is a fine collection of old steam engines, stationary and locomotive and wonderfully maintained and—as if all this were not enough—the Bressingham Light Railway, which runs over a track of 750 yards, has a 4-6-2 Pacific type locomotive, carries children and has been known to carry adults too!

Farther west are the **Lophams, North** and **South**.

To see South Lopham church tower for the first time is to be carried back with something of a shock to the austere, military, and somehow terribly alien world of the Normans. It is very early twelfth century, logically proportioned, massive, powerful, and excellently preserved. It is said to have been put up by William Bigod. It is hard to believe that more than eight centuries have passed over it. More have passed over the little circular window in the nave west of the north door, for this is Anglo-Saxon. The chancel is Decorated, and the whole church unusual, interesting and extremely beautiful.

The weaving industry survived at North Lopham right into this century. At the Bridewell Museum, Norwich, is to be seen a Jacquard loom from Lopham of staggering complexity. The 'Jacquard', of course, was invented by a man of that name in Lyons in the early nineteen hundreds to weave figured fabrics.

Just south of the Lophams are the headwaters of both the Little Ouse and the Waveney. Would that some mad millionaire would join these two headwaters (they are separated by the breadth of the road), lock the streams farther down, and thus join by water the important Broads system and the 2,000 miles of the waterways of England.

North of the Lophams stands **East Harling** which has a very fine church indeed, with a spire—which is unusual for Norfolk where spireless towers abound (it is a short lead spire similar in shape to St Peter Mancroft's, Norwich). There are two important fifteenth-century monuments: one to Sir Robert Harling and one to Sir Thomas Lovell. There is brilliant glass in the west window—put there by Sir Robert Wingfield and Sir William Chamberlain who can be seen at the foot of the window kneeling comfortably on cushions. These two knights were the husbands, one after the other, of Anne Harling, whose tomb (with Sir William) is in the church, much carved with shields and heraldry. The Harling Chapel was built by Anne's father, Sir Robert, who soldiered with Henry V and was thus probably one of the 'happy few' at Agincourt. But the way to see this church, and get the greatest impact from it, is to go down to the River Thet, nearby, climb down from the road, and look back through the trees.

We are on the eastern edge of the Brecklands now—about which more later. We can work our way northwards on the border of this sandy, empty quarter, to see **Stow Bedon** in the churchyard of which lies buried a man who died very recently. Until age seventy this man was a miller, until age 100 a very hard working farmer, and at age 104 he died.

Near **Thompson** is Thompson Water, one of the Breckland meres and a fine coarse fishing ground—a forest-encircled lake. Thompson has a beautiful little thatched pub, set among woods. Most of this country belongs to Lord Walsingham, but much has been taken over by the army for use as a 'battle area'. Several villages have been evacuated and are in ruins, and you can only officially visit them if you are being buried there, and can prove that, in life, you were a local man. To visit them, in life, and unofficially, is frightfully melancholy, but beware of live mortar bombs (both lying on the ground and flying through the air), charging tanks, and parachutists falling from the skies.

Watton has a long and attractive village street. Wayland or Wailing Wood is nearby, in which the wicked uncle, of nearby Griston Hall, had the Babes in the Wood dumped. Their wails can still be heard at midnight, by the faithful and their grave can still be seen in the wood.

Shipdham Church has the finest Tudor wooden lectern in the world and must be visited for that alone. There are said to be ancient books up over the porch.

South-east would bring us to **Hingham**, which is a very lovely large village where Mr William Cooper plays the dulcimer. The place is somehow rather lost and lonely, but full of fine Georgian and Queen Anne houses. Abraham Lincoln's ancestor, Samuel Lincoln, was a weaver at Hingham, and was baptized in the church in 1622. With many other Nonconformist Hingham weavers he fled across the Atlantic for freedom of conscience, and was followed by the parson, Robert Peck, who first destroyed the altar rail in Hingham church because he thought it was idolatrous.

There is a bust of Abraham Lincoln in the church, presented by Hingham Mass., and a mounting block in Hingham Mass., we are told, presented by Hingham, Norfolk. This is said to have an inscription on it which says that it 'was known to the Forefathers before the Migration'.

The church is Decorated, and fine, with soaring tower arch and arcades. It contains an enormous redstone monument to Lord Morley, Baron of Rye and Marshal of Ireland, who died in 1434, said to be one of the grandest monuments in England. It may have been designed by the same man who designed Erpingham Gate, in Norwich.

Attleborough is a small town notable for cider and turkeys. The former is made at Messrs Gaymers' works, the latter reared in the countryside around, and often sold in Attleborough. Until very recently there was a great annual turkey fair, at which one would see thousands of these birds and practically be deafened by their gobbling. They were carried in open trucks under wide-meshed nets, so that their heads stuck up through the latter and they surveyed the passing countryside in a most disconcerting manner.

In Defoe's day they travelled differently. Defoe was told by a man at Stratford St Mary, in Suffolk, that every year some 300 droves of Norfolk turkeys crossed the Stour there with some 500 birds per drove, and that many more crossed at Clare and Sudbury. The birds started walking in August to get to the London market in time for Christmas dinner, but they were fed and fattened on stubble fields all the way (one presumes with a small payment being made to the farmers). The story goes that these birds were made to walk over hot pitch occasionally, so as to coat the soles of their feet with this substance and thus harden them for the long walk. But change was creeping in in Defoe's day, and already birds were being carried Londonwards in wagons. The light land stretching from Attleborough to the Brecklands was turkey country in Defoe's day: it still is, although now the turkeys are kept by the most modern methods. Tens of thousands of white ducks, too, may be seen crowded into vast concentration camps.

The great spectacle of Attleborough, which is otherwise not a very distinguished little place, is its church with a great screen and rood loft, the grandest and most complete rood loft in England, stretching as it does right across both nave and aisles. There are large and interesting wall paintings over the screen. The church is strangely cut off, because the Norman tower was once in the middle of a much larger building, and is now in the east end of what remains. The old choir, which was east of the Norman Tower, belonged to the College of the Holy Cross, founded by Sir Robert Mortimer in the late fourteenth century and pulled down at the Dissolution.

Breccles Hall, west of Attleborough, is Tudor, with streams and water gardens.

If the stranger should ask me where he should go to see a Norfolk country town at its best, I should be tempted to say **Wymondham**.

Wymondham, pronounced 'Windam' by rich and poor alike, has so many fine houses in it that to mention them all would take many pages. There is the Guild Chapel dedicated to St Thomas à Becket, shortly after his murder, and rebuilt in the fourteenth century. Two monks were installed here to pray for the soul of the Earl of Arundel. It is now the County Library. Next door is the Green Dragon, famous with visiting Americans and defaced by a hideous petrol pump (I like the Cock much farther down on the road to Hingham), also a Market Cross, of 1617, and there is the **Abbey**—one of the great buildings of Norfolk and of England.

A Benedictine priory was founded at Wymondham by the William d'Albini who built the castle at Old Buckenham—the king's ex-butler. In 1834 lead coffins were excavated from close by the High Altar containing the remains of the founder's daughter-in-law, Maud, and her prematurely born baby. D'Albini intended that the church should serve both gown and town, but for some reason monks and townspeople could never agree very well, anywhere; and the history of this church was one long story of childish quarrelling. In 1249 the Pope, no less, had to be called upon to arbitrate, and he awarded the nave, north-west tower and north aisle to the people and the rest to the monks. This arrangement worked no better than the first. The monks walled off the nave from the choir of the church —denying thus the view that the people had formerly enjoyed of the great High Altar—and the people (after prolonged wrangling and litigation) built the present great west tower in 1445. The monks objected to the people having bells, because these disturbed their meditations. They built for themselves the lovely octagonal tower that survives—now at the east end of the church—but originally in the middle, for the monks' choir, to the east of it, has all been pulled down. It was, incidentally, a direct descendant of William d'Albini, Sir Andrew Ogard, who, together with Sir John de Clifton who then lived in New Buckenham Castle, gave support to building the new west tower and managed to overcome the opposition of the monks to do so.

Not only could the monks not agree with the townspeople—they could not agree with their mother abbey either—St Albans. There were the most fascinating Trollopian intrigues as Wymondham sought to sever the connection and become an abbey in its own right, instead of a priory and a mere cell of an abbey. Then came the Dissolution, dissolved the whole lot of them, and the whole of the east end of the great church was pulled down but not, fortunately, the strangely lovely octagonal tower.

So the townspeople won in the end, and they still have this wonderful building, with its massively Norman nave, aisles and towers of the fifteenth century and later, and odd pieces of ruined monastic buildings outside. The present-day parishioners seem to be resolutely 'High Church', and the modern fittings are lavish. Sir Ninian Comper's screen is a many-splendoured thing. As there was no east window (the octagonal tower making such a window impossible) he was able really to go to town on it.

While at Wymondham Abbey we may well consider the brothers Kett, because one of them—William—was hanged alive in chains on one of the towers and there left to rot, while Robert, his brother, was similarly accommodated on the walls of Norwich Castle. They were Wymondham men, so here may be the place to review their triumph —and their downfall, and perhaps one cannot understand the present-day spirit of East Anglia without considering the brothers Kett.

On 20th June 1549 there was a riot at Attleborough, aimed against the new land enclosures, and fences were pulled down which had been illegally erected by one Squire Green on common land. On the 7th of July—a Sunday—fell the annual Feast at Wymondham, during which the old guild play of St Thomas was wont to be performed. A large crowd collected, speeches were made, and the next day a great body of people went and threw down fences which a man named Flowerdew had illegally erected round common land. (It was Flowerdew who had stolen most of the lead from the old Abbey of Wymondham.)

Kett came out, confronted the mob, and listened to their grievances. He was convinced by them, and according to Nevylle's *De Furoribus Norfolciensum*, written immediately after the time, he said: 'Whatsoever lands I have enclosed shall again be made common unto ye and all men, and my own hands shall first perform it.' He then led them in pulling down his own fences.

Without Kett the rising would quickly have been suppressed, like many in other parts of England; but Kett, believing that he was fighting *for* the law, and not *against* it (for nearly all the enclosures and depopulations were illegal) proved to be a born leader.

A manifesto was drawn up (one would guess by Kett) which began:

The pride of great men is now intolerable, but our condition miserable.

These abound in delights; and compassed with the fullness of all things, and consumed with vain pleasures, thirst only after gain, inflamed with the burning delights of their desires.

But ourselves, almost killed with labour and watching, do nothing all our life but sweat, mourn, hunger, and thirst . . .

The present condition of possessing land seemeth miserable and slavish—holding it all at the pleasure of great men; not freely, but by prescription, and, as it were, at the will and pleasure of the lord. For as soon as a man offend any of these gorgeous gentlemen he is put out, deprived, and thrust from all his goods . . . The lands which in the memory of our fathers were common, those are ditched and hedged and made several; the pastures are enclosed and we are shut out. Whatsoever fowls of the air or fishes of the water, and increase of the earth—all these do they devour, consume, and swallow up; yea, nature doth not suffice to satisfy their lusts, but they seek out new devices, and as it were, forms of pleasure to embalm and perfume themselves, to abound in pleasant smells, to pour sweet things to sweet things. Finally, they seek from all places all things for their desire and the provocation of lust. While we in the meantime eat herbs and roots, and languish with continual labour, and yet are envied that we live, breathe, and enjoy common air! Shall they, as they have brought hedges about common pastures, enclose with their intolerable lusts also all the commodities and pleasure of this life, which Nature, the parent of us all, would have common, and bringeth forth every day, for us, as well as for them? . . . Nature hath not envied us other things. While we have the same form, and the same condition of birth together with them, why should they have a life so unlike ours, and differ so much from us in calling?

The complete manifesto, in modern English can be read in *The Rising in East Anglia in 1381* by Edgar Powell.

Kett led his men to Mousehold Heath, north-east of Norwich, where other rebels had been before him. There they made camp, and before long twenty thousand people had come to their standard. Twenty thousand men and women driven to such a state of desperation that they joined this assembly of outlaws knowing full well that by doing so they made it inevitable that they would be hanged if they were caught.

Under Robert Kett's leadership they were peaceable enough. True they sent foragers about the country to requisition food from big landowners, true that wherever they went they threw down illegal enclosures, and true they took some enclosing landlords prisoner. But they murdered nobody. They took no life except later on and in fair battle. Nobody remembered this when they were being slaughtered in their thousands in Norwich market place and outside the city.

The king sent a herald to Norwich to order them to surrender, and offering a free pardon if they did so. Kett answered him: 'Kings and Princes are wont to pardon wicked persons, not innocent and just men.' Kett insisted from first to last that he was there to uphold the law, not to break it.

The rebels by then had control of most of Norfolk, and also of Norwich. But after Kett's rebuffal of the king's herald, Thomas Cod, Mayor of Norwich, who had been on good terms with Kett, barred the city to him.

This angered the rebels and they stormed the walls. The citizens manned the defences and showered Kett's men with arrows, but 'vagabond boys, naked and unarmed, came among the thickest of the arrows, and gathered them up, and plucked out the very arrows that were sticking in their bodies, and gave them, all dripping with blood, to the rebels who were standing by, to fire again against the city.'

No fortress could withstand such spirit, the rebels swam the Wensum, stormed the walls, and took the city.

After this Mayor Cod was imprisoned, and Austen Steward (whose house we have noticed in Tombland in the chapter on Norwich) was made Mayor instead. He also managed to keep on fairly good terms with the rebels. Cod, though in their hands, was not harmed.

Even after this violence Kett's leadership was equal to restraining his followers, there was little looting, and no damage was done to the city. The rebels assumed that the city people would be with them, but by and large they were not.

On the return of York Herald to London the Marquis of Northampton set out with 1,500 soldiers to deal with the outbreak. This army occupied the city, the rebels attacked, Lord Sheffield was slain near the cathedral (a plaque still marks the spot), and the army fled back to London.

But the Government was gathering its powers. The Earl of Warwick was sent against Norwich with 12,000 trained troops, many of them German mercenaries with firearms. He arrived at Norwich —a herald was sent forward—and again rejected. The rebels told him that the pardon offered was nothing but 'barrels filled with ropes and halters'. Warwick occupied the city, and prepared to attack the rebel camp. His artillery train took a wrong turning and fell into the rebels' hands, but they did not know how to use it. Kett had one good gunner—Miles, who shot the king's master gunner and captured yet more of Warwick's artillery. In spite of the arquebuses of the Germans it looked as if the rebels would have the ascendancy.

But on Monday, 26th of August, 1,400 more Germans came to join Warwick, and it was on that day that Kett made his fatal mistake. Persuaded by some religious fanatics among his followers, who claimed that they had had visions, he burnt his camp on Mousehold, marched out of his strong defences there, and down to the low ground near the Wensum. There he took up a defensive position.

On the 27th Warwick attacked him. Miles, Kett's excellent gunner, managed with an iron ball to kill the king's standard-bearer. But then the mercenaries fired a terrific volley from their arquebuses, Warwick's cavalry charged, the rebels broke and fled and England was safe for the big landowners for another four hundred years.

Some of the rebels rallied and held their ground, were offered pardon, and knowing it to be worthless refused it and were killed fighting. They were the fortunate ones. The pursuit spread for miles. Kett fled with the others, and was found hiding in a barn at Swannington, eight miles from Norwich. The hangings started and went on for days. The enclosing landlords whom Kett had imprisoned (and not in one case physically harmed) clamoured for blood and more blood until even the bloodthirsty Warwick had to cry out: 'Is there no place for pardon? Shall we hold the plough ourselves, and harrow our own lands?'

Lest this should happen some labouring people had to be spared. William Kett, as we have seen, was hanged alive from one of the towers of Wymondham Abbey, and Robert from Norwich Castle walls until his body completely disintegrated from corruption. On Norwich Castle now hangs a plaque on which is written:

IN 1549 AD ROBERT KETT YEOMAN FARMER OF WYMONDHAM WAS EXECUTED BY HANGING IN THIS CASTLE AFTER THE DEFEAT OF THE NORFOLK REBELLION OF WHICH HE WAS THE LEADER. IN 1949 AD FOUR HUNDRED YEARS LATER THIS MEMORIAL WAS PLACED HERE BY THE CITIZENS OF NORWICH IN REPARATION AND HONOUR TO A NOTABLE AND COURAGEOUS LEADER IN THE LONG STRUGGLE OF THE

COMMON PEOPLE OF ENGLAND TO ESCAPE FROM A SERVILE LIFE INTO
THE FREEDOM OF JUST CONDITIONS.

A descendant of a Wymondham man, Samuel Huntington, signed
the Declaration of Independence on behalf of the State of Connecticut. His ancestor, Simon, founded the towns of Windham and
Norwich, in that state.

CHAPTER 11

King's Lynn and the Great Ouse

The most romantic town in England is **King's Lynn.**

Few towns have been as single-minded as Lynn, and Lynn's mind has always been firmly fixed on *trade*. What is surprising is that this commercial-mindedness has not led to the ruin of the old town, the pulling-down of everything not immediately profitable. Lynn has perhaps the finest collection of medieval merchants' combined houses and warehouses in England, still being used (although for other purposes than that for which they were built), still in good repair, and not too spoiled by being converted to modern employments. They remain, not because they have been consciously preserved by anyone (although the King's Lynn Preservation Trust is beginning to do good work in this direction), but because they were so well built in the middle ages, so adequately maintained and discreetly altered in later centuries, that they are as useful as they were when they were first built.

Lynn still has the smell of Old England about it: and the smell, too, of voyages to Iceland, and the Baltic, and Italy, and Spain, the New World and the Low Countries and the Greenland whale fishery. It is in no way a 'show town' or tourist resort, trading consciously on its antique character. Its modern flavour is given it by the Wash fishermen who lived in its North End (but have now, alas, been planted out in council houses like cabbages, but are Wash fishermen still), by the farmers who throng its very large cattle market, by Fenland men and women who come in to spend money made ploughing and sowing and reaping in the richest fields on earth, by merchant sailors—British and foreign—who come roaming off the ships in its modern docks, and by merchants who are the very descendants of the ones who built so much of the Lynn we see, back in the Middle Ages.

220 yards

In the very early Middle Ages Lynn and Boston (over the other side of the Wash) competed with each other for half the trade of England. The reason for the commercial ascendancy of the Wash ports was that they were the outlets to the sea of the richest hinterland of England: the cornlands of Marshland and Fenland, the Derbyshire lead mines, the Lincolnshire and Norfolk salternes, and above all the sheep and wool country of the East Midlands. The imports that came back from foreign countries were at first such exotic articles as furs from Novgorod (in 1245 the king's tailor went to Lynn and bought £174 17s 1d worth of 'greywork' from Edmund of Gothland; 'Greywork' was the fur of the Arctic squirrel, taken in winter), gerfalcons from Iceland, hawks and lesser falcons from Norway, wood and madder from Picardy, wine from Gascony, and the rarer Flemish and Italian cloths. Edward III banned the cloth, and instead imported Flemish weavers and got them to weave the cloth in England, and thus sprang up the great East Anglian weaving industry. After the ban on cloth-import, wool and woven woollen cloth became the biggest exports from Lynn. As time went on such aristocratic requirements as furs and gerfalcons declined, and articles of more mundane use came in: 'stockfish' (salt or dried cod) from Iceland, more and more wine, and the Baltic countries supplied ever-increasing quantities of forest products: rafters and deal boards, masts and spars for ships, furniture, wax, pitch, resin, tar and potash. This trade with the northern forests goes on to this day, as a stroll round Lynn docks will quickly show.

Lynn as a port is on the up-grade, its prosperity being assured by the partial seizing-up of the Port of London owing to poor labour relations. Ocean-going ships that would have docked in London and railed their goods to the Midlands now dock at Rotterdam, tranship into little Dutch motor coasters, and Midlands-bound goods are brought to Lynn, Wisbech, and Boston, and sent inland from there. And Lynn is re-developing trade with all her traditional markets. All the Baltic flags are to be seen in the wet docks, German, Belgian and Dutch, and more and more the Hammer and Sickle.

The proper way to approach a seaport is from the sea—in the case of Lynn in from the Wash and up the Great Ouse. If the traveller does this the first opening into the land that he will see, on the Lynn side of the river, is a narrow creek, that dries out to steep mud banks at low tide, called the **Fisher Fleet**. This, according to the Lynn fishermen, was presented to them for ever by King John. It is crowded with fishing boats, old and new; and should be visited even by the land-bound. There are virtually no fish in the Wash. The reason for this is that the Wash is a great breeding nursery for seals, and any finned fish that poked his nose into it would be snapped up immediately. So the Lynn fishermen go almost exclusively after shell fish: shrimps, cockles and mussels. The shrimps are boiled on board, as soon as they are caught: the mussels and cockles are raked up from the sand or mud by fishermen who have 'landed' on the sea-bottom from stranded boats. The smacks are anchored over the fishing grounds at high tide—far away in the Wash, miles from land—and the fishermen wait for the tide to go down. When it does they jump overboard on to the drying sand and rake out their cockles or harvest their mussels. Lynn fishermen still incline to such medieval-sounding names as Fyshe, Bun, Pegg, Rake, Benifer and Hornigold. They are an ancient race.

The Fisher Fleet was once twice the length that it is now, but in the 1880s it was cut in half to make the new Bentinck Dock. A boom was placed across the Fleet, and a fisherman has just died who could tell of the scene when this was done, by a gang of men protected by policemen and councillors in tall hats; but the fishermen made at least a gesture of defiance—pitching the Chief Constable's hat into the water and covering some of the top-hatted gentlemen with mud.

There was a good little boat-yard just south of the Fleet, where the Brothers Worfolk built wooden boats by traditional methods, but it has now been taken over by a larger firm. Just through the dock gates is the old fishermen's quarter that has recently been so ruthlessly pulled down to make room for worse things, but there is still the Tilden Smith, and the Fishermen's Arms, both good pubs (the Fishermen's Arms has been rebuilt, however). **St Nicholas Chapel**, in St Ann's Street, is in fact a large church although officially it is a 'chapel of ease' to St Margaret's. The fishermen claim that this, too, was given to them by King John. The church is Perpendicular, with an Early English tower and a Victorian lead spire (the first one fell down); I find it grand but rather gloomy, but there is a bench-end that is well worth going there to see. On it is carved a fifteenth-century ship with a furled square mainsail and a furled lateen mizzen (a new-fangled invention at that time), one of the ships that was being built at Lynn in the 1400s (by the ancestors of the brothers Worfolk?) for the profitable Iceland trade.

Near St Nicholas is a modern ship's chandlers and a new Port

Officials School in a very ancient building in St Ann's Street. Walking past the gate of the Austin Friary, past several very ancient half-timbered houses, and past a vast timber shed, you come to the **Tuesday Market**, as grand a non-collegiate urban open space as there is in East Anglia. Here is the exuberant corn exchange, built in 1854, and described by Pevsner as 'Jolly and vulgar'! There are plenty of good Georgian and Early Victorian buildings, and the big hotels. The Duke's Head is a fine place, put up in 1683 for the use of visitors to the new Merchant's Exchange by a Lynn vintner. The Maid's Head was much frequented by American airmen when nearby Sculthorpe was still a very big air base.

One should, wherever possible in Lynn, cut down to the River Great Ouse. Many streets lead down to the river but most of them come to a dead end there and one has to retrace one's steps. The reason for this is that it is down to the river that the great merchants' warehouses go. The pattern of these was a road running parallel to the river, the merchants' houses on this road, and at the back of the houses long narrow courtyards, flanked on either side by warehouses and cut off from the river by a further warehouse with its private wharf at which the goods, from the Baltic and elsewhere, were landed. It is these private wharfs which still impede walking along the shore of the river. The great houses along the Strand in London once stood in a similar relationship to the Thames.

One of the first buildings that we come to in **King Street** (King Street was once called *Stockfishrow*) is the famous St George's Guildhall, which was a theatre in Shakespeare's time and it is known that his company once played there (and once again was paid by the corporation *not* to play there—in an outburst of beastly puritanism), and there is no reason to think that Shakespeare was not among them. Thus it is the only building in England in which it is possible—nay likely—that Shakespeare appeared upon the stage. After long use as a warehouse it is now a theatre again and the centre for the very lively annual King's Lynn Festival.

King Street has in it not a building but what is of interest and beauty. At the end of it is the Customs House. This was built in 1683 not as a Customs House but as the Merchants' Exchange by the same man who built the Duke's Head, and designed by Henry Bell, twice Mayor of Lynn and architect of many of its buildings. The lavish use of stone in it in this stoneless country was made possible by the fact that the stone could be shipped direct down the Nene, across the

Middle Level Navigations, down the Great Ouse, and up Purfleet right to the very site of the building in Fen lighters. It is a very pretty building indeed and is adorned with a statue of Charles II.

Cut down riverwards to **King's Staithe Square** and its lane (*staithe* is Norfolk for wharf: thus there are staithes all over Broadland). Bank House, which has Charles I on top of it, is very fine. Samuel Cresswell, the grandson of Elizabeth Fry the prison reformer and one of the great Gurney family (see Norwich, p95) returned there to his home after a five-year voyage of exploration to discover if there was such a thing as the North-West Passage. There was. Farther on there are some more ancient warehouses.

Clifton House, in **Queen Street** (formerly called *Wyndgate*) is a splendid example. The dwelling house, on Queen Street, was rebuilt about 1708, but the splendid tower in the courtyard is Elizabethan, the warehouses that reach back to the river older, and the undercroft fifteenth century if not earlier. Recently a fourteenth-century pavement of Clare tiles has been uncovered in it: 'the most substantial secular pavement of this date preserved in position in England.' Thoresby College, farther south, was founded in 1502 by the Mayor, Thomas Thoresby, for training priests, but the house was turned into a merchant's house and warehouses at the Dissolution. What stands now is mostly seventeenth century, but in the great hall down by the river is a marvellous hammerbeam roof.

Continuing south are more merchants' houses, including the 'Steelyard', or 'Hanseatic Warehouse' opposite the church: here the dwelling house on the street (St Margaret's Plain) is eighteenth century, but the warehouses at the back much earlier; parts may go back to 1475 when the building was first put up. Hampton Court, farther south, is another great block of a merchant's house—counting-house, warehouses and apprentices' quarters. It has been restored by the King's Lynn Preservation Trust. Farther south, in Nelson Street (formerly *Lath Street*) are more of these superb domestic and industrial buildings. King Street, Queen Street, St Margaret's Plain and Nelson Street contain, between them, a great wealth of medieval industrial building, and it is most important that it should be preserved, for there is nothing else like it in England.

St Margaret's Church is of great interest to the architectural detective. Here again we see the result of good water-borne communication, for the very large building (what is left of it is over 230 feet long and it was built as a priory church and had more to it) is all limestone, brought from Northamptonshire. The church was founded by de Losinga over 800 years ago, as a part of his penance for the sin of simony (as was Great Yarmouth St Nicholas and Norwich Cathedral), but there is little Norman work left in it: some at the base of the south-west tower. There is a glorious early thirteenth-century chancel and an arcade and a fifteenth-century clerestory. The whole church is a cocktail of the work of different periods: from Norman down to Victorian Gothic—even Sir Gilbert Scott had a go at it. The south-west tower alone has in it, besides the Norman base already mentioned, some Transitional work, Early English, Decorated bell stage, eighteenth-century battlements. It has a clock-work moon dial of 1681. The north-west tower had to be rebuilt in Perpendicular times because it leaned. It now contains ten bells. By the west door are flood marks, the highest of them being that recording the flood of 1953.

Inside, the reason for the rebuilding of the north-west tower in the fifteenth century can be seen in the leaning of the Norman tower arch. The nave was rebuilt in 1745 after a spire had fallen through it in a gale in 1741. The arcade is very early Gothic revival. The organ is by Snetzler and its case of Grinling Gibbons-style wood carving. In the organ the dulciana stop is said to have been used for the first time. The chancel is fine Early English, there are the original stalls and good misericords. The pulpit is delicately inlaid and carved and most beautiful.

But the pride of the building, and the two things that make it from one point of view pre-eminent, are the two great brasses: one to Adam de Walsokne and his wife Margaret (Adam died 1349) and the other to Robert Braunche and his two wives, Letitia and Margaret, who look so alike as to appear twins. Braunche died in 1364. Both brasses are nearly ten feet long, the figures are life-sized, and all the surrounding brass is filled with the most exquisite engraving. At the base of de Walsokne's is a scene of country life, with a vintage, and a man carrying corn to a windmill. At the base of Robert Braunche's is the picture that gives this brass the name of 'The Peacock Feast'. A banquet is depicted, at which a roast peacock features, and at which twelve guests are sitting down to a groaning table. The twelfth guest is in such a hurry to get at the victuals that he is depicted as leaping over the table. At the flanks stand musicians. It is known that Braunche, while Mayor, gave a mighty banquet to Edward III in 1349.

11. *Above*, KING'S LYNN. *Left*, Low tide at the Customs House, originally a Merchant's Exchange. *Right*, Clifton House is one of the splendid Merchant's combined houses and warehouses that back on to the Great Ouse. *Below*, WISBECH. The north "Brink" of the river Nene

12. Blakeney (*above*) and Brancaster (*below*) share the lonely charm of that strange interlude of the English coast: the tidal 'harbours' of North Norfolk. Here the land is broken into by the sea, or the sea invaded by the land, so that there is an extensive no-man's-land of sand, mud, mussel beds and saltings, with sand dunes such as Blakeney Point and Scolt Head protecting it from the open sea

Lynn's mayor and corporation still give feasts and banquets: the last time I looked into the Guildhall there was a simply splendid affair going on. In 1215 King John was feasted at Lynn (it was known as Lynn Episcopi then—but by the locals no doubt as it is now—just plain Lynn) and again peacocks were featured in the menu. On the 12th October, after the banquet, the surfeited monarch left to cross the Fens. On the 13th his baggage train was overwhelmed by the tide—with a great treasure and his private shrine and all. People are still looking for it. John went on without his goods, reached Newark Castle, and there died, whether from over-eating at Lynn or from a broken heart one does not know.

Peacocks frequently used to feature in Lynn's great feasts, and it is interesting that there is still a tradition of keeping peacocks in Fenland. Mr and Mrs Bill Holman, at Southery, still have a fine flock and so do several other people.

The organ in St Margaret's is of marginal interest to literary historians, for it was installed there at the instigation of the organist who happened to be Dr Burney, the father of Fanny, the novelist. Fanny was born at Lynn in 1762. When her novel *Evelina* eventually came out it was a *succes fou*: Dr Johnson roared over it, Jane Austen mentioned it with warm praise in *Northanger Abbey*, and Sir Joshua Reynolds had to be fed by attendants while he was reading it, because he could not put it down. Fanny, when she heard of its success, was so pleased that she danced round the mulberry tree. Fanny was afterwards introduced into society, was appointed Keeper of the Robes to Queen Charlotte but didn't like it and got ill, and then married a French refugee, General d'Arblay and lived quietly until she died.

St Margaret's, like the rest of Lynn, was knocked about by Oliver Cromwell (in person almost for, as Colonel of Horse, he was for a time in command of the siege of the town). During the cannonade an eighteen pound cannon ball came from the other side of the river and through the window over the west door of the church, smashed a pier, and scattered the congregation. Eighty lives were lost in the town during the bombardment. Oliver Cromwell moved off to other battles, leaving the Earl of Manchester finally to storm and reduce the town. Lynn was one of the very few places in East Anglia to stand for the king: Lowestoft was the only other of any size, and *she* went Royalist simply to annoy Great Yarmouth, for it was unthinkable that the two places could be on the same side. As one generally assumes that it was the trading and commercial classes that sided with Parliament it is strange that such a resolutely commercial place as Lynn should have sided with the king.

North of the church is the **Saturday Market**, which has been a market at least since de Losinga's time and still is one. A minute of the corporation records of 1427 rules that Jews should no longer be permitted to sell meat in Jew's Lane 'unless it be near the church'—in other words unless it be in the place where the church could draw revenue from the transaction. Jew's Lane is now Surrey Street. I have not seen it, but there is said to be a tiny Jewish cemetery near the old library. In the Middle Ages Lynn had a strong Jewish community.

Overlooking the Saturday Market is the famous **Guildhall**, one of the choicest municipal buildings in the country. The Guildhall itself was built for the Guild of Holy Trinity in 1421, in fine flint and freestone chequer-boarding. Behind it is a big Assembly Room, designed by William Tuck who was a carpenter and Thomas King who was a bricklayer in 1766 (thus proving that in an age of good taste the best buildings need not be architect-designed—what would we expect of a big public building designed by a carpenter and a bricklayer in this year of grace?) and on your left as you face the Guildhall is an Elizabethan addition which acts as the entrance hall and is a most jubilant building with no less than *two* great royal coats of arms up above the door (the upper of the two brought from St James's church when this was pulled down). Farther along Queen Street but adjoining is the Town Hall proper, built in 1895 but well in keeping with the rest.

The regalia kept inside the Guildhall is simply astonishing. London itself has nothing to beat the sumptuous gold and enamel 'King John's Cup' (not King John's because it dates from 1340). This has been said again and again to be the finest cup in the country. It speaks for the lightness with which people in places like King's Lynn bear the great weight of history that until recently this cup was commonly taken home by the reigning Mayor, for his personal use at his private parties. It is said that it was once sent along the street by a messenger to have some minor repairs carried out by a local jeweller. There is also 'King John's Sword' which may indeed have been given to the town by King John, when he gave Lynn its first charter in 1204. It is a little like Oliver Cromwell's Pipe though, in that it had new silver ornamentation in the sixteenth century, and a new blade in the seventeenth. For three centuries the bishops of Norwich unrightfully kept it from Lynn, there were legal proceedings in 1520 to get it back, but it was not handed over (at the town bounds) until midsummer 1535. There is a complete set of charters down from John's time, and one of the time of Knut or Canute. There are town seals, chains of office, and maces. Most interesting of all there is the famous 'Red Book of Lynn'.

This records commercial activities with the Hansa towns and the Baltic ports, and squabbles between Lynn and Denmark and with Iceland: one of the latter caused by Lynn men having kidnapped '3 male and 2 female boys' and selling them into slavery. The complaint came from the Bishop of Iceland. There is an entry of 1394 which records that—ten years before that—citizens of Wismar and Rostock attacked the Lynn settlement in Bergen, and Henry IV had to pay 5,318 nobles to ransome the Lynn men. For centuries Lynn maintained factories or enclaves in Scandinavian and Hansa ports and there were foreign trading posts in Lynn.

Working our way inland from the river there is a good little **museum** in Baxter's Plain with some nice relics of the Greenland Whale Fishery in which Lynn men were once prominent (competing with men of Whitby). There is a lovely painting of the SS *Bedford*, a Lynn whaler homeward bound, a painting of the Fisher Fleet by Henry Baines as it looked in 1862 before it was cut in half to make the Bentinck Dock, and much else.

In Bridge Street there is a building still called the *Greenland Fishery*, originally a merchant's house, built by John Atkin in 1605, thereafter a pub, and now, alas, an office. The **South Gate** (early sixteenth century) through which the reader will probably have driven if he came overland in a carriage, is one of the few remaining parts of the town's walls. In the splendid public parts known as The Walk is **Red Mount Chapel**, built after 1485 (it is said by a man named Robert Corraunce). This contained a relic of the Virgin, and was taken in by pilgrims who had landed from ships at Lynn on the great pilgrimage to the Holy House at Walsingham, as a kind of spiritual *hors d'œuvre*. It is a building of the strangest shape, and has a perfectly lovely fan vaulted ceiling in the little chapel up above: the tracery of it has been compared with that of King's College Chapel, Cambridge.

In Norfolk Street is Fiddamans Hotel, with fine Victorian façade, opposite Mr Donaldson, the Queen's Fishmonger. By the cattle market is an exuberant building with the title 'Electric Theatre'.

But one could wander for a week in Lynn, and always be finding something rich and strange. Go there soon, though. The little town has agreed to accept an influx of 10,000 Londoners under what the local people will persist in calling the 'Overswill Scheme', and soon the distinctively East Anglian character of the place will be lost for ever. The more notable of the old buildings will no doubt be preserved, like flies in amber; but the streets and streets of less noteworthy old buildings which really give the place its charm will go. The pubs will be 'tarted up' and fitted with juke-boxes, the chain stores will come, so will acres and acres of glass and concrete factories, and the lovely pungent Norfolk speech will give way to watered-down Cockney.

Little pieces of Lynn history that are of interest. In 1885 Frederick Savage of Lynn, took out a patent for a machine called 'galloping horses' (the first roundabout), a model of which may be seen in the museum of Leek, Staffordshire. In 1330 the first-ever voyage of exploration to the Arctic set out from Lynn. George Vancouver was born in the yard of the Quaker Meeting House. He sailed as a boy with Captain Cook and later commanded a ship of his own, made extensive discoveries along the south-west coast of Australia, in New Zealand, the Gulf of Georgia, mapped the coast north of San Francisco for the first time, and discovered Vancouver Island in Canada, returning to England in 1795. He got into trouble after all this for flogging poor Lord Camelford and having him clapped in irons, but the boy was a midshipman and probably deserved it.

The first autobiography ever written was written by a Lynn woman, Margery Kempe, née Brunham. Daughter of a mayor of Lynn, she married a merchant, bore him fourteen children and after this went slightly strange in the head. She had visions, went on pilgrimages, but wherever she went she was avoided by fellow pilgrims on account of her intolerable habit of *weeping*. Her eyes gushed like the Great Ouse. She was born in 1364, but did not dictate her autobiography until after 1400. I have not read it, but am told that it casts fascinating light on the times.

Here we might consider the **Great Ouse** and the **Fen waterways**. King's Lynn owed its prominence as a seaport in the early Middle Ages, and its survival at all as one later, to the fact that it is at the mouth of a very extensive system of navigable waterways. The

Great Ouse may not compare in size with the Amazon or the Mississippi, but it and its tributaries and connected waterways drain a country that has for a great many centuries been highly productive of the goods which men want, and also well to the forefront of civilization.

The Great Ouse itself was navigable as far as Bedford, taking in on the way Ely, St Ives, Huntingdon and St Neots, while Cambridge, and that older place Grantchester, are on a tributary and Bury St Edmunds and Thetford, the old capital of East Anglia, on others. Nor is this all. The Fen Middle Level Navigations not only covered the whole of the rich Fen country with water roads but they also provided a link with the River Nene which comes right down from the heart of the East Midlands. It is now possible (the author has done it) to travel by inland waterway from King's Lynn to Birmingham, Liverpool and London and, in fact, most other places of importance in the kingdom. In the Middle Ages it was possible too—but with short portages overland.

Boston vied with Lynn, but for part of the Middle Ages the Roman-dug Foss Dike Canal, which connects Boston's river to the Trent, was silted up, thus giving Lynn the advantage, for Lynn had the Nene.

This inland water traffic to Lynn survived until a couple of decades ago, and even now the last of the Fen lighters—as grand a breed of boat in their way as the Norfolk wherry—lie rotting up by a quarry on the Nene.

The Fen lighter overcame the disability of having to be small (to pen through the tiny medieval locks of the Fens) by working in trains, or 'gangs', of four or five boats each. The gang was pulled by a horse, which was trained to leap the fences that ran down to the water's edge (see Constable's painting 'The Leaping Horse', only that was on the Stour) and trained to jump aboard one of the lighters in order to be ferried across a river, or to be carried up or down one when the wind was fair and a sail could be set; or the gang could drive with the tide. The lighters were connected together by 'fest poles', which were short bow-sprits held fast to the quarters of the barge in front by the 'fest ropes'—which had to be adjusted by the agile crew when the 'gang' was going round a corner. The gangs were, indeed, steered by these 'fest ropes', and had no rudders.

There is a good model of a Fen lighter, fest pole and all, in the home of Mr Vic Jackson, Standground Creek, Peterborough. Mr

Jackson is the last of the old 'Fen lightermen' and can tell a thousand stories about the life. He is the last of a tradition that goes back, certainly, into pre-Christian times.

There is no longer any goods-carrying on the waterways (save one little tanker that carries diesel oil to the pumping stations) but, strangely, there is a kind of renaissance. Pleasure boating is causing the old waterways to be opened up again. In 1964 the Well Creek, from Salter's Lode into the Middle Level, was opened up again after years of disuse, and even now volunteers are working to make the Great Ouse navigable again as far as Bedford. And, in spite of weed and low bridges, it is still possible to penetrate to most parts of Fenland by the Navigations, and a fascinating experience it is too (although not as *pretty* as the Broads, by any means).

The Great Ouse at King's Lynn looks fairly uncompromising. The river is wide and artificially straight, and the water the colour of the worst kind of transport-café coffee. High banks wall the Ouse, as they do most of the Fenland rivers, and at high tide the water stands within them much higher than the surrounding countryside. The tidal range in the Wash is great (18 feet) and the speed of the tide is daunting: up to 7 knots. Until you gain Denver Sluice in fact, and non-tidal waters, the Great Ouse is not for the learner navigator.

A new phenomenon has grown up (or rather down) alongside the Great Ouse. In 1959 the Tail Sluices of the great new Relief Channel were opened. They stand up just south of King's Lynn looking colossal, which indeed they are: it has been said that they are the biggest drainage sluices in Europe. The mighty Cut-off Channel has since been dug, and was opened by the Duke of Edinburgh on the 19th September 1964. This runs parallel to the Great Ouse, to the east of it, starting near Mildenhall, and it thus cuts off all the water that drains down from the high land of Norfolk and Suffolk and prevents this from running either into the Great Ouse, or over it into the Fens. By ingenious inverted syphons the tributary rivers, Little Ouse, Lark and Wissey, run over the new channel regardless—the channel goes underneath them in concrete pipes—but in times of flood the tributaries can be diverted into the Cut-off Channel and thus prevented from joining their parent river. Thus it is hoped to avoid another disaster such as that of 1947, when 70,000 acres of Fenland was flooded by the Great Ouse breaking its banks, and Ely was temporarily made an island again. The Cut-off Channel is $27\frac{1}{2}$ miles long and with its attendant works cost £3,000,000.

It protects from flooding half a million acres of land. It is hoped that it will prevent for all time that recurring terror of the Fens: burst banks and flooded country.

King's Lynn looks its best from out on the waters of the Great Ouse, when the sun is setting in Fenland splendour at your back. The town then resembles some splendid medieval city, or one of the ancient ports of the old Zuyder Zee: Enkhuizen or Stavoren, or Hoern the Golden.

King's Lynn to Houghton Hall

The country between King's Lynn and Hunstanton is some of the most distinctive and beautiful in East Anglia. The chalk uplands of north-west Norfolk here tumble down to the low marshlands by the Wash, giving way first to sandy, heathy country, and this heathland has been extensively afforested by wealthy landowners—not least among them the Queen and her royal forebears.

South Wootton just, out of Lynn, is a straggle of suburban houses about which it is hard to say anything nice except that they don't straggle far. But to the east of it, along a track, is **Reffley Wood**, in which there is said to be a temple built in 1789 by the members of a Royalist society. This society was founded in the secrecy of this wood during the Commonwealth time (in 1651 to be exact) and was limited to thirty members as this was the greatest number that it was lawful should meet together. The society still exists, there are still thirty members, they still meet in Reffley Wood, they still smoke churchwarden pipes, their chairman is still a direct descendant of the first chairman, and I have no doubt they are still Royalists.

At **North Wootton** is the Red Cat Inn, a fine place where one can put up for the night, and in the bar of which the Queen's Fishmonger very often holds forth, very sensibly, too.

And a couple of miles across Ling Common is **Castle Rising**, which is one of the most interesting places in England for lovers of that strange and foreign race, the Normans. The castle still stands massive and proud inside a giant earthwork, and the Norman church is one of the finest small Norman churches that there is.

The keep, or great tower, of the castle, stands in a high ring of earth, with the remains of a gatehouse and a bridge in front of it, and the foundations of a Saxon and Norman chapel partly buried in the earthwork to the north. The chapel was long suspected to be Saxon:

recent excavations have proved that it is. The keep is wonderfully preserved, and second in size and importance as a Norman keep to Norwich Castle. It is wider than it is high—a 'hall keep', not a 'tower keep'—well built and lavishly decorated. There is a custodian who is well informed, and willing to show the visitor around. At the time of writing the top of the walls (there is no roof) is not officially accessible, but it is worth asking the custodian to unlock the door at the top of the north-east staircase to get out on them, for the fine view of the wooded heathlands, and the old village below, and the marshes stretching away towards the Wash, and also for the sense one gets of the commanding strength of this fine fortress.

For the rest—the walls are up to 9 feet thick, there are two stories, there is intersecting arcading in the forebuilding, a marvellous great staircase going under Norman arches (over it is an interesting passage-way to a sally-port), a vestibule at the top of the staircase with a vaulted ceiling and a fireplace that was once the main door into the Great Hall and is now backed with some rather nice medieval tiles, dug up nearby but nothing whatever to do with the castle. In the south-east corner upstairs are two smaller rooms—one an elegant chapel. There are three turrets, two of which are accessible. The south-west, one of the two that have staircases in them, is not open at the moment, but one wonders at the perfect condition of the winding steps in it after so many centuries. There is a fascinating gallery in the north wall.

The earthworks, round about, are supposed to have been originally Roman, and may even have started earlier. Rising is now a tiny place, and one may wonder at these signs of its great importance in times past; but for the geographical changes of the Wash shore Rising might have become the great port that Lynn became.

No doubt Roman and Norman ships came up the estuary of the Babingley Brook, and Rising was once very near the sea. Now the sea has receded—four or five miles away—but who can say, in the Wash, where land ends and sea begins? Whereas Lynn, by virtue of the Great Ouse, still has deep water access.

Little is known about Rising history until after the Normans came. The first owner recorded was Stigand, Archbishop of Canterbury. The Conqueror gave the manor (and the huge surrounding deer forest) to his brother-in-law, Odo, Bishop of Bayeux. When Odo rebelled William gave it to his butler, William d'Albini, who built Old Buckenham and married Matilda Bigod. D'Albini's son, also

William, built the castle. This William married Queen Adeliza, widow of Henry I, and thus added Sussex to his titles and Arundel Castle to his properties. He built Rising about 1150. The fifth (and last) William d'Albini (or else his brother Hugh) obtained a charter for Rising at about the time when Lynn got its charter. Rising was a Rotten Borough until the Reform Bill, returning two members to Parliament. The corporation of this dwindled place was dissolved in 1838.

When Hugh, the last of the d'Albinis, died, the castle went to his sister who married Roger de Montalt. From the Montalts it went to the Crown. From 1331 to 1356 Queen Isabella was immured there, by her son Edward III, because he was angry with her for her suspected complicity in the murder of his father. It was a fairly liberal kind of open arrest, however, because Isabella (the 'She-wolf of France') moved around England fairly freely, and was visited by her son, and often received large sums of money from him. The Black Prince then held the castle, then Richard II, but he exchanged it in 1397 with John le Vaillant, or de Montford, Duke of Brittany, for the Duke's castle of Brest. No doubt le Vaillant used it as a hunting box, for this was one of the prime sporting estates of the realm.

After le Vaillant the castle was uninhabited and began to fall into decay. In 1544 it went back to a descendant, in the female line, of the founder; for Henry VIII exchanged it with his uncle, Thomas Howard, Duke of Norfolk, who could trace his ancestry back to the Conqueror's butler. The 7th Duke sold it, in 1695, to his cousin Thomas Howard (a nephew of the poet Dryden) and to this day it is in the Howard family, although looked after by the Ministry of Works. The current Howard lives part of his time in a modest house in the village, and when he is in residence the Custodian flies the Howard flag from the top of the keep.

There is a lively account in the King's Lynn records of a Robert de Montalt, once an owner of the castle, going into Lynn to collect the revenues and tolls from the port and market of Lynn, to which the lords of Rising were legally entitled. But a man named Nicholas de Northampton and other Lynn worthies disputed this entitlement, and they advanced on de Montalt with 'banners unfurled and in a warlike manner'. They insulted de Montalt, nay drove him into his dwelling house in Lynn, broke down the doors, beat him and his men, carried away certain arms, swords, spurs, purses of money and jewels to the value of £40. They then bore him off to the house of Robert Costin and forced him to release all actions that he was taking against the Mayor and Commonalty of Lynn. All this, however, availed Lynn nothing; for in the subsequent legal action it was adjudged that Lynn must pay de Montalt £4000 damages, and he was still entitled to purloin the harbour and market tolls.

Lynn had its own back in the end though: if the courts favoured Rising geography and history favoured Lynn:

> *Rising was a seaport when Lynn was but a marsh.*
> *Now Lynn it is a seaport town and Rising fares the worse.*

As for Rising Church, a person in a hurry might look at two things: the west end and the font.

The west end is one of the finest pieces of Norman blind arcading in the country. The font is squat and primitive, and from its west side evil-looking faces leer out. This speaks a different language from any heard in the western world today. There is a noble Norman west tower arch, inside. Much of the church is Victorian.

Across the road from the church is the Hospital of the Holy and Undivided Trinity, or the Howard Bede House.

The Earl of Northampton founded it, the second son of the poet, Surrey. It cost him £451 14s 2½d. This Howard was first educated by the Protestant Foxe, the Martyrologist, but then he came under the influence of the Bishop of Lincoln and he 'poped', or joined the Church of Rome. He fell out of favour with his cousin Queen Elizabeth, and intrigued against her in favour of James VI of Scotland, and when James came to the English throne found himself in favour again. He was said to have been treacherous and un-scrupulous, but learned, artistic and charitable. His charities included the hospital at Rising, which he built in memory of his grandfather Thomas Howard 3rd Duke of Norfolk who had been imprisoned by Henry VIII (see Framlingham, p51), one at Clun in the wilds of Shropshire, which was in memory of his brother, Thomas the 4th Duke, who was beheaded by Queen Elizabeth, one at Greenwich in memory of his father the Earl of Surrey, beheaded by Henry VIII, and one at Shotesham, in Norfolk, because that was where he was born—when his father and mother were unsuccessfully fleeing from the forces of the king.

The rules that he laid down for the hospital included provision that the Governess and eleven inmates should be of 'honest life and conversation, religious, grave and discreet, able to read if such a one may be had, single, 56 at least, no common beggar, harlot, scold, drunkard, haunter of taverns, inns or alehouses'. The place still functions as it did, and one of the sights of Rising is that of the twelve ladies (whom one is sure are all that the Founder said that they should be) walking across the road in procession to church dressed in their red cloaks with the Howard badge, and their steeple hats. They are impervious to being photographed, like the maidens of Volendam. The hospital is old and attractive, and the original Jacobean furniture is still within.

For the rest—Rising has dwindled through the centuries, as the sea receded from its wharves and the great departed from its castle. Some of Kett's men gathered in what is still called 'Kett's Castle'— an earthwork in the fields—before they drew away to Watton and thence to Mousehold to join their leader. In 1643 the great deer chase had been practically denuded of timber, and the next year the deer were systematically killed off and the countryside 'deparked' and turned to agricultural uses. Now it is a country of huge estates, where the pheasant is king.

The nicest thing about **Wolferton** is its railway station. I should have mentioned before that the whole of this country is *Norfolk carr* country. The carr is a rusty-red ironstone, or sandstone containing iron, fairly hard and a reasonable building material, the only example in East Anglia of a suitable native building stone with the exception of flint and—if you can consider it suitable—chalk. Wolferton railway station is Victorian-Gothic, as all good railway stations should be, and built of this warm, honey-coloured stone, but the special thing about it is that it is all done up for the Queen. The platform lamps are surmounted by crowns, and the whole place is specially decorated by good old British Railways and kept tidy, lest Her Majesty should decide to pay a visit to Sandringham by rail. (Alas, since this was written, no longer so. Her Majesty, like most of us, now goes by car.)

This little railway, from King's Lynn to Hunstanton, is perhaps one of the most charming branch lines in England, and well worth making a trip along. It runs between the marshes and sandy uplands all the way, through lovely heathy and wooded country, and the ancient sea-shore of Sandringham Warren is most strange: a saw-edge of steep grass-covered dunes. The engine driver goes through an elaborate ritual, all the way, of exchanging large rings with men who wait for him along the track.

Sandringham hardly exists as a village, but it is a very large estate. The countryside for many miles around in fact belongs to the Queen. The estate was bought by Edward, Prince of Wales in 1861 (in preference to Houghton, which was offered to him as well) and the present Sandringham House built after 1870. It is very ugly— like a huge and grandiose Victorian seaside hotel, Jacobean in style, of red brick and stone. The gardens are fine, particularly the fruit and vegetable gardens; and one can visit them between 11 am and 5 pm provided that no member of the Royal Family is in residence. There is a little church, set in the great parkland trees nearby, old but completely Victorianized, with much silver and gold in it presented by a Mr Wanamaker who lived nearby, and an early Greek Christian font lying on the ground at its west end, the gift of one royal brother to another.

Whether the Queen is in residence or not the visitor is struck by the relaxed and informal atmosphere of the place. If there *are* any security police about—they are well hidden. People living in the locality preserve a tradition of leaving the Queen in peace, and she can ride about the country on one of her many horses with a scarf over her head just like any other horse-loving woman, and in winter the woods echo to the report of the Duke of Edinburgh's shotgun— as pheasant after pheasant bites the dust.

Dersingham is a large village, mostly of carr stone, and inhabited largely by wealthy retired people, some of whom, it is rumoured, settle there to be near the Queen. There are several large pubs which put people up, one of them entirely decked out with objects of the Horse Cult: not an image or a pattern or a gadget in the place but has some equine association.

Down towards the railway lives Mr Jimmy Laws, one of the last two or three professional wildfowlers in England. Within living memory the fishermen of the Wash all turned to fowling in the winter time, when ducks and geese were plentiful and fish were scarce, and there were plenty of men who—like Jim Laws—lived by fowling for as many months as they could and got whatever casual work there was in the summer. The chief methods of taking wildfowl were, firstly, *punting*. This involved going out on the sea in a tiny flat punt, pointed at both ends, painted grey for camouflage, with a huge gun—a cannon, no less—mounted on the foredeck. On sighting duck or geese the fowler would lie down flat behind his gun and propel the craft towards the quarry by short paddles or 'setting sticks'. When in range he would fire—and maybe kill a hundred birds, for his gun fired anything up to two pounds of shot! Much smaller shots were the rule, though, and if he got a shot in a week he was lucky, and this only after lying about night after night in freezing weather, and probably soaking wet. Secondly there was *flight-netting*. Mr Laws still has flight nets, but he uses them to cover up his strawberries, because flight-netting is illegal now. The nets—hundreds of yards long and made of fine cotton—were set up along the tide-line, in time for the evening or morning 'flight'—when ducks and teal love to fly very fast and very low up and down the shore. The birds would fly into the nets. Thirdly there was *swivel-gunning*, which was the mounting of a huge gun like a punt gun on a swivel ashore—and letting drive into the 'brown' of a big flight of duck or geese as they flew by. Mr Laws still has—and uses—what may well be the last swivel-gun in England.

Wildfowling is one of the most ancient activities of men in East Anglia, and up until the age of 'broiler chicks' provided an important source of food for country people, and a way of livelihood for men. There are still many thousands of grey geese (mostly pink-foot) on the Wash every winter, and even more widgeon, teal, and mallard. Hundreds of 'shore gunners' go after them, hiding behind the sea walls at flight time with small shoulder guns, but the number of birds they kill is negligible, simply because they are amateurs and wild-fowling in the Wash is a highly professional business. Mr Laws still shoots hundreds of birds a year, and to supplement his income takes parties of amateurs out shooting. When Mr Laws takes amateurs shooting, when they reach the sea wall he waves his hand inland—towards the Queen's estates—and says: 'That side the birds are all *hers*. This side' (waving his hand towards the empty wastes of the Wash) 'they're all *mine*!'

The only other professional wildfowler in the Wash known to me is Mr MacKenzie Thorpe, of Sutton Bridge, and he also takes parties.

In Dersingham Church is one of the most beautiful carved chests I know. **Snettisham** has a marvellous church—doubly marvellous (in Perpendicular East Anglia) because it is of the Decorated style. The tower, with its high stone spire (the latter unusual for East Anglia too—Northamptonshire is the 'county of squires and spires') was once a crossing tower, in the middle, but the old chancel, which was to the east of it, has been removed. The glory of the place is its west window: Decorated at its most free and exciting—lovely flowing tracery—lacework in stone! A Celtic torque was found here with a Belgic coin in it.

A road goes from Snettisham down to **the Wash**, and here might be a good place to go to contemplate this extraordinary arm of the sea. At Snettisham beach, if you are lucky, you may well see that strange phenomenon, horse-and-cart fishermen. People still drive out over the sands at low tide (they can easily go two or three miles there) in carts, rake cockles out of the sand, load them into the carts, and carry them back and sell them.

The sands of the Wash, at low tide, stretch for miles and miles: one could play a game of cricket on hard sand seven miles from the shore! But the *strand-looper* or sand roamer wants to know what he is doing, for the tide comes back again very very quickly and it is easy to get cut off. There are plenty of deeper guts and gullies in the sands, which one may cross without noting them when they are dry —only to find them racing water when one wishes to get back. The sands have ancient and evocative names, like Pandora, Thief, Blackguard, Seal, the Westmark Knock and the Gat. To navigate a boat among these sands requires great skill, for when the water covers them you cannot see them, yet your keel feels them all too easily. Nor are they stable—they shift about. Two decades ago the deepwater channel to King's Lynn was five miles to the west of where it is now.

Nor must it be thought that the Wash is a calm, inland sea. A very common wind in these parts comes from the north-east, and when the wind blows north-east or northerly the Wash is anything but placid, but a raging ocean; not for nothing is the light-float in the middle of the Wash named 'the Roaring Middle'. But to people who know it the Wash is a sea of enchantment. On summer days it can be a place of mirage. Lines of houses and bunches of trees can be seen—apparently hovering above the horizon. On other, very clear days 'Boston Stump'—the tower of Boston parish church—can be seen from twenty miles away, sharp and clear, and so can Hunstanton's banded cliffs. In calm weather the water has a silky, oily sheen on it, and as the tide recedes from the sand-banks these become inhabited by hundreds of seals as they flounder up out of the water to lie and bask in the sunshine. And it is fine, when the northeaster is blowing, to bring your boat to anchor in the lee of some drying sand-bank and lie there in peace while the great waves crash to death just over on its windward edge. For the walker there are fifty miles of lonely and deserted shoreline round the Wash—certainly the longest unbuilt-over shoreline in England.

Alas—the Wash is threatened with a barrage and 'development', when it will have all the lonely charm of a sewage works.

Heacham (it is a fine walk along the shore to it from Snettisham beach) is where a party of Royalists landed from sailing keels from the Humber, in the time of the Commonwealth. Sir Hamon Le Strange—the man who commanded King's Lynn for the Royalists before Manchester stormed it—took them home to his big house of Hunstanton Hall and gave them food and ale, and afterwards had to answer for it, for he had only been allowed to go free after King's Lynn on condition that he stayed out of politics. Another Le Strange, Sir Roger, made an attempt to take Lynn back from Parliament, failed and was sentenced to death, but fled to France. He came back at the Restoration, went to London, and became the most savage of the Restoration pamphleteers, making a bitter attack on Milton among other people. But he also translated into English, for the first time, Aesop's Fables. The Le Stranges are no newcomers to Hunstanton Hall. One of them came into the place by marrying an Anglo-Saxon woman just after the Conquest and there have been Le Stranges there ever since.

Hunstanton (pronounced Hunston by most of the people who live there) is a railway-age seaside resort, with some big hotels and many smaller ones, a pier, a view of the sunset over the sea (unusual for East Anglia, but Hunstanton is the only East Anglian resort that faces west across the sea) and it is far less unattractive than it might have been because many of its Victorian and Edwardian buildings are built of carr stone. Now, alas, the reach-me-down in the form of the universal Peterborough brick is creeping in: Hunstanton ought to ban it here and now. The place is famous for its triple-banded cliffs, made of successive layers of carr stone, red chalk and white chalk. East of a line drawn from Hunstanton to Stoke Ferry lie the chalk uplands of Norfolk—a continuation of the Chilterns and the Gog and Magog Hills. West of the line are older rocks: carr stone, red chalk, and gault clay. Hunstanton gives a fine view over the Wash. Often a group of Russian or other steamers may be seen, lying out at anchor, waiting for the Lynn pilot (and, incidentally, the tide).

Old Hunstanton, now overwhelmed by its full-blown daughter, has the ruins of a church which is said to have been built at the spot where St Edmund landed from over the sea in Schleswig Holstein to come and be king of the East Angles.

Holme-next-the-Sea is special in being the terminus of the Peddar's Way, and also of the Icknield Way. The latter is said to have been a Roman Road, and also a Pre-Roman road; and Holme to have been an especially holy place amongst the British. Certainly the Way is dead straight, after the manner of Roman roads, and peters out to the south somewhere in the Brecklands. Before it peters it gives the impression that it is heading in the direction of Colchester, or Camulodunum. But all is shrouded in the fog of conjecture. Was it indeed Roman—and why did it go to Holme? The Romans certainly had a biggish naval base and fort five miles to the eastward—why would they have a station at this place? One conjecture, as good as the next, is that the Romans had a ferry service from Holme across the mouth of the Wash to Lincolnshire. This would seem to be possible, if only because, in the days when much of Fenland was flooded it would otherwise have been a very long way by land from Caistor-by-Norwich, or Brancaster for that matter, to Lincoln or even York. The sea-trip would have cut off weeks: you can still sail from Norfolk to Naburn Lock, just short of York on the Yorkshire Ouse, in two tides, if you have a fair wind and hit your tides right.

Holme marks the end of the Wash coast, and the beginning of another shore of the greatest interest and charm, far more charming, in fact, than the Wash coast which, to be honest, is pretty bleak and uncompromising, and for devotees only. From Holme to Cley the sea is separated from the dry land by wide, drying sands and by a series of natural bays, or harbours, protected from the sea by banks of sand-dunes and flanked by miles of saltings and salt marsh. This coast is the very paradise of bird lovers, of fishermen, of small boat sailors, and of lovers of wild places. Nowhere else in England is there a piece of coast remotely like it, and it has a broken, sandy, windswept beauty quite unsurpassed.

Thornham is the first of these natural harbours, a small one and less used and known than the others. The channel into the harbour, from seaward, is not well marked nor easy of entrance. The little village itself is built largely of chalk, both red and white (chalk for building is called *clunch* in Norfolk). Here and there is a little flint. But this is the transitional country between the carr stone, that occurs only in a narrow belt near the Wash and south through Downham Market, and the great flint area which stretches all the way along that coast as far as, perhaps, Mundesley.

Brancaster is the next of the harbour villages. It straggles now, with plenty of modern houses, many of them very ugly, for it has grown quickly as a golfing, sailing, and holiday centre. If you go into the Jolly Sailor (which serves marvellous food) you may hear one Norfolk voice among twenty Midlanders. There is a golf course out on the marshes next to the sea. **Brancaster Staithe** has a vigorous sailing club. The harbour is bigger than that of Thornham, and much more used: the entrance is well buoyed (but the channel inside terribly tortuous and confused by small buoys laid to mark mussel-laying), there are one or two professional whelking boats, and on fine week-ends, when the tide is high, the wide natural harbour is busy with scores of racing boats performing their weird gyrations. Across the harbour is **Scolt Head**, a wild and lonely island belonging to the National Trust, a bird-watchers' and botanists' paradise but restricted as to landing.

Brancaster was the Branodunum of the Romans. On Rack Hill, between Brancaster and its staithe, is the site of the Roman fort, with practically nothing to see. It is interesting to speculate what the geography of the harbour was when it was built. Certainly this was a naval base, and a fort of the Saxon shore.

And so we come to the Burnhams, seven. About **Burnham Deepdale** there is little to say, except that its church has an Anglo-Saxon tower and perhaps the most interesting Norman fort in England. The font, of Barnack stone (Barnack Church has a Saxon tower too) is decorated with the Months of the Year, and I know of no representation of this theme that I like better. In January a bearded man is about to drink from a horn; in February he warms himself in front of a fire, and if anybody has experienced a February south-easter at Burnham Deepdale he will know why; in March he digs his garden, in April he looks as if he is pruning—although I should have said much too late, he should have attended to that instead of doing all that quaffing and fire-warming. In May the books say he is beating the bounds, but I should say that was any-body's guess. At any rate he is doing something with a flag near a tree. In June he looks as if he is pulling out an enormous weed—probably fat-hen, I should imagine. In July he is mowing with what looks like a primitive scythe, though one is always taught that the scythe wasn't invented in those days. In August of course he is harvesting: in fact binding a sheaf of corn. In September he is into it straight away with his flail—no waiting months to thresh for better prices. In October he is probably grinding corn with his stone hand-mill, in November he is bringing in his pig for slaughter, and in December he is enjoying the fruit of all this labour: he is having himself a good feast. And what an amiable old fellow he looks too! Lions, or other wild beasts, creep about in the jungle over his head, perhaps symbolizing the perils and dangers that beset a man, unless kept at bay by steadfastness and vigilance.

Burnham Norton also has an Anglo-Saxon church tower and a Norman font. It has two pulpits—one Jacobean and used, the other fifteenth century with paintings of the Four Doctors of the Church and also the donors. To the east of Norton Church are some remains of a White Friary.

Burnham Overy is a most charming village, with a fine windmill and also a watermill over the River Burn. The latter, with its good adjoining buildings, is National Trust and very fitting and beautiful it is too. Overy was once called 'Overy Town' and was certainly much bigger than it is today. Probably it was a port, before the sea receded and Overy Staithe had to be built. The Burnhams were, collectively, a considerable port; but the coast has advanced hereabouts many miles, by reason of the tides bringing thousands of tons of sand and shingle from the Yorkshire coast and dumping it here. As the sea receded **Overy Staithe** was built, one of the prettiest little villages of all, with a fine range of granaries and maltings, also cared for by the National Trust. Plenty of barges, schooners and brigs and brigantines came into Overy Staithe until the railways came and knocked them out. Now there is small boat sailing. No commercial fishing, except for a few mussel layings. The late Captain Richard Woodget, Master of the *Cutty Sark*, lived at Overy Staithe. Overy Church is strange, with a squat Norman tower (once higher) and remains of north and south transepts. As population fell away, and the little seaport town became a tiny agricultural village, the church was truncated. The church still doesn't seem to be able to make up its mind which side of the tower it wants to be: it has had several goes at each. (Map, p215).

Nearly everybody thinks that the name *Overy* comes from sheep. It is far more likely to come from the Anglo-Saxon *Offer*, meaning a river bank. The old spelling of Overy was *Offrey*.

Burnham Market is a most handsome little town, with a great wide main street that bifurcates and splendid Georgian houses. There is an old steam organ of some renown, which is privately owned but can be seen.

Two miles south brings us to **Burnham Thorpe**, and the birthplace of Lord Nelson.

The traveller will have noticed that he is in Nelson country, if only because for miles around the pub signs have all proclaimed such names as The Nelson, The Victory, The Trafalgar, The Hero, or The Norfolk Hero. Horatio Nelson was born in Burnham Thorpe Rectory, and has given rise to a small local literary industry given over to producing such suppositious statements as 'when he was a boy Horatio must have . . .' (wandered in these field, climbed this tree, strolled along this footpath many times, etc.). He must have indeed.

But two things strike the curious traveller in Burnham Thorpe. One is the quiet, but very profound, pride of the ordinary working villager in the fact that Nelson was a local man. Nelson was the only commander ever really to have captured the love of the ordinary working Englishman. The other is the complete absence of any 'Nelson Industry', other than the perfectly harmless literary one just noticed. There is no 'Nelson Café' selling Trafalgar buns to the curious—nowhere you can get a cup of tea, in fact. (This absence of public tea places is common to many East Anglian villages, and is in very great contrast to the conditions that prevail in, say, Devon.) There are no shops selling little china Horatios or prints of the Death of Nelson—no picture postcards even in Burnham Thorpe itself. As Nelson was, after Shakespeare, the greatest Englishman this is either very strange—or else a comment on the East Anglian character. Look what has happened to Shakespeare's birthplace! Instead, it is Burnham Market which thrives on Nelson souvenirs.

The pub ('Nelson used to sit on that bench over there') has a nice atmosphere in its tap room, with plenty of Trafalgar oleographs and other contemporary relics and except for these probably much the same as it was when Nelson drank beer in it. But the saloon bar—alas—this has recently broken out with a juke-box, hideous decorations—and a *dire* mural. One prays that this *décor* does not spread to the rest of the inn.

Next door to the pub there is a huge flint barn—and Nelson may well have been born in it, according to local legend, and not in the Vicarage at all. The story is that his mother was taken short on a drive in a pony-cart and just didn't make it to home. But see the barn in any case: it is fine, with a great timber roof. The Burn, now a little stream, flows by it, but once was tidal and navigable for ships (or at least lighters) and it is likely that the great barn was a wharf-side warehouse.

At Nelson Hall, a house near the church, you can see many Nelson relics and exhibitions are often arranged there. The church and Nelson Hall between them contain, of Nelsoniana: his medicine chest, his silver goblet, the crest of a modern HMS *Nelson*, a tattered White Ensign, one vast replica of the flag flown on *Victory* at Trafalgar (sometimes flown from the church tower), some Nelson letters, graves of members of his family, Nelson's signature in the marriage register witnessing the marriage of a friend (he spelt 'Horatio' wrong and was made to do it again) and the tree in the church-yard up which the child Nelson is said to have climbed to show how brave he was. His birthplace has been pulled down—to make way for the present very undistinguished rectory (it is instructive to compare the latter with the pictures of the former to see how tastes have 'progressed'), but there is a pond in the lovely old vicarage garden said to have been dug by Nelson when he was home on half pay. That is all. The Reverend Cecil Isaacson, the former incumbent of the church who has moved now to the parishes of Burnham Westgate, Sutton and Norton, is a Nelson enthusiast, and although an extremely busy vicar is very willing to show the relics to the truly interested. Lavender seedlings and yew cuttings from the old rectory flourish in the Maryland Naval Academy, USA.

Burnham Thorpe Church is far from the village, incidentally (there is a perfectly lovely old farmhouse over the lane from it—the Norfolk farmhouse at its tenderly beautiful best) and the fields round about are hummocked with what are thought to be the remains of old cottages. It is believed that when the Black Death raged through the little place the inhabitants, in panic, fired their houses and fled to the site of the present-day village where they built new ones.

South a mile is **Creake Abbey**, which is a thirteenth-century ruin. Enough remains to make it worth going off the road to look at. Abbey Farmhouse, next to it, is all mixed up with the remains of the cloister and conventual buildings, and part of the choir and crossing of the abbey church remain.

The two Creakes are charming villages, strung out in the valley of the Burn. The blacksmith in **North Creake** is a farrier, and will shoe your horse (and his son, who works with him, will too) and he has records showing that a forefather shod Nelson's. North Creake has a good church with a hammerbeam roof with angels painted on the hammerbeams. **South Creake** has an even finer church, also with hammerbeams and carved angels up aloft. South Creake is largely a fifteenth-century building. The Creakes are a mixture of flint and chalk—the forge at North Creake for example is a chalk building. When the old people, locally, suffer from acid stomach some of them still gouge a piece from the wall of the nearest house and eat it.

On the way back to Lynn one might well look at **Houghton Hall**, although one can only do so by arrangement with Lord and Lady Cholmondeley. This was the home of the Walpole family from very early times (the Cholmondeleys are their descendants) and is a place of great importance to students of eighteenth-century architecture. It is the largest country house in Norfolk, and extremely grand, and was designed by Colin Campbell, a great student of the Palladian style. It contains a collection of paintings and tapestries and would contain more if the 3rd Earl of Orford hadn't sold so many to pay for his eccentricities. They went to the Czarina of Russia, so you must go to the Hermitage, in Moscow, if you wish to see them. Sir Robert Walpole, England's first Prime Minister, the longest to hold this office, and probably the most corrupt, had the place built. His son Horace, the epicure, letter-writer, and occasional novelist (*The Castle of Otranto*) preferred to live at Twickenham, where he built the delicious Strawberry Hill. When he did come to Houghton for a visit he wrote to a friend that he went to the church, where the congregation was divided with men one side, women the other. There was some talking, and when the parson glared a woman said: 'Sir—it is not among us!' 'So much the better,' said the parson. 'It will be the sooner over.'

Houghton Park is a product of the vast new wealth amassed by a few people early in the eighteenth century, and you either like it, or you don't.

Sir Robert, for aesthetic reasons, had the village of Houghton pulled down, and put up again somewhere else. It is said that the ruins of the old village inspired Goldsmith to write *The Deserted Village*. Sir Robert's attitude to the villagers on his estate when he pulled their village down about their ears and put it somewhere else, to improve his view, is very typical of the man and his times.

There is said to be a natural phenomenon at Houghton Park: a herd of white fallow deer.

CHAPTER 13

King's Lynn to Fakenham

We must arrive at **Holkham Hall** between 2 and 5 pm on any Thursday between the second week in June to the third in September, or else on any Monday in August excepting Bank Holiday. To view the house costs adults three and six: children two shillings; there are refreshments and a free car park.

Holkham Hall is the most perfect example of a great house built in the Palladian style as it returned to England after that Baroque period which followed the death of Inigo Jones. It stands there, massive, precise, severely classical, and almost exactly as it looked when it was finished in 1762. Considered by itself alone, divorced from its countryside, it is a work of art. Considered within its countryside it is incongruous. There is nothing of Norfolk or East Anglia about it any more than there is about Houghton Hall, its earlier rival.

Holkham was the product of the great wealth of the Coke family, combined with the vast enthusiasm of the 1st Earl of Leicester, combined with the diligence and genius of William Kent, a coachpainter from Yorkshire. Kent had been sent to Italy to study art by a patron and had returned to work with Lord Burlington as an architect. He made an intensive study of Palladio's *Book of Architecture* and of the work of Inigo Jones, and developed a style which was the culmination of that style known as Palladian. The working plans, and on-the-spot detailing were attended to by another architect, Matthew Brettingham.

The Coke (pronounced *cook*) family is an example of a family which rose to wealth and greatness during the upheaval which followed the Reformation. Edward Coke, the founder of the family's prosperity, was the son of a Norfolk barrister practising in London: by his merits he became Speaker of the House of Commons, Solicitor

General, and Attorney General, by his marriages (one to a Paston and the other to a Hatton) he acquired a huge holding in land. We may blame him for leading the prosecution of Sir Walter Raleigh, but we must praise him for opposing James I when that monarch tried repeatedly to set aside the law, and for his opposition to Charles I when he tried to do the same. James imprisoned him for a time in the Tower. Coke died before the Civil War, but his work was part of

the movement that was leading towards it. He bought the Holkham Estate from the Armigers in 1610; one of many similar purchases.

The Coke family managed to stay afloat during both the Civil War and the Restoration. Thomas Coke succeeded to the estates in 1707 when he was ten years old, and shortly afterwards he set out on the Grand Tour, accompanied by his chaplain and a retinue of other officers. He encountered Lord Burlington in Italy and became fired with a great enthusiasm for Italian art and architecture. He made a great collection of paintings and sculptures, returned to England and devoted the rest of his life to the building of Holkham Hall.

He never lived to see the Hall completed. Whatever satisfaction he derived from it was in the building; and his enjoyment was girt with brick kilns and builders' rubble. His great collection of works of art remained wrapped up for most of his lifetime, for he had nowhere to put it. Holkham Hall was to become a museum to house his collection, and a library to house his great accumulation of books. (The present Lord Leicester has recently given many of the books to the newly-formed Norwich University). Thomas Coke died, and his widow completed the building of the house in 1762: it had taken twenty-eight years to build, and decades of thought, discussion, and research before that. Thomas Coke had first watched Burlington House go up, and he, Burlington, and William Kent had spent years in studying and discussing the architecture of the classical world, and of contemporary Italy.

So Coke died, the great house was completed, and 'Capability' Brown was called in to do the garden. Thomas Coke, who when he died was 1st Earl of Leicester, left no heir; but the estates were left to a nephew who took on the name of Coke. This man died in a year, leaving the place to his son, also Thomas Coke, who became famous in England as 'Coke of Norfolk'.

'Coke of Norfolk' was, off and on, a Member of Parliament for over fifty years, a Whig, and bitterly opposed to the war against the American colonies. Also he was one of the great 'improving landlords' of the eighteenth and early nineteenth centuries. It is often said that he invented the 'Norfolk four-course rotation'. This is not so ('Turnip' Townshend of Rainham Hall came nearer to it), but he applied it on his home farms and imposed it on the many tenants of his 50,000 acre estate. He managed during his life to raise the rent he extracted annually from his tenants from £2,000 a year to £20,000. He experimented with the newly emerging breeds of sheep, cattle and pigs (he imported Italian pigs as his great-uncle had imported Italian works of art), and in many ways he was an agricultural innovator. The marl pits which dot the North Norfolk plain are mostly due to him, for he caused his tenants to marl their light soil (that is apply dressings of clay mixed with chalk dug up from selected pits). He made them improve fertility by gradual increase of stocking rates, by the 'golden hoof' (the folding of sheep on arable land), by the adoption of rotation farming instead of the old wasteful method of bare fallowing.

By attending Court in country dress he led a revolution in dress style: the Regency 'dandies' who came after him copied his country Norfolk clothes. His agricultural ideas spread over England by means of the annual 'sheep-shearings' that he held in his barn (still standing), and that were attended by his tenantry, neighbours, and by agriculturalists from all over Britain. It was on one of these occasions that one of his tenants got up and admonished the others: 'Do you do as his Lordship do you'll do better you do do!' The first of these Norfolk 'dos' can be translated as 'if' and the fourth and last as 'prosper'. The East Anglian 'do' (pronounced *dew*) can have many meanings.

When 'Coke of Norfolk' (now Lord Leicester of the second creation) died his neighbours erected, by subscription, the great column which stands to the north of the house and which has such peaceful emblems on it as a wheatsheaf at the top, and cows and sheep and other beasts of the field about the plinth.

The severity, not to say plainness, of the exterior of the house does not prepare you for the magnificence of the Marble Hall.

First you enter an **ante-hall,** which is embellished by busts of such illustrious departed as Homer, Alexander the Great, and the 2nd Earl of Leicester in terracotta, and four marble busts by Nollekins of, respectively, Francis Duke of Bedford, Charles James Fox, William Windham and the Marquis of Hastings. On the left is a Thomas Tompion clock, made in 1676 for Greenwich Observatory and wound up once a year.

Then you step into the vast colonnaded interior of the **great hall,** and great it certainly is, by any standards: 60 feet high. All seems to gleam with marble and alabaster and gold. Busts of various Earls of Leicester look down at you from on high: at the foot of the stairs is a bust of 'Coke of Norfolk' by his friend Sir Francis Chantrey and another of the 1st Earl, first creation, also by Chantrey but from a model by Roubilliac. The founder of the house is also represented by a bust by Roubilliac over the doorway, looking in. There is a bas-relief by Chantrey of William IV signing the Reform Bill, with Coke of Norfolk standing there to see that he does it, the Trial of Socrates by Westmacott, Death of Germanicus by T. Banks RA (a poignant spectacle indeed!) and the delivery-up of the gates of Florence to Cosmo the Great by Pietrino da Vinci, all bas-reliefs. And at the end of the gallery, round to the right, is a plaque, carved by Sir Francis Chantrey, of two woodcock—slain by Sir Francis Chantrey in one shot in 1829. Two woodcock killed in one shot is unusual to say the

least of it—can it be that these birds were sent to their final rest at a
moment of mutual tenderness?

The **north dining-room** is a perfect cube, with a ceiling from a
design by Inigo Jones. There is a superb head of Aphrodite over one
of the fireplaces said to have come out of the Parthenon, there is a
huge bust of Lucius Verus discovered when clearing the harbour of
Nettun, and there are classical busts of Geta and Marcus Aurelius,
with marble drapery added to them in the seventeenth century. The
carpet—probably an Axminster—echoes the Inigo Jones design of
the ceiling.

The great **statue gallery** and **tribunes** (the three rooms are
105 feet long and cut across the house almost at its narrowest part,
which gives some idea of the scale of the place) contain an astonishing collection of classical statuary: many a museum of world fame
would find it hard to match. From the left, as you go into the North
Tribune, are Athene, Thucydides (a copy of a bronze original which
was described by Professor Poulson as the earliest individual portrait
in Greek art. Certainly looking at the bust we feel we know the man),
Dionysius, Diana—said to have been owned by Cicero and bought
by the 1st Earl in 1717 for which act he only just escaped imprisonment by the Italian authorities—Venus Genetrix, a bust of Apollo
(over the fireplace), Lucius Verus over the niche and the Pythian
Apollo in it, Meleager, a wonderful statue of Silenos, Poseidon, bust
of a man called Sulla of Hadrian's reign, a brace of young satyrs, in
uneasy juxtaposition with them a Roman lady of Hadrian's time, the
head of an empress of the time of Elegabalus, a bust of Seneca, a bust
of an old man and a statue of Ceres. The furniture is all contemporary with the house and was made by Goodison from designs of
William Kent, the chief architect of the house.

To the right, from the South Tribune, are private apartments, for
the 5th Earl lives in the house, although he does not now occupy the
principal rooms. But to the left is the **drawing-room,** with a full-
length portrait of Nell Gwynne by Kneller, four landscapes by
Orizonti, Numbers 84 and 85 are emblematical representations of
King William's wars by Hondecooter, there is a storm by Poussin, a
Madonna *in Gloria* by Pietro da Pietri, Apollo flaying Marsyas by
Claude Lorrain, portrait of Henry Rich, Earl of Warwick, by Van
Dyck.

Next the **saloon,** hung with the original Genoa velvet, and with
two lovely mosaic tables found in Hadrian's villa near Tivoli.

Furniture made to Kent's design and covered with Genoa velvet. Pictures are: The Artist's Daughter by Maratti, the Holy Family by Rubens, A Lady playing on a Spinet by Maratti, Coke of Norfolk, aged twenty-eight—wearing the famous country clothes that he wore when presenting the address to George III asking for the independence of the American colonies, the clothes which inspired the accepted regency style—by Gainsborough. Portrait of Fox by Opie—commissioned by Coke of Norfolk, William III by Kneller, Duc d'Arenberg by Van Dyck, Lord Chief Justice Coke by Cornelius Johnson.

The **south dining-room** is also hung with Genoa velvet, and the fireplace is from a design by Inigo Jones. Pictures from left to right: Sir Thomas More after Holbein, copy by Andrea del Sarto of the Raphael in the Uffizi Gallery of Pope Leo X, Cardinal Guilio de Medici and his nephew Cardinal de Rossi, A Venetian Lady by Titian, A Venus—said to be Princess d'Obilo—with a portrait of Philip of Spain after Titian, A Sunset by Swanavelt (copied from a Claude), a still life by Hondecooter, St John baptizing Christ by F. Bolognese, Archbishop Laud after Van Dyck, Joseph and Potiphar's Wife by Guidi Reni, Sir A. Talmarsh by Sir Peter Lely. The blue porcelain is Sévres, 1792–1804, chairs by Chippendale.

The **landscape room** contains a fine collection of Claude Lorrains. Lorrain was said to have been the 1st Earl's favourite artist, and you would go far to find such a good collection of his work. There are also pictures by Nicholas and Gaspar Poussin.

The **green state bedroom** is hung with three panels of Brussels tapestry by Auwere, representing Europe, Africa and America, and a fourth panel, representing Asia, by Saunders of Soho. This room was slept in by Queen Victoria in 1835, and George V in 1912. Over the fireplace is the 1st Earl in the robes of the Bath, and over the door are the four seasons by Zucharelli.

In the **brown state dressing-room** is the only copy ever made of the cartoon which Michelangelo designed for one side of the hall of the Great Council of Florence, before it was maliciously destroyed by Baccio Baninelli. It is by Bastiano di San Gallo. There is also a fresco on stone by Annibale Caracci, and paintings by Maratti, Bassano and Giordano.

The **brown state bedroom** has velvet of 1910, Coke of Norfolk over the fireplace in fancy dress by Battoni and presented to Coke by Louise, wife of Charles Edward the Young Pretender. The fancy dress was worn at a ball given in honour of Charles Edward's marriage in Rome, painted by order of the bride (with whom Coke danced), and the statue in the background, of the lovelorn Ariadne, is said to be an actual likeness of Louise. There is James II by Lely and portraits of early Cokes.

The **state sitting-room** has Brussels tapestry, a ceiling designed by Lord Burlington (who took a great interest in the building of the house of course), portraits of the 1st Earl's great-grandparents, the Duke and Duchess of Leeds by Kneller.

Many large museums could envy the Holkham collection. Considered as a home, which is for what it was designed, I cannot think of anything more uncomfortable than Holkham Hall. Considered as a piece of East Anglia it is of course absurd, being a piece of Italy. But as one of the finest of the collections amassed by the English noblemen in their eighteenth-century raids on Italy and the classical world it is of the first interest.

The park at Holkham is one of the finest in the country: Canada, and other wild and semi-wild geese, flock on the big lake, deer graze within sight of the great house, and the collection of trees, which extends for miles, is most famous. Cuttings from the many fine ilex trees are sent to London to feed the giraffes at the zoo.

The Leicesters who followed Coke of Norfolk were all notable sportsmen, and shot uncountable numbers of pheasants, and more particularly partridges, on the great estate. Record after record for the slaughter of these birds was set up: in 1905 when 2,000 brace of partridges were shot in four days—1,670 birds on one beat on 7th November—a record was set up which has never been beaten. There is an extraordinary story told about when the famous Colonel Hawker went to Holkham and challenged one of the Cokes to shoot partridges against him. Hawker won, but his opponent would not admit it. The present Coke, the 5th Earl (second creation) is also a great sportsman and helped to win the Worplesdon Mixed Foursomes Golf Tournament in 1936. His Countess runs the Holkham Pottery, in a wing of the house, which employs a number of local people. The pottery welcomes visitors. There is a circular earthwork here, thought to be an Iron Age fort: possibly defensive to a harbour.

Wells-next-the-Sea is one of the most splendid little towns in England, but it carries its unawareness of its quality and uniqueness to the point where both are being damaged. Street after street of flint housing (and flint houses become rarer and rarer as more are pulled down every year and none are put up) have been bulldozed to clear land for 'development', and what the development is can too well be imagined. Characterless brick and concrete building that will eventually make Wells just another seaside town like a thousand others, and not the little flint jewel that it has been, and in part remains.

Wells has one of the most distinguished waterfronts in England. Great eighteenth- and nineteenth-century warehouses loom up over the waterfront road, and there is hardly an intrinsically ugly building along the whole front, although several have been *made* ugly, hideously so, by their owners trying to copy the lowest of the pin-table-and-Bingo culture. A fisherman once said to me, as we were coming up on the tide to the whelk boiling sheds: 'Blackpool has its "golden mile"—well Wells has its "golden hundred yards" anyway!' The marvel is that people who have good enough taste to want to go to Wells, should want to see this fine waterfront cheapened and vulgarized.

Coasting shipping still comes up to the Wells Quay. Very often a small Dutch coaster can be seen discharging fertilizer, or cattle cake, or chemicals.

There are two little fishing fleets. One consists of a small fleet of tiny decked motor trawlers locally known as 'the spratters'. These belong to a firm of enthusiasts who originally started 'pair fishing' (dragging one net between two boats) for sprats from Whitstable, in Kent. They became migratory, following the fish wherever these were to be found, but now they seem to have settled in Wells. They still catch sprats when there are any, but more often these days 'roka', as skate are called in East Anglia (like many East Anglian words this is of Dutch, and Low German, derivation). They trawl for these with small orthodox otter trawls.

But the traditional Wells fleet consists of the 'Wells whelkers'. Most of these are open clinker-built boats built much on the lines of the Sheringham crabbers but twice as big. There are, too, a couple of ex-RNLI lifeboats (of the 'Liverpool' type), converted to the fishery.

A trip to sea in a whelker is a great experience, particularly if a nor'-easter is blowing. The boats generally leave very early in the morning—any time after midnight. They get over the bar in the mouth of the Wells river as late as they dare on the ebb tide, and often they leave it a little fine and *bump* hard as they go across the drying sand and meet the breakers. Once out over that bar they have

13. CASTLE ACRE PRIORY, the grandest monastic ruin in East Anglia. *Above*, seen from the air. *Below left*, the great West Front, its Norman blind arcading broken into for the 15th century window that gapes above the door. The Prior's Solar (*right*) was later still, Tudor, and a comfortable dwelling house

14. East Anglian Windmills. *Above*, grinding mills at Denver – the summit of the mill-wright's art – and at Cley-next-the-Sea. *Below left*, the pumping mill at Thurne, one of the greatest windmills that drained the Broads country. Saxtead Green mill (*right*), is a post mill; the whole body turns with the wind and all the grinding machinery with it

the scarcely comforting thought that they cannot get *back* again—come Hell or high water—until many hours later, for they must wait until the tide recedes, and returns, and covers the bar with enough water to float them. They head straight out to sea, and may go anything up to thirty miles.

Here they sight their 'dan buoys', small sticks bobbing about on the waves with flags flying from them. Then comes the business of hauling the 'shanks' of whelk pots, which is much the same as hauling crab pots except that it is done with a power winch, and from much deeper water. Soon the man whose job it is to empty the pots is standing knee-deep in whelks and cannot move his feet. Another man works hard at rebaiting the pots with salt herring and flinging them overboard.

When all the pots have been handled and shot again—many hours of very hard work—the boats head for home. They all assemble outside Wells Bar, and bob about waiting for enough water. If a gale has blown up meanwhile they must just stay and face it—there is nowhere they can go for shelter. Finally one boat tries it—bumps hard on the hard sand bar amid sheets of spray—gets over—the others cautiously follow—and they all go running up the calm river to the boiling sheds, where the whelks are unloaded and put straight into the coppers. Nearly all the whelks in England go over the Wells Bar. There is good money in it for the fishermen, but it is hard and dangerous work, and each little family firm has thousands of pounds invested in boats and gear. A Russian trawler can come along (one often does) and roll up and completely destroy a whole shank of pots worth a couple of hundred pounds in a few minutes.

David Cox is Coxswain of the lifeboat, and one of the most active and respected of the Wells fishermen. His brother, Jack, is an accomplished landscape and seascape painter, in perhaps rather an academic style, besides being a full-time fisherman, avid wildfowler, first-class gardener, and owner of a donkey. He paints and sells many scores of pictures of Wells and its surroundings. The Shipwrights is a very good pub, much frequented by fishermen.

Wells' lifeboat is stationed right out near the bar and is launched beyond it into the open sea. You get there by walking along a mile of straight river wall, or driving along the road behind it. At the beginning of the wall is a memorial to the eleven members of the crew of the boat when she capsized in 1880. There is a big caravan camp behind the wall, and a beautiful sandy beach backed by a belt of sand dunes planted with Corsican pines (by the 2nd Lord Leicester).

Wells is a beautiful small-boat harbour, with plenty of fascinating little creeks in the saltings to explore.

Going east we come to **Stiffkey** (pronounced Stiffkey, and not as journalists insisted in the great days of the immortal rector—*stukey*—although in William the Conqueror's time it was spelt Steuekai) and this is a little village of complete charm. Charm tempered perhaps by the fact that the A149—that curse of the North Coast of Norfolk—goes right through it.

Here all is flint. The little River Stiffkey runs right behind the village (the tidal surge of 1953 turned it temporarily into a salt water creek again). Mr Philip Green, who lives in the middle of the village with his two stalwart sons, takes people fishing in boats if they want to go, and acts as guide for those wishing to probe the mysteries of the marshes.

Morston is the embarking place for the boats which carry passengers out to **Blakeney Point**, which is a National Trust nature reserve. Mr Ted Eeles is Warden of this, and owns motor boats for taking people out to it. People are welcomed there, as well as birds; and in the spring time the place is rowdy with dive-bombing terns, and oyster-catchers and other nesting waders. The point is wild and sandy, with high dunes covered with coarse grass and other flora, sea hammering it on one side and lost creeks and mud-flats on the other. Sunk down amid the sand-dunes is a weird old lifeboat house, now used as a hostel by various groups of people who go and camp there. The point is not an island, like Scolt Head, but one can walk there from Cley. Sometimes the bird-watchers outnumber the birds, and then the only thing to do is to watch the bird-watchers.

Blakeney is perhaps the most beautiful village in Norfolk. Its beauty is carefully preserved, though, by the wealthy people who have bought up nearly all the little cottages, and converted them either into holiday homes or else houses to retire to. This has happened all along this flint coast: the retired, commuters, and 'summer residents' have snapped up most of the old cottages and houses that once belonged to fishermen, seafarers and farm workers, and the latter classes have had to move off to council houses (like the ones in that vast estate that defaces Wells), or else to towns where there are cheaper houses and more work. Certainly no fisherman could afford to buy a 'fisherman's cottage' today. Cottages that would have been considered dear at £50 before the Second World War now go for £3,500. But the charm of this coast is that it was built up by farmers and their men, and by fishermen, sailors and wildfowlers.

Blakeney is now what is called 'select', meaning that many of its inhabitants have a lot of money. There is no 'pin-table-and-Bingo culture' there. And the wealthy inhabitants care for the flint cottages and houses excellently: had they not bought them most of them would have fallen down. There is a Blakeney Housing Trust that has bought up and repaired many of them—alas that there is not an equivalent in Wells.

Blakeney has a superb natural harbour, protected from the sea by Blakeney Point, with a perfectly sheltered deep-water anchorage called 'The Pit' about three miles downstream from Blakeney Quay. Blakeney is perhaps the best place of all from which to enjoy the unique mixture of open sea, and dunes, saltings, mud-flats, salt marshes and creeks of this fascinating coast. There can be few stretches of country anywhere which arouse such passionate love and enthusiasm in the people who know it and live there. A man could spend his life in getting to know it.

Blakeney Quay is always crowded with yachts and boats so that it is difficult for a stranger to find a berth. Most of the big white-painted open motor boats used for taking passengers out to Blakeney Point belong to Mr Stratton Long, the uncrowned Harbour Master, who has recently opened a well-stocked yacht chandlers in the beautiful great warehouse that comes down to the quay. Mr Long founded his fortunes by salvaging 'Queen Bee' target planes from the sea for the Americans. Blakeney was once a considerable commercial port: it still has the remains of a Guildhall. The church—up on the hill—is very fine, though much restored inside. Besides the very high fifteenth-century west tower there is another, and unique, turret at the east end, with a staircase in it which leads to a small room above the chancel. Needless to say this tower is supposed to have been built as a 'beacon' to guide sailors up the creek. Just over the road to the north of the churchyard is a large garden, the gateway into which is adorned with a most beautiful carved wood panel of West African origin: not to be missed.

East again, over the Glaveney River, is **Cley-next-the-Sea** (Cley is pronounced Cly). Another lovely flint village, smaller than Blakeney now but it was once, as Blakeney was, a thriving port and the eighteenth-century Custom House still stands at the east end of it. A Custom House of this size indicates a big trade with the Continent, and indeed Cley has a Low Country air about it, with Dutch gables over its hotel. Even allowing for the deeper draught of ships the Glaven Estuary must have silted up seriously since that Custom House was built: certainly no coasting vessel could get up there now.

Cley Church merits the epithet 'great'. It speaks of enormous prosperity in the fourteenth century when most of the church was rebuilt. Cley, then, was probably the exporting port for at least half of north Norfolk's sheep country: thousands of tons of wool must have gone out of it to be sailed away to Europe.

The nave is marvellous, and very grand. The chancel is much smaller: the building is commonly supposed to have been stopped by the Black Death. The projected great west tower never got built. I sometimes wonder if it was not only the Black Death that interfered with this: was it not also the importation of Flemish weavers by Edward III which changed the traffic from exporting raw wool to exporting finished cloth, and the source of the exports from the sheep country of north Norfolk to the weaving centres in south and east Norfolk and in Suffolk?

The fifteenth-century south porch is extremely beautiful. There is a nice arcade on the south of the nave with good carving under it, and there are some good bench-ends. It is a church not to be missed, standing as it does—a great work of art—on the edge of nowhere. There is a large and well preserved windmill at Cley, as there is at Overy Staithe.

Salthouse is yet another coastal flint village, also with a fine church. The village was much bashed by the 1953 tidal surge.

Cutting inland, and south-west, we cross the Glaven again and quickly climb up on to the high and windy chalk uplands and come to **Binham**. Binham is an example of the many little flint villages that back this wonderful coastline. These villages are generally compact, standing amid miles of empty country, and generally built around one or more huge farmsteads rather as villages tend to be in northern France. Everything is flint—even the massive barns and the cattle yards.

The cattle yards of these East Anglian farms were built to house fattening bullocks in the winter—bullocks fed on the straw and mangolds grown in the huge fields. Dairying is a new industry in

East Anglia, introduced originally by Scots farmers who flooded in and bought up farms during the depression of the 1920s. The great barns were the temples of High Farming, the sort of farming Coke of Norfolk encouraged. All these great East Anglian barns are built upon the same plan, a huge rectangle with two opposing transepts in the middle, like the transepts of a church, each containing very large doors. The purpose of the opposing doors was to allow a through wind to winnow the grain after threshing. The threshing-floor was in the middle, at the crossing. Here men battered the sheaves, the winter through, with their flails (or 'frails' as East Anglians call them), and the flails—a long and a short stick joined together—were joined together by eel skin, this being considered the toughest material for this exacting task. The eel catchers of East Anglia made more by selling their eel skins than they did from the eels inside them. The common way of catching eels along this coast was by *pritching*. The *pritch* is a barbed Neptune's trident, which is stabbed into the mud where the eels are hoped to lie. Another, rather barbarous, fishing engine exclusive to North Norfolk is the 'butt drag'. This is an iron bar set with big barbed cod hooks which is dragged through the mud so that the hooks impale the 'butts' as dabs are called in East Anglia.

But back to Binham. The priory church here is one of the most atmospheric buildings in Norfolk. The west end of it is Early English (not well represented in East Anglia) and the great (alas bricked-up) window has been described by Pevsner as 'the paradigm of Geometrical tracery at its purest'. The window is so large that there is hardly any wall. The splendid Norman triforium and clerestory have been described as surpassing even Norwich in excellence. The former aisles have been knocked off and the whole place truncated and mutilated, and it has obviously suffered—and no doubt still suffers—from a lack of money and attention: and how could such a fine great place not do so supported as it is by a tiny population around two or three farms? The wonderful Early English west front was the work of Prior Richard de Parco, early thirteenth century. It is a premature example of 'geometrical' tracery.

De Parco was a good prior, and much given to building. A successor, William de Somerton, was the medieval equivalent of a horse-player: he was an alchemist, and he sold most of the priory's valuables to obtain money for his researches. He fled to Rome in the end, leaving the priory much in debt. But Binham would have gone down anyway: it had no relics to compete either with Bromholm with its Holy Rood, or Walsingham with its Holy House. It was a cell of St Albans, and like that other cell of St Albans, Wymondham Abbey, its history is one of constant bickering with its mother abbey. In fact one wonders how the monks ever found time for any prayer or meditation so constant was their quarrelling and their litigation. In 1212 or so, Robert Fitz Walter suddenly laid claim to the patronage of the place, and besieged it with troops. 'By God's Feet!' said King John. 'Either I or Fitz Walter must be King in England!' And he sent soldiers to chase Fitz Walter away.

The ruins of the priory buildings, and the great east end of the church pulled down at the Reformation, still have much old masonry to see, and the place should be visited, alone, on a fine night with a full moon. The experience is transporting.

From Binham it is but a short step to Walsingham, perhaps the most successful religious house of all. We come to Great Walsingham first, which has a beautiful fourteenth-century church with lovely window tracery. But it is **Little Walsingham** which is really the greater of the two.

> *As ye come from the holy land*
> *Of Walsingham,*
> *Met ye not with my true love*
> *By the way as ye came?*

In the reign of King Edward the Confessor the wife of Walsingham's lord of the manor, named Richeldis, dreamed that the Virgin Mary appeared to her and asked that a replica of the House of the Annunciation should be built in the village. The site for the shrine would be revealed by the appearance of a fresh spring of water. The lady Richeldis awoke from her dream, found the new spring of water, and built over it a small and simple shrine. The fame of this rapidly spread, and the place came known as 'England's Nazareth', and so great were the numbers of pilgrims to it that the Milky Way in the heavens, with its myriad stars, became to be known as 'the Walsingham Way' and it was said to point to Walsingham. For centuries it was the greatest goal for pilgrimage in England, not excluding even Canterbury. To visit it, indeed, was the equivalent of visiting the real Nazareth in the Holy Land. The Normans took the shrine over from the English, and every king from Richard I to

Henry VIII made pilgrimage, the latter walking barefooted from Barsham Manor (as many pilgrims do today). The vast wealth of the shrine caught Henry VIII's eye, however, and at the Dissolution he sequestered all, and had the image of Our Lady of Walsingham (which had appeared miraculously in the original shrine) taken to London and burnt in Cromwell's London house at Chelsea, so that 'the people should use no more idolatrye unto it'.

> *In the wrackes of Walsingham*
> *Whom should I chuse*
> *But the Queen of Walsingham*
> *To be guide to my muse?*
>
> *Then thou Prince of Walsingham*
> *Grant me to frame*
> *Bitter plaintes to rewe they wrong*
> *Bitter wo for thy name.*
>
> *Bitter was it oh to see*
> *The seely sheepe*
> *Murdered by the raveninge wolves*
> *While the sheephards did sleep.*
>
> *Bitter was it oh to vewe*
> *The sacred vyne*
> *While the gardiners plaied all close*
> *Rooted up by the swine.*
>
> *Bitter, bitter oh to behould*
> *The grasse to growe*
> *Where the walls of Walsingham*
> *So stately did shewe.*
>
> *Such were the works of Walsingham*
> *Where she did stand*
> *Such are the wrackes as noe do shewe*
> *Of that holy land.*
>
> *Levell levell with the ground*
> *The towres doe lye*
> *Which with their golden, glitteringe tops*
> *Pearsed once to the sky.*

Where weare gates no gates are nowe,
  The waies unknowen,
Where the press of peares did pass
  While her fame was far blowen.

Oules do scrike where the sweetest himnes
  Lately were songe,
Toades and serpents hold their dennes
  Where the palmers did throng.

Weepe, weepe O Walsingham,
  Whose dayes are nightes,
Blessings turned to blasphemies,
  Holy deeds to dispites.

Sinne is where our Ladie sate,
  Heaven turned is to hell,
Sathan sittes where our Lord did swaye,
  Walsingham oh farewell.

I make no apologies for printing these beautiful verses, for firstly they are the most moving expression of the intense horror which the Reformation caused to the faithful over all the land, and secondly they are supposed to have been written by an East Anglian, Philip Howard, Earl of Arundel.

It speaks for the thoroughness with which the Reformation was carried out that so very little of this 'Holy Land of Walsingham' remains. Once, besides the huge abbey church, there was a great complex of religious houses, hostels which could house thousands of pilgrims, hundreds of merchants and palmers and other commercial hangers-on selling holy relics and images to the devout.

For anything equivalent existing today one must go to Madura, or Ramaswaram, or Badrachalam, or other of the great shrines of South India, in their times of especial holiness: places thronged with people—people pious, merry, credulous or just commercial—people laughing, jostling, friendly, sometimes open-mouthed with religious wonder—but all enjoying every moment of their religious holiday. Nothing that we see at Walsingham today gives any hint that such things could have been. The pilgrimages have begun again, but they are very decorous and English affairs.

The Augustines founded their priory in 1149. All that remains of the great church is the fifteenth-century east window which still stands up in the abbey gardens backed by great beech trees, some parts of the old monastic buildings incorporated in the big eighteenth-century house, a Norman doorway and two wishing wells. The gardens are visitable on Wednesdays and Bank Holidays from 10 am to 5 pm all the year round, on Sundays from May to September in the afternoons only, on Mondays and Fridays in August in the afternoons, and other times by arrangement with the Estate Office, Walsingham.

Parties of Roman Catholics sometimes hold services in the abbey gardens. They also have the Slipper Chapel, in the adjoining parish of **Houghton St Giles**. This is an originally fourteenth-century building, much extended and restored, and taken over by the Roman Catholics as their contemporary Walsingham shrine. It was the last stage on the ancient pilgrim's way, where pilgrims removed their shoes to make the rest of the journey barefoot.

Anglicans have their own shrine in Little Walsingham. In 1931, the Rev. Hope Patten—the incumbent of the parish—started the building of a replica of the Walsingham Holy House, which was itself a replica of the Holy House of Nazareth. The original Holy House of Walsingham was visited by Erasmus, in 1511 (when he resided at Cambridge) and he describes it thus:

> The original chapel is built of wood and pilgrims are admitted through a narrow door at each side. There is but little or no light but what proceeds from tapers yielding a most pleasant and odoriferous smell, but if you will look in you will say it is the seat of the gods, so bright and shining it is all over with jewels, gold and silver . . .

The new Holy House is of the same dimensions as the original, but is built of brick and not wood. The story of the selection of the site for it is that Hope Patten, together with a band of enthusiasts including the late Duke of Argyll, walked out of the parish church and knelt down in the main street of Little Walsingham to pray for a sign. No sign was forthcoming, but later Hope Patten sited the shrine on a convenient plot by the cross-roads, and as the foundations were being dug a filled-in well was found, and this is taken to be the original holy well of the Lady Richeldis.

Now, the new Holy House is enclosed within a large pilgrimage church, and the well is incorporated within the wall. A replica of the original Virgin of Walsingham (which had appeared miraculously) was made at Chelsea where the other was burnt and installed within the shrine, and is the chief object of pilgrimage. In addition to the altar in the Holy House, and the High Altar, there are sixteen other altars in the church, most of them in small dimly lit shrines with round brick domes over them, and there is a chapel of the Eastern Orthodox Church in which Orthodox priests come to celebrate their liturgy. Within the church are two pieces of the True Cross, a relic of St Vincent and one of St Thomas, a statue of St Charles the Martyr (otherwise Charles I) numerous pieces of (very 1930s-looking) statuary, murals, and a great wealth of icons and reliquaries, and vestments. In the garden are the Stations of the Cross, and a replica of Christ's sepulchre.

It is unfortunate that the shrine church was built when it was, for this was not a peak of excellence in English architecture, and the plastered exterior has all the distinction of a hundred pre-1940 suburban churches and fits very ill in Little Walsingham which otherwise hasn't got an undistinguished building in it. The interior is more impressive, and probably very meet for its purpose. The whole inside is a complex of round brick arches, giving mysterious vistas in every direction, with many glimpses into dimly lit chapels—all very richly furnished. The Holy House itself is a strange building, its walls set with stones from other religious foundations in the British Isles and hung with petitions from the faithful and also thanks for material and spiritual benefits received. One can purchase bottles of the water from the well. A large addition is now planned for the church.

In the ancient and beautiful college buildings beside the new shrine three or four priests live, and there is a small nunnery. The nuns run a hostel for pilgrims, and also a shop selling religious objects. Pilgrims come in great numbers, at least 100,000 every year, and recently they included the Bishop of Southwark.

The Russian Orthodox Church has its own shrine in the shrine church, and their Brotherhood of St Seraphim of Sarov has taken over Walsingham's abandoned railway station for a centre.

The parish church of Little Walsingham should not be missed in all this excitement, for it contains the finest 'seven sacrament' font in East Anglia, which is famous for this kind of font. It is richly carved but, alas, defaced. The cover to it was presented by Sir Henry Sidney and his wife: Sir Henry was cousin to the famous Sir Philip.

Great Snoring should be visited, not only because it has such an extraordinary name, but because it has a lovely late Tudor rectory and the Four Last Things (Heaven, Hell, Death and Judgement) on the commandment board in the church. **Little Snoring** has a wonderful Norman font.

East Barsham is famous for its manor house (with a nice pub opposite). This is one of the best examples there is of early Tudor carved and moulded brickwork and is really a most spectacular and theatrical building, lavishly decorated, said to have been built by Sir William Fermor in Henry VIII's reign. It looks superb from the top of the hill in the Fakenham direction, especially in winter when the bare hills are covered with snow. It can be seen inside from July to September, when there is no snow, by special appointment only (telephone Walsingham 286). There is a free vigour about this highly decorative use of brick in late medieval and early Tudor times that we may well envy at this present day, when 'brick' is another word for dullness. East Barsham manor was inhabited by a member of the Hapsburg family up until the last war.

Thorpland Hall, just north of Fakenham on the River Stiffkey, is another typical North Norfolk wool king's mansion, also of Tudor brick with a pinnacled gatehouse, mullioned windows, and wonderful moulded chimneys.

Fakenham has some good brickwork too, including nice Victorian maltings and a big flour mill. There are good eighteenth-century brick houses too around the market place, and it is an attractive little country town, on the River Wensum. The church is large, very restored, but has a Decorated clerestory and beautiful Decorated east window tracery (with Victorian glass). The best things are the sedilia and piscina, late fourteenth century and extremely graceful.

CHAPTER 14

King's Lynn to Swaffham

The **River Nar**, which debouches into the Great Ouse at King's Lynn through a squalid creek, was once called Norfolk's 'Holy River': there were so many religious foundations along it. Near its mouth now lie the rotting remains of a Humber Keel: one of those highly specialized vessels of north-eastern waterways, reminding us of the once strong commercial ties between North Norfolk and the Humber area.

First upstream is Blackborough Priory, founded by the Benedictines but chivalrously handed over to nuns and with now practically nothing to see. **Narborough**, farther upstream, stands below the fifty-foot contour and may well have been the head of navigation of the river. John Braine, a monk of Thetford in Henry IV's time, wrote that Narborough was a city in the reign of the British king Uther Pendragon, in AD 500, but was captured by Waldy and razed to the ground. It was razed to the ground again quite recently, in an ill-advised 'improvement' move, which destroyed all the houses along the river, which had made it one of Norfolk's outstandingly beautiful villages, and erected a soulless housing estate instead.

From nearby starts Devil's Dyke, and as nobody knows anything about this we may as well leave it to the Devil. **West Acre** had a very large Augustinian priory, of which significant fragments lie each side of the river, most of them mixed up with a modern farmyard. The Stag Inn is a nice building, of a fine mixture of flint, carr stone and old brick, with a spirited inn sign depicting what looks more like a stag at rut than one at bay, and the landlord is a small farmer too and, in this land of vast estates, ploughs a lonely furrow: the yeoman is almost extinct in this part of Norfolk. Mr Fred Softly, who sometimes has a pint in the Stag, can remember burning lime in the big lime-pits over the river.

Narborough Hall, just downstream of West Acre, is a vast hall with its villageless church standing in its park as though God were the personal property of the squire, and there are notable Scots pine plantations in the park. The Hall was built by the father of Sir Andrew Fountaine, who was knighted by William III and was Vice-Chamberlain to the Prince of Wales. Sir Andrew travelled in Europe and collected a great quantity of majolica ware. The whole village had been bought by the Fountaines at the end of the seventeenth century. They were an offshoot of the ffunteyens of Salle. There is a lake, trout, and wildfowl.

Castle Acre is the greatest place in East Anglia for ruin-lovers. This area of Norfolk, high on the chalk uplands, may strike the traveller as being desolate and depopulated. The country, with its light grey-looking chalky soil which blows away in such vast dust storms every spring, is given over to big farmers who have bulldozed away every hedge and spinney, leaving only the little clumps of beech trees that stand up on the rounded hills like scalp-locks on the shaven pates of Red Indians—and they have left those simply because they are growing on old marlpits which are unploughable. The practice of marling, now no longer in use, was the digging-out of mixed chalk and clay from pits and the spreading of this on the land. It was practised in Roman Britain, revived by eighteenth-century agriculturalists (notably Coke of Norfolk, who owned most of this land), condemned by the Suffolk farming writer Arthur Young as being useless, and thereafter discontinued.

There is something very medieval, yes and foreign, about Castle Acre. It reminds one of a big agricultural village in northern France. This is due to its compactness, lack of straggle, hill-top site. Instead of living in cottages scattered over the countryside as farm-workers do in other parts of England, such of the inhabitants of this stretch of countryside as are still farm-workers live in this town-like village and travel anything up to five miles to work. In the carrot-digging season, which lasts from late summer right through the winter, you will see large gangs of men and women strung out over the prairie-like fields, with cars parked in scores by the road-side.

As you enter Castle Acre, you will notice the vast earthwork of the castle up on the hill and wonder at the tremendous effort it must have taken to have thrown it up. These very massive castle earth-works, such as this and the one at Thetford, are sometimes supposed to have been pre-Norman—pre-Saxon even. They may well date from the Iron Age. Castle Acre is on the track of the Peddar's Way, which was a Roman track, and before that a Celtic one. The Normans built the mound, as they always did on such eminently defensible sites. William de Warrenne, 1st Earl of Surrey, who also founded the priory at Lewes, was the builder. The whole village of Castle Acre is in the outer bailey of the castle, which is what gives it its fine fortified appearance. In the middle of the village is a fine eleventh-century gateway, under which goes one of the village streets.

The priory, the finest ruin in East Anglia, stands low down on the green fields by the north bank of the River Nar. It is in the care of the Ministry of Works, admission is one and six a head for adults, and it is open all day on weekdays, and on afternoons on Sundays.

William de Warrenne, and his wife Gundreda who was a daughter of William the Conqueror, visited the great abbey at Cluny in Burgundy, and on coming to England established the Cluniac Priory of St Pancras at Lewes, where the de Warrennes had their chief castle. The order spread over England from there, and houses were opened at Wenlock, Northampton, Bermondsey, Daventry, Pontefract and Thetford. Castle Acre was formed as a daughter priory of Lewes, and in her turn had four daughters: Bromholm (p146) with its relic of the True Cross, Normansburgh and Slevesholm in Norfolk, and Mendham in Suffolk, very little of which remain to be seen.

The 2nd Earl of Sussex richly endowed Castle Acre Priory: the churches of Acre, Methwold, Wickmere and Trunch were some of the East Anglian properties devoted to the priory, to say nothing of '15 acres of land and 2,000 eels' at Methwold, and a serf named Ulmar 'along with his garden'. For centuries there was an uneasy relationship between the English Cluniac houses and the Chapter-General in France. In 1283 one William of Shoreham actually fortified the monastery and refused to admit Benedict of Cluny, who had been appointed by Cluny Prior in his place. There was friction between the foreign mother-house and the kings of England. Edward I heavily taxed the 'alien priories', including Acre, as did Edward II and Edward III. In 1373 the priors were naturalized British by Letters Patent, thus severing connection with the foreign mother-house. In 1401 the monks bought an Indulgence of the Portiuncula from Pope Boniface IX, which brought penitents and presumably their money to the priory on the 1st and 2nd of August every year, on which dates this Indulgence was effective. The biggest draw the priory had, though, was the arm of St Philip; but even this, in 1533, only brought in ten shillings. And on 22nd November 1537 the Reformation came to Acre, and the last prior, Thomas Malling, signed the place away to Henry VIII, who gave it to Thomas Howard, Duke of Norfolk, from whom it was taken away by Elizabeth I and given to Thomas Gresham. Eventually, with the surrounding countryside for many miles it came into the hands of the Coke family, and the present Earl of Leicester handed it over to the Ministry of Works.

The existing ruins are marvellous to behold, with the west front of the priory church standing up high and gaunt, and ornamented with the most elaborate Norman blind arcading anywhere to be seen: indeed some might think a superfluity of embellishment. The site, on green green lawns on the low riverine marshes away from the village, adds to the enchantment.

We enter through the fine early sixteenth-century gatehouse, which has two entrances, one for vehicles and one for foot passengers. Under what were the upper windows (big square Tudor-looking windows they must have been) are, from left to right, the arms of Fitzalan quartering Warrenne (the Yorkshire family of Fitzalan was long connected with the priory), the Royal Arms, de Warrenne, Maltravers, with the arms of the priory underneath over the pedestrian door. The arms, now very defaced, are thought to have been those of Mowbray.

The church was a copy of the second church of Cluny when it was built in the eleventh and twelfth centuries. It originally had five apses, for there was an apsidal chapel to the east of each transept, an apse to each chancel aisle, and one to the chancel. The foundations of these apses are clearly to be seen on the grass. In the fourteenth century the east end was pulled down and a square-ended presbytery built and a south chapel. In the fifteenth century the north chancel aisle was enlarged to make a big square-ended chapel.

But it is the wondrous west front that astonishes the beholder, and has something of the impact of Tintern Abbey when seen for the first time as one rounds the bend of the road. It is a classic example of how each age ruthlessly imposes its taste on the buildings of the past, and completely undervalues the achievement particularly of the immediately preceding age. Those two Early English pointed windows high up on the south side of the façade—surely any builder of sensibility would have retained the Anglo-Norman tradition in adding-on to that vast pile of round arches? But no. E.E. was the latest thing, and E.E. the windows had to be. And as for the huge Perpendicular west window: the whole fabric of the Norman work was torn asunder to insert that—and nobody can think that it looks anything but incongruous. In so many great buildings the builders 'got away with' such additions to older styles: triumphantly, for example, at Norwich. But at Acre their enthusiasm outran their taste.

The foundations of the priory have been well excavated and can easily be followed: the two vanished towers that were flush with the west front, the transepts with the early apsidal chapels already mentioned, the dormitory, with a vaulted undercroft, which runs south from the chapter house, the large and well-preserved *necessarium* to the south of it again—the size of it leading us to wonder whether all the monks used to want to employ it at once. The prior's house is still in perfect order, very pretty Tudor with a bay window and a gabled roof, more like the dwelling of a wealthy merchant than that of a religious. It has a private chapel upstairs, with the ghosts of wall paintings.

Do not neglect Castle Acre **parish church**. On the pulpit are representations of the Four Doctors—placed there from a screen over an aisle. They are: Augustine, Gregory, Jerome and Ambrose.

The screen is of a quality nearly to equal Ranworth. The uncle of the present incumbent of the church, J. Hague Bloom (the present vicar is Rev. Harvey Bloom) wrote a book: *Castle and Priory at Castleacre*.

A Saxon burial ground was dug up at Acre, with over a hundred urns, and two great stone coffins were discovered in the Nar, in Victorian times, when a new bridge was being built, and the parson ordered that they were to be carried up to the church. He did not provide the workmen with sufficient *beer* money, however, for such an exacting task, and they accordingly threw the coffins back again, where they rest today. Nobody has yet gone to the trouble of looking for them. It is possible that they were the coffins of William de Warrenne and Gundreda. It was the custom for such grand people to keep coffins for themselves in all of their various residences throughout the country in case death might come to them while they were in residence.

North-east, still voyaging up-Nar, we quickly come to **Newton-by-Castleacre**, which has a church with a very fine Saxon crossing tower with four Saxon-looking windows (map, p200). It is strange that, in a land where there is very little Saxon work left, there is a little group here of four Anglo-Saxon churches: this one at Newton-by-Castleacre, **East Lexham** (read the brass plate west of the altar rail here), **West Lexham** (but a picture inside of 1891 shows the place completely in ruins, so it is a reconstruction) and **Great**

Dunham. The latter (a couple of miles south of East Lexham) is most certainly worth going to see. Its church stands next to a lively school, it has plenty of Roman tiles in its arches, it has long-and-short work in its tower and naves and typically Saxon windows. It *looks* Anglo-Saxon and very ancient. Why this profusion, in this little group of villages, of Anglo-Saxon remains? This area must have escaped even Norman rebuilding: could it have been so unprosperous? Or was it because the great monastic house at Castle Acre overshadowed all else? Now the whole area is one of huge estates and practically depopulated, and so these tiny churches are more than adequate for the population.

Litcham is a fine little town, administrative centre for a district, and very attractive with much tarred flint. Down by the river is an old pilgrim's resthouse now occupied by a county councillor who is also an antique dealer, and who incidentally has a large collection of 'country by-gones', especially domestic utensils. He does not scorn to collect even such things as early tin-openers and lemonade bottles.

North (beyond the source of the Nar) are the **Raynhams**, and here is the greatest-ever collection of 'by-gones', in the spacious farm buildings of Hall Farm, the home of Mr Dick Joice. The great buildings are filled to overflowing with old farming, forestry, warreners', poachers', keepers', mole-catchers', and country tradesmen's tools and implements. There are steam engines, traction engines, ancient motor cars, some particularly fine fire engines, and domestic utensils of all kinds. This is a truly remarkable collection and probably the best in the country, but permission should be obtained from Mr Joice before visiting.

Raynham Hall is another of Norfolk's splendid seventeenth-century houses. The Hall, which is at East Raynham, was built by Sir Roger Townshend who started it in 1622. The house has given rise to much discussion as to who designed it, some plumping for Inigo Jones, others for Roger Platt, and yet others for Sir Roger himself, together with his master mason William Edge with whom Sir Roger had gone touring in the Low Countries. Certainly the great gables have a Netherlandish look, and seem scarcely a pure enough Palladian for Inigo Jones. Most of the interior of the house was done by William Kent, of Holkham fame. The house is a great block of brick and stone, standing amid flat lawns; and it looks as if it would be far more comfortable than either Holkham or Houghton, despite its size there is something homely and comely about it.

The Townshends were another family risen to wealth in the law courts. The first, Sir Roger, was a justice of the Court of Common Pleas and he has an exceedingly sumptuous monument in the form of an Easter Sepulchre in the church—he died very late fifteenth century. He was lawyer to the letter-writing Pastons and bought much land off them. A later Townshend, Charles, 2nd Viscount, married a sister of his illustrious neighbour Sir Robert Walpole and became politically prominent. More useful he became agriculturally prominent, and played a great part in the introduction of the turnip into England—thus earning a title for himself much grander than that of Viscount: 'Turnip' Townshend. Turnip cultivation (followed by that of the mangel-wurzel or cattle-beet) took the place of the old wasteful bare fallow in the rotation of ploughlands. It was a cleaning crop (i.e. its cultivation eradicated weeds) and it allowed sheep and cattle to be kept, and even fattened, in the winter. It led the way to the 'Norfolk Four Course Rotation' that spread all over England, and which itself gave rise to the great era of High Farming which only ended with the repeal of the Corn Laws.

'Turnip's' grandson, George, took over command from the dying Wolfe on the heights of Abraham and led his troops to victory. Later he became Lord Lieutenant of Ireland. In the First World War another Townshend, Sir Charles, led the defence of Kut in Mesopotamia. After a long siege by vastly superior Turkish forces he had to surrender, with 9,000 men.

South again: **Swaffham**. Here is a most elegant town, a little rural Paris, once called 'the Montpelier of England'. It was the product of more wealth, better horses and carriages, and better roads in the late eighteenth century and Regency times, all of which factors permitted the gentry to drive long distances to a social centre, to attend routs and balls, concerts and *soirées*, and to bring their daughters in for the season and to marry them off. Many elegant eighteenth- and early nineteenth-century houses remain, including the large Assembly Room (Hamond's Grammar School opposite) which must have been the hub of it all and was built in 1817. Swaffham is the finest predominantly Regency town in East Anglia. There was once a lively theatre there (W. B. Rix, in his book *Swaffham*, records that 'In 1806 Earl and Countess Nelson with their daughter, Lady Charlotte, Lady Bolton, Miss Horatio Nelson Thompson and Lady Hamilton stayed in Swaffham and bespoke the play "She Stoops to Conquer" '. Many county families took houses in

Swaffham for 'the season', and many country clergy gathered there to live, so much so as to give rise to anxiety by the Bishop who maintained that they ought to live in their parishes. Some of them replied that—at any rate—they could *see* their parishes from the high ground of Swaffham!

A great activity of Swaffham in Regency times was hare coursing. In fact it was only the lack of hotels that prevented the town from becoming the venue for the Waterloo Cup. The Swaffham Club, which was a coursing association, was formed by Lord Orford in 1776, and it was on the heaths around Swaffham that his Lordship coursed Czarina—the ancestor of every true-bred greyhound in the world today. He coursed Czarina forty-seven times and she was never once beaten. In her last match Lord Orford worked himself up into such a passion about it that he fell from his horse and died.

But Swaffham existed before the eighteenth century, as one can see from the church, which is fifteenth century and magnificent. The lavish use of Barnack stone in it tells of great wealth when it was built, for the stone must have been carried overland for several miles from the River Nar. The particularly splendid north aisle, with its seven bays and its clerestory with thirteen Tudor-arched windows, is said to have been paid for by the Pedlar of Swaffham. This man (whose story is told in detail in *Folklore as an Historic Science* by Sir L. Gomme but is much repeated by the people of Swaffham) went to London and met a stranger on London Bridge (some versions have it that the Pedlar had gone to the bridge to throw himself off it). The man told him of a dream that he had had—that he had gone to a remote Norfolk town called Swaffham, and gone to a certain garden (and here he described the Pedlar's own) and dug in it and found a great treasure. The Pedlar kept his council, went straight home, dug in his garden—and hence the north aisle of Swaffham Church. There is a library over the vestry, with a fine fifteenth-century *Book of Hours*.

I was once travelling in remotest Yorkshire and I came to a village called Gargrave. I went into a cobbler's to have a shoe mended. The cobbler spoke with a powerful Norfolk accent, and when I asked him (in a Suffolk one) whence he had come he said: 'I come from Swaaafham where they dew three daaays thraaashin' fer naaathin'' (where they do three days threshing for nothing). I was able to give him the correct reply: 'Well thass saaathin'!' (well that's something). Not since Stanley accosted Livingstone at Ujiji has there been such an encounter.

The Market Cross cost £400 in 1783. There is a very good little market, one of the excellent surviving old markets where you can buy a second-hand washing machine, a dozen white rabbits, or a goat.

South-west is **Oxborough Hall**, built in 1482 (at least that is when he received licence to crenellate) by Sir Edmund Bedingfeld, and Bedingfelds have lived in it ever since. Originally from Bedingfeld in Suffolk (which manor they took after the Conquest and kept until recent times) they came into Oxborough by marriage: one Edmund Bedingfeld marrying Margaret Tuddenham of the family that held Oxborough. About 1460 Sir Thomas Tuddenham, brother of Margaret and the owner of Oxborough, was executed for being on the wrong side in the Wars of the Roses, but Margaret, having married a Yorkist, was allowed to inherit. On Margaret's death in 1474 Oxborough went to her grandson, Edmund, who, as we have seen, received licence to build a fortified house in 1482 from Edward IV, and he built Oxborough Hall: in essence the same as we see it today although differing in many details: much of it was rebuilt in Victorian times. Henry VII slept in what is now called the King's Chamber over the gateway. Queen Elizabeth may or may not have slept in the room above: it is still called Queen's Chamber. Mary, Queen of Scots, certainly did.

The history of the Bedingfeld family has been one of consistent loyalty to two causes: that of Rome, and that of the Crown of England. The family rose to great favour with the Crown until the Reformation; but after that, remaining resolutely Catholic, led a precarious existence far from the paths of power. A Bedingfeld, Edmund, served Henry VIII in his wars, and was entrusted with the custody of Catherine of Aragon when that lady was divorced. Edmund's son, Henry, was entrusted by Catherine's daughter, Queen Mary, with the custody of the future Queen Elizabeth, when that princess was immured in the Tower and later at Woodstock. When Elizabeth became queen she quickly dismissed Sir Henry from his office—some writers record with a tart remark while others say that she bore him no grudge. As her reign went on, and Protestantism became more firmly established, families like that of Oxborough fell from prominence and power and were subject to penal laws.

The Civil War greatly damaged the family for of course it was Royalist: the Sir Henry of the time and three of his sons were captured, the fourth son was killed, and the Hall was occupied and severely damaged by the Roundheads. A Royalist family in the middle of Roundhead East Anglia was precariously placed. But the family clung on to its estates, became prosperous again at the Restoration, and in 1775 the Sir Richard of the day (a baronetcy had been bestowed on the family by Charles II) had enough money and enough time, alas and alas, to pull down what must have been the marvellous medieval Great Hall and Great Kitchen that formed the south side of the quadrangle of the Hall. The Sir Henry of the nineteenth century (who married one of the last of the Paston family) built the Roman Catholic chapel in front of the Hall in about 1835, also the tower at the south-east corner, the turreted kitchen-garden walls. The charming French *parterre* gardens were laid out about 1845, when also the delightful garden buildings were built.

Oxborough is one of the most charming of the great country houses of England, and the little village that lies next to it is charming too. There is a feeling of great remoteness about the place, far from any important road, far from a town, near the Fens but not of them, near the desolate Brecklands but also not of them: a small corner of fertile English countryside hemmed in between Fen and Breck. The view through the gate in the great surrounding wall is breathtaking: the mighty mellow brick mass of the Hall with that marvellous fortified gatehouse across the moat; the gatehouse seven stories high and almost exactly as it was when it was built nearly five hundred years ago, when machicolations were carefully provided so that substances heavy and hot could be poured through them on to the heads of attackers. Pugin called this gatehouse 'one of the noblest specimens of the domestic architecture of the fifteenth century' and so it is, if indeed we do not classify it as military architecture. Transitional the Hall may have been between purely defensive building and the undefended domestic building of Tudor times, but Oxborough was still meant to be defended, if never from a full-scale siege at least from robbers or marauders or unfriendly neighbours. That wide moat was not just dug to keep fish in.

The bridge over the moat is eighteenth century, replacing a drawbridge. The finest thing inside the gatehouse is its brick stairway: a marvel of constructing in brick what is normally constructed in stone. The roofs of the gateway itself, and of the adjoining armoury, have fine brick vaulting. The brick fireplace of the King's Chamber, on the first floor, is noteworthy. The moulded beams and the panelling in this room are modern.

But it is the King's Chamber that contains the wonder of Oxborough. And this is the Oxborough Hangings, ranged around the bed. These, of green velvet, were made some time about 1570 as wall hangings, and they contain over a hundred panels of needlework executed by Mary, Queen of Scots, during her endless imprisonment, and also by Elizabeth, Countess of Shrewsbury, or 'Bess of Hardwick'. When Queen Mary was incarcerated in Tutbury Castle it was reported of her that all day she 'wrought with hir Nydill, and that the diversitie of the colors made the worke seme lesse tedious, and contynued so long at it till veray Payn made hir to give over'. The chief impression of the needlework panels is a powerful one of organic wholeness. The themes are animals and plants, mostly cribbed in fact from books of natural history, but the total effect is of the work of people in close sympathy with a world of life and living things: it is a humbling experience for a modern man to stand before it. *Virescit Vulnere Virtus* stitched Mary: Virtue is strengthened by wounds. Certainly Mary's deep and bitter wounds strengthened her feeling for colour and form, and for life. The gatehouse is opened to the public at specified times, as are other rooms.

It is interesting to discover that the original township of Oxborough was situated, as one would have expected it to have been, at Oxborough Hythe, meaning the port of Oxborough, down on the River Wissey. There is nothing left of this at all, but when it existed it made Oxborough part of the world of the Fenland rivers: linking it closely with Cambridge and King's Lynn, and—with Cambridge —with metropolitan culture and civilization.

Oxborough's parish church is in ruins. Its tower which was no less than 150 feet, fell on top of it in 1948 and wrecked it pretty thoroughly; but not, fortunately, the amazing Bedingfeld chapel, which is unfortunately kept locked at the time of writing, but one can see quite a lot through the windows if indeed one does not have time to seek out the vicar and ask for the key. The fame of this place are the two terracotta monuments, Italianate in style and most spirited. There are other Bedingfeld monuments in the chapel. The Roman Catholic chapel, hard by the gate of the Hall, is 1835, and notable for the Flemish altar retable, early sixteenth century, various pieces of old stained glass, two Bedingfeld monuments for lovers of Victoriana.

Continuing southwards we reach a strip of country that I always consider as an inland shore, for it runs along where the higher country of the Breckland ends, and the flat Fens begin. It is a coastline from which the waters have receded and left it high and dry. I here have to warn the reader to discount some of what I say in praise of the villages along this 'shore'. I think they are marvellous; but to many eyes they would no doubt appear to be just villages. They are by no means Lavenhams, but then in the summer their streets are not choked by charabancs.

Northwold is the most northerly village of this ancient shore, and like the others it is a fascinating mixture of chalk 'clunch', flint, carr stone and old brick. The church is Decorated and beautiful, with marvellous thirteenth-century piers, each looking almost like four pillars although in fact all of a piece, and with stiff-leaf capitals. The tower is Perpendicular, late fifteenth century. The great thing is the Easter Sepulchre, perhaps the best in East Anglia, with four Roman soldiers startled and disturbed among the olive trees. This lovely piece of sculpture makes you feel the spirit of the fourteenth century when it was made, and it is very hard to forgive Cromwell's zealots who so savagely defaced it.

Methwold is the next of the border villages, almost a small town in fact, with big farmsteads all mixed up in it: all chalk, carr stone, flint and brick again like Northwold. Unusually for Norfolk the church has a steeple, a most beautiful slender octagonal one. The east window decorated, with a sort of tracery which makes one wish that the Perpendicular style had never been invented. It was, though, and the rest of the church is in it. The brass inside to Sir Adam de Clifton (died 1367) is famous. It was sold to a tinker in 1860, broken into 130 pieces, but put together again in 1888. There is a sixteenth-century vicarage, with a chimney up the middle of its stepped gable. Methwold, like other of these border places, had its river port, Methwold Hythe. Fenland reclamation has cut this off from its navigation, it is now two miles from its river—the Wissey. It is a charming group of buildings, sited right between the flat Fens and the chalk upland. The great new Cut-off Channel runs hard by it, blue and cold. Down the lane to it a fine view can be had across Fenland. There is a fine farmstead there: the house green-washed and the buildings of clunch.

At Methwold started the East Anglian outbreak of the Peasant Rising that ended, as we have seen, in drawings and quarterings at

North Walsham. It was at this time that Parson Ball composed the verse:

> *When Adam delved and Eve span*
> *Who was then the Gentleman?*

Methwold Manor, belonging then to the Duke of Lancaster, was invested by the rebels, Methwold Court Rolls were burnt, but otherwise no lives were lost nor damage done.

There is the site of a Roman villa half a mile north-west of Methwold. The Romans, or Romano-Britons, undoubtedly conquered large areas of Fenland, which were left to go back to swamps and waters when the Romans retired.

Feltwell is much overwhelmed by an airbase. There are two churches: a big St Mary's with a splendid Perpendicular tower and much Decorated work, and a smaller St Nicholas which had a carr stone tower which was being repaired by workmen in 1898. The workmen went next door to the Chequers, for a well-earned pint or two, and while they were there the pub was shaken by a terrible rumbling—and when they ran to the door and looked out the tower had crumbled into ruins. The pub, fortunately, still stands. St Nicholas is still used as a chapel, and has Norman elements. Not only has it lost its tower, but it has lost its chancel too, the latter having been pulled down by the Reverend Edward Bower Sparke in 1862, in order to use some of the material to build another aisle on to St Mary's. Sparke drew revenue from four fat livings, and so could afford to indulge in such activities.

Sparke's north aisle in St Mary's is lush indeed, and so are the windows he installed: much of the glass by Didron, of France, and in better taste than much glass of the period (certainly in better taste than the great spate of glass of the early twenties with all those knights in armour with Rupert Brooke's face). The benches are well worth looking at, and there are interesting brasses.

Apart from the great Perpendicular west tower, with its pinnacles and ornate parapet, most of this church is Decorated. And the question arises: why, in predominantly Perpendicular East Anglia, is there so much work of the Decorated style left in the churches of this ancient shore of the Fens? Can the reason be that these villages reached their prosperity in the great sheep-rearing period but *before* the great cloth weaving era initiated off by the importation of Flemish weavers into East Anglia by Edward III? These villages were well placed to enjoy the wool-exporting boom; with access, as they had, to the sheep-walks of the Brecklands and also the lush meadows of the Fens, and with water connection from their hythes with King's Lynn, one of the greatest of English ports trading with the Continent. But the whole area, King's Lynn included, got left behind in the weaving boom of late medieval and Tudor times, when Lavenham and the villages about it, and Worstead and Norwich and the east Norfolk villages, boomed as weaving villages, and the estuaries and river ports of east Suffolk and Norfolk exported the finished cloth and outstripped King's Lynn as Continental ports. And then, when the Fens were effectively drained in the seventeenth century, it was done by Metropolitan financiers and Methwold and the other border villages did not share in this prosperity. Hence they remained as backwaters, and have so remained ever since; and their churches, built in the Decorated style popular in the days of the raw-wool boom, were never pulled about and rebuilt in the late middle ages as were the great Perpendicular churches of the weaving parts of East Anglia.

Hockwold cum Wilton has a Tudor hall built on the E plan of red brick, and **Wilton** Church has a stone spire, nice benches, and a monument to Cyril Wyche by John Ivory, of Norwich.

Just south of Hockwold the road crosses the great new Cut-off Channel (for details see p198) and here the interested traveller should turn left off the road (east) and follow the channel up-stream until he comes, after a short walk, to the inverted syphon by which the Channel is carried down under the River Little Ouse. The Little Ouse is allowed to flow on regardless (it can have no way of knowing that there is a Cut-off Channel there) until time of flood, when its waters can be diverted through a sluice into the Cut-off Channel and thus prevented from going on to join the already-swollen Great Ouse. The water of the Channel still has that cold, eerie, blue colour of water flowing over chalk. Nature has scarcely had time to assert herself in the form of water weed and many fish.

Just north of Lakenheath Station is an odd-looking factory with many chimneys. This is England's chicory factory. Chicory is grown about the Fens and brought to this place to be ground up and roasted to be put in coffee, mostly of the bottled essence variety. Chicory takes the place of sugar-beet in places where eel-worm infestation makes the cultivation of the latter unprofitable.

North-west, towards King's Lynn again, **Stoke Ferry** is an old river port on the Wissey, and important trading centre in the days of the Fen Lighters and still accessible by small boats. The Bull Inn, down by the river, has a staithe to tie up to and will provide accommodation.

At **Denver** George William Manby was born. He went to school with Nelson and later—after having stood on Yarmouth beach watching a great ship perishing in the surf with the loss of all hands —he invented first a mortar, and then a rocket life-saving apparatus, the latter, streamlined and modified, still in use today. By 1823 his apparatus had saved 229 lives and Parliament awarded him £2000. He is buried at the big river port of **Hilgay** nearby. Denver has a well-maintained grinding windmill—the finest for miles, also Denver Hall with its beautiful east gable which is early sixteenth century and pretty gatehouse of 1570.

It also has Denver Sluices, old and new. The Old Sluice was built by Vermuyden to limit the run of the sea tides up the Great Ouse. It was destroyed by the Fen Tigers—men who made a living from eeling and wildfowling and didn't want the Fens to be drained— and was opposed strongly by sailors and traders, one of whom pointed out that 'whereas of old ships from Newcastle were wont to make 18 voyages in the year to Cambridge with sea coal, now, since the blocking of the stream at Denver and the diversion of its waters at Earith, they can make but 10 or 12, whereby the price of fuel has increased by half'.

The sluice was 'blown up' again by a high tide in 1713, and there were loud rejoicings by its opponents. But it was rebuilt again, and then again—much bigger and stronger—by Sir John Rennie, who also built Old Waterloo Bridge. Since Rennie's time it has been remodelled and has had steel gates fitted. It will be noticed that it is a double lock—that is that at low tide a vessel passing through it goes down-hill from south to north, but at high tide up-hill. The tidal river, north of Denver, varies greatly in height with the tide, the fresh water south of it remains constant. Through this sluice the water draining from 800,000 acres of land used to pass: now that the Cut-off Channel has been opened this load is lightened. The New Denver Sluice was opened in 1959, and it either passes or restrains the waters of the Cut-off Channel.

Over the river, and just downstream (i.e. north) from the old Denver Sluice the New Bedford Drain, which is tidal, debouches into the Ouse. If you follow it upstream it rejoins the Ouse far up near

Earith. Just downstream from its mouth is Salter's Lode, where a single sluice gate lets the Old Bedford Drain into the Ouse. All water traffic from the Great Ouse system bound for the rest of England must go through this gate, or else the other sluice gate of the recently repaired Well Creek just by it. These gates can only be used when there is 'a level', i.e. when the salt tidal water outside is level with the fresh non-tidal water inside. This condition is only obtained for a few moments twice a day.

Downham Market is a great place for lovers of the Norfolk carr stone, for it is the most considerable town to be largely built of it. It has a charm and mellowness all of its own, and a couple of fine old and comfortable hotels and big mills down by the railway. Downham was once a very big river port, but was first cut off from the river by the railway, and since that again by the Riley Channel, which carries the waters of the Cut-off Channel to the main river at King's Lynn. This has left a narrow strip of new grassland between the Channel and the Great Ouse, along which it is very pleasant to walk northwards to the Wiggenhalls, strolling now westwards to the ancient river, now eastwards to the new canal. Horses graze on the grass, and for the naturalist it is interesting to see how life, vegetable and animal, is beginning to colonize the great new gash.

Quite recently the citizens of Downham Market were split in two by a controversy which raged over the public lavatory there, which was shaped exactly like a Chinese temple. Alas, the iconoclasts won (as they generally do) and this extraordinary building was razed to the ground. Talbot Manor, at Fincham, has a large and remarkable garden, where thrive many tender plants.

The Wiggenhalls are four villages of the Norfolk Marshlands. The **Marshlands** are not to be confused with the Fens. The Marshlands, nearer the sea than the Fens, are of slightly higher land, not so subject to flooding, and have been inhabited from the earliest times. In the true Fens, excepting on the 'islands' of high ground such as Ely, there is hardly an old building. In Marshland the villages are ancient, and of an ancient prosperity. The Wiggenhalls cluster along the Great Ouse, which has not changed its course thereabouts for many centuries, and they have a charm about them not to be found in the graceless villages of the raw Fen.

Wiggenhall St Mary Magdalen has a most distinguished church with fifteenth-century glass in the windows of its north aisle: a 'must' for the saint-knower, for in the long gallery of saints depicted are many uncommon ones. There is a fine old pub crouching under the river bank by the bridge. The brother of the young landlady is the Great Ouse's last remaining professional eel catcher. Mr Gagen has a smack on the river, and from this he sets a 'stow-net' (a bag-net which hangs down from the boat while she is at anchor, so that the fish are driven into it by the tide). With this he catches small fish for bait, and he baits a great number of *grigs*, or *eel-hives*, which are traps with a one-way entrance. He sends many tons of eels up to Billings-gate. He also catches *smelts* which are a delectable tiny fish that smell most strongly of cucumber when they are being fried. Unfortunately England's total consumption of these fish is about a hundredweight a week and therefore the market is restricted. They are a royal delicacy, and until recent years the kings of England arranged for a special supply from the Great Ouse. Now hardly anybody has heard of them, and Mr Gagen has to throw most of them back.

There is a most pleasant walk (two miles) down the east bank of the river, past **Wiggenhall St Peter,** which has a church in fascinating ruin hard up against the high river bank, to **Wiggenhall St German.**

The latter is a most picturesque small Marshland village, with no less than three pubs: so many because at one time it was a great mooring-up place for Fen lightermen who were such thirsty fellows.

The church is strongly redolent of the spirit of the Middle Ages. No doubt there is much to see here besides the benches, but I can never see it for I cannot take my eyes off the superb wood carving of these latter.

They are fifteenth century, heavy and dark-looking, with intricate carving. The backs are carved, but it is the astonishing collection of bench-ends that makes such compulsive viewing. The aisle carvings are modern ones, and very good too; although they cannot, of course, quite capture that style and spirit that only comes from the Middle Ages. The nave bench-ends are an astonishing collection: sinners being swallowed by huge jaws, sinners committing away their sins, saints standing under their canopies straight from the age of faith and innocence, a monkey blowing a trumpet, weird beasts and animals.

The series of carvings depicting incidents of the life of St German in the north aisle is Victorian. He was, of course, the Duke of Bur-gundy, and a great hunter and he lived from AD 380 to 448. He hung trophies of the chase in a tree but a local bishop cut the tree down.

The bishop then had a dream which caused him to entice the angry duke into his church and there he forcibly ordained him. Afterwards German was acclaimed bishop. He came to England twice in order to refute the Pelagian heresy (which denied the doctrine of Original Sin).

At **Wiggenhall St Mary the Virgin**, just over the river, is an even more complete and perfect collection of benches, and less restored. But somehow they don't give one quite that feeling of having dropped back five hundred years. There is also a fine brass lectern, 1518. The great Elizabethan hall in a muddy field just before you get to the church is in fact mid-nineteenth century, only the entrance and the stable block are original.

Between St German and St Mary the Virgin the biggest pumping station in England lifts water from the Middle Level Main Drain up into the Great Ouse.

CHAPTER 15

The Norfolk Marshland

Perhaps the best thing about **West Lynn** is the view from it of East Lynn. Ferry Square has its own charm (and the above fine view), there is a vast canning factory, and the church has a good Decorated tower and a nice nave roof.

Terrington St Clement is a big and very ugly village north of the A17 (the trunk road between East Anglia and the Midlands and North and one of the most congested roads in the country: narrow, winding and crammed with heavy traffic) and there is hardly a nice-looking building. There is, however, a most gracious farmstead just south of the church.

And the church is magnificent even for East Anglia: it is often called 'The Cathedral of the Marshland'. The impression it conveys is one of width and massiveness: probably because of the depth given to it by its squat and heavy detached tower: Perpendicular and ashlar-faced and supported by heavy diminishing diagonal buttresses. This tower has had its uses: it served as a refuge both in 1613 and in 1670, when the sea broke through the dikes and came rolling over the Marshlands. The inhabitants of the parish had to remain in the tower and be fed from King's Lynn by boats.

The west front is very fine, with a great west window, niches to left and to right of it (and one above). There is a splendid clerestory, with flying buttresses—although obviously not as many as were intended. There are transepts, also not brought to completion and smaller than they were meant to be.

The later Perpendicular porch makes a fine entrance, with its sumptuous panelling. There is a sundial in it.

The interior of the church is very grand. Immediate view into the main body of the church is barred by a big eighteenth-century west screen, which once supported a musicians' loft. This may spoil the vista, but it also adds charm and intimacy. Through it the great crossing arches greet the eye. They were built to support the tower; but when it came to the point the nerve of the builders failed them and they decided to place the tower, campanile fashion, without the church. The quaking silt of the Marshland could not be trusted with such a weight.

Between the windows up in the clerestory are sea-creatures and men and animals, and the string-course has heads and angels. The chancel has a clerestory too, only of brick. The great five-light east window has glass in it as a memorial to the hundred men who died in the 1914–18 war. There are four ancient and interesting altar-slabs in the chancel, an Early English door to the vestry, a lovely sixteenth-century font cover with windows that open to reveal the most delightful primitives of scenes from the life of Jesus. There are great Creed and Commandment boards (1635), a fine Early English graduated sedilia and a double piscina south of the sanctuary. There is part of a chancel screen still undefaced. Why did the Marshland churches escape so much of the attentions of the Crom-wellian church-bashers? The Marshlands and Fens were solidly pro-Parliament (except the Royalists in King's Lynn and in Crow-land Abbey), and even now they are staunchly Nonconformist—so far as those prosperous and materialistic areas are anything. Why did the churches of the area escape defacing?

The church is almost all of Barnack stone. Can it be that one reason for the grandeur of the Marshland churches, and their fine state of preservation, is the absence of flint in their locality? This cheap material could not be used, and so freestone had to be floated down the Nene from Northamptonshire, and with this more am-bitious buildings could be attempted within a given budget. I am not decrying flint: the wonder of it is that, in the flinty parts of East Anglia, such magnificent buildings were constructed of what is, after all, a very difficult building material. As we range into Marsh-land, and south into Cambridgeshire, we shall find less flint and more dressed limestone. We shall miss perhaps the rough tweedy texture of the flint walls, and find that the churches have more affinity with those of the southern Midlands than with those of the eastern parts of East Anglia.

The remains of a Roman sea-wall can be seen close to the north and east of Terrington St Clement, looking no different from any

15. Four of the marvellous roofs of East Anglian churches. *Above left*, spandrels at Mildenhall; *right*, one of the carved angels at Blythborough. *Below left*, Neston; *right*, the "angel roof" at March

16. *Above*, Breckland: that area of sandy heath country once called the 'desert of East Anglia' and now containing the second largest forest in Britain. *Below*, part of the Cambridgeshire Fens: the most fertile soil in Britain. Here Hereward the Wake defied the Normans, long before the land was drained and made habitable

other sea-wall. There is a hamlet called Orange Row north of the village, so named because the Prince of Orange stayed there, as a refugee from the French, with a countryman named Baron Feagle. They must have felt at home, in this Dutch-type country. Another Hollander, Count Bentinck, saved the village in 1607 by building a bank—there is still a Bentinck's Farm north-east of the village, and Count Bentinck was a benefactor of the church until he died of Fen-fever. The reason that the altar of the church is raised up is that there is a Bentinck vault underneath it.

Terrington St Clement was founded on sheep, for at the time when that great tower was built, and most of what now stands of the church, the plough behind those old sea-walls had given way to grass and sheep grazed thick on the lush pastures. No good looking for sheep pastures now—the plough holds sway again over nearly every acre of Marshland as it does of Fenland, although there is a nice green meadow to the east of the great church on which fat Herefords graze all summer long.

To the south is Lovell's Hall, which is Early Tudor, and very impressive amid such uncompromising surroundings.

Sutton Bridge is in Lincolnshire, the home of the 'Yellowbellies' as Lincolnshire Fenmen have long been called (on account of their alleged propensity to turn yellow with the quaking ague. There is now, fortunately, no such distemper left in the Fens: draining has put an end to it). We shall hardly venture to claim Lincolnshire as East Anglia: it certainly isn't linguistically; perhaps nowhere in England is there such a sharp division in the common speech of the people in such a short distance as there is between Sutton Bridge and King's Lynn: the inhabitants of the two places hardly speak the same language. The very distinctive and most mellifluous Norfolk dialect gives way quite abruptly to that extraordinary harsh Lincolnshire brogue with its strong affinity with the Midlands and North.

There are two good old Boston-built fishing smacks in Sutton Bridge, which both go down the fiercely tidal Nene to trawl for the little brown shrimps that are found in the Wash close in to the sandbanks. (The much larger, but less delicate, pink shrimps—locally miscalled 'prawns'—are found in the much deeper water in Lynn Deep, and are fished for by the more powerful smacks which operate from Boston.) Tom Lineham, the master of one of the smacks, is ever ready to assist the visiting boatman, and is perhaps the most accomplished pilot for the Wash: there is hardly a nook or cranny of its labyrinthine channels that he does not know. For wildfowlers, Mackenzie Thorpe, who lives in the council houses, is the local authority and guide, and very good pink-foot shooting can be had in the winter time. The Bridge Hotel is an excellent place to stay in good solid comfort, and the drive to the mouth of the Nene—along the east bank—here the Nene is a wide, straight, artificial river—is interesting if hardly picturesque. It has views over the Wash at the end, and there are two little lighthouses—never used for their proper purpose although Peter Scott learnt much of what he knows about birds while living in one of them, with Mackenzie Thorpe for his guide.

It is interesting to notice, as one drives down the Nene, how sea-wall after sea-wall has been built, to enclose yet another slice of the Wash. Looking out to sea from the last one ('to sea' may seem a euphemism, for unless it happens to be the top of a very big spring tide the sea will be nowhere in sight: it may well be three miles away), one realizes that this process of accretion may continue. Now the saltings are being heavily colonized by marram grass, introduced on purpose to hold the silt together and speed up the accretion of new dry land. Sir John Rennie, builder of Denver Sluice (No 2) and the old Waterloo Bridge (to say nothing of Plymouth Breakwater) proposed a scheme for uniting the mouths of the four Wash rivers out at Lynn Well, and reclaiming, or 'inning', all the sea-bed in between, thus acquiring 150,000 new acres. He even obtained Acts of Parliament to do it, but more is required to accomplish such work than Acts of Parliament. Recently the idea has been put forward of building a great dam right across the mouth of the Wash thus turning the water of the Wash from salt to fresh and overcoming the growing water shortage of Eastern England. The Wash, by the supporters of this scheme, is often compared to the Zuider Zee. But the two seas are not really comparable. The Zuider Zee is protected from the fury of the North Sea by the Zeeland Islands and the sands of the Wadde: the Wash is not. The Wash has a tidal range of 19 feet or so: the Zuider Zee, before it was inned, a mere three or four. Also the water in the mouth of the Wash is far deeper than that in the mouth of the Zuider Zee. It seems more likely that Sir John Rennie's scheme will be achieved, by slow accretion over many years, and every few decades the inning of another few hundred acres, and one day the four rivers may indeed share a common outlet—out near

THE WASH

SEAL
SAND

Big Annie

PANDORA
SAND

Wolferton

A149

LYNN CHANNEL

BREAST SAND

Old lighthouses

North Wootton

Castle Rising

A148

Terrington Marsh

Lutton

A17

LONG SUTTON

A1101

Bentinck Farm

Orange Row

Sutton
Bridge

Terrington St. Clements

West Lynn

KINGS LYNN

Tydd St. Mary

RIVER NENE

Roman Bank

Lovell's Hall

A47

A10

A47

Tilney
All Saints

Walpole St. Andrew
Walpole St. Peter
Terrington
St. John

Tydd St. Giles

Walpole
Highway

Wiggenhall
St. Mary The Virgin

Wiggenhall
St. German

Setchey
River Nar

West
Walton

Marshland

A134

Gorefield

Middle Level Drain

RIVER OUSE

New Cut-Off Channel

WISBECH

B1441

Marshland Fen

Emneth

Stow Bardolph

A1122

Wisbech Canal (derelict)

Friday Bridge

Stow Bardolph Fen

A47

Outwell

Upwell

A1122

Salters Lode

DOWNHAM MARKET

West Dereham

R. Nene (Old course)

Three
Holes

Popham's Eau

Popham's Eau

A1101

Nordolph R.

Denver

Denver
Sluice

A10

Old Bedford

New Bedford

River

0   miles   4

the Roaring Middle. (Although when one considers the new Dutch 'Delta Plan', the inning of the Zeeland estuaries, one wonders whether anything is impossible to engineers, particularly Dutch ones.)

Botanists will notice the increasing poverty of the flora as they pass towards the sea down successive sea-walls, due, of course, to the fact that terrestrial plants have not yet had time to colonize these areas won from the saltings.

If you go to Sutton Bridge in a boat, by the way, you had best tie up at Tom Lineham's jetty (with his permission) for there is practically nowhere else to tie up to; and there is a twenty-foot rise and fall of tide, which is formidable. Ashore, there is a golf course, and this is interesting because it is in the bottom of a large harbour basin. The harbour was built in the 1880s, and would have been a very large and elaborate wet dock had it ever been completed. Even now, the masonry of the quays, and of the great lock chamber in the entrance, gives an idea of the vast amount of labour that went into it all. If it had been completed it would certainly have killed Wisbech as a port, and probably taken a lot of trade from Boston and King's Lynn. As it was a spring of water under the foundations of the great lock chamber caused part of this to subside, the company ran out of money, and the whole thing came to nothing. In 1953 the great tidal surge came over the outer lock gates—and the road along the Nene —and flooded the dock again, incidentally carrying a big steel lighter right over the top and dumping her in the old dock, where she was to be seen until recently.

Back safely in Norfolk, and East Anglia proper, we may travel southward to the Walpoles.

Walpole St Andrew has a strange local industry: the searching for King John's treasure, for it is supposed that it is in this parish that King John's baggage train subsided into the raging waters of the incoming tide. Recently a professor from Nottingham University made test borings, and brought up some metal, but people engaged in this strange quest are reticent with information. Walpole St Andrew Church has a hermit's cell in the base of its brick tower, and a mysterious chamber half-way up it.

At **Walpole St Peter** we are back among the very great churches of the Norfolk Marshlands. This is certainly a rival of Terrington St Clement, to many eyes far more stately and graceful: in fact it is one of the very beautiful parish churches of England. It is the Queen of the Marshland, and inside and out it is completely sumptuous: if the visitor to Marshland sees no other church—at least let him see this one.

The tower is about AD 1300 (which itself replaced a Saxon one) and was the first stage of the complete rebuilding of the Norman church. The nave was then constructed, and is very early Perpendicular: almost transitional in fact between Decorated and Perpendicular; this gives the arches inside a grace missing in later Perpendicular work, and the tracery of the aisle windows has a freedom and beauty not present in the later work—for example in the big Perpendicular east window. The chancel is pure Perpendicular. The tower is not as sumptuous as the rest of the church, and too small for it. The rood turrets and the bell-cote on top of the east end of the nave make a fine group: the bell-cote still has its sanctus bell. Under the High Altar (which is literally high as a result) is a sort of tunnel, or passage, called 'the bolt-hole'. It is said to have been built in to the church to conserve an ancient right of way; but was more probably to allow ceremonial circumambulation on consecrated ground (compare the pierced porch of Aldeburgh Church). It has some good carvings in it, and rings for tethering horses.

The south porch is richer than many an entire church: the bosses require an hour or more to study. There are sinners being swallowed, dog killing hare, fox and goose, pelican in her piety, sundry dragons, the Assumption of Our Lady with God looking on, the Last Judgement in which the fate of sinners is made to look very dire. There is a Pietà in the north-west corner—rare in England: the Madonna holding the dead Christ.

Inside, the church is beautiful indeed. Partly this is because of the great clear windows, the large seventeenth-century brass chandelier and the six smaller Victorian ones, but mostly it is due to excellent proportions and the absolute perfection of the arcades and of the lofty clerestory. There is a fine Jacobean font cover, with doors that open to the font, the west screen is good, and about 1630, and there is some old carving in the pews of the nave. The lectern is early Tudor, in the shape of a very fierce eagle. In this building nowhere does the eye alight without pleasure.

The Walpole family, from which came the first Prime Minister of England, left this village in the reign of King John. The village has its own saint, Godric, who must have been something of a big landowner in Anglo-Saxon times, for it is recorded of him that in

AD 970 he gave Turingtonea (now Terrington) to the Abbey of Ramsey, and that he made a pilgrimage to the Holy Land. In the church is a statue possibly of Hickathrift, the giant of the Marshland, about whom still tales are told.

I must here ask the traveller to make a strange detour: to take the road to Walpole Highway out of Walpole St Peter—thence nearly in to Wisbech—and then north again to **West Walton**. The reason for this diversion is that it is most important to approach West Walton from the south, for this gives the best view of the marvellous Early English tower standing up from its little clustering hamlet from the dead-flat fields of light-brown earth.

And here is yet *another* glorious church and for lovers of the Early English period one of the most important churches in all East Anglia.

The great detached tower is pure Early English, and a masterpiece. The west front of the church itself has had its polygonal Early English buttresses (which would have echoed the tower) pulled down and replaced by later ones, and, alas, only one original aisle window remains—in the south-east of the church—all the rest have been replaced by Perpendicular (leading one to reflect that the 'restorers' of the Perpendicular age did as much harm, in their way, as those of the Victorian).

But inside much is original thirteenth century, and there is a fine, very ancient, feel about the building. The circular piers of the nave have four detached shafts each of Purbeck marble (in places replaced in a reach-me-down manner with wood), and the piers have some of the finest stiff-leaf capitals in the country—very delicately done, and the arches above them are finely moulded. The clerestory, which is also original Early English, is unusual and noteworthy, and there are paintings between the windows—also mid-thirteenth century. There are also below the clerestory painted the emblems of the tribes of Israel: Dan, Gad, Asher, Naphtali and Joseph on the north side, and Issachar, Zebulun, Judah, Levi and Simeon on the south. These are seventeenth century—touched-up in the nineteenth.

One of the most interesting things in the church is the 'Flood Board'. This records that on 1st November 1613 the sea overflowed all Marshland, on 23rd March 1614 'this Country was overflowed with the fresh', and on 12th and 13th September 1670 'againe overflowed by the Violence of the Sea'. But now:

> *Heavens face is clear, though the Bow appeare*
> *Reader nerefear, there is no Arrow neare.*

The 'fresh' of course refers to fresh water. Thus in 1953 part of Marshland was overflowed by the sea—but in 1947 very much of it —and Fenland too—was overflowed by 'the fresh'—the fresh water in the swollen rivers bursting the banks. There is also the verse:

> *Surely our Sinns were tinctured in graine,*
> *May not we say, the labour was in vaine*
> *Soe many Washings, still the Spotts remain.*

And so we go south to **Walsoken**, now but a suburb of Wisbech, and this has the grandest Norman church of Norfolk. Thus says Dr Nikolaus Pevsner. And so many people miss it, because who goes looking in the *suburbs* for grand buildings?

The course that I should advise is to walk into the building and straight up to the splendid font. Spend some time contemplating this, and then set about looking at the rest of the church. Not that the latter is not noteworthy—simply that the font might get neglected for the church if a special move is not made to notice it.

The arcades, late Norman, are splendid, the piers slenderer than is found in earlier Norman work—their arches richly carved with zigzags. The capitals are varied and beautiful. The great chancel arch is interesting—a trifle later than the arcade arches—pointed and not round and yet in much the same style. Here Early English is separated from Norman by a hair's breadth. The tower (marvellous) is right into the Early English period. Inside the church there is fine carved timber up aloft, with paintings of angels, in both aisles there are carved screens: that in the south aisle having especially delicate tracery. There is some good wood carving on the bench-ends.

Terrington St John, not to be forgotten, has a beautiful church, with an interesting passage connecting the tower to the nave, and an unusual clerestory. **Tilney All Saints** is Norman and noteworthy. And that, finally and completely, is the end of my list of the great Marshland churches—unless the insatiable traveller wishes to include Tydd St Giles and Tydd St Mary.

The 'Marshland Series' is far less known than it deserves to be. For every person who makes the Marshland tour, a thousand probably make the tour of the West Suffolk wool villages. True we do not see in Marshland the absolute soaring perfection of the Perpendicular style, as we see at Long Melford or Lavenham, or in the tower arch of Stoke-by-Nayland; but here we have a great variety of medieval architectural styles including the earlier ones not otherwise well represented in East Anglia, a rich variety of building materials and an atmosphere and feeling of medievalism quite unique. If anyone can look at the bench carvings of Wiggenhall St Germans, or Wiggenhall St Mary the Virgin and not come away with a greater awareness than he had had before of the mind of the medieval Englishman, then he had better address himself to the science side.

Wisbech claims to be the Capital of the Fens. Certainly it would be a good centre from which to see Fenland, and Marshland too; and it is a seaport, and a river port, and set amid orchards. Furthermore it is a most pleasant small town.

The comparatively roadless wedge of country, with its apex on Wisbech, seen on the map to the north of the town, was once an arm of the sea. That, in Wash terms, means that the sea used to overrun it at high water: at low it would have been sand-flats or quaking mud. Thus Wisbech was built as a seaport town, and a transhipment port into river lighters. The present course of the River Nene is artificial (the old Nene ran miles to the east of it) and the process which is still going on—the embanking of the successive mouths of the Nene—has left Wisbech ten miles from the sea.

Ships still go to Wisbech, however, and the visitor can generally see some quite large coasters lying alongside the long quays which have been built each side of the river. The berths are very tidal and at low water, which appears to be most of the time, the ships are hard and fast aground on the mud. Russian timber ships seem to predominate, but there are Dutchmen (of course), Belgians and West Germans and sometimes even an English ship. Two sailing barges, with auxiliary engines, trade regularly up the Nene to Peterborough, carrying grain from Hull. Wisbech has come into her own again in the last couple of years as a transhipment port: once again ships are unloading timber into narrow boats (canal boats 70 feet long and 7 feet wide) for shipment up the Nene to Northampton and beyond —even as far as Leicester. But this revival of an old traffic is still only in the experimental stage.

The important parts of Wisbech are solidly Georgian, and are centred on the river, and on the old Wisbech Canal which has been most foolishly and reprehensibly closed down and filled in. But it is obvious that most of what we see of Wisbech was paid for by shipping, and in the eighteenth and early nineteenth centuries. A very large fleet of coasters was based there then, mostly 'billyboys' of the Yorkshire type, and much of the trade was, indeed, with the North. When we admire the gracious Georgian buildings of Wisbech, or explore Peckover House, let us remember the old ships which paid for it all.

The two Brinks of Wisbech—North and South—are together one of the most perfect and beautiful Georgian ensembles in England. The River Nene has been used here as the Dutch use rivers: as the prime embellishment of the town, not something to be stuck away out of sight along the backs of slummy houses. The sober and stately mansions of the two Brinks gaze across the wide river at each other in mutual admiration. The north Brink is the finer of the two: possibly the wealthier of the citizens preferred their houses facing south.

Peckover House looks grander from the rear than from the front: or perhaps one should say from the garden than from the street. The garden is Victorian, and very peaceful, and has a very big maidenhair tree in it. The house is the result of great wealth married to Quaker restraint and austerity in the early mid-eighteenth century. True, the restraint and austerity let go a little indoors, and there is a lavishness of carved wood and moulded plaster all in the very best of taste: the rococo wood carving over the fireplace in the drawing-room is superb. The house was built in 1722, and bought by Jonathan Peckover at the end of the century. He had come from Fakenham in 1777, and founded the local banking firm of Gurney, Birkbeck and Peckover (which merged with Barclay's in 1896). The house is open from Easter every Wednesday, Thursday, Saturday and Bank Holiday, until the end of September from 2 to 5 pm, adults 1s 6d.

William Godwin was a Wisbech man. The son of a Calvinist minister he at first preached Hell-fire but then came to the conclusion that 'Not God himself has the right to be a tyrant' and later became an atheist. He wrote *Political Justice* in which he extolled pacific anarchism and he said that 'generosity is a duty, not a virtue. It is impossible for me to confer a favour on any man. I can only do him a right,' and also that 'marriage is the most odious of all monopolies'. He enjoyed this monopoly though, marrying Mary Wollstonecraft after she had been deserted by her lover and left to support her daughter Fanny. Godwin's daughter by her, Mary, married Shelley (the mother died in childbirth). Shelley's *Prometheus Unbound* was based on Godwin's creed.

And here, at the 'capital of the Fens', it would not be a bad time to discuss just what **the Fens** are. From Bedford to Hunstanton, from Lincoln to Cambridge, lies the Great Level, and on it is produced a quarter of the food grown in England. The Great Level is really a kind of multiple inland delta: the four Fenland rivers, Wissey, Welland, Nene and Great Ouse, all run down into it, and through it, depositing their silt as they sluggishly creep to the sea. Their exit into the Wash is complicated by the very high tidal range of that part of the ocean. At high tide the sea forces itself high up the rivers: in medieval times it went very much farther than it does now, for now it is limited by such flood-bars as Denver Sluice on the Great Ouse. When the tide is high, and at springs, the fresh water running down the four rivers—which are the drains of a large part of England—cannot reach the sea, and it is then that they are inclined to burst their banks: as they did most recently in 1947, when the great snow of that year melted, and in 1953, when there was the phenomenal tidal surge.

The Great Level is not, in fact, quite level; although you might think it is were you standing, say, on the high ground between Newmarket and Bury St Edmunds looking north-west—for it then looks as if the whole world is as flat as a billiard-table. But in fact the area nearest the sea—particularly in the east—is higher than the areas inland: in fact the inland areas are below mean-sea-level, and this, of course, also leads to complications in draining. Formerly the Fens proper—the island areas—were a great swampy lake, here fresh water and there brackish, but with islands rising from it as at Ely, Thorney and Ramsey, where the monks took refuge and built their abbeys and cathedrals, and the *roddans*. The latter are interesting. They are winding banks of land slightly higher than the encompassing Fens, and often roads or villages are constructed on them. They are composed of a different soil from the Fen: the latter is the black peat, the Roddans are riverine sands or gravel. In fact the roddans are the old beds of rivers, which were once lower than the surrounding Fen. Now the Fen has shrunk, with the decomposition of the peat, leaving the harder beds of the old rivers standing higher.

North of Southery **the Marshlands** begin. Here the land is above mean-sea-level, and not peat, as the Black Fens are, but a silty loam. This land was laid down under salt water, whereas the Fens were laid down by fresh. When Corbett toured the Marshlands, early in the nineteenth century, 'the land was covered with beautiful grass, with sheep lying upon it as fat as hogs stretched out sleeping in a stye'. The Marshlands are now nearly all under the plough, for this land, although to a slightly lesser extent than Fenland, is pure gold.

The Marshlands have long been dry land (although always subject to occasional flooding by 'salt or fresh') and therefore they were inhabited from earliest times. The wonderful churches were the products of this habitation. The Black Fens, however, are new country, born in the seventeenth century and after, and except for their islands have no old buildings on them.

The Romans drained part of the Lincolnshire Fens, and the presence of the Roman villa we have seen at Methwold (p248) leads us to suspect that they at least started draining the Norfolk Fens; but in the Dark Ages all went back to swamp. To see what it was like (better than reading Kingsley's *Hereward the Wake*) we can go to the Biesbos area of southern Holland—though this too will soon all be 'inned' and drained by the indefatigable Dutch. But the Biesbos at the time of writing is almost certainly almost exactly as Fenland was in the Middle Ages. The men of the Fens (the 'Fen Tigers') were a semi-aquatic race (like the present-day '*Polderjongen*' of the Biesbos) who lived on low swampy islands and threaded the winding channels through the high reeds in flat-bottomed boats. In the Middle Ages the monks came to the larger islands and began the work of enclosing and draining on a small scale. But it was not until the seventeenth century, when the great wealth released by the Dissolution was causing an upsurge of capitalistic development all over England, that Dutchmen were imported from Holland with their skills of land reclamation and the task was tackled properly. Then the rivers were canalized—their windings straightened out—and often they were duplicated or even triplicated by great artificial drains like the Forty Foot (or Vermuyden's Drain), the Sixteen Foot, the Twenty Foot, Morton's Leam, the Old Bedford, the New Bedford, the Middle Level Main Drain. High banks were built along these artificial rivers and often the water in them runs high above the countryside and water has to be pumped up into them from the field drains. This was at first done by windmills—often several in series—each one raising the water a few feet. Then came steam, then diesel, and now electrical power.

Men with capital, then called 'adventurers' (there is still at least one 'Adventurers' Fen') sunk great fortunes, and men like Cornelius Vermuyden came from Holland to supervise the work. The Duke of Bedford and Charles II were two major capitalists. The 'Fen Tigers' bitterly resented the intrusion: they saw their old hunting and fishing grounds being destroyed and themselves being reduced to the status of landless labourers, and they made frequent attacks on the new works. The first time Vermuyden built Denver Sluice (p251) the Fenmen blew it up; but he built it again, and in time the wild tigers were tamed.

The land thus laid dry was rich beyond any other land in England, for it was pure peat—many yards deep. Without any fertilizer wheat grew as no wheat had ever grown before, and so did any other crop: it needed no manure because it *was* manure. But as the land was drained and ploughed and cropped it began to be noticed that it was sinking, it was getting lower in relation to mean-sea-level. The windmills that had to pump the water out of the fields up into the high embanked rivers had to pump higher and higher, and more and more windmills had to be placed in series to do it. We have already noticed, when discussing the Broads, that in the Fens none of these pumping windmills survives (there is actually one—at Wicken Fen) and that this is because they were temporary structures, of wood and not of brick, so that they could be moved about as occasion demanded.

But the land sank until no combination of windmills could cope with the draining, and in the nineteenth century steam came in the nick of time to save the Fens. Then the Fen lighters had to thread every navigable ditch carrying coal to the new steam engines, and one by one the little brick buildings with the tall chimneys that still dot Fenland were built. Nowadays great pumps driven by diesel power or electricity spin night and day to pump the Fenlands dry.

In 1851 one of the iron columns that held up the Great Exhibition building was driven down through the peat of Whittlesey Mere until its top was level with the surface of the ground. This with the intention of measuring the shrinking and sinking of the peat. Now the top of the pillar is twelve feet from the surface of the ground: and it must be remembered that this is in woodland, which has never been ploughed: on ploughland the shrinkage has been much worse. This shrinkage is due to three things: the contraction of wet peat as it dries out, wind and water erosion of peat constantly being ploughed, and the actual *using up* of the peat, which is an organic substance, by its decay, and by its being taken up by growing plants. Every ton of wheat or sugar beet or carrots sent away out of Fenland takes with it a little topsoil.

Thus the task of the engineers grows harder, as the land sinks in relation to the sea. And thus the task of the farmer gets harder, as—now only here and there in places—but the places are increasing every year—the sterile yellow clay begins to show on the surface, as its layer of peat has been stripped away. The Fens are a wasting asset.

But meanwhile the Fen farmers get richer and richer, and any able-bodied man or woman can earn good money in Fenland; making enough in the summer to live out the winter at leisure. The Fenlands are one of the last refuges of the Travellers, or Gypsies, who go there in thousands, all motorized now and most with television sets in their smart trailer caravans. Most Fenland farmers are self-made, having worked their way up from labourers. Most labourers have an acre or two of land on which they can work in their spare time: and two acres of Fenland, one of sugar beet and one of strawberries, are traditionally said to give a man a living. The Fen people work as no other people in England work: just about all the time. They live for work.

You are often told by a Fenman: 'There are no gentlemen in the Fens.' Of course the truth of this depends on what you you mean by 'gentleman': rather I would say that *all* are gentlemen in the Fens. But certainly nobody ever went there to 'retire', or to set up a country seat. There is no 'county society' in the Fens, and 'ladies of the manor' are not encouraged. Who would go for pleasure to a country as flat as a board, nearly as treeless, over which for nine months of the year a wind from Siberia cuts like a knife?

I can see a strange desolate charm about the little brick farmsteads standing like ships out at sea in the miles and miles of dead-flat black Fenland, generally at the ends of long muddy tracks. But more and more Fenland farmers are deserting these and going to live in hideous modern villas in the towns, to farm their distant fields from afar like Punjabi peasants.

The Fenmen are fiercely independent—but also interdependent. Each farmer knows that only by the communal effort of keeping up the river banks and drainage channels can his fields be kept dry: and meanwhile the great River Boards, disposing of millions of pounds, fight their never-ceasing battle to get the inland waters safely across Fenland to the sea. As for independence, it is evident from the completely egalitarian relationship between master and man, the complete absence of 'forelock pulling': and did not Cromwell draw the best and most resolute of his Ironsides from the Great Level?

South-east of Wisbech **Emneth** is notable for me for its Swan Inn, which should be visited during the strawberry-picking season. It is one of the pubs in the Wisbech fruit-growing district that does *not* display the racialist (and illegal) sign: NO VAN DWELLERS, and consequently it is one of the pubs in which a good time may often be had. Here we may hear songs that have been sung in England for hundreds of years, and the playing of the melodian, and see the dancing of the old step-dance—often in competition and for wagers. The White Swan at Outwell (p271) is another such 'Travellers' Pub'.

That Emneth is in Marshland and not in Fenland is shown by the fact that it has an ancient church (mostly Perpendicular but the chancel is Early English). There is a nice carved coffin lid in it, said to be thirteenth century, so Emneth has been above the waters for a long time.

In 1774 Lord Orford sailed with a fleet of nine ships through Outwell and Upwell and described them as 'populous towns'. Presumably his Lordship took the course of the Old Nene. Now we can still sail through them, with a fleet of *boats* if not with one of ships, thanks to the exertions of the Fen Watermen's Association (headquarters in March) in opening up once again for navigation the Well Creek, that joins the Old Nene with the Great Ouse at Salter's Lode.

The Well Creek crosses the Middle Level Main Drain on an aqueduct, with sluices under it. The sluice-keeper supplements his income by catching eels, which he does by lowering 'hives' (p253) into the water—not the old-fashioned kind woven from withies, but wire netting over a framework. Hard by here, in a small farmhouse, lives Peter Doubleday, champion long-distance skater of England. Fenland skating has a long tradition and is still very much alive. In ancient times Fenmen made skates of bone, and the freezing of the waters made travel easy for them where before it had been difficult: King Canute is supposed to have been wont to skate to Ely, preceded by a very heavy man named Pudding to test the ice for him. Now, as soon as the waters freeze up, many young farmers pull out their skates, and they skate long distances at great speeds, from one town or village to another. There is hardly an inhabited place on the Great Level which is not accessible in this way. Incidentally, Peter Doubleday's brother, Louis (11 Cemetery Road, Outwell) is the best pilot you can obtain for the Middle Level Navigations and anyone wishing to take a boat anywhere in the Middle Level is well advised to talk to him.

There is a big and very ancient drain just south of Upwell called Popham's Eau. There are several Eaus about Fenland. Eau is pronounced *ee* by the cognoscenti, and derived from Anglo-Saxon, not French as is commonly supposed.

Upwell and **Outwell** are in effect one long village, and make what must be one of the longest villages in England. They are strung out along the Old Nene (here a stagnant ditch), the Wisbech Canal, and Well Creek: the streets and houses are arranged each side of the waterways with a very Dutch effect. Coal shoots and other unloading and loading gear may be seen decaying along the waterways, and not-so-old men can remember the days when Fen Lighters brought all the bricks to build these villages from the Peterborough brick works, coal straight from the ships in Wisbech, fertilizer and animal feeding stuffs, and took away grain and other farm produce. The 'Fen Tramway' runs through the streets of the villages, a branch railway that runs along the open roads. Alas, it is going the way of the water navigation: into oblivion.

A light is thrown on the Fenland character by a farmer who lived in one of these two villages, Outwell, until he was murdered by burglars in 1967.

He was born a farm-worker's son in a cottage with one room up and one room down. He lived at the end in a big old Tudor farm-house, with a cluster of 'Traveller' caravans in the back yard all through the strawberry season, farming perhaps a thousand acres of Fen of which fifty were down to strawberries (average crop four tons per acre—average price to the jam factories £100 a ton). And he amassed what was almost certainly the best collection of Dresden china outside a museum in England, and one of the foremost collections in the world. To walk into the rooms in which this great collection was displayed was like walking into some fantastic cave of treasure.

March might be called the Crewe of the Fens, and truth to tell there are parts of it with about as much charm as the real Crewe. The railway traveller from East Anglia to the Midlands, if he has the great hardihood to go 'cross country' and not via London, is apt to find himself shivering for long periods on the open platforms of March as the unimpeded north-east wind howls at him over the flat Fen (map, p435).

But the best way to go to March is by water, for the Old Nene runs right through it. From the deck of your boat you get a glimpse of the spire of the Town Hall, and if you climb up the bank to have a closer look at the latter you will find a Palladian building which might well have made Palladio turn in his grave when it was built in 1900. But March Church must be visited, if only for its absolutely splendid double hammerbeam roof with a massed choir of wonderful carved angels with outspread wings. The effect is breath-taking. So too, but in a different way, is the cast-iron memorial fountain to George V's coronation at the top of Broad Street.

Three miles south-east of March is **Stonea Camp**, a very large and rambling Iron Age earthwork, right in the back of beyond. The imagination kindles at the idea of Bronze Age men living on what must have been a tiny island amid the reed swamps and quaking bogs. South of it, at **Honey Hill**, was a Roman encampment. This must have been one of the Empire's remotest trading posts, for—make no doubt of it—we are here in the deep black heart of Fenland. If the traveller wishes to plumb the very depths of it— let him go to Manea, Welches Dam, and Purl's Bridge.

Around **Manea** all through the autumn and winter you will see long lines of men, women and children, picking up carrots from the rich deep black peat soil. Most of these carrots, by the way, go to the jam factories, for carrots are an 'acceptable substitute' for fruit in factory-made jam. Standing on Manea station and looking along the line you can see the curvature of the earth. At **Welches Dam** is a lock, or 'staunch', which will lift a boat from the Forty Foot (or Vermuyden's Drain) up into the higher Old Bedford River. Both waterways are as straight as rulers for miles and miles, and the Forty Foot, all summer, is terribly weeded up. ('Staunch' is the Fenman's word for lock, and 'slacker' is his word for lock-paddle.)

At **Purl's Bridge** there is indeed a bridge, over the Old Bedford, but it is home-made, of planks fixed on top of floating oil drums. (A 'purl' is a tiny stream.) When a boat comes by the bridge it has to be cast adrift—and made fast again after the boat has gone through. The bridge-builder is Mr J. W. Barnes, who is a man of many parts. He is primarily an eeler of the old school, and not only sets but makes his own 'hives', out of withies that he grows himself. He also makes—and uses—the other sort of hives, bee ones. He grows withies on the 'washland' over the Old Bedford, and cuts them for thatching broatches (pegs—pronounced brortches), and he also sets a great net like a football goal with long wings out on each side for the fat silver eels in the winter time, on the flooded washland.

If you cross Mr Barnes's floating bridge you will find yourself in a very long strip of grassland, perhaps nineteen miles long but under a mile wide, between the Old Bedford River and the New Bedford; and this is a *washland*, and plays a very important part in the life of the Fens.

There are many washes, or washlands, in Fenland. They are areas of low country kept uninhabited, but down to grass and grazed by cattle and horses in the summer time, and in winter they are used as safety valves, or reserve buoyancy, for the Fens. When the pressure of water in the rivers becomes too great and the latter threaten to burst their banks, sluices are opened which allow some of the water to cascade into the empty washlands—thus relieving the pressure in the rivers. The wash between the two Bedford Rivers is apt to be flooded every year, and it is then that Mr Barnes catches his fat silver eels, as they work their way seawards—fattened on the millions of earthworms that come to the surface of the ground of the flooded lands—trying to find their way back to the Sargasso Sea to breed.

Another man, Mr 'Josh' Scott, who lives across the two rivers on the Downham side, also makes his living from the washland. During the summer he looks after the big herd of cattle belonging to different owners turned out on the washland to fatten: in winter he fares forth with a gun punt and big gun and shoots many hundreds of duck. He is one of the few people left who lead the lives of the old Fen Tigers before the big drainings: his only concession to the post-draining world is that he herds his cattle on a motor-cycle.

Nordelph is a little village that not only sounds Dutch but looks Dutch, and probably once *was* Dutch, for this countryside was much populated by the *polderjongen* imported from his own country by

Companion Guide to East Anglia

Cornelius Vermuyden. From the road between here and Downham Bridge you get a good idea of the precariousness of Fenland, for the road runs many feet below the water in the rivers, particularly in the Great Ouse at high spring tide. There are little cottages crouching below the river wall that seem to have their roof-tops below the level of the water.

CHAPTER 16

The Brecklands

The Breck country was once called the great East Anglian Desert. It is a stretch of country quite as distinctive in its way as the Fens are in theirs, or the Broadlands in theirs. It is an area of wind-blown sand covering the underlying chalk, sometimes with a layer of glacier-borne boulder clay in between, and the chalk is very rich in flints. In days gone by the sand blew with the wind, forming large moving sand-dunes, and in 1677 John Evelyn wrote: 'The Travelling Sands . . . that have so damaged the country, rouling from place to place, and like the Sands in the Deserts of Lybia, quite overwhelmed some gentlemen's whole estates.' He advocated the planting of trees to contain them.

But it was not always a desert. In Neolithic times areas of very light land with few trees such as the Breckland were the most sought after for farming; for this land could be easily worked without much tree-felling or draining, and with primitive ploughs. Thus Breckland was early a place of settlement. In Anglo-Saxon times, and later during the Dane Law, Thetford, capital of Breckland, was one of the very important places in England. It was the capital—not only of East Anglia—but at times of eastern England. It was then a great city, with palaces and many religious houses. Such a city could never have arisen in a desert, and there can be no doubt but at that time the sandy lands of Breckland were fertile and fruitful, as parts of them have been made again today. It was the sheep boom of the Middle Ages that destroyed Breckland. The hooves of the sheep, called 'golden hooves' when these animals are confined within hurdles on arable land for the great good that they do, were hooves of destruction when they were allowed to wander at large over a depopulated countryside, for the country had (with the rest of the lighter lands of Norfolk that were suitable for sheep grazing) been practically cleared of human beings. The vegetation—the comparatively fragile vegetation of arable land which had been allowed to tumble down into grass—was overgrazed by the sheep, and trodden out by their sheep hooves. The same process may be seen going on in a hundred countries in Africa and Asia today.

At the beginning of this present century life in Breckland was at a very low ebb. Villages had all but disappeared. Thetford was a small impoverished town and the countryside was given over entirely to the pheasant cult, a cult that was as destructive to the land and its inhabitants as the cult of grazing sheep had been, for the one thing the pheasant-preserver does not want is *people*.

Tenant farmers scrabbled for their rent in the interstices between the more desolate brecks—their cropping plan compulsorily decided for them by their landlords to suit, not good farming, but game preservation. The sparsely covered open countryside moved and crept with rabbits, which were, in fact, the only profitable crop. (In 1922 the Forestry Commission had to kill 83,000 rabbits before they could plant trees in their first 6,000 acres.)

Where the gamekeepers would let them in it was a great place for naturalists. The great bustard lived here until 1838 when the last pair were shot, and the stone curlew, a lesser relative, still survives. There are still rare plants. The Spanish catchfly (*Silene otites*), the maiden pink (*Dianthus deltoides*), the field gentian (*Gentian campestris*) and the dwarf orchis (*Orchis ustulata*) are still to be found, and a friend of mine tells me that *Orchis militaris* is common in a certain wood but torture would not drag from him which one.

There are still corners of Breckland which convey an idea of what this countryside was like before the trees took over. Rolling, seldom quite flat but never hilly, with heather and ling and gorse and bracken and soft rabbit-cropped grass and sand-sedge, with occasional large fields of grey dusty soil planted with rye or perhaps with turnips or mangolds or nowadays sugar beet, with, on the better farms, sheep enclosed on turnips inside hurdles manuring the arable land and consolidating it beneficially with their hooves (in this case 'golden' ones), with tall grand Scots pines growing in belts or else grandly alone with spreading branches warped by the wind, with lonely, often ugly and box-like, flint farmhouses or gamekeepers' or warreners' cottages. A desolate countryside, but a countryside fiercely loved by its few inhabitants.

Now nearly all of it is completely altered. The Forestry Commis-

Barton Bendish
Beechamwell
Cockley Cley
South Pickenham
Ashill
Shipdham
Oxborough
Hall
Hilborough
Great Cressingham
WATTON B1108
Stoke Ferry
R. Wissey
Little Cressingham
Wayland Wood
Griston
Merton
Hall
Northwold
A1065
Thompson
Methwold
Tottington
Stow Bedon
Methwold Hithe
Cranwich
Lynford Hall
Stanford
Thompson Water
B R E C K L A N D
Mundford
West Wretham
Nickle Mere
Feltwell
Grimes Graves
East Wretham
Hockwold
Weeting Castle
B1106
B1110
Fowl Mere
Home Mere
Priory
Little Ouse
Santon Downham
Santon
Lang Mere
Ring Mere
BRANDON
A134
A1065
Brandon Park
B1107
St. Mary's Priory
Bridgham
Lakenheath
Castle
THETFORD
R. Thet
Lakenheath Warren
A134
A1088
A1066
Seven Hills
Eriswell
Elveden
Thetford Heath
Barnham
Euston Hall
Little Ouse
War Mem.
Barningham
Mildenhall
A11
A1101
Icklingham
Honington
Stanton
Barton Mills
Little Livermere
Troston
A143
Walsham le Willows
West Stow
Ampton
Great Livermere
Ixworth
Icknield Way
Ingham
Flempton
Hengrave
Fornham St. Genevève
Stowlangtoft
Fornham All Saints

0   miles   4

sion has planted over fifty thousand acres with Scots and Corsican pine. This may not sound much, but if you stand on an eminence in Breckland (such as the top of one of the Commission's fire-watch towers) you look over an apparently limitless expanse of dark green tree tops, and you might well imagine yourself in the pine forests of Poland or Pomerania. Pine trees are what you see and pine trees are *all* you see and as *far* as you can see. Down below you can, though not officially, walk along dark rides through the forest, and the bracken is a sickly green in the middle-aged forests and absent altogether in the older ones. You can wander all day, only occasionally crossing a road, and seldom do you get more than a glimpse of the sky and you are unlikely to see any other person. You will certainly meet red squirrels (grey have not arrived yet: East Anglia is still relatively free from them), you will probably meet a roe deer or two, very likely a herd of red deer, which are common, and you may see some crossbills in the trees—large finches which have their bills crossed to make them useful for extracting the seeds from pine cones. The flora and fauna of the pine forests is not very rich: few animals or plants can survive in that darkened land where the ground is a thick carpet of sterile pine needles. The most beautiful thing in Breckland, indeed one of the most beautiful in the world, is the golden pheasant (*Chrysolophus pictus*). I have seen five cocks together, a most rare sight, for although these birds are common, they are very retiring. In the forest dusk they seem to flame with a fantastical brilliance of vivid colour; their gold far outshines any precious metal.

The only way to see pristine pre-forest Breckland now is to brave the terrors of the **'Battle Area'**, west of East Wretham, although not legally, and not illegally either if the red flags and manned barriers show that the area is being used, for then we are likely to have a paratrooper land on our heads or—worse—a mortar bomb. Then also there is Thetford Heath south of Thetford, Lakenheath Warren, a beautiful but tiny area around Grime's Graves, apt to be invisible under sightseers in the summer time, and one or two other odd corners here and there. A fascinating feature are the meres. There is a scattering of these around the Wrethams, one at Stanford, one at Tottington, a fascinating little one at West Tofts (all in the Battle Area), lovely Thompson Water without it. The level of water in these is quite mysterious. Sometimes they are full—at other times a mere will quite suddenly empty. They seem to be governed by some unexplained movement of the water within the underlying chalk.

In the Battle Area are lost villages, empty and desolate and smashed by shell-fire. The only way you can visit them legally is to claim to be a native and die and be buried there. If the former inhabitants cannot return to them to live—at least they can go home after death, for funerals are allowed.

The great pine forest is broken here and there by rectangular clearings, generally some open land left around one of the far and few flint farmsteads. The Commission followed the enlightened practice of leaving such farms and smallholdings unplanted, and renting the houses and land to part-time forest workers who worked their holdings in their spare time. In spite of some failures there have been some successes; and scattered about the great forest are a number of successful and happy small farmers.

Thetford is a most fascinating small town.

It has a long history, and it is moving forward into future history with what local people insist on calling an 'overswill' scheme: London factories, together with their workers, moving down into the country. There are already factories and housing estates, but so far Cockneys and council houses seem fairly well swallowed up in the forests.

One of the oldest man-made erections in Thetford is the Castle. This is simply a mound, but a big one (it *was* 100 feet high and of 784 feet circumference at the base), there was once a parapet of clunch (chalk) round the top and wooden ramparts (now all gone), it is now a very steep hill up which children race and play, and it is crowned with great trees. A fairish view over Thetford and the forests may be had from the top of it.

Nobody knows the date of the castle, and modern research places the earliest occupation at Thetford in the 8th century. Camden identified Thetford with the town of Sitomagus, and believed that the Romans had heard of it in the 2nd century B.C., but was probably wrong.

Being at the point where the Icknield Way crosses the Little Ouse, which was navigable to there, it is likely that Thetford was of early importance, and the fact that little in the way of Roman or pre-Roman remains have been found does not rule out the possibility that both the Romans and the Celts may have used this place. There is no evidence to show that the huge castle mound was not originally Iron Age (although indeed there is no evidence to show that it was.

Thereafter the Anglo-Saxon Chronicle is full of references to the town, mostly references to the sacking and burning of it by the Danes which at least indicates that there was something there to sack and burn.

In 838 the Danes attacked the town and failed. There are eight tumuli at a place called the Slough, between Thetford and Rushford, where according to a folk tale, the dead from this battle are supposed to have been buried.

> *Hringmara heath*
> *Was a bed of death;*
> *Haarfager's heir*
> *Dealt slaughter there*

Hringaram is modern Ringmere. In 866 the Anglo-Saxons foolishly allowed the Danes to winter in Thetford, but before that, in 820, the Danes under Ingua and Hubba had made their attack and defeated King Edmund at the battle of Euston: the seven tumuli on the high ground west of Snarehill are where the Danes are said to have buried their dead while the Angles buried theirs at Barnham Cross Common.

In 871 the Danes again sacked Thetford. It was rebuilt by the late Anglo-Saxons in 873 but the Danes, under Sweyne, burnt it again in 1004, and again in 1011, and by 1012 the Danes had command over the whole of East Anglia. Sweyne, who was King of all the Danes, made Thetford his capital, and died there in 1014. In 1015 Canute, or Knut, made it his capital, and in his reign there was peace. In 1020 the nunnery and monastery of St George was founded in the town of Urius—Camden claims to celebrate the battle in which King Edmund was beaten.

And then came the Conquest, and for centuries Thetford retained a certain amount of importance.

Arfast, the Conqueror's chaplain and chancellor, deposed the Saxon bishop of East Anglia (Egelmar who had his seat at North Elmham), and chose Thetford to be his bishopric: he enlarged the church of Great St Mary to be his cathedral. He schemed hard to add the great abbey of Bury St Edmunds to his possessions: it was still under Saxon control and he hoped that he could depose the abbot as easily as he had done Bishop Egelmar. But the Conqueror would not let him. If Arfast had succeeded it is probable that the face of East Anglia would now be very different: Thetford might well have remained the chief city, and the capital instead of Norwich.

Galgagus, raised by William I, succeeded Arfast (the chronicler says that he was 'learned and benevolent'), and was himself succeeded by de Losinga, who, as we have seen, committed the sin of simony to achieve the bishopric, went to Rome to confess, and was ordered by the Pope to remove his see to Norwich, build the cathedral there, and incidentally new churches at King's Lynn and Great Yarmouth.

This removal of the seat of the bishop might have been expected to have dealt a great blow to the town, but strangely it did not. For by then Roger Bigod had founded the great Priory of Our Lady.

In 1107 Henry I held his court in Thetford, and laid the foundation stone of the priory with great ceremony. Roger Bigod died soon after. He had willed his body to be buried in his new priory, but Bishop de Losinga forcibly moved it to Norwich and had it buried there.

The priory was manned by Cluniac monks from Lewes, as indeed was the Priory of Castle Acre (p238). At first they used the cathedral of Great St Mary, recently vacated by the bishop, but in 1114 they were ready to move into their new buildings. And Thetford continued to flourish as a religious centre: the list of the names of great men who were buried there gives some idea of its importance:

Roger Bigod, 2nd Earl of Norfolk, buried in 1218 but removed to Norwich.

Hugh, son of the above, died 1225.

Roger, the 2nd Earl's second son, killed by a tilting spear 1269.

Roger, last of the Bigods and Earl Marshal of England, died 1306.

John Lord Mowbray, Duke of Norfolk and his Duchess, 1460.

John Lord Mowbray, Earl Warren, died 1470.

Sir John Howard, created Duke of Norfolk by Richard III and killed at Bosworth Field 1485.

Henry Fitzroy, son of Henry VIII, died 1536.

Thomas Howard, died in the Tower 1537.

In 1540 Thomas Howard the Duke of Norfolk and his wife Agnes, their son Thomas, and Henry Fitzroy, were dug up and removed to Framlingham, where we have seen their tombs. Thetford's day was over, and even the dead were deserting it.

But Thetford had retained its importance right up until this time, the Dissolution. John o' Gaunt founded an Augustinian priory there, at what is now Ford Place. Henry VIII granted the town a charter in 1534, but in 1539 he struck the mortal blow: he dissolved the priory, along with the rest of the monastic houses of England, and sold the buildings to the Duke of Norfolk who promptly pulled some of them down. But even so, the town continued to prosper for a few years, for when Queen Elizabeth I made a state visit to it on 25th August 1578, it was reported that there were still forty butchers trading there.

The death of the priory, and the other religious foundations, would not have proved a death blow to the town had it still been the centre of fertile and prosperous countryside. But the great raw wool boom had come and gone, the peasantry had been cleared away as the land had been enclosed for sheep, and the sheep had left the country-side a desert of drifting sand. Thetford never engaged in the great industry of weaving and finishing woollen cloth for export to the Continent: this trade went to Norwich and the East Suffolk towns: towns with a readier access to the ports from which ships sailed across the North Sea. Belatedly, in 1669, the Little Ouse was made reliably navigable to Thetford (it must have been navigable for shallow-draught at certain times before that) but by then King's Lynn, with which the town was thus connected, had declined as a Continental port though it was still busy as an entrepôt.

Thetford survived as a modest country town. There was a regular service of one train of Fen lighters to King's Lynn once a week, and with the coming of the railways in 1845 (Thetford is on the main London-Norwich line) more life returned to the place. In the early eighteen hundreds an attempt was made to turn it into a 'Chalybeate spa' and a book was written extolling the efficacy of the waters, but not much came of it.

What is there to see in Thetford today, of all the past grandeur and magnificence? Of the great Priory of Our Lady, to the north of the town, west of the railway station, once one of the 'most splendid speciments of Norman architecture this country could boast', little remains. Like the even greater abbey at Bury it was torn down after the Dissolution: after that event architecture was to glorify not God, but rich men. The Holkhams and the Ickworths were to be the great buildings of the future.

We have already looked at the other Cluniac foundation at Castle Acre, and there were similarities between the two buildings. Both were derived, in plan, from the second abbey church of Cluny—the mother house of the foundation. At Thetford was the same proliferation of blind arcading. The priory church, which was half as big as Norwich Cathedral (the nave was 121 feet long) has been excavated, and the foundations have been clearly revealed. As at the original Castle Acre church the chancel ended in a semi-circular apse, and there were chancel aisles each with apses too. But in the thirteenth century the chancel was lengthened eastward, thus eliminating the original apses (same story at Castle Acre only it happened there later) and a lady chapel was added—part of the window of which still remains. A chapel for the memorial to the 1st Duke of Norfolk was built on the north aisle in the fifteenth century and sacristies were erected late in the century. Outside the church a full range of monastic buildings was constructed, over many centuries.

Now only ragged-looking, at night rather ghostly, crags of flint remain, but to the imaginative they can convey something of the scale of what must have been a large and rich community. The remains are now cheek by jowl with a new bungalow estate, and to the west the forest presses in: only the fourteenth-century gatehouse, now mixed up with farm buildings, stands up high and proud.

Of other monastic remains in Thetford, at a place called the Canons, on the right of the road as you turn off to Brandon, stands what is left of the early twelfth-century Augustinian priory of St Sepulchre. There is a big flint barn not, however, part of the monastery, but few remains of the original work. What is left of John o' Gaunt's Nunnery and Monastery of St George is now a barn: there is still a fine arch, with Norman responds, so there was an older building there, with another blank arch in line with the east wall, and a large oblong building running north to south. It is all mixed up with a fine Tudor farmhouse. The Grammar School, a famous one, on the London Road, has at the back some Early English remains of a friary which was taken over by the Blackfriars in 1335.

The present town has charm, given it by plenty of flint building, also some good timber frame houses—the Bell Hotel is such, rambling and Tudor but recently much enlarged. The Ancient House, round the corner, is timber frame, now a museum, and it has in it one of the loveliest carved beam ceilings in existence. It is well worth going into the museum just to see this. Down by the river (or rivers, for here the Little Ouse is joined by the Thet) there is great charm, with a huge watermill of white brick, willow trees, swans and anglers. There is a pleasant no-man's-land between the two rivers.

There is a brilliant statue in front of King's House (behind which is a pleasant public garden) of Thetford's most brilliant son, Thomas Paine. It is given to few men to influence world history as much as this one did, by thinking, writing and talking. Paine was born at Thetford on the 29th January 1737, son of a Quaker staymaker, and was educated at the Free Grammar School. In 1774 he went to the American colonies at the suggestion of Benjamin Franklin, with whom he had been corresponding about scientific matters. It is inconceivable that a man such as Paine could have lived his life out under the Norfolk squirearchy: if America had not existed he would have had to have invented it.

He became editor of the *Pennsylvania Gazette*, and he published a pamphlet called 'Common Sense' which advocated the complete independence of the American colonies and the formation of a North American republic. This is said to have had great influence in expediting the American Revolution. After independence had come, in fact, the States voted him £500 and a grant of 500 acres of good land and appointed him Clerk to the Committee for Foreign Affairs.

But in 1787 he went to France, and thence back to England. There he published *The Rights of Man* in answer to Burke's *Some Reflections on the French Revolution* and to avoid subsequent action for sedition he had to go to France again.

He was met at Calais with great acclaim, and made a Citizen of the Republic. But he voted against the death sentence on the former French king, which annoyed the Jacobins so that in 1793 they immured him in the Luxembourg. After the fall of Robespierre he was released and published *The Age of Reason, Decline and Fall of the System of Finances in England* and *Agrarian Justice*, and his influence on France is said to have been as great as that on America. In 1802 he left France, as a protest at the Christian religion having been officially re-introduced, died in America, in 1809, and was buried on his own farm. William Cobbett, who much admired him, disinterred his remains and—at great trouble—brought them back to England to be buried here.

His statue, brilliantly gilt, was done by Charles Wheeler, President of the Royal Academy, and presented to Thetford by the Thomas Paine Society of the United States. It says much for the broad-mindedness of the burghers of Thetford that they have allowed it to be put there, though not without bitter controversy, for Paine was a Freethinker, and it can be said that to the Government of his country he was a traitor. But he was never a traitor to Humanity; and governments come and go. Thetford has given its name to a distinctive school of early medieval pottery: Thetford Ware.

A splendid long walk from Thetford is down the banks of the River Little Ouse to Brandon. Forests hem the little clear river and its narrow green valley in on both sides, the river is fine for canoeing, and there are ancient timber *stanches* at intervals: flash weirs of primitive design for taking the place of pound locks for navigation.

The river runs by **Santon**, where—as often happens in Breckland —there is a church with no village. The church is Victorian, but built on an ancient site and it still has original Early English components. There is a permanent camping site there, and an isolated farmhouse.

Santon Downham, farther downstream, was another of the dead villages of the Breckland; but it has been revived by the Forestry Commission, which has built an entire new village there, mostly of timber houses prefabricated in Scandinavia. It is fitting that the Commission should put up timber houses, but a little alarming that it should have to import them from Scandinavia. The old church is Norman, with two Saxon doorways, and if you approach the place not from the river but the road you find it deep in the forest, and down long avenues of marvellous old linden trees which clearly indicate that Breckland *can* grow other things besides Scots and Corsican pine!

Approached from the river Santon Downham has the aspect of a river settlement in some wild and foreign land. There is a big seed extraction plant, where most of the conifer seeds used in England are extracted from their cones by being placed on wires over hot pipes. There is a big timber-treating plant, where poles and posts are pressure-treated with creosote. In the old block of estate buildings left are the headquarters of the Thetford Chase section of the Forestry Commission. In the wooden hutted offices typewriters click, in the sheds and barns timber lorries come and go, tractors and mobile cranes come in for service, Her Majesty's Foresters, wearing their green coats, knee breeches, and Crown badges, come driving in in their Land-Rovers.

And here we might discuss the great new industry which has grown up in the Breck country. Planting started by the Commission in 1922, at the beginning of the great agricultural depression. At that time it was impossible for any farmer to make a living in Breckland, particularly as nearly all the farmers were tenants, and had to find their rent before they could think of anything else. Farmers and landowners were only too glad to sell their deserted fields to the Government.

Since that time new land has been taken over and planted up every year, first mostly with Scots pine but now more and more with Corsican which proves quicker growing in that climate. This Breckland climate has been described as Continental. The winters are very cold, the summers very hot, and the rainfall the lowest in England.

The forest is now over seventy square miles in extent, the second biggest in England, and an increasing harvest of timber is coming from it. The production is still mostly from thinnings, and goes for pit-props, fencing wood, pea-drying poles, or pulp wood; but already the first trees that were planted are forty-seven years old and some timber big enough for the saw-bench is being produced. As time goes on a larger and larger proportion of the crop will go to the sawmills to be sawn into planks. Surprisingly at first glance the Commission is already clear-felling some of its forests in Breckland, although the trees are immature. Surprisingly, until one realizes that to 'farm' a forest economically it is necessary to have some blocks of forest at every stage of growth, so that ultimately every year some mature timber is clear-felled, and every year another block is planted.

The young trees are planted with the spade in shallow plough furrows at the rate of 2,150 to the acre, and a good man will put in half an acre a day. In 1927—the peak year—eight million trees were planted in Breckland. After twenty years the first thinnings must be taken, about 350 trees are cut out of each acre. Thereafter there is a thinning about every five years until the mature trees are clear-felled eighty years after they were planted. This at least is what will happen to most of the forest.

Fire, in this land of long dry springs, is a great danger; and in the war years and before, great acreages of forest were lost to this cause. Now fire-fighting is so well organized, there is such a good network of forest roads, and such good watch is kept from on top of the many watch towers, that the risk is much smaller. But people should not smoke in the forests, and there should be no open fires at all.

Farther downstream we come to **Brandon**, a pretty little Suffolk town, or big village, built largely of flint. Most of what is there now probably grew up about the river navigation, for until the Little

Ouse was improved farther up, Brandon must have been the port of
Thetford. Now it is the centre of the new forest products industry.

The Produce Depot at Brandon may be one of the biggest in the
country: acres and acres of wood-piles. It has its own railway siding
built to rail pit-props to the Midland coal fields, but unfortunately
this is no longer used: such pit-props as go, now go by privately-
owned road transport on the overcrowded roads. As the forest
belongs to the Government, so do the Produce Depot, the railway
and the coal mines, it is a little difficult to see why this should be
so. Great quantities of pit-props still go, although unfortunately steel
is taking the place of wood in many collieries, and this market for tree
thinnings is smaller than it was. Most of the wood goes now for paper
or chip-board or pulp—to places as far away as Sunbury-on-Thames:
again, all of it by road.

South of Brandon is Brandon Park, wherein is a plantation of
Scots pines 145 years old, which are a magnificent sight. They are
busily and successfully regenerating themselves, and small trees are
growing up among them.

But perhaps the most interesting place in Brandon is an ugly pub
called the Flint Knappers Arms. In the back yard there are, indeed,
flint knappers, and they carry on a trade that was old in the Old
Stone Age, certainly one of the oldest industries in the world. Two
or three leather-aproned men sit behind a huge pile of flint chippings,
though not now all the year round, hitting big flints with their
hammers to strike off chippings for gun flints, or else dressing flints
into square blocks for building. To date the gun flints have mostly
gone to Africa, to supply the muzzle-loaders of poachers the length
and breadth of the continent. But more and more go to the United
States, to the 2,000 'Old Gun Clubs' in that country. The residue
of chippings is sent to Stoke-on-Trent to be ground up for pottery
bodies and glazes.

At the time of Waterloo there were twelve knappers working at
Brandon, and they were making a great deal of money, in fact they
were bringing great prosperity to the little town. The Battle of
Waterloo was won in the flint knapperies of Brandon rather than on
the playing fields of Eton.

While concerned with flint we might go north-east to **Grime's
Graves**: one of the most interesting places in England, and of the
world. Grime's Graves are a series of shallow circular depressions in
a 34 acre open space amid the pine forests, and why they are called

Grime's Graves nobody knows. In 1869 the Reverend Canon Greenwell, of Durham, dug down in one of the depressions to a depth of thirty-two feet and found that it was an old mine shaft that had been filled in. Among the rubble he found some bones of *Bos longifrons*, bones of both roe and red deer, a bone pin and an artistically worked piece of chalk. He gave it as his opinion that he had re-opened an ancient flint mine.

Later more shafts were opened up, and it was found that the shafts had been sunk through the chalk to what is known as the 'floor stone', a layer of enormous and very hard flints at a depth underground of about twenty-six feet. From the bottoms of the shafts tunnels had been driven out radially, and these roads or tunnels had connected with those from other shafts thus providing better ventilation. Eventually the area had become pock-marked with shafts, and honeycombed by the interconnecting galleries down below. The chalk hanging-wall would not support itself in big spans, and pillars of floor stone had had to be left to support it: a miner might wonder how many Stone Age men were trapped underground by roof falls while trying too greedily to 'rob the pillars'.

In the bottom of one shaft (and it was a shaft in barren ground: the floor stone happened to be absent at that point) a little idol of a fertility goddess was found behind a rude underground altar. It is thought that the miners were sacrificing to the Goddess of Fertility to ask her to intercede for a better crop of flint. Red deer antlers are to be found in profusion, and sharpened bones for picks: in one mine alone 200 antler picks were found, their points worn out or broken, and on some of them the actual fingerprints of the miners could be observed, as fresh as those of last night's burglar. Drawings on flint, of elks and other animals, were found: one wonders what more lies underground in wait for people who have the time to excavate farther.

There were 366 of these mines: a considerable army of full-time professional miners must have been engaged at this skilled and specialized job. And all this up to the late Neolithic periods—radio-carbon tests indicate 2100 BC—when some of us might think of men as 'cave men', and hardly higher than the apes.

The Ministry of Works now cares for the site, and two shafts are kept open for public inspection, one with a glass roof over it and an iron ladder down it to give access. It is a strange experience to climb down there, and see the apparently quite fresh marks of the antler-picks of the miners of four thousand years ago in the chalk, and crouch in the low galleries and imagine the Dawn Men, hacking away by the light of little lamps carved out of chalk, with animal fat for fuel. Surely it should be the aim of every miner to make the pilgrimage to Grime's Graves, the very cradle of his craft.

Weeting, in which parish the mines are, has the ruins of a castle in it, moat-surrounded and rather beautiful in its lovely parkland, not far from the little Decorated church. There are round barrows here also.

North through the forest, **Mundford** is a large and attractive village, though now rather spoiled, and east of it, at Lynford Hall, the Forestry Commission runs a Forester Training School. **Cranwich**, to westward towards Northwold, has a quite genuine Anglo-Saxon round tower to its church with a circular window and circular sound holes, possibly Norman; it stands in the middle of a huge circular churchyard—unkempt and tree-begirt. There are lovely parklands all along the River Wissey, which runs through a most beautiful valley, well worth following up. You may thus walk to **Hilborough**, but you may have to argue yourself past gamekeepers. Hilborough has a fine church.

A pleasant circuit to the east might be made, skirting the wild and forbidden Battle Area, through the Cressinghams, Watton, Merton, and on south.

Great Cressingham has a fine church, with several details exactly the same as the ones at Hilborough. It also has some remains of a sumptuous brick house used as a priory. **Little Cressingham** has the romantic ruins of a church, and some barrows nearby in one of which an Early Bronze Age burial was unearthed complete with a crouching skeleton, a gold plaque, amber and gold beads, bronze knife and dagger.

Merton is the home of the de Grey family, with Lord Walsingham at its head and Dick de Grey the popular manager of its lands and estates. There is a good brass in the church to a William de Grey, either late fifteenth or early sixteenth century, depicting William as a young and handsome knight in armour with his two wives and two large families of long-haired children. The church has a round Norman tower, on possibly Saxon foundations, stands prettily in the great park, and has a beautiful fourteenth-century nave. For a stranger to enter it is rather like entering a private house: it feels so much the private property of this ancient family. The nicest thing at Merton is the fine walled kitchen-garden, still worked by partially disabled ex-servicemen helped by a miniature tracked tractor.

Edward Fitzgerald died at Merton Rectory, while he was staying with his old friend George Crabbe, the grandson of the poet.

East Wretham is a farouche little village in wildest Breckland, with the very nice Dog and Partridge Inn, a large camp for soldiers training in the Battle Area, and one of the largest chicken-factories in England. For those whose stomachs are strong enough to take it, to visit this is an extraordinary experience. There are huge open-air duck farms nearby, to the eastward, where ducks live bereft of water.

Bridgham is a charming tiny riverine village, and the woods to the south of it demonstrate that oaks and hard woods can, indeed, be grown on Breckland soil, for there are some fine stands of oak underplanted with beech.

Garboldisham is a lovely big village with an attractive church, and some of the cottages there are built of *clay lump*, a building material once very common in south Norfolk and north Suffolk, consisting of large blocks of unfired clay, such as are known in Southern Africa as 'Kimberley brick'. It will last for ever, but only if kept dry. A section of Devil's Ditch runs to the west of the village: another of the various works of the Devil in this part of the world, although a more recent theory has it as Anglo-Saxon: a frontier work between East Anglia and Mercia. There are several unopened tumuli nearby (map, p173).

Euston, across the Little Ouse and thus in Suffolk, is an example of a village built entirely for the comfort and aggrandizement of one family. The place is perfectly preserved, with much thatch, much 'estate Gothic', and no jarring note. The village was moved to where it is in the seventeenth century because it spoiled the view, and thus the church was left standing out alone in the great park. The church is very interesting, having been almost completely rebuilt from medieval beginnings in 1676 by an architect obviously conversant with the churches of Christopher Wren: William Bell? It has period fittings and copper gilt plate.

The Hall, which is big enough to swallow up the entire village, church and all, and several neighbouring villages as well, stands in its enormous park behind the River Black Bourn which has been canalized to form a wide and placid ornamental waterway. The park and gardens were designed by Kent, of Holkham fame, the trees planted under the direction of John Evelyn in 1671, who was here years before Kent.

Lord Arlington, a member of the notorious Cabal ministry (he paid the king £10,000 to make him Lord Chamberlain), had the Hall built in the 1660s, but it was enlarged and altered in the 1750s to bring it more into line with the Palladian tradition.

The Hall passed to Henry FitzRoy, son of Charles II and the Duchess of Cleveland, the king's mistress. Charles created FitzRoy 1st Baron of Sudbury, then Viscount of Ipswich, then Earl of Euston, and finally Duke of Grafton; but he was killed at the siege of Cork by a stray bullet in 1690.

In his life Grafton was a great hunting man, and kept one pack of hounds at Euston and another at Croydon so that he could hunt while he was living in London. To reach the latter he had to cross the Thames by ferry, and this so annoyed him that he pushed a bill through Parliament to allow Westminster Bridge to be built.

The French traveller de la Rochefoucald dined at Euston in 1784, as he did in many other great houses through East Anglia, and he wrote thereafter: 'The sideboard is furnished with a number of chamber pots and it is common practice to relieve oneself whilst the rest are drinking; one has no kind of concealment and the practice strikes me as indecent.' The pictures of horses in the study are notable. The Hall is not open to the public.

Charles II used to stay at Euston, and his widow, Catherine of Braganza, lived there. Her confessor, Father Diaz, wrote: 'the place is very pretty, and has all the conveniences that we can desire, except that there are no cows.' Now there are cows.

Defoe said in 1722: 'a place capable of all that is pleasant and delightful in Nature, and improved by Art to every extreme that Nature is able to produce.'

Near Euston is **Honington**, now an airfield, and here was born Robert Bloomfield, the 'Suffolk Poet', on the 3rd of December 1766. His father was the village tailor and his mother kept the dame's school. He wrote *The Farmer's Boy* and *The Horkey*, besides much other verse, and was kept alive by subscriptions from local gentry. *The Farmer's Boy* gives a good insight into Suffolk country life of this period. The church has a good font, and Norman south doorway.

We may round off our tour of Breckland by a visit to **Elveden**, surely one of the more exotic phenomena of East Anglia.

Admiral Lord Keppel, who died in 1786, lived in the house that stood on the site of the present Sikh palace, and it was he who planted the wind-driven countryside with a positive chequerboard of wind breaks of Scots pines. In 1801 Lord Albemarle was living there, and farming no less than 4,000 sandy acres; but he sold the estate in 1813. A subsequent owner was the king of the Sikh nation Maharajah Duleep Singh.

The Maharajah, banished from his court at Lahore and from India by Queen Victoria for his part in the Sikh wars, was allowed to live his life out at Elveden, where he consoled himself, aided by the enormous wealth of the Punjab, by setting out to out-squire the English. He once—*himself*—shot 789 partridges in a day—*partridges*, and again 2,350 of these elusive birds in nine days. In one year over 19,000 pheasants were slaughtered by the guns on his estate.

In the 1860s he employed the Victorian-Gothic architect John Norton to turn the original modest Georgian mansion into a vast oriental palace with a copper dome, richly scalloped onion-shaped arches within, ornamented ceiling vaults, beaten-copper-covered doors, and tons and tons of Carrara marble intricately carved by Italian craftsmen imported into Elveden for the purpose. In importing Italian craftsmen, he was being faithful to the tradition of his ancestors: most of the great North Indian palace builders imported Italians for stone carving and mosaic work. There were 350 men working full time for three years on the place. The effect is fantastic.

After the Maharajah's death the wealth of the Liffey replaced that of the Ravi. Elveden was bought by the family that owned Guinness's Brewery. The Lord Iveagh of the time employed William Young to enlarge the place yet again, giving it a new Italianate front of brick with stone dressings, three stories high and with twenty-five bays, a massive domed portico, and yet more work inside, this time copied from the Taj Mahal!

As for the medieval parish church, the Maharajah, quite willing to flirt with Christianity, had already had a go at it, but Lord Iveagh really got down to the job. He employed the architect Caröe to add a north nave and chancel, and later a detached tower joined to the church by a roofed walk, or cloister. The tower has lavish flush-work —but every bit of the surface of the new work is so adorned with a lushness of completely unorthodox Neo-Gothic decoration that it looks like some fantastic film set. In fifty years' time it will no doubt be considered a gem.

The towering Corinthian column two miles down the Newmarket

road is a war memorial to the men of the estate. It is 113 feet high and has 148 steps and a view from the top.

As for the present Lord and Lady Iveagh, they sensibly live in a modest and comfortable house and leave the Sikh-Irish palace to its strange memories. Lord Iveagh farms, with the help of a huge staff, some 10,000 acres, keeps more than 2,600 cattle, grows 700 acres or so of sugar beet and has proved that cattle and alfalfa, or lucerne, are of great value in the reclaiming of the wasted soils of Breckland. He is farming very profitably where, since the Middle Ages, nobody thought farming was possible.

CHAPTER 17

Bury St Edmunds to Ickworth

To conclude an account of Suffolk, and not to sing the praises of Bury St Edmunds, would offend every creature of Suffolk birth; even at Ipswich, when I was praising that place, the very people of that town asked me if I did not think Bury St Edmunds the nicest town in the world.

As it was in Cobbett's day, it is now. **Bury St Edmunds** escaped the fate of Ipswich by not rising to undue prosperity in Victorian times. A wave of prosperity earlier, in the eighteenth century, fronted most of the earlier timber and lath and plaster buildings over with decent brick, or plaster inscribed to resemble stone; but there was none of that wholesale sweeping away of everything good, and replacing it with everything bad, that happened in the capital of East Suffolk. The eighteenth century was a good time for a town to be prosperous in: the nineteenth century, at least the last half of it, a bad. And what shall we say about the first half of the twentieth century? As for the second half, Bury becomes a London 'overswill' town, and is soon to be surrounded with mile upon mile of suburban-type dwellings, like a pearl in a bad oyster.

But Bury was great a very long time ago.

Sigebert, great-grandson of the pagan Wuffa—founder of the great Wuffinga dynasty that gave us Sutton Hoo—started a small monastery here in the seventh century. King Canute established a community of Benedictines in 1020, and from then on, until the Reformation, Bury was a town of the greatest importance.

It is strange that it was Canute, a Dane, who should have founded a monastery in honour of St Edmund, an English leader who was slain by the Danes. But then Canute was the first Dane who called

himself King of England; and what were the Danes but a later wave
of the Angles and Saxons who invaded England after the going of the
Romans? Wuffa, the first big-time English invader, after all came
from Sweden, via Angeln in Denmark.

King Edmund, later a saint, may have been crowned at Bures on
Christmas Day in about 850. He was influenced by the pacifism of
early Christianity, but when the Danes landed and began to ravage
his kingdom in that happy way they had he was at last, too late,

persuaded to rally an army and go and fight them. The army was
beaten, Edmund was captured, tortured and beheaded. Just why,
out of all the English beaten and killed by the Danes, he should have
been selected to be canonized remains something of a mystery.
Brithnoth had a much more heroic record, but was perhaps not so
saintly. But it is recorded, by Abbot of Fleury, who heard the story
from Dunstan, who heard it from the lips of Edmund's armour
bearer who actually saw him die, that the king refused to renounce
his faith, though scourged, shot full of arrows and finally beheaded;

and that the story of the armour bearer moved King Aethelstan to tears.

Edmund was killed in 870, at a place called Haegelisdun. One school of thought places this at Hoxne, another at Halgeston which existed near Sutton Hoo (the burial place of the Wuffinga kings) and which was mentioned in Domesday but which no longer exists, and another at Hellesdon near Norwich. A writer of 1100 says that the body was buried at Suthtune, now identified (by the Halgeston-believers) with Sutton. Personally I favour Hoxne, not because there seems to be a shred of evidence to indicate that Edmund was killed there, but because Hoxne has so little else to give it fame—why deprive it of this? They even have a plaque there to say that Edmund was killed under Goldbrook Bridge. They will show us an old tree from which arrow-heads were removed. And is there not that marvellous description of Edmund's martyrdom by the road-mender of Hoxne in *Suffolk Scene* by Julian Tennyson? And as for Halgeston—it no longer exits.

Edmund's head and body were flung into a wood, and later a wolf miraculously led the bereaved English to the spot and was found holding Edmund's head: hence the numerous carvings of a wolf and a head in Bury St Edmunds and other places which remember the saint (such as St Mary's, Hadleigh).

Thirty years after his death Edmund's remains were removed to what is now Bury St Edmunds but was then called Bedericsworth. Sweyn Forkbeard, Canute's father, was miraculously struck dead by the spirit of St Edmund (no longer pacifist apparently) in 1014 because he would have rifled the shrine. But his son Canute, Christianized, gave a charter of liberties to the shrine, Edward the Confessor gave great possessions, and the abbey rose to be one of the greatest in the kingdom, a goal of pilgrimage to people from all over Europe, and the Abbey Church a very great building.

And now what is left? 'Alas, how like an old osseous fragment, a broken blackened shinbone of the old dead ages, this bleak ruin looks out. It is dead now and dumb; but once it was alive and spake.' Thus Thomas Carlyle.

The Abbey Church was something of the shape of Ely, but slightly shorter (it was 505 feet long, Ely is 537). There is a painting, belonging to the borough, painted by an architect in 1880, which is supposed to show what the church looked like. Very possibly it does, more or less; although the artist's conception of the pre-Dissolution fields is far out: he has merely reproduced the post-Enclosure hedged fields that exist today (but which are rapidly being bull-dozed together to suit combine farming—we are going back to the 'open field' system with a vengeance). A reproduction of this painting hangs within the Abbey Gate.

The Normans, here as elsewhere, were forced to take over the English shrines and their saints, and they confirmed the liberty of the monks and did not even immediately replace the current abbot.

Abbot Baldwin, who died in 1097, built the eastern part of the church: the west end was completed under Abbot Samson in 1182.

Samson had a long struggle with King John, which the abbot won. In John's reign, or just after it, when the French Dauphin had landed in England to attempt to drive John off the throne, the sacred body of St Edmund was stolen, and taken to Toulouse, where it was recently unearthed—an entry in the Toulouse Abbey inventory giving away its whereabouts.

An intriguing situation has now arisen about this. Bones were discovered, and brought to England; but their authenticity was doubted and they were taken by the Duke of Norfolk to Arundel Castle and there they remain. In 1965 documents came to light indicating that they really were the bones of St Edmund. There are also some relics of St Edmund in the Roman Catholic Church.

The abbey was dissolved in 1538, and now little remains except some most romantic ruins in the midst of a pleasant public garden. There is a wooden shed in which can be seen (by permission of the Foreman of Works) several shelf loads of carved stone fragments. The despoilers made a thorough job, and the stones of the abbey are now to be found scattered about in domestic walls in Bury St Edmunds or, in greater quantity, buried in their foundations.

There have been recent excavations, and pointing of the un-covered stonework so as to preserve it, and the foundations of the monastic buildings can clearly be traced. There is a plaque, on the site of the High Altar, recording the fact that on 20th November 1214 the barons of England swore at this place that they would obtain from King John a ratification of Magna Carta. On 15th of June, the next year, they did so at Runnymede. The rose garden to the west of the cloisters was paid for from the proceeds of a book called *Suffolk Summer*, written by an American airman John Appleby of Arkansas. He achieved most notably that hard thing: an under-standing of the East Anglian character by a foreigner. Or was he a foreigner? The great majority of early English settlers to North America were East Anglians: perhaps John Appleby was an East Anglian come home?

There is the Norman Gate, next to St James's Church, a splendid campanile built by Anselm after 1120; there is the abbey gate—a lovely and yet massive example of the work of the Decorated period; there are some dwelling houses built into large lumps of the ruined west front of the Abbey Church in the eighteenth-century 'Gothick' manner; there is the Abbot's Bridge, late twelfth century, over the Lark (or Linnet?).

The town itself was laid out by the Normans (under Abbot Baldwin), and is an example of early town planning as is New Buckenham in Norfolk, and Ludlow in Shropshire. Like those other places (and New York) it is laid out on the grid system.

There are two great Perpendicular churches: St James and St Mary.

The latter is the finer of the two, although there is, indeed, a spacious magnificence about St James with its lovely arcades.

The nave of St James may well have been designed by John Wastell, who helped to complete King's College Chapel, Cambridge, and was a Bury man. The chancel was rebuilt by Scott in the 1860s. Both St James and St Mary are parish churches set in what was the perimeter of the old abbey. In 1914 a bishopric was created at Bury for the diocese of St Edmondsbury and Ipswich; and St James was chosen to be the cathedral. Currently large sums of money have been devoted to building late-Gothic-style accretions around it in an attempt to turn it physically as well as officially into a cathedral: a cloister has been constructed, a chancel and choir are built, a chapter house is to follow and there were grandiose plans for transepts and a hideous tower which have prudently been shelved owing to lack of enthusiasm from the people who were supposed to pay for it all. The new work is the object of much controversy. In a land as packed with Gothic architecture as East Anglia is it may seem unnecessary to add more, and much that is genuine and original will fall down if money cannot be spared for its maintenance.

The first window from the west in the south aisle is worth seeking out. It is Flemish and early sixteenth century, and depicts a 'Tree of Jesse'—always an intriguing subject—and the Story of Susanna and the Elders. The rest of the glass is Victorian, but good of its kind.

St Mary, just along the street, is a lovely church—inside and out it is breath-takingly beautiful, and it is a blessing that it was St James, and not it, that was chosen to be embellished as a 'cathedral'.

The piers of the arcades are slender and perfect, the angel roof of the nave is superb and original, the roof of the chancel has a blue and gold 'wagon roof' with carved bosses on its panels—one of them depicting that favourite subject of the medieval satirist: a fox in the guise of a priest preaching to poultry.

To the left of the altar is the tomb of Mary Tudor, sister of Henry VIII, and Queen-Dowager of France.

She died in 1533 and was buried in the Abbey Church, but moved here after the Dissolution. We have seen her, and her husband Brandon, disporting themselves in the woods around Butley Priory. The east window of the south wall shows scenes from her life: it was presented by a distant relation, Queen Victoria.

The Suffolk Regimental Chapel, in St Mary's, is the best thing of its kind in England, and was designed by Sir Ninian Comper in 1935. The Suffolk regiment was raised in 1685 as the 12th of Foot, was centre of the Line at Dettingen in 1743 (the last battle in which an English king took part), stormed Seringapatam in 1799, and the Suffolks can wear the Minden Rose. Now, alas, the regiment is merged with the new Royal Anglian Regiment and so has lost its identity. The depot is on the Newmarket Road and looks rather like a Beau Geste fort.

The Notyngham Porch of St Mary's is noteworthy, half-way along the north side of the church. It was built mid-fifteenth century and paid for by John Notyngham, a local grocer (but a grocer in those days was more an importer of food-stuffs than just a shop-keeper). The porch has a beautiful ceiling of fan tracery.

There is a memorial in the church to those who lost their lives aboard HM Troopship *Birkenhead*. She struck a reef just west of Danger Point off South Africa and went down with several hundred men. The troops were paraded on deck when it was seen that none could be saved, and the one or two survivors reported that not a man broke ranks until the ship had disappeared beneath the water. The bank that the ship struck is named after her, and is a famous place among Cape Town line fishermen for catching a kind of fish named the 'seventy-four' from its alleged resemblance to a 74-gun man-of-war (also kabaljau and steenbras).

In the churchyard, which is to my mind the most beautiful in any town of East Anglia, is a granite pillar commemorating the burning of fourteen Protestant martyrs.

In front of the Abbey Gate is Angel Hill, which would be a fine open space were it not for the fact that it has been turned into a vast car park.

The Angel Hotel, on the west side of the square, is a most splendid building, designed by Redgrave in 1779 but built on the site of an inn going back to 1452 for certain and probably far earlier, and named at different times the Castle, the Angel, and the Bear. The cellars of the building are very old indeed and have been well converted into a sort of crypt-restaurant, in which very good food and wine may be had.

The Athenaeum stands at the south end of the Hill, a rather plain Palladian building by Francis Sandys, that architect of another Palladian place—Ickworth. Plain it may be outside but it is sumptuous within; and nothing more incongruous can be imagined than an all-in wrestling match in the great Assembly Hall: sweat and bone crunching under the chandeliers. It was not always thus: we are told in Norman Scarfe's excellent guide that in 1818 great balls were held, attended by 'numbers of the first rank and fashion; but tradespeople, however respectable, are always rigorously excluded'. Balls are still held there—but more democratic.

At the other end of Angel Hill is a lovely Queen Anne house called Angel Corner, now used as a clock museum. Frederick Gershom Parkington left his collection of time measuring instruments, one of the best in the world, to Bury corporation as a memorial to his son who was killed in World War Two. There is a great array here of instruments of many kinds, from a perfect Tompion bracket clock (note particularly the engraving on the back plate) to such esoteric devices as a 'nocturnal' inscribed 'For both Bears', meaning, not that this instrument is designed for the use of bears in telling the time at night, but that it is so constructed that the time can be told by it from sighting at the Great and Little Bear constellations of stars.

Walking south we come to Honey Hill, a most distinguished place; with the old town house of the Earls of Bristol (just why people living at Ickworth, in the suburbs almost of the town, should also need a town house in Bury, is hard to discover). Now this is offices. There are several good Georgian buildings and a modern library, and the police headquarters—brand new—are in what I for one think one of the most successful modern buildings about.

Farther down is St Mary's Square, pleasantly Georgian and how nice it would be if the A45 did not go slap through it. When, oh when, is Bury St Edmunds going to be by-passed?

In Westgate Street is the Theatre Royal, the only Regency theatre left in England, built in 1819 to the design of William Wilkins. Famous in its day it was closed in 1925, used as a warehouse, but now miraculously restored and put to use again as a theatre by the St Edmundsbury Theatre Royal Trust. Its small size makes it doubtfully profitable to run as a theatre, but delightful to be entertained in. It is helped by grants, and by the enthusiasm of local theatre-lovers. It has professional and efficient stage machinery behind the curtain, and elegant décor in front, and so far since its restoration has had produced in it a series of well-acted and well-produced plays.

Not far away is the Roman Catholic church, built 1837 and said to be one of the earliest buildings in this country put up especially for this purpose since the Reformation. It is Grecian, all Grecian, and most elegant within. It is here that the bones of St Edmund will be lodged, if, indeed, they are not already lodged here now.

The centre of Bury, the central grid laid out so systematically by the Normans, is most attractive, with hardly a bad thing in it. The shop fronts, at least the old ones, are charming. Notice the sixteenth-century posts carved as Henry VIII with a lady friend in the chemist's shop in Abbeygate Street, and the frontage of Ridley's grocer's shop and the wine merchants in the seventeenth-century Cupola House. The chain stores will doubtless come but at the time of writing this is a lovely town, and is still here to be enjoyed. The old Tudor pubs, unspoiled inside and frequented by farmers and malting men and true East Anglian country folk, are so numerous that it would challenge the strongest liver to make a complete tour of them. The grey Woolpit brick, cold and unattractive though it may be in Victorian buildings, suits the urbanity of the late eighteenth century, and was used to clothe the old timber-framed houses, so that behind the civilized and precisely constructed fronts are rough Tudor interiors, with great oak beams, and beds that have to have wedges of wood shoved under one leg to make them stand level. The Town Hall, by Robert Adam, is famous; and for lovers of Renaissance building who do not mind the use of brick in what should so palpably be of stone it is most satisfying. The Old Corn Exchange (now the Library) and the new, hard by it, are also classical. Next is Boots the Chemist—a huge and grandiose Victorian-'Tudor' extravaganza, and just beyond it Stead and Simpson's, one of the most vulgar modern buildings you could find in England and in a key position too.

Round the corner is Market Square, with a bronze wounded soldier of the Boer War (we may well wonder now what he was wounded for) surrounded by the stalls of higglers. And Moyse's Hall, a superb Norman dwelling house and now the Bury Museum.

In the other direction, down Guildhall Street, is the Guildhall, with a thirteenth-century door and a fifteenth-century porch.

Bury has a big cattle market, and the largest sugar factory in England. It also has the biggest factory for the manufacture of 'malt extract', the substance that much beer is made out of nowadays instead of the whole malt.

Bury, in its greatness, was a cultural centre and produced many works of art. The twelfth-century 'Bury Bible' is one of the first examples of English illuminated manuscripts. A volume of it is in Corpus Christi Library, Cambridge. The Metropolitan Museum of New York recently paid £90,000 for the 'Suffolk Cross', made at Bury: a small ivory cross, exquisitely decorated with relief, but relief which depicts, alas, among other things, the gory and unlikely tale of the martyrdom of William of Norwich. This cross was offered to the British Museum; but the British, squeamish to the last, would have nothing to do with it suspecting that it might be stolen property so it had to go to America. It was made in the twelfth century for Bishop Samson.

Of famous men Bury has had several. Sir Francis Bacon was the son of Nicholas, the Abbey sheep Reeve.

A mere three miles from Bury, south-west, is **Horringer**, where stand the gates of **Ickworth**. Ickworth is the eighteenth-century English equivalent of one of the pyramids of Egypt, a vast monumental edifice put up by a very rich man for his self-glorification. And besides being a very grand neo-classical building, it contains a considerable collection of works of art. It would have housed a much larger collection had not its builder been captured by the troops of Napoleon, when that military man invaded Italy in 1798, and had all his artistic possessions taken away from him. As a place to live in—it hardly looks cosy; and the effort to *complete* it, to say nothing of having to maintain it, has been a drain on generation after generation of the Hervey family, and is now one on the National Trust (map, p321).

The Hervey family came into the Manor of Ickworth by marriage in 1485, and were among the families which managed to weather the storms of Reformation, Counter-Reformation, Commonwealth, and Restoration: each time with their estates not only intact, but expanded. A Hervey was created Earl of Bristol in 1714 because he supported the Protestant Succession, and he married not one, but two wealthy heiresses. His son John married Molly Lepell, Queen Caroline's beautiful and witty Maid of Honour and became a great favourite with the queen herself (he wrote vivid memoirs about it all). He became Vice Chamberlain and later Lord Privy Seal to George II, and his son became Lord Privy Seal to George III and also Minister at Turin and Ambassador to Spain and absentee Viceroy of Ireland. Much of the famous family silver was collected by him. His brother, who succeeded him, was a Vice-Admiral of the Blue and Viceroy of Ireland, and he also wrote memoirs of war afloat and love ashore, both of which activities he indulged in to the full. Yet a third brother succeeded him to the Earldom, Frederick Augustus; and it was this man who started the building of the present Hall in 1796.

Frederick Augustus Hervey, 4th Earl of Bristol, had received a bishopric or two in Ireland from the hands of his brother when the latter was Viceroy there, and had managed to extract no less than £20,000 a year out of the diocese of Derry. With this he was able to build a couple of grandiose houses in Ireland, both since pulled down, and travel extensively on the Continent. When his brother died and he came into the Earldom he added a further £20,000 to his annual income, was able to travel even more extensively (there are scores of 'Hotels Bristol' named after him in France and Italy), make his great collection of works of art which was confiscated by Napoleon, and build Ickworth Hall.

It was on a viist to his Suffolk estate in 1792 that the Earl-Bishop decided to build a mansion there, so he appointed an architect, Francis Sandys, and imported craftsmen from Italy.

He died in 1803, long before the mansion was completed, and he died not in one of his enormous houses but in the out-house of a wretched Italian peasant who would not admit the dying man into his dwelling because the latter was a heretic, and a bishop at that.

The 5th Earl was later created Marquess, grander yet; he completed the east wing of the house as a residence for himself, and he did enough to the great central Rotunda to make it suitable for entertaining. He thus reversed his father's plan, which was to live in the Rotunda, and use the wings as museums. The family moved into the house for the first time in 1830.

For over seventy years little further work was done to the enormous white elephant; but then the 4th Marquess married a railway heiress, Theodora Wythes, and she spent a great part of her fortune on trying to complete the house.

On the 4th Marquess's death, in 1956, the hall and park were taken over by the Government in lieu of death duties, and handed over to the National Trust. The present Marquess still lives in the east wing, and has recently been involved in an ambitious but so far abortive effort to turn his estate at Shotley, at the confluence of the rivers Stour and Orwell, into a vast bungalow estate and 'marina'.

This mansion (it is 600 feet long and 104 feet high—Ely Cathedral is 537 feet long and 215 feet high) is so hidden by great belts of tall trees that we do not see it until very close by. It then suddenly reveals its enormous bulk between the trees.

Entering the front door from the Ionic portico (itself bigger than many a house) we are treated to the sight of a man named Athamas engaged in throwing his children in the sea—their mother not unnaturally trying to restrain him. This is a group of statuary commissioned by the Earl-Bishop from Flaxman in 1790, in Rome, for 600 guineas. But before we go to look more closely at this we should observe the parallel scores on the end of the long table to the left on which guide books are sold, generally by the excellent Mr Honeyball who will take our three and sixpences. This table was brought up from the Servants' Hall in the basement, and the parallel scores are shove-ha'penny marks. It is instructive, by the way, to look at these basements (which are not normally open to the public), and to compare the amenities down there with those of the living quarters above.

On our left are the embroidered purses of the Privy Seal, which belonged to the two Herveys who held this office, and above them is a dashing portrait of John, Lord Hervey, father of the Earl-Bishop, depicted holding one of the privy-seal purses in his hand. Over the fireplace is the Earl-Bishop himself, by Angelica Kauffman, and other Herveys. High up above the stair-landing is St Jerome in the

Last Communion by Ribera after Domenicino. There is a baby carriage, and two sedan chairs which have, inside, a pungent odour of the eighteenth century.

To the right is the Dining-Room, with Herveys all round the walls, including Theodora as a child in the 1880s between her two daughters at about the same age, and very fresh and charming they look too and the paintings are typical period-pieces. One can almost hear their nanny calling them in for nursery-tea. The chandelier, of about 1820, came from the Bristols' London house in St James's Square, and there is massive silver on the table. One of the candelabra was presented in 1840 to the Marquess of the day by his tenants for waiving their rents during the hungry 1830s when they could not have paid them anyway. Note the four magnificent soup tureens. Two are Italian, and two are in the same style by Frederick Kandler.

The next room—we are walking round the Rotunda, which is really an oval—is the Library.

The segmental shape of this room, made necessary by the shape of the building, is disguised in some parts by four great marble pillars: not marble really, but scagliola, from Coade's Ornamental Stone and Scagliola Works in Lambeth. They cost £216 18s 0d in 1822. The curtains are fine: three pairs from the early nineteenth century by the Gainsborough Silk Weaving Company and two pairs replaced by the same company in the first years of this century. All these curtains were dyed with vegetable dyes, and the replacements are indistinguishable from the originals. The chair covers on the other hand were replaced more recently by the same firm, and were aniline dyed, and the difference is lamentable.

Besides much splendid furniture there is a most charming hawk in the Library—Ch'ien Lung and porcelain; there is a sensuous chimney piece by the Italian, Canova; and of paintings there is a portrait of a son of Philip IV of Spain by Velasquez—a tubby little boy with a dog, a splendid conversation piece of the 3rd Earl and Vice-Admiral of the Blue saying goodbye to his mother (née Molly Lepell) and his two sisters and their husbands before rejoining his ship which lies waiting in the background.

But the *pièce de résistance* is another conversation piece by Hogarth, of the Holland House Group: the Whig *cabal* that ran the Government of the day. Here are John Lord Hervey, the two Fox brothers, and my Lords Ilchester and Holland. A luckless parson, perched on a chair looking at a fat living in the background through a telescope,

is oblivious of the fact that Hogarth is having a little joke with him—
he is just about to topple into the lake. Evidently he was not
preferred after all. The chandelier in this room was added by Lady
Theodora in 1908.

As we walk into the Drawing-Room we face, at the other end of it,
Augustus John Hervey, the gallant Vice-Admiral whom we have
just seen taking leave of his mother. Painted by Gainsborough he
assumes a swaggering pose leaning on the fluke of an anchor,
standing on a sail, holding a telescope, and in front of a ship, lest
there can be any doubt as to his calling. Nearby, on a table, is a
Gainsborough of a most charming and sensitive boy, the Vice-
Admiral's natural son. Alas he was killed, at the tender age of
thirteen, while serving as a midshipman at the Siege of Gibraltar in
1782. There is another Gainsborough of a nephew of the Admiral's,
John Augustus. The Herveys were well served in having Gainsborough as their local portrait painter.

There is a Reynolds of Sir Charles Davers, muzzle-loader on arm
and dog leaping up at him, with his seat, Rushbrooke Hall, in the
background. It was the sister of this man who married the Earl-
Bishop, who apparently did not love her very much as he left her in
the old house at Ickworth and seldom saw her. Their daughter,
painted by Romney, leans on a harp and looks beautiful, soulful, and
very nice. There is a Lawrence of her husband.

There is a most lively portrait of the Earl-Bishop himself by his
very close friend Madame Vigee le Brun. He looks a merry bishop
indeed, and furthermore very likeable. There is a gay and summery
Lady Elizabeth Foster by Angelica Kauffman. She was the daughter
of the Earl-Bishop who later became the Duchess of Devonshire.

But the two really distinguished pieces of furniture are the two
eighteenth-century commodes, one each side of the fireplace. The
one on the right, which is Louis XV, is a flamboyant piece of work.
The overmantel has mosaic work made with marble from all over
Italy.

In the Ante-room to the East Corridor is a dinner service made in
China (Ch'ien Lung) and decorated with the arms of Augustus
Lord Hervey and his wife, née Drummond, made for their marriage
in 1779. This is an interesting result of the trade between England
and China in the eighteenth century: Chinese potters turning out
china to the design of English patrons, with English armorial
patterns on them: lease-lend for the Willow Pattern.

In the East Corridor are small family portraits (surely it must have been oppressive to have lived in a house so *covered* with representations of one's relatives?)—one or two of them simple, old, and charming, like that of Isabella Carr Hervey with a bird. There is, on a stand, a 'Boy and Dolphin' by Nollekeins. The story goes that Nollekeins used to make these and bury them and have them dug up again to sell to English Grand Tourists as unearthed antiques. There is also a copy of Le Sueur's statue of Charles I, such as used to have two removable heads—the correct one, of the Martyr King, for wearing when the Roundheads were not about, another for when they were.

In the Smoking Room, which now contains a state bed of William IV's time, is a Titian, 'Portrait of a Man', a lovely self-portrait by Madame Vigee le Brun of 1791, the friend, and some say mistress, who painted the Earl-Bishop in the drawing-room (and one admires the Bishop's taste on making friends with such a lady), and there is Benjamin West's hackneyed 'Death of Wolfe'. He reproduced this picture several times; with the faces of the people grouped about the dying hero varying according to whom he intended to sell the picture. There is Sir Robert Davers by Pompeo Battoni, in the full regalia of the Grand Tour, i.e. dressed up like Charles I, or a grown-up Little Lord Fauntleroy, with the various tools of the culture-hunter around him: the eighteenth-century equivalent of mini-camera, guide book, and sun-tan lotion.

At the end of the corridor are children's toys. A doll's school of 1800, with the wooden 'Dutch dolls' that were so soon to be replaced, alas, with those mawkish wax horrors that have offended sensitive Daddies ever since; there is a splendid Victorian grocer's shop; there is the Old Woman who lived in a Shoe; there is a clockwork frog which, wound up, hops every few minutes and which evidentally hopped once too often because it bears the teeth-marks of a Victorian dog, and there is a simple doll's house made in 1907 by Mr Marriott who lived in Horringer, nearby.

Back to the Rotunda we go across to the West Corridor. Here is the Bristol silver, one of the most dazzling private collections in the country. Among the serried ranks of sumptuously ornamented ware a quite unadorned but very beautiful silver stewpan of 1716 stands out like an honest man in a group of courtiers. And do not miss the wall cases containing majolica earthenware plates of about 1550.

The Pompeian Room, right at the end, is decorated in *trompe d'œil* style, the 'Pop Art' of the Romans, and later of the Italian Renaissance. Weird clear-cut architectural effects with an almost surrealist feel about them. The basis of these murals is a series of coloured engravings made from late classical frescoes for the Earl-Bishop: the central panels derive from the Villa Negroni on the Esquiline near Rome. John Dibdee Crace (the man incidentally who decorated the staircase of the National Gallery) introduced a nice touch here by using local Suffolk small birds and animals in the dado instead of classical creatures. Within the house is a big portfolio of watercolours of these motifs, peopled principally by voluptuous boys. Beyond the Pompeian Room is a collection of fans accumulated by Geraldine, wife of the 3rd Marquess.

Through the Pompeian Room we come to the Admiral's Room, hung with sea pieces by Dominic Serres of the third Earl's naval engagements. More of Serres' work can be seen at Melford Hall. Serres was a semi-official naval artist in the 1760s. Here are also two French 'love seats' of *c.* 1750 and a Louis XV lady's desk of exquisite delicacy and complete impracticability, signed by P. Roussel. Beyond the new Exhibition gallery in the old Engine Room is the Orangery, cool and green with semi-hardy trees.

The inside of the Rotunda has never been completed. It was meant to have a u-shaped staircase winding up the centre of the house and into the dome, but this was never built, and the present rectangular staircase by Arthur Blomfield is a compromise of 1908. There is a ceiling of glass on iron grids half-way up the dome—and above this great masses of raw and naked brickwork, reminiscent of Liverpool Street Station, support a huge inverted bowl of timber, built like a wooden ship, and with massive tie-beams to hold it together. An iron spiral ladder leads to the outside on top, and from the lantern above we get a great view over the Ickworth estates and beyond, and from here also we get an impression of the gigantic scale of this house, a scale more fitting for the capital of an American state than for the home of an English family.

The Tudor-Craigs, the charming and learned custodians of Ickworth, currently encourage many cultural activities in the house.

CHAPTER 18

North of Bury St Edmunds

East-nor'-East of Bury St Edmunds is **Pakenham**, notable for its two mills, one a water and one a windmill, and both working and grinding corn. The windmill is a tower mill (the latest and most developed type to be built before the end of windmills) and she has been completely restored by her owner, Mr Bryant, a grand miller and enthusiast, with help from the Historic Buildings Council, the County Council, and other bodies. Mr Bryant also has a notable collection of steam traction engines (map, p348).

Near Pakenham is Newe House, nicely Jacobean, and famous for the fact that 'American Reeve' lived here.

Reeve was a married smallholder of Pakenham, but he ran away with a young Pakenham girl to the USA. He went to Dodge City, ran a team of buffalo hunters and flayers (frequently killing a hundred buffalo a day with his own rifle) and made so much money out of the hides of these animals that he came back to England a rich man. Not content he bought a herd of Aberdeen Angus cattle, shipped them to the States, and drove them himself down the Chisholm Trail to sell to the ranchers to improve the blood of their Spanish longhorns. This proved profitable, and he brought out many another load, once having to jettison a whole flock of sheep in mid-Atlantic because the captain told him that the ship was sinking, and it was either sheep or ship.

He became famous in the West, dressing and acting the part; and it is reported that he would flick his pretty young mistress's ankles with his stock whip if he thought she was lifting her skirts too high while crossing the road and thus providing an unearned treat for the local loungers. When he had made a very big fortune he returned to Pakenham, went to the auction of Newe House, and dropped the first bid of £10,000: far higher than anybody else would have thought of going. He bought a London house also, in which his wife mostly lived (his first smallholding wife having died, he married his mistress), and settled down to being a country squire.

But although he bred pheasants with the best of them, the local gentry would not come and shoot them, and nor would they invite him to go and shoot their own feathered creatures. He was never 'accepted'. But he was extremely popular in the village, and small boys used to pepper the hedgerows with bottles and follow him about to watch him immolate these targets with his six-shooter as he rode about the lanes.

Packenham Rectory has a blocked-up window on which Rex Whistler painted a be-wigged eighteenth-century parson, sitting at his window looking out over the apple trees. Whistler was stationed near here and this was in payment for hospitality.

North we go to **Ixworth**, which is a great place for both bird and priory lovers. It is a beautiful place, near the edge of the Brecklands. There is a watermill, a long street of ancient and unselfconscious houses, a priory, and a waterfowl farm.

The latter belongs to Colonel Johnson MC, and is a most complete collection in a perfect setting—the birds in wire-netted paddocks all along the River Black Bourn. Over a hundred and twenty species are represented, from common barnyard ducks to black-necked swans at £50 the pair, and peafowl and ornamental pheasants, capercailzie and grouse. The place is a very considerable avian zoo, and there are Jacob and St Kilda sheep running about there too.

Ixworth was a Roman station, later the site of two Anglo-Saxon manors, and at the Conquest was handed over to the Blount family. The Blounts endowed a community of Augustinian canons, according to some accounts they started this in about 1100, according to other accounts 1170. At any rate it was a big enough priory to build a cruciform Norman church 220 feet long, very little of which now remains.

At the Dissolution Henry VIII, wishing to give his new wife Anne Boleyn a new toy, built Nonsuch for her; and as he wanted a certain site for this he had to dispossess the existing owners, the Coddington family. So he gave them Ixworth in exchange. As he had got Ixworth for nothing, by stealing it from the canons, he made a pretty good bargain.

After this Ixworth Abbey, as the place came to be known, had many owners, and the present ones run a small school in it for French girls, who may sometimes be seen flitting about the ruins. The present house, which is very large, is a great mixture of ages and styles. The owners show people around, and even serve teas at certain times of the year, and explain very charmingly and knowledgeably what there is to be explained. Ixworth Abbey is a very pleasant place to go and see (map, p277). **Ixworth Thorpe** church has good bench ends.

South-east to **Stowlangtoft**. Here you must go into the church, for the nine fifteenth-century Flemish carved wooden panels are not to be missed at any price. Bought from a junk shop in Ixworth for an old song by Henry Maitland Wilson, the then owner of the Hall, in 1850, these panels of oak, now set in somewhat reach-me-down frames in front of the altar, are most moving and beautiful. Note such tender details as the footprints of Jesus on the ground behind him, as he leaves the earth in his ascension! These panels repay close study, and time should be set aside for them: they are very remarkable.

The late fifteenth-century carved bench-ends are noteworthy. There are over sixty carved figures in all, most lively and sensitively done. Note especially the 'owl-man', a pig playing a harp, and a man with pen and ink who is supposed to represent 'scandal'; and there are many birds and animals. There is a fine iron-bound door to the belfry. The church outside has chequered flush-work, and is very clean-cut and block-like. It looks good from the west, from the Vicarage garden, with a huge cedar before its tower (map, p277).

Church lovers should go north to **Stanton** and south to **Norton**, the former for fourteenth-century tomb canopy, the latter for its font (map, pp277 and 349).

Walsham-le-Willows is as attractive as its name; and a useful place to go if you are a farmer looking for cheap materials, for here is a big dealer in Government-surplus stores. There is said to be an ancient carving of a man with his head trapped under a portcullis under the book-rest of one of the stalls in the church, but you need a light to see it and I have never had one.

North is **Wattisfield**, which had a pottery in Roman times and still has one. A Roman kiln, unearthed nearby, can still be seen in Henry Watson's Pottery, and there is reason to believe that pottery was made here long before the Romans: by the Beaker Folk in fact, 4,000 years ago. The Watsons once built a kiln on the Roman model and fired Roman-type pots in it, in conjunction with Ipswich Museum. Their present pottery is a very modern affair though, using much refined clay from Stoke-on-Trent for their more finished articles, but local clay for their great variety of garden ornaments. The family will take people around, but it is best to telephone them first: Walsham-le-Willows 239.

Barningham Church should be visited for its bench-ends, and for its screen.

Troston has a very fine Elizabethan Hall. This was the home of Edward Lefft who was an editor of Shakespeare and published a ten volume edition of the Plays. His nephew, Capel Lefft, helped the poor village poet Bloomfield (see Honington) and also helped Wilberforce put an end to the slave trade. The church has a good Early English chancel, faded but evocative paintings around the wall, and the remains of a rood loft.

The **Livermeres** (Great and Little) were bought by a Baptist who won a state lottery in 1722 and they have a grand park with a fine mere for waterfowl. Skeat claims that the name Livermere comes from *laefer*, meaning the plant known as a flag, or flag-iris (map, p277). Beside the mere are the melancholy remains of what was a 'Strawberry Hill Gothic' church: the only one in West Suffolk.

Ampton Hall, over the water, was the home of Captain Robert Fitzroy RN, who in 1828 sailed in HMS *Beagle* on the first of his two voyages to explore the Magellan Straits. On the second of these he took Charles Darwin. Fitzroy captured some Tierra del Fuegans and brought them back to England. He became very attached to one girl child, and was heart-broken when she died. The remainder he took back on his second voyage, with some missionaries, but the natives robbed the missionaries and left them destitute and the mission was not a success. Fitzroy was the first weather-forecaster, and a father of meteorology.

There are many fine Calthorpe monuments in the church, and Chilean pines ('Monkey puzzles'), cork trees and tulip trees among the more ordinary specimens in the fine woods. The village is very pretty.

Ingham has a Roman graveyard, which was brought to light when the railway was cut through it. The railway is now a ghost, too (map, p277).

West Stow Hall has a splendid gatehouse of brick, built in the 150s by Sir John Crofts, Master of Horse to Mary Tudor, in the

English style of building the classical style of the Renaissance. In a room above the gateway are murals, including a hunter carrying an enormous hare with the writing 'Thus do I all the day', a man embracing a wench with 'Thus do I while I may', an older man watching him saying 'Thus did I while I might', and a very old man: 'Good Lord, will this world last for ever?' A sequence hardly likely to cheer us up.

The ground around West Stow is almost indecently full of Iron Age, Roman, and Saxon remains. There was a big first-century Roman pottery on the Lark, a mile upstream from West Stow (map, p277). At the time of writing Mr Stanley West is excavating a pagan Saxon village of some seventy houses covering five and a half acres.

The **River Lark** was made navigable to Bury St Edmunds, and there are still locks along it. It is still navigable as far as Isleham for vessels of 88 feet length, 14 feet 6 inches beam and 4 feet 6 inches draught, and above Isleham for vessels of 2 feet 6 inches draught.

North-west across the heathland is **Icklingham** (all these places the names of which start Ick or Ix are near the Icknield Way), and to this place we must go to look at one of its two churches: All Saints. St James is dull.

All Saints is thatched, large, and very impressive. On Norman foundations (there are blocked Norman windows to the north) the church is predominantly early fourteenth century with a most beautiful east window to the south aisle and near it a cinquefoiled piscina and two elaborate niches. The south aisle is very wide, the floor of the church is tiled and bare, the few benches are ancient and rude, there are ancient hassocks to kneel on cut out of reed turf from the fen! The church is virtually unrestored (the Victorians let themselves go on St James's) except for the glass in the east window, and the place seems to speak of an older, grander, simpler, and more fundamental religion. This church was not built to the glory of Man. It has fine architecture, uncluttered by trivialities. There are fourteenth-century tiles in the chancel and a sumptuous chest bound with wrought-iron by some master blacksmith of that time. On a smaller scale it has something of the bareness and simplicity of Blythburgh.

We may now take the right fork to Lakenheath, another of the 'shoreline' settlements between Fen and Breckland.

Just north of Lakenheath we find the great modern **Cut-off Drain**, and across this out towards the Fen a tiny pub called High Bridge—and high the bridge beside it is—all of five feet above sea-level. This pub was once a roistering resort of Fen lightermen, for they brought their floating trains up the Eriswell Lode from the Little Ouse, to Lakenheath which was then a port. Now, since the opening of the Cut-off Drain, the Lode is dry, but the little pub carries on and is a good place to go and have a drink. Farther out into the great sea-bed of the Fens is Burnt Fen, so named because it really did burn, for years. Once the black peat is ignited it is very hard to put it out. Feltwell Anchor, miles out there if you can find it and nowhere near Feltwell, is the loneliest little pub in the world. I have not been to it for several years but hope that it is still there and unchanged.

Lakenheath is next to the biggest American airbase in all East Anglia, and in many ways the little town is transatlantic. Like the other towns and villages of the 'Breckland Shore' it is built of a strange mixture of old brick, chalk 'clunch', flint, carr stone and limestone—the limestone having been carried by water to it down the River Nene and across the Middle Level. Note the wall of the churchyard to the north with its enormous flints: such as we have seen in the 'floor stone' down the flint mines called Grime's Graves. The tower of the church is a fantastic geological mixture: the base limestone—the rest a cocktail. The west end of the nave is topped with that unfortunate Woolpit brown brick (which the Earl-Bishop of Ickworth called 'a brick that looks like a sick, pale, *jaundiced* red brick, that would be red brick if it could . . .' The south aisle has lots of carr stone, and I have read that there is a septaria in the chancel. It is as though the builders, over their many centuries, just shoved in whatever came most handy.

As for the church as a building, it is one of the most interesting in Suffolk (map, p277).

St Etheldreda owned the church in the seventh century, but the earliest part of the building that we can recognize now is Norman: the chancel arch that was probably the west arch of a crossing tower. The chancel is Early English (thirteenth century), the base of the tower very early Decorated (maybe end of thirteenth century) and so we may assume that the Norman crossing tower fell, or was pulled down, late in the twelve hundreds.

The roof is most famous, and may have been done by the same master carpenter as those other 'shore' churches: Methwold and Mildenhall. There are sixty wooden angels up there, sixteenth century, and stone angels on the corbels which support it. Take field glasses if you have them—it is a sumptuous roof. There is woodwork down below, too: a fifteenth-century pulpit mounted on a stem, most rare bench-ends with acrobats and giant fish, and that silly tiger who gazed into a looking-glass either from the sheer vanity of looking at her own reflection, or thinking she could see her cubs there, while zoo-questers of the ages gone took her real cubs away from her. The font is the choicest thirteenth-century font in England and there is a wall painting of St Edmund, and scenes from the life of Christ— all growing organically out of a tree.

Numerous Kitcheners are buried outside the church; and inside is an inscription to the Lord Kitchener of the First World War.

During the Peasant Rising of 1381 (for which see under North Walsham, p149) John of Lakenheath and Chief Justice Cavendish were killed near here by the rebels, together with the Prior of Bury Abbey, and their heads stuck on the ramparts of Bury St Edmunds. Cavendish nearly escaped by jumping into a boat on the Fens, but before he managed to get into the vessel a woman pushed it away from the shore with her feet and he was apprehended. It was Cavendish who was trying with great severity to enforce the Statute of Labourers, which was passed after the Black Death to prevent the surviving peasants from exploiting their scarcity value.

We may now go south to the old river port of **Mildenhall**. But to see one of the glories of this place we will have to go to the British Museum, for here is exhibited the Mildenhall Treasure, turned up in a field by a ploughman during the war: a collection of late Roman silver dishes, most perfectly preserved. A glory that has not yet been removed to the Museum is the church, an even grander one than that of Lakenheath, 170 feet long, tower 120 feet high, and with a roof of carved timber that beggars description.

The chancel and north chapel are Early English. The east window is Decorated, most strange, and in fact quite unique. It has been much praised, but for me, alas, it does not quite come off. I can imagine it in a Victorian railway station, surrounded by red brick. There is a great north porch with a Lady Chapel over it, as at Fordham. Walk around the church outside to look at the stone carving.

But it is that roof inside that is so marvellous, lavishly carved, and the whole vault above us seemingly filled with angels. The angels are said to be riddled with the shot of the Puritans—what could they have thought they were achieving? The roofs of the aisle, too, are superb: that of the north aisle a surpassing masterpiece of medieval wood carving, and in the south aisle are the swan and antelope of Henry V, saints, birds and beasts galore: the sublime mixing on the happiest of terms with the humorous and the farcical. To me this church far surpasses in interest and beauty many of the far more famous and no doubt more 'perfect' churches of the 'wool villages' in the south of the county.

Under the tower is the altar-tomb of Sir Henry de Barton, Lord Mayor of London in the year after Agincourt. He is said to have been the instigator of London's street lighting, and he fathered this very simply by ordering people to hang lanterns outside their houses after dark. There are other interesting tombs, for Mildenhall was once a great deal more important than it is now. There is still a lively street market, around a market cross said to be sixteenth century.

Down by the River Lark is a great mill, still working although not driven by water, and a gas-works with a certain period charm. Beside it is the old navigable river with a lock pen, now, unfortunately and most reprehensibly, closed to navigation by having been shut off with a fixed weir. Let us hope that before long the authorities will be found with enough sense to open the river for navigation again as far as Bury St Edmunds. At High Lodge, near Mildenhall, a late Clactonian Palaeolithic site was recently re-excavated by the British Museum.

At **Worlington** (Early English chancel) is the Worlington Herd of Pedigree Welsh Pigs (Messrs C. R. Reeder and Son), reminding us that the modern 'Welsh' pig has been much modified by East Anglian breeders, who were the first to cross it judiciously with the Swedish Landrace to give it that extra length beloved of the bacon curer, and to produce that most excellent animal for the outdoor pig keeper: a long white pig, hardy, the ears of which hang over its eyes and prevent it from fence-breaking by obscuring its vision.

Barton Mills has the fine Bull Inn beside its bridge, and the Rev. Tylor Whittle informs me that *Orchis militaris* grows in a wood near here but wild horses will not drag from him which wood.

After the Reformation the Manor of Barton Mills came into the hands of the Steward family, a member of which, Elizabeth, married the corn reeve of Ely to become the mother of Oliver Cromwell. Barton Mills may not seem to be in the centre of world politics now;

but in the thirteenth century it had for its rector Jacobus de Scabellis, or Savelli, who became a cardinal, a papal prefect, and ultimately Pope Honorius IV. By then he was so racked with gout that he had to have a mechanical contrivance to raise his hands up at the moment of the Elevation of the Host. The living of Barton Mills is in gift of the Crown and is peculiar in that the rector is not under the bishop of the diocese in which his parish lies.

Back along the main road towards Bury we get **Flempton** (map, p277) which once had a parson named Mr Blastus Godly and still has a west window celebrating the reception of Queen Victoria in Heaven, and then **Hengrave**, with an important house (map, p277). Hengrave Hall is now the Convent of the Assumption, and a school for Roman Catholic young ladies whose parents can afford it. By arrangement by telephone it is possible to be shown over the Hall, and its accompanying church, and as the nuns who show visitors around are most charming it can be a very pleasant experience. You approach the Hall through a plantation of fiercely pollarded lime trees, about thirty-five years old, which make an impressive sight and a strange pattern when looked upon from the windows of the Hall above. There is an avenue among the limes called 'The Nuns' Walk', because during the French Revolution the Gages, who lived here, lent the Hall to the refugee canonesses of St Augustine, from Bruges. The superior of this community incidentally was Mother More, a direct descendant of Sir Thomas.

Hengrave Hall was one of the great houses of England held by a recusant family; and Mary Tudor came to it during her flight from Wimpole on her way to Framlingham, before she secured the crown. In Thomas Kytson's time, however, when Elizabeth I stayed at the Hall, she knighted Thomas on condition that he promised to end his recusancy, and accept the Church of England. He promised all right, but back-slid, and his wife even went to prison for recusancy.

Penelope, a daughter of the family who was courted all at the same time by no less than three men, contrived to marry them all: one at a time, of course. They were Sir George Trenchard, Sir John Gage and Sir William Hervey whose picture we saw at Ickworth. Hengrave passed to her second husband's son, thus to the Gage family. Edward Gage was made a baronet by Charles II, and Gages held Hengrave for nine generations and were all Roman Catholics. Their motto was '*Bon temps viendra*'. The Gages ended, the Hall was sold and after passing through the hands of several owners is in

Catholic hands again and as we have seen a convent and a girls' school.

The house, of stone and brick, was built by Sir Thomas Kytson between 1525 and 1538 and it cost him £3000. The south front of the house is magnificent Tudor, with mitred turrets similar to those on top of King's College Chapel, and has a fine bay window over the doorway (dated 1538) on which are painted in florid colour and sumptuously carved the arms of the Kytsons, which include three fish: not, we are told, because the Kytsons, although City merchants, were fishmongers; but because the family held some ancient rights of fishery in the River Lark.

This bay window, as indeed most of the house, is pure Gothic in feeling; but the coming of the Renaissance is felt in the treatment of the coat of arms, and the putti that support it.

Inside the house is an enclosed courtyard surrounded on three sides by cloisters. The courtyard has a pretty wrought-iron Etruscan well-head, with a lady and a unicorn with its head on her lap.

The glory of the house is the Oratory, still used by the nuns, which has one of the most beautiful and complete stained glass windows in East Anglia. The glass is of 1527 and later, Gothic in feeling (we remember again that this was a Roman household—not given to embracing too readily Renaissance ideas) and it does repay close study.

The bedrooms upstairs all have names, and one is named 'Wilbye'. Here lived John Wilbye, the man born in Diss in 1574 who composed madrigals which are still popular today. There is a great room on the north-east side of the house (the occupants call it north) with a rather macabre Elizabethan design around the fireplace, of mysterious origin and unpleasant effect. But the visitor, unless a burglar, is unlikely to enter this house without the escort of one of the charming inmates, so I will describe no more.

The little church, right up against the house, has a Saxon tower. The rest of it was added to the tower towards the end of the fourteenth century by Sir Thomas de Hengrave and his mother, and the Lady Chapel was added in 1540. The little church is notable for its monuments, which remained undesecrated throughout the iconoclastic ages because this was no longer a public church then but a private family one. Now it is the church of the convent. The fine arcades, the miniature clerestory, the slightly skew-whiff appearance of the chancel arch, give the building an unusual and beautiful appearance; as does the fact that it is in use as a Catholic place of worship and therefore richly decorated. There are engaging angels on the capitals of the north arcade, a piscina in the porch, with ist own little arch, and the family monuments are noteworthy, but self-explanatory. There is a hopeful poem on the tomb of Thomas Darcy.

On the road to Bury there are **the three Fornhams**: All Saints, St Genevieve, and St Martin's. Little remains of St Genevieve, save the memory of the battle between Beaumont, Earl of Leicester, Hugh Bigod, and ten thousand imported Flemish mercenaries on the one hand, and the king's troops under Humphrey Bohun, the King's Constable, on the other. Hugh Bigod got away, of course, but the Flemings perished, it is said to a man. Whether they did or not, bones, weapons and pennies of Henry II's time have certainly been dug up here, and when in 1826 a great pollarded willow was over-thrown forty skeletons were unearthed beneath it, lying face upwards in a circle, their feet towards the centre, and their skulls showing traces of violent death. Also found at this time was a gold ring with a ruby in it.

Fornham St Martin has a village hall presented to the village by the Sultan of Johore, who was a great friend of the Squire.

Fornham All Saints has a fine range of flint farm buildings at the cross-roads, with freestone inserts, and some not undistinguished Neo-Georgian council houses, another very pretty farmhouse painted Suffolk-pink, and a very workmanlike row of long thatched cottages. There are many things of interest in the church, such as carved heads in the stonework, gargoyles, nice poppyheads, and the comforting thought that on Saturday, the 2nd of June 1927, in 2 hours and 50 minutes, a Peal of Grandsire Doubles of 5,040 changes, being 42 six-scores in ten different callings, was rung on the bells.

CHAPTER 19

South West Suffolk

West of Bury St Edmunds, past orchards is **Little Saxham** which has a splendid Norman round tower to its church and also a curious modernized house with its lawn running down, fenceless, to the roadside like an American 'yard'. **Great Saxham** has good foreign sixteenth-century glass in its east window, and a memorial to John Eldred, the fabulous merchant adventurer who lived in Nutmeg Hall nearby, and whose adventures we have described under New Buckenham where he was born. Saxham Hall (1779–88) has an Angelica Kauffman ceiling and a Moorish temple.

Heading for Barrow we find ourselves coming into splendid country, hilly and wooded, but a country of large farms and rich men. This is the northern and western edge of the high country of south-west Suffolk.

Barrow has, so far as I know, England's only lady hurdle-maker, and it also has Mr Arthur Valliant, who will paint you a picture of a horse or a dog rivalling the work of Grandma Moses if you give him a photograph to work from. He is sometimes to be found in the Horseshoes. Barrow has Broom's Barn Experimental Station which is an offshoot of Rothampstead and where research into sugar-beet culture is carried out. The buildings are modern, and of good design, with good big pitched roofs (the flat roof is alien to East Anglia and quite unsuitable to our climate). The original Broom's Farm, incidentally, was used as a small-pox hospital in 1882.

The brick tower standing so forlornly opposite the Weeping Willow is all that remains of a Salvation Army Citadel. The housing estate of tile-hung houses near the village was erected in fifteen weeks flat by T. H. Johnson (Building Systems Ltd) of Doncaster. Tile-hung walls are a South-of-the-Thames expedient, and have nothing whatever to do with East Anglia, except where introduced by people who ought to know better.

There is a map of Barrow in 1597 in the County Records Office at Bury, often studied by people interested in the Open Field System.

The land was divided into *furlonges* which were approximately 200 yards square, and the furlonges into strips 22 yards wide. The strip was what a team of oxen could plough in a day, and was thus long in order to save the bother of turning the long team too often. The furlonges on this map have names like 'Nether Lightly', 'Wallopes Wentte' and 'Priests Pightel'.

Dalham is a little show village, and now we are getting near Newmarket where are rich people, and show villages abound. Dalham runs along both banks of the River Kennet, there are green strips along the banks with little white footbridges over and the whole place is too pretty for words. There are two mills, neither working, and one is a smock mill.

At **Moulton**, north, and another pretty Surrey-like village, is a famous pack-horse bridge, spanning a stream in which there is hardly any water. The size of the bridge, which is fifteenth century, shows that there was much more water once and is yet another sign of the desiccation of East Anglian streams. There is another fifteenth-century bridge in the village, farther up.

Kentford is unfortunately pierced by the A45, but the church is fine Decorated, up on a high bank, though the visitor is unlikely to go and see it for there is nowhere nearby where he can park his horseless carriage. Here is the *Small Animals Centre* of the Animal Health Trust.

And so we come, across the famous Heath, to **Newmarket**. The great industry of Newmarket is catering for absentee horse owners. A person buys a race horse (or more often has one bought for him or her by somebody who knows how to do it), and places the horse with a Newmarket trainer. The owner may see his horse several times a year—he may see it more seldom: it is most unlikely that he will ever ride upon its back. The trainer enters the horse for various races up and down the country, and the horse sometimes wins, and sometimes loses; but in the nature of things, there being more than two horses in each race, it most probably loses. If it wins the owner may make some money, if it loses he will certainly lose some; but whether it wins or loses he will certainly be faced with a hefty weekly bill for its training and upkeep.

Newmarket was new, indeed, in 1227, when the old market, down at Exning, was closed up because of a plague. The place rose to great wealth and fame in Charles II's time owing to the passion for racing of that monarch, but James I had come there before him to hunt, hawk, course and race.

The Earl of Bath, writing in 1753, conveys something of the excitement that the sport of horse-racing has for its addicts:

Now the contention becomes animating; 'tis delightful to see two, or sometimes more, of the most beautiful animals of creation struggling for superiority, stretching every muscle and sinew to obtain the prize and win the goal! To observe the skill and

address of the riders, who are all distinguished by different colours
of white, blue, green, red, or yellow, sometimes spurring and
whipping, sometimes checking and pulling to give fresh breath
and courage! And it is sometimes observed that the race is won as
much by the dexterity of the rider, as by the vigour and fleetness
of the animal.

James I built the King's House here, and conferred no less than
ninety-nine knighthoods in the intervals of his sporting activities.
Charles II built a great house which was pulled down to make way
for the present Congregational Chapel: a notable change of use. The
Rutland Arms is still there, a noble coaching inn (this was on the
main road between Norwich and London, and Norwich and Cambridge, and so an important staging post). Otherwise there is little of
architectural interest, unless we are interested in the great flowering
of pseudo-Tudor in the reigns of Edward VII and George V, and in
very large and expensive-looking villas put up by sporting gentlemen.
Newmarket is a landlocked Cowes. The Jockey Club, by Richardson,
is admired.

The Devil's Dike offers traditionally the only free grandstand
view of the racing. Small aeroplanes come and go with great
frequency all during race meetings—taking highly-paid jockeys from
one meeting to another up and down the country. The juke-box
cafés in the town are filled with 'stable lads', who are a race apart,
and the Rutland Arms is patronized by tweed-clad trainers and
senior jockeys.

If you go early in the morning to the heathland slopes to the west
and north-west of the town you will see some hundreds of stable lads,
all looking much alike, riding an equivalent number of horses, all
looking exactly alike. They are going for their morning training
walks. There is a statue of a horse on the Snailwell Road, and one
expects to see little votive offerings of oats placed before it. At
Tattersalls, the great sale ring over towards the station, if you hear
the auctioneer saying 'fifteen' he does not mean fifteen *hundred*
guineas. He means *thousand*. This tip may save you a lot of money if
you are thinking of buying a horse.

Exning, north-west, is now a very expensive suburb. Here was
once one of the palaces of the Wuffinga dynasty; and Queen
Etheldreda, later Saint and the founder of Ely, was born here, and
baptized in St Mindred's Well. The latter was a place of pilgrimage,

and is still to be seen, a little spring on land belonging to the Jockey Club.

We can cut back into the main part of Suffolk, via Ashley to **Ousden**, which has a strange little Norman church. The north door could not make up its mind whether to be Norman or Early English (it is half one and half the other). The chancel is under the tower, and the Norman tower arches are impressive. The Fox, just up the road, is a cheerful pub, and Mr Fred Myson, a gamekeeper who sometimes puts in there, is a mine of information about country matters. The Queen's ratcatcher lives at Ousden.

Lidgate has a brass in its church to John Lydgate, a poet who followed just after Chaucer and wrote a prodigious number of lines, with some good grain to be found among an unconscionable amount of chaff.

Wickhambrook is a large parish, scattered over hilly country (hilly for East Anglia, remember) with several large halls and farmhouses. But all of this country is suffering now a little from its proximity to London: the semi-commuters are beginning to move in. But at least they do stop the old thatched cottages from falling down. The cottagers (such as are left of them) move into the council houses, and the Londoners move into the cottages, which they can appreciate. Although one can see the sense of the man who says: 'I would rather live in an ugly house and look out at a pretty one, than live in a pretty one and look out at an ugly one!'

Badmondisfield Hall, two miles to the north of Wickhambrook, is a moated hall, most of it sixteenth century (although some earlier), but ferociously restored. The church is mostly Decorated, with Saxon carving outside the south wall.

Great Bradley should be visited by all brickmakers; for the bricks of its south porch are said to have been made by the King's Brickmaker in Henry VIII's time. There is a fireplace inside the church, said to be for baking the wafers of the Eucharist. (It may be of interest that the Thomian Christians of South India have had arrangements inside their churches for baking their holy bread since AD 50; but they use leavened bread; and they claim that the yeast that leavens it is the living descendant of yeast handed to St Thomas by Christ himself.) There is a bell at Great Bradley that has rung for 600 years and looks as if it may go on ringing for another 600. There is some *corking* glass in the east window—of a Rupert Brook-type young soldier in the trenches. It will be a collector's piece in fifty years' time.

Little Bradley has one of the very few predominantly Anglo-Saxon churches left standing in England. It has a round tower, thought to be tenth century, and long-and-short work in the nave and chancel. It is impossible for an Englishman to stand in such a building without awe.

John Daye, the great printer, was buried here; and there is a brass to him, with a wife and six sons and five daughters and two babies under the table. This was nothing—he had as big a tribe by another wife! He still found time for a great deal of printing, however; he published Foxe's *Book of Martyrs*—lodging John Foxe in his house while he wrote it, and printed the works of the Anglo-Saxon Abbot Alfic to please Archbishop Parker, the Master of Corpus Christi who collected the great library of that college. Daye cut an Anglo-Saxon type-face to do the latter work, and he was the first Englishman to cut a face for the printing of music. He was also the first to print the Psalms in English.

> *Here lies the Daye that darkness could not blynd*
> *When Popish fogges had overcast the sunne . . .*

There is a window to him in the church put there by the Stationers Company in 1880, and his name is perpetuated by the publishers, John Day of New York. They still use his emblem: an angel in front of the sun.

Withersfield has some distinguished and unusual carved benches, and is a very pretty village. And so we come, if come we must, to **Haverhill**. Haverhill is pronounced variously 'aver'il (we are getting near London where they drop their aitches) 'avvril', 'hayvril' and 'havvrill'; and most of the present town is late-Victorian, for the town shot forward at that time, rebuilt after a fire, as a sort of rural Leeds. It shoots forward again, or at least in some direction, into the Age of 'Overswill', and is already quite overwhelmed by factories and council houses. There is a very modern factory, designed by Messrs E. D. Mills and Partners, for the good old East Anglian firm of Polak and Schwarz. Nathaniel Ward, a parson from Haverhill, founded Haverhill in Massachusetts.

Kedington, east-nor'-east, called Ketten by the knowing and Kitten by the even more knowing, has a church of extraordinary interest. On its east gable is an Anglo-Saxon crucifixion at least 900 years old, which was dug up in 1860; there are Roman bricks in the church and Roman foundations under it; and it is now the mausoleum of the Barnardiston family, which has inhabited this place for twenty-seven generations!

To enter the church, when it is empty of people, is like walking into some silent dormitory, with stone figures sleeping all about, or kneeling beside their beds in prayer. Sir Thomas's tomb is particularly fine, with his two wives and his fine armour. He died in 1503. There are several later Sir Thomases—one a great fat Falstaff of a fellow with a lion at his feet; there is Nathaniel who outdid his fellow Puritans in piety; and a mere stone inscribed to Sir Samuel, who gave the Puritans their name of 'Roundheads' (the Queen looked out of her window at a Puritan riot and said: 'See what a handsome round head is there!' looking at the handsome Sam, and the name stuck). He kept his round head well down in the Civil War, though, so much so that Charles II knighted him when he got the throne back.

There are finely carved pews in this church, mostly seventeenth century for it was then that the family seems to have flourished the most. There is a most notable Puritan pulpit, from which the famous Fairclough thundered. There is an hour glass and a wig pole, and Addison tells us that John Tilletson, who hung his wig on the latter, was the first parson ever to wear a wig, God bless him.

Sou'-east to **Stoke-by-Clare**, which should be visited by all misers, pulpiteers and windmill-lovers. The church has the most beautiful pulpit in England, paid for in 1498, but so small as to be inadequate for a really well-fed incumbent. As for windmills—there is a depiction, in fifteenth-century stained glass, of a post mill in a window of the south transept. There is a Doom on the east wall. Misers will revere this place because John Elwes lived in the priory here in the eighteenth century. His wealthy mother starved herself to death, and John, who incidentally became a Member of Parliament, was so mean that he would not have his boots cleaned lest it wear them out, and when he injured both his legs would only pay the doctor to heal one: he healed the other himself by copying what the doctor did to the first.

Elwes's house had been a college of priests which started at Clare about 1090 but was transferred to Stoke-by-Clare in 1124. Matthew Parker was at one time Dean of it. It is now a college again, or at least a school.

Clare, which Stoke is by, is a fascinating little town, most beautiful, and still substantially unspoilt. And the resort here of many Londoners of money and good taste will probably keep it that way, externally at least; although it will become less and less of a farming centre and more of a dormitory.

Down by the railway station is a large castle mound, with a fragment of keep on top of it—the mound cut into along the bottom to make way for the station yard. While the Victorian excavations were going on a cross was found—a reliquary cross of great beauty and value, of gold set with large pearls on a gold chain and a remarkable Christ figure on it, and it was thought to have contained a portion of the True Cross. It was presented to Queen Victoria by a loyal railway company, and it may well have been her property, in a way, for later research points to it once having belonged to Edward III, and that Edward's second son, Lionel, Duke of Clarence, gave it to his daughter Philippa who lived in Clare Castle. It makes us wonder what more treasures have been flung down among the nettles.

In the early Middle Ages Clare was a very important military stronghold. It was the fort that commanded passage along the Icknield Way. It was in a position that could effectually bar passage along that ridge of high well-drained ground that connected East Anglia to the rest of England, and which had the impassable forest-swamps of Essex on one side of it, and the Fens on the other.

It may then be wondered why the castle was not built actually astride the Way. The answer to this is that stone could not have been got to such a site without the almost impossible task of dragging it overland. Clare was the nearest point to the Way on a navigable river (the Stour) up which stone could be carried from Normandy, to this stoneless country. The Normans early saw the strategic importance of the site. The first mention of the castle is in 1090, twenty-four years after the Conquest. William had given the Honour of Clare to Richard Fitzgilbert, and by the reign of King John Gilbert, 7th Earl of Clare, was one of the most important men in England.

But the de Clare that we hear most of was Elizabeth. She was the daughter of yet another Gilbert de Clare, the 9th Earl, and her mother was Joan of Acre, the daughter of Edward I. Joan was born at Acre, when her father was on his crusade; and when Gilbert married her he was three times her age. They had four children: a boy who got killed at Bannockburn, Elizabeth of whom we write, and two daughters who became wards of Edward II who married them off to his two 'creatures', Piers Gaveston and Hugh Despenser.

Elizabeth inherited Clare Castle and other vast estates, for her father had been one of the richest men in England. She married three times, and each time was widowed; by the age of twenty-eight she was a widow for good. There is a story that one of her husbands was killed before her eyes while participating in a joust to celebrate their wedding. She settled down at Clare and there lived in great style, keeping apartments always ready for her cousin Edward III, and entertaining constantly two other cousins and friends: Marie de Valance, Countess of Pembroke, and John, Duke of Lancaster. The former founded Pembroke College, the latter Corpus Christi, and the latter's steward, Edmund Gonville, founded Gonville and Caius: thus this group of friends founded four of Cambridge's colleges.

The massive church of Clare stands bang in the middle of the village. The heavy tower is thirteenth-century Early English, the body of the church remodelled in the fifteenth century (but the chancel later, in the seventeenth). Fortunately the seventeenth-century builders did not despise the style of their ancestors and used good Perpendicular: no worse than that of earlier ages. We may wonder what would have happened had Englishmen not gone whoring off into Italy, but had allowed their architecture and art to go on developing naturally from the Gothic style that they had so triumphantly developed, instead of making that wild jump backwards to the Classical ages again.

There is a very fine 400-year-old brass lectern, and eagle with dogs at foot, probably Flemish and said to be the gift of Queen Elizabeth. There is Tudor heraldic glass in the east window (Dowsing smashed 1,000 'superstitious pictures' in these windows but spared the heraldic glass); good Jacobean stalls; and Roman bricks among the flint of these walls. The church has an ancient look, and seems to crouch down amid the little town around it.

Over the Stour is Clare Priory, the first Augustinian foundation in England. The religious house originally established at Clare was of Benedictines; but as we have seen these were removed to Stoke-by-Clare in 1124. They came originally from Bec, in Normandy.

In 1248 Richard de Clare, grandson of Fitzgilbert, brought the Austin Friars from France, the first Augustinians to arrive in England. They spread from here all over the country, and to Ireland

17. Lavenham, the most spectacular of the 'wool villages'. *Above*, the church; *below*, timber-framing in the village

18. Long Melford church. Here most of the area of the walls is glass, buttresses support the roof, and the East Anglian art of 'flush work' or alternating flint and free-stone is seen at its perfection

where they persisted after the English Reformation, and from where they have since reached out as missionaries to many parts of the world, and now they have come back to Clare, for Clare was again made an Augustinian priory in 1953. There are five or six friars living there now, and their purpose is to teach novices to the order; but when I went there in 1965 they had no novices to teach. In 1298, when we may suppose that the community was at its zenith, there were twenty-nine friars and novices, and it is recorded that Edward I, when he visited the place, gave them one *solidus* each.

The monastery had a large church with cloisters on the south side and infirmary and reredorter on the east. The infirmary building is still standing and in use as an out-house, and extensive remains of the walls of the church are still standing. There is a tomb-recess believed to be that of Joan of Acre, who is known to have been buried at Clare. There is a grave in the chancel thought to be that of Lionel, Duke of Clarence, son of Edward III, who was buried here in 1377. One of the walls of the cloister garth still stands to almost its full height.

The main building still existing, though, is the seventeenth-century dwelling house which was built among the ruins of the Prior's House and Cellarer's Hall. This still has windows and buttresses of the late fifteenth century, and a fine doorway in the west wall of the early fourteenth century. The big house has great charm, and is a jumble of bits of different periods. The priory grounds are almost surrounded by the River Stour, which was diverted by the monks for that purpose, and there are noble trees.

Clare village itself contains many beautiful old houses and cottages, and some of the best *pargetting* in the world. The Ancient House, near the church, has the date 1473 on its pargetting, but undoubtedly this was the date of the house and not of the pargetting, for pargetting was a later art: most of it done in the seventeenth century, about the time of Charles II. Much of this work (the application of moulded plaster) was done to old timber-framed buildings, which probably had to be plastered anyway to cover up the draughts caused by the shrinking of the timbers over the centuries. To see the art at its finest we must go to the Ancient House, Buttermarket, Ipswich.

Following downstream along the Stour we come to **Cavendish**, where is a Sue Ryder Home behind the Old Rectory for victims of Nazi persecution. Here is one of the most attractive village greens in Suffolk. There is a fine church here (we are coming now into an area in which fine churches are ten a penny, and so the one at Cavendish may well get disregarded). But observe the noble clerestory of the fifteenth century, Roman bricks in the south aisle and Flemish tiles in the north, a ringing chamber in the tower which was once lived in and has a fireplace, the fourteenth-century door with its original ironwork, the fifteenth-century eagle lectern, the fourteenth-century chest and the seventeenth-century altar table. The chancel was built with money from Sir John Cavendish who had his head cut off by rebels of 1381 because his son had treacherously killed their leader, Wat Tyler, after the king had given the latter amnesty. Sir John's old house is on the green.

Glemsford is for some reason or other called 'Little Egypt'. During every war Glemsford has a flax factory, and Suffolk farmers devote part of their acreage to growing linseed for flax. The factory is turned into a plastics factory now, a sign of the times no doubt; but no doubt again the country will be glad enough to grow and work flax again if there is another 'emergency'. But at the moment West Suffolk farmers seem to grow nothing but barley, owing to the big subsidy on this crop, and the fact that it can be harvested, in the depopulated countryside, with practically no labour whatever.

But as Glemsford has for so long been famous for flax, and as so many people living here have worked in the flax factory, it might be of interest to include a note about it. The flax is cut by reaper-and-binder, stacked, and later sent to the factory. Here it is *rippled*, which consists of combing the seed out of it, and this seed is crushed for the linseed oil which puts such a bloom on fattening cattle. The stems of the plant are then *retted*, which means that they are laid in warm water for a few days. You can see coconut husks being subjected to the same treatment in India and Ceylon. This softens the flesh clinging to the fibres and enables it to be got off, by *scutching* (at Liston, nearby in Essex, there is still a pub called The Scutcher's Arms). The fibre, thus cleaned, goes for linen, the shive as the inferior fibre scutched from it is called, for tow, and the chaff scutched out of the stems goes for cattle food; so that nothing of this most excellent and economical crop is wasted.

There is also a factory in Glemsford, owned by Messrs Arnold and Gould, which is still working processing horsehair. The hair is simply prepared here for other manufacturers. There is a factory for making machines that break down coconut fibre, or coir. The latter used to be done here, but now only the machines are made for export to the

Malabar Coast. And there is Glemsford Silk Mills Ltd. Here silk, imported from China with a little from Japan, is woven into scholastic and other silk robes for London robe-makers, who hire these robes out to the wearers on great occasions. The factory is highly automated, and is said to run all night completely unattended. Mr Piper, the manager, is always glad to show anybody who is truly interested around the works.

Glemsford has been a weaving town for a very long time, and in the Middle Ages had its own peculiar cloth, called Gleynforths. The Angel pub has a fifteenth-century wood carving of the Archangel Michael for its sign, the church is fine, with a notable fifteenth-century font, and George Cavendish, Wolsey's biographer and his faithful servant until his downfall, is buried within the church. Without it is buried James Albion, died 1791, with this on his stone:

> *In ringing ever from my youth*
> *I always took delight.*
> *My bell is rung and I am gone*
> *My soul has took its flight.*
> *To join a choir of heavenly singing*
> *Which far excel the harmony of ringing.*

Let us hope that his bell-ringing was better than the scansion of his commemorator.

Boxted, north-about, has a small church standing behind the gamekeeper's cottage, and there are Poleys everywhere in it. There are Poley windows, Poley slabs, Poley monuments, even a Poley family tree engraved on marble on the wall. Poleys have lived in the nearby Hall for five hundred years, a Poley gave his life for his country on the 15th of September 1942, and Major John Weller-Poley still lives at the Hall.

In the church are two lovely *oak* Poleys, lying down, William and Alice, of 1587, and really sensitively carved: most fine. But the *coup d'œil* is Sir John, who died in 1638 but the statue was later. It is most spirited: Sir John stands in his armour, his hand jauntily on his hip, looking extremely pleased with himself. He has a frog hanging in his ear, said to be a Danish honour, for Sir John served the King of the Danes for twenty years and also fought the Spaniards under Elizabeth. The song *Froggie would a'wooing go* (Roley, Poley, Gammon and Spinach) is thought to refer to Sir John Poley, the Rowleys of Stoke-by-Nayland, the Bacons and the Greenes, all families of this area. There is a little old glass in the Poley chapel; but the east window of the church is in what I can only call the *marzipan* school of glass painting.

Whepstead is of interest if only to the saint-knower. The church is dedicated to St Petronilla, the only one in England so to be. This saint was, of course, long thought to have been the daughter of St Peter; but the opening of her tomb in Rome in 1873 showed that she was in fact the daughter of a Roman nobleman, and suffered martyrdom. There is nothing now, beyond some pretty little villages, to stop us from getting back to Bury St Edmunds.

CHAPTER 20

The West Suffolk Wool Villages

We now embark on what some people will regard as the most rewarding section of our tour of East Anglia: the inspection of the famous West Suffolk 'wool villages', and we will take the bull by the horns and go straight to Lavenham, the most famous of them all.

It is best to approach **Lavenham** from the west, south-west or south. For thus you drive across the gently rolling Suffolk fields, suddenly to see, very far away, a really large apparently rectangular *block* standing up on the horizon. It is quite alone, there is no other object near it, and at first sight you may take it for a water tower. Almost immediately, though, you notice a slight tapering about its shape and it is borne in upon you that here is no water tower, but significant form. This is Lavenham church tower (map, p348).

As you get nearer the tower becomes more distinct and beautiful; until quite suddenly you swing round a corner and there it is, Lavenham Church, right in front of you, and from that direction unhindered by any other building. An edifice that, no matter what we may find wrong with its proportions, could not be more beautiful were it studded with diamonds.

But let us keep on past it and have a look at the town first.

This town was built in the period preceding the seventeenth century, when it was a weaving town, and we may suppose that most of the buildings were put up in the fourteen and fifteen hundreds, for it was during a decade or so each side of 1500 that the large amount of money needed to rebuild that splendid church was found, and so that is when Lavenham's prosperity was at its height, and when the greatest amount of rebuilding probably took place. Before 1400 we may suppose the clothiers lived in rude houses. After that they were able to put up houses so substantial, and so well-built and long lasting, that they are still considered highly desirable, four hundred years old though they may be. After 1600 Lavenham began to decline, and then very few houses were built. The reason why it declined was the development of water power for the laborious business of fulling cloth. The weaving industry moved to the west of England, and the north, where hill streams provided power. The invention then of power looms and spinning-jennies knocked East Anglia out completely, for these machines also depended on water power. The application of coal then to provide the power for them knocked out the west of England too; the north became all supreme and East Anglia was spared the horrors of the Industrial Revolution.

In Lavenham there are streets and streets practically solid with timber-framed building. Whether these houses originally displayed their timber framing to the view is debatable: certainly some of them did not always, as *pecking* on the timber tells us: this pecking was done to form an anchor for plaster. Whether the plaster was put on when the house was built as a protection for the timber, or afterwards to block up draughts, it is hard to say. Now most of the plaster has been stripped off by timber-lovers, so that the attractive black and white pattern results. East Anglian timber framing differs from that of the Midlands and Cheshire in that the verticals are closer together than the horizontals. When these houses were put up timber framing was by far the cheapest method of building a big house. In 1965 when Trust Houses Ltd put up some new timber framing to enlarge their Swan Inn and to incorporate within it the old Wool Hall next door, it cost them £170,000: such is the cost of oak now (they needed 400 tons of it) and the cost of craftsmen. It will be noticed, incidentally, that iron fastenings are not used in good timber framing: the members are held together by wooden pegs, 'dowls' or 'pins'. Thus there is no iron to rust and in so doing split the timber, and the houses do not become 'nail-sick' as do iron-fastened ships; they will last as long as the timber lasts, which appears to be for ever.

The Swan, by the way, is a very fine example of Elizabethan timber framing (and some Elizabeth II timber framing as well) and is a big and very good hotel. The incorporated Wool Hall was actually pulled down in 1913, when such buildings were only beginning to be valued; but it was rescued by the Reverend Henry Taylor and the Society of the Preservation of Ancient Buildings and put together again.

It is interesting, and sad, that one of the old weaving families kept on—a family of Huguenot descent, as many of the weaving families were—until a few years ago, when the last weaver (Mr Jarvis) died and his son decided not to carry on the business. Their looms have been taken over, though, and a non-Lavenham family still weaves cloth on them and runs a shop on the Hadleigh Road. The cloth they produce may be a very little dearer to buy than factory cloth, but it is so very much better, and so much longer lasting, that there can be no comparison about its value.

In Shilling Street is Shilling Grange, a very fine house, and in it lived Jane and Anne Taylor who wrote songs for children (Jane wrote 'Twinkle, Twinkle, Little Star'). Their portrait, painted by their Dad, hangs in the National Portrait Gallery. Father was an artist and a Dissenter, and his house was attacked once by a mob. When he moved to Lavenham in 1786 his rent was 6s a year. Since then rents have gone up here. A secret room was discovered in this house, in modern times, with medieval murals.

De Vere House, on Water Street, is fifteenth century and on a Saxon site, and it was also pulled down once by vandals but re-erected by preservationists. It has new brick-nogging (infilling of bricks in the spaces between the timber framing—the bricks often laid diagonally).

In the Market Place, which has good Georgian building besides Tudor, is the spectacular Guildhall, built by the Corpus Christi Guild soon after this was formed in 1529. At this time John de Vere, 15th Earl of Oxford, gave Lavenham a charter. Notice the splendid porch of this building and its carved corner posts—one with John de Vere holding a distaff and the charter of the Guild—and the oriel windows. When Howard visited it in 1784 the place was a prison—'dirty and unsafe and lacking straw and water'. The martyr John Taylor was held here on his way to the burning pyre at Hadleigh.

But it is best, in Lavenham, simply to wander round the streets, for there is not one of them that does not have splendid building in it. Note the timbered houses in Church Street with pargetting on them depicting tools of the wool industry, the Old Grammar School in Barn Street, and Mullet House near it, and the house called Woolstaplers in Prentice Street. Note the names of the streets. And so back to the church, which is the product of collaboration of the mercantile class with the aristocracy.

Lavenham was one of a group of wool towns, and just as mercantile rivalry was intense among them so was rivalry in other things, and particularly in the building of churches. The rivalry, and the prosperity to support it happened to come in a period of high architectural accomplishment: the period of the Late Perpendicular. Here at Lavenham the landed aristocracy (descendants of William the Conqueror's fellow armed robbers), in the form of John de Vere, 13th Earl of Oxford, combined with the weavers, in the persons principally of Simon Branch and the Spring family, to rebuild the old church on a scale that they hoped would pip Stoke-by-Nayland and Long Melford. They first built a tower that certainly pips the lot: it is 141 feet high and it would have been higher, the story goes, if the master-builder had not fallen from the top of it. They then had the good sense to allow this vast weight of stone to settle before they attached the rest of the church. Meanwhile they were pulling down the ancient nave, and holding their services in the chancel.

Most of the tower was built by 1495, of Barnack limestone and knapped flint—note the unique limestone plinth at the base of it. A rich clothier, Thomas Spring the Second, paid for most of the cost, and it is a little touching that when his son, Thomas Spring the Third, completed the top of the tower he had his coat of arms—which had just been given him—depicted on it no less than thirty-two times! Here was a family of 'base blood' buying itself into the ranks of the gentry by the profits of industry, and enormously proud of its new position!

The new nave was added around 1513, and fortunately the lovely little crocketted sanctus turret, Decorated and of unknapped flint, was left and not pulled down. This church tells us something more about the history of the English cloth trade. The chancel was never rebuilt. It had been intended, once the new nave was complete and services could be held there instead of in the old chancel, to pull the latter down and rebuild it. Not to do so must have been a terrible loss f face. But it was not rebuilt. It can only be because the sands were running out: the weaving industry was dying, Lavenham was eking a precarious living by spinning wool for the looms of Norwich —and even Norwich was beginning to feel the pinch and was soon to dwindle as a cloth town and go over to making shoes. And then, of course the Reformation came and put an end to grandiose church building.

We enter the church through the De Vere Porch, which is most beautiful. The porch was paid for by the 13th Earl, and there are de Vere arms all over it. There are also wild boars—a pun on the name de Vere (*verres* being Latin for boar), and there is the de Vere Star, which was awarded to Albericke de Vere by his fellow crusaders when Albericke had recovered the standard of St George from the Saracens after this had been lost during a battle. 'They gave him a star of silver to beare in the first quarter of his Shield, because a certain star did shine so clerely that the Christian Armye at darke midnight did overcome the Saracens.'

Albericke's father had come to England with the Conqueror (he actually held lands here before the Conquest), and Albericke's son was created 1st Earl of Oxford. The 20th Earl, who was descended in direct male line, died with no heir in 1703, just five hundred years later. Twenty successive Earls of Oxford in half a thousand years! The Oxfords were lords of the manor of Lavenham, and greatly enriched by the cloth trade, and thus they worked with the weavers to build the church; and wonder beyond wonders—Aubrey, the 15th Earl—married the daughter of a clothier—a niece of Thomas Spring the Third, who was known as 'the Rich Clothier'! An indication of the standing that the mercantile classes had already achieved by the sixteenth century.

The interior of the church is breath-taking. And yet for me it is lacking in mystery: I feel the cold breath of Reason and the Reformation fast approaching when this church was built. It is all so well-designed, so rational. Those great windows let in so much light.

There is a clean-cut magnificence about it. The decoration, cut in Castleton stone, is so sharp and perfect that it is hard to believe that it is not new; the panels, for example, on the spandrels of the arcades. The piers are slender and most beautiful, with their flowered Tudor capitals. The aisles are wide and spacious: the whole building of lovely proportions. Alas and alas that Dowsing smashed all the glass. These windows need to be a picture gallery to impart colour and warmth, and the Victorian glass that is in a few of them is fairly horrid.

The tower arch is splendid, if not so soaringly moving as the one at Stoke-by-Nayland. And the bells—the eight bells of Lavenham—are famous. The tenor, in particular, which weighs a ton and three hundredweight, is said to be the sweetest bell in all England, and every year a special peal is rung in honour of its birthday, which was the 21st of June 1625. It was cast by Miles Gray of Colchester.

The Spring Chantry, at the east end of the north aisle, has a splendid parclose screen: intricately carved woodwork of Renaissance style, with a lovely dark patina as if smoked by incense. The chantry was built for the souls of Thomas Spring III and his wife Alice. Saint-knowers will scarcely need to be told that the figures of St Blaise are here, together with those of St Catherine to whom the chantry is dedicated, because St Blaise was the patron saint of wool-combers. He was *combed to death* during the Diocletian persecutions.

The Branch Chapel is north of the chancel. It is about 1500. The Oxford Chantry (east end of south aisle) is similar to the Spring Chantry, but slightly different in style, a little earlier, a purer style, perhaps? It is to the 13th Earl, who died in 1513. In the Branch Chapel also are lively fourteenth-century misericords, a Pelican in her piety, a man squeezing a pig under his arm (surely the precursor of the bagpipes?) and other subjects. In front of the altar is a brass to a tiny baby, Clopton d'Ewes, which is bound to wring a tear from any mother. The Dister brass is interesting, mainly for the inscription that is on it.

William Gurnell was Rector here from 1644, and he wrote *The Christian in Complete Armour*, which I have to confess I have not read.

Every year, in May and June, Lavenham runs a modest Festival of Music and the Arts, with lectures, concerts, and exhibitions.

Long Melford, Lavenham's chief rival perhaps, is about five miles to the south-west. It is long, and we should start at the south end of it, and walk northwards. We thus traverse one of the grandest village streets in England, even though it has none of the purity of Lavenham. It is by no means solidly Tudor: there is much eighteenth-century building and, alas, some nineteenth. Since Long Melford was a wool town just as Lavenham was we may well ask ourselves why? And the reason is that Long Melford was a river port and thus shared in Georgian and early Victorian prosperity (map, p321).

As we walk northward the street widens and has tree-shaded greens along it, and there is a great mixture of architectural styles until we get to the Bull Inn, very grand, and Melford Green (one of the many 'finest greens in Suffolk'). The Victorian school is fun, with a turret echoing the great Hall over the road. The houses on our left, after the school, stand well back and are a quiet and dignified row. The people who live in them are to be envied, with that great green in front of them and those mighty elm trees.

Standing out in the green is a strange edifice called the Conduit, which had something to do with the conveyance of water to **Melford Hall**, although quite what nobody seems to know. Hard by the

Conduit is the gateway to the hall itself. This is one of the very fine Elizabethan houses of England, and now belongs to the National Trust, although it is lived in by its family. It is open to the public.

Before the Reformation the Hall belonged to the Abbots of Bury St Edmund, who used it for the strangely secular purpose of a hunting lodge. For these holy men liked to hunt the stag, as well as higher truth. After the monastery was dissolved the Hall fell into the hands of William Cordell (Cordle is still a farming name in Suffolk, and among the Cordle clan are several notable Baptists). William was one of the men of Henry VIII's time who rose from obscurity to affluence by the practice of the Law (at a time of many shipwrecks the sharks flourish) and like hundreds of other smart operators he managed to acquire the sequestrated Hall and lands from the king, firstly for a rental, and then for nothing; as King Henry realized that he could not go on drawing rents from a third of England in perpetuity. Cordell became Solicitor-General, Master of the Rolls, and Speaker of the House of Commons. He managed to adapt his faith to the varying changes of religion, and to keep both his job and his head during the reigns of Mary and Elizabeth. In 1578 he entertained the latter queen at a vast banquet, being the first Suffolk man to do so during her Royal Progress; and it is said that he set such an example of lavishness as practically broke the rest of the county, who had to follow suit. '. . . there was in Suffolke suche sumptuous feastinges and bankets as seldom in anie parte of the worlde there hath been seen afore.'

After Cordell various people occupied the Hall, until it came to the present family, the Parkers. Sir Harry Parker, 6th Baronet, bought it in 1786. Sir Harry had come from a family of sailors: Sir Hyde, 5th Baronet, sailed round the world with Anson, became Vice-Admiral of the Blue, and commanded the British fleet at St Lucia on the famous 25th March 1780, and at the Dogger Bank on the 5th of August 1781. On being offered a peerage by George III he gruffly refused it, as he said he was dissatisfied with the way the navy was being run. Unfortunately he was posted to the East Indies, to take command of the fleet there, and went down with HMS *Cate*, which was lost with all hands in 1782.

The second Hyde Parker was knighted for forcing the boom across the Hudson River in the American War while in command of a squadron of frigates, and it was to his signal, later, that Nelson put his telescope to his blind eye—for he commanded the Baltic Fleet at Copenhagen. He was also in command of the West Indies Fleet. Nor were his sons less martial: one of them left a leg at Waterloo—the other was killed at Talavera.

Sir Richard Hyde Parker, 11th Baronet, lives in the Hall today, having restored it after the depredations of the military during the Second World War, farms his large estates on the wheat-and-barley-prairie system forced on large farmers by cost of labour, and collects old weapons. He also collects old navigational instruments, and models of farm machinery and has a surpassingly interesting model of the first reaping machine, built by Smith of Deanstone, a Scottish cotton king. It would cut an acre in an hour with its revolving knife, but its manufacture was discontinued owing to the hostility of the Luddites. Sir Richard is pleased to show these collections to visitors to the house.

The Hall itself stands in grand grounds behind a large brick wall (note the nice topiary visible from the road south of it) and is large, early Elizabethan if not indeed pre-Elizabethan, and stands on three sides of a square. There is an old drawing of it when it stood on four sides, forming one of those gloomy and sunless courtyards beloved of the Elizabethans (what could they do in them?) and there are other drawings of it open on one side but with a crazy bridge across the opening which served as a grandstand for the ladies to watch the hunt! Under the present Hall are medieval vaults, indicating that this, indeed, was the hunting lodge of the abbots. The house is of brick made from clay dug up in Melford Green (the hole is still there) and the earlier work is distinguished by the brickwork being in 'English bond' (alternate layers of stretchers and headers) instead of the 'Flemish bond' introduced later.

The classical porch of the house originally led to a Screens passage, like the Screens of Cambridge colleges, with kitchens to the left and Great Hall to the right. The Great Hall remains, although embellished (or not, as the taste might run) with columns put up in 1740 (rather like the ones in the Library at Ickworth) with eighteenth-century moulding, relief painting high up on the walls, and a great fireplace in the style of William Kent. Oh that the eighteenth century could have left well alone! But it is a fine room all the same, and a room in which one could be comfortable and at home.

There are portraits in the Great Hall, of various Parkers, and their predecessors too; for when Sir Harry bought the Hall he surprisingly bought some portraits of former owners with it. There is a set of andirons in the fireplace said to have belonged to Abbot Samson in the eleven hundreds, which have portraits of Samson killing the lion. They have new feet though, with the cockatrice of the Cordells, dated 1559. If 1559 is new.

Most of the glass in the windows is German armorial glass collected by the 9th Baronet; but there is some local glass, including the arms of John Winthrop, first Governor of Massachusetts and a Groton man. There is good and well-fitting furniture in the Great Hall, including some ivory figures carved by Portuguese in Goa: part of the loot from the *Santissima Trinidad* which the 5th Baronet captured while she was sailing from China laden with gifts from the Emperor of China to the King of Spain. There is plenty of loot in Melton Hall, and the house seems to accommodate it quite nicely.

The Hyde Parker Room, into which we next go, used to be the Cordell Room. It was burnt out with the rest of the north wing by the billeted troops during the Second World War. This disaster was not without its benefits, to the Parker family, for it enabled them to build new rooms in the north wing, smaller and more convenient for modern living. In the Hyde Parker Room are more family portraits, and fine Regency furniture.

The Blue Drawing-Room escaped the fire, and therefore still has Georgian decoration in the style of William Kent. Very nice Dutch paintings: there is much of Low Country origin in the house, for the old admirals traded with the Hollanders, besides fighting them at the Dogger Bank. There is some Chinese porcelain from the *S. Trinidad*.

In the Library is a Romney portrait of the 5th Baronet, every inch a sailor, and a collection of paintings of the various naval battles the 5th Baronet engaged in, including the Dogger Bank, all done by Dominique Serres, the Gascon painter employed by George III as his official war painter and the man who made the similar paintings at Ickworth. Serres was the forerunner of the war-photographers of the present day; and we may be sure his paintings are pretty authentic: it is most unlikely that the 5th Baronet would have tolerated so much as one staysail-halliard in the wrong place!

There are books in the Library, too, which nobody ever reads. If they did they would find that they were a most splendid collection of seventeenth- and eighteenth-century works of topography and exploration; there is a priceless collection of eighteenth-century sea

341

charts, too: the working charts used by the sailing Parkers themselves.

On the staircase is more *Santissima Trinidad* loot, and the 'Miser's Wedding' by Pieter Brueghel. In the Gallery is a window depicting Elizabeth I, and a portrait of one of the Hall's owners: Countess Rivers, who lost it and her other possessions for adhering to the Catholic Faith at the wrong moment. Some of her needlework hangs below.

There is a tiny chapel upstairs with an exquisite Goanese Madonna which has twice been looted: once from the *Santissima Trinidad* and once again by a burglar (may we hope not an East Anglian?) who was mean enough to break her fingers and her ears in order to steal the gold rings and earrings.

The grounds are beautiful, with rare trees, topiary, and other delights, including a charming and most uncommon Tudor garden pavilion.

South of the Hall grounds is a river, the Chad Brook; and a pleasant short stroll along it ends at a fish weir. By the river is a round concrete block with a steel bar sticking up from it, which may well puzzle the curious of the younger generation. It is a spigot mortar base. The spigot mortar would fling a bomb as big as a football at unfriendly tanks, and during the Second World War East Anglia was peppered with them. This is one of the few that survives.

Whether it was Melford Hall or one of the other two great houses of this parish, according to George Borrow it was at the 'Great House' of Long Melford that his girl friend Isopel Berners was brought up. A lass of aristocratic origins and heroic proportions, she supported the author on her knee while he rested in between bouts with the Flaming Tinman: that mighty bruiser whom Borrow managed to rout. He lived with the girl in a Dell, but we gather platonically.

Over the great and noble Green stands the Trinity Hospital; built by Sir William Cordell in 1573 but since altered. Past it we go (there used to be a branch of Doctor Barnardo's hard by) and suddenly we are confronted by the great church—which many people consider to be the grandest building in all Suffolk. We are too near to it, when we see it, for it to have its fullest impact.

Certainly it is long, large, noble, and Perpendicular. The tower is a bad let-down: the original one fell down, was replaced in 1725, and covered with stone in 1903. At the opposite end is the great Lady

Chapel, impeccably enough 1496 but it doesn't fit the rest of the
church at all. It is quite the wrong shape, and seems to be (in fact is)
a separate building. And yet Long Melford Church would lose a lot
of its distinction without it. But the chunk in between: this part is
very grand and beautiful indeed: the late-Perpendicular 'glass-
house' ideal, superbly carried out. If people say that this is the finest
church in Suffolk who is to argue with them?

LONG MELFORD CHURCH

KEY TO PLAN

A Porch and South Entrance
B Tower and West Entrance
C Belfry Turret
D North Door
E Rood Turret
F Clopton Chapel
G Clopton Chantry Chapel
   and Lily-Crucifix
H Founder's Tomb
I Cordell Monument
J Jesus or Martyn Chapel
K Choir Vestry
L Priest's Vestry
M Lady Chapel
N British Legion Chapel
O Children's Chapel

Unlike most of our churches Long Melford's was built nearly all
at one go (except the tower), in the last two or three decades of the
fifteenth century. The rich weavers and cloth-finishers were able to
sweep away what went before and put up a complete new building.
Long Melford is not the product of the slow accretion of the centuries,
and this fact gives it purity, its period gives it grandeur and perfection, but—like Lavenham—it lacks the *mystery* of many older
churches, and its *ninety-seven* windows let in a vast amount of light.
The builders of the modern shrine at Walsingham knew what they
were doing when they kept it practically pitch dark.

343

The interior is staggering. The slenderness of the piers of the arcades, the delicacy of the moulding of the arches, the loftiness of the clerestories which they support, the high proportion of glass to stone: this is most skilful engineering—not just architecture. We are made to feel that reinforced concrete could do no more—nay not as much, than this cut and dressed limestone is doing. Stone building can be carried no further than this.

After recovering from the general effect, walk to the north aisle and look at the glass. The salvaging of the scattered remnants of the old glass was financed by the Pilgrim Trust; and the fragments (some of which had actually been re-inserted paint-to-weather!) have been re-arranged, and placed in order. Some time must be devoted to their study, for here is an important collection. Note the lovely *Pietà* over the north door: Our Lady of Pity in the middle, St Peter on her right, St Francis on her left, and three rabbits, sharing the same three ears, and said to be a symbol of the Undivided Trinity. But these windows, painted and fired by Flemish glaziers when the church was built, are a picture-gallery of mayors, judges, citizens, prior and priests.

Let into the north wall, beyond the windows, is an alabaster relief, which do not miss. It is a most sensitive depiction of the Adoration of the Magi. Poor Joseph, looking understandably wronged, sits at the foot of his wife's bed holding a pair of crutches. It is a lovely piece and thought to be of *c.* 1350, thus antedating the present church.

In the north aisle too is a carved piscina with ogee arch: the tomb of Sir William Clopton who died in 1446 (thus also before the main part of the church was rebuilt), and was the father of John, who bore the expense of most of the rebuilding. There are many Clopton brasses.

The Clopton Aisle leads to the Clopton Chantry, through a tiny priest's room in which is a fireplace, and which obviously was the cell in which lived the chantry priest whose sole job in life was to chant, for ever, masses for the salvation of the Clopton souls. This room is roofed with solid slabs of stone, carved to make them look like a fan vault, but simply in fact stone beams, like the roof of a Hindu *adyta*, of the times before the introduction of the dome by the Moguls.

The chantry, into which this leads, has an Easter Tomb, delicately carved and with antique paintings on it: one of them of the risen

19. Blickling Hall (*above*), was built in the early 17th century where was once a manor of King Harold of England. The house is much bigger than it looks from this picture, because it is deeper than it is wide. Holkham Hall (*below*) one of the most lavish exercises of the Palladian in England

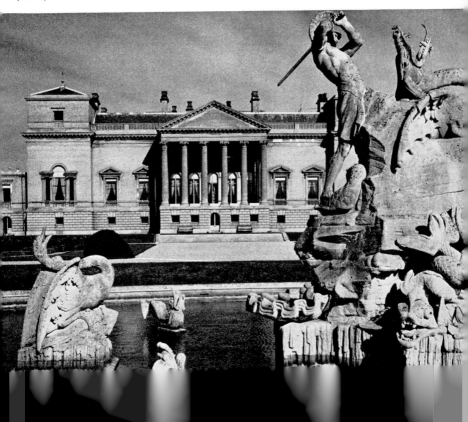

20. A complete absence of building stone (save flint) forced the eastern counties to develop brick to a high art. *Top*, Melford Hall. *Centre*, Oxborough. *Below*, Hengrave Hall

Christ with the text above him: *Omnis qui vivet et credit in me non morietur in aeternum.* The whole chantry was once surrounded by texts and hymns, said to have been written by John Lydgate, the monkish poet of Bury who died in 1450, forty-six years before the chantry was built. But the glory of this chantry is the east window, which contains the tiny but splendidly mystical Lily Crucifix: a depiction of the Lily of the Annunciation with the Crucifixion visible within it, the End within the Beginning.

The chancel of the church is completely dominated, so that one feels that the altar itself is about to be edged out, by a monstrous monument to Sir William Cordell, the lawyer, Master of the Rolls, etc, who so lavishly entertained Elizabeth when she made her Royal Progress. It was this man who presumably built Melford Hall, and the hospital by the church gate. The knight rests his feet on a cockatrice, his emblem. His mighty monument is completely classical, vulgarly so to my taste, and it fits ill with the rest of the church. Sir William takes up far more than his fair share of space, in death as he no doubt did in life.

The Lady Chapel, which is quite a separate building, although reached from the body of the church *via* the south-east door of the Martyn Chapel (east end of south aisle) is unique. It has an indoor cloister, or ambulatory, right round it, and going behind the shrine. The cambered roofs are charming, and the whole chapel has an air of sanctity and antiquity. It was for centuries used as a school.

Back on the main road, and farther north, and on the right, is Mrs Adam's Bakery. This is one of the only two faggot-fired bakeries known to me in East Anglia, and Mrs Adams, now a widow, and her two daughters, bake and deliver two hundred loaves a day. They put their dough to rise overnight (unlike modern factory-bakers, who put it to rise an hour or two before it is baked), and in the evening fill their still-hot oven with faggots, which come from hedge-cuttings about the countryside. In the morning a match is put to the oven-dried faggots, which explode into flame; and when the fire has burned down the glowing ashes are drawn out and put into a little grate next to the oven. The oven is then white-hot; and the loaves are put into it, not in tins but straight on the oven-floor, by the use of a long-handled 'slice', or a series of them, for as the back of the oven is filled slices with shorter handles have to be used. To watch Mrs Adams loading her oven is to watch an exhibition of great skill and dexterity: speed is important, lest the oven cool. The time the bread stays in the oven is a matter for nice judgement (not constant openings of the door!), and varies very much according to the weather. The resulting bread is so superior to the wrapped-pap of the factories that it seems another substance altogether.

Acton, two miles east, is an ugly village (that 'bus garage'!) but its church has the most famous military brass in England: that of Sir Robert de Bures. This is one of the five chain-mail effigies of England dated as early as 1302, and is the most perfect of them. Sir Robert is cross-legged (i.e. a crusader), wears reinforced chain-mail common in the period 1250–1325, with knee-pieces made of *cuir-bouilli* (boiled leather), and over his armour he has a long surcoat with a girdle round his waist. His mail hood and hauberk are separate from the body armour, his shield, slung over one shoulder, is charged with the Bures arms. There is an ornamental bawdrick on his hips, and on his thigh the silk pourpoint worn beneath the armour can be seen. He wears pryck spurs. He gives the impression of being very much a warrior and old campaigner, veteran of many camps; and not just a lawyer or a businessman wearing armour to look grand on his monument. Many brasses are best seen from rubbings. This one not. It is most important to see the actual brass (map p349). There is another excellent brass and an important eighteenth-century tomb.

CHAPTER 21

From Sudbury to Woolpit

Described by Dickens in *Pickwick* as Eatanswill, **Sudbury** is a very ancient town, and the biggest of the 'wool towns', or weaving towns, of Suffolk. Weaving is still carried on here, in several factories weaving silk. It does not contain the antique charm and purity of some of the other wool towns, because it continued to be a manufacturing town long after they did, and still is one, making, amongst many other things, and for some extraordinary reason, ship's propellers. (Why here? So far from coal—so far from iron—so far from a ship?) And there are big chalk and lime works. It continued thus in manufacturing importance because it developed as a big river port, and so remained until the railway came.

Thomas Gainsborough was born in Sepulchre Street in 1727, now called Gainsborough Street. The house where he was born, No 46, is a museum.

Gainsborough was the youngest of the nine children of a Non-conformist woollen crêpe maker, and when he was fourteen his father sent him apprentice to the engraver Gravelot in London. He returned to Sudbury and took up portrait painting, and also married a girl of rare beauty, Margaret Burry, who brought with her a dowry of £200 a year.

He moved to Ipswich, and set up there as a portrait painter and landscapist. He was helped by patrons, including Richard Thicknesse, the Governor of Landguard Fort, and the brewing Cobbold family (the latter relationship is described vividly in *Margaret Catchpole*). He moved to Bath, and became the most famous painter of his age.

There is a bronze statue of him on Sudbury Market Hill, clutching a palette and brush in case we should be in any doubt as to what his profession was. It is by Sir Bertram Mackennal.

The other important man in Sudbury was Simon Tybald, who is notable for having had his head cut off by Wat Tyler's men during the Peasants' Revolt. He was Archbishop of Canterbury; but this did not stop him from also holding the office of Chancellor of England. As the former he excommunicated John Ball, the parson who was trying to secure help for the wretched poor; as the latter he imposed a savage poll tax on the labourers, and advised Richard II to keep them in subjection. He urged the utmost severity on the people he called 'barefooted rebels'.

All this led to Wat Tyler leading 10,000 'barefooted rebels' to London in 1381, treating with the king, and dragging the hated Tybald out of the Tower where he was hiding and executing him. His head is now in the vestry of St Gregory's Church, Sudbury, for all to see, or at least his skull is, and St Gregory's is the church that Tybald helped to build.

The church has a marvellous telescopic font cover (over a modern font), very ingenious and lavish. By the tower arch is a picture of a knight booting the Devil. Not applying the toe of his boot to any part of the Devil's person, but confining the Devil in a boot. This is one interpretation: another is that he is conjuring the Devil *out* of the boot—of a person who had the gout.

The other church, St Peter's, is a grand building, standing right up out of the street on Market Hill amid milling traffic, with fine traceried doors, seventeenth-century nave roof panelled in blue and gold, good carved sixteenth-century chairs, a good rood screen with saints and a famous piece of fifteenth-century embroidery still used at the funerals of aldermen; but at the time of writing St Peter's is closed for repairs. A third church, All Saints, has a rare oak pulpit, well preserved, and three notable screens.

Thomas Dawes came from Sudbury. It was he who set the lantern in the tower of Old North Church, Boston, Mass., to signal to Paul Revere to make his famous ride: thus a Sudbury man set the first match to the American Revolution.

The town owes much of what it is to the River Stour Navigation. In 1705 (Queen Anne) an Act of Parliament was passed for improving the navigation, the Undertakers to get 5s per chaldron of coals, or ton of other merchandise, between Manningtree and Sudbury. Millstones, however, and other materials for mills, were to be allowed up free. Sudbury had shot ahead commercially as a port; in 1724 Defoe could say that the Navigation was not paying its opera-

tors. By the mid-nineteenth century the proprietors desperately tried to sell out to the all-conquering railway, the offer was refused, and in 1913 the company went into liquidation: in 1930 the last barge went to Dedham.

The barges used are familiar to us by having been so often painted by John Constable—he even painted one being built. They worked in pairs, took fourteen hours to get upstream to Sudbury from the sea-going ships at Mistley, and during this voyage the horse had to cross the river thirty-three times, which he did by being 'boated': i.e. carried across in the boat. The horse also had to be trained to jump the stiles across the tow-path (as did the horses of the Fen lighter trains) and Constable's famous painting 'The Jumping Horse' shows one doing this, with a boy on his back.

The barges were 27 feet long, 9 feet beam and 3 feet draught when carrying 26 tons. In the heyday 12,000 tons of coal a year went to Sudbury in them. Gainsborough held shares in the Navigation, and John Constable Senior, the painter's father, was to have 50s a year in perpetuity in compensation for the closing up of a ford of his, and the Undertakers had to build a bridge instead, which is still there and maintained by the East Suffolk County Council.

Boxford is east, and away from the river. It is a compact and attractive village, once a much larger place, and in 1600 it had four weavers' guilds, eleven clothmakers, thirty-seven weavers, four dyers, two fullers and six shearmen; but these, we presume, were mastermen: there were far more workers. In 1684, in fact, one employer of Boxford is known to have been employing 200 people.

The church is fine. The fourteenth-century north porch of it is of wood, and thus probably the oldest timber porch in England. The south porch is of stone from Caen and is very elaborate. There is a plaque inside the sanctuary that would wring a tear from any mum and not a few dads—to little David Birde, who died in 1606. There he is, a little boy in a great big bed, with his shoes tidily put underneath it. There is also the sad story of Elizabeth Hyams: 'for the fourth time a widow, who by a fall, that brought on a mortification, was at last hastened to her End, on the 4th May, 1748, in her 113th year.'

Groton, north, is remarkable for its 'Jiving Vicar'. The Reverend Brian Bird encourages 'swing' in his church, and is himself no mean exponent. His choir's syncopated rendering of 'Holy, Holy, Holy' is quite something to listen to.

John Winthrop was a Groton man. He sailed to North America aboard the *Arabella*, 300 tons with a crew of fifty, in the company of three smaller vessels. They carried 200 cows, 60 horses and 700 human beings, and landed at Massachusetts Bay in 1630. Seventy of the animals had died at sea, 200 humans died then or soon after landing, and 100 basely returned to England. But the rest stayed on, Winthrop became Governor of Massachusetts and his son of Connecticut. John Winthrop's *Life and Letters* was recently edited by a descendant, Robert Charles Winthrop. There is a window in Groton Church to him. The church hides behind an old farmhouse, on a hill, and in pretty country. The Fox and Hounds is an attractive country pub (or was when I wrote this—but you never know, these days).

South to **Nayland**, again on the Stour. Most charming. Old weavers' cottages and houses, a willow-shaded loop in the Stour, locks, a watermill which was converted in the early days of electricity to generate it, good pargetting and timber framing, and Alston Court, in the middle, a fine house that it would be an adventure to live in. Its east wing is fifteenth century, the rest Tudor, superb barge-boards. The porch of the church (very fine, but restored in Victorian times) was paid for by Wm. Abel, clothier, in 1525, and he also built the bridge over into Essex. (The word clothier did not mean as it does now a seller of cloth, but a manufacturer of it.)

Stoke-by-Nayland has another mighty church, with a particularly marvellous tower. The little town (a village now, much reduced) is on a hill and the brick tower is 120 feet high and the result is that it is a landmark for many miles around. Thus it was much painted by Constable, who put it in very many of his landscapes (often moving it from one side to the other for better effect). His 'Stoke-by-Nayland Church' is famous, and a painting of great drama: nobody else, save perhaps a Blake or a Palmer, could have got away with that rainbow.

Like all the 'wool churches' this is predominantly fifteenth century; although the south porch is Decorated. Note the bosses in the roof of the latter, and in particular the south door with its fine and original wood carving. The west door is noteworthy too. The setting of the church, in a close of lovely Tudor houses and with green grass and great trees on the little hill, is marvellous. Inside, the glory of this glorious building is the tower arch—a soaring masterpiece. The whole church is beautiful, and undervalued compared with Lavenham and Long Melford. The organ has just been restored and has the sweetest tone. There are some good monuments: to the Howards, Tendrings and others.

Of the splendid houses near the church the Guildhall and the old Maltings are the most noteworthy: timber framing and lath and plaster in excellent repair. Outside the village, Thorington Hall, a mile and a half east-south-east, is of the sixteenth and eighteenth centuries: an important house. And Tendring Hall, of which only the park remains, and a fishing lodge, was one of the very mighty houses of England, but was used as a prisoner of war camp during the Second World War and afterwards pulled down. Its history, though, is interesting. It was owned in 1285 by William Tendring, and at the end of the fourteenth century went by marriage into the Howard family. After three generations a Howard, John, was created 1st Duke of Norfolk. Later, when Thomas Howard was beheaded by Queen Elizabeth for trying to marry Mary Queen of Scots and filch the crown (see p52) Tendring Hall came into the hands of Sir Joshua Rowley, Vice-Admiral of the White, and he had Sir John Soane design a great new house for him in 1784.

The most interesting thing that remains of all this is *The Household Book of the Duke of Norfolk*, 1481 which can be seen in the Library of the Society of Antiquaries, and which gives much day-to-day detail of the life of a great fifteenth-century house. An ox then was worth a pound, a lamb 1s 1d, wheat 6s 8d a quarter, a goose 2d, a chicken a penny, eggs 11d a hundred and it cost 4d to get a horse shod—thus a chicken a leg: what it costs now.

Gifford's Hall, two miles east-north-east of Stoke-by-Nayland, is described by Pevsner as 'one of the loveliest houses of its date in England, neither small nor overwhelmingly grand; warm and varied, happy in scale and in the proportions between its materials'. Its period is Henry VII and Henry VIII but it has alterations of the early eighteenth and late nineteenth centuries. It is not open to the public.

Polstead, north, the 'Place of Pools', still has a pool, an artificial lake in which witches used to be 'swum', and into which once a coach and four horses, having been bewitched, plunged headlong. This pool is at the bottom of a hill, and a little green at the top of the hill (you can walk from the pool at the bottom to the green at the top by a pleasant village footpath on your left instead of by the road) would rank high in my list of the prettiest village greens of East Anglia. It has the Cock public house with its fine inn sign and the Cock Farm nearby it. The Reverend John Whitmore, in the early nineteenth century (he came to Polstead in 1795) had to exorcize ghosts. The spirit creation had its own back though, for the reverend gentleman was himself to be seen, after death, driving a horse and trap down the rectory lane *sans* head.

At Domesday there was a Hall, sixty-two villeins, fifteen caracates (plough teams) and one poor wretched serf. There were 650 souls in the parish. The custom of 'Borough English' prevailed at Polstead Manor, which meant that the youngest son, and not the eldest, inherited.

Polstead became nationally famous in that most certain of ways to achieve fame in England—a good grisly murder. You can still see the thatched cottage where Maria Marten lived, down Marten Lane; but the famous Red Barn has since been burnt down, and it is no good looking for it. But crowds of morbid sightseers—charabanc loads of them from London and the Midlands—*still* go and look at where they think it was.

William Corder, the man who brought all this fame to his little parish, was a rich farmer's son, and he lured Maria, a mole-catcher's daughter, to the Red Barn to persuade her to don male attire (Victorian melodrama loved 'male attire') and then run away with him and get married. Maria was never seen alive again. Corder went away, writing to the girl's father to say that they were happily married. But Maria's mother kept having dreams about the Red Barn. She kept dreaming about one particular spot in it. She finally persuaded her husband to go and dig there, and dig he did, and found Maria's body, shot and bashed, in the very position his wife had dreamed about. Corder was found, in Brentford of all places, where he had married a lady of means whom he had discovered through a matrimonial advertisement. They were keeping together, most unsuitably one might think, a school for young ladies. Corder was hanged, in August 1828, in Bury St Edmunds before an estimated 10,000 spectators. The rope used to do it was sold by the hangman for a guinea an inch, a book about his trial was bound in his skin, which the prison doctor thoughtfully took off for the purpose, and it is still supposed to be in Bury Museum, and his skeleton is in West Suffolk General Hospital. If his ghost could only draw royalties on all the performances of *Maria Marten and the Red Barn* that have been staged it would buy him a most sumptuous apartment down below.

Polstead Church is hidden up a hill behind great trees, west of the road at the bottom of the hill; and it is architecturally most interesting. The church inside is Norman, primitive, and simple. The outside gives no indication of this Norman work inside (compare—and in other ways too—Ickleton in Cambridgeshire). The Norman arches are of *brick*. This is a most peculiar circumstance, since the Normans were not supposed to have used brick. These bricks are a different size from Tudor bricks ($9'' \times 4\frac{1}{4}'' \times 2\frac{1}{4}''$) and were once thought to be Roman—but then they are a different size from Roman bricks ($5\frac{1}{4}'' \times 2\frac{1}{2}'' \times 1\frac{1}{4}''$). The inference then is that they were made by the Normans who built the church (at least by the English who built it during the 'Norman' times) and are thus the earliest bricks known to have been made in England since the Romans made bricks: earlier even than the bricks at Coggeshall in Essex. Fibre-glass enthusiasts should examine the font cover, which was made of this material by a nun from the Community of St Clare, in 1964. It has a dove on top of it, a fibre-glass dove. It is believed that under the whitewash of this church are wall paintings. Some good Elizabethan ones were found in the lovely house next door.

In the churchyard is a young oak whose parent was the Gospel Oak, now a mere rotting remnant. The oak was supposed to be 1,000 years old, and Saxon missionaries under St Cedd are said to have preached under it in the seventh century. As old as this or not (as enthusiasts we may believe—as arboriculturalists we may doubt) the oak, before its decline, was 36 feet in girth, so it was a very old tree.

There are cast-iron monuments in the churchyard—a fleeting fashion of the late eighteenth and early nineteenth centuries (although perhaps not so fleeting—there is one as early as 1619 at Burrington in Herefordshire), but Maria Marten's stone has been quite chipped away for souvenirs by the morbid.

At **Layham**, at Holly Lodge Farmhouse, is a small pottery, open to visitors. **Hadleigh** was one of the more important of the wool towns. Its position on the River Brett gave it water-power, water for washing wool and fulling cloth, and transport. It has suffered less than others from having all its houses snapped up by wealthy 'old-

Tudor' enthusiasts, and is still very much an ordinary country commercial town and you can still hear the birds singing above the clicking of the camera shutters.

The pleasantest part of Hadleigh may well be thought to be down at the old mill weir, near Sun Court, at the north end of the town; but if we walk from there south along the main street we will find pleasant houses to the left and to the right.

The church is surrounded by spectacular houses. The Deanery Tower is very grand indeed, a small edition of the great gate-tower of Oxburgh. It was the grandiose entrance to the ecclesiastical palace built in 1495 by Archdeacon Pykenham, who evidently did not approve the injunction to Christians to embrace poverty like a bride. His palace has since been pulled down, the present Deanery, scarcely less magnificent although much truncated in recent years, was built in mock-Tudor in 1831. But the splendid fifteenth-century gate-tower remains.

The Guildhall, south of the church, is a magnificent timbered building. The church itself is large, but it has none of the architectural purity of the great Perpendicular wool churches. Its tower is too narrow for it, and possibly of Norman origin but of Decorated completion. The walls of the body of the church are of the Decorated period, but the windows in them, and the clerestory above, are Perpendicular. Here was not the wholesale sweeping away of the old and the replacing it with the latest fashion that we find at Long Melford and Lavenham. The result is something of a jumble. The great lead spire of the tower is distinctive, and the Angelus bell which is said to be one of the oldest in England. It has Lombardic characters on it: *Ave Maria Gracia Plena Dominus Tecum*—but they were cast in mirror-image by mistake and are therefore backwards! The bell is said to be 600 years old.

Inside is a noble 'ringers' gotch', or bell-ringers' ale jug; for in the olden days, as in ours, bell-ringing was acknowledged to be thirsty work.

Guthrum, King of the Danes, had his headquarters here in the ninth century. Asser records that this king was conquered and converted to Christianity by Alfred the Great and buried in the royal town of Hadleigh. There is a tomb canopy in the south wall of the church, inside, which is still called 'Guthrum's Tomb'. Actually the design of the canopy, which is Decorated, makes it just five hundred years too late; but who is to say that it was not erected in the fourteenth century in place of an older tomb, pulled down? Folk memory, in these matters, is seldom found to be wrong.

The Manor of Hadleigh was given by Brithnoth, the heroic leader of the East Angles killed at the Battle of Maldon, to Canterbury at the end of the tenth century, and such is the tenacity of tradition in England that it was not until 1838 that the practical effects of this were terminated. Until the latter year Hadleigh was a 'peculiar' of Canterbury, and it did not come at all under the spiritual dominion of the bishops of East Anglia. The rectors of Hadleigh had the title 'Dean of Bocking', for Bocking, in Essex, was another Canterbury Peculiar.

In the vestry of the church are many prints and pictures connected with the affair of Dr Rowland Taylor. The most likeable of all Protestant martyrs, Taylor was not an East Anglian but a Northumbrian (much the same stock). He was born at the beginning of the sixteenth century, and thus born a Catholic, but he early heard the preaching of Hugh Latimer, and then became chaplain to Cranmer and a Protestant. Cranmer appointed him to be 'Dean of Bocking', and Taylor became the enormously popular parson of Hadleigh. On the crowning of Mary Tudor, however, Taylor heard the bells ringing in his church, and they were ringing without his consent. He strode into the church, where he found a Catholic priest celebrating Mass. He thrust him forth, and was himself forthwith arrested. He was taken before Bishop Gardiner who badgered him, had him stripped of his garments and re-arrayed as a Catholic priest. Bishop Bonner then came to deprive him of his priestly office. But when Bonner came to strike him in the chest with his crozier, as part of this edifying ceremony, Taylor, who was a huge man physically, warned him that if he did do he would strike him back, and Bonner waived this part of the ceremonial.

Taylor was taken back to Hadleigh (being locked up in Lavenham Guildhall on the way), and amused his guards—the sheriff and other officers—by asserting that he, and many others in Hadleigh, were to be deceived. When they asked in what way, expecting no doubt another argument about doctrine, he said: 'I am, as you see, a man that hath a very great carcass, which I had thought to have been buried in Hadleigh churchyard, if I had died in my bed, as I well hoped I should have done. But herein I was deceived; and there are a great many worms in Hadleigh churchyard, which should have had a jolly good feeding upon this carrion, which they had looked for many a day.'

He was taken on to Hadleigh, where he arrived at night; but in the darkness he was recognized and his wife and children came out to greet him and the people turned out to cheer him on; even three of the four yeomen who were guarding him were in tears for his sake. He was burnt next morning, on the 9th February 1555, on Aldham Common (then still a common but stolen from the people by the enclosers in 1729). A stone was placed there afterwards with this inscription:

1555

D. TAYLOR. IN DE
FENDING. THAT WAS GOOD
AT THIS PLAS LEFT
HIS BLODE.

In 1819 a new monument was erected, which is still there (we can see it by going about a mile along the main Ipswich road, where there is a sign, and we get to it by walking across a field), and this monument has a poem, very moving I think, written by the Reverend Dr Hay Drummond in 1818.

Kersey is very much on the chara-route. It is so picturesque that it would do, untouched except for wires, for a period film set. The classic view of it is from the church, which is on a steep hill (steep by East Anglian standards) to the south of the village. From here we look down on the roofs of the village (many of them of red tiles or the big Suffolk pantiles but some, alas, of Caernarvon slate), and we see the street running down the hill to the ford at the bottom, and then up again steeply the other side. For Kersey runs down into, and out of again, the valley of a tributary of the Brett.

The church, in this most lovely position, is architecturally very interesting; although much visited by bashers in the seventeenth century and restorers in the nineteenth. The building of the Decorated nave was evidently interrupted by the Black Death. The tower, pure Perpendicular, is all of flint: an intractable material for building such a large edifice, but Kersey is a long way from a water navigation and freestone would have been very expensive if hauled to it overland. The south porch is noteworthy, with a lovely ceiling. There is much in the church to admire, but not the east end of it.

Kersey gave its name to a cloth, and Shakespeare speaks of '... russet Yeas and honest Kersey Noes' which contrast with courtly prevarication. **Lindsey**, a village hard-by which washed its wool in the same stream, gave its name to *Lindsey-woolsey*, another kind of honest cloth. Nearby is St James's Chapel, thirteenth century, full description inside.

Brent Eleigh, north-west, has the best tool dealer in Suffolk, and if Len Arthur (Lavenham 442) hasn't got a tool, and cheaper than you can get it elsewhere, then you can give up hunting for it.

In Brent Eleigh Church was recently discovered a mural of the greatest interest and importance. On the left of it are two kneeling angels, busy censing a blocked-out figure (Mary?), and with fine wing detail. In the centre is a crucifixion, with John on the right and Mary on the left. On the right is Doubting Thomas, a figure of Christ holding a vexillum (standard), a kneeling figure variously interpreted as being the monkish donor of the church or else Mary Magdalene, and a beautifully painted jug and barrel—almost certainly a pun on the donor's name. The painting has been dated by Caiger-Smith as 1400, but by Dr Tudor-Craig much earlier: 1290 in fact. The church is rich in other ways too, particularly in woodwork. The only Victorian imprint is the gorgeous cast-iron stove in the library.

The Hall, hard by the church, has been painted the colour of peas boiled with cooking soda—a bilious green.

Bildeston, nor'-east, has a church stuck out in the fields to the west of it; there is a pleasant footpath leading across the fields to the church from Chelsworth, and along this it should be approached. In the church is a tablet to Captain Edward Rotherham who commanded the *Royal Sovereign* which was Head of the Line at Trafalgar. In the churchyard is a tombstone to George Whittel, who died in 1884, aged eighty-three:

> *These tuneful bells for seventy years*
> *He rang, he tolled, he chimed full well.*
> *Births, weddings, deaths he thus proclaimed*
> *And others now have tolled his knell.*

The village, which is worth looking around, is very pretty, and not infested with coaches.

At **Hitcham** is buried John Henslow, who angered local farmers by starting country schools about the country, in which were taught such inflammatory subjects as botany, which of course rendered them unfit for the stations that they had been called to in life; but he

later endeared himself to them again by discovering the use of
Suffolk Crag: those deposits of fossilized fish dung which provided a
rich source of phosphate manure for many years. Henslow was a
botanist and a naturalist who had great influence on Charles Darwin.
He suffered great fears lest Darwin should develop doubts about the
Book of Genesis if he put into his hands Lyall's *Principles*, but nevertheless he was honest enough to do so, trusting in Darwin's piety that
the doubts should not prevail. They did, though; and led to *Origir
of Species*. Hitcham church has fifteenth-century angels on its screen,
in feathered tights, carrying the instruments of the Passion.

Woolpit is supposed to have been named for wolves and not wool,
and the last wolves in England are said to have been killed in a pit
there: probably, we might suppose, a pit-trap. There are pits still:
the remains of vast brick quarries; for here is the source of 'Woolpit
brick': the grey-brown bricks from the gault clay of which much of
nineteenth-century West Suffolk, and Cambridgeshire too, is built,
and it is said the White House, Washington! If the latter piece of
information is true then it must be supposed that ships carried the
bricks up the Chesapeake and Potomac as ballast for it can scarcely
have been economic to ship them over as freight. Certainly they were
much in demand, and samples were ordered to be sent to Petersburgh
by the Emperor of the Russias, and that was in 1820.

Woolpit Church is a very noble one. It has a spectacular Victorian
spire, flying buttresses and lettering done in flush-work and all, and
perhaps the most sumptuous porch in Suffolk, of 1435–55. Most of
the rest of the church is Perpendicular too, except the chancel and
south aisle which are earlier, and all is grand within and without.
The hammerbeam roof is noteworthy and so is the early sixteenth-
century eagle lectern.

There is a legend, fostered in its persistence no doubt by the fact
that Camden related it, having read it in the writings of William of
Newburgh who lived in the twelfth century, that two green children
came out of the ground at Woolpit during harvest time. They were
taken to the house of Sir Richard de Calne, where at first they would
eat nothing but green food, but at length they took to meat and
bread and lost their green colour. They were both baptized but the
little boy died soon afterwards. The girl grew up though, and
married a Lynn man and had children. After the green children had
learned to speak our language (or at least that of our forebears) they
told how they had lived in a country called St Martin's Land, where

CHAPTER 22

Cambridge: the Colleges

The site of **Cambridge** had to be important, for it was the best practicable crossing of the River Cam, or Grant, for many miles. To the north lay the Fens: to the south many miles of riverine swamps; but at the site of Cambridge there was hard ground right to the river on both sides and here a ford could be established, and later a bridge, and a great castle mound to prevent the wrong people from crossing it, and a city grew up. The name may have come from *cam*, crooked, and *rhydd*, ford: both words in the Ancient British language and in the modern Welsh.

As is necessarily often the case in rivers, the head of navigation in the Cam coincided with the lowest ford; and Cambridge was early a port, and a port far inland, which last factor was always of great use in days of poor land communications. In Roman times Cambridge was thus an important staging post on a trunk road, a river crossing, a port, and a base from which to set out to conquer the denizens of the watery Fens.

To the East Angles, when they came, it was more: it was also a frontier town. For the Kingdom of East Anglia may have met the Kingdom of Middle Anglia and later of Mercia along the Cam, and as Cambridge was the only practicable crossing it followed that it was the most important place of interchange between the two nations. The more powerful state of Mercia occupied the Castle on the western bank, and the East Angles built a settlement on the western, of which at least one building survives: St Benet's Church, although this they built under Danish rule.

When the Normans came they used Cambridge as the base for their operations against the English rebels under Hereward the Wake, and in 1068 William built a castle on the Castle Mound, destroying twenty-seven houses to do it. William actually lived here while commanding the long-drawn-out operations against Hereward. At the time of Domesday it was an important place: 400 *masurae*, or homesteads.

And, but nobody knows just when (King John gave a charter in 1211) an annual fair grew up near Cambridge which in its day was the biggest in Europe, surpassing even the Fair of Nijni Novgorod.

Fuller, writing in the sixteenth century, asserted that 'Stourbridge Fair' as it was called was started by Westmorland cloth merchants on their way to Norwich to sell cloth. From Westmorland to Norwich was an enormous journey, but Norwich was one of the wool staples in England, and with its great export trade to the Continent a firm enough market to make such a journey profitable.

But when they reached the bridge over the Cam a great rain storm came on, making it necessary for the merchants to open their packs and spread their merchandise out to dry. And before it was fairly dry they had sold the lot, and so, thereafter, the Westmorland merchants never bothered to go as far as Norwich again.

But it was inevitable that Cambridge should become a centre of trade, for it was the nearest point on the Fenland waterways system to London. We read of wealthy East Anglian families in early Tudor times sending to Stourbridge Fair to buy Continental wine and goods that had been shipped in to London, and no doubt much of the country produce of East Anglia found its way to London in exchange *via* Stourbridge Fair. For anyone who has sailed a motorless boat around the coast of East Anglia it is easy to see that there would be a strong tendency for shippers sending goods from the north of England to London to by-pass the perilous slog round East Anglia by sending their ships straight into the Wash, up the Cam, and then hauling overland to London. It is easy and safe to sail from York to Cambridge, but hazardous and uncertain to sail from York to London.

Carter, the Cambridgeshire historian, writing in 1753 gives a very full description of the Fair. He describes the great procession on St Bartholomew's Day, when the Fair was set out by the Mayor and Corporation of Cambridge, how the site was a cornfield (meaning of course an open field common to all strip-holders, for this was before the Enclosures) a field from which, according to ancient custom, all the corn had to be harvested before the date of the Fair otherwise it would be trodden underfoot, and all the Fair tackle had to be removed by the stall-holders, by Michaelmas Day at noon,

otherwise the ploughmen could drive their ploughs over it, how the booths were set out in rows with names like Garlick Row, Booksellers' Row, Cooks' Row, Cheese Fair, Hop Fair, Wool Fair, and the Duddery. There is still a street called Garlick Row in Cambridge.

At the Duddery were sold woollen manufactured goods, and within a week £100,000 worth of these might change hands there, and vastly more be sold unseen. One single stall in this Duddery, dealing in Norwich goods only, carried £20,000 worth of stock. Hops were sold in values nearly as great, and it being the East Anglian herring season, then as now, and there being an R in the month vast quantities of oysters from Colchester and fresh herrings from the coast were consumed on the spot.

The 14th of September was the greatest day of all: the Horse Fair. Defoe gives a lively description of the Fair in *Tour through the whole Island of Great Britain*, and Bunyan parodied it as the 'Vanity Fair' of his *Pilgrim's Progress*.

Quite why or when a university started at Cambridge nobody knows. Alfred the Great is known to have founded a college of priests at Ely, and the monks of Ely certainly established schools at Cambridge: why at Cambridge and not at Ely is hard to understand. Possibly because Cambridge was the bigger place, nearer to London, and they did not wish to have their devotions at Ely disturbed by a lot of undergraduates. An Augustinian abbey was founded at Barnwell, just outside Cambridge, Augustinians came to the Hospital of St Johns, and Benedictine nuns to the Priory of St Radegund, now Jesus College. This is all fairly conjectural.

It is said that there was a university at Oxford before there was one at Cambridge. There was certainly one at Paris, and in 1229 some students were expelled from it and may have come to Cambridge, and there was certainly some sort of a centre of learning here then. But for a long time there was no kind of university organization: merely halls in which this or that teacher held a school for boys for payment. The boys might lodge with their master, or find private lodgings in the town. A Chancellor was referred to in 1226.

But early in the thirteenth century there was a well-developed university organization; with a chancellor, masters, and 'clerks'. The latter were the scholars. The purpose of all education was to train for the priesthood, or rather, for all the duties, including those of the civil service, then undertaken by clerics. All the members of the university were under clerical law, to be tried for any misdemeanours by

'Courts Christian', and not subject, whatever they did, to the death penalty.

In 1281 the first proper college was founded, Peterhouse, and after this colleges were founded in the following order:

Peterhouse	1281	(received charter in 1284)
Michaelhouse	1324	(since merged into Trinity College)
Clare	1326	(originally called University Hall)
King's Hall	1317	(received charter in 1377 and later merged into Trinity College)
Pembroke	1347	
Gonville Hall	1348	(since merged into Gonville and Caius)
Trinity Hall	1350	
Corpus Christi	1352	
King's	1441	
Queens'	1448	
St Catharine's	1473	
Jesus	1496	
Christ's	1439	(received charter in 1443; refounded in 1505)
St John's	1511	
Magdalene	1428 and 1542	
Trinity	1546	
Gonville and Caius	1557	
Emmanuel	1584	
Sidney Sussex	1596	
Downing	1800	(received charter)
Girton	1869	(moved to Girton 1873)
Newnham	1871	
Selwyn	1882	
Fitzwilliam	1887	
New Hall	1954	
Churchill	1961	
Darwin	1964	
University	1965	

A guide to the Cambridge colleges would have to be a very long book of its own; so that all we can do here is to give the briefest outline of what there is to see in the most interesting buildings. Most of what is noteworthy is contained in a small space, perhaps half a mile by a mile; but it is not a bit of good trying to see it all in a day. A week would give one a better chance, and indeed in that time a fair idea might be had of the externals of Cambridge, which is certainly one of the most beautiful and interesting cities in the world.

For the student of English architecture Cambridge is a complete education in itself; for it contains monumental buildings of every style from Saxon down to the most 'advanced' of the present day; and nor will it stop here for the colleges and the university are expanding rapidly and all the time.

Before we embark on a tour of the buildings it might be as well to include a few notes on the more curious customs of the place, most of which have been handed down from the very early Middle Ages.

Fellows are men who have been elected by existing fellows to their fellowships. Corporately they are the owners of the college with the Master and Scholars. They can live in rooms in college and are now paid a salary, although in former time it was a 'dividend' and the surplus on the income of the college endowments. Fellows may dine in Hall every evening (scholars may too). The fellows, and others not *in statu pupillari*, eat at the High Table, the rest in the body of the hall. The master lives in his own lodge, which is within the precincts of the college.

The room or rooms of fellows and undergraduates are grouped behind an outer oak door which is called 'the oak' and over the 'oak' is painted the denizen's name. When this door is shut the inmate is said to be 'sporting his oak' and is not to be disturbed. Undergraduates, and other gentlemen, were traditionally waited upon by men servants called 'gyps', but now many are served by women 'bedders' and are not waited upon much at all.

At night an official of the university called the 'Proctor' prowls the town, accompanied by two men called 'Bulldogs' or 'Bullers'. One of the latter used, in days gone by, to carry a truncheon and the other a stick for measuring butter but now of course they don't. The duty of this triumvirate is to care for, and if necessary apprehend, any undergraduate who is drunk or otherwise disorderly, and try and prevent, if possible, any undergraduate from getting into trouble with the police. Wrong-doers may be fined 6s 8d, or multiples of this sum, which was half a mark—a monetary denomination long since extinct in England. Or a sinner may be 'gated', meaning that he cannot leave his college at night, or even 'sent down'. 'Up' means towards the university: 'down' means away from it.

The gates are shut at midnight in some colleges, 2 a.m. in many, and after this an undergraduate cannot lawfully get out of his college, although he may lawfully be admitted into it, having his name taken by the porters, and subsequently reported to his 'tutor', the don responsible for directing his studies. No undergraduate has ever, though, been deterred by these circumstances: every college can be 'climbed into' or 'climbed out of', and is every night, despite the elaborate defences erected by the authorities—spikes and *chevaux de frise* and all the rest of it (the more barbarous of these defences recently somewhat mitigated)—to prevent it. There is a story of a kindly policeman who seeing a figure late at night pacing up and down the pavement outside a college wall said: 'Can I give you a leg up, sir?' The figure turned out to be that of the master of the college, having a late night stroll.

The great sporting and social event at Cambridge is called 'May Week'. It is not in May but in June, and not a week but nearly a fortnight.

Entry into colleges by the general public is, by courtesy, at most times free and unhindered. You can wander into any college, go into the chapel if it is open, the hall if a meal is not being served in it (or an examination being held), wander through any court ('court' in Cambridge is the same as 'quad' in Oxford, a space surrounded by college buildings), see the library in some colleges if it is open, but it is better to ask permission. You may not go up any of the stairs leading to living quarters without invitation by somebody who lives there, or into any private rooms.

The master of a college keeps his dwelling in the lodge, and this is, of course, quite private: private, too, his garden and, generally, the Fellows' Garden. In the Porter's Lodge, by the main gate, are always porters (one wonders what they do all the time), and they are extremely courteous men, generally well-informed about their colleges, and very eager to help visitors. Cambridge men are proud of their colleges, and not at all averse to having them looked over by appreciative strangers.

Do not try to see Cambridge by motor car. The traffic congestion is intolerable, parking places full, and the traffic wardens of the city have eagle eyes and stony hearts. Park your car well outside the centre of the town, or in that extraordinary multi-story car park in Park Street, and resolutely leave it. Walk, bicycle, or take a taxi—but do not try to drive.

The perfect way to approach Cambridge, as indeed to approach

most English towns and cities, is by water. The voyage up the Great
Ouse and Cam from Ely (where cabin cruisers can be hired from
Messrs Appleyard, Lincoln & Co, telephone Ely 2244) is quite
delightful (craft of 100 foot length, 14 foot beam, 4 foot draught and
9 foot briggage can get to Cambridge), and thus approaching the city
we avoid the dreary outskirts, for Cambridge has allowed herself to
become surrounded by suburbs of a dreariness which simply passes
belief.

Our ship moored, or our car parked, we will take ourselves to
Emmanuel College, on St Andrew's Street. Emmanuel because it is
at one end of a horse-shoe route which will take us through most of
the more interesting colleges of Cambridge. As we can never hope to
see even the colleges in one day I will deal with colleges first, and
other buildings afterwards.

Emmanuel was one of the later colleges, founded in 1584 for the
same purpose that Sidney Sussex was founded: to combat popery.
It was founded by Sir Thomas Mildmay, a courtier of Queen
Elizabeth and her Chancellor of the Exchequer, and it was built on
the site of a Dominican friary which Sir Thomas bought for £550.
The site must have been healthy, for the first master, Laurence
Chaderton, lived to be a hundred and three.

Being so strongly Puritan the college contributed many alumni to
the settlements in America. John Harvard was one of them. He
sailed, for consciences' sake, in 1636 (the *Mayflower* had sailed in
1620), died of consumption at the age of thirty-one, bequeathing
half of his estate (£779 17s 2d) and 320 books to found Harvard
College.

So Protestant was Sir Thomas the founder that he turned the old
church of the Dominicans into a refectory and their refectory into a
chapel, and the latter ran north and south which was so contrary
to Catholic practice as almost to constitute black magic. However, another chapel was built later to the design of Sir Christopher
Wren, and it is still there, and it runs east and west in the accepted
fashion.

Wren's chapel was built between 1668 and 1674, and is less
strictly classical than the earlier Wren chapel at Pembroke. The
plaster ceiling within is especially fine (by John Grove, who worked
under Wren), and there is good woodwork of 1676, organ case of
1686 by Father Schmidt, reredos 1687 which has in it the Return of
the Prodigal Son by Jacopo Amigoni and is early eighteenth century.

The stained glass is of 1883. The general impression that one gets from the chapel and its furnishings is that it is all very civilized and elegant; but has little to do with the searing religious convictions of former ages.

The rest of the college is architecturally undistinguished; but the gardens are superb. There is an enormous oriental plane tree, a large ornamental pond (and a smaller one, but guarded by fellows—the larger one once the fish-pond of the friars), private swans, a swimming pool and a large and flourishing example of *Metasequoia glyptostoboides*: the 'fossil tree' from that desert-surrounded area of West China in which both plants and animals were protected for so many millennia from outside competition. The tree is a deciduous conifer, and was, until discovered in China, thought to have died out in Cretaceous times.

North-west along St Andrew's Street is **Christ's College**, founded in 1439 by William Bingham and then called God's House but refounded, in 1505, by Lady Margaret Tudor (née Beaufort) the pious mother of Henry VII. This lady used to keep chambers in the college. If Bishop Fisher's sermon preached at her funeral was the truth then she must have been a truly noble noblewoman, at a time when arrogance and insensitiveness were the common qualities of the rich. 'Bounteous she was,' said the Bishop, 'and liberal . . . of singular easiness to be spoken unto . . . of marvellous gentleness to all folk . . . unkind to no creature, nor forgetful of any service done to her (which is no little part of very nobleness) . . . All England for her death have cause for weeping.' It seems consistent with this character that she is supposed to have leant out of the window of her chamber in Christ's College on seeing a boy being beaten by a master and shouted: 'Lente! Lente!' Students were much younger in those days than undergraduates are now, a tender thirteen or fourteen.

Milton was at Christ's from 1625 to 1632, and there is a venerable mulberry tree in the garden under which he is said to have written *Lycidas*, and which is still called 'Milton's Mulberry Tree'.

The Gateway is a relic of Lady Margaret's time. On the street side there is a brilliant display of heraldic carving supported by beasts called *yales* which have goatish heads. In medieval Indian temples there are animals called *yalis* very similar in feature. The *yalis* have round stones carved out of the rock inside their mouths so that the stones can never be removed without breaking the *yali*: a piece of virtuosity unknown among the *yales* of Cambridge.

The Hall, much altered, alas, by Sir Gilbert Scott but with fine tracery in the two tall windows, has portraits of the pious foundress, Bishop Fisher, Field-Marshal Jan Smuts, Quarles, Paley who wrote *Evidences of Christianity*, Charles Darwin who wrote evidences of quite another sort, and other notables who went to, or were connected with, the college. There is some very good Tudor plate in the Buttery (not normally on view). The Fellows' Building is mid-seventeenth century, vast, idiosyncratically but well and beautifully designed. The chapel, with a brick turret with a pretty eighteenth-century top to it, embodies the original fabric of the former chapel of God's House. There is existing a document dated 12th December 1506, signed by James Stanley, Bishop of Ely, giving permission to the master, fellows and scholars of the college to celebrate divine service. The north vestries are from the original building, as are the moulded beams in the ante-chapel, and some other beams beneath later panelling—some of which have been opened up to the view. The brass eagle lectern is famous: early sixteenth century and very beautiful. The windows of the north side have good fifteenth- and sixteenth-century glass, well worth noticing. In the most easterly window of this north range is Edward the Confessor and the foundress at her prayers. In the Master's Lodge is a fine Tudor bay window.

The gardens of Christ's are famous. There is a fine collection of irises in the Third Court; the Fellows' Garden is a notable winter garden—well furnished with evergreen shrubs and trees; there is a *Stachyrurus praecox* on the west side (so lovely in early spring when its flowers precede its leaves); Milton's mulberry tree supported by its large mound, another *Metasequoia* but a lesser one than that of Emmanuel (ground not wet enough here?) and nine hives for the honey bee. The bees do better here than their sisters of the open countryside owing to the absence of poisonous sprays in the city. These bees seem to confute the commonly held theory that hives must never be placed under trees. The fellows eat the honey and it is held to sweeten their tempers.

Farther along Sidney Street we come to Jesus Lane, on the right, and whatever we do or do not do in Cambridge we should go and look at **Jesus College**. It was founded in 1497 by Bishop Alcock, of Ely, after he had himself, as visitor, closed the Benedictine nunnery of St Radegund's on the site because there were said to be only two nuns left there and one of these was *infamis*. Persistent legend has it, in fact, that Maids' Causeway, not far distant, was so named in ironical reference to the fact that the nuns of St Radegund's used to go there to meet their gentlemen friends, and in the fellows' garden there is still said to grow a herb with which these naughty nuns anticipated the pill.

The entrance to the college is a long walled paved walk called by undergraduates the 'Chimney' (from *cheminée*) (the church over the road they call 'St Ops' because it is opposite). Going through the chimney we then walk through a building which is basically twelfth century, i.e. very early, but much altered by Bishop Alcock in the fifteenth century. He used white brick—the earliest use of this unfortunate material in Cambridge colleges. We then find ourselves in a biggish courtyard, open to the west which gives a fine sense of air and space and is one of the most fascinating courts in Cambridge. The range of buildings to the north of it is seventeenth century but it fits well with the earlier monastic buildings to the east. In fact this open-sided court is quite impeccable and most attractive.

The beautiful carved doorway in the east range, which gives access to the cloisters, is original, but was moved to its present position in Alcock's time. We pass through it into the cloisters, one of the most magical places in Cambridge.

There are blackbirds in many Cambridge courts, and there are here; they sing most beautifully and the acoustics of the court seem to favour them. The cloister is the original one of the nuns of St Radegund's, altered and enlarged by the founder of the college and it thus has some of the bishop's early white brick in it.

In the north-east of this most charming and peaceful square is an odd alcove—the floor of which has sunk below the level of the present-day cloister (or perhaps remained where it was while the cloister has risen) which was once an entrance to the chapter house of the nunnery. It is a doorway with a window each side of it; about 1230 and Early English in its purest and most lovely form, with stiff-leaf capitals and composite shafts of central pillars surrounded by rings of slender shafts. The latter remind one irresistibly of the 'chiming pillars' of South Indian temples, pillars which when struck emit clear bell-like notes of different pitch. But these at Jesus emit no such notes and are not to be struck. The English, unlike the Indians and the Romans and other peoples, did not build monolithically.

The timber ceilings of the Cloisters must be noticed: these again are Bishop Alcock's work. His rebus—the cock—may be seen carved here and there on them: his cockerel, here as at Ely and several parish churches, is carved around with a profusion that is most exhibitionist.

The Combination Room is in what was the chapter house of the nunnery, and has a most noteworthy ceiling. The hall, north of the cloisters, is where the hall of the nuns was, or their refectory; in other words it has been continuously used for eating in for nearly nine hundred years. St Radegund's was founded at the beginning of the eleventh century. St Radegund herself was a queen of the sixth century when the world was filled with saints: daughter of Berthram Prince of Thuringia, queen of Lotharius King of the Franks.

The Hall is a fine one. Particularly note the beautiful bay window, built about 1500 with such delicate carving in its tracery, and also in its walls and vault. The fine massive hammerbeam roof of the hall is original. But St Radegund's Church, which still survives as the chapel of the college, is one of the great things in Cambridge.

We enter this from the south cloister walk—through a door that was once the arch that joined the north aisle of the church to the north transept; for Bishop Alcock lopped the north aisle off the church to enlarge his cloister, and then used the old arch as his door from the outside. The bishop was Comptroller of Works to Henry VIII, and so he knew a thing or two about building.

The chapel inside is Norman in plan: i.e. cruciform with a central tower; but nearly everything in it is very early Early English: in fact the whole building is of this style.

Restored it has been—Pugin went over it about 1850—but restoration was needed; many thirteenth-century details had been obliterated and had to be replaced. The chapel that we see today is the chancel of the nuns' chapel, and the old nuns' nave and transepts are now an ante-chapel. Perhaps the present ante-chapel has been less restored than the chapel. It was a much bigger church once: Bishop Alcock cut a lump off it to turn into the Master's Lodge.

The chapel is exciting, not only for lovers of the Early English style, but also for admirers of the pre-Raphaelites. Morris designed the ceilings put in between 1864–67, and most of the stained glass in the ante-chapel was made by Morris to the design of Burne-Jones; but there is some glass (the lower scenes in the west window of the south nave and the south window on the east side of the south transept) by Ford Madox Brown. The Burne-Jones windows are brilliant and vivid, utterly unlike medieval glass but strangely fitting very well in this early medieval chapel. There are the nine orders of angels in the south transept, with man in the tenth place; there is a gallery of blessed saints with Bishop Alcock thrown in for good measure, there are the Four Evangelists, each attended by a very pagan Sibyl; and in the tower lights are the Incarnation, Passion, Resurrection and Ascension. The south nave windows have patriarchs and prophets, and the north the Virtues, busy trampling underfoot their contrary vices. It is interesting to compare the Ford Madox Brown glass with that of Burne-Jones.

There is much nineteenth- and twentieth-century building round about this medieval nucleus. The big outer court to the east of the cloisters resembles a block of workers' dwellings put up on a bomb-site by an unenlightened town council. There are two angels supporting a coat of arms in the south-east corner, on Morley Horder's building, which immediately strike the eye. They are by Eric Gill. But like his Prospero and Ariel (which he tells us he secretly meant for God the Father and the Son) stuck on the front of London's Broadcasting House the building that supports them does not do them justice.

Cranmer, the archbishop burnt by Bloody Mary because he recanted against his acknowledgment of Catholic doctrine and the supremacy of the Pope, was a Jesus man. Although he prevaricated all his life at least he showed fine hardihood in his death, holding his right hand out into the flames of his pyre to be burnt first because it had offended by signing the wrongful document.

In the library of Jesus there is the autograph copy of the first edition of the first Bible ever printed on the American continent. It is written in the Mohican tongue. The Bible was printed in Cambridge, Mass., in 1663, the Corporation of London paying for this extraordinary enterprise, and the translator was a Jesus man, John Eliot, of Nasing, who took his degree in 1622, joined the Non-conformists nine years later and sailed to the American colonies—to convert untold numbers of Red Indians.

Samuel Taylor Coleridge was also here from 1791 to 1793. He distinguished himself by tracing the words 'Liberty and Equality' on the grass of a court in gunpowder and setting fire to them. This did not endear him to the authorities, who neither endorsed the sentiment nor liked having their lawn branded. The wrought-iron gate of Jesus was recently replaced by an exact copy of the original one by Mr Frank Lewis, of Yelling, on the Huntingdonshire border.

On Jesus Green, the Reverend John Hullier, Vicar of Babraham, was burnt alive in 1556 for being a Protestant. His pyre was made up of Protestant books.

North of Jesus College is that part of the River Cam where the racing eights are housed in large boat-houses, and where the 'bumping races' are held. The latter are a form of race made necessary by the fact that the river is too narrow for eights to navigate two abreast, and therefore have to race in line ahead. If a boat manages to bump the boat ahead she *goes up*, by changing places with it—and if she is bumped by the boat astern she *goes down*. The leading boat is called Head of the River, and may be rowed back to her boat-house with her flag flying.

Magdalene College was founded in 1542, as a hostel to house young monks from the Benedictine abbey of Crowland, in the Fens; and later the monks of Walden, Ramsey and Ely contributed to it money and students. It can be understood that these religious foundations wished their novitiates to benefit by the more sophisticated education that Cambridge afforded, but did not wish them to come into too close a contact with secular students. Thus a separate college, or hostel, was necessary for them. As Henry Stafford, 2nd Duke of Buckingham, contributed to the building of the college it was at first called Buckingham College; but in 1542 Thomas Audley, Lord Chancellor to Henry VIII and some would say his creature, refounded the college on a larger scale with some of the money that he had grabbed from the monasteries at the Dissolution. The nomination of the master of the college is yet within the gift of Audley's descendants.

The most interesting and beautiful thing to see, by far, in this college is the Pepysian Library.

The building was started in the 1670s. Certainly it has somewhat the plan of a Tudor manor house, but with an Italianate colonnade and other seventeenth-century features externally: as a building no doubt it can be faulted and it lacks unity; but nevertheless it is a lovable and beautiful building and attractively idiosyncratic.

The books, the choicest of their day, are as Pepys left them: kept in his own 'book presses', with each book hoisted on a block of wood so that the tops of all the books are level! This system at least has the virtue that, over the centuries, the books have been kept in order. There are some 3,000 books, many of the greatest value and interest; and the famous Diary was discovered among them, written in the short-hand cypher that Pepys invented for himself. It was transcribed into long-hand by a student of St John's College and published in 1825. The range of the other books in the library gives some idea of the catholicity of Pepys's interests, and of the lively and enquiring climate of his times.

For the rest, Magdalene is not one of the architecturally great colleges, although it has some comely buildings of clunch.

Charles Kingsley was a Magdalene man, and used to climb out of the college in the small hours of the morning in order to go fishing in the Fen country, about which he wrote so vividly later on in *Hereward the Wake*. Kingsley's portrait is in Hall, so is Pepys's by Lely, T. S. Eliot by Wyndham Lewis, and a copy of Holbein's Lord Audley. While in the hall note the carved bunches of fruit and other flora behind the High Table. These are Tudor, although the rest of the wainscoting is eighteenth century. Sir John Vanbrugh is thought to have designed the stairway and gallery to the Combination Room.

When leaving Magdalene note Benson Court, nearby. A group of charming Tudor houses standing on what was Fisher Row—a medieval staithe. They were very well restored by Sir Edward Lutyens and David Wyn Roberts. The big timber-framed house is sixteenth century and was once the Cross Keys Inn.

St John's College was founded, like Christ's, by Lady Margaret Tudor (or Beaufort). She founded it after she had founded Christ's and it was not built until after her death. The building of it was entrusted to Bishop Fisher, Lady Margaret's confessor and a man in whom she placed great confidence. It was Fisher who had the great gatehouse of red brick and stone built between 1511 and 1516, after the foundress's death. But the college stands on the site of a much earlier foundation: that of the Hospital of St John, which was founded before 1200. The few surviving fragments of the old chapel of the hospital appear to be mid-thirteenth century.

St John's is a vast college, the second largest in Cambridge; and we can here but describe its salient features. The gatehouse, already mentioned, is lofty, turreted, magnificent. On the street side of it is a brilliant, and brilliantly painted heraldic display such as that at Christ's College, the arms also supported by yales. The statue of St John was placed there in 1662, replacing an older version.

The first court is much spoiled by Sir Gilbert Scott's monstrous Victorian-Gothic chapel, which rises up on the north side of it, not really joining the other buildings to form part of them—just rearing up its great bulk to be admired, or not admired, as may be the case. The east range of this first court is the hall, kitchen and buttery. The passage that divides hall from kitchens in Cambridge colleges (as in medieval manor houses) is called the Screens. Here the Screens passage is beautiful, with a smaller heraldic group with Lady Margaret presiding over it, carved Tudor screen and original carved beams.

The hall is splendid, with a massive hammerbeam roof, most of it Tudor, and much original linenfold panelling. There is a fine portrait of Lady Margaret, a much smaller one of Bishop Fisher, and a long gallery of famous men including Herrick, Wordsworth, William Cecil, Wilberforce, Herschel the astronomer, Lord Palmerston, and a Romney portrait of Sir Noah Thomas. There is also a portrait of Edward Henry Palmer, orientalist, and Arabic, Persian and Urdu scholar. He taught himself these languages in Cambridge, without visiting the lands where they were spoken, by his friendships with undergraduates who came from them. He became so good that fairly obscure Urdu papers used to commission him to write poems for them. He did eventually spend some time in the East, and was eventually sent to Egypt on a political mission, and was killed by unfriendly Arabs near the Suez Canal.

The Combination Room is the finest in Cambridge, 100 feet long with transomed windows and a plaster ceiling, the latter said to be by the hand of the same Italian craftsmen who made Trinity fountain; the room is contemporary with Trinity Great Court. There are two fine fireplaces: the east one originally where it is—the west one brought here from a house in Cambridge. Its date is 1594. There is a magnificent set of Chippendale chairs.

The library forms the north side of third court, and ends right on the brink of—almost in—the river. It is an interesting building, built 1624 but most unusually for this date very Gothic-looking Evidently the architect was what we would call a traditionalist, and his building is none the worse-looking for that. The rest of the third court came shortly after the library. The library is best seen from a boat, for there is a splendid oriel window carried right over the water, and the letters J.L.C.S. carved very big and lavishly over the window with the date, the initials being for Johannes Lincolniensis

Custos Sigilli, meaning the Dr John Williams, Bishop of Lincoln, who gave the money to build the library. He gave it anonymously, but it leaked out. Lady Mary Cavendish also gave money anonymously, to build the north side of the second court, but that leaked out too.

There are two bridges here across the Cam: one, the more upstream of the two, having been started after the turn of the century by Grumbold, after Christopher Wren's idea; and the other the famous 'Bridge of Sighs', named after the real one in Venice, built 1831. Students of military architecture will be interested to note in all the college bridges the lengths to which the authorities have gone to keep in—or keep out—undergraduates at night. Lengths, it may be said, entirely unavailing: there is not one college that cannot be climbed in and out of by the student of ordinary accomplishment: the present writer, no alpinist, has been in and out of many of them.

What shall we say of St John's new court over the river? It is vast, and a fine Victorian-Gothic cocktail. It might well have been designed as a screen set for a Walt Disney extravaganza and is commonly called 'the Wedding Cake'. By virtue of its size and position it dominates the Backs. The gilded vane at the top of the fantastic flying-buttressed and be-pinnacled lantern in the centre of the great pile was decorated, in the 1880s, with one of the scarlet 'blazers', or flannel sports jackets, of the Lady Margaret Boat Club. In those pre-helicopter days it took the authorities much effort, and several days, to remove the indignity, and one marvels at the virtuosity of the undergraduate—who was probably well primed with beer—who put it there in the first place.

The scarlet jacket of the St John's oarsmen, incidentally, is said to have been the first ever of the genus 'blazer', and it gave its name to all of those egregious garments.

A new range of building, called Cripps, won the RIBA bronze in 1968.

Trinity College is the largest college in Cambridge, bigger than many an entire university and in output of great men it has surpassed many an entire nation. In a short list of poets of Trinity one can include George Herbert, Cowley, Suckling, Marvell, Dryden, Byron, Macaulay, Tennyson, Edward Fitzgerald, Housman, Iqbal. Of public men half a dozen Prime Ministers of Britain, the Earl of Essex, John Winthrop of New England, William Smith O'Brien of

Ireland, and the Marquis of Granby, who earned undying fame by not stopping to retrieve the wig which blew off his bald head during a cavalry charge, and for this remarkable feat of restraint had some hundreds of inns named after him, the length and breadth of the land. Of great men of science there is a list many pages long; but Newton, Sedgwick the geologist, Rutherford who split the atom with such unfortunate results, Eddington and Jeans will have to do. Sir James Frazer, Macaulay, G. M. Trevelyan and Lord Acton are among its famous writers of prose, and Vaughan Williams among its writers of music.

Henry VIII founded the College of the Holy and Undivided Trinity in 1546, a year before his death. He did it by knocking together nine existing foundations or hostels, including Michaelhouse and King's Hall, which were two of the biggest colleges in Cambridge. Michaelhouse had been founded in 1324 by Edward II's Chancellor of the Exchequer Hervey de Stanton: King's Hall by Edward III in 1336; so that although Trinity may seem at first sight to be an upstart college only 420 years old, in fact it can claim that, in part at least, it dates from 1324.

The Great Gate, finished 1535, was built to commemorate Edward III, but his statue was removed from it and Henry VIII's put there instead. Edward's was moved to the clock tower by the chapel.

The other buildings that were gobbled up by Henry VIII were: St Catherine's Hostel, Physwick Hostel, Crutched Hostel, Gregory's Hostel, Tyled Hostel, Oving's Inn and St Gerard's Hostel—commonly called 'Garret' Hostel (there is still Garret Hostel Lane nearby). Henry was able to appropriate all of these institutions, including tne church of St Michael, because being monastic they fell to the Crown on the Dissolution. He also, of course, appropriated all their endowments, and these, together with the endowments of many other religious houses, were devoted to the great college that was to perpetuate his memory. The Tudor sovereigns looked upon the founding of colleges much as the Pharaohs of Egypt looked upon building pyramids: as imperishable memorials. Henry VIII got his very cheaply.

We enter Trinity through the Great Gate, which was in fact built as the gate for King's Hall between 1519 and 1535, but is on such a scale that it was obviously built with the idea that it should become the gate of a much bigger college. But when Henry VIII died the college had only just been founded, and the Great Court was not conceived until Queen Elizabeth's time. Under Mary was built the chapel and other of the buildings surrounding the court.

But it was Dr Thomas Nevile, Master of Trinity in 1593 and a favourite of Queen Elizabeth, who really built the college as it stands today.

He shifted King Edward's Tower (or the Clock Tower) from its former position due west of the Great Tower and moved it to where it is today—in line with Mary's chapel. He pulled down most of Mary's buildings, and built new ranges to suit his plan: which was to build the biggest and grandest court in either Oxford or Cambridge, and one of the most impressive urban open spaces in the world.

The Great Gate is grand enough, although Henry VIII's statue on one side of it, and James I and his wife and son on the other, seem uninspired. Turn right through the gate and we face the chapel, massive and Marian Gothic, the kind of over-civilized late Gothic of which Mary Tudor was so fond: a Gothic persisted in after the rest of the world had gone over to the styles of the Renaissance. It was built 1555-64, and although individually not a great building it fits in very well indeed with the composition of the Great Court.

Walking into the ante-chapel the breath is taken away by the perfectly white, cold, silent chamber into which one is plunged, in which sit or stand six over-life-sized statues. There is a feeling that these great men have been holding commune with each other, and that one has interrupted their discourse. The famous one is Newton, by Roubiliac, often considered the finest thing in Cambridge and one of the best pieces of stone portraiture since the Greeks. It inspired the lines in Wordsworth's *Prelude*:

> *Newton with the prism and silent face,*
> *The marble index of a mind for ever*
> *Voyaging through strange seas of thought, alone.*

The others are Bacon by Weeks—Bacon in splendid stage Elizabethan costume, but I cannot believe that the original looked quite so miserable; Barrow, the Master who had the library built, by Noble; Whewell, the Master who built Whewell's Court, by Woolner; Macaulay by Woolner; and Tennyson by Thorneycroft, in a fine theatrical pose. There are also a number of busts about the walls.

The lavish screen, holding the organ and dividing the chapel from the ante-chapel, was put up in Bentley's time. Bentley was the most unpopular master any college ever had, even if a great classical scholar. He impoverished his college by putting up grandiose works to embellish the chapel and his own lodge, he used publicly to call his fellows 'asses', 'dogs', 'fools' and 'sots' and even other—yet more scurrilous—names. Masters of Trinity are appointed by the Crown, not elected as in other colleges; and no doubt they are very hard to get rid of. Bentley finally was degraded by orders of the University Senate, was reinstated and died in 1742 after having been master for forty-two most unhappy years. Where a great Perpendicular window was in the east end of the chapel he had a huge reredos raised: gorgeous but somehow the wrong shape.

Tacked on to the west of the chapel is the Clock Tower, or King Edward's Tower, which was originally the gateway to King's Hall and was built 1427–33. The statue of Edward was put in it in 1601. Wordsworth mentions the clock in it in his *Prelude*, and undergraduates try to race the chiming of it at midnight by running right round the Great Court: a feat that can be accomplished by a good athlete.

West of the tower is the Master's Lodge, built by Nevile but enlarged at great expense by Bentley. Then come the hall, kitchens and butteries and all the rest of it. The gate over in the middle of the south range is the Queen Elizabeth Gate with a statue of Elizabeth I in it, and the south-east corner of the Great Court is known as Merton's (or 'Muttonhole') Corner, and is notable for the fact that Lord Byron used to keep his tame bear in it (students being forbidden to keep dogs). When asked by a fellow what he intended to do with the animal he said that it should sit for a fellowship. There is a story that Byron was finally sent down (expelled) from the college because he would insist on bathing naked in the fountain in the centre of Great Court. This fountain, which is very beautiful, was built by Italian craftsmen in 1602.

The visitor will notice that the Great Court is quite asymmetrical: it is far from being even a perfect rectangle, or even straight sided. Like all really surpassingly beautiful concourses of building it has grown up organically, over the centuries, each new component being fitted into the older ones, and thus has unity in diversity. One cannot help wondering just how well a modern building of any kind we like to think of would fit in to Trinity Great Court. Is ours the first age that could not conceivably contribute?

The steps up into the Hall are, like the chiming of the clock, a challenge to undergraduates. Some of them can, but others cannot, jump down them in a leap: others, but few indeed, can jump up them.

The Hall was built by Nevile, with his own money.

It is one of the finest halls there is, and is modelled on the hall of the Middle Temple in London and is 103 feet long. The old hall of Michaelhouse was on the other side of the Screens, i.e. where the kitchen and buttery now are. The kitchens of Trinity are vast and highly organized, like the kitchens of a really great hotel; and in the old kitchen turtle shells, engraved with the dates on which their occupants made soup on great occasions, are hung on the steaming walls.

The screen of the Screens is a most exuberant piece of carved and painted woodwork, reminding one strongly of the decoration of some of the less restrained modern Hindu temples of North India, and obviously the work is influenced by the Elizabethan artists' idea of the Georgeous East. Awareness of the Orient was coming to England in Tudor times: witness the splendid date palms carved on the west door of King's College Chapel.

The hall, which has a fine hammerbeam roof, is dominated by the famous portrait of that very dominating monarch, Henry VIII, by Holbein. To his right is his unhappy daughter, Mary Tudor, looking crabbed and dissatisfied (compare her portrait as a young girl in Sawston Hall done before all those executions looking innocent and happy). The Mary in Trinity is by Antonio Moro. There is the Duke of Gloucester, in fancy dress, by Sir Joshua Reynolds, Lord Tennyson by Watts, a contemporary painting on wood of Francis Bacon, and a portrait of Nevile, who had it all built, near the entrance. Look up to see the beautiful lantern in the roof, which was originally to let the smoke out, for the hall was heated by a huge centrally-placed open brazier.

Out into the Screens again we turn right and walk out into Nevile's Court. Right opposite is the Wren Library, designed by Sir Christopher and built in 1675, in Isaac Barrow's mastership. Wren was a close friend of Barrow and the latter persuaded him to design the library for nothing. It is a superb building within and without, built of a lovely glowing stone from Ketton in Rutland, and raised above a cloister. To balance the library, on the other side of the court, Wren had a tribune built: a blind and purely ornamental feature with a platform, staircases, columns and niches.

The library itself is a building of fine classical purity and simplicity. The insides of the book cases, designed by Wren, are embellished by busts of Trinity men by famous sculptors, and much enriched by wood carvings of Grinling Gibbons—the greatest master of this art since medieval times. These carvings well repay some study. Some of the busts are pretty run-of-the-mill, but the first Coke (the Lord Chief Justice) by Roubiliac, and also this artist's Cotton, Barrow, Bentley, Newton and Bacon, and each side of the entrance the naturalists Ray and Willoughby, are fine, and so is Woolner's bust of a beardless Tennyson. The great statue by Thorwaldsen of Byron was offered to Westminster Abbey, but the Dean and Chapter refused it because of the poet's morals. It lay in the cellars of the London Customs house before it was rescued by Byron's old college, which apparently had forgiven him for his bear and his bathing. There are other Byron relics in the library. Byron's morals, incidentally, besides leading him into the enormities that we have already spoken of, are also said to have caused him to climb up on the roof of Trinity Library and lewdly embellish the statues up there. (There is a book, incidentally, written in the last century, called *The Roof-Climber's Guide to Trinity College*. Recently a more comprehensive guide has come out, *Night Climbers of Cambridge*, which is to be bought in any Cambridge bookshop. The sport is still a very popular one.)

In the library also are Newton's death mask and his telescope, some priceless illuminated manuscripts, manuscripts of Milton, Macaulay, Thackeray and Tennyson, and a fifteenth-century Roll of Carols said to be the earliest known manuscript of musical harmony.

Back in Nevile's Court the long cloister on the north side is interesting; for it was in this that Newton worked out his theory of sound. If you stand at the west end and stamp your foot you can hear the clear and very sharp echo which Newton timed to measure, for the first time, the speed of sound.

The New Court is of interest mostly to botanists, or at least gardeners; for it has a distinguished collection of creepers on its walls. Bishop's Hostel is small and very atmospheric. It was paid for in 1667–71 by the Bishop of Lichfield (the man who dammed up Well Creek thus cutting off the navigation between Wisbech and King's Lynn, for which folly he found himself in trouble).

From New Court to the River Cam there was once a mighty avenue of lime trees, planted in 1672. They were all cut down recently because of an heroic decision made by the master and fellows of Trinity. These elderly men preferred that this should be done and new ones planted so that future generations should enjoy them, rather than that they themselves should continue to enjoy the old ones during their lifetimes.

If we like to cross the Cam, and then the traffic-swollen Queen's Road which latter we do at the risk of our lives, we can look through a superb wrought-iron gate down an avenue of mighty elm trees that reminds us of the piers and vaults of a cathedral.

Trinity, besides being the largest of the colleges, is also by far the wealthiest. The agricultural depression which hit England in the 1870s when cheap grain began to flood in from America hit most of the colleges badly, for their investments were mostly in land. Trinity, however, owned much of its property in the industrial north, and thus was enriched rather than impoverished.

Next to Trinity we come to **Gonville and Caius**, generally called 'Caius' which is pronounced Keys.

Gonville Hall was originally founded in some houses in Free School Lane, near present Corpus Christi, by Edmund Gonville, of Terrington, in Norfolk. He obtained his licence to build it in 1347, but died shortly afterwards, and left his executor, William Bateman, Bishop of Norwich, to finish the job. Bateman also died leaving the college in embryo, and it was not until Dr John Caius came along, in 1557, and refounded the old college as Gonville and Caius, that it really came to much.

Caius was a Norwich man, although of a Yorkshire father. The family name was, in fact, Keys, but was Latinized into Caius in the fashion of the day. He was a great and remarkable man, a student of Latin, Greek and Hebrew at the original Gonville Hall, was made a fellow at the age of twenty-three, studied medicine at Padua, was physician to Edward VI and Mary Tudor and President of the Royal College of Physicians. He was one of the first people in England to put the study of anatomy on a serious footing.

When he was offered the mastership of his new college he accepted reluctantly, refused to accept pay, and himself paid for most of the new building. Unfortunately he had a penchant for collecting Papist objects at a time when Popery was disrespectable. A mob of militantly Protestant students collected and—under the eye of the Vice-Chancellor of the University and with his approval—they broke into Dr Caius's lodge, flung his collection of missals and chasubles and other sacred objects into the court, and burnt them; and Caius was forced to retire from the college that he had founded and built and —because he had impoverished himself in the building of it and then had no other means of support—he died destitute. But his grave is in the chapel, and has on it: *Fui Caius*—I was Caius. And also *Vivit post Funera Virtus*.

The court of Caius into which we come from Trinity Street is Victorian and uninspired. We then pass under the great Gate of Virtue.

The Gate of Virtue is one of the first pieces of High Renaissance architecture to be built in England (remember Dr Caius had studied in Padua). It is thus very interesting from an architectural point of view. It is for me curiously unsatisfying, being spoilt, I think, by its windows.

The Gate of Humility, by which in the past students were wont to enter the college, has been removed to the master's garden, where no doubt it reminds the occupant of this important virtue. The Gate of Honour, however, is still there, leading the way towards the Senate House where students receive their degrees.

It is an astonishing little building. It is a splendid miniature—a little fantasia. It is a product, like the Gate of Virtue, of the first impact of classical architecture on England, when anything went: there were no inhibitions about mixing up orders or styles, or about 'purity' or anything else like that. It is really quite absurd. The Greek temple half-way up it should be on the grand scale or not at all, but it is completely dwarfed and dominated by the curious rustic phallic dome on top.

The rest of Caius Court consists of two ranges of chambers put up by Caius, of stone and very medieval-looking, with the chapel on the north. The chapel is fourteenth century (licence to celebrate Divine Office in it was given in 1339), originally of clunch faced with brick; but both are covered up now by stone, put there in 1716. The interior is very eighteenth century, i.e. more fitting for a theatre than for a place of worship. The apse at the east end was added by Waterhouse in 1870, the cross and candles on the altar are by Gerald Benney of 1958 and, for lovers of Victorian sentimentality, there is a corking *Non Angli sed Angeli* in a window, with a roguish bishop eyeing two winsome boys. The original Gonville Court is part fifteenth century.

Caius is noted for producing doctors, and also good food. Its cuisine has always had a reputation for being better than that of other

21. *Above left*, Sir John Poley's monument (see page 331); *right*, the Jennens Monument at Acton. *Below*, the lovely alabaster relief of the Adoration of the Magi in Long Melford Church

22. CAMBRIDGE. *Above left*, the portico of the Fitzwilliam Museum; *right*, the astonishing roof of King's College Chapel. The stone-work, eighty feet up, is so delicate that to stand on it would be to put your foot through it, yet every one of the bosses that it supports is said to weigh a ton. *Below left*, the chapel of Sidney Sussex College; *right*, Wren's famous Library at Trinity

colleges, although certainly the cooks of Peterhouse would dispute this hotly.

Trinity Hall has little to detain us, in its buildings at least, although the principal court is fourteenth century, but ashlared (i.e. covered with dressed stone facing) in the eighteenth. The college was founded in 1350 by the William Bateman, Bishop of Norwich, who took over the care of Gonville from his friend who founded it. Bateman was not only Bishop of Norwich, but one of the great English diplomats of the time: a papal dignitary, and an international lawyer of great renown. He died at the papal court at Avignon; and was buried with great pomp and ceremony in front of the High Altar in the Church of St Mary along with a bevy of previously departed Popes. He gave an impetus towards law in his foundation of Trinity Hall which still persists; and Trinity Hall is to law what Caius is to medicine.

The library is sixteenth century in spite of its Gothic windows, charming and flower-surrounded. There are many old books in it, some of them still chained. In the chapel is a vast painting of the Presentation in the Temple, and the college has one of the best collections of silver in Cambridge.

Clare should really be seen for the first time from over the river. First, then, we come to its perfectly lovely garden, one of the loveliest in the country; with its Perfume Garden, its Sunken Garden in which plays are performed in a most magical setting, and Clare—not to be outdone in this important matter—has a *very* fine *Metasequoia*. In the master's garden is a vast and sumptuous copper beech tree (there is a print by Ackerman showing it six feet high!), and even vaster plane trees. But then Cambridge abounds in mighty trees.

The iron gate that gives on to the bridge is one of the most beautiful in existence—delicate lace-work in iron and in perfect taste. Clare Bridge is beautiful too, with its stone balls. One of these is newer than the others—the reason being that, in an assault by the students of St John's, the balls got thrown into the river before the Clare men counter-attacked and the Johnians were thrown into a rout. All the balls were recovered save one—surely a challenge to modern frogmen? The bridge is 1640, and built by Thomas Grumbold, the great Cambridge mason. The lovely set of gates is by Warren, and is of 1714: there is another like it in the entrance to the college from Trinity Lane.

From the bridge the block of Clare presents to us a massive and most civilized building, which has often been said to look more like a palace than a college. The south side of it, overlooking King's Lawn, is of 1640 or thereabouts, the west side must have at least been influenced by Wren, but the design was by Robert Grumbold—son of Thomas who built the bridge.

The effect of this whole building is urbane and harmonious, and inside the one old court of Clare it is the same. The east range is the oldest part, by John Westley, master mason, of 1638, and showed when it was built a mixture of Gothic and the new styles coming in from Italy and, more especially perhaps, France. Thus there was a Tudor-type Perpendicular fan vault ceiling in the gateway, two oriel windows above, Perpendicular niches to each side, the whole surmounted by a classical gable. When it was built this range (and others to follow) had battlements on top of the walls, hiding the dormer windows, and Tudor-arched windows. The battlements were replaced in the eighteenth century by the present pretty balustrade; and the windows made straight-topped. The building of the whole court took from 1638 to the end of the century—the work being held up for years by the Civil War; but the feeling of unity and harmony in the court is most profound.

The chapel is of the 1760s, again much influenced by Wren. The octagonal ante-chapel is famous for its glazed cupola: it was designed by the Master of Caius, Sir James Burrough, who was an amateur architect and who had a good plasterer. The chapel proper has a barrel vault, with the same delicate plaster work, and an altar painting by Cipriani of the *Annunciation*, but like so many churches of this period absolutely no religious feeling whatever. Pull the stalls and the altar out and it is a ballroom.

Clare College was founded by Lady Elizabeth de Clare, three times widowed, and daughter of Gilbert de Clare. Of this lady more under Clare, the village in Suffolk. Suffice here that she took over the burnt-out University Hall, a college that had been founded in 1326 by Richard Badew, and refounded it as Clare Hall in 1339. She was very friendly with John, Duke of Lancaster, and his steward Edmund Gonville the Rector of Terrington who as we have seen founded his own college of Gonville Hall. Another intimate of Lady Elizabeth was the Countess of Pembroke who founded Pembroke College, so this group of intimates, or little coterie of wealthy friends did much to build up Cambridge.

There is fine plate at Clare, including many good candlesticks and a 'poison cup' which has a crystal in it which is supposed either to shatter or to discolour at the presence of poison.

There are books in Clare Library of the ninth century, made of parchment in which are warble-fly holes. It can be deduced from these that the warble-flies of eleven hundred years ago were much the same as the ones which torment our cattle today, causing them to tear round the fields in panic with their tails in the air.

Over the river is a large block of buildings belonging to Clare designed by Sir Giles Gilbert Scott and built of brick, and it is hard by the university library designed by the same man. The Clare building is inoffensive, although marred by silly bits of vestigial Georgian ornamentation: the university library is very bad. The recently built Castle Hill Hostel, designed by David Roberts, is supposed to be a good piece of modern building and meet for its purpose. But to look at the seventeenth- and eighteenth-century buildings of Clare, and then at those of the twentieth, is to wonder in which direction our civilization is travelling.

King's College is, of course, completely overshadowed by its chapel, which is one of the most famous buildings in the world and the very peak and culmination of the Gothic art.

In our tour of East Anglia so far we have seen much Perpendicular period building: most certainly East Anglia contains more choice building of this period than any other province of England; but here in King's College Chapel we have the *ne plus ultra* of the style: any further change or development could only lead to decadence.

We should, of course, attend at least one choral service in the chapel during our stay in Cambridge, for perhaps nowhere in the world is more joyous music allied to visual surroundings more sublime.

King Henry VI, who would have made a better monk than a king, decided in 1440 to found a college in Cambridge linked with a school at Eton much as William of Wykeham had done seventy years before with Winchester and New College Oxford.

The first buildings of King's were built north of where the chapel now is, in what is now called the Old Schools. But then Henry became more ambitious; and drew up a grand plan for the greatest college ever built, and he actually swept away a large part of the centre of Cambridge town, the whole of the old parish of St John Zachary—the most central and important commercial parish in Cambridge. Trading hithes on the river, scores of houses and business premises, were ruthlessly flattened, and Milne Street, one of the main streets of the city, was cut in two. During times of drought you can still see the outlines of seventeenth century paths and walls of the college gardens on the great lawn of King's: for the grass growing over the foundations dries out more quickly than that growing on deeper soil. It was 280 years, though, before any permanent buildings were built on this vast cleared area and the college began to move to the south of its chapel, as King Henry planned that it should.

The foundation stone of the chapel was laid by Henry VI on 25th July 1446. It is believed that the general plan of the chapel was that of his master mason, Reginald Ely.

Henry approved a document in 1448, which is still called his Will, in which he laid down in great detail how both chapel and college were to be built, and alas that later generations did not take more notice of it. In particular the buildings were to eschew 'superfluitie of too great curious werkes of enteille and besy moulding'. But when he died the 'busy moulding' and the 'too great curious works' crept in, and subsequent monarchs sought to glorify themselves on the pretext of glorifying God by adorning the great chapel over with their personal symbols. Thus the buttresses of the east part of the chapel, which were finished in the founder's time, are unadorned and the finer for it: those of later dates are over-embellished with royal emblems. But the grand design of the building could not be altered; and the chapel is great enough to carry these superficial details without detriment.

The work on the chapel was held up twice, the first time by the Wars of the Roses and Henry's deposition in 1461. Before this happened most of the building had been done with a magnesian limestone from Yorkshire.

Yorkshire may seem a long way to go for such a vast amount of stone, until one realizes that a sailing barge, given a fair wind, can go from Hull to the Wash on an ebb and a flood tide, and a modern motor lorry may not do much better. However, after Henry VI's time, when building was resumed by his successors, stone was brought from nearer at hand (although it may have taken just as long to get there) from Weldon in Northants, down the Nene and through the Fen waterways to the Cam.

The join between these two kinds of stone can be seen (more easily on the north side), and it shows almost exactly where the earlier work

stopped and the later began. It shows that the whole of the foundation was laid in Henry VI's time and much of the east end of the
chapel was completed. Work stopped with unseemly precipitation
on Henry's death: so much so that one stone was left half carved in
the south-east corner of the Great Court, and it lay there until it was
taken to be used as the foundation stone for the 'Gibbs' Building'
when this was started in 1724.

One important result of this long break in the building was the
fact that the roof inside was built in a different style from that
intended. Henry VI and his great master builder planned a lierne
vaulted roof, and lierne vaults are indeed to be found in two of the
side chapels which were completed before Henry's death. But the
actual main roof is fan vaulted.

In order to accommodate the planned lierne vaulting the shafts
were given seven components—whereas the fan vaulting substituted
only required five. Therefore two of the members or flutings of each
shaft were found unnecessary; and they simply stop at the top of the
shaft with no upward continuation. Undoubtedly had it not been
for Henry VI's deposition the chapel would have been lierne vaulted,
and we should not have had that soaring, spreading, delicate lace-
work in stone which is one of the wonders of the world. The imagination fairly reels when we try to think how that stone was got up there,
and fitted, and when we contemplate the utter daring of the people
who built that roof soaring up there 80 feet above our heads. There
are said to be two miles of stone ribs, the panelling itself is so thin
that you may not walk upon it or you would put your foot through,
and the bosses which hang at the conjunctions of the fans—alternate
Tudor roses with Beaufort portcullises—and which look so ethereal
and delicate from the ground—each weigh a ton.

Nor are the walls which support this tent-work of stone any less
delicate. By far the greater area of the walls is glass, in fact the chapel
is in its way a glorious glass-house. The buttresses which rise up so
gracefully between the great windows, and which are, in fact, really
all there is of the walling except the windows, do, of course, support
all the weight. The twenty-five gargantuan oak trusses, each with a
number of beams, were during the last century, suspected of thrust-
ing the walls apart; hence Sir G. G. Scott's tie-rod inserted in the
1860's above the vaulting which ties the whole thing together. Only
Fellows with their guests may ascend into the roof by the stairway in
the north-east turret. Up there the stone vaulting lies beneath one's

feet, the lead weather-roof above the head, and the twenty-five mighty beams between.

Simon Clerk, architect in most of this second period, probably intended fan vaulting: he was master mason at King's in 1476; but John Wastell, who was master mason in 1512 when the work was started, actually designed and built the vault. Wastell's master stone-carver was Thomas Stockton. Men were found, from first to last, worthy of the work they were doing: no part of the building shows craftsmanship which lets down the rest: design, masonry, stone-carving, all are perfect.

The glass was made between 1517 and the 1530's. The window over the north-west porch and some others are attributed to the king's glazier, a Fleming named Barnard Flower who lived at Southwark. This man died, and was succeeded by other Flemings, and the style of the glass is essentially Flemish-Renaissance. The study of King's windows can be a life work, rendered difficult by the fact that it is hard, from the ground, to make out the figures and background without close study. An excellent pamphlet can be got for three shillings, and a booklet listing the subjects of the pictures in the windows for threepence, at the table which sells such things in the north-west corner of the ante-chapel. Sufficient here that the upper tiers of lights in general show scenes from the Old Testament, while the lower scenes from the New which were thought by the artists to show a correspondence in some way; e.g. Job tormented above, Christ scourged below. The glass is glowing and beautiful, made at the peak of the glazier's art. On a sunny day the chapel is flooded with glorious coloured light. It is supposed to be due to Milton that this glass survives. Uncompromising Protestant though he was, Milton loved King's Chapel (he wrote verse about it) and he was a friend of Cromwell and may have interceded with him to let the windows alone. There is a record that the bursar of King's paid William Dowsing his usual fee of 6s. 8d. Was Dowsing satisfied with the fee but appalled by the labour? Or had he received orders from Cromwell to spare his hand? The Earl of Manchester, who was in command of the Parliamentary forces, was incidentally a friend of the provost of King's.

There is one window (number XXIII) which has in it the detail of a sailing ship of the early fifteen hundreds. This, depicted in perfect detail, has high fore and stern castles (the high forecastle went out in English ships soon after this period—giving the English ships an advantage to windward of the Spanish ones and enabling us to win the battle with the Armada), three masts, square courses and topsails on main and fore and lateen on the mizzen, running and standing rigging clearly shown and correct, shrouds rattled down, a boat lying alongside and another, very like a modern Yorkshire 'cog boat', pulling off to her in the foreground with white-coated figures. Whichever old Fleming painted that piece of glass knew what a ship looked like.

The quality of the wood carving of the screen and of the choir stalls of the chapel is said to be the best north of the Alps; and Pevsner pronounces it 'the purest work of the Early Renaissance style in England'. The screen and choir stalls are later than the rest of the chapel, and the fact that Anne Boleyn's initials are carved on the screen dates it between 1533 and 1536.

Placed at the east end of the chapel now is the Adoration of the Magi by Peter Paul Rubens, which was painted in 1634 as an altarpiece for the White Nuns of Louvain. This was donated by Major Allnatt in 1961, and is a princely work and very fitting for this position.

Before services candles are lighted at the places of the choristers. Then the choir files in, and—in Wordsworth's words:

> *. . . from the arms of silence—list! O list!*
> *The music bursteth into second life;*
> *The notes luxuriate, every stone is kissed*
> *By sound, or ghost of sound, in mazy strife;*
> *Heart-thrilling strains, that cast, before the eye*
> *Of the devout, a veil of ecstasy!*

For the rest, King's College has its fine Great Court, rendered the greatest in the world by being bounded by the chapel on the north side, but otherwise with the Gibbs' Building on the west (this is actually the Fellows' Building for it contains their rooms; but was designed by James Gibbs in 1723 after plans made by Hawkesmore ten years earlier had been dropped. The Provost had asked Hawkesmore to avoid ornament on the ground that "something of the nature is in the Founder's Will": thus after 400 years Henry VI's wishes were still being taken into account). The rest of the buildings of King's do not come up to Gibbs' Building: the great range to the south of the court and to the south of the even larger lawn at the Backs is Victorian and later, and so is the stone screen (Wilkins,

1823-8) that fills in the east of the Great Court along King's Parade. The later has been praised by many competent critics but I must beg to be excused. We can only be thankful that it is no bigger.

The head of King's is entitled 'Provost', and not 'Master' as in other colleges. Until 1851 King's men were not subject to the authority of the university proctors, and they were not allowed to take any footling examinations to get their degrees: these were conferred automatically. Eton men who went to King's and liked to stay on after having been granted their degrees almost automatically became fellows, and could 'keep' in fairly luxurious rooms, dine in Hall, and—unless they wanted to do so—perform no visible tasks at all. This gave rise to a splendid race of eccentrics. E. F. Benson, in his most delightful book about Cambridge, *As We Were*, describes several of these gentlemen. One in particular was of the most engaging habits. He 'never emerged except in the evening gloaming. He then shuffled out on to the big lawn, with a stick in his hand, and prodded with it at the worms in the grass, muttering to himself: "Ah, damn ye: ye haven't got me yet!" He said with Dr Faustus, "This feeds my soul," and after this physical refreshment, he returned to his rooms till the same hour the next day.'

But fellows nowadays have to prove their scholarship in order to get their fellowships, and thereafter justify themselves in some tangible way; and scholars from Eton do not automatically become fellows of King's.

After King's, **Queens'**. Some might say that this is the choicest and the most anciently beautiful of the Cambridge colleges. Certainly it contains the greatest mass of Tudor building.

It is interesting to seek a reason for this. There is a very great deal of earlier-than-Tudor and Tudor building in Cambridge colleges, but it was almost all of it ashlared, or covered with dressed stone, in the seventeenth and eighteenth centuries.

The two queens who founded it were Margaret of Anjou and Elizabeth Woodville. While her husband, Henry VI, was founding King's, Margaret of Anjou, not to be outdone, took over Queens', and she was only eighteen when she did it. Elizabeth Woodville, wife of Edward IV, refounded and endowed the college, saying that she should become co-foundress by right of succession. The man who actually did the work was Andrew Doket, Rector of St Botolph's, whose patroness Queen Margaret was, and he named the college after St Bernard.

It was built on the site of a house of Carmelite friars, who came to the place after they had often found themselves going through floods to reach Cambridge from Newnham, the present site of the famous women's college. Doket started St Bernard's in 1446, Queen Margaret took it over two years later, and Queen Elizabeth Woodville in 1465, after Margaret and her husband had been defeated in the Wars of the Roses. Margaret of Anjou wished to found a college 'to laud and honneure of sexe feminine'! What a pity she did not go the whole hog and make it *for* women. It was not until 1869 that the need of the 'sexe feminine' for higher education was realized and Girton was founded.

But if we want to know what a college looked like in the fifteenth century—or a great manor house for that matter—we can find out by going to Queens'. It is as important a monument, in its way, as the medieval warehouses of King's Lynn are in theirs. If we wish to see great houses on the plan of Queens' Principal Court still used as private dwellings we will have to go to Schleswig Holstein, in the Jutland Peninsula, for there are several (although Gifford's Hall, Stoke-by-Nayland, and Onburgh Hall, Norfolk, are not dissimilar).

The Principal Court, into which one enters from Queens' Lane through the Great Gatehouse (the latter hardly to be seen entire, because of the narrowness of Queens' Lane) is all fifteenth century, planned and built as one unit by one builder; and he is thought to have been Reginald Ely who was responsible for the beginnings of King's Chapel.

It is of clunch faced with red brick, and it makes you deplore the cold white brick—'public convenience brick'—used in Trinity Great Gate and Jesus College and used so much, alas, ever since. The old red Tudor brick is so beautiful and mellow.

The tower in the south-west is still called Erasmus's Tower, for it was at the top of it that he kept his rooms. Erasmus may have been lured to Cambridge by his friend Bishop Fisher, who, as well as Sir Thomas More, wished to broaden the barren and pettifogging teachings of the medieval schoolmen by the introduction of the classical spirit. Erasmus brought the study of Greek to the university, and something of the Greek pagan freedom of mind. Although he lived and died a Catholic his teaching led up to the Protestant Reformation; and in later years Protestants favoured him and the Catholics did not. Even to the extent that, when the Protestants

were in power in Cambridge they enforced the Erasmian pronunciation of Greek (which was quite wrong) and when the Catholics
were in power they disallowed it. As the Protestants triumphed
in the end the Erasmian pronunciation prevailed without learning
it anew.

But standing in this Principal Court, with the Great Gate behind
us, we can see what was the plan of many a great country house of
medieval times.

On our right is the old chapel, then a passage, then the library,
then round the corner—i.e. facing us—the great hall, then the
Screens passage, then the kitchens and buttery (facing us but on
the left), then the south-west corner with Erasmus's Tower then,
round another corner again, the south range which is dwelling
chambers.

The old chapel is no longer a chapel; but now a reading and
lecture room. It has some good original glass in it still. There is a
great and most curious sundial over the old chapel, early seventeenth
century, commonly credited to Sir Isaac Newton but actually there
before he was born. The present chapel is late Victorian (by Bodley),
and for a man in a hurry is not worth going to see.

Above the Screens passage are the Royal Arms of 1557. To enter
the hall is to be nearly knocked over by a blinding burst of jolly
Victorian colour, supposed to have been done, in part, by William
Morris. It is a regular fairground, but very likely the roof was
originally painted in much such a fashion. The fireplace was restored in the 1860s and the tiles above it are by Morris—the figures
designed by Ford Madox Brown. Elizabeth Woodville—a very pretty
girl although she was a queen—is in the painting behind the
president's chair. The head of Queens', incidentally, is the 'President', not the 'Master'.

Through Screens passage we come to Cloister Court, which takes
us right back into the age of the Tudors. In fact it is not a bad idea to
come to Queens' for the first time from the river side, so as to enter
this court first.

But approached from the Screens we see in front of us the
president's lodge, a most spectacular Tudor building with a brick
cloister below, and above two stories of typically East Anglian stud
timbering—the upper story is the long and spectacularly beautiful
President's Gallery. This gallery, late sixteenth century, is much like
the long gallery of many an Elizabethan great house—there is one

at Sawston. Quite what the purpose of it was is hard to see (although it is supposed to have been for exercise); it would certainly be a most uncomfortable room to sit in, although this one at Queen's is beautiful within as without.

This block of Tudor buildings is very well seen from outside the Cloister Court: from the college garden to the north. Some of the timbering, especially the curved pieces, was put in during a restoration of 1911; and it is these curved beams that to my eye at least look out of place: a consciously 'rustic' effect in what should have been a highly finished and sophisticated building: and more Midland in feeling than East Anglian anyway. Erasmus's Chair, by the way, a weighty seat for a weighty scholar, is in the President's Gallery.

The brick part of the president's lodge side, which rises straight up from the waters of the River Cam, is older than the timbered, in fact of about 1460. There are filled-in arches at water-level—surely landing bays in the days when the colleges drew their fuel (peat from the Fens), wine, and imported provender, from the Fen Lighters? Such arches can be seen in the shops of many a Dutch shop or warehouse leading into tunnels under the canal-side road in such cities as Dordrecht.

But perhaps this Cloister Court of Queens' is one of the most romantic and evocative in Cambridge (although there are so many others that could stake a claim!).

Over the Cam here there is a wooden bridge which is called the Mathematical Bridge and is sometimes attributed, like so much else, to Sir Isaac Newton. It was built in 1749, probably actually to the design of a man named Etheridge, and it was designed so cunningly that it held together with no fastenings: neither bolt, nail, nor dowel, being knitted into one by strange mathematical forces. Alas, some unhappy chap in the Victorian age took it to pieces to see how it worked and was unable to put it together again, and so now it is fastened with ordinary nuts and bolts like other, non-mathematical, bridges. The bridge upstream of it, Silver Street Bridge, is a very old-established bridge (although not as old as the Great Bridge of Magdalene Street—a modern structure now but on the site of an almost primordial bridge), replaced in 1950. For centuries Silver Street was a toll bridge, and the toll-collector was a hermit—fulfilling thus a common office of hermits in early days.

St Catharine's was founded by Robert Woodlarke in 1473. Woodlarke was then 3rd Provost of King's, and responsible for much of the administrative detail of King's Chapel. He came of a wealthy family and spent much of his fortune on St Catharine's (which he named for the Patron Saint of Learning), and he also lent much money to the king to help to build King's and we hear that he did not get it back. None of his original buildings survive at St Catharine's: most of the structure is seventeenth century or later. Robert Grumbold, who did so much of Clare, did much of this—including the chapel, which is well worth seeing for lovers of the Baroque.

Corpus Christi was unfortunately much knocked about in the nineteenth century: Wilkins, who did the stone screen along King's Parade, destroyed a chapel of 1579 to put up his tasteless battle-mented 'Gothic' buildings. But thank God he spared the Old Court: perhaps the most perfect ensemble of fourteenth-century collegiate buildings in England.

Corpus is the only college founded by the guilds: the guild of Corpus Christi and that of St Mary combining to start it. Their object was to train clergy to officiate in their own churches; and when the college was founded it had but a master, two scholars, and two servants. These medieval guilds were less trade unions, as many people suppose them to have been, than friendly societies and religious and ceremonial bodies. A guild could be composed of people from many different trades, every member contributed to it and, at real need, could draw from it. Lawsuits between members were not allowed until all the resources of the guild as mediator had failed, prices and conditions of labour were laid down, and elaborate religious ceremonial in the guild's own church was carried out. To see such guild ceremonial today we would have to go to Spain. Corpus Christi was by far the richer of the two guilds founding the college, and therefore the latter retains its name.

The original hall is now kitchens, in the Old Court. The chapel has nice French sixteenth-century glass in the windows with figures and faces of photographic realism, but the east window is Victorian. The chancel, with its blind arcading in the Early English style and its ogee arches, is by Bloomfield, 1870.

The two things to see in this college are the Old Court, and the library. The library, castellated like a fortress and with great 'Tudor' windows, contains the best collection of Anglo-Saxon manuscripts in the world, besides an incomparable selection of other very ancient books. The books were collected by Matthew Parker, Master of Corpus from 1544 to 1553 and later Archbishop of Canterbury. As head of the post-Reformation Anglican Church he was much concerned to demonstrate that Christianity was of ancient and venerable foundation in the British Isles, and not just a Roman religion; and to this end he made this astonishing collection of very early books—easy enough to make at that moment in history because of the break-up of the monasteries. He thus saved at least some priceless works from being used for lighting fires. He collected the earliest known version of the Anglo-Saxon Chronicle, the *Canterbury Gospel*—said to have been sent by Pope Gregory to St Augustine when he was coming to England to convert the heathen in AD 597, the 'Bury Bible', written and illuminated superbly by the monks of Bury St Edmunds Abbey and said to be the finest English twelfth-century book existing, and very many Celtic manuscripts.

Security in this library is, most rightly, intense. You cannot borrow the original Anglo-Saxon Chronicle and take it back to your hotel. Archbishop Parker laid it down, when he presented the books, that in the event of more than so many of them being lost the remainder should be taken away from Corpus and given to Caius, and in the event of Caius losing any then Trinity Hall should have them. Both these latter colleges, therefore, have the right of inspection in Corpus Library.

The Old Court is the prize piece of Corpus Christi. Its six-hundred-year-old walls are of clunch, but plastered, as chalk often is to protect it from the weather. The buttresses and garrets are later, about 1500. The roofs are of small multi-coloured tiles peculiar to Cambridgeshire, and which give them a warm tweedy texture. And, further, the Anglo-Saxon tower of St Benet's church can be seen over the roofs—looking so different from any later architecture that it seems to come from another world, as well as from almost another millennium, and another civilization. The Old Court is connected with St Benet's by a sixteenth-century red-brick corridor—best seen from Free School Lane.

Farther down the street **Pembroke College**. Pembroke was founded by a French girl, Marie, daughter of Guy de Chatillon, Count of St Pol, and widow of Amoryde, or Aymer, de Valence, Earl of Pembroke, in 1346. Aymer de Valence, who was a most important nobleman at the court of the first two Edwards, was about fifty when he married Marie at about seventeen. The legend is that he was killed on their nuptial night before her eyes by a (surely over-zealous) wedding guest in a friendly joust. Gray writes of:

> *Sad Chatillon, on her bridal morn*
> *Who wept beside her bleeding love.*

In fact he died three years after the wedding—probably of apoplexy. After her widowhood she became great friends with another widow of enormous wealth: the Lady de Clare who founded Clare College, and it was perhaps the latter's influence that caused this young French girl to found a college herself.

The earliest parts of the fabric of the college are on the corner of Pembroke Street and Trumpington Street: this is a fourteenth-century building, although encased in sixteenth-century brick in places and nineteenth-century stone in others. At the west end of it is the Old Chapel, now called the Old Library; the oldest collegiate chapel in Cambridge, licensed to celebrate the Office by a Papal Bull of 1354 (of course Jesus Chapel is much older, but started life as a nuns' church). It was re-faced with brick in 1663 and later converted into a library. It has a notable ceiling done in the seventeenth century by Henry Doogood, who did much stucco-work in Wren churches.

The New Chapel of Pembroke is a most important building, being the first essay into architecture by Christopher Wren.

His uncle, Dr Matthew Wren, Bishop of Ely, had for eighteen years been immured in prison by the Puritans for his religious beliefs (at least they didn't burn him up), and when he got out he said to his nephew words to the effect of: 'You're a mathematician—build us a chapel.'

And his nephew did. Then in his thirties, and never an architect, he turned his hand to the job and designed the building we see, and we see it best from across Trumpington Street from the gate of Little St Mary's, where it shows a west end of quiet, well-mannered but decorative Corinthian classicism. The other end of the building is not Wren, for the Victorians had the presumption to add a chancel on to it, the second George G. Scott doing his best with the job in 1880. Wren's part of the interior has a lovely plaster ceiling, and there is a painting of the Deposition after Barocci, with a delicate girlish face of Mary.

Pembroke has the best piece of medieval plate in Cambridge (it was always too easy to melt old silver down and turn it into something more in accord with the latest fashion). This is the Foundress's Cup, which is silver gilt and has written on it on one side 'M.V. help. at. need.' and on the other 'drenk and mak gud cher.' This is not normally on view.

Gray, Edmund Spenser and Pitt the Younger were all at Pembroke. Gray kept his rooms in Peterhouse until, legend says, he was lured out of his window one night by shouts of 'Fire!' from down below. He swarmed down a rope which he always kept in a somehow very Thurberesque way by his window for just such an occasion, for he had a phobia about fire. He 'landed', if that is the right word, in a large tub of water, placed there by the same undergraduates who had called 'Fire!' for his reception. In dudgeon he left Peterhouse, and moved across the road into Pembroke.

Peterhouse, whence the poet moved, was the very first of the Cambridge colleges. In 1281 Hugh de Balsham, Bishop of Ely and a Cambridgeshire man, founded a college for secular scholars who were to live alongside the regular canons of the old-established Hospital of St John. This arrangement was not a success—'the scholars being perhaps too wise, and the brethren possibly over-good', and the college was moved next door to what was St Peter's Church (hence 'Peterhouse') but which has now been altered to the church of St Mary the Less.

De Balsham moulded his college on Merton in Oxford (which had been founded in 1265). Hugh de Balsham died two years after the move was made, but he left 300 marks with which were bought land for the still-existing hall.

This hall, alas, was fallen upon by Sir G. G. Scott, like so much else in Cambridge, in 1868; but it still has good old tables and benches, a lovely early Tudor cast-iron fireplace with a fireback and tiles by William Morris, the walls are Morris-stencilled and there is Morris glass in the windows (made, at least, by the Morris Company but designed by Burne-Jones and Madox Ford). There is a lovely oak-panelled Combination Room, also with a Morris fireback.

Behind Peterhouse is the Grove, separated from Coe Fen and the Cam by a very ancient wall (a blocked gateway has the arms of Bishop Hotham of 1316 on it), and there is a glorious garden full of fine trees. Coe Fen is beautiful and peaceful and we hope safe from the twentieth-century. If you wish to see the old Peterhouse, unfaced with eighteenth-century ashlar, go into the churchyard of St Mary's the Less.

The chapel of Peterhouse is an interesting building half Perpendicular, half classical, completed in 1636 by the Dr Matthew Wren who asked his nephew, Christopher, to make the designs for Pembroke Chapel over the road. Dr Wren made this chapel in fulfilment of a vow which he made during his eighteen years' imprisonment by the Puritans. The chapel was originally brick, but was faced with stone in the 1660s, and much altered then too. The inside is gorgeous: golden suns in the ceiling, old panelling in the walls, vivid coloured glass—galumphing German of the 1850s in most of the windows but Flemish of 1639 in the east window which is said to be from a design by Rubens for his *Crucifixion*.

North of the chapel, abutting the street, is a fine Palladian building by Burrough of 1738–42. The Principal Court is civilized and urbane, without a jarring note in it: nicely carved barge-boards over fifteenth-century building at east end of south range.

Peterhouse was the college of the notorious Dr Perne, who was master through several reigns and changes in religion. He was 'of such accommodating breadth of view' that he was able to switch from one religion to another at the drop of a hat—or at the accession of a sovereign. In Edward VI's reign he was so Protestant that he burned many of the books in the university library because they were too Catholic, in Mary Tudor's reign he was so Catholic that he went to the trouble of digging up the interred bodies of two German Protestant scholars—Bucer and Fagius—and burning them on Market Hill because they were too Protestant, and when Elizabeth came to the throne he was once more convinced of the rightness of Protestantism and preached the sermon at the service in which the two Germans were re-instated in respectability, albeit that their bodies couldn't be buried again having been burned up. He gave rise amongst the undergraduates to the pseudo-Latin verb *pernare*, to change one's opinions; and a weathercock in Cambridge with his initials A.P. on it the letters were taken to mean 'A Protestant' or 'A Papist' whichever way the wind blew.

Fitzwilliam Street brings us to **Downing College**, if we want to go there, which is Grecian, Grecian, all the way by that versatile man William Wilkins (who died in 1839).

There are even newer colleges. There is **Churchill**, on Madingley Road, by Messrs Richard Sheppard, Robson and Partners (we have gone a long way from the illiterate master mason!) and it is brick and fortress-like, simple and workmanlike, and much praised by good critics.

Fitzwilliam House, of Huntingdon Road, has a hall which, although it might look more at home in Fatehpur Sikri than in East Anglia, is a splendid and exuberant piece of architecture. Nicholas Taylor, in that very good little book *Cambridge New Architecture*, describes it as 'a riot of sculptural invention'.

New Hall, the new college for women, has a hall that looks rather like an atomic reactor pile surrounded by ventilators of the London Underground. We have come a long way from King's College Chapel.

CHAPTER 23

Cambridge: University and Town

Having made our circuit of the colleges, we can now make another one of the churches, museums, and other public places, and of the buildings of the university proper.

Of the latter there is the **Senate House**, best seen from the tower of Great St Mary's, from where it looks like a splendid model. From below, as indeed from above, it appears a most accomplished piece of early Georgian Classicism, and was designed by James Gibbs and built in 1722. Here are held the 'Congregations' of the Senate which rules the university. A proposal for new legislation—called a 'grace' —was until recently read aloud by the proctor dressed in his robes. If any member, opposing it, said 'Non placet' the proctor cried 'Ad scrutinum!' and the 'Placets' and 'Non-Placets' then divided and were counted.

Part of the **Old University Library**, rather hidden to the west of the Senate, was built in 1836–42 by the architect C. R. Cockerell in a rather free Grecian style; but the building which stands at right-angles to the Senate, thus forming a rough open-sided quadrangle with the Senate and King's College Chapel, is pure and pretty Palladian by Burrough, about 1754.

Behind it are the **Old Schools**, for long the only buildings belonging to the university and not to a specific college. The most interesting thing about them is the Great Gatehouse which was once the gatehouse of King's College, before its translation to the other side of its chapel. Now, alas, the gatehouse is set in a vast Victorian pile—the university offices. The Great Gatehouse of King's was the second great gateway built in Cambridge, the first of course being the 'Clock Tower', or King Edward III's Tower, of Trinity.

Most of the books of the old library (and its beautiful old book-cases) have gone to the hideous new library over the river; but there

402

is still a thirteenth-century Life of Edward the Confessor, the illustrations of which have been used to help with modern coronations; and one of the very earliest manuscripts of the Gospels.

Of museums, the **Fitzwilliam** is one of the best museums in the country. Certainly it is one of the pleasantest and most delightful; and there are not enough hours in the day to spend in it.

It is massive Victorian Greek, or Neo-Greek, or Neo-Neo-Greek, in Trumpington Street. Viscount Fitzwilliam made his bequest in 1816; but the building did not get finished until 1875 and by then it had cost a cool £115,000. Inside it is one of the best collections of works of art that may be seen anywhere. It is far far beyond the scale of any 'provincial museum', and in the scope of this book it would be impossible more than to hint at the contents. Since David Piper took over the directorship, incidentally, changes have been made.

There is a noteworthy Egyptian section, a fine collection of Turner watercolours, a wonderful collection of medieval illuminated manuscripts from all over Europe (almost too many, one might think). Of things which I feel it would be wrong to miss there is, perhaps first of all, the fifteenth- and sixteenth-century Print Room. Dürers and other German draughtsmen—note the detail of *Christ Carrying the Cross* by Martin Schongauer; the loveliest Renoir of all, *Le Retour des Champs*, in the Impressionist Room, Room No V. In Room VI, the Upper Marley Gallery, the two spirited *Siege of Troy* pictures, all in Renaissance costume, by Biagio di Antonio, fifteenth century (numbers 44 and 45), and the much-reproduced *St Sebastian* by Lorenzo de Credi.

In the Italian Room, Room VII, the lovely bright Canaletto-like *Grand Canal* by Bellotto and the actual Canaletto *Interior of the Doge's Palace*, and do not miss the majolica ware in the side cases. There is also a most moving *Virgin and Child with Saints and Doves* by Marco Basaiti.

In the Flemish Room, Room X, there is a transporting early sixteenth-century reredos, *The Deposition*, and an unforgettable *Village Fête* by Brueghel the Younger (after the Elder) with the story of the pedlar being enacted on an outdoor stage (where the wronged husband gets carried home inside the pedlar's basket and, while thus hidden catches his wife *flagrante delicto*). In the next room (Room XI No 73) is another *Village Fête* by Jan Steen—note the fellow communing with the pig in the gutter which reminds us of the song which ends: 'And the *pig* got up and walked away.'

Above it is a picture of a Dutch frigate seriously taken aback—either the officer of the watch was lax, or very unlucky. And the horrific *Arctic Adventure* by Honduis, nearby.

In Room LX, the Octagon, some lovely small Turner water-colours, a couple of little Cotmans for Norfolkmen, some Constables including a study for *The Lock* which takes you back with a jolt to the Essex-Suffolk border country, a fine, colour-glowing, Samuel Palmer (that most underrated artist), a Blake *Ascension*.

The Spanish Room, No VIII, has a stunning *Road to Calvary* by Antonio and Diego Sanchez, late fifteenth century, with a clean-shaven Christ. There are two large Murillos—the *Vision of Fra Lauterio* particularly notable. In Room II are some good English School: a big Reynolds, *Near Norwich* by James Stark, Constable's *Hampstead Heath*, some Blake manuscripts and watercolours in glass cases, which miss not, and the famous *Last of England* by Ford Madox Brown.

In the Central Gallery are some Hogarths (including some, not to be missed, in a glass case) and there are some more Gainsboroughs. In Room I my eye is always taken by the Sickerts, the Christopher Wood, some Stanley Spencer suburb-scapes, a Graham Sutherland *Deposition*, and *Thomas Hardy* by Augustus John. Also most note-worthy Epsteins—the loveliest being *Oriel Ross*, and there is *Einstein* by Epstein.

These items that I have mentioned are a drop in the ocean in this great museum—idiosyncratic choices of my own. To walk into the Upper Marley Gallery (Room VI) is to plunge into a great bath of golden colour—to run a gauntlet of transcending glowing works of art—it is an almost overwhelming experience. There is so much to see in Cambridge that people are apt to miss the Fitzwilliam on the grounds that, well after all many cities have a museum but how many have a thirteenth-century university? This is a mistake, and perhaps a special journey should be made to Cambridge to see the Fitzwilliam alone.

There is another little museum, the **Folk Museum** in Castle Street over Magdalene Bridge, which is a good one of its kind. Near it, behind Northampton Street, is the **School of Pythagoras**, never a school, nothing to do with Pythagoras, but late twelfth century and thus perhaps the oldest dwelling house in this country, but now a theatre and part of St John's College. This was bought by Merton to found the first English college in, but unfortunately he thought better of it and went to Oxford instead and founded it there, not realizing at the time that he was founding it in what was to become a vast and suffocating motor-car manufacturing conurbation. Near the School of Pythagoras is a different establishment—the Cambridge College of Hairdressing.

Castle Mound, nearby, is worth climbing for the view.

Of churches there is **St Benet's**, hard by Corpus Christi College, and connected to it, as we may have seen, by a covered passageway. The tower of this is one of the most complete pieces of Anglo-Saxon building in this country, and was possibly the parish church of the East Anglian settlement on the east of the Cam, when the Mercians occupied the castle on the other bank. (There are grounds, though, for dating the existing building to the reign of Canute, the Danish King of England; but this does not make it any less East Anglian, for it would have been built by the Christianized East Anglians and not by the recently pagan Danish invaders.)

The tower is an astonishing Saxon survival. It has the typical long-and-short work in its corners (alternate vertical and horizontal stones which cannot have had much binding-power—a fact which may be one of the reasons why there is so little pre-Norman work left standing beyond the round towers which had no corners, apart from the corner of the nave and some walling of the chancel) and it has double sound-holes of a strange shape. The tower arch, inside, is a most barbaric piece of architecture—very reminiscent of medieval Ethiopian cave-sculpture, with the mouldings of the arch springing from the backs of the most strange beasts, and long-and-short work, again, in the jambs. The rest of the church has been altered in various ages; but there are still Saxon components to be seen. The church today is unusual in that it is a parish church, but served by Anglican Franciscans sent from their mother house at Cerne Abbas in Dorset. A former Clerk of this parish was Fabian Stedman, born 1631, who was 'the Father of English change ringing', i.e. he invented the art of ringing bells as we know it today.

Great St Mary's is a big and grand Perpendicular church, which Cambridge people like to compare with the greatest wool churches of Suffolk and Norfolk (it's very fine but it doesn't *really* compare!), and it is well worth while climbing to the top of the tower for the best view that you can get, short of hiring a helicopter, of the city. The church may have been designed by Wastell, who worked on Lavenham church as well as King's Chapel.

Great St Mary's is the university church; and for centuries has been bound up with the life of the university. For years it was used for all sorts of secular uses, as indeed churches all were and churches should still be. Scholars disputed in it to gain their tripos (a B.A. had to sit on a three-legged stool to deliver a satirical speech—hence the name); in the Puritan age a great gallery was built on which the fellows sat at ceremonials with their backs to the east end (in refutation of both *east-worship* and *table-worship*); and there are even now ugly galleries over the aisles, for spectators at university ceremonies. Twice a term, still, the university sermon is preached—by a select preacher invited from afar for his learning. To have 'Select Preacher' after your entry in Crockfords is much desired by prominent divines. When the Assizes are held in Cambridge, an Assize Sermon is preached, with great pomp and ceremony, and, incidentally, the Judge has right of residence in the Master of Trinity's Lodge, the Master having to move out to make way for him.

There is a sensitive wood carving of the Madonna and Child near the south door, and Christ in Majesty in gilded wood by Alan Durst over the altar, splendid and effective, but not as big perhaps, and as commanding, as a Majestas should be. This was done in 1960.

But the things that are really striking to the eye about this church are the great late Perpendicular arcade (although spoilt by the galleries already mentioned), the clerestory, and the wide and generous chancel arch.

St Mary the Less, or **Little St Mary's**, hard by Peterhouse, is a little gem of the Decorated period, a period for which Cambridgeshire is famous.

It has a simple, barn-like plan, and has a fascinating chapel down in a crypt. Richard Crashaw, the poet, was a parson here in 1639, and there is a monument to Richard Washington who was incumbent here at the beginning of the eighteenth century. His coat of arms was the Stars and Stripes and his crest an Eagle, and it was an illustrious member of his family who gave the USA her flag and emblem.

Holy Sepulchre, the Round Church, opposite St John's, might be the most fascinating building in England, but unfortunately the Victorians visited upon it the full wrath of their restoration. They were egged on by the Camden Society; and it seems almost unbelievable that Salvin, their architect, should have chosen to build on to this glorious and purely Norman building a chancel in imitation Decorated!

The church was built about 1130, on the plan of the Holy Sepulchre in Jerusalem. It is probable that the design was influenced by the returning Crusaders. And, restoration or not, it is still a good experience to stand inside 'the Round', as the nave of the church is called, after having put sixpence in the little box by the door to switch on the lights.

Over Magdalene Bridge is the fascinating little church of **St Peter**. This may well have been the Christianized Mercian answer to the East Anglian St Benet's over the river, and it is said to stand on the site of an earlier fane, a temple to Diana. The door and the font are Norman, the latter wildly barbaric, with Mermen with twin tails. There is nothing much *to* this little church, which was practically rebuilt in 1781; but its yard—a slight hill in that flat land—shaded by sycamore and chestnut trees, is a place of such perfect peace and refreshment that it is a good place for the weary sightseer to retire to.

Finally, but not least, **St Mary Magdalene** on the Newmarket Road, just over the railway lines. This is bang in the deplorable suburb of Barnwell, is dumped by the railway tracks, and is in just about the most degrading and slummy position imaginable. This setting simply adds to the wonder of it—the traveller, bounding unwitting in his horseless carriage into Cambridge from the Newmarket direction through the crummy outskirts of the city, is suddenly struck and delighted by this vision of better things.

It is solidly Norman and amazingly unspoiled. The roof and east window are new, but fitting: the rest is original; and the church is not only real Norman but the choicest kind of Norman at that. It is said that it was originally the chapel of a leper hospital at Stourbridge, endowed by King John with money from the mighty Stourbridge Fair.

In hot weather, as the visitor will speedily find, **the 'Backs'** (area between the big colleges and the River Cam) are places of great delight, and furthermore a boat can be hired at any of the boat-hiring staithes and punted, paddled, or sculled gently up and down the river. Surely this must be one of the most civilized strips of water in the world; and the voyage up to Grantchester in the right weather and the right company surpasses all expectations.

Another resort in hot weather, or in very cold for a different reason, is the **university botanic garden**. In cold weather this is fine because of its hot houses—particularly the Tropical House which makes one long for better climes. This latter is the place to resort to when the freezing winds come whistling across the flat Fens from the equally flat steppes of Siberia.

Outside there is a very good rock garden, a scented garden, a terrace garden, a winter garden, a fine collection of trees and shrubs and herbaceous plants, and a chronological bed in which we can see at what date different plants were discovered by explorers.

In going through Trumpington Street towards the botanic gardens we will have noticed two little rivers running in the gutters each side, making the newcomer think of burst hydrants. These are the 'Rivers' Pem and Pot, or Pet. They are exactly like the *jubes* in Tehran in Persia, but as you will in Persia you will not in Cambridge notice people washing the baby upstream in them while other people draw water for their tea downstream. If we follow them up, and trace their courses underground, we will eventually come to Hobson's Conduit, a cheerful monument of 1614 to Thomas Hobson the originator of the expression 'Hobson's Choice'. Peterhouse is irreverently called 'Pothouse' because of its nearness to the 'River Pot' as much as because of the fame of its beer.

Hobson, many times Mayor of Cambridge, was also owner of a big carrier's business and livery stable. In the latter he kept no fewer than 'forty good cattle', but if you wanted to hire one you had to take the one he chose for you and not necessarily the one you wanted yourself: hence the immortal expression. He lived from the reign of Henry VIII to that of Charles I, has a street named after him, his portrait is in the Guildhall, and he made possible the scheme (actually thought of by the famous Dr Perne) to bring the waters of a brook into Cambridge, and run them along the street in the 'jubes' we have noticed.

CHAPTER 24

North East Cambridgeshire

If we leave Cambridge on the Newmarket Road we shortly come to **Stow Cum Quy**, where there is little to see excepting a military brass of John Ansty, 1460.

Bottisham looks good across the flat land from the Newmarket Road, because it is well set back from it, and is seen as a compact village dominated by a lovely and most interesting church.

To understand the series of villages that we are now setting out to see, it must be realized that they are 'shore' villages: they were, when they were built, along the shores of the watery Fens, just as are the Norfolk and Suffolk villages that we have already seen—between Mildenhall and Northwold. And just as the Norfolk and Suffolk 'shore' villages each has a 'hythe', or satellite port village, to which ships or Fen lighters could come, so each of these Cambridgeshire equivalents has its 'lode'. The lode hamlets are set at the heads of long artificial cuts from the River Cam: their parent villages are built on the drier and firmer chalk uplands and connected to their ports by road. The word 'lode' refers to the watercourse.

Bottisham is a large village, alas being made larger by much very undistinguished modern building; but the centre of the village is still attractive, with good old Cambridgeshire houses. Here is the second of the experimental 'Village Colleges' of Cambridgeshire, architecturally dull but no doubt culturally lively. North of the churchyard is a very attractive group of dwellings called 'The Arch', which was originally a parish rehousing scheme of about 1840. The dwellings are set about a courtyard of mellow brick roofed by Suffolk pantiles and are most distinguished architecturally. This block could well serve as a model for designers of council houses, who, with few exceptions, sorely need a model of some kind.

The church is very interesting, as indeed are most of the churches of the old Fenland shore. Being thirteenth and early fourteenth century much of it is transitional between Early English and Decorated. These shoreline churches speak of great prosperity in the Decorated period—before the great cloth export boom which turned trade away from the Wash ports to Norwich and Ipswich. The nave, dated c. 1310, is very fine and there is a lovely arcade of the most vigorous period of English Gothic, and there are blind arcades, both inside and out, on the aisle walls. There is a Perpendicular rood screen of stone (the vicar dates it 1474), and two quite lovely Decorated parclose screens. Note the fluting around the clerestory and also the sedilia and piscina. There is a monument to Sir Roger and Lady Jenyns, which depicts them both sitting on the grass apparently just about to have a picnic.

Bottisham has its lode, and this one is just called Lode, *tout simple*. **Lode** is an interesting little place, with much thatch (a material right on the doorstep, because it could be floated up from Wicken Fen in punts), and Cambridge white brick. A long straight 'cut', or canal, runs to it, the lode itself, and next to this is a road, and if we drive down this we get a good view, on our right, of the real 'black peat' of the Fens: the soil is nearly as black as soot, soft and friable and people say that it is worth its weight in gold. At the end of the track is a most lovely Fenland farmhouse with a roof of very small pantiles, and there is an ancient wooden sluice-gate of great interest to sluice-gate lovers.

Lode would be a fine place to lie in a boat if one wishes to visit, or even to work in, Cambridge. The willow-hung canal could be very attractive. South-west of Lode is **Anglesey Abbey**, now National Trust. It is the remains of an Augustinian priory founded in the twelfth century and since made into a private house, and has a grand eighteenth-century-type garden stretching to the Fens, with good statuary and ornaments, and 'Emperor's' and 'Warrior's' Avenues started in 1926. It is open to the public and worth a visit.

Swaffham Bulbeck is another big village, and it also has its lode with its port-hamlet called **Commercial End** at the top of it. The size of Commercial End is an indication of its past importance as a port. There is a magnificent tiled warehouse down the most northerly lane leading to it, and several other buildings connected with storing cargoes.

Swaffham Bulbeck has beautiful green and extensive grasslands, willow-bordered, between it and the Cam. The church is mostly built of clunch with an Early English tower and the rest of it mostly fourteenth century, i.e. Decorated. There is a magnificent chest within, or rather a travelling altar: the lid opens to form a reredos and is embellished with good and most interesting carving. This is Italian, probably fifteenth century. There is also good fifteenth-century carved woodwork in the church: arm rests and poppy-heads with weird beasts and fishes.

The vicar of Bulbeck for the greater part of the nineteenth century was Leonard Blomefield, alias Jenyns. He was a close friend of Charles Darwin, and gave up his place in the *Beagle* to let Darwin go instead. He wrote Darwin's book of fishes for him when he got back, and otherwise acted as his amanuensis, and he also edited Gilbert White's writings and is said to have known *Selborne* practically off by heart. He and Darwin used to go for long nature rambles together, and one can imagine that in their days Swaffham Bulbeck would have been a good place for the job, with the Fens on one side, Newmarket Heath on the other, and the Brecklands not far away.

Swaffham Prior has two windmills, alas no longer working, one a tower mill in very good condition but hemmed in between a hideous water tower as high as itself, and a group of council houses. The village also has two churches in the same churchyard.

The churches are most interesting and impressive. Quite why there are two of them nobody seems to know. The lower one of the two, St Mary's, was once in the gift of Ely Abbey having been granted to it by Brithnoth in the reign of Ethelred the Unready. As we shall discuss later, while dealing with Ely, this East Anglian hero gave Ely many gifts of churches and land as he was on his way to fight the disastrous Battle of Maldon. The church has a square Norman base to its tower with an octagon above it, and on top of that an Early English octagonal top with lancet windows. The lantern which was once at the top of it all was struck by lightning in the eighteenth century.

But by the time of the lightning strike the body of the other church had been pulled down, and the church was decayed. But the superstitious parishioners took the lightning as an omen, and they would no longer worship in St Mary's Church. Nothing would do but they must move to the other church, and build a rather undistinguished Georgian nave to it. St Mary's won in the end, however; for its ruins were restored at the end of the nineteenth century, and now it is Saints Cyriac's and Julitta's which is being given over to the bats, swallows, and courting couples. St Cyriac died under the Diocletian persecution as a small boy while his mother, St Julitta, encouraged him to face martyrdom before she was herself immolated: at least that is one version of their story.

St Mary's is very notable for its strange tower, which is grand and impressive from within or without: note the vast thickness of the white clunch walls as seen through the tower arch. There is some early twentieth-century glass of strong period interest (its vogue will come!) with strong scenes from the trenches, the mountains of Switzerland, Wicken Fen, an ammunition factory, and other somewhat unrelated matter.

Baldwin Manor, near the village, is a wonderfully preserved and very beautiful Tudor timber-framed house which can be seen from the road: the goal aimed at, in fact, by every 'Detached Tudor

Period Villa' on a hundred by-passes, and so signally missed. It is not open to the public.

Half a mile north-east brings the road to what looks like a long straight abandoned railway embankment. This is in fact the **Devil's Ditch**, which can be seen at this place to perfection. There is nothing to see, beyond what I have described; but, if one knows what it is, this earthwork is romantic, and is well worth going for a walk along.

It is a colossal earthwork. The total length is 7 miles, from the bottom of the ditch to the top of the bank is 60 feet and the width of bank and ditch together is 40 yards. Surely a vast amount of shifted earth, and the product of tremendous labour. Some archaeologists have dated it as pre-Roman, others as Roman and others even as Anglo-Saxon, but post-Roman it most probably was.

If we walk north-west along Devil's Ditch, or else take the road due north from Swaffham Prior (past, incidentally, the site of a Roman villa) we come to the northernmost end of the Ditch at Reach.

The Ditch here comes arbitrarily to an end. At one time it butted on to Reach Lode, a canal certainly dug by the Romans; but it was cut off, for I know not what reason, between 1743 and 1768 (a traveller visited it on both those dates—on the first it was intact—on the second cut).

Reach Lode was dug, one would imagine, for two purposes: for navigation like the other lodes of this old 'coast', and to form a defensive extension to Devil's Ditch.

Now **Reach** is the strangest little place, set around a wide irregular green, all quite unspoiled through not being quite beautiful enough for Cambridge commuters to want to come and live there. It is the remains of a much larger place, and is said to have once had its own fair which rivalled that of Stourbridge.

Roman remains have been dug up from the peat all down Reach Lode, the skull of a wild bull with a flint axe-head embedded in it was found there (my theory is that the wild bull got away with the axe-head in its head and subsequently fell in a swamp—otherwise why would not the hunter have recovered his weapon?); fossil remains of forests have been unearthed—layer upon layer as though forest after forest was destroyed by a new submergence of dry land. Many trunks of 'bog oak' have been dug up; one, discovered in 1909, was 130 feet long. The trees, falling into the swamp, have been perfectly preserved; as have the bones of bears, wolves, wild boars, aurochs, and wild cattle.

Reach was important beyond the other lodes of this inland 'shore', because here the navigable 'cut' runs right into the chalk, and so Reach has a very big clunch quarry where the Romans dug clunch, and whence came the clunch to build the Lady Chapel of Ely and half the Cambridge colleges.

The Church of England church at Reach is so screamingly ugly that it might quite well engender a headache in a moderately sensitive person. It is a product of 1860. In complete contrast is the quiet and well-mannered little Nonconformist chapel: a pleasant building, and most meet for its purpose. Reach is a remote-feeling and self-contained little place, and there is an atmosphere of great antiquity and peace there.

Burwell, hard by, is a big village—nay a small town; and it must have had prosperity after most of the other Cambridgeshire villages had fallen on harder times, for its church is Perpendicular and very grand. It is still prosperous industrially, with a vast factory employing over 400 people making Tillotson's corrugated carboard cases. In the recreation garden of the factory is a circular pavilion like the Tea House of the August Moon, looking very exotic and charming, and completely un-East Anglian.

Burwell Church has a glorious roof, inside, and most of it original; with the liveliest carvings of angels and winged creatures and animals of a kind that we will never recognize as akin to the ones we see in the zoo. Over the altar steps is a fine boss carved as a pelican, from which used to hang the pyx containing the Reserved Sacrament. In the chancel are lavishly carved niches, and a fine roof, with corbels carved as angels playing stringed instruments. There is a brass to John Lawrence de Wardeboys. This divine had his brass made before his death, as many people did; and he had it engraved with a portrait of himself arrayed in a mitre and the fine robes of the Abbot of Ramsey, which at that time he was. However, came the Reformation, and the Dissolution, and de Wardeboys received a pension from Henry VIII for his eagerness in handing over his abbey for dismantling; and so he had the brass cut in half, and half of it turned over and another portrait of himself engraved on it—in humble clerical garb: more fitting for the changed conditions. To add to the confusion the original brass itself was purloined from another use, for the reverse of the canopy shows a much earlier portrait of a deacon.

There was a castle at Burwell: now earthworks only, outside which one of the great rebels or outlaws who took refuge in the Fens was killed by an arrow. This was Geoffrey de Mandeville, who flourished as an outlaw and bandit during the nineteen years' war between King Stephen and Queen Matilda.

Burwell had a great disaster. In 1727 a company of strolling players, on their way to Stourbridge Fair, gave a performance in a Burwell barn. So many people clamoured for admittance that the doors were nailed up to prevent any more getting in, the place caught fire and eighty-two people were burned to death and buried in one pit in Burwell churchyard. In 1774 an old man confessed on his deathbed that it was he, for some small spite, who had started the fire.

Fordham is the next of this series of fine Cambridgeshire 'coastal' villages: the tiny river Snail comes down to it from **Snailwell** which has a church with a Norman round tower and some lovely Decorated tracery.

But Fordham itself has its navigation, for it could be reached by Fen lighter from Soham Lode. It has a fine and most unusual church, with a Lady Chapel placed as is the Lady Chapel of Ely Cathedral in relation to the church, with a vaulted, crypt-like, lower story which acts as a porch for the church, and another chapel above it with very beautiful Decorated windows. There are Norman windows in the west end of the north aisle, a restored Early English chancel, the eastern piers of the arcades are Early English—the rest are splendid Decorated, and the most glorious arcades they are, with painted spandrels. There is a splendid soaring tower-arch, and more painted decoration within it.

Landwade, just south of Fordham, has a most unspoiled church in a semi-private park, full of monuments to departed Cottons. Good screen and glass fragments.

If we take the Soham Road and turn first left we come to Wicken, and, more especially, to Wicken Fen.

Wicken itself is a pretty village with much reed thatch, where—at least until recently—the white poppy was grown in the gardens. The heads of this flower were boiled in days gone by to make an infusion which was drunk for 'Fen ague'. No doubt it had some effect, as it must have been rich in opium.

Wicken Fen is nearly the only piece of primordial Fenland left in approximately its old condition; and so is of first interest to naturalists and ecologists. It is preserved in this state because, some of it at least, was bought by the National Trust as far back as 1899, and the rest in 1911, and it is still preserved by the Trust as a strict nature reserve, and has a resident staff. It is open for anybody to walk in, but you are always asked to sign the visitors' book.

The Fen cannot, in fact, be left quite to nature: waterways must be kept clear, water pumped *up* into the Fen because the surrounding cultivated land has shrunk and the Fen has not, alder and buckthorn must be prevented from colonizing the drier land. As far as possible it is kept as sedge and reed growing fenland, and there are giant mare's tail, hart's-tongue fern, flowering water plantain, bog bedstraw, forget-me-not, loosestrife, hemp agrimony, marsh pea, water parsnip, willow-herb, angelica, meadowsweet and many orchids, including the sundew which entraps flies. There are plentiful fish in the waters including the unusual eel-pout, which resembles a catfish.

The *pièce de resistance* of the Fen, though, is the swallowtail butterfly. This disappeared during Hitler's war, when much of the Fen was drained and turned into cultivated land (by Alan Bloom, whom we have met at Bressingham in Norfolk). But the Fen was restocked with swallowtails from the Norfolk Broads, when it was certain that the distinct variety of the Fenlands was completely extinct. There are warblers, water fowl of all sorts, and, on warm summer nights, the moth-collectors make interesting watching. They put up sticky screens and attract the moths into them with lights.

Part of Adventurers' Fen (there are several Fens named like this—'adventurers' were groups of financiers similar to later joint stock companies who got together to drain the Fens: we also find 'Undertakers' Fen') which was ploughed up during the war was returned afterwards to the Trust, and an old pumping windmill that was on it has been renovated, and removed to Wicken Sedge Fen, and there it still is—probably the only working pumping windmill in Fenland. Incidentally when Adventurers' Fen was ploughed up great numbers of huge bog-oaks were found in it, some of them over 100 feet long. They were all lying in a north-easterly direction, as though all felled together in some monstrous south-west gale. Could it have happened that, their roots submerged in the waters by some subsidence of the

23. ELY CATHEDRAL, looking West along the Choir. Above is the famous Lantern, built by Alan of Walsingham in the 14th century to replace the huge Norman Tower which fell in ruins and smashed the Chancel as it fell. Alan stood amid the ruins on the night when the tower fell and 'knew not whither to turn'. But he recovered his courage, 'set his hand to the work', and produced his masterpiece

24. Hogweed, fescue and bent – Potter Heigham railway station

land, they were all drowned together and then some savage gale—or series of them—laid them low?

Wicken Fen is by now eight feet above the surrounding cultivated land, and this distance will go on increasing until all the surrounding peat has been used up and eroded by cultivation. The pumping windmill, for this reason, is used for pumping water up into the Fen and not out of it.

Apart from the interest of its flora and fauna, Wicken Fen gives some idea of the utter impenetrability of the aboriginal Fenland to all excepting Fenmen. The ditches and lodes are too shallow to swim in, too wide to jump, and too soft-bottomed to wade. To attempt the last would be to court death. To travel by boat, if you were a stranger, would be to get lost and stranded into the bargain. We can here see why William the Conqueror, and other invaders, had such a difficult time in conquering Fenland.

Beyond Wicken is **Upware**, alas a place of memories now that the dear old 'Five Miles from Anywhere' or 'No Hurry' Inn burned down.

This was a splendid riverside pub, the resort of both Fen lightermen and undergraduates who used to row down from Cambridge, where these two diverse breeds of men used to meet on common ground. The undergraduates formed here the 'Upware Republic' in which was done much debating, smoking, and drinking of beer. Samuel Butler was a prominent member. The old pub burned down not many years ago and not a brick remains to show us where it was; but there is an ancient lock nearby: a splendid place to picnic on the river's brink.

A mile west of Wicken is Spinney Abbey, a farmhouse to which Henry Cromwell, the Protector's second son, retired from his great offices at the Restoration of the monarchy. Charles II took a notion to visit him in his retirement, and one of Charles's courtiers had a fancy to walk before Cromwell carrying a pitch-fork as he had previously carried a mace when Henry was Lord Deputy of Ireland. Henry Cromwell was a man of high intelligence, and great dignity and integrity.

Back eastwards to **Soham** there is yet another splendid church of the ancient shoreline.

Built upon a promontory of the chalk into the old Fens, Soham was one of the earliest places in East Anglia chosen by a monastic community. St Felix, the Burgundian missionary who landed at

Companion Guide to East Anglia

what is now Felixstowe to convert the East Angles under the reign of
Sigebert (or reconvert them, for Redwald, Sigebert's father, as we
have seen, at least had a Christian altar in his temple even if it was
alongside a pagan one) had his bishopric at Dunwich, but he set up
an abbey at Soham, and in this was burned in AD 634. Soham, then,
was the farthest flung of the East Anglian kingdom—for the people
west of it were Britons, or Celts, and already Christianized by the
Romans.

But Soham Abbey, like Ely, was destroyed in the great Danish raid
of 870. Ely rose again: Soham did not, and the remains of St Felix
were removed to Ramsey.

Soham's present church has a high Perpendicular nave, window
tracery of lovely flowing Decorated, a noble arch to the east of the
nave (there is a crossing) with delicious moulding, and a fine
hundred-foot tower with East Anglian flush-work at the top of it.

Isleham is somewhat out of our way; but as it is one of the line of
'shore' villages we have been following we might as well look at it
now.

If we take the most direct road from Soham we may well come to
believe the story that the old East Anglian road-makers liked to work
with the wind at their backs, and the wind kept a 'changing!'. This
wayward lane, incidentally, takes us past the foundations of a
Romano-British villa.

Isleham has some very early Norman remains of a Benedictine
priory. Its present church is like all these 'shore' churches: early
fourteenth century, high-standing with its lofty clerestory and short
in proportion to its great height. The tower is new, and although
critics have damned the candle-snuffer roof to it I must admit it
comes as a rather pleasant surprise to be greeted by this poking up
from the Fen-surrounded island village, taking us in feeling to
France.

This is an important as well as an interesting church; but in a
land crammed with interesting churches it is likely to go unnoticed.
But no-one should miss the brasses and monuments: particularly the
brass to Thomas Peyton who died in 1484, with his elaborate and
comical-looking plate armour with huge elbow guards, and his
pair of wives, most elegant: the one in the lovely flowered dress is
Margaret, née Bernard, who brought Isleham into the Peyton family
in the first place. Thomas Peyton was a fine fellow: High Sheriff of
Cambridgeshire and Huntingdonshire. There are several lush-

looking Peyton monuments, and some brasses to the earlier Bernard family. There is a brass to Sir Geoffrey Bernard (probably), who went to the Crusades with Prince Edward—later Edward I. The figure on the brass can be seen to be a Crusader, for his legs are crossed; and he can be dated to about 1275 by the type of tailed surcoat that he is wearing over his armour. Thus this is a very early brass indeed. The moulding of the canopy over the figure on the brass is said to resemble almost exactly the moulding that Edward I had done on the Coronation Chair in Westminster Abbey.

If we wind our way back to Soham now, and embark on the road to Ely, we will be embarking on the causeway built over the flooded Fens by Hervey, first Bishop of Ely, and its abbot. St Edmund appeared in a dream to a man of Exning telling him to go to this bishop and tell him to build this causeway, and this the man did, and the bishop followed the suggestion. (A parallel of this legend concerns the building of the famous *Pont d'Avignon* over the Rhône.) Apart from a temporary causeway built by William the Conqueror during his campaign against Hereward this was the first dry land communication between Ely and the rest of England.

The Causeway used the little island of **Stuntney** as a stepping-stone. *Stunt* still means *steep* in the Cambridgeshire dialect, and Stuntney is a steep-sided place, and from it can be had a grand view of the goal of our pilgrimage: Ely itself.

The Isle of Ely stands high up above the flat Fenland (I am using 'high' in an East Anglian sense—expect no snow-capped mountains!), and until Bishop Hervey built his causeway it was only to be approached by boat and then only by a boatman who knew the channels. It was thus a refuge for the oppressed; and Celtic Britons lingered on there long after the rest of the country was Anglo-Saxonized; and thus probably kept alive a spark of Christianity before St Felix converted the heathen English.

CHAPTER 25

Ely

First the name. When St Dunstan, who was so insistent on the celibacy of the priesthood, came to **Ely** he found that many of the monks were married, or at any rate, the next best thing. So he miraculously changed all the married monks into eels, and there have been eels in the waters of Ely ever since: hence the name Ely—Eel Island.

The story of the founding of the abbey there is this. Etheldreda was born at Exning, near Newmarket, one of the palaces of the Wuffinga kings of East Anglia—as we have seen, Rendlesham was probably the chief one—and her father was Anna, the king who was slain by the pagan Mercians at Blythborough, and who was buried there. Anna was blessed with a bevy of saintly daughters. Etheldreda was sent to her aunt at Whitby, Hilda, Abbess of Whitby Abbey, and there she decided to embrace the holy life. Her father, for reasons of state, married her off to a British prince: Tonbert, lord of the wild Girvii, the Celtic tribe that still inhabited the Fens.

But Etheldreda would not let Tonbert consummate his marriage, and Tonbert eventually died, leaving to his somewhat unsatisfactory wife his domains in Fenland, including the Isle of Ely.

In 671 Etheldreda was again forced into marriage, this time with Egfrid, King of Northumberland. From this time onwards, her story is carved, for all to follow if they have a powerful pair of field glasses, on the fourteenth-century corbels half way up the eight great piers of the Octagon of Ely Cathedral.

King Egfrid was as unlucky as his predecessor had been: consummation was denied him. After twelve years he permitted Etheldreda to go to Coldingham, in Berwickshire, to another aunt there, Ebba, the Abbess. Bishop Wilfrid of York came and administered the veil of *sanctimonialis femina* to her, and after this it was unthinkable that she would return to her husband. However, Egfrid had other ideas. He gave chase to her, a year later, as she was making the journey back to her dominions in Fenland. He would have caught her too, had he not been miraculously stopped by a high tide at Abb's Head, and Etheldreda got by, a virgin. After this she stuck her staff in the ground and it miraculously took root and put forth branches.

She got to Ely, and there founded a nunnery of which she became Abbess, and it was a monastery too, for there were men as well as women; and Etheldreda ruled them both alike. She practised severe austerities, and eventually died of a tumour in the throat: said to be due to her venal love of wearing necklaces when a girl.

Sexburgha, Etheldreda's sister, took over, and sixteen years after Etheldreda's death her sister had her remains (needless to say uncorrupted) buried in a shrine in the chapel; in a white marble sarcophagus of Roman make which was discovered in what is now the Fellows' Garden at Magdalene College.

Etheldreda was canonized; and became one of the greatest saints of the English, and Ely benefited by the oblations of the pilgrims. And it was not poor in the first place, for Etheldreda, after all, was still Queen of the Girvii. Miracles occurred—not the least when, in 870, the Danes plundered Ely, and a Dane tried to rifle the saint's tomb. His eyes fell out of his head.

Etheldreda's name became shortened to 'St Audrey', and St Audrey's Fairs were held once a year all over England, and at them trinkets were sold including 'St Audrey's necklaces'; and our word *tawdry* comes from the fact that much tawdry rubbish came to be sold at these fairs: particularly, as we have seen, the fair at Woodbridge.

In 970, after many vicissitudes and burnings by the Danes, a new Benedictine abbey was founded at Ely by King Edgar, as part of the great revival of monasteries then going on. Then came the Conquest; and Ely held out long after the rest of England; and became the refuge, under Hereward the Wake, of many dispossessed Anglo-Saxons. It might possibly have held out for good, and become a rallying-point for an English counterblast against the Normans. But, alas, the cause was betrayed by the Abbot himself, who secretly made a peace with William and had him shown the way to the island when Hereward was away on a raid. When Hereward got back it was to find the Normans in occupation, and he had to flee for his life.

The monks, if they thought they were going to get off lightly by their treachery, were disappointed. William rode up to the abbey church when they were all at dinner. Without giving them warning he strode up to the shrine of St Etheldreda and flung a small piece of money on it as an offering, and then walked out and rode away. One of his knights strode into the refectory and shouted: 'Ye wretched drivellers! Can ye choose no better time for guzzling than this when the King is here, yea, in your very church?'

But William had gone; and the monks had to run three miles to Witchford (through which place he had built the causeway to attack the isle) to catch him, and he thereupon imposed a huge fine on them for not greeting him in a proper manner, and moreover he billeted on them a great body of knights, one for each monk, to keep an eye on them, and subsequently he doubled the fine because he alleged that some of the coin (they had to set up a mint to cast the treasure of the abbey down into coin to pay their fine) was under-weight. William was not a conqueror who wore kid gloves.

Of course it was not long before a Norman was appointed Abbot. Simeon, the brother of Wakelin, Bishop of Winchester, took the job, and with it all the revenue from the old kingdom of the Girvii; and he began to build the mighty church that we see today: the cathedral that ranks among the most glorious and sumptuous buildings of Christendom. The main part of the cathedral took just the 268 years to build, and was finished in time for the Black Death which put an end to so much building.

In 1083 Simeon, then an old man, laid the foundations of the north and south transepts which stand to this day, and of the central tower which has since collapsed.

The choir was built, and the remains of St Etheldreda were brought thither from the old Anglo-Saxon church (the Normans found that they could not do without the Anglo-Saxon saints. Perhaps they did this to consolidate their grip on the conquered race: perhaps because they had so few saints of their own.) Her sister Sexburgha was laid at her feet and on each side of her a second sister and a niece who had both followed her as Abbess. Old King Anna may seem to us to be a semi-legendary figure lost in the pagan past; but in one generation his family had established firmly its immortality and moved from the pre-history of ship-burials at Sutton Hoo into the history of precise dates and carefully documented facts, and of great buildings which are still standing today.

At the request of Henry I the Pope made the Abbot of Ely a bishop, and to this fact we owe the continued existence of the cathedral, for had it not been a cathedral as well as a minster it would have been pulled down at the Dissolution. Hervey, the causeway-builder, was the first bishop, appointed in 1109. This first Norman bishop took over the 'Franchise and Liberty' of the Isle of Ely, which had been handed down from St Etheldreda herself as Queen of the Girvii, and even today the results of Etheldreda's marriage to the wild King of the Girvii remain: the 'Isle of Ely', although part of Cambridgeshire, is still a county of its own with its own county council, although now a battle rages between people who wish to extinguish this ancient entity, and those who wish to retain it.

When seen from far across the Fens the cathedral stands up enormous, dominating everything; and when no detail can be seen it resembles some vast barn, with turrets, standing up alone in the flat fenny country. As we get nearer, from north or south—i.e. from a side view we have the impression of a vast ark or ship, riding the hill of the Isle of Ely as a great wave. But it is from the east that the impression of sumptuousness presents itself.

From here the place looks like a gigantic fairy castle, or a magic palace. The foreshortening of the Octagon and the mighty West Tower, the proliferation of pinnacles and Gothic towers, make for a jumbled mass of upward-striving detail. It has been compared by the unsympathetic to 'a great Gothic wedding cake'; but to the more discerning it 'comes off' entirely: an entirely satisfactory *tour de force* of architecture: an attempt of almost inconceivable boldness that completely and brilliantly succeeds.

The building history is briefly thus. Simeon, and the Normans who came after him, built transepts, nave, and a small Norman apsed chancel, and also a huge Norman central tower which fortunately did not have strong enough foundations.

The Norman chancel was, as usual, not big enough for later needs; and the chancel and chancel aisles were lengthened under Bishop Northwold in the thirteenth century, thus in the Early English style, and we see today a glorious and lofty Early English east end. Henry III and his son Prince Edward came to the dedication of this chancel in 1252.

The king and his son came in peace then; but fifteen years later they came in war, for, after the defeat of the barons at the Battle of

Evesham and the death of Simon de Montfort a group of the defeated who called themselves 'The Disinherited' made Ely their refuge; and it was not until the king himself, with Scottish troops, had constructed bridges and causeways and attacked the island, that the rebels yielded.

But the abbey and the minster went on unchanged; and the Benedictine monks continued to rise at two in the morning to say Mattins and Lauds, and say or sing offices at frequent intervals during the day, and sit shivering in the cloisters copying books, and go once every six weeks to the Infirmary for the routine blood-letting, and fill any spare time which they may have had with tending the vineyards (for which Ely was noted) and gardens, and draining the marshes.

The minster appeared at that time to be complete. But early in the fourteenth century, that lovely time of English Gothic, it was decided to add a Lady Chapel.

Alan of Walsingham, the Sacrist, discussing the general idea with his assistant, Brother John, who:

> . . . betook himself therefore to prayer, and thereafter called his mates together, some being monks, some, likewise, being seculars. And them he besought to meet at a certain hour, and help him in digging out a square trench which might serve as a foundation for the whole fabric.
>
> At the appointed time, accordingly, they met one night, and began to dig, each separately in the place assigned to him . . .
>
> And when the whole night was well nigh spent, and in the earliest dawn, a small rain came on, to the annoyance of those digging. Calling then his mates from their work, he said: 'Brethren mine, and fellow labourers, yea, most heartily do I thank you for your long and well-wrought task. And good it is to pause a little after your work. Therefore I commend you to God. And may He pay you a full worthy wage for your labour.'

But Brother John, unknown to the other diggers, had struck a crock of silver in his digging, which he concealed under his bed, and with its contents he subsequently paid for much of the building.

And thus rose up the Lady Chapel, and—with all our tower cranes and bulldozers and pre-stressed reinforced concrete—what can we build today to touch it?

But—disaster. No sooner than the chapel had been started—than the great central tower of the old cathedral built two hundred years before by the Normans, collapsed on to the roof of the Norman choir, itself in ruins and bringing ruin as it fell.

Fortunately the Sacrist, Alan of Walsingham who was then quite a young man, happened to be perhaps the most inspired builder that England has ever possessed. He 'rose up by night and came and stood over the heap of ruins, not knowing whither to turn. But recovering his courage, and confident in the help of God and His kind Mother Mary, and in the merits of the holy virgin Etheldreda, he set his hand to the work.'

Inspiration came to him. In the place of the square tower, with its insufficient foundation, he set up a mighty Octagon, cutting boldly into the fabric of the building to accommodate it, and crowning it with a wooden lantern: the whole piece a work in the Decorated style at its most free and inspired and beautiful. The building took twenty-six years, which is amazingly little; even the removal of the mighty mass of rubble from the ruined tower and choir must have been an enormous work. We read of John Attegrene the Master Mason, John of Burwell the Master Woodcarver, William Shank the Chief Decorator, William Hurle the inspired Carpenter and even Ralph le Goldbeter who beat the gold coin donated by the Sacrist himself for the embellishment of the interior. Their names should be preserved.

As for the Lady Chapel, John of Wisbech, who dug during the night, finished it just before he died in the Black Death of 1349.

The West Tower, which soars over everything else—it is 215 feet high—is embellished with tier upon tier of Early English arcading, which gets later in style as it gets higher owing to the time-lag in its construction. The octagon at the top of the tower is a later addition. There is a transept south of the tower, said to be of the finest Norman work in England: the corresponding transept to the north collapsed.

The west porch, or Galilee ('Behold I go before you into Galilee!'), thus named some people say because it is farthest from the altar as the real Galilee is farthest in the Holy Land from Bethlehem, but others have it that it is called Galilee because, in ceremonial circumambulations of the building the deacon who led the procession would cry out: 'Behold—I am come unto Galilee!' before entering the church. This Galilee, Early English like the west tower, has columns of Purbeck marble, the hard fresh-water limestone from Dorset. Note the slenderness of the shafts on each side supporting their ogee arches. They are much decayed, and some of them have been replaced by a Devonshire marble.

As we walk through the inner door of the Galilee the view that greets us is breathtaking. The more so because Mr Essex, in 1769, simply swept away the whole of the stone screen, or pulpitum, the

ELY CATHEDRAL

LADY CHAPEL

1 W. TOWER   NAVE   5   28   29

CLOISTER GARTH

1 Gallilee Porch, c.1215
2 St. Catherine's Chapel, rebuilt 1848
3 Prior's Door, c.1140
4 Ovin's Cross, late 7th. C.
5 Alan of Walsingham's Tomb, 1364
6 Monk's Door, c.1140
7 Chapter Vestry, 1090
8 Library, 1090
9 Presbytery, c.1234
10 Site of St. Etheldreda's Shrine, 1252
11 High Altar
12 Sir Mark Steward, 1603
13 Sir Robert Steward, 1570
14 Bishop Heton, 1609

15 Bishop Gunning, 1684
16 John Tiptoft, Earl of Worcester, 1470
17 Bishop West's Chantry, 1533
18 Cardinal de Luxembourg, 1443
19 St. Etheldreda's Chapel, 1952
20 Bishop Alcock's Chantry, 1488
21 Bishop Northwold, 1254
22 Bishop Kilkenny, 1256
23 Bishop Redman, 1505
24 Bishop Nigel, 1174
25 Dean Caesar, 1636
26 St. Edmund's Chapel, restored 1898
27 St. George's Chapel, " 1920
28 Octagon & Lantern, 1342
29 Choir, 14th. century

only Norman stone screen in England, in his 'restoration' work. The eighteenth century could be far more destructive when it came to Gothic buildings than the nineteenth. At least the nineteenth century loved the Gothic—if they often loved it to death. The eighteenth century hated it as the work of barbarians, and said so, and would sweep it away whenever it felt like it.

But the fact that there is no screen means, unlike at Norwich, the whole great vista of the cathedral presents itself. There are the massive Norman arcades of the nave, the equally clean and massive Norman triforia of double arches, with, above them, the treble arched clerestories. The nave roof, 105 feet above our heads, may be a disappointment: it is painted wood. The two Victorians who painted it did their best and one of them, at least, was a Norfolk man: Henry Styleman Le Strange of Hunstanton Hall. He adapted his design from the wooden roof of St Michael's, Hildesheim, in Germany. The nave and the transepts never got to be roofed in stone: the Black Death intervened.

If we move down the nave and to the right, the south aisle, we come to the Prior's Door, and this we must see from the outside. It presents to us a wealth of strange and barbaric Norman carving: an art more akin to the art of pagan and very early Christian Celtic art than to that of the Middle Ages. There is a primitive but terrifyingly effective Christ on the tympanum above the door. It is worth while to spend same time making out the rest of the carving. Human life is depicted down one side of the door, and the animal creation down the other. The fact that the two men in the rowing boat are pulling against each other would not have been lost on the monks of Ely, for every one of these was perforce a waterman.

Inside again, a little way down the aisle to the east, is Ovin's Cross, or, more properly, Owen's Cross. Written on the base of this is: Lucem tuam ovino da deus et reqvie(m) Amen.

There is but the base and the shaft left of this: it was smashed at the Reformation; but it takes us back to Saxon times if not, indeed, earlier. Owen, later sainted himself, was Saint Etheldreda's steward, and probably a member of the Girvii tribe, i.e. a Celt, hence his Welsh name. He is mentioned by Bede, who tells us that when Queen Etheldreda no longer required his services he walked to Lichfield monastery, clad in a plain garment and carrying a pick and a bill-hook to indicate that he had not come to live in idleness, and there became a monk. On down the nave we come to the transepts: the one on the right being the oldest part of the cathedral: Bishop Simeon's work, begun in 1083.

But we may find it hard to contemplate this Norman work because of our pleasure and amazement at what goes on over our heads: Alan of Walsingham's octagonal tower is the wonder of the cathedral, and indeed of medieval building in England. It soars above us: eight lofty pillars branching out into splendid palm leaves, the ribs of which apparently support the eight-sided lantern, the walls of which are offset to the eight walls of the tower below. The effect is momentous. We cannot begin to understand how the mighty lantern (it is said to weigh 400 tons) can be held up there by those slender ribs, and yet, somehow, there is no feeling of insecurity by this arrangement. We are not to know, of course, that it is not held up by the ribs at all—but by a cunningly concealed arrangement of mighty beams of oak. For these beams eight trunks had to be found absolutely straight and without a fault, and 64 feet long, 3 feet 4 inches wide by 2 feet 8 inches thick when adzed down (imagine the job of adzing them!). Eight were found—in Bedfordshire, and each one, adzed, weighed 10 tons. We may wonder how they were got to Ely, until we realize that the Great Ouse runs right through Bedfordshire—they *had* to come from Bedfordshire. We may then wonder at the engineering skill, or at least the skill of the riggers who got them up to that height and put them in position. What did the army of monks and labourers sing as they hauled on the falls of the tackles?

Whether Alan intended in the beginning to roof his Octagon with stone we do not know, but this would have involved vaulting a span of 74 feet at a height of 86 feet, something never before achieved. But the solution that he found, or was driven to: the poising of this magnificent wooden lantern at the top of it all, was the happiest that there could have been. The lantern is surrounded with windows, and is full of light; and walking out underneath it after the claustrophobic massiveness of the Norman nave is like moving from a sombre age of militarism and dungeons into a new age of sunshine and wonder and delight.

It is here that we can admire the scenes from the life of St Etheldreda, as imagined by fourteenth-century stone carvers, on the corbels half way up the eight shafts of the Octagon.

The screen is Victorian; but beyond it the choir stalls are fourteenth century, and so are the next three bays of the building: built by Alan of Walsingham to replace the ones smashed by the collapse of the tower. The Bible scenes carved with such a heavy hand (compared, that is, to the hand which carved the delicate woodwork surrounding them) are Belgian, and nineteenth-century insertions. But the rest of the woodwork is medieval, and there are no less than fifty-four medieval miserere seats of the most surprising variety and interest: the strip-cartoons of the Middle Ages. Nor should the 'Ely Imps' be neglected—at the join of the first two arches of the choir on the south side, in stone: the one on the other's back.

We proceed eastwards into the presbytery which was fortunately missed by the tower as it fell and so still stands. It was completed by Hugh de Northwold in 1232. Etheldreda's shrine, the purpose of the whole building, was beneath the two bosses in the vaulted roof: one carved with the Virgin being crowned, the other with the Saint. The shrine was destroyed by Bishop Goodrich in the reign of Henry VIII: the same bishop who desecrated the Lady Chapel. It is interesting that this so zealous Protestant found himself able to turn an equally zealous Catholic when Mary came to the throne.

There are a number of tombs in the choir aisles, which we have not the space to describe, and in any case they are all clearly labelled. Do not miss the stark effigy of Bishop Kilkenny in the north aisle, and to the north of the choir the weird carving on the monument of a bishop thought to be Nigel—of the Angel Gabriel carrying the bishop's little soul up to Heaven, about 1150, and made of marble by the craftsmen in Tournai in Belgium—like the font of Winchester Cathedral.

In the south-east of the presbytery is Bishop West's Chantry, built in the high Perpendicular style just before the Dissolution of the monastery and built internally of clunch: a stone which lends itself to exuberant carving. There are touches of Renaissance decoration among the lush embellishment: an Italian feel about it, and the whole thing is secular in feeling rather than religious. More sumptuous still is Bishop Alcock's Chantry (1488) in the north-east corner: an absolute fairy palace of clunch, like a cave of ice or of stalactites, with a fan vault of the utmost splendour, a mighty boss in the middle dripping with leaves and grapes. This chapel is best seen through the restrained and dignified Early English arch outside it— the contrast is terrific. Alcock was the man who founded Jesus College, and as we have seen his rebus there—the cockerel—so we see it here too.

Perhaps a harder and more intransigent rock than chalk would have led to more restrained carving than we see in these two chantries, but all the same they are nothing if not *fun*.

The chapel in between the two chantries of the merry bishops is dedicated to St Etheldreda herself, and is a memorial to the 'men of

Grantabryggeshire' who stood firm in 1939–46, as their ancestors did nine hundred years before on Ringmere Heath.

In Bishop West's Chantry, incidentally, lie the bodies of seven East Anglians who were dug up from various parts of the cathedral and moved here. They include the heroic Brithnoth, Alderman of East Anglia under Ethelred the Unready; who met and at least withstood the Danes at the Battle of Maldon, when he was killed.

> *Then drave from each hand*
> *Full starkly the spear,*
> *Showered the sharp arrows,*
> *Busy were bows,*
> *Shield met shaft,*
> *Bitter the Battle.*

Brithnoth's headless body (the Danes got away with his head) was brought back to Ely by the monks and buried here. The story is that, on his way to the battle, Brithnoth put in to the Abbey of Ramsey and asked for food. The monks said that they could entertain him and a few picked companions, but not his whole force. He replied: 'Tell my Lord Abbot that I cannot fight without my men, neither will I feed without them!' and he proceeded to Ely, where men and leader were alike entertained, and to requite this hospitality he bestowed upon the Abbey, there and then, no less than nine manors only stipulating that his body should be buried there, which it still is.

The next great thing to see is the Lady Chapel: the foundations of which were laid out by Brother John and his mates in that night which ended in 'a small rain'. To find this we have to search for a small door in the north-east corner of the north transept.

We walk into the chapel as into a bath of light. It is Late Decorated work of the most splendid, although the tracery of the east window is just beginning to verge on the coming Perpendicular discipline. The span of the vaulted roof is 46 feet—the widest in England. The interior is lined on all sides with the most exquisite carving in clunch (all this chalk was brought down the river from the great quarry at Reach), but unfortunately the statues that were held by these seemingly innumerable niches were ravaged by the iconoclasts, and only one small example remains out of hundreds. Thomas Goodrich made it his business to destroy this great heritage of medieval art because he considered them 'works of Mariolatry', and as we look around the chapel now we may well feel that the strong and simple faith that kept Brother John and his mates digging through the night until that small rain came has gone from the building just as surely as have the statues which embellished those empty niches.

But there is still enough splendour to keep us entranced for days. The white rock has been carved with inconceivable intricacy and great delicacy; with none of the vulgarity which we may feel compromises the chantries of those two jolly bishops; the lovely lierne vaulting soars above our heads, the generous clear windows, bereft of their original coloured glass, dazzle us with the flowing brilliance of their tracery.

It now remains for us to do one last thing, and that the most strenuous. We must climb the 215 feet of the West Tower. On the journey upwards we receive a conception of the almost inconceivable amount of stone that went into a great cathedral: a vast volume of massive masonry, all hidden away behind the scenes. From the top we look down at the tweedy-textured tiled Georgian roofs, the careful flower gardens and fruitful vegetable plots of the clergy, all professional gardener-tended, the playing fields of Kings' School, the jumbled old houses of the city and beyond it all the far-stretching Fens, the Great Ouse winding through it, and if it is clear enough the spires of Cambridge to the south and the hazy waters of the Wash to the northward.

Of monastic buildings, there are the cloisters—nothing like so complete as those at Norwich, the Prior's House and the Bishop's House built in what was the monks' refectory, Prior Cauden's Chapel, now the chapel of Kings' School, which was built by Alan of Walsingham and is therefore very unusual and beautiful and not to be missed on any account at all—it is one of the choicest pieces of building at Ely, the Ely Porta, or great gate of the monastery, and beyond it the tythe barn, now a gymnasium for Kings' School.

Kings' School (two kings were involved in it, hence the placing of the apostrophe) was founded before the reign of Edward the Confessor, for he was a scholar at it. It was, in fact, founded by Alfred the Great after his defeat of the Danes at Ethaldune, as the 'College', and to this day what would be called 'the Close' in other cathedral cities is here called 'the College'.

These things are of note at Ely, the Lantern, and Chapel of Mary,
A windmill too, and a vineyard that yieldeth wine in abundance.

Know that the Choir before you exceedeth all others in beauty,
Made by Alan our brother, Alan the wise Master Builder;
Alan the Prior, forget not, here facing the Choir lyeth buried.
He, for that older Tower which fell one night in the darkness,
Were erected, well-founded, the Tower that ye now are beholding.

(Latin inscription on the brass over Alan of Walsingham's grave, translation by Conybeare.)

As for Ely 'the city' of itself: it is an unspoiled little market town and river port. There are streets of old houses, mostly Georgian, its own brewery, an interesting river-front. It is unindustrialized and still a good example of a predominantly Georgian East Anglian country town.

The Cutter Inn, down by the river, is a good place to tie up beside in a boat, and Messrs Appleyard, Lincoln and Co not only hire out cabin cruisers but build them too, in a big yard they have built across the river and which is accessible by a chain ferry. Mr Appleyard was of old a great builder of Fen lighters, and he comes from a line of Fen watermen. Mr Lincoln, at present the leading partner in the firm, has brought it up to date, and has done more than anyone to open up the Fenland rivers for pleasure cruising.

Oliver Cromwell's grandfather was Steward, or tythe-farmer, for the Dean and Chapter of Ely; responsible for collecting every tenth sheaf in the harvest fields of the Isle of Ely and far beyond and storing, some of it at least, in the great tythe barn now used as a school gymnasium. Oliver, born at St Ives, succeeded his grandfather in this office and accordingly came to live in Ely, in the Steward's House. When the Civil War broke out Cromwell came to drill his Ironsides on St Mary's Green. He sent a message to Canon Hitch, who was then responsible for the services in the cathedral, telling him to give up his popish practices; and when the message had no effect led a body of troopers into the cathedral during Holy Communion and 'drave out' both priest and communicants. He must have had a soft spot for the building, though, for he did not allow it to be pulled down during the Commonwealth.

There is a Chinese restaurant in Fore Street.

At **Prickwillow**, a tiny village north-east of Ely, is a pumping station that lifts the waters of the River Lark a great height so that they can flow into the lofty Great Ouse, and a church with Victorian carpentry in it resembling that of Leiston, in Suffolk. The most noteworthy object in this otherwise quite unprepossessing little church in this tiny and undistinguished Fen village (not that the *people* are undistinguished—far from it, they are famous men) is the font. This is a marble bowl of urbane and sophisticated eighteenth-century workmanship, quite incongruous in its bucolic surroundings.

From here we can circle through the black Fens, where celery and onions grow in endless weedless rows down hedgeless billiard-table fields, to **Littleport**, remembered for its martyrs. In 1816 there was widespread hunger in the Fens owing largely to the enclosure of common land. When their children were starving the unemployed farm workers of Littleport were obliged to watch trains of Fen lighters being loaded in their village with the grain that would have kept them alive—grain grown in their own parish and being sent away to London to make profits for the already extremely wealthy farmers. Wages, for the few that had any, were 9s a week: wheat was £5 5s 0d a quarter.

They rioted. They marched to Ely armed with bill-hooks and scythes, and covered by a predecessor of the tank: a farm wagon on which were mounted four great punt-guns. They fired no shot, killed nobody, and after some window-breaking and lawlessness retired home.

The military were sent for, and invested the district, and after weeks of searching and interrogating eighty men were arrested and taken to Ely to be made an example of.

They were tried by judges selected by the Bishop of Ely, for in this 'Liberty and Franchise' he had this power. Five men were publicly hanged (with great difficulty, for the Bishop could not for a long time get anybody to lend him a cart for the job), five were transported for life, and the rest all put in prison for long periods. The bishop then marched into the cathedral in a great procession with fifty men of Ely carrying white wands, his sword being borne before him by his butler, and everybody singing 'Why Do the Heathen Rage?'

This miserable exhibition was the last exercise of temporal power by the Bishops of Ely: a power handed down to them in direct line from the ancient British tribe of the Girvii, in the Fens 1,146 years before.

433

North West Cambridgeshire

We now embark into the drained Fens north of Cambridge, first coming to the two villages of their ancient shore, Landbeach and Waterbeach.

At **Waterbeach** Carr Dyke is to be seen south of the village, a Roman canal. This navigation of the Romans is traceable all the way to Lincoln, where it joined the Foss Dyke, another Roman canal, at Breyford Pool. Vessels were thus able to go from just north of Cambridge for York, to carry Fenland grain to the Military Zone in the North of England, via Carr Dyke, Foss Dyke, down Trent, and up the Yorkshire Ouse. The Carr Dyke, incidentally, is mostly obliterated by later Fenland draining: the Foss Dyke is still easily navigable, and much used by motor keels carrying grain from Hull to Lincoln.

North of Waterbeach is the site of Denny Priory, where the widowed Countess of Pembroke, who founded Pembroke College, Cambridge, founded a nunnery. Parts of the refectory and fragments of the chapel are left.

Landbeach is notable for its angel lectern, seventeenth century and very dashing, supposed to have been the support to a Dutch pulpit.

Stretham is across the Old West River. The Old West is the original course of the Great Ouse, before Vermuyden cut his two Bedford rivers thus cutting off the great corner, much as Bishop Morton dug his Leam to cut off the corners of the River Nene centuries before. The Old West is still navigable, although somewhat weeded up in summer time, and it has a great charm of its own: a natural winding watercourse in a land of straight artificial ones. It joins the Cam at Pope's Corner, where is the Fish and Duck Inn, a hostelry only approachable by water or by land over a track over the

Fens: a marvellous place to moor a boat, or to stay ashore for a holiday of complete retirement.

But Stretham is remarkable for its Old Engine. This was installed by the Waterbeach Level Draining Commissioners in 1831, and is a 60 HP Boulton and Watt beam engine, erected by the Butterley Company of Derbyshire. It cost £400, and when first installed drained 5,600 acres, taking over from a great many windmills. That is, it lifted the water from the lower Fens into the higher Old West River between its banks. The engine originally drove a scoop wheel of just over 30 feet in diameter, which had to be increased to 33 feet in diameter in 1849 owing to further shrinking of the peat and consequent subsidence of the land, and again to 37 feet 2 inches in 1896, which it is now.

The engine is still in perfect working order, having worked for a hundred years and stood mostly idle for another thirty, for a diesel has now taken over its task. It is in the care of the Stretham Engine Preservation Trust, by which the above details were supplied, and the Trust depends upon public support. It is hoped to establish a museum of Fenland drainage here. The engine looks most impressive and beautiful in its lofty house, and can be appreciated as much for its beauty by laymen as for its technical and historical interest by engineers.

West from Stretham we rise into a spur of the Isle of Ely to **Wilburton**, the church of which is interesting to saint-knowers, for there is a faded mural, besides the usual Saint Christopher, of St Blaise, who was of course Bishop of Sebaste, martyred in 316, and the patron saint of wool combers, and of Saint Leodegar, Bishop of Autun in France during the seventh century. Wilburton also has a lovely red-brick manor house of 1600 called the Burystead.

Haddenham is a large village, and we are now becoming aware that we are no longer really in East Anglia at all. Although built on a spur of the Isle of Ely this place has a Midland air about it: we might be in Huntingdonshire or Bedfordshire. The church has been severely dealt with by the Victorians, who rebuilt the tower in its original style of transitional between Decorated and Perpendicular. This church was founded by our old friend Owen, Latinized to Ovin, whose cross is in Ely Cathedral. The cross was set up here as an object of veneration until the Reformation, when it was smashed and made into a mounting-block.

South-west of Haddenham is the hamlet of **Aldreth**, which is historically interesting because from here to Willingham runs the first ever Fen causeway to Ely, set up by William the Conqueror.

But north from Haddenham we drop sharply down into the Fen again, to below sea level in fact—North Fen on our left and Grunty Fen on our right. In Grunty Fen were dug up a bronze sickle and ornaments of twisted gold, on the other side of Haddenham spur a great hoard of bronze weapons was found, as though tipped out of a canoe, also gold money, a Celtic urn and the bones of an aurochs. We traverse only a narrow strip of Fenland here, though, to rise again to another spur of the Isle on which stands Sutton.

Sutton has an unforgettable church, all Decorated, with a tower which soars so high on its hill that on a misty day travellers, from afar, have taken it for Ely. The church was started by Bishop Barnet of Ely in 1366, thus after the Black Death and the tower was obviously inspired by Ely Octagon. It is in fact one octagon perched on top of another and the lower perched on a square tower. The whole church is interesting and beautiful: the last lovely flourish of the Decorated before the Perpendicular came in, and a product of the great wealth of Ely in the fourteenth century before it suffered the eclipse that lasted until the Great Drainings of the seventeenth century. Note the ceiling in the tower, the tower arch, the corvels south of the nave, the lovely Decorated window tracery. Fresh Cambridgeshire cheese is sold just south of the church, and east of it is a most charming brick gabled farmhouse. Sutton is a lovely village, on its peninsular jutting out into the dry seabed of the Fens, and its orchards.

Mepal has little to attract the stranger, save the 'Three Pickerels Inn' down by the waters of the two Bedford Rivers, with some charming waterside buildings. Beyond the rivers the road runs along Ireton's Way: a causeway built by Ireton, the great Roundhead general, during the Civil War.

Doddington was once the site of a palace of the Bishops of Ely (they had many, including Ely Place in the City of London, where the Liberty and Franchise of Ely extended so that the city authorities could not enter without permission, and where is still to be seen St Etheldreda's Chapel) and here Christopher Tye was rector: a man who composed much music, including the air to 'While Shepherds Watch their Flocks by Night', an anthem which has been much paraphrased by small boys. When rebuked by Queen Elizabeth for playing music out of tune he told her Majesty that it was her ears that were out of tune. The east window in the north aisle of the church is early William Morris.

Benwick, to the west, has a pub called The Five Alls. The spirited sign depicts a lawyer: 'I Plead for All', a parson: 'I Pray for All', a soldier: 'I Fight for All', Queen Victoria: 'I Rule All', and underneath them all a man at the tail of a plough and the legend in larger letters: 'I PAY FOR ALL'.

There is a funny little Victorian church built of Norfolk carr stone —a long way to bring this rather unsuitable building material but presumably done to make the church look 'rustic'. Rustic it looks. The Old Nene, hard beside the church, is navigable, and below the level of the land (most Fenland rivers are above it) and has a pleasant natural appearance.

The road from Benwick to **Whittlesey** takes us across the drained bed of Whittlesey Mere, which was the biggest of the open waters of Fenland. Big sailing vessels once sailed its waters: one of them which had sunk with a freight of stone was discovered when the Mere was drained in 1850—and the draining extinguished the last of the Great Copper butterflies of this country. In the woodland near Holme there is an iron column, originally one of the supports of the Great Exhibition of 1851, which was, after the draining of the Mere, driven down so that its top was level with the ground. It now stands up 11 feet above the surface, and this in woodland which is not cultivated and is therefore not shrinking as fast as the cultivated land.

Whittlesey is an attractive small town, and the source of a very large part of the material which makes up London; for here are England's biggest brick works, with sky-raking 'shafts' (chimneys) and vertical-sided pits deep down into the gault clay. It is from here and from Fletton near Peterborough that the cheap red moulded bricks that make up so much of modern England come in such prodigious quantities. Whittlesey's St Mary's Church has one of the finest spires in Cambridgeshire—we are getting very near to North-amptonshire, the county of squires and spires.

North we cross **Morton's Leam**, which was dug by the order of Bishop Morton, Abbot of Ely, in 1480, the first of the really radical Fen drainage works. It cut off a great corner of the River Nene from Peterborough to Wisbech thus allowing the river to precipitate its water more quickly into the sea. The Bishop's plan was quite sound, although in later centuries the work itself proved inadequate and another great cut was made, and this we cross shortly after having crossed Morton's Leam, and which simply parallels it. This is navigable as far as Peterborough for quite large vessels (two auxiliary sailing barges still trade regularly between Hull and Peterborough Mill with cargoes of foreign grain), and in fact you can go up this river, past Peterborough and right up to Northampton and thereafter by a flight of narrow locks into the Grand Union Canal and the whole waterways system of England. Just downstream of where we cross is the 'Dog in a Doublet Sluice': the big modern lock which keeps the tide from going any higher, just as Denver Sluice does on the Great Ouse. This sluice is named after the very fine inn nearby.

North again and we come to **Thorney Abbey.** After King Wulfhere of Mercia (who, incidentally, was married to one of St Etheldreda's sisters—the seed of old King Anna had Christianized even the pagan Mercians who killed him) had endowed the Abbey of Peterborough with great possessions 'the Abbot prayed of him that he would give him whatsoever he should ask. And the King granted him. Then said the Abbot: "Here have I God-fearing monks, who would fain live as hermits, knew they but where. And there is an island which is called Ancarig" ' (modern Thorney). 'And my boon is that we might there build a Minster, to the glory of St Mary, so that they who would lead a life of peace and rest may dwell therein.' The king acceded to his request and Thorney was founded in 657, when a small abbey was built, not much more than the abode of anchorites. In the devastating Danish raid of 870, described so vividly in the 'Crowland Chronicle', the much greater foundations of Crowland and Peterborough were utterly destroyed —every building burnt and every monk who would be captured tortured and killed—all except one, a young boy 'fair in form and face', who was taken on by a Danish chief as a pet but who later escaped to tell the tale. Thorney was used as a refuge for the few who fled from Crowland, but the probability is that it later suffered in its turn.

Thorney Abbey was refounded by the Benedictines in 972, by Ethelwold, Bishop of Winchester. It became important, and William of Malmsbury wrote of it, about 1135: '. . . a little paradise, delightsome as Heaven itself may be deemed, fen-circled, yet rich in loftiest trees, where water-meadows delight the eye with rich green, where streamlets glide unchecked through each field. Scarce a spot of ground lies there waste: here are orchards, there vineyards. Nature vies with culture, and what is unknown to the one is produced by the other. And what of the glorious buildings, whose very size it is a wonder that the ground can support amid such marshes? A vast solitude is here the monks' lot, that they may the more closely cling to things above. If a woman is there seen she is counted a monster, but strangers, if men, are greeted as angels unawares. Yet here none speaketh, save for a moment; all is holy silence . . . From its dense thickets it is called Thorney.'

The Abbey Church was spared by Henry VIII on condition that it became the parish church, and its remains are still parochial. All that still stands is 117 feet of its nave with the aisles shorn off it and the east end cut away too. The west end still has a certain grandeur (the 'Perpendicular' inserts, such as the west window, were Perpendicular revival of 1638) and there is a ravaged beauty about the Norman arcades and triforia within.

The village around it is quite un-Fenlike, owing to the fact that this countryside fell to the Earls of Bedford in the great Fen Drainings of Vermuyden's day, and still remains in the Bedford family, and they have made of Thorney a model estate village. There are pretty estate houses and the country is planted with trees in a most un-Fenlike manner: your true Fenman only has one reaction when he sees a tree—he reaches for his axe.

A strange thing is that the Bedfords allowed Huguenot refugees to settle at Thorney in the seventeenth century, and right until 1715 French pastors were ministering in the church. In the churchyard are many French graves; and there is much French blood in the people of Thorney.

We might cut back to Cambridge through foreign territory: the Huntingdonshire villages of Ramsey and St Ives.

Ramsey is approachable by boat from the Forty Foot Drain, and we can see by its main street that the canal once ran straight through it, but alas it has been filled in and turned into a long car park. How extremely delightful the place would look if this had not been done, and the little place were once again main-streeted by a waterway like a Dutch village, and yachts lay alongside its quays.

St Ives is a charming place, and a wonderful port of call for a boat on the Great Ouse, and there is a good boatyard run by Mr L. H. Jones. At **Holywell**, just downstream, is the famous thatched Ferry Boat Inn, which was selling beer in 1068 and has been selling it ever since, and which may thus dispute with the Trip to Jerusalem of

Nottingham the claim to be the oldest licensed house in England. Its age is pre-Conquest, in fact, for there are documents which mention it as early as AD 980. The inn serves the finest food, which should however be booked in advance: telephone St Ives 3227. There is a specimen of bog-oak in the bar, and ask Dave Forrest, the landlord, to show you the grave slab of poor Juliet Tewsley.

This young lady hanged herself on a tree by the river nearby on 17th March 1050, because a woodcutter named Thomas Zoul spurned her away as she waited for him on his way home from work with a bunch of flowers. Ghost-lovers may wish to visit the pub on St Patrick's Day when, if they drink enough beer, they may hope to see her walk.

Farther downstream is another good inn: the Pike and Eel at **Overcote Ferry,** and here again is first-class food; the telephone number is Swavesey 225. It is pretty, with weeping willow by the river.

Earith is at a great meeting place of the waters. Here the Old and the New Bedford Rivers take off from the Great Ouse, to cut as straight as two rulers across the Fenland to Denver Sluice. The Old was cut in 1630: the New in 1650. The Old is tideless, being cut off from the tidal Great Ouse below Denver Sluice by a sluice of its own. The New is tidal, and, at High Springs, the tide may even get up it as far as Earith.

It was here, on the Old Bedford, that a bizarre experiment was conducted to prove to an incorrigible Flat-Earther that our planet is, indeed, round. The Flat-Earther was a man who went about lecturing under the *nom-de-plume* Parallax, proving to one and all that the earth was flat. He supported his claim by offering to lay a heavy wager with anybody who was willing to prove otherwise. A man took him up, and an experiment was carried out on the Old Bedford River, this being the longest straight stretch of perfectly calm water in the kingdom (the Victoria Canal on the Coast of Coramandel would have done better, this being 300 miles longer than the Old Bedford). Three vessels were moored, having their cross-trees at the same level above the water. These Victorian gentlemen then clambered to the cross-trees of one of them and aimed a telescope at the cross-trees of the other two. If the earth was flat—then these should be in line. If round then they should not. Perhaps not un-expectedly the Flat-Earther found they were but everyone else found they were not, and Parallax lost his money.

441

Over has a grand and lavish church with the most engaging gargoyles this side of Notre Dame de Paris: they should certainly be visited on a rainy day to see them in full gush. But everything about this church is beautiful. It is lavishly built of Barnack stone, Early English tower and chancel (although the latter has Perpendicular windows inserted), Decorated the lovely south porch, which has a weathered sculpture believed by most people to be Christ in Glory but in fact Our Lady in Glory, a much rarer subject, a sanctus bell in its turret over the eastern gable of the nave—again a rare survival as nearly all these bells and turrets were especially obnoxious to Protestants since they tolled at the moment of the Elevation of the Host. There is lovely woodwork within, old misericords from Ramsey Abbey, a Decorated roof and most of the window tracery; this is a fine church, full of quality and good workmanship.

Willingham is a big village, and to the east of it rises the pre-historic fortification known as Belsar's Hill. Belsar was the general of William the Conqueror who built the causeway to the Isle of Ely to give access for the final attack on that place. The church at Willingham again is a superb one (we are again here on that magic line—the ancient shoreline of the Fens: the villages of which were all prosperous, having extensive common rights on the drier parts of the Fen for summer grazing) with a massive hammerbeam roof almost as glorious as the one at March and the most fascinating chapel off the chancel with a lovely stone roof of very unusual design: Decorated as is most of the rest of the church. Can it have been a rising in the waters of the Fens in the fifteenth century, making it impossible to graze sheep, that accounts for the existence of so much Decorated in these 'shoreline' churches? The resulting impoverishment would have prevented the rebuilding that went on in the rest of East Anglia during the Perpendicular period that followed. Or can it be another explanation: the build-up of liver-fluke, inevitable in marshy grazing overstocked with sheep?

Swavesey, south of Over, had a Benedictine priory founded by Alan de la Zouche just after the Conquest, and it later turned Carthusian, but there is nothing to see of it. The church, like that of Over, is another of this magnificent group on the south side of the Great Ouse Valley. With its splendid cedars and larches it looks fine when approached from the village, with something very clean-cut and blocky about it like a good modern building. It has lovely Decorated tracery in its windows, sumptuous south doorway inside its Perpendicular porch and the nave has a notable array of bench-ends, some of them very good Victorian copies. Some of the benches are tiny, evidently for children.

Long Stanton has not one, but two interesting churches. St Michael, mostly Early English although the chancel is Victorian-rebuilt, has a notable double piscina and a twelfth-century oak chest. All Saints is cruciform, mostly Decorated and has monuments to the Hatton family which bought the manor from Queen Elizabeth after that monarch had filched it from the Bishop of Ely. When he protested she said: 'Obey my pleasure or I will forthwith unfrock you!'

On a former occasion Elizabeth was entertained by the same bishop at his palace at Long Stanton, and an embarrassing event occurred. Some Cambridge undergraduates, wishing to show the queen their Protestant zeal, performed a masque before her in which a dog, presumably a Protestant one, danced before Her Majesty with a consecrated Host in its mouth. When the Queen saw what was going forward she swept from the room in disgust—ordering all the lights to be put out and leaving the wretched undergraduates to find their properties in the pitch dark as best they could and make their way back to Cambridge.

Oakington would be a place of pilgrimage to Nonconformists, if, indeed, Nonconformists were given to making pilgrimage. Here is a graveyard in which are buried the bodies of Francis Holcroft, Joseph Oddy, and Henry Oasland. These three were leaders of the Non-conformist movement that survived the Restoration of Charles II, losing their Anglican livings for it under the Act of Uniformity of 1662, and thereafter preaching clandestinely up and down the land.

Histon is more a town than a village, with many modern factories including one which makes Chiver's Jam. The place is not attractive, although it has a church very interesting to lovers of the Early English—very similar to St Radegund's, in Jesus College.

Girton is famous for its women's college, which moved here from Hitchin in 1873. Except for the lovely grounds, and many pretty girls, there is nothing to go and see.

Madingley has a huge and very beautiful Tudor mansion, set in a great park in which, in summer, Herefords fatten. The house was built by Mr Justice Hinde in Henry VIII's time, partly with material he took from the church of St Etheldreda in Histon when he pulled this down. He filched the fine Norman font when he did so, but this

443

has now been removed from the house and placed in Madingley Church. Edward VII lived at Madingley when he was an under-graduate at Trinity, and Charles I is supposed to have hidden there when he had escaped from the army at nearby Childerley Hall. The army had captured him in order to exert pressure on Parliament to meet its demands, but he escaped, and Madingley was owned by Sir John Coton, a Royalist. King Charles is said to have banged on his door in the middle of the night, disguised as a peasant, but the troopers soon came after him, and the whole incident was hushed up. The Hall now belongs to Cambridge University.

On the A45 nearby is a very pretty little post mill, brought here and set up as an ornament, and well looked after. Nearby is the American War Cemetery, in which are buried thousands of American dead.

CHAPTER 27

South West Cambridgeshire

Cambridgeshire has shown us one of the loveliest cities in the world, the most sumptuous of all English cathedrals, and the magnificent line of great churches along the old Fenland shores. Surely it can be excused from not having so very much more to offer, and indeed the south of the county, although in odd corners quietly pretty, has little to show to equal the great Suffolk wool villages.

Grantchester is traditionally approached from Cambridge in a punt, with a pretty girl reclining on the cushions, but it may be achieved by other means. And however one gets there the place has its enchantment, a fact that Byron, Tennyson and Rupert Brooke alike acknowledged, and even Chaucer mentioned the place. There are several large pubs here now; and the village itself has got itself the stigma of a 'beauty spot'; but surprisingly the lovely river side is seldom overcrowded for long, and on a sunny day reclining beneath one of those enormous willow trees and watching the punts being slowly poled up from Cambridge is to be convinced that Grantchester is all that Rupert Brooke cracked it up to be. There is a most pleasant walk, too, to Cambridge along the river.

The mill . . .

> *And laughs the immortal river still*
> *Under the mill, under the mill.*

. . . is a mill, alas, no longer; having been burned down in 1928. If the church clock still does not stand at ten to three somebody ought to be shot, the church has Roman bricks in its walls, there is a window that may be a Saxon one, and one of the most lovely chancels of the Decorated style in the country.

The rector of **Hardwick** in 1644 being a man blessed with a wife and seven children was accused of being a man devoted to 'many superstitious ceremonies, and commonly useth altar-worship, east-worship, and dropping-worship, and after the sermon came out of the pulpit and there made an end of his ill-worship'. He was ejected and sequestrated. He might have taken a tip or two from the celebrated Dr Perne (see p400) or from the Vicar of Bray for that matter.

Toft has some alabaster fragments in its church of sculptures which were smashed by Dowsing in 1663 for which service, with other destruction, he was paid 6s 8d. St Hubert is recognizable among these fragments, the patron saint of hunters. He was, of course, converted to Christianity by meeting a hart in the forest with golden antlers and was given a key by St Peter which has the power of curing hydrophobia. The fragment here shows him, headless, thanks to Dowsing, but with the key, a hound, and the golden hart, all very sensitively carved.

Bourn is a pretty little place, with the River Bourn flowing through it, and what is supposed to be the oldest windmill in England. This is a post mill with an appearance rather of a sentry-box set up on wooden legs, and it was built in 1636. It was bought and repaired and presented to the Cambridge Preservation Society with funds raised at an exhibition, in Cambridge, of Epstein's *Genesis*!

There is an Elizabethan mansion at Bourn, built on the site of a former castle which itself was built by Picot, Sheriff of Cambridgeshire under the Conqueror. The church is noteworthy, cruciform, Norman and Early English, with noble arches inside and on the floor of the tower there is a maze, most rare in England now although there is a recently-made one in Ely Cathedral. At one

446

time, like maypoles, they were widespread and had a mystical significance.

Eltisley, where the higher greensand ridge from Cambridge begins to peter out into the Valley of the Great Ouse, is of interest to the saint-knower. Here are buried two blessed saints of great obscurity: St Pandiana, who, Leland tells us, was a Scots princess (meaning at the time that she lived in Ireland, where the Scots came from) and that she fled all the way to Eltisley to escape the importunities of her suitors and there founded a nunnery which perished at the Conquest. The other is St Wendreda, who has a well near Newmarket and the great church of March.

At Eltisley in 1234, according to Roger of Wendover, there was a great famine; and it caused the poor of the parish to invade the fields and devour the crops. The farmers 'who ever from their avarice look upon the poor with an evil eye' went to the parson and asked that the poor should be excommunicated; but one farmer 'adjured him in God's name to pronounce such sentence for *his* crops'. A great gale blew up, which blew down every man's corn excepting that of the good man who did not grudge the starving poor.

From here we might cut south through foreign (Bedfordshire) territory to **Gamlingay**. This has a grand and very big cruciform church, built of red ironstone, and about as un-East Anglian looking as a church could be. There are daunting gargoyles below battlements, a fine and individual west tower, and from the outside the church reminds one of a fortress. In a field nearby are several thatched barns being allowed to fall down in the name of Profit, there is a range of two storied seventeenth-century almshouses, unusual in being of a size big enough to live in and very good-looking, there is a good modern school, and, east of the village, a noteworthy timber-framed farmhouse, really well restored, and with no obnoxious 'olde-Tudor' knick-knacks slung about it.

By **Croydon**, south-east, we are in lovely and atypically Cambridgeshire country: rolling uplands with extensive woods in places. Truth to tell South Cambridgeshire is scenically uninspiring for the most part, and is these days being brought very much under the bulldozer; but there are the delicious corners to be come upon unexpectedly well away from the main roads. Croydon is a little hamlet near an actual *hill*, that anybody would recognize as a hill; and there are woods and trees about, and the Queen Adelaide was a noble little pub until it was all done up inside with plastic tiles and wallpaper printed to make it look like Cotswold oolitic stone-work.

At Croydon lived the Downing family. The first of the name was a sort of James Bond of the Commonwealth and Restoration period. His mother was a sister of John Winthrop, the Governor of Massachusetts, and he spent his childhood in the American colonies, returned to England to act as head spy for Cromwell, became Ambassador to France and Holland, while at the Hague managed to ingratiate himself with Charles Stuart by giving away Commonwealth secrets to him and thus stayed in favour at the Restoration. He double-crossed everybody, forced England into a war with Holland for his personal profit, starved his aged mother and built Downing Street. His grandson founded Downing College in Cambridge, with the money left by his grandsire's childless cousin.

Wimpole lies in even nicer country: chalk downlands, woodlands and a fine variegated landscape. The place is entirely given over to the enormous park and mansion.

The mansion, built in the seventeenth century by the Chichele family, was the home of the Earls of Hardwicke in the eighteenth. The first of these, Philip Yorke, rose from being an obscure lawyer to the post of Lord Chancellor, amassed in this office a great fortune, condemned the Highland rebels of the '45 to death, and enacted a law forbidding the Scots to weave the tartan. The house is now occupied by the late Mr Rudyard Kipling's daughter, and is not open to the public. It will one day, though, come to the National Trust. Wimpole church has several fine monuments.

Orwell has orchards around it, embellishing the chalk downland. The church has a clunch tower, originally Early English, a light and airy Perpendicular chancel, also of clunch and really lovely, there is what looks like a Celtic cross inside the porch and the great treasure is the early fourteenth-century Calvary, now in the south chapel, with Christ nailed to a tree-trunk. This was hidden by being embedded in the south-east spandrel of the north arcade at the Reformation to save it from destruction, and was not re-discovered until 300 years later.

Melbourn is much cut through by the London-Cambridge road. It has a fine very new-looking church which is in fact not new as some of it is thirteenth century, there are fourteenth-century arcades and a fifteenth-century clerestory and roof and there is said to be one of Bishop Alcock's many cockerels on a tie-beam up there. There are saint niches in the south transept, the tower arch is strangely assymetrical with the west window behind it, the east window is most distinguished Perpendicular. It is over the road from the Pink Geranium, a most genteel licensed restaurant where you can get a very good steak, and can sip your sherry first in a pretty garden.

To the east, stretching between Fowlmere and Heydon is the Bran Ditch, one of the several defensive works athwart the Icknield Way. Skeletons of Romano-British soldiers have been unearthed here, with their bones broken as if in war. This whole district is rich in Iron Age, Roman, Saxon and other pre-Conquest remains. The chalk ridge between Essex forests and Fens was well inhabited in ancient times. Bran, in Welsh, means crow or raven.

Ickleton, one of the many villages with names influenced by the Icknield Way, has a church which is really worth going far to see.

Do not be put off by the undistinguished exterior, for this is just a shell over a Norman church the equal of which it would be hard to find. There are very stark and simple arcades, very early Norman with some of their arches resting on monolithic Roman pillars. Traces of colour show that there was once painted decoration on this otherwise quite undecorated stonework.

Some people assign these arcades to earlier-than-Norman times. They have a very strange, almost Byzantine, look about them. Without doubt the piers are Roman: monoliths of Barnack stone which must have been brought to this locality with enormous trouble. They could have been floated up the River Granta for some way but the river is very small for some distance below Ickleton. Some authorities believe that the piers were brought to the church from nearby Chesterford, in Essex, where there was certainly a Roman station. Others, though, believe that the Romans set them up where they are now, and that this was a Roman villa where the church now is. The plan of the church suggests that this might have been so—the pillars having stood each side of the Roman central open court, and having been roofed over by the Saxons, not the Normans, who built the existing clerestory (which indeed looks very Saxon) to admit light. The Saxons did not take over many Romano-British buildings for their own uses, being as a rule more concerned with burning them down; but there is no reason why this should not be the exception that proves the rule. It is a strange experience to stand within this church.

North to **Duxford**, where are three sacred buildings, one the old chapel of St John's Hospital, for long employed as a barn.

These 'hospitals' were not institutions for the care of the sick; but rest houses put up for travellers by the charitable, exactly as are the *choultries* of India today. This English-style *choultry* was, in its day, endowed with sixty acres of meadow land and a watermill in the thirteenth century and is a very good-looking building.

Pampisford has some of the biggest maple trees, Norway and Common, in the British Isles.

It has a Norman tympanum over the west door of its church which reminds us at first glance of the moon stones found in Sinhalese palaces at Polunaruwa. There is a lovely row of thatched and white-washed cottages near the church, one of them the Chequers Inn, with the date 1599 on its wall.

And so we come to **Sawston**, with its famous Hall. The nicest thing about Sawston Hall used to be the charming couple that lived in it. The Huddlestons lived in this house for just under five hundred years (although not the present pair) and they lived there until last year when they, alas, sold the house. The family is Catholic and it is this fact—this adherence to the old faith—that explains why the Hall has remained virtually unchanged since Elizabethan times when it was built. The family, constantly impoverished by the heavy fines that it had to pay for being of the wrong religion, and denied all chances of office, never had the money to carry out 'improvements' as all other country magnates were doing in later centuries. Thus instead of having some concoction of the Renaissance, more Italian or pseudo-Italian than true English, we have this lovely Elizabethan mansion in its four-square simplicity and good sense and lack of pretension.

The house is built of clunch, or chalk, and demonstrates the endurance of this soft rock so long as 'you keep its head and its feet dry'. In any case it has stood there since 1584, when the house was finished, and it looks as good as new, and some of it is earlier than 1584, for the present house was built within the walls of a much earlier mansion.

When the first settlers came from Angeln, in the Jutland peninsula, after the withdrawal of the Romans from Britain, they sailed into the land via the Wash, made their ways up the Wash rivers, and settled along their banks. These settlers turned their backs on the sea, burned their boats metaphorically if not physically, and it was not until the Wuffinga kings came over, probably from Uppsala in Sweden, that, as we have seen, East Anglia became united into a single kingdom.

Sawston, then called Salsingetune, or the town of Salsa, was one of the scattered settlements of these early settlers, and thus Sawston Hall has a very early antecedent.

Sir Edmund de la Pole, Captain of Calais and Sheriff of Cambridgeshire and Huntingdonshire, became owner of the manor of Sawston in 1377, and it was a great great great grand-daughter of his who married a Huddleston shortly after 1500, and thus the Hall came into the Huddleston family. William Huddleston, the man she married, had a great grandfather who fought at Agincourt.

The great crisis in the life of the Hall was when Edward VI died and Mary Tudor, his half-sister, was sent for from where she had been more or less a prisoner at Hunsdon, to go to London. On the way she was warned that her summons was a plot by the Duke of Northumberland, who had every intention of having her executed so that his daughter-in-law, Lady Jane Grey, should be queen instead of her. She fled to East Anglia, towards her own house in Kenninghall in Norfolk, and as we have seen while discussing Framlingham she eventually reached the latter place and there rallied a sufficient force to secure the Crown for herself.

But while on her way she arrived at Sawston Hall, on 7th June 1553, and was entertained for the night by John Huddleston. Early the next day some of Northumberland's troops, under Lord Robert Dudley, another of his sons, and a Cambridge mob, came and attacked the Hall. Princess Mary left by a back door disguised as a dairymaid, riding pillion behind a servant and escorted by her host. Without doubt John Huddleston saved her life, and thus assured the present royal line of England.

They fled to the Gog Magog Hills, and looking back saw the sky smudged with flames: the mob, balked of their quarry, had set fire to Sawston House. Princess Mary said to John Huddleston: 'Let it blaze! When I am Queen I will build Huddleston a better house.' And when she was queen she knighted him, and made him Captain of the King of Spain's (her husband's) guard, and allowed him to take away the stone from Cambridge Castle to build a new house. And it is the new house which we see now.

The house was built between 1557 and 1584, taking so long because the family had to go into hiding during part of Elizabeth I's reign, on account of its recusancy. Things looked up with Charles I, for the Huddlestons of course were staunch Royalists, but they looked very gravely down during the Commonwealth when most of the Huddleston lands were sequestrated. Better with the Restoration, for it was a Huddleston who hid Charles II when he hid in the Boscobel Oak after the Battle of Worcester, but rough after Charles's death, when heavy fines were imposed on recusants. Better again now, as thousands upon thousands of people flood through the house in the summer, paying their half-crowns, have tea in the lovely grounds, and buy the excellent little guide from which I have extracted many of the above facts, and also the fascinating little book: 'Recipes and Remedies of Sawston Hall', which tells you how to cook many strange dishes, and cure many strange diseases with even stranger remedies.

The house today is quite unchanged and unaltered, despite the ravages of the armed forces during the Second World War (quite unbelievably this completely unspoilt Elizabethan mansion was seized by the army during the war for billeting troops: in the Butler's Pantry, until recently the living-room of Captain and Mrs Huddleston, are photographs of the complete devastation they caused): it is still very much of a private home, and does not seem spoiled or altered by people who go to look at it.

We enter the Great Hall, with the original fireplace and oak panelling. The panelling has been 'grained' to make it look like walnut. Apparently this was done at a time when walnut panelling was fashionable but unobtainable: walnut was reserved by law for the making of musket-stocks. There is a fine portrait of Mary Tudor looking young and happy: compare it with the picture in Trinity College Hall, where she looks unhappy and bad tempered, after some years of her disastrous reign. There is a piece of fourteenth-century glass with the arms of the de la Pole family, legal documents with seals attached, and some fine furniture. The Drawing-Room has a harpsichord, made in 1773 by Jacobus Kirckman, in London, and bought for £27 2s od, and some family portraits (including one of a lovely twelve-year-old girl); the staircase, beyond, has working drawings and sections of eighteenth-century ships of great interest, a grand 'French prisoner' ship model, in a Chippendale case, a portrait of Charles I by Van Dyck and an oyster table. It leads to the Little Gallery, built about 1800 to by-pass the bedrooms, because, like many Tudor houses, people could only get from one bedroom to another by going through a third: a circumstance which might well have its disadvantages. In the Little Gallery, the windows of which look down on the central courtyard, are several *objets d'art*, including a fine fifteenth-century Flemish triptych.

The Panelled Bedroom, I feel, is exactly as a bedroom of Jacobean times would have been. There are portraits, and the Royal Proclamation exempting Father John Huddleston (the priest who hid Charles in the oak tree—and afterwards shrived him at his death) from banishment for being a priest, fine Stuart furniture, solid and comfortable, a Flemish four poster bed, Restoration stool, pewter washstand.

The Tapestry, or Haunted Bedroom, is the one slept in by Mary Tudor on the fateful night, and since then it has been slept in—or perhaps *not* slept in—by innumerable ghost-hunters. Captain Huddleston has finally had to put a stop to ghost-watching in the bedroom: it is one thing to have your home haunted by ghosts, but another to have it haunted by ghost-watchers. There is the actual bed that Mary slept in and a most marvellous set of Flemish tapestries, about 1500, showing scenes from the life of King Solomon. One lively scene of the 'Building of the Temple' which must have resembled the building of many a great Renaissance building in Europe at that time, with one of the masons obviously being given the sack by a Master of Works who is measuring up a stone he has carved and found it the wrong shape.

The Long Gallery is long indeed, 100 feet, and, once again as always with these Tudor long galleries, I wonder what it was for. Certainly it is now an uncomfortable and draughty place to sit. Tudor and pre-Tudor domestic architecture is in other respects so comfortable and practical. There is a theory that it was built as a walk for ladies in bad weather.

But the gallery is a beautiful room, in spite of its lack of 'cosiness', and has some good portraits and tapestries, a fascinating collection of relics in a glass case—one of them a silver paten which was found in the moat in 1929—obviously having been flung there to hide it from Protestants at one time or another. Note the French king's mistress, in the fine hunting-scene tapestry, making eyes at a courtier behind his back.

There is a tower, probably antedating the rest of the house, which leads to the Priest Hole, the most famous priest hole in the country, and certainly the best. This is hollowed out of the solid masonry of the tower, in such a way that it could never be discovered from ordinary observation. It has an air-vent into the central courtyard, most cunningly disguised, a cover that fits in perfectly with the floor of the chamber above it and can be fastened from within so that it would withstand not only close inspection but a battering-ram, and there is now electric light in it, and iron steps, and it can be inspected by small boys. It was designed by that greatest of all priest-hole makers, Nicholas Owen, or 'Little John', a Jesuit who made priest holes all over England and was finally captured by the Government and tortured in the Tower to make him reveal the whereabouts of his work. When asked by Cecil what information had been extracted from him, the Governor of the Tower had to admit none at all and he added: 'The man is dead, he died in our hands.'

In the attic is a hidden chapel—the paten and chalice of which are now on loan to the Victoria and Albert Museum. The present chapel is an elegant one, and was used by local Catholics as a parish church until a new church was built in the village.

In Sawston is the first of the Cambridgeshire village colleges. It was designed by Dunn and built in 1930, and is Neo-Georgian. Although Neo-Georgian is a naughty word it is very good-looking, and excellent for its job, and makes me wonder if we should not have gone on developing our architecture step by step, as we had done for the previous few thousand years, rather than taking wild leaps into the dark.

Sawston Church is very high, the Sacrament is reserved. There is a fascinating squint from the south aisle to the chancel, the piers are of very hard clunch, and on Monday, 15th November 1948, in 2 hours 47 minutes, a peal of 5040 chimes in Bob Minor was rung by the men of the parish.

Babraham has a fine park in the Granta valley at the foot of the Gog Magogs in which is an ugly great Victorian mansion and a church with Saxon work in its walls. The predecessor of the present hall was built by a fine swashbuckling character, Horation Palavazene, a Genoese sailor who came to England and commanded a ship against the Armada. In Queen Mary's reign he had the job of collecting 'Peter's Pence', the penny a year that every householder had to contribute to the Vatican. He collected a vast amount but, providentially, he had not actually sent any of it to the Vatican when Queen Mary died and he didn't have to. Instead he lent it to Queen

Elizabeth, who certainly wasn't going to send it to any Pope, and this gave rise to his epitaph, which goes:

> *Here lies Horation Palavazene,*
> *Who robbed the Pope to lend the Queen.*
> *'He was a Thiefe.' 'A Thiefe? Thou liest;*
> *For why? He robbed but Antichrist.*
> *Him Death with besom swept from Babram*
> *Into the Bosom of old Abram.*
> *But then came Hercules with his Club,*
> *And struck him down to Beelzebub.*

We might perhaps be tempted to think that the last two lines were added by a Roman Catholic: we are, after all, next door to Sawston Hall. A vicar, John Hullier, was burnt as a Protestant (see p374).

The **Shelfords, Great** and **Little**, have fine and interesting churches but all this country between Sawston and Cambridge has been so smothered with dreary twentieth-century building that I cannot imagine any traveller wishing to go there. But go he should to Trumpington.

To **Trumpington** if only to see the Trumpington Brass, to Sir Roger, who died in 1289, and the second oldest brass in England. He is splendidly attired in chain-mail, with a dog biting the scabbard of his great sword, his shield slung on his shoulder, his mailed hands pressed together in prayer and his rugged soldierly face forced into what one might suspect was a rather unwonted expression of piety although he did sail to the Crusades with Edward I.

The church is very noble, and nearly all in the best Early English style. There is an inscription to an officer killed in 1914 by Eric Gill, and the village war memorial is also by Gill. In the village, The Green Man is a magnificent timbered pub.

East of Cambridge, **Cherry Hinton**, now swallowed up, has an Early English chancel to its church of the greatest beauty—if only somebody hadn't knocked a late Perpendicular window in its east end! It is important to go inside this chancel for the inside is better than the out, and note the piscina and sedilia, and in the body of the church the arcading, the priest door, and the carved coffin lid in the west wall of the tower.

The road from Cherry Hinton to Fulbourn is dead straight, but is not, as one might suppose, a Roman road. It is a 'furrow-drawn' road. When the common lands were enclosed in various ages before the eighteenth century new roads were often made across the common fields, and these were generally drawn out by the best ploughman of the parish with his plough.

Fulbourn has a (very restored) church of interest to saint-knowers, for it is dedicated to St Vigor, the only church in England to be so excepting the one at Stratton on the Fosse, in Somerset. Needless to say St Vigor was Bishop of Bayeux in AD 514, but only a real saint-knower will know how he came to be patron of Fulbourn in Cambridgeshire, and I do not.

There are five brasses in the church and several lavish tombs: the one to John Careway, 1433, grisly indeed and not to be shown to the children. The brass to Canon William Fulburne, 1380, is said to be the earliest known brass of a priest vested in a cope. There is a fine fourteenth-century oak pulpit with painted panels.

South-east of Fulbourn we hit the A11, the main London-Norwich road, and if we turn left along it soon come to where it traverses **Fleam Dike**. The road is historically interesting (if dull) in that it follows the course of the Icknield Way. This was an ancient trackway running, roughly, from the Wiltshire downlands to the uplands of West Norfolk. These two comparatively well drained and treeless areas were ideal for settlement by people without iron axes and ploughs: it was not until the Belgians came, shortly before Julius Caesar, bringing their heavy iron wheeled ploughs, that men began to conquer the heavy clay lands of Suffolk and Essex.

The Way, which is supposed to be 8,000 years old, was not a road but a wide droving-way, like the overland routes that superceded diesel road-trains of cattle trailers in the Australian Outback. Anyone who has driven cattle along established droveways in road-less countries (such as parts of South West Africa) will know that a narrow track is impracticable. The cattle, or small-stock such as sheep and goats, must forage as they go; and to do this each flock or herd must spread out beyond ground tramped over by its predecessors—and spread widely itself as it grazes along at from eight to ten miles a day (at eight miles a day in good bush cattle will fatten). The Icknield Way runs along the dry well-drained chalk ridge between the Essex clay, which was densely forested, and the impassable Fens, and was thus the only possible route for men to drive their animals between East Anglia and the rest of England.

If we stand on top of Fleam Dike, near the A11, we have a most impressive view of the Way, which was in constant use for cattle

droving from these very early times to the Enclosures at the beginning of the nineteenth century. Over the rolling hedgeless Cambridgeshire fields, whose only crop nowadays is barley, we can see the soil
changed in texture, the underlying chalk churned up in it, the very
crops themselves modified in tone by this broad belt trodden and
kicked up by the hooves of countless animals over thousands upon
thousands of years.

And Fleam Dike, on which we stand, was the Maginot Line of the
Celts living in East Anglia against incursions of hostile tribes along
the Icknield Way; but like the Maginot Line and other linear
defence works it succumbed to attack by a superior force.

When the Romans invaded Britain in AD 55 the ruling people in
East Anglia were the Iceni, who were traitors to the extent that they
co-operated with the Romans in order to free themselves from the
domination of Cymbeline who called himself King of Britain. As the
English discovered later on when they drove the Celts from England
and afterwards conquered Scotland, Ireland and Wales, it was
always possible to persuade half the Celts to fight against the other
half. But, after the Roman victory, when the Romans asked the
Iceni to hand over their arms, the Iceni refused, and manned their
Fleam Dike, on which we now stand. The Roman general Ostorius
came upon them suddenly with his light auxiliary troops only.
Not waiting for his regulars to arrive he attacked the Dike along the
whole of its length—flung the Iceni back—and slaughtered them as
they tried vainly to clamber up their second line of defence: Devil's
Dike across Newmarket Heath.

It must be remembered that these great earthworks were crowned
by wooden palisades.

The survivors of the tribe were disarmed, and accepted the Roman
yoke. But twelve years afterwards, goaded beyond endurance by the
legions, they made their heroic stand under Boadicea and slaughtered
a vast number of Romans—but unfortunately not enough, for the
Romans counter-attacked and wiped the Iceni off the face of the
earth: there was never afterwards a single mention of them in
history.

But Fleam Dike today is much more peaceful, and the last resort
in Cambridgeshire of many chalk-loving plants that the selective
weed killers have wiped out elsewhere, such as the rare Pasque
Flower (*Anenome pulsatilla*)—that grand anenome that is supposed
to flower at Easter time.

Linton is an outstandingly pretty village, or tiny town, which straggles along each side of the Granta, and here again is a Cambridgeshire village college.

Bartlow has three great tumuli, alas excavated in 1835 when excavating wasn't what it is now—on top of which the finds were kept in a house which burnt to the ground; but there were walled graves with enamel-ware, bronze and glass. Bartlow Church has a round tower, certainly Norman and perhaps earlier as to its base. It has been conjectured, in fact, that this tower was the 'minster of stone and lime' raised by Canute to celebrate his victory over the English at Assundon, which has been identified with the modern Ashdon in Essex. The English, in this battle, were betrayed by one of their nobles: Edric, who had been promised by Canute that if he did this he would be raised up higher than any of the other of the English nobility. He was: after the battle his head was cut off and raised to the highest turret of the Tower of London.

Castle Camps, where is little to see, had a castle, now earthworks. It was built by de Vere, Earl of Oxford, soon after the Conquest.

Balsham, the highest place in Cambridgeshire, all of 400 feet up in the clouds, has an important and interesting church. The tower is Early English but so shored up with massive buttresses that the west door and old pointed windows have been obscured. Inside is that rare thing—not only a rood screen, but a rood loft. How this escaped the Reformation, and the Puritans, is hard to understand. John de Sleford added the nave and aisles to the earlier tower and chancel, and he died in 1401, and his sumptuous brass is still in the church for all to see—nine foot long and with saints embroidered all down his cope. This man was Master of the Wardrobe to Edward III, Canon of Ripon, Archdeacon of Wells, Chaplain to the Queen as well as Rector of Balsham. There is another fine brass to another barefaced pluralist: John Blodwell, Rector here in 1439 besides being Dean of St Asaph, Canon of St David's, Prebendary of Hereford and Prebendary of Lichfield. It is to be feared that, in those days of slow travel, he could not have discharged all these duties very conscientiously, particularly as among his activities he numbered assisting at the prosecution of Joan of Arc.

De Sleford paid for the excellent carvings of the chancel stalls, which none should miss; and a recent rector carved, with his own hands, the font cover, altar rails and alms box, and taught wood carving to his parishioners.

There is a simply corking east window by A. K. Nicholson, and a possibly even more sentimental chancel window by Christopher Webb. As an antidote to this seek out the Anglo-Saxon coffin lid which was dug up in the graveyard.

In Anglo-Saxon times the entire population of Balsham was wiped out, save one man, by the Danes after the terrible battle of Ringmere Heath when Svend Forkbeard overthrew the English hero Ulfcytel so that 'all England did quake before him like a reed bed rustling in the wind'. The men of Balsham put up a stiff resistance and so were made an example of; but one man took refuge in the doorway to the tower of the church and defended himself to such good effect that the Danes retired and left him alone. This may well be the same doorway that we can stand in today.

Hugh de Balsham, who founded Peterhouse, comes, as his name suggests, from Balsham.

At **West Wratting**, in 1877, a man named Frost built a flying machine powered by steam, but it did not fly. At **Weston Colville** are two good brasses: Robert Leverer of 1427 in armour amid flowers, wife in flowing headdress and son between them; and Abraham Gates, 1636, with wife at a *prie-Dieu*, cherubs, skulls, angel flying away with a trumpet to announce his arrival to St Peter, the lot.

Westley Waterless also has a brass, and a good one, to Sir John and Lady Alyne Creek. He is in chain-mail with a surcoat known as a cyclas, she in a lovely dress. Their faces remind one of many a young well-bred couple at a Hunt Ball. The brass, being 1324, is a very early one.

Kirtling has Kirtling Tower, of which only the gateway is old, the mansion having been pulled down in the last century. The gatehouse is 1530, brick, and pretty grand with turrets—more for show than for defence. The house was built by the first Lord North, Chancellor to Henry VIII. His son entertained Queen Elizabeth at Kirtling Towers and it is even rumoured that she was hid there during part of Mary Tudor's reign. Both father and son have lavish tombs in Kirtling church. The 3rd Lord died in the Fire of London. He is credited with the startling discovery of the health springs of Tunbridge Wells, and was a close friend of Charles II. The church has a really fine south doorway, well carved, with Norman ironwork on the door, Norman arches in the south arcade, and it is, though small, very interesting and evocative (map, p410).

Kirtling 'Beehive' is a delicious country pub, although corrugated iron replaces thatch on the roof. Here, in a Sunday lunchtime session, you will hear the liveliest conversation, full of East Anglian pithiness and wit (if you can understand it), and the young men sit in too with the good and natural relationship that existed between the age-groups in pre-juke-box days. We are really back in East Anglia now, after our excursion across the Cam. This is a good place to savour, besides good beer, the rich East Cambridgeshire dialect.

Cheveley has a cruciform church with a crossing tower and a fine Decorated oak screen and a very beautiful Early English chancel. Noble arches support the crossing tower: their piers said each to have been the property of a trade gild, and on which that gild kept its light burning (map, p410).

Wood Ditton is so named for having been at the 'wood', i.e. the forest, end of Devil's Dike. There is a rather defaced brass in the church of a knight wearing *camail* armour: steel discs sewn to boiled leather. This is to Henry Englissh and his wife, 1393.

We have missed one place out in Cambridgeshire. The **Gog Magog Hills.** These do not need crampons and ice-axes to ascend, being no more than 220 feet of very gentle chalk slope; but they make a good walk out of Cambridge, and from them a good view of the city can be had, and, on a clear day, the Fens as far as Ely. There are several theories as to the derivation of the name—the most intriguing being that the Emperor Probus quartered gigantic Vandal auxiliaries there, and the much shorter Celts gave to them the names of giants—Gog and Magog. Hence, also, the name Wandlebury, which is still used for the great earthwork on the summit of these tiny mountains. Lethbridge believed that this was a sacred Iron Age site, and that great figures of gods were cut in the chalk (now no longer visible).

The East Anglian Voyage

By far the most rewarding way to see the East Anglian coast is to approach it, as the first East Anglians did, by water. The present writer has cruised the Suffolk and Norfolk coasts in everything from a fourteen-foot dinghy to a 175 ton sailing barge loaded with wheat, and entered every enterable harbour in his own thirty-four ton Dutch *hoogaerse* (when he had one), and landed on nearly every beach with a *coble*. The coble had the enormous advantage that she could be beached, and thus places like Cromer and Winterton were accessible, which would not have been the case with larger vessels.

The coast of East Anglia is not for the inattentive navigator. Between Harwich and the Wash, harbours are not only few but extremely difficult, and in some cases impossible, to enter. If anyone has ever tried sailing into Lowestoft in an on-shore gale they will know what I mean. If you cannot enter these harbours (and sometimes you cannot) there is *no shelter*, anywhere, and there are dangerous off-shore shoals like the Haisborough, the Scroby and the Whiting. The North Norfolk coast is ferocious in a north-easterly gale, and admittance into its tiny unmarked harbours difficult at any time and impossible at low water. The Wash is a refuge, but only to the good navigator: it is a death trap to the unwary. The next stop north is the Humber, and that is an inhospitable place for the small boat if ever there was one.

I am not trying to put the mariner off the East Anglian Voyage. I am merely warning him that he must know what he is doing before he makes it. In summer weather, with a good forecast, good sails and gear (it is the mariner who trusts to an engine who generally comes to grief), the East Anglian coast can provide as good cruising as there is to be had in the world. True, you do not get the lofty mountain or fiord scenery that you do in the Highlands or Norway, but the company you meet ashore in the little fishing or old barging places is superb, and where else can the sailor moor his vessel in

the shadow of buildings like King's College Chapel or Norwich or
Ely Cathedrals? The rewards of the East Anglian voyage are enormous. And the Londoner, pressed for time, can leave his boat at a
railhead in a dozen places, catch a train back to London, and come
back again when the chains are loosened to fare farther on.

In providing a few notes on the East Anglian Voyage I do not
intend to offer a Pilot's Guide. Plenty of these are available, and I
trust that nobody will venture along this coast without an Admiralty
chart, or at best one of those coloured yachtsmen's charts made for
people who cannot afford a pair of parallel rulers.

By starting the Voyage in the south I am not making the bland
assumption that nobody exists north of the Wash. But I have got
to start at one end or the other, and I do recognise that more people
live in London and all those even more foreign places across the
Channel than in the North of England and Scotland, and therefore
we shall begin our voyage at Harwich: its harbour being the first
one on the East Anglian coast that we can enter on any tide and in
any weather.

Harwich itself is a splendid old English town, and not very much
changed since Nelson was based there. There are great pubs down
by the quayside—the Angel is the biggest and grandest and much
used by Harwich fishermen, but the Globe, next door, is very good
and do not neglect the Alma—round the corner from the Angel
and inland a bit. There is a depot of the Brethren of Trinity House
here, with a yard full of huge sea buoys lying awaiting painting
themselves and also painting by artists, and out in the river you
sometimes see light vessels with such evocative names as 'Shipwash'
or 'Galloper' painted on their sides: resting for a spell from their
stormy stations.

The trouble with Harwich is that it is a very uncomfortable place
for the yachtsman to lie. The harbour itself is exposed, if he moves
round into the Stour he is in the way of the fast Parkeston ferries
to the Continent, and if he tries to get into that tiny harbour enclosed by wooden jetties just in front of the Angel he is moved constantly by Trinity House or other working boats. The only thing for
him to do is to anchor in a couple of fathoms of water inside the
Guard Buoy (Heaven help him if he anchors outside, or to the north
of it: he will be run down by a ferry rushing back from the Hook of
Holland) and go ashore in his dinghy. He will find nowhere to leave
the latter and may well get his rowlocks pinched.

If he wants a quiet night he had better go on up-Orwell and anchor at **Stone Heaps.** This is an anchorage perhaps a few hundred yards up-stream from Shotley Point, on the Shotley side. There is deep water there, good holding ground, it is sheltered from all winds and for centuries barges used to lie there waiting for a fair wind for London or 'down North' (all East Coast seafaring men talk of 'down North' and 'up South'—the tides run that way). Stone Heaps is so named because in the days of the 'cement stone' trade —when septaria was dredged up from the seabed to be taken to the cement factories—it was dumped ashore here by the 'stone drudgers' (sailing smacks used for the job) before being loaded into barges.

The shore delights of Stone Heaps are negligible (it's a long walk to the Bristol Arms, down at **Shotley Ferry)** so soon the voyager will decide to go up-river to **Pin Mill.**

Just round Collimer Point comes Butterman's Bay, where the ocean-faring windjammers used to lie while lightering their cargoes into sailing barges. The first house on the port hand is Hare's Creek, a double cottage, with one half occupied by a customs officer and the other by William Empson, the poet. The next is The Clamp, where is now a small sailing school. The voyager should here think seriously about looking for an anchorage, for the nearer he gets to Pin Mill the more difficult it will be for him to find one.

If he anchors at 'Foxhole', a cleft of the hill on his port hand, he will have this fine wooded hill to shelter him but a longish pull in his dinghy to Pin Mill Hard which will give him a thirst to be slaked at the Butt and Oyster, that doyen of waterside pubs. Pin Mill is a famous place. Bob Roberts, master of the last trading sailing barge, lives there, Norman King does too—a famous builder of really high-class fishing and pleasure boats—none of your plastic rubbish—and the Webbs who are the last barge-wrights. The Pin Mill Sailing Club is most hospitable. Jack Ward sells chandlery and petrol, and George Burrows is the retired harbourmaster and uncrowned king, and honour to him should be paid (he likes rum and dark-and-mild and knows more about the Orwell than anybody else).

Up-stream is **Woolverstone,** with its famous Cat-house (not the kind of establishment that usually goes under that name) and the Royal Harwich Yacht Club, all apparently lost in the forests. Farther up again, through lovely sylvan reaches, **Ipswich** heaves into view, and we come to **Lavender Bay,** one of the few places in the world where we can navigate by *nose* (it is here that Ipswich discharges her unwanted material) past a very hospitable and vigorous sailing club to port near Bourne Bridge—the Orwell Yacht Club— with a fair but drying-out anchorage in not very salubrious water and then we can lock into Ipswich Wet Dock (for a fee), where we can take on fresh water or anything else. It is a very busy commercial harbour but there is plenty of room still alongside its wharfs. The centre of Ipswich is not far away, and how better to see it than from your own floating hotel? Whitmores, near the Custom House, is a fine yacht and ship chandler and a sail maker of the first class: particularly of heavier sails.

Down-river again there is always Felixstowe Dock, to port, enterable at any stage of the tide but there really isn't room for yachts in there. Since the partial strangulation of the Port of London these little ports have become enormously busy.

Around Landguard Fort, where the Ipswich Fencibles drove off the Dutch, stand well out if you don't want to hit a submerged Roman castle, and head for the **Deben.** Here pull out your pilot's guide, or get a real live pilot (the Newson family, ashore, will generally either flag you in—or come out in a boat and lead you), and get inside where you will find a lovely anchorage in all weathers and a good steep clean landing place for a dinghy on the Felixstowe side (better than all that mud at Pin Mill), and a good pub, the 'Victory', run by one of the Newson family. The Newsons are professional fishermen and barge people, catch lobsters, and are very helpful.

The Deben, up-stream, is as lovely a river in its way as the Orwell but much shallower so beware the gripeing mud. **Ramsholt,** to starboard, has an, alas, tarted-up pub (it used to be a justly famous waterside pub in the great days of the Brinkleys), and a very beautiful anchorage and landing. And let no one dispute your right either to anchor or to land. **Waldringfield,** farther up and to port, is another Pin Mill-type place, yacht club, boat builder, splendid pub, miles from anywhere. The owner of a large yacht might be advised to achor or moor there and go farther by tender: **Woodbridge** is accessible to deep-keeled craft at high tide but it is very crowded and dries right out at low—unless you pay to enter the new yacht harbour built in the old pound of the tidal mill. Woodbridge is a lovely place to lie for a long period though, and to winter in: good facilities ashore, civilised company, and fast trains to London.

The stretch farther up, as far as **Melton,** I think we may leave to the dyed-in-the-wool mud-crawler. If he gets there at all Harry Cuthbert (Eyke 367) will provide him with the most excellent oven-ready roasting fowl, and furthermore deliver it to his boat in person.

The next estuary north, the **Ore,** is easier to get into than the Deben (in both rivers there is a buoy outside and leading marks ashore, but, in both rivers I disclaim all responsibility). There is a part-time coastguard at **Shingle Street,** just by the entrance, whom the Felixstowe Coastguard will put you on to, and he will sometimes flag you in or come out in a small boat. Scenically the Ore is a boring river. **Butley Creek,** to port, is a pretty diversion, with a good anchorage below the old oysterage at Ferry Cottage where Mr

Richard Pinne still sells oysters to say nothing of smoked salmon, but it is miles from anywhere. A dash in the dinghy up to Butley Mill is delightful, with reed-covered marshes, saltings, huge rafts of widgeon in winter, pheasants galore ashore (and gamekeepers!) and wild loneliness. But beware the mud.

Havergate Island, which we can circumnavigate if we wish, is an RSPB reserve and the nesting-place of avocets, and you will see these birds winging their way up and down on their occasions. Mr Partridge, of Orford, is their warden.

The Jolly Sailor Inn at **Orford,** is another noble waterside pub (I am tempted to say my favourite of all) and Mr Sid Harper the landlord and his charming wife Minnie will do anything to help anybody. They will telephone to Mr Dick Elliot, in his shop in Pump Street just off the Market Square, and that gentleman will deliver stores, and bring them aboard for you himself very likely as he has a boat and is a keen fisherman. You can anchor either below or above the jetty, land on the jetty for temporary reasons, or drag your dinghy up the clean shingle beach just up-stream from the jetty for longer trips ashore, but not on the concrete slipway there because it is constantly used by the landing craft of the boffins who go to the Atomic Weapons Research Station on 'The Island', which isn't an island at all, over the river.

A long straight boring run takes you to **Aldeburgh,** where you will be a hundred yards from the sea as the mariner spits but ten miles as his boat sails. Here good anchorage above the yacht club and hard over the other side of the river, easy dinghy landing. A fine small but rather exclusive yacht club ashore (you have to be the child of a member to become a member—rather like London dockers), a short walk to a splendid little seaside town and what better way to attend the Aldeburgh Festival than go there in your own yacht? Cables and Burrells and Wards and others make up a vigorous fishing community with a fine life-boat record, and some practise as boatmen in the summer down at the river landing (notably Mr 'Jumbo' Ward), and everything can be found in Aldeburgh that a reasonable man's heart could desire.

Higher up the river is for mud-crawlers only, and if you even get as far as **Iken** I admire your pertinacity. This is a beautiful sylvan and deserted place, with a tiny river beach and an anchorage that you will never forget afterwards (even if you can forget getting stuck on the mud getting to it). **Snape Maltings** has a very good wharf to tie up to (with permission ashore), a drying out berth of course, and incidentally it's fun to paddle in your dinghy under the horrible new bridge and a mile or so up into the fresh-water river (the Alde here of course); a thing very few people have thought of. At Snape Maltings are cultural junketings: as I write this 'Jazz at the Maltings' is one.

Down-stream and out at sea again we round **Orfordness** and the mariner should heed the old bargeman's saw:

> 'Wind from the West
> One foot on deck—one on the Ness',

the significance of which is that there is deep water right up to the point and it behoves you to stay up-wind so you don't have to fall away from the coast too far on rounding the Ness. The huge concrete monstrosities ashore are the Atomic Weapons Research Station.

We sail by Aldeburgh, which looks lovely from the sea, and Thorpeness, and along a beautiful deserted coast which for many miles is spoiled only by that bloody power station at Sizewell—and Dunwich (where if it be midnight we should hear the bells ringing from the drowned churches under the sea)—and then in at **Southwold Harbour.** And again be warned. It is a difficult harbour to enter with a strong cross-current at the entrance and much submerged jagged concrete inside.

I have sailed into Southwold in my 34-ton Dutch barge (when I had one) with a strong on-shore wind, at low tide, with a huge sea running into the entrance and the harbour master waving frantically to me from the pier-head not to come in because he couldn't believe that such a big boat could only draw three feet (she was flat bottomed). It was a most exhilarating experience and the sense of quiet when I got inside reminded me of Mrs Patrick Campbell's commendation of 'the peace of the marriage bed after the hurley-burley of the *chaise-longue*!' I had all sail set and only just managed to scramble it off and get an anchor down before colliding with the Bailey bridge. This brought me up just opposite the Harbour Inn and it couldn't have brought me up at a better place. I would be hard put to think of a nicer pub, in the world, than the Harbour Inn at Southwold. It's a long walk from here to the town, and stores, but if you can't find a lift in the Harbour something has gone wrong somewhere as Southwold has a vigorous little long-shore fishing fleet and the nicest lot of fishermen imaginable.

To sea again, north again, along a deserted and wooded coast —endless deserted beaches—past Covehithe (non-existent), **Kessingland,** where are beach 'punts' and professional fishermen and a good place to beach if you are in a beaching boat, and on into the grand harbour of **Lowestoft.** Turn sharp left inside and into the Yacht Basin.

This can be crowded, and has the Royal Norfolk and Suffolk Yacht Club whose Secretary forgot to reply to Queen Victoria's letter saying he could be Royal so that it took years of lobbying by the Prince Consort before she would allow him to become Royal again. But if I were going to spend some time in Lowestoft I think I would get them to swing the bridge for me and go farther up the river towards Lake Lothing—industrialised, but more room. Yachts are not really welcomed in any of the fishing basins, which are extremely busy ones, and, by the way, trawlers swoosh in and out of the harbour mouth as if their lives depended on saving a second so beware collision.

Great Yarmouth is easier to get into, although here again is a narrow entrance and fierce cross-currents and many ships have come to grief trying to make it. Large sailing vessels that have to run in before a gale can bring themselves up by rounding to starboard inside and putting themselves ashore on the Spending Ground, a beach of sand hard round the corner.

The **Yare** is long, busy with big shipping but there is plenty of room to tie up to the long quays on either side and ashore every delight and every facility for the ship's husband. Great Yarmouth is a magnificent place to be, and it is, of course, the gateway to the Broads. Without even lowering your mast you can get to **Norwich,** tying up at **Reedham** and **Brundall** on the way and seeing a typical broad at **Rockland** (where is the New Inn with a shelter with rings for tying horses, and Mr Fudgey Stone—a knowledgeable man about the Broads, and nearby Mr Ted Ellis, one of the best naturalists in the country and certainly the best in Broadland). You could, instead of going up-Yare, go up-**Waveney** instead, to **Beccles,** taking in **Burgh Castle** *en route*. If you can get your mast down, and don't draw more than six feet, you can enter the 'North River' from Great Yarmouth and thread your way into the classic Broadland country: but that is another story.

When you put to sea from Yarmouth, northward bound, you want a good weather forecast; for you have eighty miles of coast before you which is to all intents and purposes harbourless. For forty-five miles it is completely harbourless—there is not a hole or cranny into which you can get. Then comes **Blakeney Harbour,** for which you need high water, fine weather, and a knowledge of what you are doing. There is a fine big anchorage in **The Pit,** inside Blakeney Harbour, but a very long pull up to the village. It is here that you feel the need either for a sail on your dinghy and a fair wind, or else one of these new-fangled outboard motors. If you know it, or can find it, there is a footpath leading across some miles of saltings to **Morston,** where is Mr Ted Eeles a boat-man and warden on Blakeney Point: he and Mr Philip Green of Stiffkey know this coast as well as any. Incidentally you must make a landing on **Blakeney Point,** a bird reserve—beware treading on terns' nests—but a place of great charm and interest, particularly in the winter. There is splendid bird-watching on this coast, good fishing, and wild-fowling in winter, and Blakeney village is almost impossibly pretty. If you do take your yacht up there you will find the river terribly crowded and much opposition to your taking a big boat there at all, and the only thing to do is to plonk yourself down and say 'shift me!' which nobody can legally do. But, after all, the people who live there should have priority. Blakeney is inhabited by very nice people, and Mr Stratton Long has a good yacht chandlery.

Wells-next-the-Sea is hard to get into (if you get there in an on-shore gale and see the buoy marking the harbour entrance— *high up on a sand bank* it inspires no confidence), but once in it is fine and you can tie up within a few yards of a pub, or a shop for that matter. You will soon be asked to move on though, by the harbour master, for this is a busy little fishing port and there are some Dutch coasters. You may be allowed to lie awhile tied up to the quay, or you can go over the river and anchor by the saltings, or farther up, to the whelk boiling sheds, and throw yourself on the mercy of the Cox family: either Jack or David will tell you where to lie. The Shipwright's Arms is a splendid pub, but like most water-side pubs better in the winter than in the summer.

Burnham Harbour is even trickier than Wells, but **Overy Staithe** is charming when you get there. A pub, not many facilities, but interesting walking to the Severn Burnhams, in Nelson country.

Brancaster, around **Scolt Head** (another bird-watcher's para-dise) is another fiendish place to get into (although there is more water over the bar there than there is at Wells). The village is not attractive, but the Jolly Sailor is famous for its food and, for those who like them, there is a golf course.

Thornham Harbour I have never been into.

These harbours were all busy shipping harbours once, and within living memory there was a busy trade of Billyboys, which sailed from the Humber loaded with coal, selling the coal to farmers and merchants who came with carts to the ship-side to get it, then loading gravel from the banks outside and sailing that back to Yorkshire.

You have now nowhere to run, really, until you get right round into the **Wash** and up-river to King's Lynn. You could of course anchor for a while off **Hunstanton,** but if a northerly gale springs up you might wish you hadn't. The **Lynn Channel** is well marked, but tortuous, and remember that the Wash is for the competent mariner. If you are not—get a pilot.

At **King's Lynn** really the only sensible thing to do is to lock into the Wet Dock. The gates only open at high tide, so tie up alongside a lighter if you can, by the mouth. If you make friends with the fishermen they may allow you to tie up to the staging inside their **Fisher Fleet,** where the mud dries out steep at low tide—it's a most interesting place to lie but you will be *very* privileged if you are allowed to lie there—though you will be safer, and more comfortable, inside the Wet Dock, where you must pay up like a man, and where you will be afloat all the time, can step ashore dry-shod, and be right near the centre of one of the most interesting towns in England. The two Wet Docks are not pretty places (unless you like ships, cranes, and piles of Baltic timber) but they are convenient. I cannot understand why yachtsmen flock to the South Coast in such numbers, to all those crowded, commercialised and basically very uninteresting places, and ignore a coast that has King's Lynn. Here is something *worth* sailing a few hundred miles to see.

Up-Ouse you must have a lowering mast and a good sense of rivermanship. The tidal **Great Ouse** is really a horrid river. If you anchor you have to land from your dinghy in steep and sticky mud —and when you want to go aboard again your dinghy will either be high and dry or else upside down or carried right away. There is a sluicing tide—it can be seven knots—so you need good ground tackle. But anchor just the same—to see the **Wiggenhalls**—which are dealt with in the text of this book.

Navigable Rivers
Unnavigable Rivers
Navigable Canals
Unnavigable Canals
Locks

Lincoln
Horncastle
WITHAM
Revesby
Stickford
Thorpe Culvert
MEDLAM
HOBHOLE
SLEAFORD
Sleaford
Boston
THE WASH
BLACK SLUICE
Fosdyke
Surfleet
Sandringham
GLEN
Spalding
Castle Rising
KINGS LYNN
NAR
Castle Acre
Bourne
WELLAND
Market Deeping
Stamford
NENE
Wisbech
NEW CUT OF DRAIN
PETERBOROUGH
Outwell
Wisbech
Downham
Denver
Stoke Ferry
TWENTY FOOT
March
OLD NENE FOOT
SIXTEEN FOOT
OLD BEDFORD
WISSEY
Southery
LIT. OUSE
Wilton
FORTY FOOT
Holme
Little-port
LARK
Brandon
Lakenheath
Thetford
NENE
Ramsey
NEW BEDFORD
Prickwillow
West Row
Mildenhall
Thrapston
Earith
St. Ives
Ely
OLD WEST OUSE
Houghton
Huntingdon
Brampton
Godmanchester
CAM
Burwell
Reach
BURY ST. EDMUNDS
Rushden
OUSE
St. Neots
CAMBRIDGE
0 miles 10
BEDFORD
Tempsford

Beware **Denver** Bridge. I once wrote that the builder of this
bridge should be put in a sack and chucked off it—but then I *met*
the builder, who was a most charming man named Charles Slade
(alas dead now) who lived in a house at Hammersmith Mall which
was hung all over inside with portraits of himself done by Augustus
John, and so I hereby retract my statement. It is a fine bridge, no
doubt, for the landsmen who have to go over it, but not for the

boatman who has to go *under* it. My advice is to go up on the flood tide but turn round to face the flood and let this drop you slowly astern through the bridge (the most westerly opening is the one to choose) while your engine goes slow ahead to give you steerage. Like this, if you hit anything, at least you won't hit it hard.

At **Salter's Lode** you can, if you wait for the **exact** moment when there is a tidal level, pen through into the **Old Bedford River,** or else **Well Creek,** newly opened up again by the Fen Waterman's Association, headquarters **March.** Either of these waters give you access to the whole intricate network of the Fenland **Middle Level Navigations.** These are not to everybody's taste. They are for the most part dead straight, very weeded up, with the water well below the banks so you can't see anything without getting out of the boat. To the initiated they are quite fascinating because they lead through the country of the Fenmen who are such fascinating people. It is the people here who are everything, and to enjoy this country you must meet them. Loo Doubleday, of 11 Cemetery Road, **Outwell,** is your best guide to the Middle Level.

But, if you by-pass these labyrinths and keep up-Ouse, you almost immediately come to **Denver Sluice** (you could, if you had the hardihood, carry on up the tidal **New Bedford River** to **Earith:** I have never done it). Pen through the great double locks and you enter placid, clean, non-tidal water; the river is a natural one and slightly winding, you *can* see over the banks, and there is marvellous coarse fishing (and it's complete nonsense that coarse fish taste 'muddy'—they taste delicious, and it would improve river fishing enormously if more of them were eaten: all our rivers suffer from over fish-population) and you can, if you draw not more than three foot six inches, turn up the **Wissey** as far as **Stoke Ferry** where is the Bull Inn (**Hilgay,** on the way, is a fine big Fenland village— well worth a Saturday evening visit), and, farther up-Ouse, you can penetrate the **Little Ouse** as far as **Brandon Staunch** (but this really *is* ditch-crawling). But keep on up-Great Ouse and you get to **Ely.** This is one of the nicest places to lie. You are within not many yards of the Cathedral, there are good wharfs to tie up to (you can see that this was once a throbbing river port), good shops within spitting distance, the 'Cutter' is a fine inn, and Messrs Lincoln and Appleyard run a good boatyard and will even build you a boat if yours sinks, or else charter you one.

Up-stream at the confluence of the Great Ouse (here called the

Old West) and the **Cam** is the **Fish and Duck Inn**—and what a
marvellous place! Just the Fish and Duck Inn and absolutely nothing
else. Not even a road. If you take the right fork you can get right
up (along an increasingly beautiful and un-fenlike river) through
St Ives and **St Neots,** and the locks are being repaired as far as
Bedford. But if you turn left at the Fish and Duck you will come
to **Upware,** where you should shed a tear as you land for the old
'Five Miles from Anywhere—No Hurry Inn', now, alas, burnt down,
with a short walk to **Wicken Fen,** a National Trust Nature Reserve
and one of the last pieces of unchanged Fenland. This was what it
was like in Hereward the Wake's day. Up-stream very light-draught
boats can get to lovely villages like **Wicken, Burwell, Reach** or
Swaffham Bulbeck (I have never tried it) or you can keep on up
to Cambridge.

There are three locks to **Cambridge,** and they have lock keepers,
and these gentlemen will tell you how far towards the middle of
the city you can decently go without getting in everybody's way
and where to tie up. Much depends on how many boats are already
there. There are fees.

The sea voyage from the Great Ouse to the **Nene** is very difficult,
for there are tortuous sands and channels to navigate. You might
well go 'overland' through the Middle Levels achieved through
Salter's Lode. If you go by sea and want a pilot you might telephone
Mr Tom Lineham (Sutton Bridge 453) who may be able to put
you on to one: he probably won't be able to make it himself—he
and his young son Tommy are far too busy fishing. If you go through
the Middle Level you will come out at **Stanground,** near **Peterborough.** If you take the sea way you will run up-stream to **Sutton
Bridge** (if you haven't run aground outside at Big Annie) and there
the only thing to do is to tie up to Mr Lineham's jetty. You cannot
lie to anchor because of the big ships going up to Wisbech.

You can get up to **Wisbech** with your mast up. Here you can tie
to the long quays on either side of the river, but remember you will
dry right out at low tide, there is a terrible rise and fall, so you must
have long warps out and look to them. Or if you can get permission
to do so hang on to one of the floating pontoons various people have
moored in the river, or else to the side of a coasting vessel. Wisbech
is a fine place to see from a boat, although a difficult place to lie
(the fools filled in their canal—which would have made such a good
yacht harbour. But how were people of limited imagination to know

The East Anglian Dialect

In Norfolk, Suffolk, North Essex and Cambridgeshire east of the River Cam a dialect is spoken which is recognisably East Anglian and quite distinct from the language spoken anywhere else. An East Anglian can notice a great difference between, say, a North Norfolk man and one from South Suffolk, but they speak basically the same dialect and one can understand the other perfectly well. Perhaps nowhere in England is there a sharper dividing line between two dialects than there is between King's Lynn, in Norfolk, and Sutton Bridge in Lincolnshire. The former is pure Norfolk—the latter strong Midland without an East Anglian element in it. The Essex men are recognisably East Anglian until you come near to the Thames, where they become abruptly and completely Cockney (people from both side of the Thames Estuary can be recognised by their use of the word 'fur' for *far*).

The East Anglian does not drop his aitches. He talks with a singsong intonation that is very difficult to copy. No 'foreign' (i.e. non-East Anglian) actor has ever been able to master the tongue: as witness all the performances of Arnold Wesker's play *Roots*. Few educated East Anglians indeed can do it. The true East Anglian countryman can talk the Queen's English as well as anybody (although he can never hide the fact from a fellow countryman that he comes from East Anglia) but also, if he wants to, he can talk in such a way that the Londoner or other 'foreigner' will never understand him.

I list here, with Mrs Claxton's very kind permission, some of the many hundreds of words and phrases included in *The Suffolk Dialect of the Twentieth Century*, by the late A. O. D. Claxton, published by Norman Adlard and Co. of Ipswich. I have only taken words which I have heard used myself (and many of which I have, unconsciously, used). Many of the words are received English words: it is their use by the Suffolk person that is peculiar. Although these words were collected in Suffolk most of them will be recognisable to the Norfolk 'Dumpling' too: and to the man from East Cambridgeshire. West Cambridgeshire tends more to the South Midland dialect and intonation. I have not always stuck to Claxton's interpretations of examples.

Abroad. Out of doors. Seamen use it for 'out at sea'. Said by an old man on his last legs: 'Oi'll sune be sleeping abroad.'

Addle. To thrive, flourish.

A'doin'. Same as addle. 'He's a'doin'!' means he's getting on not too badly. It also might mean he's doing a piece of work well.

A-huh. Lop-sided. 'Whoi, missus, yar hat's all of a-huh.'

Airy-wiggle. Earwig.

Annind. On end. Of a horse—'he reared right up annind.'

Antic. Play the fool.

Arse-uppards. Regularly used for upside down—even in polite society!

Arternune—getting into the . . . Getting old. Of an old dog—'Oi doubt he's a'gittin' into the arternune.'

Babbing. Catching eels or crabs with a bunch of worms or a piece of meat but no hook.

Bachelors' Buttons. White campion.

Back-us. The scullery at the back of a farmhouse. Every farmhouse once had its 'back-us boy'.

Bagging iron. Instrument like a sickle but with a smooth edge—not serrated.

Bait. Food. To 'bait the hosses'—to feed them. Commonly used for a snack in the fields.

Barley Bird. Nightingale.

Bawk. Balk. Ridge left in ploughing. (Old English—*balca*—a ridge).

Becket. A knife sheath. A man who keeps his hands in his pocket is called 'Beckets'.

Beevers. Afternoon snack in the fields. (also 'fourses').

Betsy. Tea kettle.

Betty. A womanish man—one who bustles about the house. 'Stop you a'bettyin' about!' Stop fussing.

Bezzle. Booze.

Bibble. Ducks bibble in the mud. Babies bibble (dribble). To tipple.

Billy-buster. A blusterer—or a large dumpling.

Billywitch. Cockchafer.

Binger. 'Tha's a binger'—that is finished. A goner.

Bishop Barnabee. Ladybird.

Blare. To cry—to shout. 'He was a'blarin' away there!'

Blood Olp. Bullfinch.

Blowbroth. Busybody.

Bodge. Mend clumsily.

Bolsom. Humbug. 'Oi don't want to listen to yar owd bolsom!'

Bonka. Fine, strapping, when applied to kids.

Bop. To curtsey.

Bor. An extremely common term of familiar address in East Anglia. Not to be confused with 'boy' which is used too, but quite differently. Bor has been derived from *neighbour*—Old English *neahgebur*—and Low German—*bur*—countryman. I favour the latter.

Botsy. Rabbit.

Bowne. To wind-dry fish. Done to small 'butts' or flounders to prepare them for lobster bait, as well as sprats for human consumption.

Brackly. Brittle.

Braft. Work.

Brand. Smut in wheat—a fungus disease.

Brawtch. Pointed flexible twig for holding down thatch.

Bread-and-pull-it. A piece of dry bread with a smaller piece a'top of it. Of a poor person—'all he's got to eat is bread-and-pull-it.'

Breeder. A whitlow, or any sore without visible cause.

Brew. Claxton just gives 'the edge of a ditch away from the hedge' but I've heard it also as 'the brew of a hill'—the *brow* of a hill. 'Just over the brew there.'

Brawk. To belch.

Brung. Past tense of 'to bring'. East Anglians have a lot of these special past tenses! 'She brung me some bread and cheese.'

Brush. To beat coverts to drive out game. To trim nettles, etc.

Buck. The body of a wagon or tumbril.

Bullfice. (I've heard it *bullfist*). Puff ball. Powder stops wounds bleeding.

Bulley. Man who stands half-way up a stack to pass on hay or sheaves passed from below.

Bulley-hole. Hole in which the above stands.

Bush. A thorn. A Suffolker never has 'a thorn in his finger'—always 'a bush'. I knew a man who got a 'bush' in his eye whereat the 'jelly' inside ran down his face. He cycled six miles into Ipswich hospital, had his eye out, and cycled back again in time to milk his cows.

Butt. Dab or flounder.

Butterwitch. Cockchafer.

Buzzhawk. Nightjar.

Cade. Measure of herrings.

Cadman. Smallest pig in litter.

Cankers. Hips of the dog rose.

Carnser—carnsey. Causeway over wet ground.

Chaits. Scraps or leavings. (Also called 'mungey'—there's a horrible story about the skipper of a yacht who went below to eat his dinner, it was dark in the fo'c's'le, and when he remarked on the toughness of the steak the Third Hand shouted out: 'Blast bor—you're eatin' the Mate's mungey!'

Chance one. The odd one. When asked if he had docks in his field a farmer might say: 'Well—chance one.'

Chance time. Occasionally.

Charley. Toad.

Chice. A small quantity—a taste.

Cis (pronounced sis). A poor attempt. 'Oi've made a rare cis o' that, Sir!' (I've made a mess of it).

Cley. A narrow draining spade.

Clip. A hit. 'I'll give you a clip o' the lug do you don't stop a'blarin'!'

Clung. Shrunken, shrivelled, of fruit or roots.

Clunk. To whet a blade on a stone.

Cob. Wicker basket to carry on arm for baiting animals.

Cob. Chaff from threshing clover for seed.

Cobble. A fruit stone.

Cock Ulf. Cock bullfinch.

Come-backs. Guinea-fowl (from their cry).

Conjuration. A weird contrivance. Claxton doesn't give this but he gives 'combustibles' for 'a bundle of sundry things.'

Coop-wee. Cry to a horse to make it go to the left (*see* 'Wardee')

Cow mumble. Cow parsley.

Crabb. A capstan on a boat.

Crank. A heron (*see* harnser).

Cringle. To shrivel up.

Crome or croom. Any crook or hook.

Cruddle. To nestle—to lie close.
Cuckoo Barley. Barley planted too late.
Cuckoo Flower. Early purple orchis.
Cuckoo's Mate. Wryneck.

Dag. Dew.
Dan. A yearling lamb.
Dawzled. Stupid. Confused.
Dead. Death in the sense of: 'Oi'm worrit to dead!' (i.e. worried to death).
Debble (according to Claxton—I think it's 'dibble'). Wooden tool for making holes for putting in plants.
Deek (Claxton—I've always heard 'Dick'). A ditch. (Old English—*dic*).
Delf. Claxton gives 'A dug drain or small hole'. I've heard it only used for the ditch behind all sea and river walls. (Dutch—*delft*. All sea-wall makers' tools are still called by Dutch names).
Dickey. Donkey.
Didall (long *I*—as 'dide-al'). Spade for digging out ditch. Also a huge shovel used on Broads—hauled up by a tackle—for dredging channels. I have seen the same thing—with nearly the same name —used in Randstat Holland.
Diddle. Duck.
Dills. Teats.
Dilly. Small cart on two wheels used as trailer.
Ding. To throw—hurl. The past tense is *dung*. 'He hully dung that at me!' Or hit. 'He give him a ding about the lug-hole!'
Dinger. An even larger 'ding'.
Do. Now this is the most overworked word in the East Anglian dialect. It can have all the meanings it has in received English, but it can also mean: ('do that rain we's'll get wet'), *a command*: ('do you come along o' me!') *prosper*: ('That øl owd sow do well on that grub'. 'You'll do boy!' 'He's a'doin'!'), *or*: ('You come with me do you'll get lost!').
Don't. Used like 'do' but negatively. Thus: 'Do you hurry up don't you'll miss the 'bus.' But sometimes you also hear: 'Do you hurry up do you'll miss the bus.' Learning the various ramifications of the word 'do' is half-way to understanding East Anglian.
Dodman. Snail (*see* hodmedod).
Dog in a Blanket. Roly-poly pudding.

479

Dog weed. Wild cornel.

Dorhawk. Nightjar.

Dow (rhymes with cow). Wood pigeon.

Dreening. Very wet.

Drift. Rough private roadway.

Drindle. To trickle. A tiny stream (*see* grindle).

Drug. A 'timber drug'—vehicle for carrying timber.

Dudder. Shake.

Dun billy. Crow.

Dunk. House sparrow.

Dunt. Wallop on the head.

Dussn't. Dare not.

Dutfin. Bridle of a cart horse.

Duzzy. Euphemism for damned.

Dwile. Wiping-up flannel. (Dutch *dweyle*).

Eel pritch. Spear with several barbed prongs. (Also *butt pritch*).

Elevenses. Mid-morning snack in fields.

Fang. To grab.

Fare. (Very common)—to seem—to appear. 'That fare to be going to rain.' 'That don't fare very hot to me.' Also used as 'do'— 'How do you fare today bor?' Claxton quotes an old man who has been on a switchback as saying: 'That fare t' make me fare hully duzzified.'

Fare thee well. Or farewell. Commonly used for 'good-bye' still. In other cases the second person (thou, thee, thine) is seldom used in East Anglia, in contrast to the North of England.

Fetched. Reached. 'Oi fetched the pub a'fore closing toime.'

Few (good). Not a few.

Filla (or thiller). Shaft horse.

Fist. Claxton gives 'to make a fist of a job is to do it awkwardly.' But I have always heard: 'He made a good fist o' that' or 'he didn't make much of a fist of it!'

Five fingers. The ox-lip. Also the star fish.

Flash. To trim the side of a hedge or a bank.

Flee. To skin. 'My missus allus flee a teal afore she cook it. Thass quicker'n featherin' of it.'

Fleet. Shallow. 'Plough that a bit fleet' (don't plough too deep). East Anglian sailors also say: 'Fleet the cable round the drum,' meaning: let the cable run out slowly checking itself on a windlass drum.

Fleet. To skim cream off milk. A cream skimmer is called 'a fleeter'.

Floaters. Dumplings. I've also heard them called 'sinkers'.

Fog nightingale. Frog.

Fold pritch. A heavy iron bar for making holes in ground for stakes of sheep hurdles.

Frawn. Frozen. ('Oi be hully frawn!').

Fulfer. Fieldfare.

Funny. Very. ('That do funny rain.')

Gainer. Cleverer or better.

Gambrel (I've heard gambel). The steel or wooden cross-piece you hang a pig up with.

Gay. Picture. Still commonly used. 'Gimme the paper—I just want to look at the gays.'

Gnew. Past tense of gnaw. Claxton quotes: 'That duzzy owd hog gnew a hole in th' stye.'

Gon. Past tense of to give. 'He gon me a pint.'

Goslins. Willow catkins.

Grindle. Same as drindle—a tiny stream. (Also called a *purl*).

Grunt. 'What a lot o' grunt they put in the papers nowadays!' Rubbish.

Guler. Yellow bunting.

Gull. A deep channel in the saltings.

Hake. Kettle-crane in fireplace. Or iron in front of plough on which whipple-tree is hooked.

Happen. Haps. Perhaps. 'Happen he will—happen he won't.'

Harnser. Heron. ('I know a hawk from a handsaw'—Shakespeare). It is said that when a harnser swallows an eel the eel wriggles right through. Therefore the harnser backs up against a gatepost before swallowing it.

Hayjack. Reedwarbler.

Haysel. Hay harvest.

Hew. Past tense of to hoe.

Hewd. (pronounced *howd*) past tense of to hold. 'Oi hewd on hud!'

Hin. Yonder.

Hob gob. Nasty short sea.

Hodman or *Hodmedod.* Snail.

Hopnetot. Frog.

Horkey. Harvest home supper. Once a great thing—now no more.

Hornpie. Lapwing.

Hoss needle. Dragonfly.

How: *hud* Or howd yew hud. 'Hold hard'—stop talking.

Housen. Plural of house. (I have heard *cown* as plural of cow).

Hulk. To gut a rabbit.

Hully (rhymes with fully). Means *wholely* and is a very much used word. Claxton gives: 'Oi felt hully ill.' 'That fare to be hully cowd(cold).' 'That hully rained last night.' 'Tha's hully a nice dawg.' 'Oi wuz hully stammed(confounded).'

Hulver. Holly.

Hurdle (pronounced huddle). To thread one leg of a rabbit or hare through the hamstring of another to carry it (*hock* in received English).

Jacob. A toad.

Jasper. Wasp.

Jereboam. Chamber pot. ('Oi hully drunk some beer las' night—that was 'thumbs awash!'.

Jowlies. Young herring.

Kedgy. Alert.

Kiddle. To cuddle, embrace.

King Harry. Goldfinch.

Knap Kneed. Knock kneed. (The opposite is: 'He couldn't stop a pig in a passage!').

Largesse. Gifts to harvesters for their harvest beer. An old custom.

Larn. To teach.

Leece. Plural of louse.

Leet. Crossroads.

Lijahs. Or Elijahs. Leggings.

Mardle. To gossip.

Mash. Marsh.

Master. Very. Claxton gives: 'Owd Rubbud ha' got a master grut hog.' 'Yow take a master long time a'dewin' that job.' 'Tha's a master rummun!' (rummun=rum one—i.e. peculiar).

Maw. Term of address for young girl.

Mawkin. Scarecrow.

Mawther. A girl, either ready for courting or else a little girl. 'She's a rare dear little mawther.'

Meetiner. A Non-conformist. (One who attends the meeting house).

Mew. Past tense of to mow.

Moithered Up. Claxton gives 'cluttered up' but I've heard 'Do you stop a'moitherin' me!' meaning stop worrying me.

Mockbeggar's Hall. A poor, or mean, household. (There are several Mockbeggar's Hills about—one just before Orford. There is a 'Drag-arse Hill' just west of Wickham Market. It is down this hill condemned men used to be led to the gallows).

Mort. Can be *dead*, or can be *plenty*. (Old Norse—*morgt*=much.).

Nab Nannies. Lice.

Neezen. Plural of nest.

Olp. Bullfinch.

Onsensed. Stunned.

Owd. Old, but used as a diminutive or endearment. 'Good owd boy!' a very common term of approbation, or 'Good owd gal!' 'My little owd dawg.' Used for nearly everything you like or are used to, including very *young* things: 'Moi little owd babby.'

Owd Sarah. Hare. 'My little old larcher hully hustled owd Sarah about!' (larcher=lurcher=a hunting dog.)

Paigle. Cowslip. 'Paigle wine' is very common.

Pea-make. A hook for harvesting (i.e. *making*) peas.

Phoebe. Very often used for the sun. 'Owd Phoebe begin to show!'

Pipman. Like *pitman*—runt. Smallest pig in litter.

Polliwog. Tadpole.

Pritch. A pointed instrument.

Pudden-e-poke. Long-tailed tit.

Railing. Trolling for mackerel. (Now surplanted by 'the feathers').

Ringle. Ring in pig's snout (to stop it *grunnying*). To insert such ring.

Roker. Skate.

Rug. Past tense of to rig.

Rum. Peculiar. 'He's a rummun' means he's strange—possibly untrustworthy. 'Thass a rummun!' constantly used for any peculiar circumstance. 'That fare a bit rum to me!'

Sarnick. To loiter. Claxton gives: 'Whoi, bor, how yow dew go a'sarnickin' along!'

Sew (rhymes with few). Past tense of to sew or to sow.

Shotten herring. Herring that's spawned (and 'in't na good').

Shruk. Past tense of to shriek. 'Oi hully shruk!'

Shug. To shake. 'I shug this har cask and I could hear that a'swugglin'.'

Silly. Excessively. 'You don't want that silly tight.'

Snew. Past tense of to snow. 'That snew!'

Solomon Grundy. Pickled herrings.

Sowja (soldier). A red herring.

Sparling. Sprat.

Spreed. Always used for *spread*. 'Oi've bin a'spreedin' o' muck.'

Squit. Nonsense. 'Thass a lot o' squit what he talk.'

Stam. To astonish. (Old English *stamm*).

Staunch (pronounced starnch). To dam a river. (Launch is pronounced larnch).

Sukey. Tea kettle.

Swift. Newt.

Swounded. Swooned.

Tewk. Redshank. (Claxton didn't get *that* one!).

That. Always used for *it*.

Thow. To thaw. (Past tense *thew*, past participle *thowed*).

Togither. Claxton says this is the plural of 'bor'. It is constantly used when addressing several people. 'Come along yew togither!' 'How are yew togither?' 'Oi hully enjoyed myself—how did yow enjoy yourselves togither?' 'Oi don't know about you togither but Oi'm a'gooin' hoom!'

Wurr-de. Command to a horse to go right.

Published in 1830, and now reprinted by David and Charles, *The Vocabulary of East Anglia* is another useful book dealing with this subject.

Bird Watching

East Anglia is still one of the best places for the bird watcher. The large Suffolk estuaries, cut off from humanity by miles of roadless marshes, the Suffolk beaches too, shingle or sand, also well insulated from the roads (try even *reaching* the sea in most parts of Suffolk!), the unique North Norfolk coast with its many deserted inlets from the sea, its sand dunes and its saltings, the Wash, still, thank God, unenclosed and un-'improved' in any way, one of the great wild goose habitats in Britain, the Broads and the Fens, the Sandlings and the Breckland. All attracting their own bird populations, and providing miles of quiet sanctuary—for bird and bird-watcher alike. The Great Bustard may have been slaughtered to extinction by pre-Victorian 'sportsmen'—but the stone curlew still haunts the Breckland, the avocet which came back to Havergate Island has been protected there by the R.S.P.B., the goldcrest and the crossbill are discovering new habitat among the Forestry Commission pine forests, and the bittern still booms away in the eastern marshes.

Mr R. S. R. Fitter has very kindly allowed us to quote the relevant passages from his book *Collins Guide to Bird Watching*. This is certainly one of the most useful and practical books for the bird lover in the British Isles that there is: by relating birds strictly to where they live it is of far more interest and use than a mere list of birds jumbled in together. In fact with this and *Collins Pocket Guide to British Birds*, by the same author and Mr R. A. Richardson, in his pocket and a pair of binoculars, the bird watcher is splendidly equipped.

P   = Permit needed
PF = Permit needed away from footpath
NP = No permit needed

CAMBRIDGESHIRE

HABITATS

Woodland (B/1): Borley Wood, Linton; Ditton Park Wood, Wood Ditton; Eltisley Wood; Camlingay Wood; Hall Yard Wood, Fordham; Hayley Wood, Long Stowe; Wandlebury; Chippenham Fen; Wicken Fen.

Heaths and Downs: Gog Magog Hills, Newmarket Heath.

Marshes: Chippenham Fen; Ely Beet Factory; Fulbourn Fen; Nene Washes, Peterborough to Guyhirn; Cuse Washes, Earith to Denver; Quy Fen, Stow-cum-Quy; Teversham and Wilbraham Fens; Wicken Fen.

Fresh Water: Nene Washes; Ouse Washes; Gravel pits at Fen Drayton, Hauxton, Landbeach, Mepal, Milton, Waterbeach and Wimblington, Wicken Fen.

Heronries: Chettisham, Guyirn.

Gull roosts: Cambridge sewage farm, Ouse Washes.

Museum: Cambridge.

SPECIAL BIRDS

Long-eared owl: breeds at Wicken Fen and several isolated fen woods.

Heronries: Chettisham, Guyhirn.

Bewick's swan: regular on Nene and Ouse Washes, the latter its main haunt in England.

Pink-footed goose: Fens.

Pintail: Ouse Washes are most important winter haunt in eastern England.

Little ringed plover: breeds at several gravel pits.

Dotterel: still one fairly regular migration halt, at Melbourn, and less regular ones on chalk in S.E.

Stone curlew: breeds on the chalk.

Gull roosts: Cambridge sewage farm, Ouse Washes.

Black-headed gullery: Ely sugar beet factory.

Quail: breeds on the chalk.

Red-legged partridge: common.

RESERVES AND SANCTUARIES

Chippenham Fen (Nature Conservancy; P).
Fulbourn Fen (Cambridgeshire and Isle of Ely Naturalists' Trust).
Hall Yard Wood (C I E N T).
Hayley Wood (C I E N T).
Ouse Washes (Royal Society for the Protection of Birds; P).
Welches Dam (C I E N T).
Wicken Fen (National Trust; NP).

SOCIETIES etc.

Cambridgeshire and Isle of Ely Naturalists' Trust.
Cambridge Bird Club.
Madingley Ornithological Field Station, Cambridge University.

LITERATURE

Cambridge Bird Report, annually (Cambridge B.C.).
The Birds of Cambridgeshire, by David Lack (1934).
Adventurer's Fen, by E. A. R. Ennion (1942), is about Wicken Fen.
The Birds of the Letchworth Region, by A. R. Jenkins (1958).

NORFOLK

HABITATS

Woodland (B/1): Blickling Woods; Fellbrigg Great Wood; North-repps Hall Woods; Thursford Woods; Westwick Woods.
Woodland (conifer): Breckland; sep. Thetford Chase.
Heaths: Breckland, inc. Cockley Cley Warren, Croxton Heath, E. Harling Heath, E. Wretham Heath, Garboldisham Heath, Gooderstone Warren, Santon Warren, Thetford Heath, Weeting Heath, Buxton Heath, Hevingham; Dersingham Heath; Holt Lowes; Kelling Heath and Warren, with Salthouse Heath; Roydon Common, with Grimston Warren, King's Lynn.
Marshes: Barton Broad, Bure Marshes, Hickling Broad, Horsey Mere, Ranworth Broad, Hoveton Broad, Alderfen Broad;

Waveney Valley; Yare Valley; Surlingham Broad; sewage farm at Wisbech; Welney Washes.

Fresh Water: Breckland: Didlington Park, Fowlmere, Langmere, Micklemere, Ringmere, Shadwell Park, Standford Water, Thompson Water; *Broads:* Alderfen, Barton, Ranworth, Cockshoot, Decoy, Hoveton, S. Walsham, Upton, Ormesby, Rollesby, Filby, Hickling, Martham, Heigham, Horsey, Rockland, Surlingham, Bayfield, Park, Holt; Blickling; Gunton; Holkham Park; Narford, Swaffham; Scoulton Mere; Sea Mere, Hingham; gravel pits at Snettisham and Welney; Welney Washes.

Estuaries: Blakeney Harbour, with Morston and Stiffkey Marshes; Brancaster Harbour; Breydon Water, with Halvergate Marshes; Cley and Salthouse Marshes; the Wash, esp. Heacham, Snettisham, Ouse Mouth and Terrington Marsh; Burnham Overy Marsh; Wells Harbour, with Warham Marshes; Holme next the Sea; Thornham Harbour.

Seashore: Hunstanton; Blakeney Point; Scolt Head Is.; Holkham; Palling to Gt. Yarmouth, inc. Winterton Dunes.

Migration Watch Points: Blakeney Point, Cley East Bank, Hunstanton, Scolt Head Is.

Heronries: Buckenham, Denver Sluice, Earsham, Holkham Park, Islington Kimberley Park, Mautby Hall, Melton Constable, Snettisham, Wickhampton.

Gull roosts: Breydon Water, Blakeney Harbour, Hickling Broad, Thompson Water, Wroxham Broad, The Wash, Ouse Washes (Welney).

Bird Collections: Cromer, Kelling, Great Witchingham.

Museums: King's Lynn, Norwich, Thetford.

SPECIAL BIRDS

Crossbill: breeds in Breckland.

Snow bunting: regular in winter on north and east coasts.

Lapland bunting: fairly regular in winter on north coast.

Shore lark: Regular in winter between Scolt Head and Salthouse.

Bearded tit: breeds in Broads area and on Cley Marshes.

Spoonbill: fairly regular on migration at Breydon Water and Cley.

Heronries: Buckingham Carrs, Denver Sluice, Earsham, Holkham Park, Islington, Kimberley Park, Mautby Hall, Melton Constable, Snettisham, Wickhampton.

Bittern: breeds Broads and Cley Marshes.

Greylag goose: feral flocks from Woodbastwick and Rackheath visit Breydon Water, Broads and north coast.

Canada goose: breeds in Broads, Breckland and Holkham Park.

Brent goose: Blakeney Harbour, Scolt Head Is., the Wash.

Egyptian goose: feral breeding colony in Holkham Park, often seen on nearby marshes.

Shelduck: breeds inland, Wisbech sewage farm.

Gadwall: breeds (originally introduced) in Breckland; has recently spread to the Broads and Cley Marshes.

Garganey: breeds regularly, the Broads and Cley Marshes.

Eider: winter flocks at Heacham and Hunstanton; summering increasingly along north coast.

Fulmar: breeds on cliffs near Sheringham.

Collared dove: original British breeding colony still exists near Cromer.

Stone curlew: breeds fairly commonly in Breckland.

Ringed plover: breeds sparsely inland in Breckland.

Knot: up to 50,000 winter in the Wash; a flock of *c.* 30,000 feeds off Snettisham and roosts at Thornham.

Purple sandpiper: regular on South Hunstanton mussel beds in winter and on front at high tide.

Terneries: Blakeney Point, Scolt Head Island, Scroby Sands.

Gull roosts: Breydon Water, Blakeney Harbour, Hickling Broad, Thompson Water, Wroxham Broad, the Wash.

Black-headed gulleries: 14, mainly on North coast, but large ones inland at Cantley and Wissington sugar beet factories and Alderfen Broad.

Arctic skua: regular on migration in the Wash and along north coast.

Golden pheasant: frequent in Breckland.

Red-legged partridge: common.

RESERVES AND SANCTUARIES

Breckland: East Wretham Heath (Norfolk Naturalists' Trust; NP). Weeting Heath (N.N.T. and Nature Conservancy; P).

Broads:
Alderfen Broad (N.N.T.; P).
Barton Broad and Barton Turf Marshes (N.N.T.).
Bure Marshes (Ranworth, Cockshoot and Decoy Broads) (Nature Conservancy and N.N.T.; P).
Hickling Broad (Nature Conservancy and N.N.T.; P).
Horsey Mere (National Trust; PF).
Martham Marshes (N.N.T.).
Surlingham Broad and Bargate Fen (N.N.T.).

COAST

Blakeney Point (National Trust; NP).
Cley and Arnold's Marshes (N.N.T. and National Trust; PF).
Holkham (Nature Conservancy; PAF).
Holme-next-the-Sea (N.N.T.).
Scolt Head Island (Nature Conservancy, N.N.T. and National Trust; NP).
Winterton Dunes (Nature Conservancy; PF).

ELSEWHERE

Blickling Woods (National Trust).
Blo Norton Wood (N.N.T.).
Bulfer Grove (N.N.T.).
Thursford woodlands (N.N.T.).

SOCIETIES, ETC.

Norfolk Naturalists' Trust.
Norfolk and Norwich Naturalists' Society.
Norfolk Wildlife Park (Ornamental Pheasant Trust), Great Witchingham (collection of pheasants, waterfowl, etc.).

LITERATURE

The Norfolk Bird and Mammal Report, published annually by Norfolk and Norwich Nat. Soc.; and notes on the Wash and Fen areas in *Cambridge Bird Report*.
A History of the Birds of Norfolk, by B. B. Riviere (1930).

A Check List of the Birds of Cley, by R. A. Richardson (1961).
In Breckland Wilds, by W. G. Clarke (1925).
Broadland Birds, by E. L. Turner (1924).
Bird Watching on Scolt Head, by Miss E. L. Turner (1928).
Birds of Norfolk, by M. J. Seago (1968).

SUFFOLK

HABITATS

Woodland (B/1): Combs Wood; Fakenham Wood, Euston; Staverton Forest and the Thicks, Butley; woods around Bentley; Redgrave and Lopham Fens.
Woodland (conifer): Breckland.
Heaths: Breckland, inc. Cavenham Heath, Horn and Weather Heaths, Lakenheath Warren, Thetford Heath and Tuddenham Heath; coastal heaths, inc. Aldringham Common; Black Heath, Wenhaston; Blaxhall Common; Hollesley Common; Knodishall Common; N. Warren and Hazelwood Common, Aldeburgh; Rushmere Heath, Ipswich; Sutton Common; Tunstall Common; Walberswick Common; Westleton Heath.
Marshes: Benacre Broad, Easton Broad, Dunwich to Walberswick, Minsmere Level, Redgrave and Lopham Fens, Thorpeness, Tuddenham Fen.
Fresh Water: Benacre Broad, Covehithe Broad, Easton Broad, Fritton Decoy, Livermere, Culton Broad, gravel pits at Benacre Ness.
Estuaries: Alde-Ore, inc. Havergate Is.; Blyth, Deben, Breydon Water, Butley River, Orwell, Stour.
Seashore: Orfordness, Benacre Ness, Shingle Street, Lowestoft Ness.
Migration Watch Points: Lowestoft, Walberswick.
Heronries: Benham, Livermere, Methersgate Hall, N. Cove, Snape.
Gull roosts: Breydon Water, Orewell estuary.
Bird Observatory: Walberswick.
Bird Collection: Bury St Edmunds, Lowestoft.
Museums: Bury St Edmunds, Ipswich.

SPECIAL BIRDS

Hawfinch: at least as common as in any other county.

Crossbill: breeds in Breckland.

Bearded tit: breeds coastal marshes, esp. Minsmere.

Long-eared owl: Herringfleet area.

Short-eared owl: coast, breeds Havergate Island.

Marsh and Montagu's harriers: coastal marshes, esp. Minsmere.

Spoonbill: fairly regular on migration, Breydon Water.

Heronries: Henham, Livermere, Methersgate Hall, North Cove, Snape.

Bittern: breeds coastal marshes, esp. Minsmere.

Canada goose: breeds Breckland.

Shelduck: breeds inland, Butley Thicks.

Gadwall: breeds coastal marshes.

Stone curlew: breeds Breckland and coastal heaths.

Ringed plover: breeds inland, Breckland heaths.

Avocet: Havergate Island and Minsmere are the only breeding places in British Isles.

Sandwich tern: Havergate Island; North Weir Point, Orfordness.

Gull roost: R. Orwell, Breydon Water.

Black-headed gull: large gullery on Havergate Island; three smaller ones, two on coast, one at Bury St. Edmunds.

Kittiwake: nests on South Pier Pavilion, Lowestoft.

Golden pheasant: frequent in Breckland.

Red-legged partridge: common.

RESERVES AND SANCTUARIES

Cavenham and Tuddenham Heaths (Breckland) (Nature Conservancy; P for part only).

Havergate Island (Royal Society for the Protection of Birds; P).

Horn and Weather Heaths (Royal Society for the Protection of Birds; P).

Minsmere (RSPB; P).

North Warren, Thorpeness (RSPB; NP).

Orfordness-Havergate (RSPB and Nature Conservancy; P for part only).

Redgrave and Lopham Fens (Suffolk Naturalists' Trust).

Thetford Heath (Norfolk Naturalists' Trust and Nature Conservancy; P).

Westleton Heath (Nature Conservancy; PF).

SOCIETIES, ETC.

Dingle Bird Club.
Flatford Mill Field Centre, East Bergholt (Field Studies Council).
Suffolk Naturalists' Society, Ornithological Section.
Suffolk Naturalists' Trust.
Walberswick Ringing Station (Dingle Bird Club).

LITERATURE

Annual bird report in *Transactions* of Suffolk Nat. Soc.
The Birds of Suffolk, by C. B. Ticehurst (1932).
RSPB pamphlets on Minsmere and Havergate.
In Breckland Wilds, by W. G. Clarke (1925).
The Birds of Suffolk, by W. H. Pain (1962).

Hotels in East Anglia

CAMBRIDGESHIRE			Telephone No.
Cambridge	Blue Boar		63121
	Garden House		55491
	Royal Cambridge		51631
	Station		59295
	University Arms		51241
Ely	Lamb		2204
March	Griffin		2517
Whittlesford	Red Lion	Sawston	3344
Wisbech	Rose and Crown		3187
	Ship		2614
	White Lion		3221

SUFFOLK			
Aldeburgh	Brunenell		2071
	Wentworth		2312
	White Lion		2720
	Uplands		2420
Barton Mills	Bull Inn	Mildenhall	3230
Beccles	King's Head		2147
	Waveney House		2270
Beck Row	Bird-in-Hand	Mildenhall	3247
		(see Mildenhall)	
Brandon	Great Eastern		229
Bungay	King's Head		377

Telephone No.

Bury St Edmunds	Suffolk	3995
	Angel	3926
	Everards	5384
	Square House	5337
Clare	Bell	430
	Nethergate	279
Copdock	Copdock House	260
Felixstowe	De-Novo	2809
	Orwell	2142
	Cavendish	2696
	Waverley	2811
	Highcliffe	2503
	North Sea	2103
	Ordnance	4276
Framlingham	Crown	521
Hadleigh	White Lion	3256
Halesworth	Angel	3356
Haverhill	Rose and Crown	2043
Ipswich	Great White Horse	56558
	Belstead Brook	52380
	Crown and Anchor	38506
	Golden Lion	52523
Lavenham	Swan	477
Long Melford	Bull	494
	Crown Inn	366
Lowestoft	Harbour	2931
	Hatfield	5337
Mildenhall	Bird-in-Hand	3247 (see Beck Row)
	Bell	2134
Needham Market	Limes	305

495

Telephone No.

Newmarket	Bedford Lodge		3175
	Rutland Arms		3016
	White Hart		3051
Orford	Crown and Castle		205
Oulton Broad	Wherry	Lowestoft	3521
	Golden Egg Motel	Lowestoft	2157
Saxmundham	Bell		2331
Shottisham	Wood Hall		283
Southwold	Swan		2186
	Crown		2275
Stowmarket	Fox		2798
Sudbury	Four Swans		2793
Thorpeness	Dolphin Inn	Aldeburgh	2681
Walberswick	Anchor	Southwold	2112
Wickham Market	White Hart		203
Woodbridge	Melton Grange		3439
	Seckford Hall		2678
	Crown		2917

NORFOLK

Blakeney	Blakeney	Cley	343
	Manor	Cley	241
Caistor St Edmund	Caistor Hall	Framingham Earl	246
Cromer	Albany		2297
	Colne House		2013
	Hotel de Paris		3141
	Links	West Runton	413
	Cliff House		2445
	Monksmead	West Runton	265
	Overstrand Court	Overstrand	282
	West Parade		2443

Telephone No.

	Cliftonville		2543
	Red Lion		2737
	Regency		2526
Dersingham	Feathers		207
Diss	Park		2244
	King's Head		2016
Acle	Fishley Manor		377
Dereham	Phoenix		2276
	George		3119
Fakenham	Crown		2010
Gorleston-on-Sea	Cliff	Great Yarmouth	62179
	Seacliffe	Great Yarmouth	62869
	St Edmunds	Great Yarmouth	62119
Great Yarmouth	Carlton		55234
	Star		2294
	Central		2356
	Royal		2698
	Two Bears		3198
	Burlington		4568
	Imperial		2057
	Marine View		2879
Harleston	Magpie		211
	Swan		221
Holkham	Victoria	Wells	469
Holt	Feathers		2318
Horning	Petersfield House		365
Hunstanton	Golden Lion		2688
	Le Strange Arms		2810
	Lodge		2896
	Driftwood		2241
	Garden House		2295
Ingoldisthorpe	Ingoldisthorpe Manor	Snettisham	380

Companion Guide to East Anglia

Telephone No.

King's Lynn	Duke's Head		2234
	Cozen's		2156
	East Anglian		2732
	Globe		2617
	Oakwood Guest House	Watlington	256
Mundesley-on-Sea	Continental		271
	Ship		448
	Royal		350
North Walsham	Scarborough Hill		2151
Norwich	Castle		24283
	Lansdowne		20302
	Maid's Head		28821
	Royal		28434
	Bell		21256
	Town House		35212
	Cumberland		34550
Overstrand	Overstrand Court	Overstrand	282
		(see Cromer)	
Overy Staithe	Moorings	Burnham Market	239
Sheringham	Burlington		2224
	Dormy House		2006
	Beaumaris		2370
	Southlands		2679
	Two Lifeboats		2401
Stalham (Sutton)	Sutton Staithe Country Club	Stalham	244
Swaffam	George		238
Thetford	Bell		2055
	Anchor		3329
	Central		2259
Titchwell	Manor	Brancaster	221

Telephone No.

Tottenhill (*King's Lynn*)	Oakwood Guest House	Watlington	256
Wells-Next-The-Sea	Crown Victoria	Wells	209 469
		(see Holkham)	
West Runton	Links		413
		(see Cromer)	
Weybourne	Maltings		275
Winterton-on-Sea	Hermanus		216
Wroxham	King's Head		2429
Wymondham	Abbey		2302

Index

Principal references are in **bold** type

Certain specialist interests are listed in the Index for the enthusiast. These lists are not necessarily complete. The subjects thus listed are:

Castles
Cathedrals, pro-cathedrals and great churches
Churches, outstanding
Fen Lighters
Fisheries
Fonts, Font covers and Baptistries, outstanding
Houses, outstanding
Mills, Tidal
Mills, Water
Mills, Wind
Monastic Buildings and Remains
Museums

Porches, church, outstanding
Romans
Royal National Lifeboat Institute
Sailing Barges
Screens and Retables, outstanding
Thatch
Tombs and Brasses, outstanding
Towers and Spires, outstanding
Wherries
Wildfowling
Wood-carving, outstanding
Wool and Weaving Industries.

Index

Index

Index

Index

Index